SPANISH-ENGLISH ENGLISH-SPANISH DICTIONARY

SPANISH-ENGLISH ENGLISH-SPANISH DICTIONARY

LUCEM LIBRIS DISSEMINAMUS

GEDDES&
GROSSET

Contents

Abbreviations · Abbreviaturas

abrev	abbreviation	abreviatura
adj	adjective	adjectivo
adv	adverb	adverbio
art	article	artículo
auto	automobile	automóvil
aux	auxiliary	auxiliar
bot	botany	botánica
chem	chemistry	química
col	colloquial term	lengua familiar
com	commerce	comercio
compd	in compounds	usada en palabras compuestas
comput	computers	informática
conj	conjunction	conjunctión
dep	sport	deporte
excl	exclamation	exclamación
f	feminine noun	sustantrivo femenino
fam	colloquial term	lengua familiar
ferro	railway	ferrocarrilero
fig	figurative use	uso figurado
gr	grammar	gramática
imp	impersonal	impersonal
inform	computers	informática
interj	interjection	interjección
invar	invariable	invariable
irr	irregular	irregular
jur	law term	jurisprudencia
law	law term	jurisprudencia
ling	linguistics	lingüística
m	masculine noun	sustantivo masculino
mar	marine term	vocablo marítimo
mat, math	mathematics	matemáticas
med	medicine	medicina
mil	military term	lo militar
mus	music	música
n	noun	sustantivo
pej	pejorative	peyorativo
pl	plural	plural
pn	pronoun	pronombre
poet	poetical term	vocablo poético
prep	preposition	preposición
quim	chemistry	química
rad	radio	radio
rail	railway	ferrocarilero
sl	slang	argot
teat	theatre	teatro

tec	technology	téchnica, tecnologia
TV	television	televisión
vb	verb	verbo
vi	intransitive verb	verbo intransitivo
vr	reflexive verb	verbo reflexivo
vt	transitive verb	verbo transitivo

Spanish-English Dictionary

A

a *prep* to; in; at; according to; on; by; for; of.

abadía *f* abbey.

abajo *adv* under, underneath; below.

abalanzarse *vr* to rush forward.

abandonado, da *adj* derelict; abandoned; neglected.

abandonar *vt* to abandon; to leave: —~**se** *vr* ~ **a** to give oneself up to.

abarcar *vt* to include; to monopolise.

abarrotado, da *adj* packed.

abarrotar *vt* to tie down; (*mar*) to stow.

abastecer *vt* to purvey.

abatido, da *adj* dejected, low-spirited; abject.

abatimiento *m* low spirits *pl*, depression.

abatir *vt* to knock down; to humble.

abdicar *vt* to abdicate.

abdomen *m* abdomen.

abdominal *adj* abdominal.

abecedario *m* alphabet; spelling book, primer.

abeja *f* bee.

aberración *f* aberration.

abertura *f* aperture, chink, opening.

abeto *m* fir tree.

abierto, ta *adj* open; sincere; frank.

abismal *adj* abysmal.

abismo *m* abyss; gulf; hell.

ablandar *vt, vi* to soften.

abnegado, da *adj* selfless.

abogacía *f* legal profession.

abogado, a *m/f* lawyer; barrister.

abogar *vi* to intercede:—~ **por** to advocate.

abolir *vt* to abolish.

abollar *vt* to dent.

abonado, da *adj* paid-up:— *m/f* subscriber.

abonar *vt* to settle; to fertilise.

abono *m* payment; subscription; dung, manure.

aborrecer *vt* to hate, abhor.

abortar *vi* to miscarry; to have an abortion.

aborto *m* abortion; monster.

abotonar *vt* to button.

abovedado, da *adj* vaulted.

abrasar *vt* to burn; to parch:—~**se** *vr* to burn oneself.

abrazar *vt* to embrace; to surround; to contain.

abrazo *m* embrace.

abrebotellas *m invar* bottle opener.

abrelatas *m invar* can opener.

abreviar *vt* to abridge, cut short.

abridor *m* opener.

abrigar *vt* to shelter; to protect.

abrigo *m* shelter; protection; aid.

abril *m* April.

abrillantar *vt* to polish.

abrir *vt* to open; to unlock.

abrochar *vt* to button; to do up.

abrumar *vt* to overwhelm.

absolución *f* forgiveness, absolution.

absoluto, ta *adj* absolute.

absorber *vt* to absorb.

absorción *f* absorption; takeover.

absorto *adj* engrossed.

abstemio *adj* teetotal.

abstracción *f* abstraction.

abstracto, ta *adj* abstract.

abstraer *vt* to abstract:—~**se** *vr* to be absorbed.

absuelto, ta *adj* absolved.

absurdo *adj* absurd.

abuela *f* grandmother.

abuelo *m* grandfather.

abulia *f* lethargy.

abultado, da *adj* bulky, large, massive.

abultar *vt* to increase, enlarge:—*vi* to be bulky.

abundante *adj* abundant, copious.

aburrido, da *adj* boring, bored.

aburrir *vt* to bore, weary.

abusar *vt* to abuse.

acá *adv* here.

acabado, da *adj* perfect, accomplished; old.

acabar *vt* to finish, complete; to achieve:—~**se** *vr* to finish, expire.

academia *f* academy; literary society.

acaecer *vi* to happen.

acallar *vt* to quiet, hush; to soften, appease.

acalorado, da *adj* heated.

acampar *vt* (*mil*) to encamp.

acanalado, da *adj* grooved; fluted.

acaparar *vt* to monopolise; to hoard.

acariciar *vt* to fondle, caress.

acarrear *vt* to transport; to occasion.

acaso *m* chance:—*adv* perhaps.

acatarrarse *vr* to catch cold.

acceder *vi* to agree:—~ **a** to have access to.

accesible *adj* attainable; accessible.

acceso *m* access; fit.

accidentado, da *adj* uneven; hilly; eventful.

accidental *adj* accidental; casual.

accidente *m* accident.

acción *f* action, operation; share.

accionar *vt* to work.

accionista *m* shareholder.

acebo *m* holly tree.

acechar *vt* to lie in ambush for; to spy on.

aceite *m* oil.

aceituna *f* olive.

aceitunado, da *adj* olive-green.

aceleración *f* acceleration.

aceleradamente *adv* swiftly, hastily.

acelerar *vt* to accelerate; to hurry.

acento *m* accent.

aceptar *vt* to accept, admit.

acera *f* pavement, sidewalk.

acerca *prep* about, relating to.

acercar *vt* to move nearer:— ~**se** *vr* ~ **a** to approach.

acero *m* steel.

acertar *vt* to hit; to guess right.

acertijo *m* riddle.

achacar *vt* to impute.

achaque *m* ailment; excuse; subject, matter.

achicar *vt* to diminish; to humiliate; to bale (out).

achicharrar *vt* to scorch; to overheat.

aciago, ga *adj* unlucky; ominous.

ácido *m* acid:—~, **da** *adj* acid, sour.

acierto *m* success; solution; dexterity.

aclamar *vt* to applaud, acclaim.

aclaración *f* clarification.

aclarar *vt* to clear; to brighten; to explain; to clarify.

acobardar *vt* to intimidate.

acodarse *vr* to lean.

acoger *vt* to receive; to welcome; to harbour:—~**se** *vr* to take refuge.

acogida *f* reception; asylum.

acometida *f* attack, assault.

acomodar *vt* to accommodate, arrange:—~**se** *vr* to comply.

acompañar *vt* to accompany; to join; (*mus*) to accompany.

acompasado, da *adj* measured; well-proportioned.

acondicionar *vt* to arrange; to condition.

acongojar *vt* to distress.

aconsejar *vt* to advise:—~**se** *vr* to take advice.

acontecer *vi* to happen.

acontecimiento *m* event, incident.

acoplar *vt* to couple; to fit; to connect.

acordar *vt* to agree; to remind:—~**se** *vr* to agree; to remember.

acorde *adj* harmonious:—*m* chord.

acordeón *m* accordion.

acorralar *vt* to round up; to intimidate.

acortar *vt* to abridge, shorten:—~**se** *vr* to become shorter.

acostar *vt* to put to bed; to lay down: —~**se** *vr* to go to bed; to lie down.

acostumbrar *vi* to be used to:—*vt* to accustom:—~**se** *vr* ~ **a** to become used to.

acotar *vt* to set bounds to; to annotate.

ácrata *m/f* anarchist.

acreditar *vt* to guarantee; to assure; to authorise.

acreedor *m* creditor.

acribillar *vt* to riddle with bullets; to molest, torment.

acta *f* act:—~**s** *fpl* records *pl*.

actitud *f* attitude; posture.

actividad *f* activity; liveliness.

activo, va *adj* active; diligent.

acto *m* act, action; act of a play; ceremony.

actor *m* actor; plaintiff.

actriz *f* actress.

actuación *f* action; behaviour; proceedings *pl*.

actual *adj* actual, present.

actualizar *vt* to update.

actuar *vt* to work; to operate:—*vi* to work; to act.

acuarela *f* watercolour.

acudir *vi* to go to; to attend; to assist.

acuerdo *m* agreement:—**de** ~ OK.

acumular *vt* to accumulate, collect.

acurrucarse *vr* to squat; to huddle up.

adelantado, da *adj* advanced; fast.

adelantar *vt, vi* to advance, accelerate; to pass.

adelante *adv* forward(s):—*excl* come in!

adelanto *m* advance; progress; improvement.

adelgazar *vt* to make thin or slender; to discuss with subtlety.

además *adv* moreover, besides:—~ **de** besides.

adentro *adv* in; inside.

aderezar *vt* to dress, adorn; to prepare; to season.

adeudar *vt* to owe:—~**se** *vr* to run into debt.

adherir *vi*:—~ **a** to adhere to; to espouse.

adiestrar *vt* to guide; to teach, to instruct.

adiós *excl* goodbye; hello.

adivinar *vt* to foretell; to guess.

admirar *vt* to admire; to surprise:—~**se** *vr* to be surprised.

admitir *vt* to admit; to let in; to concede; to permit.

admonición *f* warning.

adobar *vt* to dress; to season.

adobe *m* adobe, sun-dried brick.

adobo *m* dressing; pickle sauce.

adolecer *vi* to suffer from.

adolescencia *f* adolescence.

adónde *adv* where.

adoptar *vt* to adopt.

adoquín *m* paving stone.

adorar *vt* to adore; to love.

adormecer *vt* to put to sleep:—~**se** *vr* to fall asleep.

adornar *vt* to embellish, adorn.

adosado, da *adj* semi-detached.

adquirir *vt* to acquire.

adrede *adv* on purpose.

aduana *f* customs *pl*.

adueñarse *vr*:—~ **de** to take possession of.

adular *vt* to flatter.

adulterio *m* adultery.

adulto, ta *adj, m/f* adult, grown-up.

advenedizo *m* upstart.

advenimiento *m* arrival; accession.

adversidad *f* adversity; setback.

advertencia *f* warning, foreword.

advertir *vt* to notice; to warn.

aerodeslizador *m* hovercraft.

aeronave *f* spaceship.

aeropuerto *m* airport.

afán *m* hard work; desire.

afanar *vt* to harass; (*col*) to pinch:—~**se** *vr* to strive.

afear *vt* to deform, misshape.

afección *f* affection; fondness, attachment; disease.

afectar *vt* to affect, feign.

afectuoso, sa *adj* affectionate; moving; tender.

afeitar *vt*:—~**se** *vr* to shave.

aferrar *vt* to grapple, grasp, seize.

afianzar *vt* to strengthen; to prop up.

aficionado, da *adj* keen:—*m/f* lover, devotee; amateur.

afilado *adj* sharp.

afilar *vt* to sharpen, grind.

afín *m* related; similar.

afinar *vt* to tune; to refine.

afincarse *vr* to settle.

afirmar *vt* to secure, fasten; to affirm, assure.

aflicción *f* affliction, grief.

aflictivo, va *adj* distressing.

aflojar *vt* to loosen, slacken, relax.

aflorar *vi* to emerge.

afluente *adj* flowing:—*m* tributary.

afónico, ca *adj* hoarse; voiceless.

afortunado, da *adj* fortunate, lucky.

afrenta *f* outrage; insult.

afrontar *vt* to confront; to bring face to face.

afuera *adv* out, outside.

agacharse *vr* to stoop, squat.

agarradero *m* handle.

agarrar *vt* to grasp, seize:—~**se** *vr* to hold on tightly.

agasajar *vt* to receive and treat kindly; to regale.

agenciarse *vr* to obtain.

agenda *f* diary.

agente *m* agent; policeman.

ágil *adj* agile.

agilidad *f* agility, nimbleness.

agitar *vt* to wave; to move:—~**se** *vr* to become excited; to become worried.

aglomeración *f* crowd; jam.

agobiar *vt* to weigh down; to oppress; to burden.

agolparse *vr* to assemble in crowds.

agonía *f* agony.

agorar *vt* to predict.

agostar *vt* to parch.

agosto *m* August.

agotado, da *adj* exhausted; finished; sold out.

agotar *vt* to exhaust; to drain; to misspend.

agradable *adj* pleasant; lovely.

agradar *vt* to please, gratify.

agradecer *vt* to be grateful for; to thank.

agradecido, da *adj* thankful.

agrandar *vt* to enlarge; to exaggerate.

agrario, ria *adj* agrarian; agricultural.

agravante *f* further difficulty.

agraviar *vt* to wrong; to offend:—**~se** *vr* to be aggrieved; to be piqued.

agredir *vt* to attack.

agregar *vt* to aggregate, heap together; to collate; to appoint.

agreste *adj* rustic, rural.

agrícola *adj* farming *compd*.

agricultor, ra *m/f* farmer.

agrietarse *vr* to crack.

agrimensor *m* surveyor.

agrio *adj* sour, acrid; rough, craggy; sharp, rude, unpleasant.

agrupar *vt* to group, cluster; to crowd.

agua *f* water.

aguacate *m* avocado pear.

aguacero *m* cloudburst, downpour.

aguado, da *adj* watery.

aguafuerte *m* etching.

aguamarina *f* aquamarine (gem stone).

aguanieve *f* sleet.

aguantar *vt* to bear, suffer; to hold up.

aguardar *vt* to wait for.

aguarrás *f* turpentine.

agudo, da *adj* sharp; keen-edged; smart; fine; acute; witty; brisk.

aguijón *m* sting of a bee, wasp, etc; stimulation.

águila *f* eagle; genius.

aguileño, ña *adj* aquiline; sharp-featured.

aguja *f* needle; spire; hand; magnetic needle; (*ferro*) points *pl*.

agujerear *vt* to pierce, bore.

agujero *m* hole.

ahí *adv* there.

ahijada *f* goddaughter.

ahijado *m* godson.

ahínco *m* earnestness; eagerness.

ahogar *vt* to smother; to drown; to suffocate; to oppress; to quench.

ahora *adv* now, at present; just now.

ahorrar *vt* to save; to avoid.

ahumar *vt* to smoke, cure (in smoke): —**~se** *vr* to fill with smoke.

ahuyentar *vt* to drive off; to dispel.

aire *m* air; wind; aspect; musical composition.

aislar *vt* to insulate; to isolate.

ajardinado, da *adj* landscaped.

ajedrez *m* chess.

ajedrezado, da *adj* chequered.

ajeno, na *adj* someone else's; foreign; ignorant; improper.

ajetreo *m* activity; bustling.

ajo *m* garlic.

ajorca *f* bracelet.

ajustar *vt* to regulate, adjust; to settle (a balance); to fit.

al = **a el**.

ala *f* wing; aisle; row, file; brim:—*mf* winger.

alabar *vt* to praise; to applaud.

alacena *f* cupboard, closet.

alacrán *m* scorpion.

alambre *m* wire.

alameda *f* avenue; poplar grove.

álamo *m* poplar.

alargar *vt* to lengthen; to extend.

alarido *m* outcry, shout:— **dar ~s** to howl.

alarma *f* alarm.

alba *f* dawn.

albañil *m* mason, bricklayer.

albarán *m* invoice.

albaricoque *m* apricot.

albedrío *m* free will.

albergue *m* shelter:—**~ de juventud** youth hostel.

albóndiga *f* meatball.

albornoz *m* burnous:—**~ de bañio** bath robe.

alboroto *m* noise; disturbance, riot.

alborozo *m* joy.

albricias *fpl* good news *pl*.

albufera *f* lagoon.

álbum *m* album.

alcachofa *f* artichoke.

alcalde *m* mayor.

alcaldesa *f* mayoress.

alcantarilla *m* sewer; gutter.

alcanzar *vt* to reach; to get, obtain; to hit.

alcaparra *f* caper.

alcayata *f* hook.

alcázar *m* castle, fortress.

alcornoque *m* cork tree.

aldea *f* village.

aleatorio, ria *adj* random.

aleccionar *vt* to instruct; to train.

alegar *vt* to allege; to quote.

alegrar *vt* to cheer; to poke; to liven up:—**~se** *vr* to get merry.

alegre *adj* happy; merry, joyful; content.

alegría *f* happiness; merriment.

alejar *vt* to remove; to estrange:—**~se** *vr* to go away.

alemán, ana *adj, m/f* German:—*m* German language.

alentar *vt* to encourage.

alergia *f* allergy.

alero *m* gable-end; eaves *pl*.

alertar *vt* to alert.

aleta *f* fin; wing; flipper; fender.

alfabeto *m* alphabet.

alfarería *f* pottery.

alféizar *m* window sill.

alfiler *m* pin; clip; clothes peg.

alfombra *f* carpet; rug.

alga *f* (*bot*) seaweed.

algo *pn* something; anything:—*adv* somewhat.

algodón *m* cotton; cotton plant; cotton wool.

alguien *pn* someone, somebody; anyone, anybody.

alguno, na *adj* some; any; no:—*pn* someone, somebody.

alhaja *f* jewel.

aliado, da *adj* allied.

alianza *f* alliance, league; wedding ring.

alicates *mpl* pincers *pl*, nippers *pl*.

aliciente *m* attraction; incitement.

aliento *m* breath; respiration.

aligerar *vt* to lighten; to alleviate; to hasten; to ease.

alijo *m* lightening of a ship; alleviation; cache.

alimentar *vt* to feed, nourish:—**~se** *vr* to feed.

aliñar *vt* to adorn; to season.

alinear *vt* to arrange in line:—**~se** *vr* to line up.

alisar *vt* to plane; to polish; to smooth.

aliviar *vt* to lighten; to ease; to relieve, mollify.

allá *adv* there; over there; then.

allanar *vt* to level, flatten; to subdue; to burgle.

allí *adv* there, in that place.

alma *f* soul; human being.

almacén *m* warehouse, store; magazine.

almacenar *vt* to store (up).

almeja *f* clam.

almena *f* battlement.

almendra *f* almond.

almíbar *m* syrup.

almirez *m* mortar.

almizcle *m* musk.

almohada *f* pillow; cushion.

almorranas *fpl* haemorrhoids *pl*.

almuerzo *m* lunch.

alocado, da *adj* crazy; foolish; inconsiderate.

alojamiento *m* lodging; housing.

alpargata *f* rope-soled shoe.

alpinismo *m* mountaineering.

alquilar *vt* to let, rent; to hire.

alquitrán *m* tar, liquid pitch.

alrededor *adv* around.

alta *f* (*mil*) discharge from hospital.

altanero, ra *adj* haughty, arrogant, vain, proud.

altavoz *m* loudspeaker, amplifier.

alterar *vt* to alter, change; to disturb.

altercado *m* altercation, controversy; quarrel.

alterno, na *adj* alternate; alternating.

Alteza *f* Highness (title).

altibajos *mpl* ups and downs *pl*.

altitud *f* height; altitude.

altivo, va *adj* haughty, proud, high-flown.

alto, ta *adj* high; tall:—*m* height; storey; highland; (*mil*) halt; (*mus*) alto: —¡~!, ¡~ ahí! *interj* stop!

altura *f* height; depth; mountain summit; altitude.

alubia *f* kidney bean.

alucinar *vt* to blind, deceive:—*vi* to hallucinate.

alumbrado *m* lighting; illumination.

alumbrar *vt* to light:—*vi* to give birth.

alumno, na *m/f* student, pupil.

alza *f* rise; sight.

alzar *vt* to raise, lift up:—**~se** *vr* to get up; to rise in rebellion.

ama *f* mistress, owner; housewife; foster mother.

amable *adj* kind, nice.

amagar *vt* to threaten; to shake one's fist at:—*vi* to feint.

amamantar *vt* to suckle.

amanecer *vi* to dawn:—**al ~** at daybreak.

amanerado, da *adj* affected.

amansar *vt* to tame; to soften; to subdue:—**~se** *vr* to calm down.

amante *m/f* lover.

amapola *f* (*bot*) poppy.

amar *vt* to love.

amargo, ga *adj* bitter, acrid; painful: —*m* bitterness.

amarillo, lla *adj* yellow:—*m* yellow.

amarrar *vt* to moor; to tie, fasten.

amasar *vt* to knead; (*fig*) to arrange, settle; to prepare.

ámbar *m* amber.

ambiente *m* atmosphere; environment.

ambiguo, gua *adj* ambiguous; doubtful, equivocal.

ámbito *m* circuit, circumference; field; scope.

ambos, bas *adj, pn* both.

ambulante *adj* travelling.

ambulatorio *m* state-run clinic.

amenazar *vt* to threaten.

ameno, na *adj* pleasant; delicious; flowery (of language).

América *f* America:—~ **del Norte/del Sur** North/ South America.

amianto *m* asbestos.

amiga *f* (female) friend.

amigo *m* friend; comrade; lover:—~, **ga** *adj* friendly.

aminorar *vt* to diminish; to reduce.

amistad *f* friendship.

amistoso, sa *adj* friendly, cordial.

amo *m* owner; boss.

amoldar *vt* to mould; to adapt:—~**se** *vr* to adapt oneself.

amor *m* love; fancy; lover:— ~ **mio** my love:—**por ~ de Dios** for God's sake: —~ **propio** self-love.

amortiguador *m* shock absorber.

amortizar *vt* to redeem, pay, liquidate, discharge (a debt).

amperio *m* amp.

ampliar *vt* to amplify, enlarge; to extend; to expand.

amplificador *m* amplifier.

amplio, lia *adj* ample, extensive.

ampolla *f* blister; ampoule.

amueblar *vt* to furnish.

anacoreta *m* anchorite, hermit.

anacronismo *m* anachronism.

añadir *vt* to add.

analfabeto, ta *adj* illiterate.

analgésico *m* painkiller.

análisis *m* analysis.

anaranjado, da *adj* orange-coloured.

anarquía *f* anarchy.

ancho, cha *adj* broad, wide, large:—*m* breadth, width.

anchoa *f* anchovy.

anchura *f* width, breadth.

anciano, na *adj* old:—*m/f* old man/woman.

ancla *f* anchor.

anclaje *m* anchorage.

andamiaje *m* scaffolding.

andar *vi* to go, walk; to fare; to act, proceed.

andén *m* pavement, sidewalk; (*ferro*) platform; quayside.

andrajo *m* rag.

anegar *vt* to inundate, submerge;.

añejo, ja *adj* old; stale, musty.

anexión *f* annexation.

anfibio, bia *adj* amphibious.

anfitrión, ona *m/f* host(ess).

ángel *m* angel.

angosto, ta *adj* narrow, close.

anguila *f* eel.

angula *f* elver.

angular *adj* angular:—**piedra ~** *f* cornerstone.

ángulo *m* angle, corner.

angustia *f* anguish; heartache.

anhelar *vi* to gasp:—*vt* to long for.

anidar *vi* to nestle, make a nest; to dwell, inhabit.

añil *m* indigo plant; indigo.

anillo *m* ring.

ánima *f* soul.

animación *f* liveliness; activity.

animado, da *adj* lively.

animal *adj, m* animal.

animar *vt* to animate, liven up; to comfort; to revive:—~**se** *vr* to cheer up.

ánimo *m* soul; courage; mind; intention:—*excl* come on!

anís *m* aniseed; anisette.

aniversario, ria *adj* annual:—*m* anniversary.

ano *m* anus.

año *m* year.

anoche *adv* last night.

anochecer *vi* to grow dark:—*m* nightfall.

anónimo, ma *adj* anonymous.

añoranza *f* longing.

anormal *adj* abnormal.

anotar *vt* to comment, note.

anquilosamiento *m* paralysis.

ánsar *m* goose.

ansiar *vt* to desire.

ansiedad *f* anxiety.

antagónico, ca *adj* antagonistic; opposed.

antaño *adv* formerly.

ante *m* suede:—*prep* before; in the presence of; faced with.

anteanoche *adv* the night before last.

anteayer *adv* the day before yesterday.

antebrazo *m* forearm.

antelación *f*:—**con ~** in advance.

antemano *adv*:—**de ~** beforehand.

antena *f* feeler, antenna; aerial.

antepasado, da *adj* passed, elapsed: —**~s** *mpl* ancestors *pl*.

anterior *adj* preceding; former.

antes *prep, adv* before:—*conj* before.

antibiótico *m* antibiotic.

anticiclón *m* anticyclone.

anticipar *vt* to anticipate; to forestall; to advance.

anticonceptivo *m* contraceptive.

anticongelante *m* antifreeze.

anticuado, da *adj* antiquated.

anticuerpo *m* antibody.

antiestético, ca *adj* unsightly.

antifaz *m* mask.

antiguamente *adv* in ancient times, of old.

antiguo, gua *adj* antique, old, ancient.

antipático, ca *adj* unpleasant.

antojo *m* whim, fancy; longing.

antorcha *f* torch; taper.

antro *m* (*poet*) cavern, den, grotto.

antropófago *m* cannibal.

antropología *f* anthropology.

anual *adj* annual.

anudar *vt* to knot; to join:—**~se** *vr* to get into knots.

anular *vt* to annul; to revoke; to cancel:—*adj* annular.

anunciar *vt* to announce; to advertise.

anuncio *m* advertisement.

anzuelo *m* hook; allurement.

apacible *adj* affable; gentle; placid, quiet.

apaciguar *vt* to appease; to pacify, calm.

apagar *vt* to put out; to turn off; to quench, extinguish.

apañar *vt* to grasp; to pick up; to patch: —**~se** *vr* to manage.

aparador *m* sideboard; shop window.

aparato *m* apparatus; machine; radio or television set; ostentation, show; (*med*) bandage, dressing.

aparcamiento *m* car park.

aparcar *vt, vi* to park.

aparecer *vi* to appear:—**~se** *vr* to appear.

aparentar *vt* to look; to pretend; to deceive.

apariencia *f* outward appearance.

apartamento *m* flat, apartment.

apartar *vt* to separate, divide; to remove; to sort;.

aparte *m* aside; new paragraph:—*adv* apart, separately; besides; aside.

apasionado, da *adj* passionate; devoted; fond; biased.

apeadero *m* halt, stopping place; station.

apearse *vr* to dismount; to get down/out/off.

apechugar *vt* to face up to.

apego *m* attachment, fondness.

apelar *vi* (*jur*) to appeal:—**~ a** to have recourse to.

apellido *m* surname; family name; epithet.

apenar *vt* to grieve; to embarrass:—**~se** *vr* to grieve; to be embarrassed.

apenas *adv* scarcely, hardly: —*conj* as soon as.

apéndice *m* appendix, supplement.

apercibirse *vr* to notice.

aperitivo *m* aperitif; appetiser.

apero *m* agricultural implement.

apesadumbrar *vt* to sadden.

apestar *vt* to infect:—*vi* **~ a** to stink of.

apetito *m* appetite.

apiadarse *vr* to take pity.

apilar *vt* to pile up:—**~se** *vr* to pile up.

apiñado, da *adj* crowded; pyramidal; pine-shaped.

apio *m* (*bot*) celery.

apisonadora *f* steamroller.

aplacar *vt* to appease, pacify:—**~se** *vr* to calm down.

aplastar *vt* to flatten, crush.

aplatanarse *vr* to get weary.

aplaudir *vt* to applaud; to extol.

aplauso *m* applause; approbation, praise.

aplazar *vt* to postpone.

aplicado, da *adj* studious; industrious.

aplicar *vt* to apply; to clasp; to attribute:—**~se** *vr* **~ a** to devote oneself to.

aplique *m* wall light.

aplomo *m* self-assurance.

apocado, da *adj* timid.

apoderado, da *adj* powerful:—*m* proxy, attorney; agent.

apodo *m* nickname, sobriquet.

apogeo *m* peak.

apósito *m* (*med*) external dressing.

aposta *adv* on purpose.

apostar *vt* to bet, wager; to post soldiers:—*vi* to bet.

apóstol *m* apostle.

apoteosis *f* apotheosis.

apoyar *vt* to rest; to favour, patronise, support:—**~se** *vr* to lean.

apreciar *vt* to appreciate; to estimate, value.

aprecio *m* appreciation; esteem.

apremiante *adj* urgent.

aprender *vt* to learn:—**~ de memoria** to learn by heart.

aprensión *f* apprehension.

apresar *vt* to seize, grasp.

apresurar *vt* to accelerate, hasten, expedite:—**~se** *vr* to hurry.

apretar *vt* to compress, tighten; to constrain:—*vi* to be too tight.

aprisa *adv* quickly, swiftly; promptly.

aprobar *vt* to approve; to pass:—*vi* to pass.

apropiado, da *adj* appropriate.

aprovechar *vt* to use; to exploit; to profit from; to take advantage of:—*vi* to be useful; to progress:—**~se** *vr* **~ de** to use; to take advantage of.

aproximar *vt* to approach:—**~se** *vr* to approach.

aptitud *f* aptitude, fitness, ability.

apto, ta *adj* apt; fit, able; clever.

apuesta *f* bet, wager.

apuñalar *vt* to stab.

apuntar *vt* to aim; to level, point at; to mark:—*vi* to begin to appear or show itself; to prompt (theatre):—**~se** *vr* to score; to enrol.

apurado, da *adj* poor, destitute of means; exhausted; hurried.

aquél, ~ la *pn* that (one):—**~ los, ~ las** *pl* those (ones).

aquel, ~la *adj* that:—**~los, ~las** *pl* those.

aquello *pn* that.

aquí *adv* here; now.

árabe *adj, m/f, m* (*ling*) Arab, Arabic.

arado *m* plough.

araña *f* spider; chandelier.

arañar *vt* to scratch; to scrape; to corrode.

arancel *m* tariff.

arandela *f* washer.

arar *vt* to plough.

árbitro *m* arbitrator; referee; umpire.

árbol *m* tree; (*mar*) mast; shaft.

arbolado, da *adj* forested; wooded: —*m* woodland.

arbusto *m* shrub.

arca *f* chest, wooden box.

arcada *f* arch; arcade:—**~s** *fpl* retching.

arce *m* maple tree.

archivar *vt* to file.

arcilla *f* clay.

arco *m* arc; arch; fiddle bow; hoop: —**~ iris** rainbow.

arder *vi* to burn, blaze.

ardilla *f* squirrel.

área *f* area.

arena *f* sand; grit; arena.

arenque *m* herring:—**~ ahumado** red herring.

argolla *f* large ring.

argucia *f* subtlety.

argumentar *vt, vi* to argue, dispute; to conclude.

árido, da *adj* dry; barren.

arisco, ca *adj* fierce; rude; intractable.

arlequín *m* harlequin, buffoon.

arma *f* weapon, arms.

armado, da *adj* armed; reinforced.

armador *m* shipowner; privateer; jacket, jerkin.

armar *vt* to man; to arm; to fit:—**~la** to kick up a fuss.

armario *m* wardrobe; cupboard.

armazón *f* chassis; skeleton; frame.

armonía *f* harmony.

armonizar *vt* to harmonise; to reconcile.

arnés *m* harness:—**~eses** *mpl* gear, trappings *pl*.

aro *m* ring; earring.

aroma *m* aroma, fragrance.

arpa *f* harp.

arpía *f* (*poet*) harpy, shrew.

arpillera *f* sackcloth.

arpón *m* harpoon.

arqueado, da *adj* arched, vaulted.

arquero *m* archer.

arquitectónico, ca *adj* architectural.

arrabal *m* suburb; slum.

arraigado *adj* deep-rooted; established.

arraigar *vi* to root; to establish:—*vt* to establish;.

arrancar *vt* to pull up by the roots; to pull out:—*vi* to start; to move.

arrasar *vt* to demolish, destroy.

arrastrar *vt* to drag:—*vi* to creep, crawl; to lead a trump at cards:—**~se** *vr* to crawl; to grovel.

arrebatar *vt* to carry off, snatch; to enrapture.

arrebato *m* fury; rapture.

arrecife *m* reef.

arreglar *vt* to regulate; to tidy; to adjust:—**~se** *vr* to come to an understanding.

arrellanarse *vr* to sit at ease; to make oneself comfortable.

arrendar *vt* to rent, let out, lease.

arrendatario, ria *m/f* tenant.

arrepentirse *vr* to repent.

arrestar *vt* to arrest; to imprison.

arriate *m* flowerbed; causeway.

arriba *adv* above, over, up; high, on high, overhead; aloft.

arribista *m/f* upstart.

arriendo *m* lease; farm rent.

arriesgado *adj* risky, dangerous; daring.

arriesgar *vt* to risk, hazard; to expose to danger:—**~se** *vr* to take a chance.

arrimar *vt* to approach, draw near; (*mar*) to stow (cargo):—**~se** *vr* to sidle up; to lean.

arrinconar *vt* to put in a corner; to lay aside.

arrodillarse *vr* to kneel down.

arrogante *adj* arrogant; haughty, proud; stout.

arrojar *vt* to throw, fling; to dash; to emit; to shoot, sprout:—**~se** *vr* to hurl oneself.

arrollar *vt* to run over; to defeat heavily.

arropar *vt* to clothe, dress:—**~se** *vr* to wrap up.

arroyo *m* stream; gutter.

arroz *m* rice.

arrozal *m* ricefield.

arrugar *vt* to wrinkle; to rumple; to fold:—**~ la frente** to frown:—**~se** *vr* to shrivel.

arruinar *vt* to demolish; to ruin:—**~se** *vr* to go bankrupt.

arrullar *vt* to lull:—*vi* to coo.

artesanía *f* craftsmanship.

ártico, ca *adj* arctic, northern:—*m* **el A~** the Arctic.

articular *vt* to articulate; to joint.

artículo *m* article; clause; point; (*gr*) article; condition.

artífice *m* artisan; artist.

artificio *m* workmanship, craft; artifice, cunning trick.

artimaña *f* trap; cunning.

artista *m* artist; craftsman.

arzobispo *m* archbishop.

as *m* ace.

asa *f* handle; lever.

asado *m* roast meat; barbecue.

asaltar *vt* to assault; to storm (a position); to assail.

asamblea *f* assembly, meeting.

asar *vt* to roast.

ascender *vi* to be promoted; to rise:—*vt* to promote.

ascenso *m* promotion; ascent.

ascensor *m* elevator.

asco *m* nausea; loathing.

ascua *f* red-hot coal.

asear *vt* to clean; to tidy.

asedio *m* siege.

asegurar *vt* to secure; to insure; to affirm; to bail:—**~se** *vr* to make sure.

asentar *vt* to sit down; to affirm, assure; to note:—*vi* to suit.

asentir *vi* to acquiesce, concede.

aseo *m* cleanliness; neatness:—**~s** *mpl* toilets *pl*.

aséptico, ca *adj* germ-free.

asequible *adj* attainable; obtainable.

aserrar *vt* to saw.

aserrín *m* sawdust.

asesinar *vt* to assassinate; to murder.

asesorar *vt* to advise; to act as consultant:—**~se** *vr* to consult.

asfalto *m* asphalt.

asfixiar *vt* to suffocate:—**~se** *vr* to suffocate.

así *adv* so, thus, in this manner; like this; therefore; so that; also:—**~ que** so that; therefore:—**así, así** so-so; middling.

asiento *m* chair; bench, stool; seat; contract; entry; residence.

asignar *vt* to assign, attribute.

asignatura *f* subject; course.

asilo *m* asylum, refuge.

asimismo *adv* similarly, in the same manner.

asir *vt* to grasp, seize; to hold, grip:—*vi* to take root.

asistencia *f* audience; presence; assistance, help.

asistir *vi* to be present; to assist:—*vt* to help.

asma *f* asthma.

asno *m* ass.

asociación *f* association; partnership.

asolear *vt* to expose to the sun:—**~se** *vr* to sunbathe.

asomar *vi* to appear:—**~se** *vr* to appear, show up.

asombrar *vt* to amaze; to astonish:—~se *vr* to be amazed; to get a fright.

aspa *f* cross; sail.

aspecto *m* appearance; aspect.

áspero, ra *adj* rough, rugged; craggy, knotty; horrid; harsh, hard; severe, austere; gruff.

aspiración *f* breath; pause.

asqueroso, sa *adj* disgusting.

asta *f* lance; horn; handle.

astilla *f* chip (of wood), splinter.

astillero *m* dockyard.

astral *adj* astral.

astro *m* star.

astrología *m* astrology.

astronomía *f* astronomy.

astucia *f* cunning, slyness.

astuto, ta *adj* cunning, sly; astute.

asumir *vt* to assume.

asunto *m* subject, matter; affair, business.

asustar *vt* to frighten:—~se *vr* to be frightened.

atacar *vt* to attack.

atajo *m* short cut.

atañer *vi*:—~ a to concern.

atar *vt* to tie; to fasten.

atardecer *vi* to get dark:—*m* dusk; evening.

atascar *vt* to jam; to hinder:—~se *vr* to become bogged down.

ataúd *m* coffin.

atemorizar *vt* to frighten:—~se *vr* to get scared.

atención *f* attention, heedfulness; civility; observance, consideration.

atender *vi* to be attentive:—*vt* to attend to; to heed, expect, wait for; to look at.

atenerse *vr*:—~ a to adhere to.

atentamente *adv*:—le saluda ~ yours faithfully.

atento, ta *adj* attentive; heedful; observing; mindful; polite, courteous, mannerly.

atenuar *vt* to diminish; to lessen.

ateo, a *adj, m / f* atheist.

aterciopelado, da *adj* velvety.

aterrar *vt* to terrify:—~se *vr* to be terrified.

aterrizar *vi* to land.

aterrorizar *vt* to frighten, terrify.

atesorar *vt* to treasure *or* hoard up (riches).

atestado, da *adj* packed:—*m* affidavit.

atestiguar *vt* to witness, attest.

atiborrar *vt* to stuff:—~se *vr* to stuff oneself.

ático *m* attic.

atinado, da *adj* wise; correct.

atizar *vt* to stir (the fire) with a poker; to stir up.

atlántico, ca *adj* atlantic.

atleta *m* athlete.

atletismo *m* athletics.

atomizador *m* spray.

átomo *m* atom.

atónito, ta *adj* astonished, amazed.

atontado, da *adj* stunned; silly.

atornillar *vt* to screw on; to screw down.

atosigar *vt* to poison; to harass; to oppress.

atracar *vt* to moor; to rob:—~se *vr* ~ (de) to stuff oneself (with).

atractivo, va *adj* attractive; magnetic:—*m* charm.

atraer *vt* to attract, allure.

atragantarse *vr* to stick in the throat, choke.

atrapar *vt* to trap; to nab; to deceive.

atrás *adv* backward(s); behind; previously:—**hacia** ~ backward(s).

atrasar *vi* to be slow:—*vt* to postpone: —~ **el reloj** to put back a watch:—~se *vr* to stay behind; to be late.

atravesado, da *adj* oblique; cross; perverse; mongrel; degenerate.

atravesar *vt* to cross; to pass over; to pierce; to go through:—~se *vr* to get in the way; to meddle.

atreverse *vr* to dare, venture.

atribuir *vt* to attribute, ascribe; to impute.

atril *m* lectern; bookrest.

atrio *m* porch; portico.

atrocidad *f* atrocity.

atropellar *vt* to trample; to run down; to hurry; to insult:—~se *vr* to hurry.

atroz *adj* atrocious, heinous; cruel.

atuendo *m* attire.

atún *m* tuna (fish).

aturdir *vt* to stun, confuse; to stupefy.

audaz *adj* audacious, bold.

audiencia *f* audience.

auge *m* boom; climax.

augurio *m* omen.

aula *f* lecture room.

aullar *vi* to howl.

aumentar *vt* to augment, increase; to magnify; to put up:—*vi* to increase; to grow larger.

aún *adv* even:—~ **asi** even so.

aunque *adv* though, although.

auricular *m* receiver:——~es *mpl* headphones *pl*.

aurora *f* dawn.

ausencia *f* absence.

ausente *adj* absent.

auspicio *m* auspice; prediction; protection.

austero, ra *adj* austere, severe.

auténtico, ca *adj* authentic.

autoadhesivo, va *adj* self-adhesive.

autobús *m* bus.

autocar *m* bus, coach.

autóctono, na *adj* native.

autodefensa *f* self-defence.

autodeterminación *f* self-determination.

autoescuela *f* driving school.

automovilismo *m* motoring; motor racing.

autónomo, ma *adj* autonomous.

autopista *f* motorway.

autopsia *f* post mortem, autopsy.

autor, ra *m/f* author; maker; writer.

autoridad *f* authority.

autorizar *vt* to authorise.

autorretrato *m* self-portrait.

autoservicio *m* self-service store; restaurant.

autostop *m* hitch-hiking.

autosuficiencia *f* self-sufficiency.

autovía *f* state highway.

auxiliar *vt* to aid, help, assist; to attend:——*adj* auxiliary.

aval *m* guarantee; guarantor.

avanzar *vt, vi* to advance.

avaricia *f* avarice.

avaro, ra *adj* miserly:——*m/f* miser.

ave *f* bird; fowl.

avecinarse *vr* to approach.

avellana *f* hazelnut.

avena *f* oats *pl*.

avenida *f* avenue.

aventajar *vt* to surpass, excel.

aventura *f* adventure; event, incident.

avergonzar *vt* to shame, abash:——~se *vr* to be ashamed.

avería *f* breakdown.

averiado, da *adj* broken down; out of order.

averiguar *vt* to find out; to inquire into; to investigate.

avestruz *m* ostrich.

aviación *f* aviation; air force.

avicultura *f* poultry farming.

avidez *f* covetousness.

avinagrado, da *adj* sour.

avión *m* aeroplane.

avioneta *f* light aircraft.

avisar *vt* to inform; to warn; to advise.

aviso *m* notice; warning; hint.

avispa *f* wasp.

avispado, da *adj* lively, brisk; vivacious.

¡ay! *excl* alas!; ow!:——¡~ **de mi!** alas! poor me!

ayer *adv* yesterday.

ayuda *f* help, aid; support:——*m* deputy, assistant.

ayudar *vt* to help, assist; to further.

ayunar *vi* to fast, abstain from food.

ayuntamiento *m* town/city hall.

azabache *m* jet.

azafata *f* air hostess.

azafrán *m* saffron.

azahar *m* orange or lemon blossom.

azar *m* fate:——**por ~** by chance:——**al ~** at random.

azotar *vt* to whip, lash.

azotea *f* flat roof of a house.

azúcar *m* sugar.

azufre *m* sulphur, brimstone.

azul *adj* blue:——~ **celeste** sky blue.

azulejo *m* tile.

B

baba *f* dribble, spittle.

babero *m* bib.

babia *f*:—**estar en ~** to be absent-minded *or* dreaming.

baca *f* (*auto*) roof rack.

bacalao *m* cod.

bache *m* pothole.

bachillerato *m* baccalaureate.

bahía *f* bay.

bailar *vi* to dance.

bailarín, ina *m*/*f* dancer.

baja *f* fall; casualty.

bajada *f* descent; inclination; slope; ebb.

bajamar *f* low tide.

bajar *vt* to lower, let down; to lessen; to humble; to go/come down.

bajo, ja *adj* low; abject, despicable; common; humble:—*prep* under, underneath, below:—*adv* softly; quietly:—*m* (*mus*) bass; low place.

bala *f* bullet.

balance *m* hesitation; balance sheet; balance; rolling (of a ship).

balanza *f* scale; balance; judgement.

balar *vi* to bleat.

balcón *m* balcony.

balde *m* bucket:—**de ~** *adv* gratis, for nothing:—**en ~** in vain.

baldío, dia *adj* waste; uncultivated.

baldosa *f* floor; tile; flagstone.

ballena *f* whale; whalebone.

balneario *m* spa.

baloncesto *m* basketball.

balonmano *m* handball.

balonvolea *m* volleyball.

balsa *f* balsa wood; pool; raft, float; ferry.

bañador *m* swimsuit.

bañar *vt* to bathe; to dip; to coat (with varnish):—**~se** *vr* to bathe; to swim.

bancarrota *f* bankruptcy.

banco *m* bench; work bench; bank.

banda *f* band; sash; ribbon; troop; party; gang; touchline.

bandada *f* flock; shoal.

bandeja *f* tray, salver.

bandera *f* banner, standard; flag.

bando *m* faction, party; edict.

bandolero *m* bandit.

bañera *f* bath (tub).

baño *m* bath; dip; bathtub; varnish; crust of sugar; coating.

banqueta *f* three-legged stool; pavement, sidewalk.

banquete *m* banquet; formal dinner.

banquillo *m* dock.

bar *m* bar.

baraja *f* pack of cards.

barandilla *f* small balustrade, small railing.

barato, ta *adj* cheap:—**de ~** gratis:—*m* cheapness; bargain sale.

barba *f* chin; beard:—**~ a ~** face to face.

barbaridad *f* barbarity, barbarism; outrage.

bárbaro, ra *adj* barbarous; cruel; rude; rough.

barbecho *m* first ploughing, fallow land.

barbero *m* barber.

barbilampiño, ña *adj* clean-shaven; (*fig*) inexperienced.

barbilla *f* chin.

barca *f* boat.

barco *m* boat; ship.

barnis *m* varnish; glaze.

barómetro *m* barometer.

barquillo *m* wafer; cornet, cone.

barra *m* bar; rod; lever; French loaf; sandbank.

barraca *f* hut.

barranco *m* gully, ravine; (*fig*) great difficulty.

barrenar *vt* to drill, bore; (*fig*) to frustrate.

barrendero *m* sweeper, garbage man.

barrer *vt* to sweep.

barrera *f* barrier; turnpike, claypit.

barriga *f* abdomen; belly.

barril *m* barrel; cask.

barrio *m* area, district.

barro *m* clay, mud.

barrote *m* ironwork of doors, windows, tables; crosspiece.

barruntar *vt* to guess; to foresee; to conjecture.

bártulos *mpl* gear, belongings *pl*.

barullo *m* uproar.

basar *vt* to base:—~**se** *vr* ~ **en** to be based on.

báscula *f* scales *pl*.

base *f* base, basis.

básico, ca *adj* basic.

bastante *adj* sufficient, enough:—*adv* quite.

bastar *vi* to be sufficient, be enough.

bastidor *m* embroidery frame:—~**es** *mpl* scenery (on stage).

basto, ta *adj* coarse, rude, unpolished.

bastón *m* cane, stick; truncheon; (*fig*) command.

bastos *mpl* clubs *pl* (one of the four suits at cards).

basura *f* rubbish; trash.

bata *f* dressing gown; overall; laboratory coat.

batalla *f* battle, combat; fight.

batata *f* sweet potato.

batería *m* battery; percussion.

batir *vt* to beat; to whisk; to dash; to demolish; to defeat.

baúl *m* trunk.

bautisar *vt* to baptise, christen.

baza *f* card-trick.

bazo *m* spleen.

beato, ta *adj* happy; blessed; devout: —*m* lay brother:— *m/f* pious person.

bebé *m/f* baby.

beber *vt* to drink.

bebida *f* drink, beverage.

beca *f* fellowship; grant, bursary, scholarship; sash; hood.

bedel *m* head porter; uniformed employee.

belén *m* nativity scene.

bélico, ca *adj* warlike, martial.

belladona *f* (*bot*) deadly nightshade.

belleza *f* beauty.

bello, lla *adj* beautiful; handsome; lovely; fine.

bellota *f* acorn.

bemol *m* (*mus*) flat.

bendecir *vt* to bless; to consecrate; to praise.

bendito, ta *adj* saintly; blessed; simple; happy.

beneficiar *vt* to benefit; to be of benefit to.

beneficio *m* benefit, advantage; profit; benefit night.

beneficioso, sa *adj* beneficial.

beneplácito *m* consent, approbation.

benévolo, la *adj* benevolent, kind-hearted.

benigno, na *adj* benign; kind; mild.

berberecho *m* cockle.

berenjena *f* eggplant.

bergantín *m* (*mar*) brig.

berrear *vi* to low, bellow.

berrinche *m* anger, rage, tantrum (applied to children).

berrinchudo, da *adj* bad tempered.

berro *m* watercress.

berza *f* cabbage.

besar *vt* to kiss:—~**se** *vr* to kiss.

bestia *f* beast, animal; idiot.

besugo *m* sea bream.

betún *m* shoe polish.

biberón *m* feeding bottle.

bibliófilo, la *m/f* booklover, bookworm.

bibliografía *f* bibliography.

biblioteca *f* library.

bicarbonato *m* bicarbonate.

bicho *m* small animal; bug:—**mal** ~ villain.

bici *f* (*fam*) bike.

bicicleta *f* bicycle.

bidé *m* bidet.

bien *m* good, benefit; profit:—~**es** *mpl* goods *pl*, property; wealth:—*adv* well, right; very; willingly; easily:—~ **que** *conj* although:—**está** ~ very well.

bienestar *m* well-being.

bienhechor, ra *m/f* benefactor.

bienvenida *f* welcome.

bifurcación *f* fork.

bigote *m* moustache; whiskers *pl*.

bilingüe *adj* bilingual.

bilis *f* bile.

billar *m* billiards *pl*.

billete *m* note, banknote; ticket; (*ferro*) ticket:—~ **sencillo** single ticket:—~ **de ida y vuelta** return ticket.

biografía *f* biography.

biología *f* biology.

biombo *m* screen.

birlar *vt* to knock down at one blow; to pinch (*fam*).

bis *excl* encore.

bisabuela *f* great-grandmother.

bisabuelo *m* great-grandfather.

bisagra *f* hinge.

bisiesto *adj*:—**año** ~ leap year.

bisnieto, ta *m/f* great-grandson/daughter.

bistec *m* steak.

bisturí *m* scalpel.

bisutería *f* costume jewellery.

bisco, ca *adj* cross-eyed.

biscocho *m* sponge cake; biscuit; ship's biscuit.

blanco, ca *adj* white; blank:—*m* whiteness; white person; blank, blank space; target (to shoot at).

blando, da *adj* soft, smooth; mild, gentle; (*fam*) cowardly.

blanquear *vt* to bleach; to whitewash; to launder (money).

blasfemar *vi* to blaspheme.

bledo *m*:—**no me importa un ~** I don't give a damn (*sl*).

blindado, da *adj* armour-plated; bullet-proof.

bloc *m* writing pad.

bloque *m* block.

bloquear *vt* to block; to blockade.

blusa *f* blouse.

bobada *f* folly, foolishness.

bobina *f* bobbin.

bobo, ba *m/f* idiot, fool; clown, funny man:—*adj* stupid, silly.

boca *f* mouth; entrance, opening; mouth of a river:—**~ en ~** *adv* by word of mouth:—**a pedir de ~** to one's heart's content.

bocacalle *f* entrance to a street.

bocadillo *m* sandwich, roll.

bocado *m* mouthful.

bocazas *m invar* big-mouth.

boceto *m* sketch; design; mock-up.

bochorno *m* sultry weather, scorching heat; blush.

bocina *f* (*mus*) trumpet; (*auto*) horn.

bocinar *vi* to sound a horn, hoot.

boda *f* wedding.

bodega *f* wine cellar; warehouse; bar.

bofetada *f* slap (in the face).

boina *f* beret.

boj *m* box, box tree.

bola *f* ball; marble; globe; (*fam*) lie, fib.

bolera *f* bowling alley.

bolero *m* bolero jacket; bolero dance.

boletín *m* bulletin; journal, review.

boleto *m* ticket.

boliche *m* jack at bowls; bowls, bowling alley; dragnet.

bolígrafo *m* (ballpoint) pen.

bollo *m* bread roll; lump.

bolo *m* ninepin; (large) pill.

bolsa *f* handbag; bag; pocket sac; stock exchange.

bolsillo *m* pocket; purse.

bomba *f* pump; bomb; surprise:—**dar a la ~** to pump:—**~ de gaso- lina** petrol pump.

bombero *m* fireman.

bombilla *f* light bulb.

bombo *m* large drum.

bombón *m* chocolate.

bondad *f* goodness, kindness; courtesy.

bondadoso, sa *adj* good, kind.

boñiga *f* cow pat.

bonito *adj* pretty, nice-looking; pretty good, passable:—*m* tuna (fish).

boquerón *m* anchovy; large hole.

boquilla *f* mouthpiece of a musical instrument; nozzle.

borde *m* border; margin; (*mar*) board.

bordear *vi* (*mar*) to tack:—*vt* to go along the edge of; to flank.

bordillo *m* kerb.

bordo *m* (*mar*) board of a ship.

boreal *adj* boreal, northern.

borracho, cha *adj* drunk, intoxicated; blind with passion:—*m/f* drunk, drunkard.

borrador *m* first draft; scribbling pad; eraser.

borrar *vt* to erase, rub out; to blur; to obscure.

borrasca *f* storm; violent squall of wind; hazard; danger.

borrico, ca *m/f* donkey, ass; blockhead.

borrón *m* blot, blur.

bosque *m* forest; wood.

bosquejo *m* sketch (of a painting); unfinished work.

bostezar *vi* to yawn; to gape.

bota *f* leather wine-bag; boot.

botánica *f* botany.

bote *m* bounce; thrust; tin, can; boat.

botella *f* bottle.

botijo *m* earthenware jug.

botín *m* high boot, half-boot; gaiter; booty.

botiquín *m* medicine chest.

botón *m* button; knob (of a radio etc); (*bot*) bud.

bóveda *f* arch; vault, crypt.

boxeo *m* boxing.

boya *f* (*mar*) buoy.

boyante *adj* buoyant, floating; (*fig*) fortunate, successful.

bozo *m* down (on the upper lip or chin); headstall (of a horse).

braga *f* sling, rope; nappy, diaper:—**~s** *fpl* breeches *pl*; panties *pl*.

bragueta *f* fly, flies *pl* (of trousers).

brasa *f* live coal:—**estar hecho una ~** to be very flushed.

bravío, vía *adj* ferocious, savage, wild; coarse.

bravo, va *adj* brave, valiant; bullying; savage, fierce; rough; sumptuous; excellent, fine:—*excl* well done!

braza *f* fathom.

brazo *m* arm; branch (of a tree); enterprise; courage:—**luchar a ~ par-tido** to fight hand-to-hand.

brea *f* pitch; tar.

brebaje *m* potion.

brecha *f* (*mil*) breach; gap, opening.

breva *f* early fig; early large acorn.

breve *m* papal brief:—*f* (*mus*) breve: —*adj* brief, short:—**en ~** shortly.

brezo *m* (*bot*) heather.

bribón, ona *adj* dishonest, rascally.

bricolaje *m* do-it-yourself.

brida *f* bridle; clamp, flange.

brigada *f* brigade; squad, gang.

brillante *adj* brilliant; bright, shining:—*m* diamond.

brillar *vi* to shine; to sparkle, glisten; to shine, be outstanding.

brincar *vi* to skip; to leap, jump; to gambol; to fly into a passion.

brindis *m invar* toast.

brío *m* spirit, dash.

brisca *f* card game.

broca *f* reel; drill; shoemaker's tack.

brocado *m* gold or silver brocade:—**~, da** *adj* embroidered, like brocade.

brocha *f* large brush:—**~ de afeitar** shaving brush.

broche *m* clasp; brooch; cufflink.

broma *f* joke.

bromear *vi* to joke.

bronca *f* row.

bronceado, da *adj* tanned:—*m* bronzing, suntan.

brotar *vi* (*bot*) to bud, germinate; to gush, rush out; (*med*) to break out.

bruces *adv*:—**a ~, de ~** face down-ward(s).

bruja *f* witch.

brújula *f* compass.

bruma *f* mist; (*mar*) sea mist.

bruñir *vt* to polish; to put rouge on.

brusco, ca *adj* rude; sudden; brusque.

brutal *adj* brutal, brutish:—*m* brute.

bruto *m* brute, beast:—**~, ta** *adj* stupid; gross; brutish.

bucal *adj* oral.

bucear *vi* to dive.

bucle *m* curl.

buen *adj* (*before m nouns*) good.

bueno, na *adj* good, perfect; fair; fit, proper; good-looking:—**¡buenos días!** good morning!:—**¡buenas tardes!** good afternoon:—**¡buenas noches!** good night!:—**¡~!** right!

buey *m* ox, bullock.

bufanda *f* scarf.

bufete *m* desk, writing-table; lawyer's office.

bufo, fa *adj* comic:—**opera ~a** *f* comic opera.

buhardilla *f* attic.

búho *m* owl; unsocial person.

buitre *m* vulture.

bujía *f* candle; spark plug.

bullicio *m* bustle; uproar.

bulto *m* bulk; tumour, swelling; bust; baggage.

buñuelo *m* doughnut; fritter.

buque *m* vessel, ship, tonnage, capacity (of a ship); hull (of a ship).

burbuja *f* bubble.

burdel *m* brothel.

burguesía *f* bourgeoisie.

burlar *vt* to hoax; to defeat; to play tricks on, deceive; to frustrate:—**~se** *vr* to joke, laugh at.

burro *m* ass, donkey; idiot; saw-horse.

bursátil *adj* stock exchange *compd*.

buscar *vt* to seek, search for; to look for; to hunt after:—*vi* to look, search, seek.

busilis *m* difficulty, snag.

busto *m* bust.

butaca *f* armchair; seat.

butano *m* butane.

butifarra *f* Catalan sausage.

butrón *m* burglary.

buzo *m* diver.

buzón *m* mailbox; conduit, canal; cover of a jar.

C

cabalgar *vi* to ride, go riding.

cabalgata *f* procession.

caballa *f* mackerel.

caballería *f* mount, steed; cavalry; cavalry horse; chivalry; knighthood.

caballero *m* knight; gentleman; rider, horseman.

caballete *m* ridge of a roof; painter's easel; trestle; bridge (of the nose).

caballo *m* horse; (at chess) knight; queen (in cards):—**a ~** on horseback.

cabecera *f* headboard; head; far end; pillow; headline; vignette.

cabecilla *m* ringleader.

cabello *m* hair.

caber *vi* to fit.

cabeza *f* head; chief, leader; main town, chief centre.

cabida *f* room, capacity.

cabildo *m* chapter (of church); meeting of a chapter; corporation of a town.

cabina *f* cabin; telephone booth.

cabizbajo, ja, cabizcaido, da *adj* crestfallen; pensive, thought-ful.

cable *m* cable, lead, wire.

cabo *m* end, extremity; cape, headland; (*mar*) cable, rope.

cabra *f* goat.

cabrón *m* cuckold:—¡~! (*fam*) bastard! (*sl*).

cacahuete *m* peanut.

cacao *m* (*bot*) cacao tree; cocoa.

cacarear *vi* to crow; to brag, boast.

cacerola *f* pan, saucepan; casserole.

cachalote *m* sperm whale.

cacharro *m* pot.

cachivache *m* pot; piece of junk.

cachondo, da *adj* randy; funny.

cachorro, ra *m/f* puppy; cub.

caco *m* pickpocket; coward.

cada *adj invar* each; every.

cadáver *m* corpse, cadaver.

cadena *f* chain; series, link; radio or TV network.

cadera *f* hip.

caducar *vi* to become senile; to expire, lapse; to deteriorate.

caer *vi* to fall; to tumble down; to lapse; to happen; to die:—**~se** *vr* to fall down.

café *m* coffee; cafe, coffee house.

cafetera *f* coffee pot.

cagar *vi* (*fam*) to have a shit (*sl*).

caimán *m* caiman, alligator.

caja *f* box, case; casket; cashbox; cash desk; supermarket check-out: —**~ de ahorros** savings bank:—**~ de cambios** gearbox.

cajón *m* chest of drawers; locker.

cal *f* lime:—**~ viva** quick lime.

calabacín *m* small marrow, courgette.

calabaza *f* pumpkin, squash.

calamar *m* squid.

calar *vt* to soak, drench; to penetrate, pierce; to see through; to lower:—**~se** *vr* to stall (of a car).

calavera *f* skull; madcap.

calcar *vt* to trace, copy.

calcetín *m* sock.

calcio *m* calcium.

calcomanía *f* transfer.

calculadora *f* calculator.

calcular *vt* to calculate, reckon; to compute.

caldear *vt* to weld; to warm, heat up.

calderada *f* stew.

calderilla *f* small change.

caldo *m* stock; broth.

calefacción *f* heating.

calendario *m* calendar.

calentar *vt* to warm up, heat up:—**~se** *vr* to grow hot; to dispute.

calidad *f* grade, quality, condition; kind.

cálido, da *adj* hot; (*fig*) warm.

caliente *adj* hot; fiery:—**en ~** in the heat of the moment.

callado, da *adj* silent, quiet.

callar *vi*, **~se** *vr* to be silent, keep quiet.

calle *f* street; road.

callejear *vi* to loiter about the streets.

callejón *m* alley.

callo *m* corn; callus:—**~s** *mpl* tripe.

calmante *m* (*med*) sedative.

calmar *vt* to calm, quiet, pacify:—*vi* to become calm.

calor *m* heat, warmth; ardour, passion.

calumnia *f* calumny, slander.

calvo, va *adj* bald; bare, barren.

calzado *m* footwear.

calzoncillos *mpl* underpants, shorts *pl*.

cama *f* bed:—**hacer la ~** to make the bed.

cámara *f* hall; chamber; room; camera; cine camera.

camarada *m/f* comrade, companion.

camarera *f* waitress.

camarero *m* waiter.

camarón *m* shrimp, prawn.

camarote *m* berth, cabin.

cambalache *m* exchange, swap.

cambiar *vt* to exchange; to change:—*vi* to change, alter:—**~se** *vr* to move house.

cambio *m* change, exchange; rate of exchange; bureau de change.

camelar *vt* to flirt with.

camello *m* camel; drug dealer.

camilla *f* couch; cot; stretcher.

caminar *vi* to travel; to walk, go.

camino *m* road; way.

camión *m* truck.

camisa *f* shirt; chemise.

camiseta *f* T-shirt; vest.

camisón *m* nightgown.

campamento *m* (*mil*) encampment.

campana *f* bell.

campanario *m* belfry.

campeón, ona *m/f* champion.

campesino, na, campestre *adj* rural.

campo *m* country; field; camp; ground; pitch.

caña *f* cane, reed; stalk; shinbone; glass of beer:—**~ dulce** sugar cane.

cañada *f* gully; glen; sheepwalk.

canal *m* channel, canal.

canalla *f* mob, rabble.

cáñamo *m* hemp.

canas *fpl* grey hair:—**peinar ~** to grow old.

cañaveral *m* reedbed.

cancelar *vt* to cancel; to write off.

cancha *f* (tennis) court.

canción *f* song.

candado *m* padlock.

candilejas *fpl* footlights *pl*.

canela *f* cinnamon.

cangrejo *m* crab; crayfish.

canica *f* marble.

canilla *f* shinbone; armbone; tap of a cask; spool.

canjear *vt* to exchange.

cano, na *adj* grey-haired; white-haired.

canoso, sa *adj* grey-haired; white-haired.

cansancio *m* tiredness, fatigue.

cansar *vt* to tire, tire out; to bore:—**~se** *vr* to get tired, grow weary.

cantante *m/f* singer.

cantar *m* song:—*vt* to sing; to chant: —*vi* to sing; to chirp.

cántaro *m* pitcher; jug:—**llover a ~s** to rain heavily, pour.

cantera *f* quarry.

cantidad *f* quantity, amount; number.

cantina *f* buffet, refreshment room; canteen; cellar; snack bar; bar.

canto *m* stone; singing; song; edge.

canuto *m* (*fam*) joint (*sl*), marijuana cigarette.

caño *m* tube, pipe; sewer.

cañón *m* tube, pipe; barrel; gun; canyon.

caoba *f* mahogany.

caos *m* chaos; confusion.

capa *f* cloak; cape; layer, stratum; cover; pretext.

capacidad *f* capacity; extent; talent.

capataz *m* foreman, overseer.

capaz *adj* capable; capacious, spacious, roomy.

capeo *m* challenging of a bull with a cloak.

caperuza *f* hood.

capirote *m* hood.

capital *m* capital; capital sum:—*f* capital, capital city:—*adj* capital; principal.

capítulo *m* chapter of a cathedral; chapter (of a book).

capó *m* (*auto*) bonnet.

capote *m* greatcoat; bullfighter's cloak.

capricho *m* caprice, whim, fancy.

captar *vt* to captivate; to understand; (*rad*) to tune in to, receive.

capturar *vt* to capture.

capucha *f* cap, cowl, hood of a cloak.

capullo *m* cocoon of a silkworm; rosebud.

cara *f* face; appearance:—**~ a ~** face to face.

cárabe *m* amber.

caracol *m* snail; seashell; spiral.

carácter *m* character; quality; condition; hand-writing.

característico, ca *adj* characteristic.

caradura *m/f:*—**es un ~** he's got a nerve.

caramba *excl* well!

carámbano *m* icicle.

carambola *f* cannon (at billiards); trick.

caravana *f* caravan; tailback (traffic).

carbón *m* coal; charcoal; carbon; carbon paper.

carboncillo *m* charcoal.

carbono *m* (*quim*) carbon.

carburador *m* carburettor.

carcajada *f* (loud) laugh.

cárcel *f* prison; jail.

carcoma *f* deathwatch beetle; woodworm; anxious concern.

cardenal *m* cardinal; cardinal bird; (*med*) bruise, weal.

cardo *m* thistle.

carecer *vi:*—**~ de** to want, lack.

cargar *vt* to load, burden; to charge: —*vi* to charge; to load (up); to lean.

cargo *m* burden, loading; employment, post; office; charge, care; obligation; accusation.

carguero *m* freighter.

caricia *f* caress.

caridad *f* charity.

caries *f* (*med*) tooth decay, caries.

cariño *m* fondness, tenderness; love.

carmesí *adj, m* crimson.

carmín *m* carmine; rouge; lipstick.

carne *f* flesh; meat; pulp (of fruit).

carné, carnet *m* driving licence:—**~ de identidad** identity card.

carnicería *f* butcher's shop; carnage, slaughter.

caro, ra *adj* dear; affectionate; dear, expensive:—*adv* dearly.

carpa *f* carp (fish); tent.

carpeta *f* table cover; folder, file, portfolio.

carpintero *m* carpenter.

carraca *f* carrack (ship); rattle.

carrera *f* career; course; race; run, running; route; journey:—**a ~ abierta**, at full speed.

carrete *m* reel, spool, bobbin.

carretera *f* highway.

carril *m* lane (of highway); furrow.

carrillo *m* cheek; pulley.

carro *m* cart; car.

carrocería *f* bodywork, coachwork.

carta *f* letter; map; document; playing card; menu:—**~ blanca** carte blanche:—**~ credencial** *o* **de creencia** credentials *pl:*—**~ certificada** registered letter:—**~ de crédito** credit card:—**~ verde** green card.

cartabón *m* square (tool).

cartel *m* placard; poster; wall chart; cartel.

cartera *f* satchel; handbag; briefcase.

carterista *m/f* pickpocket.

cartero *m* postman.

cartón *m* cardboard, pasteboard; cartoon.

casa *f* house; home; firm, company: —**~ de campo** country house:—**~ de moneda** mint:—**~ de huéspedes** boarding house.

casar *vt* to marry; to couple; to abrogate; to annul:—**~se** *vr* to marry, get married.

cascabel *m* small bell; rattlesnake.

cascada *f* cascade, waterfall.

cascanueces *m invar* nutcracker.

cascar *vt* to crack, break into pieces; (*fam*) to beat:—**~se** *vr* to be broken open.

cáscara *f* rind, peel; husk, shell; bark.

casco *m* skull; helmet; fragment; shard; hulk (of a ship); crown (of a hat); hoof; empty bottle, returnable bottle.

cascote *m* rubble, fragment of material used in building.

caserío *m* country house; hamlet.

casero *m* landlord; janitor:—**~, ra**, *adj* domestic; household *compd*; home-made.

caset(t)e *m* cassette:—*f* cassette-player.

casi *adv* almost, nearly:—**~ nada** next to nothing:—**~ nunca** hardly ever, almost never.

caso *m* case; occurrence, event; hap, casuality; occasion; (*gr*) case:—**en ese ~** in that case:—**en todo ~** in any case:—**~ que** in case.

caspa *f* dandruff; scurf.

castaño *m* chestnut tree:—**~, na** *adj* chestnut(-coloured), brown.

castañuela *f* castanet.

castellano *m* Castilian, Spanish.

castigar *vt* to castigate, punish; to afflict.

castillo *m* castle.

castizo, za *adj* pure, thoroughbred.

casto, ta *adj* pure, chaste.

castor *m* beaver.

castrar *vt* to geld, castrate; to prune; to cut the honeycombs out of (beehives).

casualidad *f* chance, accident.

cataplasma *f* poultice.

catar *vt* to taste; to inspect, examine; to look at; to esteem.

catarata *f* (*med*) cataract; waterfall.

catarro *m* catarrh; cold.

cátedra *f* professor's chair.

categoría *f* category; rank.

católico, ca *adj*, *m*/*f* catholic.

catorce *adj*, *m* fourteen.

catre *m* cot.

cauce *m* riverbed; (*fig*) channel.

caucho *m* rubber; tyre.

caudal *m* volume, flow; property, wealth; plenty.

causa *f* cause; motive, reason; lawsuit:—**a ~ de** considering, because of.

causar *vt* to cause; to produce; to occasion.

cautela *f* caution, cautiousness.

cautivar *vt* to take prisoner in war; to captivate, charm.

cauto, ta *adj* cautious, wary.

cavar *vt* to dig up, excavate:—*vi* to dig, delve; to think profoundly.

caverna *f* cavern, cave.

cavidad *f* cavity, hollow.

cavilar *vt* to ponder, consider carefully.

cazador, ra *m*/*f* hunter; *m* huntsman: —**~ furtivo** poacher.

cazar *vt* to chase, hunt; to catch.

cazo *m* saucepan; ladle.

cazuela *f* casserole; pan.

cebada *f* barley.

cebar *vt* to feed (animals), fatten.

cebo *m* feed, food; bait, lure; priming.

cebolla *f* onion; bulb.

cebra *f* zebra.

cedazo *m* sieve, strainer.

ceder *vt* to hand over; to transfer, make over; to yield, give up:—*vi* to submit, comply, give in; to diminish, grow less.

cedro *m* cedar.

cédula *f* certificate; document; slip of paper; bill:— **~ de cambio** bill of exchange.

cegar *vi* to grow blind:—*vt* to blind; to block up.

ceja *f* eyebrow.

cejar *vi* to go backward(s); to slacken, give in.

celebrar *vt* to celebrate; to praise.—**~ misa** to say mass.

célebre *adj* famous, renowned; witty, funny.

celeste *adj* heavenly; sky-blue.

celestial *adj* heavenly; delightful.

celo *m* zeal; rut (in animals):—**~s** *mpl* jealousy.

celoso, sa *adj* zealous; jealous.

célula *f* cell.

cementerio *m* graveyard.

cena *f* supper.

cenar *vt* to have for dinner:—*vi* to have supper, have dinner.

cenegal *m* quagmire.

cenicero *m* ashtray.

ceniza *f* ashes *pl*:—**miércoles de ~** Ash Wednesday.

censo *m* census; tax; ground rent:—**~ electoral** electoral roll.

censurar *vt* to review, criticise; to censure, blame.

centella *f* lightning; spark.

centenar *m* hundred.

centeno *m* rye.

centésimo, ma *adj* hundredth:—*m* hundredth.

centígrado *m* centigrade.

centímetro *m* centimetre.

céntimo *m* cent.

centinela *f* sentry, guard.

central *adj* central:—*f* head office, headquarters; (telephone) exchange.

centro *m* centre:—**~ comercial** shopping centre.

centuplicar *vt* to increase a hundredfold.

ceñido, da *adj* tight-fitting; sparing, frugal.

ceñudo, da *adj* frowning, grim.

cepa *f* stock (of a vine); origin (of a family).

cepillo *m* brush; plane (tool).

cepo *m* branch, bough; trap; snare; poorbox.

cera *f* wax:—**~s** *fpl* honeycomb.

cerámica *f* pottery.

cerca *f* enclosure; fence:—**~s** *mpl* objects *pl* in the foreground of a painting:—*adv* near, at hand, close by:—**~ de** close, near.

cercano, na *adj* near, close by; neighbouring, adjoining.

cerciorar *vt* to assure, ascertain, affirm:—**~se** *vr* to find out.

cerdo *m* pig.

cerebro *m* brain.

cereza *f* cherry.

cerilla *f* wax taper; ear wax:—**~s** *fpl* matches, safety matches *pl*.

cero *m* nothing, zero.

cerrado, da *adj* closed, shut; locked; overcast, cloudy; broad (of accent).

cerrajero *m* locksmith.

cerrar *vt* to close, shut; to block up; to lock:—**~ la cuenta** to close an account:—**~se** *vr* to close; to heal; to cloud over:—*vi* to close, shut; to lock.

cerro *m* hill; neck (of an animal); backbone; combed flax or hemp:—**en ~** bareback.

cerrojo *m* bolt (of a door).

certamen *m* competition, contest.

certero *adj* accurate; well-aimed.

certeza, certidumbre *f* certainty.

certificado *m* certificate:—**~, da** *adj* registered (of a letter).

cerveza *m* beer.

cesar *vt* to cease, stop; to fire (*sl*); to remove from office:—*vi* to cease, stop; to retire.

cese *m* suspension; dismissal.

cesión *f* cession; transfer.

césped *m* grass; lawn.

cesta *f* basket, pannier.

ciática *f* sciatica.

cicatriz *f* scar.

cicatrizar *vt* to heal.

ciclista *m/f* cyclist.

ciclo *m* cycle.

cicuta *f* (*bot*) hemlock.

ciego, ga *adj* blind.

cielo *m* sky; heaven; atmosphere; climate.

ciempiés *m invar* centipede.

cien *adj, m* a hundred.

ciénaga *f* swamp.

ciencia *f* science.

cieno *m* mud; mire.

cierto, ta *adj* certain, sure; right, correct:—**por ~** certainly.

ciervo *m* deer, hart, stag:—**~ volante** stag beetle.

cierzo *m* cold northerly wind.

cifra *f* number, numeral; quantity; cipher; abbreviation.

cigarra *f* cicada.

cigarro *m* cigar; cigarette.

cigüeña *f* stork; crank (of a bell).

cilindro *m* cylinder.

cima *f* summit; peak; top.

cimiento *m* foundation, groundwork; basis, origin.

cinc *m* zinc.

cincelar *vt* to chisel, engrave.

cinco *adj, m* five.

cincuenta *adj, m* fifty.

cine *m* cinema.

cínico, ca *adj* cynical.

cinta *f* band, ribbon; reel.

cintura *f* waist.

cinturón *m* belt, girdle; (*fig*) zone:—**~ de seguridad** seatbelt.

ciprés *m* cypress tree.

circo *m* circus.

circuito *m* circuit; circumference.

circular *adj* circular; circulatory:—*vt* to circulate:—*vi* (*auto*) to drive.

círculo *m* circle; (*fig*) scope, compass.

circunspecto, ta *adj* circumspect, cautious.

circunstancia *f* circumstance.

circunvalacion *f*:—**carretera de ~** bypass.

cirio *m* wax candle.

ciruela *f* plum:—**~ pasa** prune.

cirugía *f* surgery.

cisne *m* swan.

citar *vt* to make an appointment with; to quote; (*jur*) to summon.

ciudad *f* city; town.

ciudadano, na *m/f* citizen:—*adj* civic.

clamor *m* clamour, outcry; peal of bells.

clandestino, na *adj* clandestine, secret, concealed.

clara *f* egg-white.

claraboya *f* skylight.

clarear *vi* to dawn:—**~se** *vr* to be transparent.

clarín *m* bugle; bugler.

clarinete *m* clarinet:—*m/f* clarinetist.

claro, ra *adj* clear, bright; evident, manifest:—*m* opening; clearing (in a wood).

clase *f* class; rank; order.

clasificar *vt* to classify.

claudicar *vi* to limp; to act deceitfully; to back down.

claustro *m* cloister; faculty (of a university).

cláusula *f* clause.

clavar *vt* to nail.

clave *f* key; (*mus*) clef:—*m* harpsichord.

clavel *m* (*bot*) carnation.

clavicordio *m* clavichord.

clavícula *f* clavicle, collar bone.

clavija *f* pin, peg.

clavo *m* nail; corn (on the feet); clove.

clemente *adj* clement, merciful.

clérigo *m* priest; clergyman.

cliente *m/f* client.

clima *m* climate.

climatizado, da *adj* air-conditioned.

clínica *f* clinic; private hospital.

clip *m* paper clip.

cloaca *f* sewer.

coacción *f* coercion, compulsion.

coagular *vt*, ~**se** *vr* to coagulate; to curdle.

coartada *f* (*jur*) alibi.

coartar *vt* to limit, restrict, restrain.

cobalto *m* cobalt.

cobarde *adj* cowardly, timid.

cobaya *f* guinea pig.

cobertizo *m* small shed; shelter.

cobijar *vt* to cover; to shelter.

cobrar *vt* to recover:—~**se** *vr* (*med*) to come to.

cobre *m* copper; kitchen utensils *pl*; (*mus*) brass.

cocear *vt* to kick; (*fig*) to resist.

cocer *vt* to boil; to bake (bricks):—*vi* to boil; to ferment:—~**se** *vr* to suffer intense pain.

cochambroso, sa *adj* nasty; filthy, stinking.

coche *m* car; coach, carriage; pram, baby carriage:— (*ferro*) ~ **cama** sleeping car:—~ **restaurante** restaurant car.

cochino, na *adj* dirty, filthy; nasty:—*m* pig.

cocina *f* kitchen; cooker; cookery.

cocinero, ra *m/f* cook.

coco *m* coconut; bogeyman.

cocodrilo *m* crocodile.

codazo *m* blow given with the elbow.

codear *vt*, *vi* to elbow:—~**se** *vr* ~**se con** to rub shoulders with.

codiciar *vt* to covet, desire.

código *m* code; law; set of rules.

codillo *m* knee of a four-legged animal; angle; (*tec*) elbow (joint).

codo *m* elbow.

codorniz *f* quail.

coetáneo, nea *adj* contemporary.

coexistir *vi* to coexist.

cofia *f* (nurse's) cap.

cofradía *f* brotherhood, fraternity.

cofre *m* trunk.

coger *vt* to catch, take hold of; to occupy, take up:— ~**se** *vr* to catch.

cogollo *m* heart of a lettuce or cabbage; shoot of a plant.

cogote *m* back of the neck.

cohecho *m* bribery.

coherencia *f* coherence.

cohete *m* rocket.

cohibido, da *adj* shy.

coincidir *vi* to coincide.

coito *m* intercourse, coitus.

cojear *vi* to limp, hobble; (*fig*) to go astray.

cojín *m* cushion.

cojo, ja *adj* lame, crippled.

col *f* cabbage.

cola *f* tail; queue; last place; glue.

colaborar *vi* to collaborate.

colada *f* wash, washing; (*quím*) bleach; sheep run.

colador *m* sieve.

colar *vt* to strain, filter:—*vi* to ooze: —~**se en** to get into without paying.

colcha *f* bedspread, counterpane.

colchón *m* mattress.

coleccionar *vt* to collect.

colecta *f* collection (for charity).

colectivo, va *adj* collective.

colega *m/f* colleague.

colegial *m* schoolboy.

colegiala *f* schoolgirl.

colegio *m* college; school.

colegir *vt* to collect; to deduce, infer.

cólera *f* bile; anger; fury, rage; cholera.

coleta *f* pigtail.

colgar *vt* to hang; to suspend; to decorate with tapestry:—*vi* to be suspended.

colibrí *m* hummingbird.

coliflor *m* cauliflower.

colina *f* hill.

colisión *f* collision; friction.

colmar *vt* to heap up:—*vi* to fulfill, realise.

colmena *f* hive, beehive.

colmillo *m* eyetooth; tusk.

colmo *m* height, summit; extreme:—**a** ~ plentifully.

colocar *vt* to arrange; to place; to provide with a job:—~**se** *vr* to get a job.

collar *m* necklace; (dog) collar.

colono *m* colonist; farmer.

coloquio *m* conversation; conference.

color *m* colour, hue; dye; rouge; suit (of cards).

colorado, da *adj* ruddy; red.

colorete *m* rouge.

columna *f* column.

columpio *m* swing, seesaw.

colza *f* (*bot*) rape; rape seed.

coma *f* (*gr*) comma:—*m* (*med*) coma.

comadreja *f* weasel.

comandante *m* commander.

comarca *f* territory, district.

combatir *vt* to combat, fight; to attack:—*vi* to fight.

combinar *vi* to combine.

combustible *adj* combustible:—*m* fuel.

comedia *f* comedy; play, drama.

comedido, da *adj* moderate, restrained.

comedor, ra *m/f* glutton:—*m* dining room.

comentar *vt* to comment on, expound.

comentario *m* comment, remark; commentary.

comenzar *vi* to commence, begin.

comer *vt* to eat; to take (a piece at chess):—*vi* to have lunch.

comercial *adj* commercial.

comercio *m* trade, commerce; business.

comestible *adj* eatable:—*mpl* ~s food, foodstuffs *pl*.

cometa *m* comet:—*f* kite.

cometer *vt* to commit, charge; to entrust.

cómico, ca *adj* comic, comical.

comida *f* food; eating; meal; lunch.

comillas *fpl* quotation marks *pl*.

comino *m* cumin (plant or seed).

comisaría *f* police station; commissariat.

como *adv* as; like; such as.

cómo *adv* how?; why?:—*excl* what?

cómoda *f* chest of drawers.

cómodo, da *adj* convenient; comfortable.

compacto, ta *adj* compact; close, dense.

compadecer *vt* to pity:—~se *vr* to agree with each other.

compaginar *vt* to arrange, put in order:—~se *vr* to tally.

compañero, ra *m/f* companion, friend; comrade; partner.

compañía *f* company.

comparar *vt* to compare.

compartimento *m* compartment.

compartir *vt* to share.

compás *m* compass; pair of compasses; (*mus*) measure, beat.

compatible *adj*:—~ **con** compatible with, consistent with.

compensar *vt* to compensate; to recompense.

competencia *f* competition, rivalry; competence.

competente *adj* competent; adequate.

compilar *vt* to compile.

compinche *m* pal, mate (*sl*).

complacencia *f* pleasure; indulgence.

complacer *vt* to please:—~se *vr* to be pleased with.

complejo *m* complex:—~, **ja** *adj* complex.

complementario, ria *adj* complementary.

complemento *m* complement.

completar *vt* to complete.

completo, ta *adj* complete; perfect.

complicar *vt* to complicate.

cómplice *m/f* accomplice.

complot *m* plot.

componer *vt* to compose; to constitute; to mend, repair; to strengthen, restore; to compose, calm:—~se *vr* ~se de to consist of.

comportamiento *m* behaviour.

compostura *f* composition, composure; mending, repairing; discretion; modesty, demureness.

compota *f* stewed fruit.

comprar *vt* to buy, purchase.

comprender *vt* to include, contain; to comprehend, understand.

compresa *f* sanitary towel.

comprimido *m* pill.

comprimir *vt* to compress; to repress, restrain.

comprobar *vt* to verify, confirm; to prove.

comprometer *vt* to compromise; to embarrass; to implicate; to put in danger:—~se *vr* to compromise oneself.

compuerta *f* hatch; sluice.

compuesto *m* compound:—~, **ta** *adj* composed; made up of.

compulsar *vt* to collate, compare; to make an authentic copy.

compungirse *vr* to feel remorseful.

comulgar *vt* to administer communion to:—*vi* to receive communion.

común *adj* common, usual, general: —*m* community; public:—**en** ~ in common.

comunicar *vt* to communicate:—~se *vr* to communicate (with each other).

comunidad *f* community.

con *prep* with; by:—~ **que** so then, providing that.

coñac *m* brandy, cognac.

cóncavo, va *adj* concave.

concebir *vt* to conceive:—*vi* to become pregnant.

conceder *vt* to give; to grant; to concede, allow.

concejal, la *m/f* member of a council.

concentrar *vt*:—**~se** *vr* to concentrate.

concepto *m* conceit, thought; judgement, opinion.

concernir *v imp* to regard, concern.

concertar *vt* to coordinate; to settle; to adjust; to agree; to arrange, fix up:—*vi* (*mus*) to harmonise, be in tune.

concesión *f* concession.

concha *f* shell; tortoise-shell.

conciencia *f* conscience.

concienciar *vt* to make aware:—**~se** *vr* to become aware.

concierto *m* concert; agreement; concerto:—**de ~** in agreement, in concert.

conciliar *vt* to reconcile:—*adj* conciliar, council.

conciso, sa *adj* concise, brief.

concluir *vt* to conclude, end, complete; to infer, deduce:—**~se** *vr* to conclude.

concordar *vt* to reconcile, make agree:—*vi* to agree, correspond.

concordia *f* conformity, agreement.

concretar *vt* to make concrete; to specify.

concubina *f* concubine.

concurrido, da *adj* busy.

concursante *m/f* competitor.

concurso *m* crowd; competition; help, cooperation.

conde *m* earl, count.

condenable *adj* culpable.

condenar *vt* to condemn; to find guilty:—**~se** *vr* to blame oneself; to confess (one's guilt).

condensar *vt* to condense.

condescender *vi* to acquiesce, comply.

condición *f* condition, state; quality; status; rank; stipulation.

condimentar *vt* to flavour, season.

condolerse *vr* to sympathise.

condón *m* condom.

conducir *vt* to convey, conduct; to drive; to manage:—*vi* to drive:—**~ (a)** to lead (to):—**~se** *vr* to conduct oneself.

conducta *f* conduct, behaviour; management.

conducto *m* conduit, pipe; drain; (*fig*) channel.

conductor, ra *m/f* conductor, guide; (*ferro*) guard; driver.

conectar *vt* to connect.

conejo *m* rabbit.

conexión *f* connection; plug; relationship.

confección *f* preparation; clothing industry.

conferencia *f* conference; telephone call.

confesar *vt* to confess; to admit.

confianza *f* trust; confidence; conceit; familiarity:—**en ~** confidential.

confiar *vt* to confide, entrust:—*vi* to trust.

configurar *vt* to shape, form.

confinar *vt* to confine:—*vi* **~ con** to border upon.

confirmar *vt* to confirm; to corroborate.

confiscar *vt* to confiscate.

confitería *f* sweet shop.

confitura *f* preserve; jam.

conflicto *m* conflict.

conformar *vt* to shape; to adjust, adapt:—*vi* to agree:—

~se *vr* to conform; to resign oneself.

conforme *adj* alike, similar; agreed: —*prep* according to.

confortar *vt* to comfort; to strengthen; to console.

confundir *vt* to confound, jumble; to confuse:—**~se** *vr* to make a mistake.

confusión *f* confusion.

congelado, da *adj* frozen:—*mpl* **~s** frozen food.

congelar *vt* to freeze:—**~se** *vr* to congeal.

congeniar *vi* to get on well.

congoja *f* anguish, distress, grief.

congraciarse *vr* to ingratiate oneself.

congregar(se) *vt* (*vr*) to assemble, meet, collect.

conjetura *f* conjecture, guess.

conjugar *vt* (*gr*) to conjugate; to combine.

conjunto, ta *adj* united, joint:—*m* whole; (*mus*) ensemble, band; team.

conjurar *vt* to exorcise:—*vi* to conspire, plot.

conmemorar *vt* to commemorate.

conmigo *pn* with me.

conmover *vt* to move; to disturb.

conmutador *m* switch.

conmutar *vt* (*jur*) to commute; to exchange.

connotar *vt* to imply.

cono *m* cone.

conocer *vt* to know, understand:—**~se** *vr* to know one another.

conocimiento *m* knowledge, understanding; (*med*) consciousness; acquaintance; (*mar*) bill of lading.

conquistar *vt* to conquer.

consabido, da *adj* well-known; above-mentioned.

consagrar *vt* to consecrate.

consanguíneo, nea *adj* related by blood.

consecuencia *f* consequence; conclusion; consistency:—**por ~** therefore.

consecuente *adj* consistent.

conseguir *vt* to attain; to get, obtain.

consejo *m* advice; council.

consentir *vt* to consent to; to allow; to admit; to spoil (a child).

conserje *m* doorman; janitor.

conservar *vt* to conserve; to keep; to preserve (fruit).

conservas *fpl* canned food.

conservatorio *m* (*mus*) conservatoire.

consideración *f* consideration; respect.

considerar *vt* to consider.

consigna *f* (*mil*) watchword; order, instruction; (*ferro*) left-luggage office.

consignar *vt* to consign, dispatch; to assign; to record, register.

consigo *pn* (*m*) with him; (*f*) with her; (*vd*) with you; (*refl*) with oneself.

consiguiente *adj* consequent.

consistente *adj* consistent; firm, solid.

consistir *vi*:—**~ en** to consist of; to be due to.

consola *f* control panel.

consolar *vt* to console, comfort, cheer.

consolidar *vt* to consolidate.

consonante *m* rhyme:—*f* (*gr*) consonant:—*adj* consonant, harmonious.

consorcio *m* partnership.

consorte *m/f* consort, companion, partner; accomplice.

conspirar *vi* to conspire, plot.

constante *adj* constant; firm.

constar *vi* to be evident, be certain; to be composed of, consist of.

constatar *vt* to note; to check.

consternar *vt* to dismay; to shock.

constipado, da *adj*:—**estar ~** to have a cold.

constituir *vt* to constitute; to establish; to appoint.

construir *vt* to form; to build, construct; to construe.

consuegro, gra *m/f* father-in-law / mother-in-law of one's son or daughter.

consuelo *m* consolation, comfort.

cónsul *m* consul.

consultar *vt* to consult, ask for advice.

consultor, ra *m/f* adviser, consultant.

consultorio *m* (*med*) surgery.

consumar *vt* to consummate, finish; to carry out.

consumir *vt* to consume; to burn, use; to waste, exhaust:—**~se** *vr* to waste away, be consumed.

contabilidad *f* accounting; bookkeeping.

contacto *m* contact; (*auto*) ignition.

contado, da *adj*:—**~s** scarce, few:—*m* **pagar al ~** to pay (in) cash.

contador *m* meter; counter in a cafe: —**~, ~a** *m/f* accountant.

contagiar *vt* to infect:—**~se** *vr* to get infected.

contaminar *vt* to contaminate; to pollute; to corrupt.

contar *vt* to count, reckon; to tell:—*vi* to count:—**~ con** to rely upon.

contemplar *vt* to look at; to contemplate, consider; to meditate.

contemporáneo, nea *adj* contemporary.

contenedor *m* container.

contener *vt* to contain, hold; to hold back; to repress:—**~se** *vr* to control oneself.

contentar *vt* to content, satisfy; to please:—**~se** *vr* to be pleased or satisfied.

contento, ta *adj* glad; pleased; content:—*m* contentment; (*jur*) release.

contestador *m*:—**~ automatico** answering machine.

contestar *vt* to answer, reply; to prove, corroborate.

contienda *f* contest, dispute.

contigo *pn* with you.

contiguo, gua *adj* contiguous, close.

continente *m* continent, mainland:—*adj* continent.

contingencia *f* risk; contingency.

continuar *vt, vi* to continue.

continuo, nua *adj* continuous.

contorno *m* environs *pl*; contour, outline:—**en ~** round about.

contra *prep* against; contrary to; opposite.

contrabajo *m* (*mus*) double bass; bass guitar; low bass.

contrabando *m* contraband; smuggling.

contrachapado *m* plywood.

contradecir *vt* to contradict.

contraer *vt* to contract,

shrink; to make (a bargain):—~se *vr* to shrink, contract.

contrahecho, cha *adj* deformed; hunchbacked; counterfeit, fake, false.

contralto *m* (*mus*) contralto.

contrapartida *f* (*com*) balancing entry.

contrapelo *adv:*—**a ~** against the grain.

contrapeso *m* counterpoise; counterweight.

contraproducente *adj* counterproductive.

contrariar *vt* to contradict, oppose; to vex.

contrariedad *f* opposition; setback; annoyance.

contrario, ria *m/f* opponent:—*adj* contrary, opposite:—**por el ~** on the contrary.

contrarrestar *vt* to return a ball; (*fig*) to counteract.

contraseña *f* countersign; (*mil*) watch word.

contrasentido *m* contradiction.

contrastar *vt* to resist; to contradict; to assay (metals); to verify (measures and weights):—*vi* to contrast.

contratar *vt* to contract; to hire, engage.

contratiempo *m* setback; accident.

contrato *m* contract, agreement.

contravenir *vi* to contravene, transgress; to violate.

contraventana *f* shutter.

contribución *f* contribution; tax.

contribuir *vt, vi* to contribute.

contrincante *m* competitor.

controlar *vt* to control; to check.

contumaz *adj* obstinate, stubborn; (*jur*) guilty of contempt of court.

contundente *adj* overwhelming; blunt.

contusión *f* bruise.

convalecer *vi* to recover from sickness, convalesce.

convencer *vt* to convince.

conveniencia *f* suitability; usefulness; agreement:— **~s** *fpl* property.

convenir *vi* to agree, suit.

convento *m* convent, nunnery; monastery.

conversar *vi* to talk, converse.

convicto, ta *adj* convicted (found guilty).

convidar *vt* to invite.

convocar *vt* to convoke, assemble.

convocatoria *f* summons; notice of a meeting.

conyugal *adj* conjugal, married.

cónyuge *m/f* spouse.

cooperar *vi* to cooperate.

coordinar *vt* to arrange, coordinate.

copa *f* cup; glass; top of a tree; crown of a hat:—**~s** *fpl* hearts *pl* (at cards).

copiar *vt* to copy; to imitate.

copla *f* verse; (*mus*) popular song, folk song.

copo *m* small bundle; flake of snow.

coquetear *vi* to flirt.

coraje *m* courage; anger, passion.

coral *m* coral; choir:—*adj* choral.

corazón *m* heart; core:—**de ~** willingly.

corazonada *f* inspiration; quick decision; presentiment.

corbata *f* tie.

corchete *m* clasp; hook and eye.

corcho *m* cork; float (for fishing); cork bark.

cordel *m* cord, rope; (*mar*) line.

cordero *m* lamb; lambskin; meek, gentle person.

cordial *adj* cordial, affectionate:—*m* cordial.

cordillera *f* range of mountains.

cordón *m* cord, string; lace; cordon.

cornada *f* thrust with a bull's horn.

coro *m* choir; chorus.

corona *f* crown; coronet; top of the head; crown (of a tooth); tonsure; halo.

coronilla *f* crown of the head.

corpiño *m* bodice.

corporal *adj* corporal.

corpulento, ta *adj* corpulent, bulky.

corral *m* yard; farmyard; corral; playpen.

correa *f* leather strap, thong; flexibility.

correcto, ta *adj* exact, correct.

corregir *vt* to correct, amend; to reprehend:—**~se** *vr* to reform.

correo *m* post, mail; courier; postman:—**a vuelta de ~** by return of post:—**~s** *mpl* post office.

correr *vt* to run; to flow; to travel over; to pull (a drape):—*vi* to run, rush; to flow; to blow (applied to the wind):—**~se** *vr* to be ashamed; to slide, move; to run (of colours).

correspondencia *f* correspondence; communication; agreement.

corresponder *vi* to correspond; to answer; to be suitable; to belong; to concern:—~**se** *vr* to love one another.

corresponsal *m/f* correspondent.

corriente *f* current; course, progression; (electric) current:—*adj* current; common, ordinary, general; fluent; flowing, running.

corro *m* circle of people.

corroer *vt* to corrode, erode.

corromper *vt* to corrupt; to rot; to turn bad; to seduce; to bribe:—~**se** *vr* to rot; to become corrupted:—*vi* to stink.

cortacesped *m* lawn mower.

cortado *m* coffee with a little milk:—~**, da** *adj* cut; sour; embarrassed.

cortar *vt* to cut; to cut off, curtail; to intersect; to carve; to chop; to cut (at cards); to interrupt:—~**se** *vr* to be ashamed or embarrassed; to curdle.

corte *m* cutting; cut; section; length (of cloth); style:—*f* (royal) court; capital (city):—**C**~**s** *fpl* Spanish Parliament.

cortejo *m* entourage; courtship; procession; lover.

cortés, esa *adj* courteous, polite.

cortesía *f* courtesy, good manners *pl*.

corteza *f* bark; peel; crust; (*fig*) outward appearance.

cortina *f* curtain.

corto, ta *adj* short; scanty, small; stupid; bashful:—**a la** ~**a** *o* **a la larga** sooner or later.

corzo, za *m/f* roe deer, fallow deer.

cosa *f* thing; matter, affair:—**no hay tal** ~ nothing of the sort!

cosecha *f* harvest; harvest time:—**de su** ~ of one's own invention.

coser *vt* to sew; to join.

cosquillas *fpl* tickling; (*fig*) agitation.

costa *f* cost, price; charge, expense; coast, shore:—**a toda** ~ at all events.

costado *m* side; (*mil*) flank; side of a ship.

costal *m* sack, large bag.

costar *vt* to cost; to need.

coste *m* cost, expense.

costero, ra *adj* coastal; (*mar*) coasting.

costilla *f* rib; cutlet:—~**s** *fpl* back, shoulders *pl*.

costra *f* crust; (*med*) scab.

costumbre *f* custom, habit.

cotejar *vt* to compare.

cotidiano, na *adj* daily.

cotilla *m/f* gossip.

cotizar *vt* to quote:—~**se** *vr* ~ **a** to sell at; to be quoted at.

coto *m* enclosure; reserve; boundary stone.

cotorra *f* small parrot; (*col*) chatterbox.

covacha *f* small cave, grotto.

coyuntura *f* joint, articulation; juncture.

coz *f* kick; recoil (of a gun); ebbing (of a flood); (*fig*) insult.

cráneo *m* skull.

crear *vt* to create, make; to establish.

crecer *vi* to grow, increase; to rise.

crecida *f* swell (of rivers).

creciente *f* crescent (moon); (*mar*) flood tide:—*adj* growing; crescent.

crecimiento *m* increase; growth.

crédito *m* credit; belief, faith; reputation.

creer *vt, vi* to believe; to think; to consider.

crema *f* cream; custard.

cremallera *f* zipper.

crepúsculo *m* twilight.

cresta *f* crest (of birds).

creyente *m/f* believer.

cría *f* breeding; young.

criadero *m* (*bot*) nursery; breeding place.

criadilla *f* testicle; small loaf; truffle.

crianza *f* breeding, rearing.

criar *vt* to create, produce; to breed; to breast-feed; to bring up.

criatura *f* creature; child.

crimen *m* crime.

criminal *adj, m/f* criminal.

crin *f* mane; horsehair.

crío, a *m/f* (*fam*) kid.

cripta *f* crypt.

crisis *f invar* crisis.

crisol *m* crucible; melting pot.

crispar *vt* to set on edge; to tense up.

cristal *m* crystal; glass; pane; lens.

cristalino, na *adj* crystalline.

cristalizar *vt* to crystallise.

cristiano, na *adj, m/f* Christian.

criterio *m* criterion.

crítica *m/f* criticism.

criticar *vt* to criticise.

croar *vi* to croak.

cromo *m* chrome.

crónica *f* chronicle; news report; feature.

crónico, ca *adj* chronic.

cronista *m/f* chronicler; reporter, columnist.

cronómetro *m* stopwatch.

cruce *m* crossing; crossroads.

crucero *m* cruiser; cruise; transept; crossing.

crucifijo *m* crucifix.

crucigrama *m* crossword.

crudo, da *adj* raw; green, unripe; crude; cruel; hard to digest.

cruel *adj* cruel.

crueldad *f* cruelty.

crujiente *adj* crunchy.

crujir *vi* to crackle; to rustle.

crustáceo *m* crustacean.

cruz *f* cross; tails (of a coin).

cruzar *vt* to cross; (*mar*) to cruise:—**se** *vr* to cross; to pass each other.

cuaderno *m* notebook; exercise book; logbook.

cuadra *f* block; stable.

cuadrado, da *adj, m* square.

cuadrante *m* quadrant; dial.

cuadrar *vt, vi* to square; to fit, suit, correspond.

cuadrilátero, ra *adj, m* quadrilateral.

cuadrilla *f* party, group; gang, crew.

cuadro *m* square; picture, painting; window frame; scene; chart.

cuadrúpedo, da *adj* quadruped.

cuajar *vt* to coagulate; to thicken; to adorn; to set:—**se** *vr* to coagulate, curdle; to set; to fill up.

cual *pn* which; who;

whom:—*adv* as; like:—*adj* such as.

cuál *pn* which (one).

cualidad *f* quality.

cualquier *adj* any.

cualquiera *adj* anyone, anybody; someone, somebody; whoever; whichever.

cuando *adv* when; if; even:—*conj* since:—**de ~ en ~** from time to time: —**~ más, ~ mucho** at most, at best: —**~ menos** at least.

cuándo *adv* when:—**¿de cuándo acá?** since when?

cuánto *adj* what a lot of; how much?: —**¿~s?** how many?:—*pn, adv* how; how much; how many.

cuanto, ta *adj* as many as; as much as; all; whatever:—*adv* **en ~** as soon as:—**en ~ a** as regards:—**~ más** moreover, the more as.

cuarenta *adj, m* forty.

cuaresma *f* Lent.

cuarto *m* fourth part; quarter; room, apartment; span:—**~s** *mpl* cash, money:—**~, ta** *adj* fourth.

cuarzo *m* quartz.

cuatro *adj, m* four.

cuatrocientos, tas *adj* four hundred.

cuba *f* cask; tub; (*fig*) drunkard.

cubierta *f* cover; deck of a ship; (*auto*) bonnet; tyre; pretext.

cubierto *m* cover; shelter; place at table; meal at a fixed charge:—**~s** *mpl* cutlery.

cubo *m* cube; bucket.

cubrir *vt* to cover; to disguise; to protect; to roof a

building:—**~se** *vr* to become overcast.

cucaracha *f* cockroach.

cuchara *f* spoon.

cucharada *f* spoonful; ladleful.

cucharadita *f* teaspoonful.

cuchichear *vi* to whisper.

cuchillo *m* knife.

cuclillas *adv*:—**en ~** squatting.

cuclillo *m* cuckoo; (*fig*) cuckold.

cuello *m* neck; collar.

cuenca *m* bowl, deep valley; hollow; socket of the eye.

cuenta *f* calculation; account; bill (in a restaurant); count, counting; bead; importance.

cuento *m* tale, story, narrative.

cuerda *f* rope; string; spring.

cuerdo, da *adj* sane; prudent, judicious.

cuerno *m* horn.

cuero *m* hide, skin, leather.

cuerpo *m* body; cadaver, corpse.

cuesta *f* slope, hill; incline:—**ir ~ abajo** to go downhill:—**~ arriba** uphill.

cuestión *f* question, matter; dispute; quarrel; problem.

cueva *f* cave; cellar.

cuidado *m* care, worry, concern; charge.

cuidar *vt* to care for; to mind, look after.

culebra *f* snake.

culo *m* backside; bum (*sl*); bottom.

culpa *f* fault, blame; guilt.

culpable *adj* culpable; guilty: —*m/f* culprit.

cultivar *vt* to cultivate.

culto, ta *adj* cultivated, cul-

tured; refined, civilised:—
m culture; worship.

cumbre *f* top, summit.

cumplir *vt* to carry out, fulfil; to serve (a prison sentence); to carry out (death
penalty); to attain, reach (a
certain age):—**~se** *vr* to be
fulfilled; to expire, be up.

cuna *f* cradle.

cuña *f* wedge.

cuñado, da *m/f* brother/sis-
ter-in-law.

cura *m* priest:—*f* cure; treatment.

curar *vt* to cure; to treat,
dress (a wound); to salt; to
dress; to tan.

curioso, sa *adj* curious:—*m/f*
bystander.

currar *vi* (*fam*)to work.

curso *m* course, direction;

year (at university); subject.

curtir *vt* to tan leather:—**~se**
vr to become sunburned;
to become inured.

curva *f* curve, bend.

custodia *f* custody, safekeeping, care; monstrance.

cutis *m* skin.

cutre *adj* (*fam*) mean, grotty.

cuyo, ya *pn* whose, of which,
of whom.

CH

chabola *f* shack.

chal *m* shawl.

chalado, da *adj* crazy.

chale(t) *m* detached house.

chaleco *m* waistcoat.

champán *m* champagne.

champiñón *m* mushroom.

champú *m* shampoo.

chamuscar *vt* to singe, scorch.

chantaje *m* blackmail.

chapa *f* metal plate; panel; (*auto*) numberplate.

chaparrón *m* heavy rainshower.

chapuza *f* badly done job.

chaqueta *f* jacket.

charco *m* pool, puddle.

charcutería *f* shop selling pork meat products.

charlar *vi* to chat.

charlatán, ana *m/f* chatterbox.

charol *m* varnish; patent leather.

chasco *m* disappointment; joke, jest.

chasis *m invar* (*auto*) chassis.

chasquido *m* crack; click.

chatarra *f* scrap.

chato, ta *adj* flat, flattish; snub-nosed.

chaval, la *m/f* lad/lass.

chicle *m* chewing gum.

chico, ca *adj* little, small:— *m/f* boy/girl.

chiflado, da *adj* crazy.

chile *m* chilli pepper.

chillar *vi* to scream, shriek; to howl; to creak.

chimenea *f* chimney; fireplace.

china *f* pebble; porcelain, china-ware; China silk.

chincheta *f* drawing pin, thumb-tack.

chino, na *adj, m/f* Chinese:— *m* Chinese language.

chirriar *vi* to hiss; to creak; to chirp.

chisme *m* tale; thingummyjig.

chispa *f* spark; sparkle; wit; (rain)drop); drunkenness.

chiste *m* funny story, joke.

chivo, va *m/f* billy/nanny goat.

chocar *vi* to strike, knock; to crash:—*vt* to shock.

chochear *vi* to dodder, be senile; to dote.

chocolate *m* chocolate.

chófer *m* driver.

chopo *m* (*bot*) black poplar.

chorizo *m* pork sausage.

chorro *m* gush; jet; stream:— **a ~s** abundantly.

chuchería *f* trinket.

chulear *vi* to brag.

chuleta *f* chop.

chulo *m* rascal; pimp.

chupar *vt* to suck; to absorb.

churro *m* fritter.

D

dado *m* die (*pl* dice).

daga *f* dagger.

dama *f* lady, gentlewoman; mistress; queen; actress of principal parts.

damnificar *vt* to hurt, injure, damage.

dañar *vt* to hurt, injure; to damage.

dañino, na *adj* harmful; noxious; mischievous.

danza *f* dance.

dar *vt* to give; to supply, administer, afford; to deliver.

dátil *m* (*bot*) date.

dato *m* fact.

de *prep* of; from; for; by; on; to; with.

debajo *adv* under, underneath, below.

debatir *vt* to debate, argue, discuss.

debe *m* (*com*) debit:—~ y **haber** debit and credit.

deber *m* obligation, duty; debt:—*vt* to owe; to be obliged to:—*vi* **debe (de)** it must, it should.

debidamente *adv* justly, duly; exactly, perfectly.

débil *adj* feeble, weak; sickly; frail.

debilitar *vt* to debilitate, weaken.

decadencia *f* decay, decline.

decena *f* ten.

decencia *f* decency.

decepción *f* disappointment.

decidir *vt* to decide, determine.

décimo, ma *adj, m* tenth.

decir *vt* to say; to tell; to speak; to name.

decisión *f* decision; determination, resolution; sentence.

declamar *vi* to declaim; to harangue.

declarar *vt* to declare; to manifest; to expound; to explain; (*jur*) to decide: — ~se *vr* to declare one's opinion:—*vi* to testify.

declinar *vi* to decline; to decay, degenerate:—*vt* (*gr*) to decline.

declive *m* slope; decline.

decorar *vt* to decorate, adorn; to illustrate.

decrecer *vi* to decrease.

decrépito, ta *adj* decrepit, worn out with age.

decretar *vt* to decree, determine.

dedal *m* thimble; very small drinking glass.

dedicar *vt* to dedicate, devote; to consecrate:—~se *vr* to apply oneself to.

dedo *m* finger; toe; small bit:—~ **meñique** little finger:—~ **pulgar** thumb: —~ **del corazón** middle finger:—~ **anular** ring finger.

deducir *vt* to deduce, infer; to allege in pleading; to subtract.

defecto *m* defect; defectiveness.

defectuoso, sa *adj* defective, imperfect, faulty.

defender *vt* to defend, protect; to justify, assert; to resist, oppose.

defensor, ra *m/f* defender, protector; lawyer, defence counsel.

deferir *vi* to defer; to yield (to another's opinion):—*vt* to communicate.

deficiente *adj* defective.

definir *vt* to define, describe, explain; to decide.

definitivo, va *adj* definitive; positive.

deformar *vt* to deform:—~se *vr* to become deformed.

deforme *adj* deformed; ugly.

defraudar *vt* to defraud, cheat; to usurp; to disturb.

defunción *f* death; funeral.

degenerar *vi* to degenerate.

degollar *vt* to behead; to destroy, ruin.

degradar *vt* to degrade:—~se *vr* to degrade or demean oneself.

degustar *vt* to taste.

dehesa *f* pasture.

dejadez *f* slovenliness, neglect.

dejar *vt* to leave, quit; to omit; to let; to permit, allow; to forsake; to bequeath; to pardon:—~ **de** to stop; to fail to:—~se *vr* to abandon oneself.

del *adj* of the (contraction of *de* and *el*).

delantal *m* apron.

delante *adv* in front; oppo-

site; ahead:—~ **de** in front
of; before.

delantero, ra *adj* front:—*m*
forward.

delegar *vt* to delegate; to
substitute.

deleitar *vt* to delight.

deletrear *vt* to spell; to examine; to conjecture.

delfín *m* dolphin; dauphin.

delgado, da *adj* thin; delicate,
fine; light; slender, lean.

deliberadamente *adv* delib-
erately.

deliberar *vi* to consider, deliberate: —*vt* to debate; to
consult.

delicado, da *adj* delicate, tender; faint; exquisite; delicious, dainty; slender, subtle.

delicioso, sa *adj* delicious;
delightful.

delincuencia *f* delinquency.

delineante *m/f* draftsman/
woman.

delirar *vi* to rave; to talk nonsense.

delito *m* offence; crime.

demacrado, da *adj* pale and
drawn.

demandar *vt* to demand; to
ask; to claim; to sue.

demarcar *vt* to mark out
(limits).

demás *adj* other; remaining:—*pn* **los/las** ~ the others, the rest:—**estar** ~ to be
over and above; to be useless or superfluous:—**por** ~
in vain.

demasiado, da *adj* too; excessive:—*adv* too, too much.

demencia *f* madness.

demoler *vt* to demolish; to
destroy.

demonio *m* demon.

demorar *vt* to delay:—~**se** *vr*
to be delayed:—*vi* to linger.

demostrar *vt* to prove, demonstrate; to manifest.

denegar *vt* to deny; to refuse.

denigrar *vt* to blacken; to insult.

denominar *vt* to name; to
designate.

denotar *vt* to denote; to express.

denso, sa *adj* dense, thick;
compact.

dentado, da *adj* toothed; in-
dented.

dentadura *f* set of teeth.

dentífrico *m* toothpaste.

dentista *m/f* dentist.

dentro *adv* within:—*pn* ~ **de**
in, inside.

denunciar *vt* to advise; to denounce; to report.

depender *vi*:—~ **de** to depend on, be dependent on.

dependiente *m* shop assistant:—*adj* dependent.

depilatorio *m* hair remover.

deponer *vt* to depose; to declare; to displace; to deposit.

deportar *vt* to deport.

deporte *m* sport.

deportista *m/f* sportsman/
woman.

depositar *vt* to deposit; to
confide; to put away for
safekeeping.

depravación *f* depravity.

deprimir *vt* to depress:—~**se**
vr to become depressed.

deprisa *adv* quickly.

depurar *vt* to cleanse, purify;
to filter.

derecho, cha *adj* right;
straight; just; perfect; certain:—*m* right, justice; law;
just claim; tax, duty; fee:—
adv straight.

derivar *vt*, *vi* to derive; (*mar*)
to drift.

derogar *vt* to derogate, abolish; to reform.

derramar *vt* to drain off (water); to spread; to spill,
scatter; to waste, shed:—
~**se** *vr* to pour out.

derretir *vt* to melt; to consume; to thaw:—~**se** *vr* to
melt.

derribar *vt* to demolish; to
flatten.

derrochar *vt* to dissipate; to
squander.

derrotar *vt* to destroy; to defeat.

derruir *vt* to demolish.

derrumbar *vt* to throw
down:—~**se** *vr* to collapse.

desabrido, da *adj* tasteless,
insipid; rude; unpleasant.

desacato *m* disrespect, inci-
vility.

desacertado, da *adj* mistaken;
unwise; inconsiderate.

desaconsejar *vt* to advise
against.

desacostumbrado, da *adj*
unusual.

desacuerdo *m* blunder; disa-
greement; forgetfulness.

desafiar *vt* to challenge; to
defy.

desafinar *vi* to be out of tune.

desafuero *m* outrage; excess.

desagradable *adj* disagreeable, unpleasant.

desagradecido, da *adj* ungrateful.

desagüe *m* channel, drain;
drainpipe; drainage.

desahogar *vt* to ease; to
vent:—~**se** *vr* to recover; to
relax.

desahuciar *vt* to cause to despair; to give up; to evict.

desajustar *vt* to make uneven; to unbalance:—**~se** *vr* to get out of order.

desalentar *vt* to put out of breath; to discourage.

desaliño *m* slovenliness; carelessness.

desalmado, da *adj* cruel, inhuman.

desalojar *vt* to eject; to move out:—*vi* to move out.

desamparar *vt* to forsake, abandon; to relinquish.

desangrar *vt* to bleed; to drain (a pond); (*fig*) to exhaust (one's means):—**~se** *vr* to lose a lot of blood.

desanimar *vt* to discourage:—**~se** *vr* to lose heart.

desaparecer *vi* to disappear.

desapercibido, da *adj* unnoticed.

desaprobar *vt* to disapprove; to condemn; to reject.

desaprovechado, da *adj* useless; unprofitable; backward; slack.

desaprovechar *vt* to waste, turn to a bad use.

desarmar *vt* to disarm; to disband (troops); to dismantle; (*fig*) to pacify.

desarraigar *vt* to uproot; to root out; to extirpate.

desarrollar *vt* to develop; to unroll; to unfold:—**~se** *vr* to develop; to be unfolded; to open.

desasosiego *m* restlessness; anxiety.

desastre *m* disaster; misfortune.

desatar *vt* to untie, loose; to separate; to solve:—**~se** *vr* to come undone; to break.

desatascar *vt* to unblock; to clear.

desatender *vt* to pay no attention to; to disregard.

desatinar *vi* to talk nonsense; to reel, stagger.

desatornillar *vt* to unscrew.

desayunar *vt* to have for breakfast:—**~se** *vr* to breakfast:—*vi* to have breakfast.

desazón *f* disgust; uneasiness; annoyance.

desbarrar *vi* to talk rubbish.

desbordar *vt* to exceed:—**~se** *vr* to overflow.

descalabrado, da *adj* wounded on the head; imprudent.

descalificar *vt* to disqualify; to discredit.

descalzo, za *adj* barefooted; (*fig*) destitute.

descaminado, da *adj* (*fig*) misguided.

descansar *vt* to rest:—*vi* to rest; to lie down.

descansillo *m* landing.

descapotable *m* convertible.

descarado, da *adj* cheeky, barefaced.

descargar *vt* to unload, discharge:—**~se** *vr* to unburden oneself.

descarriar *vt* to lead astray; to misdirect:—**~se** *vr* to lose one's way; to stray; to err.

descarrilar *vi* (*ferro*) to leave or run off the rails.

descartar *vt* to discard; to dismiss; to rule out.

descendencia *f* descent, offspring.

descender *vt* to take down:—*vi* to descend, walk down; to flow; to fall: —**~ de** to be derived from.

descenso *m* descent; drop.

descifrar *vt* to decipher; to unravel.

descollar *vi* to excel.

descolorido, da *adj* pale, colourless.

descomunal *adj* uncommon; huge.

desconcertar *vt* to disturb; to confound; to disconcert:—**~se** *vr* to be bewildered; to be upset.

desconectar *vt* to disconnect.

desconfiar *vi*:—**~ de** to mistrust, suspect.

descongelar *vt* to defrost.

desconocer *vt* to disown, disavow; to be totally ignorant of (a thing); not to know (a person); not to acknowledge (a favour received).

desconsuelo *m* distress; trouble; despair.

descontar *vt* to discount; to deduct.

descontento *m* dissatisfaction; disgust.

descortés, esa *adj* impolite, rude.

descoser *vt* to unseam; to separate:—**~se** *vr* to come apart at the seams.

descreído, da *adj* incredulous.

descremado, da *adj* skimmed.

describir *vt* to describe; to draw, delineate.

descuartizar *vt* to quarter; to carve.

descubrir *vt* to discover, disclose; to uncover; to reveal; to show:—**~se** *vr* to reveal oneself; to take off one's hat; to confess.

descuento *m* discount; decrease.

descuidado, da *adj* careless, negligent.

descuidar *vt* to neglect:—*vi* ~**se** *vr* to be careless.

desde *prep* since; after; from:—~ **lue-go** of course:—~ **entonces** since then.

desdén *m* disdain, scorn.

desdeñar *vt* to disdain, scorn:—~**se** *vr* to be disdainful.

desdentado, da *adj* toothless.

desdicha *f* misfortune, calamity; great poverty.

desdoblar *vt* to unfold, spread open.

desear *vt* to desire, wish; to require, demand.

desecar *vt* to dry up.

desechar *vt* to depreciate; to reject; to refuse; to throw away.

desecho *m* residue:—~**s** *mpl* rubbish.

desembarcar *vt* to unload, disembark:—*vi* to disembark, land.

desembolsar *vt* to pay out.

desempatar *vi* to hold a play-off.

desempeñar *vt* to redeem; to extricate from debt; to fulfil (any duty or promise); to acquit:—~**se** *vr* to get out of debt.

desempleo *m* unemployment.

desencadenar *vt* to unchain:—~**se** *vr* to break loose; to burst.

desencajar *vt* to disjoint; to dislocate; to disconnect.

desencanto *m* disenchantment.

desenchufar *vt* to unplug.

desenfado *m* ease; facility; calmness, relaxation.

desenfocado, da *adj* out of focus.

desenfreno *m* wildness; lack of self-control.

desengañar *vt* to disillusion:—~**se** *vr* to become disillusioned.

desenganchar *vt* to unhook; to uncouple.

desengrasar *vt* to take the grease off.

desenlace *m* climax; outcome.

desenredar *vt* to disentangle.

desenroscar *vt* to untwist; to unroll.

desentenderse *vr* to feign not to understand; to pass by without noticing.

desenterrar *vt* to exhume; to dig up.

desentonar *vi* to be out of tune; to clash.

desenvolver *vt* to unfold; to unroll; to decipher, unravel; to develop:—~**se** *vr* to develop; to cope.

deseo *m* desire, wish.

desequilibrado, da *adj* unbalanced.

desertar *vt* to desert; (*jur*) to abandon (a cause).

desesperar *vi*, ~**se** *vr* to despair:—*vt* to make desperate.

desestabilizar *vt* to destabilise.

desfachatez *f* impudence.

desfalco *m* embezzlement.

desfallecer *vi* to get weak; to faint.

desfasado, da *adj* old-fashioned.

desfavorable *adj* unfavorable.

desfiladero *m* gorge.

desfilar *vi* (*mil*) to parade.

desfogarse *vr* to give vent to one's passion or anger.

desgana *f* disgust; loss of appetite; aversion, reluctance.

desgañitarse *vr* to scream, bawl.

desgarrar *vt* to tear; to shatter.

desgaste *m* wear (and tear).

desgracia *f* misfortune; disgrace; accident; setback.

desgreñado, da *adj* dishevelled.

deshabitado, da *adj* deserted, uninhabited; desolate.

deshacer *vt* to undo, destroy; to cancel, efface; to rout (an army); to solve; to melt; to break up, divide; to dissolve in a liquid; to violate (a treaty); to diminish; to disband (troops):—~**se** *vr* to melt; to come apart.

deshelar *vt* to thaw:—~**se** *vr* to thaw, melt.

desheredar *vt* to disinherit.

deshidratar *vt* to dehydrate.

deshinchar *vt* to deflate:—~**se** *vr* to go flat, go down.

deshonesto, ta *adj* indecent.

deshonrar *vt* to affront, insult, defame; to dishonour.

deshuesar *vt* to rid of bones; to stone.

desidia *f* idleness, indolence.

desierto, ta *adj* deserted; solitary:—*m* desert; wilderness.

designar *vt* to design; to intend; to appoint; to express, name.

desigual *adj* unequal, unlike; uneven, craggy, cliffy.

desilusionar *vt* to disappoint:—~**se** *vr* to become disillusioned.

desinfectar *vt* to disinfect.

desinflar *vt* to deflate.

desinteresado, da *adj* disinterested; unselfish.

desistir *vi* to desist, cease.

desleal *adj* disloyal; unfair.

desleír *vt* to dilute; to dissolve.

deslenguado, da *adj* foulmouthed.

desligar *vt* to untie; to separate.

deslizar *vt* to slip, slide; to let slip (a comment):—**se** *vr* to slip; to skid; to flow softly; to creep in.

deslumbrar *vt* to dazzle; to puzzle.

desmayar *vi* to be dispirited or faint-hearted:—**se** *vr* to faint.

desmedido, da *adj* disproportionate.

desmemoriado, da *adj* forgetful.

desmentir *vt* to give the lie to:—**se** *vr* to contradict oneself.

desmenuzar *vt* to crumble; to chip at; to fritter away; to examine minutely.

desmesurado, da *adj* excessive; huge; immeasurable.

desmoralizar *vt* to demoralise.

desnatado, da *adj* skimmed.

desnivel *m* unevenness of the ground.

desnudar *vt* to undress; to strip; to discover, reveal:—**se** *vr* to undress.

desnutrido, da *adj* undernourished.

desobedecer *vt, vi* to disobey.

desocupar *vt* to vacate; to empty:—**se** *vr* to retire from a business; to with-draw from an arrangement.

desodorante *m* deodorant.

desolado, da *adj* desolate, disconsolate.

desordenar *vt* to disorder; to untidy: —**se** *vr* to get out of order.

desorganizar *vt* to disorganise.

desorientar *vt* to mislead; to confuse: —**se** *vr* to lose one's way.

desovar *vi* to spawn.

despabilado, da *adj* watchful, vigilant; wide-awake.

despacho *m* dispatch, expedition; cabinet; office; commission; warrant, patent; expedient; smart answer.

despachurrar *vt* to squash, crush; to mangle.

despacio *adv* slowly, leisurely; little by little:—¡~! softly!, gently!

desparramar *vt* to disseminate, spread; to spill; to squander, lavish: —**se** *vr* to be dissipated.

despavorido *adj* frightened.

despecho *m* indignation; displeasure; spite; dismay, despair; deceit; derision, scorn:—**a ~ de** in spite of.

despectivo, va *adj* pejorative, derogatory.

despedir *vt* to discharge; to dismiss (from office); to see off:—**se** *vr* ~ **de** to say goodbye to.

despegar *vt* to unglue; to take off:—**se** *vr* to come loose.

despegue *m* take-off.

despeinar *vt* to ruffle.

despejado, da *adj* sprightly, quick; clear.

despellejar *vt* to skin.

despensa *f* pantry, larder; provisions *pl*.

desperdiciar *vt* to squander.

desperdigar *vt* to separate; to scatter.

desperfecto *m* slight damage; flaw.

despertador *m* alarm clock.

despertar *vt* to wake up, rouse from sleep; to excite:—*vi* to wake up; to grow lively or sprightly:—~**se** *vr* to wake up.

despiadado, da *adj* heartless; merciless.

despido *m* dismissal.

despierto, ta *adj* awake; vigilant; fierce; brisk, sprightly.

despistar *vt* to mislead; to throw off the track:—~**se** *vr* to take the wrong way; to become confused.

desplazar *vt* to move; to scroll:—~**se** *vr* to travel.

desplegar *vt* to unfold, display; to explain, elucidate; (*mar*) to unfurl:—~**se** *vr* to open out; to travel.

desplomarse *vr* to fall to the ground; to collapse.

despoblar *vt* to depopulate; to desolate: —~**se** *vr* to become depopulated.

despojar *vt*:—~ **(de)** to strip (of); to deprive (of):—~**se** *vr* to undress.

desposar *vt* to marry, betroth:—~**se** *vr* to be betrothed or married.

desposeer *vt* to dispossess.

déspota *m* despot.

despreciar *vt* to offend; to despise.

desprender *vt* to unfasten, loosen; to separate:—~**se**

vr to give way; to fall down; to extricate oneself.

despreocupado, da *adj* careless; unworried.

desprevenido, da *adj* unawares, unprepared.

desproporcionado, da *adj* disproportionate.

desprovisto, ta *adj* unprovided.

después *adv* after, afterwards; next.

despuntar *vt* to blunt:—*vi* to sprout; to dawn:—**al ~ del dia** at break of day.

desquiciar *vt* to upset; to discompose; to disorder.

desquite *m* recovery of a loss; revenge, retaliation.

destacamento *m* (*mil*) detachment.

destacar *vt* to emphasise; (*mil*) to detach (a body of troops):—**~se** *vr* to stand out.

destajo *m* piecework.

destapar *vt* to uncover; to open:—**~se** *vr* to be uncovered.

destartalado, da *adj* untidy.

destello *m* signal light; sparkle.

desteñir *vt* to discolour:—**~se** *vr* to fade.

desternillarse *vr*:—**~ de risa** to roar with laughter.

desterrar *vt* to banish; to expel, drive away.

destetar *vt* to wean.

destilar *vt*, *vi* to distil.

destinar *vt* to destine for, intend for.

destinatario, a *m/f* addressee.

destino *m* destiny; fate, doom; destination; office.

destornillador *m* screwdriver.

destreza *f* dexterity, cleverness, cunning, expertness, skill.

destrozar *vt* to destroy, break into pieces; (*mil*) to defeat.

destruir *vt* to destroy.

desvalido, da *adj* helpless; destitute.

desvalijar *vt* to rob; to burgle.

desván *m* garret.

desvanecer *vt* to dispel:—**~se** *vr* to grow vapid, become insipid; to vanish; to be affected with giddiness.

desvarío *m* delirium; giddiness; inconstancy, caprice; extravagance.

desvelar *vt* to keep awake:—**~se** *vr* to stay awake.

desventaja *f* disadvantage; damage.

desventura *f* misfortune; calamity.

desvergüenza *f* impudence; shamelessness.

desvestir *vt*: **~se** *vr* to undress.

desviar *vt* to divert; to dissuade; to parry (at fencing):—**~se** *vr* to go off course.

detallar *vt* to detail, relate minutely.

detener *vt* to stop, detain; to arrest; to keep back; to reserve; to withhold: **~se** *vr* to stop; to stay.

detenidamente *adv* carefully.

detergente *m* detergent.

deteriorar *vt* to damage.

determinar *vt* to determine:—**~se** *vr* to decide.

detestar *vt* to detest, abhor.

detonar *vi* to detonate.

detrás *adv* behind; at the back, in the back.

deuda *f* debt; fault; offence.

devanar *vt* to reel; to wrap up.

devastar *vt* to devastate.

devengar *vt* to accrue.

devoción *f* devotion, piety; strong affection; ardent love.

devolver *vt* to return; to send back; to refund:—*vi* to be sick.

devorar *vt* to devour, swallow up.

día *m* day.

diablo *m* devil.

diablura *f* prank.

diana *f* (*mil*) reveille; bull's-eye.

diapositiva *f* transparency, slide.

diario *m* journal, diary; daily newspaper; daily expenses *pl*:—**~, ria** *adj* daily.

diarrea *f* diarrhoea.

dibujar *vt* to draw, design.

diccionario *m* dictionary.

dicha *f* happiness, good fortune:—**por ~** by chance.

diciembre *m* December.

dictamen *m* opinion, notion; suggestion; judgement.

dictar *vt* to dictate.

diecinueve *adj*, *m* nineteen.

dieciocho *adj*, *m* eighteen.

dieciséis *adj*, *m* sixteen.

diecisiete *adj*, *m* seventeen.

diente *m* tooth; fang; tusk.

diestro, tra *adj* right; dexterous, skilful, clever; sagacious, prudent; sly, cunning:—*m* skilful fencer; halter; bridle.

dieta *f* diet, regimen; diet, assembly; daily salary of judges.

diez *adj*, *m* ten.

diezmar *vt* to decimate.

difamar *vt* to defame, libel.

diferencia *f* difference.

diferenciar *vt* to differentiate, distinguish:—**~se** *vr* to differ, distinguish oneself.

diferente *adj* different, unlike.

diferido, da *adj* recorded.

difícil *adj* difficult.

dificultad *f* difficulty.

difundir *vt* to diffuse, spread; to divulge:—**~se** *vr* to spread (out).

difunto, ta *adj* dead, deceased; late.

digerir *vt* to digest; to bear with patience; to adjust, arrange.

dignarse *vr* to condescend, deign.

digno, na *adj* worthy; suitable.

dilatado, da *adj* large; numerous; prolix; spacious, extensive.

dilatar *vt* to dilate, expand; to spread out; to defer, protract.

dilema *m* dilemma.

diligencia *f* diligence; affair, business; call of nature; stage coach.

dilucidar *vt* to elucidate, explain.

diluir *vt* to dilute.

diluviar *vi* to rain in torrents.

diminuto, ta *adj* minute, small.

dimitir *vt* to give up:—*vi* to resign.

dinamita *f* dynamite.

dinamo *f* dynamo.

dineral *m* large sum of money.

dinero *m* money.

dios *m* god.

diosa *f* goddess.

diplomado, da *adj* qualified.

dique *m* dam.

dirección *f* direction, guidance; administration; steering.

directo, ta *adj* direct, straight; apparent, evident; live.

director, ra *m/f* director; conductor; president; manager.

dirigir *vt* to direct; to conduct; to regulate, govern:—**~se** *vr* to go towards; to address oneself to.

discernir *vt* to discern, distinguish.

discípulo *m* disciple; scholar.

disco *m* disc; record; discus; light; face (of the sun or moon); lens (of a telescope).

díscolo, la *adj* ungovernable; peevish.

discordante *adj* dissonant, discordant.

discreción *f* discretion; acuteness of mind.

discrepar *vi* to differ.

discreto, ta *adj* discreet; ingenious; witty, eloquent.

disculpar *vt* to exculpate, excuse; to acquit, absolve:—**~se** *vr* to apologise; to excuse oneself.

discurrir *vi* to ramble about; to run to and fro; to discourse (on a subject): —*vt* to invent, contrive; to meditate.

discurso *m* speech; conversation; dissertation; space of time.

discutir *vt, vi* to discuss.

disecar *vt* to dissect; to stuff.

diseminar *vt* to scatter; to disseminate, propagate.

diseñar *vt* to draw; to design.

disentir *vi* to dissent, disagree.

disfrazar *vt* to disguise, conceal; to cloak, dissemble:—**~se** *vr* to disguise oneself as.

disfrutar *vt* to enjoy:—**~se** *vr* to enjoy oneself.

disgustar *vt* to disgust; to offend:—**~se** *vr* to be displeased; to fall out.

disidente *adj* dissident:—*m/f* dissident, dissenter.

disimular *vt* to hide; to tolerate.

disipar *vt* to dissipate, disperse, scatter; to lavish.

dislocarse *vr* to be dislocated or out of joint.

disminuir *vt* to diminish; to decrease.

disolver *vt* to loosen, untie; to dissolve; to disunite; to melt, liquefy; to interrupt.

disparar *vt* to shoot, discharge, fire; to let off; to throw with violence:—*vi* to shoot, fire.

disparate *m* nonsense, absurdity, extravagance.

displicencia *f* displeasure; dislike.

disponer *vt* to arrange, prepare; to dispose.

disponible *adj* available; disposable.

dispositivo *m* device.

disputar *vt* to dispute, controvert, question:—*vi* to debate, argue.

disquete *m* floppy disk.

distancia *f* distance; interval; difference.

distante *adj* distant, far off.

distinguido, da *adj* distinguished, conspicuous.

distinguir *vt* to distinguish; to discern:—**~se** *vr* to distinguish oneself.

distinto, ta *adj* distinct, different; clear.

distraer *vt* to distract:—**~se** *vr* to be absent-minded, be inattentive.

distraído, da *adj* absent-minded, inattentive.

distribuir *vt* to distribute.

distrito *m* district; territory.

disturbio *m* riot; disturbance, interruption.

disuadir *vt* to dissuade.

diurno, na *adj* daily.

diva *f* prima donna.

divagar *vt* to digress.

divergencia *f* divergence.

diversidad *f* diversity; variety of things.

diversificar *vt* to diversify; to vary.

diversión *f* diversion; sport; amusement; (*mil*) diversion.

divertir *vt* to divert (the attention); to amuse, entertain; (*mil*) to draw off: —**~se** *vr* to amuse oneself.

dividir *vt* to divide; to disunite; to separate; to share out.

divieso *m* (*med*) boil.

divino, na *adj* divine, heavenly; excellent.

divorcio *m* divorce; separation, disunion.

divulgar *vt* to publish, divulge.

dobladillo *m* hem; turn-up.

doblar *vt* to double; to fold; to bend: —*vi* to turn; to toll:—**~se** *vr* to bend, bow, submit.

doble *adj* double; dual; deceitful:—**al ~** doubly:—*m* double.

doblegar *vt* to bend:—**~se** *vr* to yield.

doblez *m* crease; fold; turn-up:—*f* duplicity.

doce *adj*, *m* twelve.

docena *f* dozen.

dócil *adj* docile, tractable.

doctor, ra *m*/*f* doctor.

documento *m* document; record.

dogma *m* dogma.

dólar *m* dollar.

doler *vt*, *vi* to feel pain; to ache:—**~se** *vr* to feel for the sufferings of others; to complain.

dolor *m* pain; aching, ache; affliction.

domar *vt* to tame; to subdue, master.

domesticar *vt* to domesticate.

domicilio *m* domicile; home, abode.

dominar *vt* to dominate; to be fluent in:—**~se** *vr* to moderate one's passions.

domingo *m* Sunday; (Christian) Sabbath.

donar *vt* to donate; to bestow.

donativo *m* contribution.

doncella *f* virgin, maiden; lady's maid.

donde *relative adv* where

¿dónde? *interrogative adv* where?:—**¿de dónde?** from where?

dondequiera *adv* wherever.

dorado, da *adj* gilt *compd*; golden:—*m* gilding.

dormir *vi* to sleep:—**~se** *vr* to fall asleep.

dos *adj*, *m* two.

doscientos, tas *adj pl* two hundred.

dosis *f invar* dose.

dotado, da *adj* gifted.

drama *m* drama.

dramatizar *vt* to dramatise.

droga *f* drug; stratagem; artifice, deceit.

droguería *f* hardware store.

ducha *f* shower; (*med*) douche.

ducho, cha *adj* skilled, experienced.

dudar *vt* to doubt.

duelo *m* grief, affliction; mourning.

duende *m* elf, hobgoblin.

dueño, ña *m*/*f* owner; landlord/lady; employer.

dulce *adj* sweet; mild, gentle, meek; soft:—*m* sweet, candy.

dúo *m* (*mus*) duo, duet.

duodécimo, ma *adj* twelfth.

duplicar *vt* to duplicate; to repeal.

duradero, ra *adj* lasting, durable.

durante *adv* during.

durar *vi* to last, continue.

durazno *m* peach; peach tree.

dureza *f* hardness; harshness:—**~ de oido** hardness of hearing.

duro, ra *adj* hard; cruel; harsh, rough: —*m* five peseta coin:—*adv* hard.

E

e *conj* and (before words starting with *i* and *hi*).

ébano *m* ebony.

ebrio, ia *adj* drunk.

ebullición *f* boiling.

echar *vt* to throw; to add; to pour out; to mail:—**~se** *vr* to lie down.

eco *m* echo.

económico, ca *adj* economic; cheap; thrifty; financial; avaricious.

ecuánime *adj* level-headed.

ecuménico, ca *adj* ecumenical; universal.

edad *f* age.

edición *f* edition; publication.

edificar *vt* to build, construct; to edify.

edificio *m* building; structure.

editar *vt* to edit; to publish.

educación *f* education; upbringing; (good) manners *pl*.

educar *vt* to educate, instruct; to bring up.

efectivamente *adv* exactly; really; in fact.

efecto *m* effect; consequence; purpose: ——**~s** *mpl* effects *pl*, goods *pl*:—**en ~** in fact, really.

efectuar *vt* to effect, carry out.

eficaz *adj* efficient; effective.

eficiente *adj* efficient.

egoísta *m/f* self-seeker:—*adj* selfish.

eje *m* axle; axis.

ejecutar *vt* to execute, perform; to put to death; (*jur*) to distrain, seize.

ejecutivo, va *adj* executive:—*m/f* executive.

ejemplar *m* specimen; copy; example:—*adj* exemplary.

ejemplo *m* example:—**por ~** for example, for instance.

ejercer *vt* to exercise;*vi* to apply oneself to the functions of an office.

ejercicio *m* exercise.

ejercitar *vt* to exercise.

ejército *m* army.

el *art*, *m* the.

él *pn* he, it.

elaborar *vt* to elaborate.

elástico, ca *adj* elastic.

elección *f* election; choice.

eléctrico, ca *adj* electric, electrical.

electrocutar *vt* to electrocute.

electrodomesticos *mpl* (electrical) household appliances *pl*.

electrotecnia *f* electrical engineering.

elefante *m* elephant.

elegante *adj* elegant, fine.

elegir *vt* to choose, elect.

elemento *m* element:—**~s** *mpl* elements, rudiments, first principles *pl*.

elevar *vt* to raise; to elevate:—**~se** *vr* to rise; to be enraptured; to be conceited.

eliminar *vt* to eliminate, remove.

eliminatoria *f* preliminary (round).

ella *pn* she; it.

ello *pn* it.

elogiar *vt* to praise, eulogise.

eludir *vt* to elude, escape.

emanar *vi* to emanate.

embadurnar *vt* to smear, bedaub.

embalaje *m* packing, package.

embaldosar *vt* to pave with tiles.

embalse *m* reservoir.

embarazada *f* pregnant woman:—*adj* pregnant.

embarazoso, sa *adj* difficult; intricate, entangled.

embarcación *f* embarkation; any vessel or ship.

embarcar *vt* to embark:—**~se** *vr* to go on board; (*fig*) to get involved (in a matter).

embargo *m* embargo:—**sin ~** still, however.

embarque *m* embarkation.

embaucar *vt* to deceive; to trick.

embeber *vt* to soak; to saturate:—*vi* to shrink:—**~se** *vr* to be enraptured; to be absorbed.

embeleso *m* amazement, enchantment.

embellecer *vt* to embellish, beautify.

embestir *vt* to assault, attack.

emblanquecer *vt* to whiten:—**~se** *vr* to grow white; to bleach.

embobado, da *adj* amazed; fascinated.

émbolo *m* plunger; piston.

embolsar *vt* to put money into (a purse); to pocket.

emborrachar *vt* to intoxicate, inebriate:—**~se** *vr* to get drunk.

emboscada *f* (*mil*) ambush.

embotar *vt* to blunt:—**~se** *vr* to go numb.

embotellamiento *m* traffic jam.

embotellar *vt* to bottle (wine).

embozar *vt* to muffle (the face); (*fig*) to cloak, conceal.

embrague *m* clutch.

embriagar *vt* to intoxicate, inebriate; to transport, enrapture.

embrión *m* embryo.

embrollo *m* muddle.

embromar *vt* to tease; to cajole, wheedle.

embrujar *vt* to bewitch.

embrutecer *vt* to brutalise:—**~se** *vr* to become depraved.

embudo *m* funnel.

embustero, ra *m/f* impostor, cheat; liar:—*adj* deceitful.

embutido *m* sausage; inlay.

emerger *vi* to emerge, appear.

emigrar *vi* to emigrate.

eminente *adj* eminent, high; excellent, conspicuous.

emisora *f* broadcasting station.

emitir *vt* to emit; to issue; to broadcast.

emoción *f* emotion; feeling; excitement.

emocionar *vt* to excite; to move, touch.

emotivo, va *adj* emotional.

empacho *m* (*med*) indigestion.

empalagoso, sa *adj* cloying; tiresome.

empalmar *vt* to join.

empanada *f* (meat) pie.

empanar *vt* to cover with bread-crumbs.

empantanarse *vr* to get swamped; to get bogged down.

empapar *vt* to soak; to soak up:—**~se** *vr* to soak.

empapelar *vt* to paper.

empaquetar *vt* to pack, parcel up.

emparedado *m* sandwich.

emparrado *m* vine arbour.

empastar *vt* to paste; to fill (a tooth).

empatar *vi* to draw.

empedernido, da *adj* inveterate; heartless.

empedrado *m* paving.

empeine *m* instep.

empellón *m* push; heavy blow.

empeñar *vt* to pawn, pledge:—**~se** *vr* to pledge oneself to pay debts; to get into debt:—**~se en algo** to insist on something.

empeorar *vt* to make worse:—*vi* **~se** *vr* to grow worse.

empequeñecer *vt* to dwarf; (*fig*) to belittle.

empezar *vt* to begin, start.

emplazamiento *m* summons; location.

empleado, da *m/f* official; employee.

emplear *vt* to employ; to occupy; to commission.

empobrecer *vt* to reduce to poverty:—*vi* to become poor.

empollar *vt* to incubate; to hatch; (*fam*) to swot (up).

empolvar *vt* to powder; to sprinkle powder upon.

empotrado, da *adj* built-in.

emprender *vt* to embark on; to tackle; to undertake.

empresa *f* (*com*) company; enterprise, undertaking.

empujar *vt* to push; to press forward.

empujón *m* push; impulse:—**a ~ones** in fits and starts.

emular *vt* to emulate, rival.

en *prep* in; for; on, upon.

enaguas *fpl* petticoat.

enamorado, da *adj* in love, lovesick.

enamorar *vt* to inspire love in:—**~se** *vr* to fall in love.

enano, na *adj* dwarfish:—*m* dwarf.

enardecer *vt* to fire with passion, inflame.

enarenar *vt* to fill with sand.

encabezar *vt* to head; to put a heading to; to lead.

encadenar *vt* to chain, link together; to connect, unite.

encajar *vt* to insert; to drive in; to encase; to intrude:—*vi* to fit (well).

encaje *m* lace.

encalar *vt* to whitewash.

encallar *vi* (*mar*) to run aground.

encaminar *vt* to guide, show the way:—**~se** *vr* **~ a** to take the road to.

encandilar *vt* to dazzle.

encanecer *vi* to grow grey; to grow old.

encantado, da *adj* bewitched; delighted; pleased.

encantador, ra *adj* charming:—*m/f* magician.

encantar *vt* to enchant, charm; (*fig*) to delight.

encarcelar *vt* to imprison.

encarecimiento *m* price increase:—**con** ~ insistently.

encargado, da *adj* in charge:—*m/f* representative; person in charge.

encargar *vt* to charge; to commission.

encariñarse *vr*:—~ **con** to grow fond of.

encarnar *vt* to embody, personify.

encasillar *vt* to pigeonhole; to typecast.

encastillarse *vr* to refuse to yield.

encausar *vt* to prosecute.

encauzar *vt* to channel.

encebollado *m* casseroled beef or lamb and onions, seasoned with spice.

encenagado, da *adj* muddy, mud-stained.

encendedor *m* lighter.

encender *vt* to kindle, light, set on fire; to inflame, incite; to switch on, to turn on:—~**se** *vr* to catch fire; to flare up.

encerado *m* blackboard.

encerar *vt* to wax; to polish.

encerrar *vt* to shut up, confine; to contain:—~**se** *vr* to withdraw from the world.

enchufar *vt* to plug in; to connect.

enchufe *m* plug; socket; connection; (*fam*) contact, connection.

encía *f* gum (of the teeth).

encierro *m* confinement; enclosure; prison; bull-pen; penning (of bulls).

encima *adv* above; over; at the top; besides:—~ **de** *prep* above; over; at the top of; besides.

encina *f* evergreen oak.

encinta *adj* pregnant.

enclenque *adj* weak, sickly:—*m* weakling.

encoger *vt* to contract, shorten; to shrink; to discourage:—~**se** *vr* to shrink; (*fig*) to cringe.

encolar *vt* to glue.

encolerizar *vt* to provoke, irritate:—~**se** *vr* to get angry.

encomendar *vt* to recommend; to entrust:—~**se** *vr* ~ **a** to entrust oneself to; to put one's trust in.

encontrar *vt* to meet, encounter:—*vr* ~**se con** to run into:—*vi* to assemble, come together.

encrucijada *f* crossroads; junction.

encuadernar *vt* to bind (books).

encubierto, ta *adj* hidden, concealed.

encubrir *vt* to hide, conceal.

encuesta *f* inquiry; opinion poll.

encurtir *vt* to pickle.

endeble *adj* feeble, weak.

endemoniado, da *adj* possessed with the devil; devilish.

enderezar *vt* to straighten out; to set right:—~**se** *vr* to stand upright.

endeudarse *vr* to get into debt.

endosar *vt* to endorse.

endrino *m* blackthorn, sloe.

endulzar *vt* to sweeten; to soften.

endurecer *vt* to harden, toughen:—~**se** *vr* to become cruel; to grow hard.

enebro *m* (*bot*) juniper.

enemistar *vt* to make an enemy:—~**se** *vr* to become enemies; to fall out.

energía *f* energy, power, drive; strength of will.

energúmeno, na *m/f* (*fam*) madman/woman.

enero *m* January.

enfadar *vt* to anger, irritate; to trouble:—~**se** *vr* to become angry.

énfasis *m* emphasis.

enfermar *vi* to fall ill:—*vt* to make sick; to weaken.

enfermedad *f* illness.

enfermero, ra *m/f* nurse.

enfermo, ma *adj* sick, ill:—*m/f* invalid, sick person; patient.

enfocar *vt* to focus; to consider (a problem).

enfoque *m* focus.

enfrentar *vt* to confront; to put face to face:—~**se** *vr* to face each other; to meet (two teams).

enfrente *adv* over against, opposite; in front.

enfriar *vt* to cool; to refrigerate:—~**se** *vr* to cool down; (*med*) to catch a cold.

enfurecer *vt* to madden, enrage:—~**se** *vr* to get rough (of the wind and sea); to become furious or enraged.

enfurruñarse *vr* to get sulky; to frown.

engañar *vt* to deceive, cheat:—~**se** *vr* to be deceived; to make a mistake.

enganchar *vt* to hook, hang up; to hitch up; to couple, connect; to recruit into military service:—~se *vr* (*mil*) to enlist.

engañoso, sa *adj* deceitful, artful, false.

engastar *vt* to set, mount.

engatusar *vt* to coax.

engendrar *vt* to beget, engender; to produce.

englobar *vt* to include.

engordar *vt* to fatten:—*vi* to grow fat; to put on weight.

engorroso, sa *adj* troublesome, cumbersome.

engranaje *m* gear; gearing.

engrasar *vt* to grease, lubricate.

engreído, da *adj* conceited, vain.

engullir *vt* to swallow; to gobble, devour.

enharinar *vt* to cover or sprinkle with flour.

enhebrar *vt* to thread.

enhorabuena *f* congratulations *pl*:—*adv* all right; well and good.

enhoramala *interj* good riddance!

enjalbegar *vt* to whitewash.

enjambre *m* swarm of bees; crowd, multitude.

enjuagar *vt* to rinse out; to wash out.

enjuiciar *vt* to prosecute, try; to pass judgement on, judge.

enlace *m* connection, link; relationship.

enladrillar *vt* to pave with bricks.

enlazar *vt* to join, unite; to tie.

enlodar *vt* to cover in mud; (*fig*) to stain.

enloquecer *vt* to madden, drive crazy:—*vi* to go mad.

enmarañar *vt* to entangle; to

complicate; to confuse:—~se *vr* to become entangled; to get confused.

enmendar *vt* to correct; to reform; to repair, compensate for; to amend:—~se *vr* to mend one's ways.

enmohecer *vt* to make mouldy; to rust:—~se *vr* to grow mouldy or musty; to rust.

enmudecer(se) *vt* to silence:—~se *vr* to grow dumb; to be silent.

ennegrecer *vt* to blacken; to darken; to obscure.

enojar *vt* to irritate, make angry; to annoy; to upset; to offend:—~se *vr* to get angry.

enorgullecerse *vr*:—~ (de) to be proud (of).

enorme *adj* enormous, vast, huge; horrible.

enredadera *f* climbing plant; bindweed.

enredar *vt* to entangle, ensnare, confound, perplex; to puzzle; to sow discord among:—~se *vr* to get entangled; to get complicated; to get embroiled.

enrejado *m* trelliswork.

enrevesado, da *adj* complicated.

enriquecer *vt* to enrich; to adorn:—~se *vr* to grow rich.

enrojecer *vt* to redden:—*vi* to blush.

enrolar *vt* to recruit:—~se *vr* (*mil*) to join up.

enrollar *vt* to roll (up).

enroscar *vt* to twist:—~se *vr* to curl or roll up.

ensalada *f* salad.

ensalmo *m* enchantment, spell.

ensalzar *vt* to exalt, aggrandise; to exaggerate.

ensamblar *vt* to assemble.

ensañar *vt* to irritate, enrage:—~se con *vr* to treat brutally.

ensanchar *vt* to widen; to extend; to enlarge:—~se *vr* to expand; to assume an air of importance.

ensangrentar *vt* to stain with blood.

ensartar *vt* to string (beads, etc).

ensayar *vt* to test; to rehearse.

ensayo *m* test, trial; rehearsal of a play; essay.

enseñar *vt* to teach, instruct; to show.

ensimismarse *vr* to be or become lost in thought.

ensordecer *vt* to deafen:—*vi* to grow deaf.

ensuciar *vt* to stain, soil; to defile:—~se *vr* to wet oneself; to dirty oneself.

ensueño *m* fantasy; daydream; illusion.

entablar *vt* to board (up); to strike up (conversation).

entablillar *vt* (*med*) to put in a splint.

entallar *vt* to tailor (a suit):—*vi* to fit.

ente *m* organisation; entity, being; (*fam*) odd character.

entender *vt, vi* to understand, comprehend; to remark, take notice (of); to reason, think:—**a mi ~** in my opinion: —~se *vr* to understand each other.

enterar *vt* to inform; to instruct:—~se *vr* to find out.

enternecer *vt* to soften; to

move (to pity):—~**se** *vr* to be moved.

entero, ra *adj* entire, complete; perfect; honest; resolute:—**por** ~ entirely, completely.

enterrar *vt* to inter, bury.

entidad *f* entity; company; body; society.

entierro *m* burial; funeral.

entonar *vt* to tune, intonate; to intone; to tone:—*vi* to be in tune:—~**se** *vr* to give oneself airs.

entonces *adv* then, at that time.

entornar *vt* to half close.

entorpecer *vt* to dull; to make lethargic; to hinder; to delay.

entrada *f* entrance, entry; (*com*) receipts *pl*; entree; ticket (for cinema, theatre, etc).

entrampar *vt* to trap, snare; to mess up; to burden with debts:—~**se** *vr* get into debt.

entrañable *adj* intimate; affectionate.

entrañas *fpl* entrails *pl*, intestines *pl*.

entrar *vi* to enter, go in; to commence.

entre *prep* between; among(st); in:—~ **manos** in hand.

entrecejo *m* space between the eyebrows; frown.

entredicho *m* (*jur*) injunction:—**estar en** ~ to be banned:—**poner en** ~ to cast doubt on.

entregar *vt* to deliver; to hand over: —~**se** *vr* to surrender; to devote oneself.

entremeses *mpl* hors d'oeuvres.

entrenarse *vr* to train.

entrepierna *f* crotch.

entresuelo *m* entresol; mezzanine.

entretanto *adv* meanwhile.

entretejer *vt* to interweave.

entretela *f* interfacing, stiffening, interlining.

entretener *vt* to amuse; to entertain, divert; to hold up; to maintain:—~**se** *vr* to amuse oneself; to linger.

entrever *vt* to have a glimpse of.

entrevistar *vt* to interview:—~**se** *vr* to have an interview.

entristecer *vt* to sadden.

entrometer *vt* to put (one thing) between (others):—~**se** *vr* to interfere.

entumecido, da *adj* numb, stiff.

enturbiar *vt* to make cloudy; to obscure, confound:—~**se** *vr* to become cloudy; (*fig*) to get confused.

entusiasmar *vt* to excite, fill with enthusiasm; to delight.

enumerar *vt* to enumerate.

envalentonar *vt* to give courage to:—~**se** *vr* to boast.

envanecer *vt* to make vain; to swell with pride:—~**se** *vr* to become proud.

envaramiento *m* stiffness; numbness.

envasar *vt* to pack; to bottle; to can.

envase *m* packing; bottling; canning; container; package; bottle; can.

envejecer *vt* to make old:—*vi* ~**se** *vr* to grow old.

envenenar *vt* to poison; to embitter.

envés *m* wrong side (of material).

enviar *vt* to send, transmit, convey, dispatch.

enviciar *vt* to vitiate, corrupt:—~**se** *vr* to get corrupted.

envidia *f* envy; jealousy.

envidiar *vt* to envy; to grudge; to be jealous of.

envilecer *vt* to vilify, debase:—~**se** *vr* to degrade oneself.

envío *m* (*com*) dispatch, remittance of goods; consignment.

enviudar *vi* to become a widower or widow.

envolver *vt* to involve; to wrap up.

enyesar *vt* to plaster; (*med*) to put in a plaster cast.

enzarzarse *vr* to get involved in a dispute; to get oneself into trouble.

épico, ca *adj* epic.

epígrafe *f* epigraph, inscription; motto; headline.

episodio *m* episode, instalment.

época *f* epoch; period, time.

epopeya *f* epic.

equidad *f* equity, honesty; impartiality, justice.

equilibrar *vt* to balance; to poise.

equilibrio *m* balance, equilibrium.

equipaje *m* luggage; equipment.

equipar *vt* to fit out, equip, furnish.

equipararse *vr*:—~ **con** to be on a level with.

equipo *m* equipment; team; shift.

equitación *f* horsemanship; riding.

equitativo, va *adj* equitable; just.

equivaler *vi* to be of equal value.

equivocación f mistake, error; misunderstanding.

equivocar vt to mistake:—~**se** vr to make a mistake, be wrong.

equívoco, ca adj equivocal, ambiguous:—m equivocation; quibble.

era f era, age; threshing floor.

erario m treasury, public funds pl.

erguir vt to erect, raise up straight:—~**se** vr to straighten up.

erial m fallow land.

erigir vt to erect, raise, build; to establish.

erizarse vr to bristle; to stand on end.

erizo m hedgehog:—~ **de mar** sea urchin.

ermita f hermitage.

erotismo m eroticism.

errar vi to be mistaken, to wander.

errata f misprint.

erre:—~ **que** ~ adv obstinately.

error m error, mistake, fault.

eructar vi to belch, burp.

esbelto, ta adj slim, slender.

esbirro m bailiff; henchman; killer.

esbozo m outline.

escabeche m pickle; pickled fish.

escabroso, sa adj rough, uneven; craggy; rude, risqué, blue.

escabullirse vr to escape, evade; to slip through one's fingers.

escafandra f diving suit; space suit.

escala f ladder; (mus) scale; stopover.

escalar vt to climb.

escalera f staircase; ladder.

escalfar vt to poach (eggs).

escalofriante adj chilling.

escalón m step of a stair; rung.

escama f (fish) scale.

escamar vt to scale, take off scales:—~**se** vr to flake off; to become suspicious.

escamotear vt to swipe; to make disappear.

escampar vi to stop raining.

escándalo m scandal; uproar.

escaño m bench with a back; seat (parliament).

escapar vi to escape:—~**se** vr to get away; to leak (water, etc).

escaparate m shop window; wardrobe.

escape m escape, flight; leak; exhaust (of motor).

escarabajo m beetle.

escaramuza f skirmish; dispute, quarrel.

escarbar vt to scratch (the earth as hens do); to inquire into.

escarcha f white frost.

escarlata adj scarlet.

escarlatina f scarlet fever.

escarmentar vi to learn one's lesson: —vt to punish severely.

escarola f (bot) endive.

escarpado, da adj sloped; craggy.

escaso, sa adj small, short, little; sparing; scarce; scanty.

escenario m stage; set.

escéptico, ca adj sceptic, sceptical.

esclarecer vt to lighten; to illuminate; to illustrate; to shed light on (problem, etc).

esclavo, va m/f slave; captive.

esclusa f sluice, floodgate.

escoba f broom, brush.

escocer vt to sting; to burn:—~**se** vr to chafe.

escoger vt to choose, select.

escolar m/f schoolboy/ girl:—adj scholastic.

escollo m reef, rock.

escoltar vt to escort.

escombros mpl rubbish; debris.

esconder vt to hide, conceal:—~**se** vr to be hidden.

escondite m hiding place:— **juego de** ~ hide-and-seek.

escoplo m chisel.

escorbuto m scurvy.

escote m low neck (of a dress).

escribir vt to write; to spell.

escrito m document; manuscript, text.

escritor, ra m/f writer, author.

escritorio m writing desk; office, study.

escrúpulo m doubt, scruple, scrupulousness.

escuchar vt to listen to, heed.

escudilla f bowl.

escudo m shield.

escudriñar vt to search, examine; to pry into.

escuela f school.

esculpir vt to sculpt.

escupir vt to spit.

escurreplatos m invar plate rack.

escurrir vt to drain; to drip:—~**se** vr to slip away; to slip, slide:—vi to wring out.

ese, esa adj that:—**esos, as** pl those.

ése, ésa pn that (one):—**ésos, as** pl those (ones).

esencial *adj* essential; principal.

esfera *f* sphere; globe.

esforzarse *vr* to exert oneself, make an effort.

esfuerzo *m* effort.

esfumarse *vr* to fade away.

esgrima *f* fencing.

esguince *m* (*med*) sprain.

eslabón *m* link of a chain; steel; shackle.

esmalte *m* enamel.

esmerado, da *adj* careful, neat.

esmeralda *m* emerald.

esmero *m* careful attention, great care.

eso *pn* that.

esos, as; ésos, as *pl* of **ese, a; ése, a.**

espabilar *vt* to wake up:— **~se** *vr* to wake up; (*fig*) to get a move on.

espaciar *vt* to spread out; to space (out).

espacio *m* space; (radio or TV) programme.

espada *f* sword; ace of spades.

espalda *f* back, back-part:— **~s** *fpl* shoulders *pl*.

español, la *adj* Spanish:—*m/f* Spaniard:—*m* Spanish language.

espantajo *m* scarecrow; bogeyman.

espantar *vt* to frighten; to chase or drive away.

esparadrapo *m* adhesive tape.

esparcir *vt* to scatter; to divulge:—**~se** *vr* to amuse oneself.

espárrago *m* asparagus.

espátula *f* spatula.

especia *f* spice.

especial *adj* special; particular:—**en ~** especially.

especie *f* species; kind, sort; matter.

especificar *vt* to specify.

espectáculo *m* spectacle; show.

espectador, ra *m/f* spectator.

especular *vt* to speculate.

espejismo *m* mirage.

espejo *m* mirror.

espeluznante *adj* horrifying.

esperanza *f* hope.

esperar *vt* to hope; to expect, wait for.

esperma *f* sperm.

espeso, sa *adj* thick, dense.

espesor *m* thickness.

espía *m/f* spy.

espiga *f* ear (of corn).

espigón *m* ear of corn; sting; (*mar*) breakwater.

espina *f* thorn; fishbone.

espinaca *f* (*bot*) spinach.

espinilla *f* shinbone.

espino *m* hawthorn.

espiral *adj*, *f* spiral.

espirar *vt* to exhale.

espíritu *m* spirit, soul; mind; intelligence:—**el E~ Santo** the Holy Ghost:—**~s** *pl* demons, hobgoblins *pl*.

espléndido, da *adj* splendid.

espliego *m* (*bot*) lavender.

espolón *m* spur (of a cock); spur (of a mountain range); sea wall; jetty; (*mar*) buttress.

espolvorear *vt* to sprinkle.

esponja *f* sponge.

espontáneo, nea *adj* spontaneous.

esposa *f* wife.

esposas *fpl* handcuffs *pl*.

esposo *m* husband.

espuma *f* froth, foam.

espumar *vt* to skim, take the scum off.

espumoso, sa *adj* frothy, foamy; sparkling (wine).

esputo *m* spit, saliva.

esqueje *m* cutting (of plant).

esquela *f* note, slip of paper.

esqueleto *m* skeleton.

esquema *m* scheme; diagram; plan.

esquí *m* ski; skiing.

esquina *f* corner, angle.

esquirol *m* blackleg.

esquivar *vt* to shun, avoid, evade.

esta *adj f* this:—**~s** *pl* these.

ésta *pn f* this:—**~s** *pl* these.

estable *adj* stable.

establecer *vt* to establish.

establo *m* stable.

estaca *f* stake; stick; post.

estación *f* season (of the year); station; railroad station, terminus:—**~ de autobuses** bus station:—**~ de servicio** service station.

estacionar *vt* to park; (*mil*) to station.

estadio *m* phase; stadium.

estado *m* state, condition.

Estados Unidos *mpl* United States (of America).

estafar *vt* to deceive, defraud.

estallar *vi* to crack; to burst; to break out.

estambre *m* stamen.

estamento *m* estate; body; layer; class.

estampa *f* print; engraving; appearance.

estampar *vt* to print.

estancar *vt* to check (a current); to monopolise; to prohibit, suspend:—**~se** *vr* to stagnate.

estancia *f* stay; bedroom; ranch; (*poet*) stanza.

estanco *m* tobacconist's (shop):—**~, ca** *adj* watertight.

estándar *adj, m* standard.

estaño *m* tin.

estanque *m* pond, pool; reservoir.

estantería *f* shelves *pl*, shelving.

estar *vi* to be; to be (in a place).

estatua *f* statue.

este[1] *m* east;

este[2], **ta** *adj* this:—**estos, tas** *pl* these.

estera *f* mat.

estéreo *adj invar, m* stereo.

estereotipo *m* stereotype.

estéril *adj* sterile, infertile.

esterlina *adj*:—**libra ~** pound sterling.

estético, ca *adj* aesthetic:—*f* aesthetics.

estiércol *m* dung; manure.

estilo *m* style; fashion; stroke (swimming).

estima *f* esteem.

estimar *vt* to estimate, value; to esteem; to judge; to think.

estimular *vt* to stimulate, excite; to goad.

estío *m* summer.

estipular *vt* to stipulate.

estirar *vt* to stretch out.

esto *pn* this.

estofado *m* stew.

estómago *m* stomach.

estopa *f* tow.

estorbar *vt* to hinder; (*fig*) to bother: —*vi* to be in the way.

estornudar *vi* to sneeze.

estos, as, éstos, tas *pl* of **este, ta; éste, ta**.

estrado *m* drawing room; stage, platform.

estrafalario, ria *adj* slovenly; eccentric.

estrago *m* ruin, destruction; havoc.

estrangular *vt* to strangle; (*med*) to strangulate.

estraperlo *m* black market.

estratagema *f* stratagem, trick.

estrato *m* stratum, layer.

estraza *f* rag:—**papel de ~** brown paper.

estrechar *vt* to tighten; to contract, constrain; to compress:—**~se** *vr* to grow narrow; to embrace:—**~ la mano** to shake hands.

estrecho *m* straits *pl*:—**~, cha** *adj* narrow, close; tight; intimate; rigid, austere; short (of money).

estrella *f* star.

estrellar *vt* to dash to pieces:—**~se** *vr* to smash; to crash; to fail.

estremecer *vt* to shake, make tremble:—**~se** *vr* to shake, tremble.

estrenar *vt* to wear for the first time; to move into (a house); to show (a film) for the first time:—**~se** *vr* to make one's debut.

estreñido, da *adj* constipated.

estrépito *m* noise, racket; fuss.

estribillo *m* chorus.

estribo *m* buttress; stirrup; running board:—**perder los ~s** to fly off the handle (*fam*).

estribor *m* (*mar*) starboard.

estricto, ta *adj* strict; severe.

estrofa *f* (*poet*) verse, strophe.

estropajo *m* scourer.

estropear *vt* to spoil; to damage:—**~se** *vr* to get damaged.

estructura *f* structure.

estruendo *m* clamour, noise; confusion, uproar; pomp, ostentation.

estuche *m* case (for scissors, etc); sheath.

estudiar *vt* to study.

estufa *f* heater, fire.

estupefaciente *m* narcotic.

estupefacto *adj* speechless; thunderstruck.

estupendo, da *adj* terrific, marvellous.

estúpido *adj* stupid.

etapa *f* stage; stopping place; (*fig*) phase.

etcétera *adv* etcetera, and so on.

eterno, na *adj* eternal.

ético, ca *adj* ethical, moral.

etiqueta *f* etiquette; label.

evacuar *vt* to evacuate, empty.

evadir *vt* to evade, escape.

evaluar *vt* to evaluate.

evaporar *vt* to evaporate:—**~se** *vr* to vanish.

eventual *adj* possible; temporary, casual (worker).

evidente *adj* evident, clear.

evitar *vt* to avoid.

evolucionar *vi* to evolve.

ex *adj* ex.

ex profeso *adv* on purpose.

exacerbar *vt* to exacerbate; to irritate.

exacto, ta *adj* exact; punctual; accurate.

exagerar *vt* to exaggerate.

exaltar *vt* to exalt, elevate; to praise, extol:—**~se** *vr* to get excited.

examen *m* exam, examination, test, inquiry.

examinar *vt* to examine.

exasperar *vt* to exasperate, irritate.

excavar *vt* to excavate, dig out.

exceder *vt* to exceed, surpass, excel, outdo.

excelente *adj* excellent.

excéntrico, ca *adj* eccentric.

excepto *adv* excepting, except (for).

exceso *m* excess.

excitar *vt* to excite:—**~se** *vr* to get excited.

exclamar *vt* to exclaim, cry out.

excluir *vt* to exclude.

excremento *m* excrement.

excursión *f* excursion, trip.

excusa *f* excuse, apology.

excusado *m* toilet.

excusar *vt* to excuse; to avoid:—**~ de** to exempt from:—**~se** *vr* to apologise.

exento, ta *adj* exempt, free.

exhalar *vt* to exhale; to give off; to heave (a sigh).

exhausto, ta *adj* exhausted.

exhibir *vt* to exhibit.

exhortar *vt* to exhort.

exhumar *vt* to disinter, exhume.

exigir *vt* to demand, require.

exiliado, da *adj* exiled:—*m/f* exile.

existir *vi* to exist, be.

éxito *m* outcome; success; (*mus, etc*) hit:—**tener ~** to be successful.

exorbitante *adj* exhorbitant, excessive.

exótico, ca *adj* exotic.

expandir *vt* to expand.

expatriarse *vr* to emigrate; to go into exile.

expectativa *f* expectation; prospect.

expedición *f* expedition.

expediente *m* expedient; means; (*jur*) proceedings *pl*; dossier, file.

expedir *vt* to send, forward, dispatch.

expensas *fpl*:—**a ~ de** at the expense of.

experimentar *vt* to experience:—*vi* **~ con** to experiment with.

experto, ta *adj* expert; experienced.

expiar *vt* to atone for; to purify.

expirar *vi* to expire.

explayarse *vr* to speak at length.

explicar *vt* to explain, expound:—**~se** *vr* to explain oneself.

explorar *vt* to explore.

explotar *vt* to exploit; to run:—*vi* to explode.

exponer *vt* to expose; to explain.

exportar *vt* to export.

exposición *f* exposure; exhibition; explanation; account.

expresar *vt* to express.

expreso, sa *adj* express, clear, specific; fast (train).

exprimir *vt* to squeeze out.

expropriar *vt* to expropriate.

expulsar *vt* to expel, drive out.

éxtasis *m* ecstasy, enthusiasm.

extender *vt* to extend, stretch out:—**~se** *vr* to extend; to spread.

extenso, sa *adj* extensive.

extenuar *vt* to exhaust, debilitate.

exterior *adj* exterior, external:—*m* exterior, outward appearance.

exterminar *vt* to exterminate.

externo, na *adj* external, outer:—*m/f* day pupil.

extinguir *vt* to wipe out; to extinguish.

extintor *m* (fire) extinguisher.

extra *adj invar* extra; good quality:—*m/f* extra:—*m* bonus.

extraer *vt* to extract.

extrañar *vt* to find strange; to miss: —**~se** *vr* to be surprised; to grow apart.

extranjero, ra *m/f* stranger; foreigner:—*adj* foreign, alien.

extraño, ña *adj* foreign; rare; singular, strange, odd.

extraviar *vt* to mislead:—**~se** *vr* to lose one's way.

extremidad *f* extremity; brim; tip:—**~es** *fpl* extremities *pl*.

extremo, ma *adj* extreme, last:—*m* extreme, highest degree:—**en ~, por ~** extremely.

extrovertido, da *adj, m/f* extrovert.

exuberancia *f* exuberance; luxuriance.

F

fábrica *f* factory.

fabricar *vt* to build, construct; to manufacture; (*fig*) to fabricate.

fábula *f* fable; fiction; rumour, common talk.

fabuloso, sa *adj* fabulous, fictitious.

facción *f* (political) faction; feature.

fachada *f* facade, face, front.

fácil *adj* facile, easy.

facilitar *vt* to facilitate.

fácilmente *adv* easily.

factor *m* (*mat*) factor; (*com*) factor, agent.

factura *f* invoice.

facultativo, va *adj* optional:— *m/f* doctor, practitioner.

faena *f* task, job; hard work.

faisán *m* pheasant.

fajo *m* bundle, wad.

falaz *adj* deceitful, fraudulent; fallacious.

falda *f* skirt; lap; flap; train; slope, hillside.

fallar *vt* (*jur*) to pronounce sentence on, judge:—*vi* to fail.

fallecer *vi* to die.

falso, sa *adj* false, untrue; deceitful; fake.

falta *f* fault, defect; want; flaw, mistake; (*dep*) foul.

faltar *vi* to be wanting; to fail; not to fulfil one's promise; to need; to be missing.

fama *f* fame; reputation, name.

familia *f* family.

familiar *adj* familiar; homely, domestic:—*m/f* relative, relation.

famoso, sa *adj* famous.

fanfarrón *m* bully, braggart.

fango *m* mire, mud.

fantasía *f* fancy; fantasy; caprice; presumption.

fantasma *f* phantom, ghost.

fardo *m* bale, parcel.

farmacia *f* pharmacy.

faro *m* (*mar*) lighthouse; (*auto*) headlamp; floodlight.

farola *f* street light.

fascículo *m* part, instalment.

fascinar *vt* to fascinate; to enchant.

fase *f* phase.

fastidiar *vt* to annoy; to offend; to spoil.

fatal *adj* fatal, mortal, awful.

fatiga *f* weariness, fatigue.

fatuo, tua *adj* fatuous, stupid, foolish; conceited.

fauces *fpl* jaws *pl*, gullet.

favor *m* favour; protection; good turn.

favorecer *vt* to favour, protect.

fe *f* faith, belief.

febrero *m* February.

fecha *f* date (of a letter etc).

fecundar *vt* to fertilise.

felicitar *vt* to congratulate.

feliz *adj* happy, fortunate.

felpa *f* plush; towelling.

felpudo *m* doormat.

femenino, na *adj* feminine; female.

feo, ea *adj* ugly; bad, nasty.

feria *f* fair, rest day; village market.

fermentar *vi* to ferment.

feroz *adj* ferocious, savage; cruel.

ferretería *f* ironmonger's shop.

ferrocarril *m* railway.

fértil *adj* fertile, fruitful.

festejo *m* courtship; feast.

festivo, va *adj* festive, merry; witty: —**dia ~** holiday.

feto *m* foetus.

fiable *adj* trustworthy; reliable.

fiambre *m* cold meat.

fianza *f* (*jur*) surety.

fiar *vt* to entrust, confide; to bail; to sell on credit:—**~se** *vr* to trust.

fibra *f* fibre.

ficha *f* token, counter (at games); (index) card.

fidelidad *f* fidelity; loyalty.

fideos *mpl* noodles *pl*.

fiebre *f* fever.

fiel *adj* faithful, loyal:—*mpl* **los ~es** the faithful *pl*.

fieltro *m* felt.

fiera *f* wild beast.

fiesta *f* party; festivity:—**~s** *fpl* holidays *pl*, vacations *pl*.

figura *f* figure, shape.

figurar *vt* to figure:—**~se** *vr* to fancy, imagine.

fijar *vt* to fix, fasten:—**~se** *vr* to become fixed:—**~se en** to notice.

fijo, ja *adj* fixed, firm; settled, permanent.

fila *f* row, line; (*mil*) rank:— **en ~** in a line, in a row.

filete *m* fillet; fillet steak.

filmar *vt* to film.

filo *m* edge, blade.

filosofía *f* philosophy.

filtro *m* filter.

fin *m* end; termination, conclusion; aim, purpose:—**al ~** at last:—**en ~** (*fig*) well then:—**por ~** finally, lastly.

finalmente *adv* finally, at last.

financiar *vt* to finance.

finca *f* land, property, real estate; country house; farm.

fingir *vt* to feign, fake:—**~se** *vr* to pretend to be:—*vi* to pretend.

fino, na *adj* fine, pure; slender; polite; acute; dry (of sherry).

firma *f* signature; (*com*) company.

firmamento *m* firmament, sky, heaven.

firme *adj* firm, stable, strong, secure; constant; resolute:—*m* road surface.

fiscal *adj* fiscal:—*m/f* district attorney.

fisco *m* treasury, exchequer.

fisgar *vt* to pry into.

física *f* physics.

flaco, ca *adj* lean, skinny; feeble.

flan *m* crème caramel.

flauta *f* (*mus*) flute.

flecha *f* arrow.

flequillo *m* fringe (of hair).

flete *m* (*mar*) freight; charter.

flexible *adj* flexible; compliant; docile.

flojo, ja *adj* loose; flexible; slack; lazy.

flor *f* flower.

florecer *vi* to blossom.

florero *m* vase.

flotador *m* float; rubber ring.

flotar *vi* to float.

fluctuar *vi* to fluctuate; to waver.

fluir *vi* to flow.

foco *m* focus; centre; source; floodlight; (light)bulb.

fogón *m* stove; hearth.

fogoso, sa *adj* fiery; ardent, fervent; impetuous, boisterous.

folleto *m* pamphlet; folder, brochure.

follón *m* (*fam*) mess; fuss.

fomentar *vt* to encourage; to promote.

fondo *m* bottom; back; background; space:—**~s** *mpl* stock, funds *pl*, capital:—**a ~** perfectly, completely.

fontanero, ra *m/f* plumber.

forjar *vt* to forge; to frame; to invent.

forma *f* form, shape; pattern; (*med*) fitness; (*dep*) form; means, method: —**de ~ que** in such a manner that.

formación *f* formation; form, figure; education; training.

formar *vt* to form, shape.

fornido, da *adj* well-built.

forro *m* lining; book jacket.

fortuna *f* fortune; wealth.

forzar *vt* to force.

forzoso, sa *adj* indispensable, necessary.

fosa *f* grave; pit.

fósforo *m* phosphorus:—**~s** *mpl* matches *pl*.

fotocopia *f* photocopy.

fotografía *f* photography; photograph.

fracasar *vi* to fail.

frágil *adj* fragile, frail.

fraguar *vt* to forge; to contrive:—*vi* to solidify, harden.

fraile *m* friar, monk.

frambuesa *f* raspberry.

francés, sa *adj* French:—*m* French language:—*m/f* Frenchman/woman.

frasco *m* flask.

frase *f* phrase.

fraternal *adj* fraternal, brotherly.

fraude *m* fraud, deceit; cheat.

frazada *f* blanket.

frecuencia *f* frequency.

fregar *vt* to scrub; to wash up.

freír *vt* to fry.

frenar *vt* to brake; (*fig*) to check.

frenesí *m* frenzy.

freno *m* bit; brake; (*fig*) check.

frente *f* front; face:—**~ a ~** face to face:—**en ~** opposite; (*mil*) front:—*m* forehead.

fresa *f* strawberry.

fresco, ca *adj* fresh; cool; new; ruddy: —*m* fresh air:—*m/f* (*fam*) shameless or impudent person.

fresno *m* ash tree.

frigorífico *m* fridge.

frijol *m* kidney bean.

frío, fría *adj* cold; indifferent:—*m* cold; indifference.

friso *m* frieze; wainscot.

frito, ta *adj* fried.

frívolo, la *adj* frivolous.

frondoso, sa *adj* leafy.

frontera *f* frontier.

frontón *m* (*dep*) pelota court; pelota.

frotar *vt* to rub.

fructificar *vi* to bear fruit; to come to fruition.

frugal *adj* frugal, sparing.

fruncir *vt* to pleat; to knit; to contract:—~ **las cejas** to knit the eyebrows.

frustrar *vt* to frustrate.

fruta *f* fruit:—~ **del tiempo** seasonal fruit.

frutal *m* fruit tree.

frutilla *f* strawberry.

fuego *m* fire.

fuente *f* fountain; spring; source; large dish.

fuera *adv* out(side); away:— ~ **de** *prep* outside:—¡~! out of the way!

fuerte *m* (*mil*) fortification, fort; forte: —*adj* vigorous, tough; strong; loud; heavy: —*adv* strongly; hard.

fuerza *f* force, strength; (*elec*) power; violence:—**a** ~ **de** by dint of:—~**s** *mpl* troops *pl*.

fugarse *vr* to escape, flee.

fugaz *adj* fleeting.

fullero *m* cardsharper, cheat.

fumar *vt*, *vi* to smoke.

función *f* function; duties *pl*; show, performance.

funcionar *vi* to function; to work (of a machine).

funcionario, ria *m/f* official; civil servant.

funda *f* case, sheath:—~ **de almohada** pillowcase.

fundar *vt* to found; to establish; to ground.

fundir *vt* to fuse; to melt; to smelt; (*com*) to merge; to bankrupt; (*elec*) to fuse, blow.

fúnebre *adj* mournful, sad; funereal.

furgoneta *f* pick-up (truck).

furioso, sa *adj* furious.

furtivo, va *adj* furtive.

fusible *m* fuse.

fusión *f* fusion; (*com*) merger.

fútbol *m* football.

futuro, ra *adj*, *m* future.

G

gabardina *f* gabardine; raincoat.

gabinete *m* (*pol*) cabinet, study; office (of solicitors, etc).

gafas *fpl* glasses *pl*, spectacles *pl*.

gafe *m* jinx.

gai (*fam*) *adj invar*, *m* gay (*sl*), homosexual.

gajo *m* segment (of orange).

galápago *m* tortoise.

galardón *m* reward, prize.

galbana *f* laziness, idleness.

galera *f* (*mar*) galley; wagon; galley (of type).

galería *f* gallery.

galgo *m* greyhound.

gallardo, da *adj* graceful, elegant; brave, daring.

galleta *f* biscuit.

gallina *f* hen:—*m/f* (*fig*) coward:—~ **ciega** blindman's buff.

gallo *m* cock.

gama *f* (*mus*) scale; (*fig*) range, gamut; doe.

gamba *f* shrimp.

gamberro, rra *m/f* hooligan.

gamuza *f* chamois.

gana *f* desire, wish; appetite; will, longing:—**de buena ~** with pleasure, voluntarily:—**de mala ~** unwillingly, with reluctance.

ganado *m* livestock, cattle *pl*:—~ **mayor** horses and mules *pl*:—~ **menor** sheep, goats and pigs *pl*.

ganar *vt* to gain; to win; to earn:—*vi* to win.

gancho *m* hook; crook.

gandul *adj*, *m/f* layabout.

ganga *f* bargain.

ganso, sa *m/f* gander; goose; (*fam*) idiot.

garabatear *vi*, *vt* to scrawl, scribble.

garaje *m* garage.

garantía *f* warranty, guarantee.

garbanzo *m* chickpea, garbanzo.

garbo *m* gracefulness, elegance; stylishness; generosity.

garganta *f* throat, gullet; instep; neck (of a bottle); narrow pass between mountains or rivers.

gárgara *f* gargling, gargle.

garra *f* claw; talon; paw.

garrafa *f* carafe; (gas) cylinder.

garrafal *adj* great, vast, huge.

garrotillo *m* (*med*) croup.

garrucha *f* pulley.

garza *f* heron.

gasa *f* gauze.

gaseoso, sa *adj* fizzy:—*f* lemonade.

gasoil *m* diesel (oil).

gasolina *f* petrol.

gasolinera *f* petrol station.

gastar *vt* to spend; to expend; to waste; to wear away; to use up:—~**se** *vr* to wear out; to waste.

gata *f* she-cat:—**a ~s** on all fours.

gato *m* cat; jack.

gavilán *m* sparrow hawk.

gavilla *f* sheaf of corn.

gaviota *f* seagull.

gazpacho *m* Spanish cold tomato soup.

gelatina *f* jelly; gelatine.

gemelo, la *m/f* twin.

gemir *vi* to groan, moan.

generación *f* generation; progeny, race.

general *m* general:—*adj* general:—**en ~** generally, in general.

género *m* genus; kind, type; gender; cloth, material:—~**s** *mpl* goods, commodities *pl*.

generoso, sa *adj* noble, generous.

genio *m* nature, character; genius.

genital *adj* genital:—*mpl* ~**es** genitals *pl*.

gente *f* people; nation; family.

gentileza *f* grace; charm; politeness.

genuino, na *adj* genuine; pure.

geografía *f* geography.

geología *f* geology.

geometría *f* geometry.

geranio *m* (*bot*) geranium.

gerente *m/f* manager; director.

germinar *vi* to germinate, bud.

gestión *f* management; negotiation.

gesto *m* face; grimace; gesture.

gigante *m* giant:—*adj* gigantic.

gilipollas *adj invar* (*fam*) stupid:—*m/f invar* wimp (*sl*).

gimnasia *f* gymnastics.

ginebra *f* gin.

ginecólogo, ga *m/f* gynecologist.

gira *f* trip, tour.

girar *vt* to turn around; to swivel:—*vi* to go round, revolve.

girasol *m* sunflower.

gitano, na *m/f* gipsy.

glacial *adj* icy.

glándula *f* gland.

globo *m* globe; sphere; orb; balloon: —~ **aerostatico** air balloon.

glorieta *f* bower, arbour; roundabout.

glosar *vt* to gloss; to comment on.

glotón, ona *m/f* glutton.

gobierno *m* government.

goce *m* enjoyment.

gol *m* goal.

golondrina *f* swallow.

golosina *f* dainty, titbit; sweet.

golpe *m* blow, stroke, hit; knock; clash; coup:—**de ~** suddenly.

goma *f* gum; rubber; elastic.

gordo, da *adj* fat, plump, big-bellied; first, main; (*fam*) enormous.

gorjear *vi* to twitter, chirp.

gorrión *m* sparrow.

gorro *m* cap; bonnet.

gorrón, ona *m/f* scrounger.

gota *f* drop; (*med*) gout.

gotera *f* leak.

gozar *vt* to enjoy, have, possess:—~**se** *vr* to enjoy oneself, rejoice.

gozne *m* hinge.

gozo *m* joy, pleasure.

grabado *m* engraving.

grabar *vt* to engrave; to record.

gracia *f* grace, gracefulness; wit:—¡(**muchas**) ~**s!** thanks (very much): —**tener ~** to be funny.

gracioso, sa *adj* graceful; beautiful; funny; pleasing:—*m* comic character.

grada *f* step of a staircase; tier, row:—~**s** *fpl* seats *pl* of stadium or theatre.

grado *m* step; degree:—**de buen ~** willingly.

gráfico, ca *adj* graphic:—*m* diagram: —*f* graph.

grajo *m* rook.

gramo *m* gram(me).

gran *adj* = **grande**.

granada *f* pomegranate.

granate *m* garnet (precious stone).

grande *adj* great; big; tall; grand:—*m/f* adult.

grandioso, sa *adj* grand, magnificent.

granel *adv*:—**a ~** in bulk.

granizado *m* iced drink.

granizo *m* hail.

granja *f* farm.

grano *m* grain.

granuja *m/f* rogue; urchin.

grapa *f* staple; clamp.

grasa *f* suet, fat; grease.

gratis *adj* free.

grato, ta *adj* pleasant, agreeable.

gravamen *m* charge, obligation; nuisance; tax.

grave *adj* weighty, heavy; grave, important; serious.

gravilla *f* gravel.

gravoso, sa *adj* onerous, burdensome; costly.

graznar *vi* to croak; to cackle; to quack.

gremio *m* union, guild; society; company, corporation.

greña *f* tangle; shock of hair.

gresca *f* clatter; outcry; confusion; wrangle, quarrel.

grieta *f* crevice, crack, chink.

grifo *m* tap, faucet; petrol station.

grillo *m* cricket; bud, shoot.

gripe *f* flu, influenza.

gris *adj* grey.

gritar *vi* to cry out, shout, yell.

grosella *f* redcurrant:—~ **negra** blackcurrant.

grosero, ra *adj* coarse; rude, bad-mannered.

grúa *f* crane (machine); derrick.

grueso, sa *adj* thick; bulky; large; coarse:—*m* bulk.

grulla *f* crane (bird).

gruñir *vi* to grunt; to grumble; to creak (of hinges, etc).

grupo *m* group.

gruta *f* grotto.

guadaña *f* scythe.

guante *m* glove.

guapo, pa *adj* good-looking; handsome; smart.

guardabosque *m* gamekeeper; ranger.

guardacostas *m invar* coastguard vessel.

guardaespaldas *m/f invar* bodyguard.

guardar *vt* to keep, preserve; to save (money); to guard:—~**se** *vr* to be on one's guard:—~**se de** to avoid, abstain from.

guardarropa *f* wardrobe; cloakroom.

guardia *f* guard; (*mar*) watch; care, custody:—*m/f* guard; police officer: —*m* (*mil*) guardsman.

guarecer *vt* to protect; to shelter:—~**se** *vr* to take refuge.

guarnecer *vt* to provide, equip; to reinforce; to garnish, set (in gold, etc); to adorn.

guasa *f* joke.

gubernativo, va *adj* governmental.

guía *m/f* guide:—*f* guidebook.

guiar *vt* to guide; (*auto*) to steer.

guijarro *m* pebble.

guiñar *vt* to wink.

guinda *f* cherry.

guindilla *f* chilli pepper.

guión *m* hyphen; (film) script.

guisante *m* (*bot*) pea.

guisar *vt* to cook.

guitarra *f* guitar.

gula *f* gluttony.

gusano *m* maggot, worm.

gustar *vt* to taste; to sample:—*vi* to please, be pleasing:—**me gusta...** I like...

H

haba *f* bean.

haber *vt* to get, lay hands on; to occur:—*v imp* **hay** there is, there are: —*v aux* to have:—**~se** *vr* **habérselas con uno** to have it out with somebody:—*m* income, salary; assets *pl*; (*com*) credit.

hábil *adj* able, clever, skilful, dexterous, apt.

habitación *f* habitation, abode, lodging, dwelling, residence; room.

habitar *vt* to inhabit, live in.

hábito *m* dress; habit, custom.

habitual *adj* habitual, customary.

hablar *vt, vi* to speak; to talk.

hacendoso, sa *adj* industrious.

hacer *vt* to make; to do; to put into practice; to perform; to effect; to prepare; to imagine; to force; (*mat*) to amount to, make:—*vi* to act, behave:—**~se** *vr* to become.

hacha *f* torch; axe, hatchet.

hacia *adv* toward(s); about:— **~ arriba/abajo** up(wards)/ down(wards).

hada *f* fairy.

halagar *vt* to cajole, flatter.

halcón *m* falcon.

hallar *vt* to find; to meet with; to discover:—**~se** *vr* to find oneself; to be.

hambre *f* hunger; famine; longing.

harina *f* flour.

harto, ta *adj* full; fed up:— *adv* enough.

hasta *prep* up to; down to; until, as far as:—*adv* even.

haya *f* beech tree.

hazaña *f* exploit, achievement.

hebilla *f* buckle.

hebra *f* thread; vein of minerals or metals; grain of wood.

hebreo, ea *m/f, adj* Hebrew; Israeli:—*m* Hebrew language.

hechizar *vt* to bewitch, enchant; to charm.

hecho, cha *adj* made; done; mature; ready-to-wear; cooked:—*m* action; act; fact; matter; event.

hectárea *f* hectare.

helado, da *adj* frozen; glacial, icy; astonished; astounded:—*m* ice cream.

helar *vt* to freeze; to congeal; to astonish, amaze:—**~se** *vr* to be frozen; to turn into ice; to congeal:—*vi* to freeze; to congeal.

helecho *m* fern.

hélice *f* helix; propeller.

hembra *f* female.

heno *m* hay.

heredar *vt* to inherit.

hereje *m/f* heretic.

herir *vt* to wound, hurt; to beat, strike; to affect, touch, move; to offend.

hermana *f* sister.

hermano *m* brother:—**~, na** *adj* matched; resembling.

hermético, ca *adj* hermetic, airtight.

hermoso, sa *adj* beautiful, handsome, lovely; large, robust.

héroe *m* hero.

herradura *f* horseshoe.

herrero *m* smith.

hervir *vt* to boil; to cook:—*vi* to boil; to bubble; to seethe.

hiedra *f* ivy.

hiel *f* gall, bile.

hielo *m* frost; ice.

hierba *f* grass; herb.

hierro *m* iron.

hígado *m* liver; (*fig*) courage, pluck.

higiene *f* hygiene.

higo *m* fig.

hijo, ja *m/f* son/daughter; child; offspring.

hilera *f* row, line, file.

hilo *m* thread; wire.

hincar *vt* to thrust in, drive in.

hinchar *vt* to swell; to inflate; (*fig*) to exaggerate:— **~se** *vr* to swell; to become vain.

hinojo *m* (*bot*) fennel.

hipo *m* hiccups *pl*.

hipócrita *adj* hypocritical:— *m/f* hypocrite.

hipódromo *m* racetrack.

hipoteca *f* mortgage.

historia *f* history; tale, story.

historieta *f* short story; short novel; comic strip.

hocico *m* snout:—**meter el ~ en todo** to meddle in everything.

hogar *m* hearth, fireplace; (*fig*) house, home; family life.

hogaza *f* large loaf of bread.

hoguera *f* bonfire; blaze.

hoja *f* leaf; petal; sheet of paper; blade.

hojalata *f* tin (plate).

hojaldre *f* puff pastry.

hojear *vt* to turn the pages of.

hola *excl* hello!

holgado, da *adj* loose, wide, baggy; at leisure; idle, unoccupied; well-off.

hollín *m* soot.

hombre *m* man; human being.

hombro *m* shoulder.

homenaje *m* homage.

homicidio *m* murder.

hondo, da *adj* deep, profound.

honesto, ta *adj* honest; modest.

hongo *m* mushroom; fungus.

honor *m* honour.

honorario, ria *adj* honorary:—**~s** *mpl* fees *pl.*

honra *f* honour, reverence; self-esteem; reputation; integrity:—**~s funebres** *pl* funeral honours *pl.*

hora *f* hour; time.

horario, ria *adj* hourly, hour *compd*: —*m* timetable.

horchata *f* tiger-nut milk.

horma *f* mould, form.

hormiga *f* ant.

hormigón *m* concrete.

horno *m* oven; furnace.

horquilla *f* pitchfork; hairpin.

hórreo *m* granary.

horrible *adj* horrid, horrible.

horror *m* horror, fright; atrocity.

hortaliza *f* vegetable.

hospedar *vt* to put up, lodge; to entertain.

hospicio *m* orphanage; hospice.

hospital *m* hospital.

hostal *m* small hotel.

hostelería *f* hotel business or trade.

hostia *f* host; wafer; (*fam*) whack (*sl*), punch.

hostil *adj* hostile; adverse.

hotel *m* hotel.

hoy *adv* today; now, nowadays:—**de ~ en adelante** from now on, henceforward.

hoyo *m* hole, pit; excavation.

hoz *f* sickle; gorge.

hucha *f* money-box.

hueco, ca *adj* hollow, concave; empty; vain, ostentatious:—*m* interval; gap, hole; vacancy.

huelga *f* strike.

huella *f* track, footstep.

huérfano, na *adj*, *m/f* orphan.

huerta *f* market garden; irrigated region.

hueso *m* bone; stone, core.

huésped, da *m/f* guest, lodger; inn-keeper.

huevo *m* egg.

huir *vi* to flee, escape.

humano, na *adj* human; humane, kind.

húmedo, da *adj* humid; wet; damp.

humilde *adj* humble.

humillar *vt* to humble; to subdue:—**~se** *vr* to humble oneself.

humo *m* smoke; fumes *pl.*

humor *m* mood, temper; humour.

hundir *vt* to submerge; to sink; to ruin:—**~se** *vr* to sink, go to the bottom; to collapse; to be ruined.

huraño, ña *adj* shy; unsociable.

hurtadillas *adv*:—**a ~** by stealth.

hurtar *vt* to steal, rob.

husmear *vt* to scent; to pry into.

I

ictericia *f* jaundice.

ida *f* departure, going:—(viaje de) ~ outward journey:—~ y vuelta round trip:—~s y venidas comings and goings *pl*.

idea *f* idea; scheme.

ídem *pn* ditto.

idéntico, ca *adj* identical.

idioma *m* language.

idiota *m/f* idiot.

idóneo, nea *adj* suitable, fit.

iglesia *f* church.

ignorar *vt* to be ignorant of, not to know.

igual *adj* equal; similar; the same:—al ~ equally.

ilegal *adj* illegal, unlawful.

ileso, sa *adj* unhurt.

ilimitado, da *adj* unlimited.

iluminar *vt* to illumine, illuminate, enlighten.

ilusión *f* illusion; hope:—hacerse ~ones to build up one's hopes.

ilustre *adj* illustrious, famous.

imagen *f* image.

imaginar *vt* to imagine; to think up:—*vi* ~se *vr* to imagine.

imán *m* magnet.

imitar *vt* to imitate, copy; to counterfeit.

impaciente *adj* impatient.

impar *adj* odd.

imparcial *adj* impartial.

impedir *vt* to impede, hinder; to prevent.

impeler *vt* to drive, propel; to impel; to incite, stimulate.

impenetrable *adj* impenetrable, impervious; incomprehensible.

impenitente *adj* impenitent.

imperdible *m* safety pin.

imperdonable *adj* unforgivable.

imperfecto, ta *adj* imperfect.

impermeable *adj* waterproof:—*m* raincoat.

imperturbable *adj* imperturbable; unruffled.

implacable *adj* implacable, inexorable.

implicar *vt* to implicate, involve.

imponer *vt* to impose; to command: —~se *vr* to assert oneself; to prevail.

impopular *adj* unpopular.

importante *adj* important, considerable.

importar *vi* to be important, matter: —*vt* to import; to be worth.

importe *m* amount, cost.

importunar *vt* to bother, pester.

imposible *adj* impossible; extremely difficult; slovenly.

impostor, ra *m/f* impostor, fraud.

impotencia *f* impotence.

impracticable *adj* impracticable, unworkable.

impreciso, sa *adj* imprecise, vague.

imprenta *f* printing; press; printing office.

imprescindible *adj* essential.

impresión *f* impression; stamp; print; edition.

impresionar *vt* to move; to impress:—~se *vr* to be impressed; to be moved.

imprevisto, ta *adj* unforeseen, unexpected.

imprimir *vt* to print; to imprint; to stamp.

improbable *adj* improbable, unlikely.

improvisar *vt* to extemporise; to improvise.

improviso, sa *adj*:—de ~ unexpectedly.

imprudente *adj* imprudent; indiscreet; unwise.

impúdico, ca *adj* shameless; lecherous.

impuesto, ta *adj* imposed:—*m* tax, duty.

impulso *m* impulse; thrust; (*fig*) impulse.

impune *adj* unpunished.

impuro, ra *adj* impure;, foul.

inaccesible *adj* inaccessible.

inadvertido, da *adj* unnoticed.

inagotable *adj* inexhaustible.

inaguantable *adj* unbearable, intolerable.

inalterable *adj* unalterable.

inapreciable *adj* imperceptible; invaluable.

inaudito, ta *adj* unheard-of.

inaugurar *vt* to inaugurate.

incalculable *adj* incalculable.

incansable *adj* untiring, tireless.

incapaz *adj* incapable, unable.

incauto, ta *adj* incautious, unwary.

incendio *m* fire.

incentivo *m* incentive.

incertidumbre *f* doubt, uncertainty.

incierto, ta *adj* uncertain, doubtful.

incineración *f* incineration; cremation.

incitar *vt* to incite, excite.

inclemencia *f* inclemency, severity; inclemency (of the weather).

inclinar *vt* to incline; to nod, bow (the head):—~**se** *vr* to bow; to stoop.

incluir *vt* to include, comprise; to incorporate; to enclose.

incluso, sa *adj* included:— *adv* inclusively; even.

incógnito, ta *adj* unknown:—**de ~** incognito.

incombustible *adj* incombustible, fireproof.

incómodo, da *adj* uncomfortable; annoying; inconvenient.

incomparable *adj* incomparable, matchless.

incompasivo *adj* unsympathetic.

incompleto, ta *adj* incomplete.

incomunicado, da *adj* isolated, cut off; in solitary confinement.

inconcebible *adj* inconceivable.

incondicional *adj* unconditional; whole-hearted; staunch.

inconfundible *adj* unmistakable.

inconsciente *adj* unconscious; thoughtless.

inconstante *adj* inconstant, variable, fickle.

incorporar *vt* to incorporate:—~**se** *vr* to sit up; to join (an organisation), become incorporated.

incorrecto, ta *adj* incorrect.

incrédulo, la *adj* incredulous.

increíble *adj* incredible.

incremento *m* increment, increase; growth; rise.

inculcar *vt* to inculcate.

inculto, ta *adj* uncultivated; uneducated; uncouth.

incumbencia *f* obligation; duty.

incurable *adj* incurable; irremediable.

indagar *vt* to inquire into.

indebido, da *adj* undue; illegal, unlawful.

indeciso, sa *adj* hesitant; undecided.

indefenso, sa *adj* defenceless.

indemnizar *vt* to indemnify, compensate.

independiente *adj* independent.

indeterminado, da *adj* indeterminate; indefinite.

indicador *m* indicator; gauge.

indicar *vt* to indicate.

índice *m* ratio, rate; hand (of a watch or clock); index, table of contents; catalogue; forefinger, index finger.

indicio *m* indication, mark; sign, token; clue.

indiferencia *f* indifference, apathy.

indígena *adj* indigenous, native:—*m/f* native.

indignar *vt* to irritate; to provoke, tease:—~**se** *vr* ~ **por** to get indignant about.

indigno, na *adj* unworthy, contemptible, low.

indirecta *f* innuendo, hint.

indiscreción *f* indiscretion, tactlessness; gaffe.

individual *adj* individual; single (of a room):—*m* (*dep*) singles.

individuo *m* individual.

índole *f* disposition, nature, character; soft, kind.

indolente *adj* indolent, lazy.

indómito, ta *adj* untamed, ungoverned.

inducir *vt* to induce, persuade.

indudable *adj* undoubted; unquestionable.

indultar *vt* to pardon; to exempt.

industria *f* industry; skill.

inédito, ta *adj* unpublished; (*fig*) new.

ineficaz *adj* ineffective; inefficient.

inepto, ta *adj* inept, unfit, useless.

inercia *f* inertia, inactivity.

inerte *adj* inert; dull; sluggish, motionless.

inesperado, da *adj* unexpected, unforeseen.

inevitable *adj* unavoidable.

inexacto, ta *adj* inaccurate, untrue.

inexperto, ta *adj* inexperienced.

infame *adj* infamous.

infancia *f* infancy, childhood.

infantil *adj* infantile; childlike; children's.

infarto *m* heart attack.

infatigable *adj* tireless, untiring.

infectar *vt* to infect.

infeliz *adj* unhappy, unfortunate.

inferior *adj* inferior.

infernal *adj* infernal, hellish.

infiel *adj* unfaithful; disloyal; inaccurate.

infierno *m* hell.

infiltrarse *vr* to infiltrate.

ínfimo, ma *adj* lowest; of very poor quality.

infinidad *f* infinity; immensity.

infinito, ta *adj* infinite; immense.

inflamable *adj* inflammable.

inflar *vt* to inflate, blow up; (*fig*) to exaggerate.

inflexible *adj* inflexible.

influir *vt* to influence.

información *f* information; news; (*mil*) intelligence; investigation, judicial inquiry.

informal *adj* irregular, incorrect; untrustworthy; informal.

informar *vt* to inform; to reveal, make known:—**se** *vr* to find out: —*vi* to report; (*jur*) to plead; to inform.

informática *f* computer science, information technology.

informe *m* report, statement; piece of information, account:—*adj* shapeless, formless.

infortunio *m* misfortune, ill luck.

infracción *f* infraction; breach, infringement.

infructuoso, sa *adj* fruitless, unproductive, unprofitable.

infundado, da *adj* groundless.

ingeniero, ra *m/f* engineer.

ingenio *m* talent; wit; ingenuity; engine: —**~ de azúcar** sugar mill.

ingenuo, nua *adj* naive.

ingerir *vt* to ingest; to swallow; to consume.

ingle *f* groin.

inglés, esa *adj* English:—*m* English language:—*m/f* Englishman/woman.

ingrato, ta *adj* ungrateful, thankless; disagreeable.

ingresar *vt* to deposit:—*vi* to come in.

inhabilitar *vt* to disqualify, disable.

inhabitable *adj* uninhabitable.

inhibir *vt* to inhibit; to restrain.

iniciar *vt* to initiate; to begin.

ininteligible *adj* unintelligible.

injertar *vt* to graft.

injuriar *vt* to insult, wrong.

injusto, ta *adj* unjust.

inmediaciones *fpl* neighbourhood.

inmediatamente *adv* immediately, at once.

inmobiliario, ria *adj* real-estate compd:—*f* estate agency.

inmortal *adj* immortal.

inmóvil *adj* immovable, still.

inmueble *m* property:—*adj* **bienes ~s** real estate.

inmundo, da *adj* filthy, dirty; nasty.

inmune *adj* (*med*) immune; free, exempt.

innato, ta *adj* inborn, innate.

innecesario, ria *adj* unnecessary.

innegable *adj* undeniable.

innumerable *adj* innumerable, countless.

inocente *adj* innocent.

inodoro *m* toilet:—**~, ra** *adj* odourless, without smell.

inofensivo, va *adj* harmless.

inolvidable *adj* unforgettable.

inoxidable *adj*:—**acero ~** stainless steel.

inquietar *vt* to worry, disturb:—**~se** *vr* to worry, get worried.

inquilino, na *m/f* tenant; lodger.

inquirir *vt* to inquire into, investigate.

inscribir *vt* to inscribe; to list, register.

insecto *m* insect.

insensato, ta *adj* senseless, stupid; mad.

insensible *adj* insensitive; imperceptible; numb.

inseparable *adj* inseparable.

insertar *vt* to insert.

inservible *adj* useless.

insignia *f* badge:—**~s** *fpl* insignia *pl*.

insinuar *vt* to insinuate:—**~se** *vr* **~ en** to worm one's way into.

insípido, da *adj* insipid.

insistir *vi* to insist.

insolación *f* (*med*) sunstroke.

insolencia *f* insolence, rudeness, effrontery.

insólito, ta *adj* unusual.

insolvente *adj* insolvent.

insomnio *m* insomnia.

insondable *adj* unfathomable; inscrutable.

insoportable *adj* unbearable.

inspeccionar *vt* to inspect; to supervise.

inspector, ra *m/f* inspector; superintendent.

inspirar *vt* to inspire; (*med*) to inhale.

instalar *vt* to install.

instantáneo, nea *adj* instantaneous: —*f* snap(shot):— **café** ~ instant coffee.

instante *m* instant:—**al** ~ immediately, instantly.

instigar *vt* to instigate.

instinto *m* instinct.

instructivo, va *adj* instructive; educational.

instrumento *m* instrument; tool, implement.

insuficiente *adj* insufficient, inadequate.

insulso, sa *adj* insipid; dull.

insultar *vt* to insult.

insuperable *adj* insuperable, insurmountable.

intacto, ta *adj* untouched; entire; intact.

integral *adj* integral, whole:— **pan** ~ wholewheat bread.

intemperie *f*:—**a la** ~ out in the open.

intencionado, da *adj* meaningful; deliberate.

intenso, sa *adj* intense, strong; deep.

intentar *vt* to try, attempt.

intercalar *vt* to insert.

intercambio *m* exchange, swap.

interés *m* interest; share, part; concern, advantage; profit.

interesar *vt* to be of interest to, interest:—**~se** *vr* ~ **en** o **por** to take an interest in:— *vi* to be of interest.

interferir *vt* to interfere with; to jam (a telephone):—*vi* to interfere.

interfono *m* intercom.

interino, na *adj* provisional, temporary:—*m/f* temporary holder of a post; stand-in.

interior *adj* interior, internal:—*m* interior, inside.

intermedio, dia *adj* intermediate:—*m* interval.

interminable *adj* interminable, endless.

intermitente *adj* intermittent; *m* (*auto*) indicator.

internado *m* boarding school.

interno, na *adj* interior, internal:—*m/f* boarder.

interpretar *vt* to interpret, explain; (*teat*) to perform; to translate.

interrogación *f* interrogation; question mark.

interrogatorio *m* questioning; (*jur*) examination; questionnaire.

interrumpir *vt* to interrupt.

interruptor *m* switch.

intervenir *vt* to control, supervise; (*com*) to audit; (*med*) to operate on: —*vi* to participate; to intervene.

intestino, na *adj* internal, interior:—*m* intestine.

íntimo, ma *adj* internal, innermost; intimate, private.

intranquilo, la *adj* worried.

intransitable *adj* impassable.

intrépido, da *adj* intrepid, daring.

intrigar *vt*, *vi* to intrigue.

introducir *vt* to introduce; to insert.

introvertido, da *adj*, *m/f* introvert.

intruso, sa *adj* intrusive:— *m/f* intruder.

inundar *vt* to inundate, overflow; to flood.

inusitado, da *adj* unusual.

inútil *adj* useless.

inválido, da *adj* invalid, null and void:—*m/f* invalid.

invencible *adj* invincible.

invernadero *m* greenhouse.

inverosímil *adj* unlikely, improbable.

inverso, sa *adj* inverse; inverted; contrary.

invertir *vt* (*com*) to invest; to invert.

investigar *vt* to investigate; to do research into.

invierno *m* winter.

invitar *vt* to invite; to entice; to pay for.

invocar *vt* to invoke.

ir *vi* to go; to walk; to travel:—**~se** *vr* to go away, depart.

ira *f* anger, wrath.

iris *m* iris (eye):—**arco** ~ rainbow.

ironía *f* irony.

irracional *adj* irrational.

irreal *adj* unreal.

irreflexión *f* rashness, thoughtlessness.

irregular *adj* irregular; abnormal.

irremediable *adj* irremediable; incurable.

irresistible *adj* irresistible.

irreverente *adj* irreverent; disrespectful.

irrisorio, ria *adj* derisory, ridiculous.

irritar *vt* to irritate, exasperate; to stir up; to inflame.

isla *f* island, isle.

istmo *m* isthmus.

italiano, na *adj* Italian:—*m* Italian language:—*m/f* Italian.

itinerario *m* itinerary.

izquierdo, da *adj* left; left-handed:—*f* left; left(-wing).

J, K

jabalí *m* wild boar.

jabón *m* soap.

jaca *f* pony.

jacinto *m* hyacinth.

jadear *vi* to pant.

jaleo *m* racket, uproar.

jamás *adv* never:—**para siempre ~** for ever.

jamón *m* ham:—**~ de York** cooked ham:—**~ serrano** cured ham.

jaque *m* check (at game of chess):—**~ mate** checkmate.

jaqueca *f* migraine.

jarabe *m* syrup.

jardín *m* garden.

jarra *f* jug, jar, pitcher:—**en ~s, de ~s** with hands to the sides.

jaula *f* cage; cell for mad people.

jazmín *m* jasmin.

jefe *m* chief, head, leader:— (*ferro*) **~ de tren** guard, conductor.

jerarquía *f* hierarchy.

jerigonza *f* jargon, gibberish.

jeringa *f* syringe.

jeroglífico, ca *adj* hieroglyphic:—*m* hieroglyph, hieroglyphic.

jersey *m* sweater, pullover.

jilguero *m* goldfinch.

jinete, ta *m/f* horseman/woman, rider.

jipijapa *m* straw hat.

jirón *m* rag, shred.

jornada *f* journey; day's journey; working day.

jornal *m* day's wage.

jornalero *m* (day) labourer.

joroba *f* hump:—*m/f* hunchback.

jota *f* jot, iota; Spanish dance.

joven *adj* young:—*m/f* youth; young woman.

jovial *adj* jovial, cheerful.

joya *f* jewel:—**~s** *fpl* jewellery.

juanete *m* (*med*) bunion.

jubilar *vt* to pension off; to superannuate; to discard:—**~se** *vr* to retire.

júbilo *m* joy, rejoicing.

judía *f* bean:—**~ verde** French bean.

judicial *adj* judicial.

judío, día *adj* Jewish:—*m/f* Jewish man/woman.

juego *m* play; amusement; sport; game; gambling.

jueves *m invar* Thursday.

juez *m/f* judge.

jugar *vt, vi* to play, sport, gamble.

jugo *m* sap, juice.

juguete *m* toy, plaything.

juicio *m* judgement, reason; sanity; opinion.

julio *m* July.

junco *m* (*bot*) rush; junk (Chinese ship).

junio *m* June.

junta *f* meeting; assembly; congress; council.

juntar *vt* to join; to unite:—**~se** *vr* to meet, assemble; to draw closer.

junto, ta *adj* joined; united; near; adjacent:—**~s** together:—*adv* **todo ~** all at once.

jurar *vt, vi* to swear.

jurídico, ca *adj* lawful, legal; juridical.

justicia *f* justice; equity.

justificante *m* voucher; receipt.

justo, ta *adj* just; fair, right; exact, correct; tight:—*adv* exactly, precisely; just in time.

juventud *f* youthfulness, youth; young people *pl*.

juzgado *m* tribunal; court.

kárate *m* karate

kerosén *m*, **kerosene** *m*, **kerosina** *m*, **kerosín** *m* kerosene, paraffin.

kilogramo *m* kilogram(me).

kilolitro *m* kilolitre

kilométrico *adj* kilometric

kilometraje *m* distance in kilometres.

kilometrar *vt* to measure distance in kilometres.

kilómetro *m* kilometre.

kilovatio *m* kilowatt.

kiosco *m* kiosk; newspaper stand = **quiosco**.

kodak *f* small camera.

L

la *art f* the:—*pn* her; you; it.

labio *m* lip; edge.

labor *f* labour, task; needlework; farmwork; ploughing.

laborioso, sa *adj* laborious; hard-working.

labrar *vt* to work; to carve; to farm; (*fig*) to bring about.

laca *f* lacquer; hairspray.

lacio, cia *adj* faded, withered; languid; lank (hair).

lacrar *vt* to seal (with sealing wax).

lactancia *f* lactation; breastfeeding.

lácteo, tea *adj*:—**productos ~s** dairy products.

ladera *f* slope.

ladino, na *adj* cunning, crafty.

lado *m* side; faction, party; favour, protection; (*mil*) flank:—**al ~ de** beside:—**poner a un ~** to put aside:—**por todos ~s** on all sides.

ladrar *vt* to bark.

ladrillo *m* brick.

ladrón, ona *m/f* thief, robber.

lagar *m* wine press.

lagartija *f* (small) lizard.

lagarto *m* lizard.

lago *m* lake.

lágrima *f* tear.

laguna *f* lake; lagoon; gap.

laico, ca *adj* lay.

lamentar *vt* to be sorry about; to lament, regret:—

vi **~se** *vr* to lament, complain; to mourn.

lamer *vt* to lick, lap.

lámina *f* plate, sheet of metal; engraving.

lámpara *f* lamp.

lana *f* wool.

lancha *f* barge, lighter; launch.

langosta *f* locust; lobster.

lanzar *vt* to throw; (*dep*) to bowl, pitch; to launch, fling; (*jur*) to evict.

lápida *f* flat stone, tablet.

lápiz *m* pencil; mechanical pencil.

largamente *adv* for a long time.

largo, ga *adj* long; lengthy, generous; copious:—**a la ~a** in the end, eventually.

las *art fpl* the:—*pn* them; you.

lascivo, va *adj* lascivious; lewd.

láser *m* laser.

lástima *f* compassion, pity; shame.

lastimar *vt* to hurt; to wound; to feel pity for:—**~se** *vr* to hurt oneself.

lastre *m* ballast.

lata *f* tin; tin can; (*fam*) nuisance.

latido *m* (heart)beat.

latifundio *m* large estate.

latir *vi* to beat, palpitate.

latitud *f* latitude.

latón *m* brass.

latoso, sa *adj* annoying; boring.

laúd *f* lute (musical instrument).

laudable *adj* laudable, praiseworthy.

laurel *m* (*bot*) laurel; reward.

lavabo *m* washbasin; washroom.

lavadora *f* washing machine.

lavanda *f* lavender.

lavar *vt* to wash; to wipe away:—**~se** *vr* to wash oneself.

laxante *m* (*med*) laxative.

lazarillo *m*:—**perro ~** guide dog.

lazo *m* knot; bow; snare, trap; tie; bond.

le *pn* him; you; (*dativo*) to him; to her; to it; to you.

leal *adj* loyal; faithful.

lebrel *m* greyhound.

lección *f* reading; lesson; lecture; class.

leche *f* milk.

lecho *m* bed; layer.

lechón *m* sucking pig.

lechuga *f* lettuce.

lechuza *f* owl.

leer *vt, vi* to read.

legado *m* bequest, legacy; legate.

legal *adj* legal; trustworthy.

legaña *f* sleep (in eyes).

legislar *vt* to legislate.

legítimo, ma *adj* legitimate, lawful; authentic.

legumbres *fpl* pulses *pl*.

lejano, na *adj* distant, remote; far.

lejía *f* bleach.

lejos *adv* at a great distance, far off.

lelo, la *adj* stupid, ignorant:—*m/f* idiot.

lema *m* motto; slogan.

leña *f* wood, timber.

lencería *f* linen, drapery.

lengua *f* tongue; language.

lenguado *m* sole.

lenguaje *m* language.

lente *m/f* lens.

lenteja *f* lentil.

lentilla *f* contact lens.

lento, ta *adj* slow.

león *m* lion.

leopardo *m* leopard.

leotardos *mpl* tights.

lesión *f* wound; injury; damage.

letal *adj* mortal, deadly.

letanía *f* litany.

letargo *m* lethargy.

letra *f* letter; handwriting; printing type; draft of a song; bill, draft:—~s *fpl* letters *pl*, learning.

letrero *m* sign; label.

leucemia *f* leukaemia.

levadura *f* yeast; brewer's yeast.

levantar *vt* to raise, lift up; to build; to elevate; to hearten, cheer up:—~se *vr* to get up; to stand up.

levante *m* Levant; east; east wind.

levantisco *adj* turbulent, restless.

leve *adj* light; trivial.

léxico *m* vocabulary.

ley *f* law; standard (for metal).

leyenda *f* legend.

liar *vt* to tie, bind; to confuse.

libélula *f* dragonfly.

liberal *adj* liberal, generous:—*m/f* liberal.

libertad *f* liberty, freedom.

libra *f* pound:—~ **esterlina** pound sterling.

libre *adj* free; exempt; vacant.

librería *f* bookshop.

libreta *f* notebook:—~ **de ahorros** savings book.

libro *m* book.

licencia *f* licence; licentiousness.

licenciado, da *adj* licensed:—*m/f* graduate.

lícito, ta *adj* lawful, fair; permissible.

líder *m/f* leader.

liebre *f* hare.

lienzo *f* linen; canvas; face or front of a building.

liga *f* suspender; birdlime; league; coalition; alloy.

ligar *vt* to tie, bind, fasten:—~se *vr* to commit oneself:—*vi* to mix, blend; (*fam*) to pick up.

ligero, ra *adj* light, swift; agile; superficial.

liguero *m* suspender belt.

lijar *vt* to smooth, sandpaper.

lima *f* file.

límite *m* limit, boundary.

limón *m* lemon.

limosna *f* alms *pl*, charity.

limpiar *vt* to clean; to cleanse; to purify; to polish; (*fig*) to clean up.

linaza *f* linseed.

lince *m* lynx.

lindar *vi* to be adjacent.

lindo, da *adj* pretty; lovely.

línea *f* line; cable; outline.

lino *m* flax.

linterna *f* lantern, lamp; torch.

lío *m* bundle, parcel; (*fam*) muddle, mess.

liquidar *vt* to liquidate; to settle (accounts).

líquido, da *adj* liquid.

lirio *m* (*bot*) iris.

lirón *m* dormouse; (*fig*) sleepy-head.

liso, sa *adj* plain, even, flat, smooth.

lisonja *f* adulation, flattery.

lista *f* list; register; catalogue; menu.

listo, ta *adj* ready; smart, clever.

litera *f* berth; bunk, bunk bed.

litigio *m* lawsuit.

litoral *adj* coastal:—*m* coast.

litro *m* litre (measure).

liviano, na *adj* light; fickle; trivial.

lo *pn* it; him; you:—*art* the.

lobo *m* wolf.

lóbulo *m* lobe.

local *adj* local:—*m* place, site.

loco, ca *adj* mad:—*m/f* mad person.

locutor, ra *m/f* (*rad*) announcer; (*TV*) newsreader.

lodo *m* mud, mire.

lograr *vt* to achieve; to gain, obtain.

lombarda *f* red cabbage.

lombriz *f* worm.

lomo *m* loin; back (of an animal); spine (of a book):—**llevar** *o* **traer a** ~ to carry on the back.

lona *f* canvas.

loncha *f* slice; rasher.

longaniza *f* pork sausage.

longitud *f* length; longitude.

loro *m* parrot.

los *art mpl* the:—*pn* them; you.

losa *f* flagstone.

lote *m* lot; portion.

loza *f* crockery.

lucero *m* morning star, bright star.

luchar *vi* to struggle; to wrestle.

luciérnaga *f* glowworm.

lucir *vt* to light (up); to show off:—*vi* to shine:—**~se** *vr* to make a fool of oneself.

luego *adv* next; afterward(s): —**desde ~** of course.

lugar *m* place, spot; village; reason: —**en ~ de** instead of, in lieu of.

lúgubre *adj* lugubrious; sad, gloomy.

lujo *m* luxury; abundance.

lujuria *f* lust.

lumbre *f* fire; light.

luna *f* moon; glass plate for mirrors; lens.

lunar *m* mole, spot:—*adj* lunar.

lunes *m invar* Monday.

lupa *f* magnifying glass.

lupanar *m* brothel.

luto *m* mourning (dress); grief.

luz *f* light.

LL

llama *f* flame; llama (animal).

llamar *vt* to call; to name; to summon; to ring up, telephone:—*vi* to knock at the door; to ring up, telephone:—**~se** *vr* to be named.

llano, na *adj* plain; even, level, smooth; clear, evident:—*m* plain.

llanta *f* (wheel) rim; tyre; inner (tube).

llanura *f* evenness, flatness; plain, prairie.

llave *f* key:—**~ maestra** master key.

llegar *vi* to arrive:—**~ a** to reach:—**~se** *vr* to come near, approach.

llenar *vt* to fill; to cover; to fill out (a form); to satisfy, fulfil:—**~se** *vr* to gorge oneself.

llevar *vt* to take; to wear; to carry; to convey, transport; to drive; to lead; to bear:—**~se** *vr* to carry off, take away.

llorar *vt, vi* to weep, cry.

llover *vi* to rain.

lluvia *f* rain.

M

maceta *f* flowerpot.

machacar *vt* to pound, crush:—*vi* to insist, go on.

macho *adj* male; (*fig*) virile:—*m* male; (*fig*) he-man.

macizo, za *adj* massive; solid:—*m* mass, chunk.

madera *f* timber, wood.

madrastra *f* stepmother.

madre *f* mother; womb.

madreselva *f* honeysuckle.

madriguera *f* burrow; den.

madrugar *vi* to get up early; to get ahead.

maduro, ra *adj* ripe, mature.

maestro *m* master; teacher:— ~, **tra** *adj* masterly, skilled; principal.

magia *f* magic.

magisterio *m* teaching; teaching profession; teachers *pl*.

magnetofón, magnetófono *m* tape recorder.

magnífico, ca *adj* magnificent, splendid.

mago, ga *m*/*f* magician.

magullar *vt* to bruise; to damage; to bash (*sl*).

mahometano, na *m*/*f*, *adj* Muslim.

maíz *m* maize, Indian corn.

majadero, ra *adj* dull; silly, stupid:—*m* idiot.

majo, ja *adj* nice; attractive; smart.

majuelo *m* vine newly planted; hawthorn.

mal *m* evil; hurt; harm, damage; misfortune; illness:—*adj* (before masculine nouns) bad.

malcriado, da *adj* rude, ill-behaved; naughty; spoiled.

maldad *f* wickedness.

maldecir *vt* to curse.

maldito, ta *adj* wicked; damned, cursed.

malecón *m* pier.

maleducado, da *adj* bad-mannered, rude.

malestar *m* discomfort; (*fig*) uneasiness; unrest.

maleta *f* suitcase; (*auto*) boot.

maleza *f* weeds *pl*; thicket.

malgastar *vt* to waste, ruin.

malhablado, da *adj* foul-mouthed.

malhechor, ra *m*/*f* malefactor; criminal.

malhumorado, da *adj* cross, bad-tempered.

malla *f* mesh, network:—~s *fpl* leotard.

malo, la *adj* bad; ill; wicked:—*m*/*f* villain.

maltratar *vt* to ill-treat, abuse, mistreat.

malva *f* (*bot*) mallow.

malvado, da *adj* wicked, villainous.

mama *f* teat; breast.

mamá *f* (*fam*) mum, mummy.

mamar *vt*, *vi* to suck.

mamífero *m* mammal.

manada *f* flock, herd; pack; crowd.

manantial *m* source, spring; origin.

manchar *vt* to stain, soil.

manco, ca *adj* one-armed; one-handed; maimed; faulty.

mancomunidad *f* union, fellowship; community; (*jur*) joint responsibility.

mandar *vt* to command, order; to bequeath; to send.

mandarina *f* tangerine.

mandíbula *f* jaw.

mandil *m* apron.

manera *f* manner, way; fashion; kind.

manga *f* sleeve; hose.

mango *m* handle; mango.

manguera *f* hose; pipe.

maní *m* peanut.

manifestación *f* manifestation; show; demonstration; mass meeting.

manifestar *vt* to manifest, declare.

maniobrar *vt* to manoeuvre; to handle.

manipular *vt* to manipulate.

maniquí *m* dummy:—*m*/*f* model.

manivela *f* crank.

mano *f* hand; hand (of clock, etc); foot, paw (of animal); coat (of paint); lot, series; hand (at game):—**a ~** by hand:—**a ~s llenas** liberally, generously.

manojo *m* handful, bunch.

manopla *f* flannel; mitten; gauntlet.

manosear *vt* to handle; to mess up.

manso, sa *adj* tame; gentle, soft.

manta *f* blanket.

manteca *f* fat:—~ **de cerdo** lard.

mantel *m* tablecloth.

mantener *vt* to maintain, support; to nourish; to keep:—**~se** *vr* to hold one's ground; to support oneself.

mantequilla *f* butter.

manzana *f* apple.

manzanilla *f* camomile; camomile tea; manzanilla sherry.

maña *f* handiness, dexterity, cleverness, cunning; habit, custom; trick.

mañana *f* morning:—*adv* tomorrow.

mapa *m* map.

maquillar *vt* to make up:—**~se** *vr* to put on make-up.

máquina *f* machine; (*ferro*) engine; camera; (*fig*) machinery; plan, project.

maquinilla *f*:—**~ de afeitar** razor.

maquinista *m* (*ferro*) train driver; operator; (*mar*) engineer.

mar *m/f* sea.

maravilla *f* wonder.

marca *f* mark; stamp; make, brand.

marcar *vt* to mark; to dial; to score; to record; to set (hair):—*vi* to score; to dial.

marchar *vi* to go; to work:—**~se** *vr* to go away.

marco *m* frame; framework; (*dep*) goalposts *pl*.

marea *f* tide.

marear *vt* (*mar*) to sail, navigate; to annoy, upset:—**~se** *vr* to feel sick; to feel faint; to feel dizzy.

marfil *m* ivory.

margarita *f* daisy.

margen *m* margin; border:— *f* bank (of river).

marido *m* husband.

marinero, ra *adj* sea *compd*; seaworthy:—*m* sailor.

marioneta *f* puppet.

mariposa *f* butterfly.

mariquita *f* ladybird.

marisco *m* shellfish *pl*.

mármol *m* marble.

marrano *m* pig, boar.

marrón *adj* brown.

martes *m invar* Tuesday.

martillo *m* hammer.

marzo *m* March.

mas *adv* but, yet.

más *adv* more; most; besides, moreover:—**a ~ tardar** at latest:—**sin ~ ni ~** without more ado.

masa *f* dough, paste; mortar; mass.

mascar *vt* to chew.

máscara *m/f* masked person:—*f* mask.

mascullar *vt* to mumble, mutter.

mástil *m* (*mar*) mast.

mastín *m* mastiff.

mata *f* shrub; sprig, blade; grove, group of trees; mop of hair.

matadero *m* slaughterhouse.

matar *vt* to kill; to execute; to murder:—**~se** *vr* to kill oneself, commit suicide.

matasellos *m invar* postmark.

mate *m* checkmate:—*adj* matt.

material *adj* material, physical:—*m* equipment, materials *pl*.

maternidad *f* motherhood.

matinal *adj* morning *compd*.

matiz *m* shade of colour; shading.

matrícula *f* register, list; (*auto*) registration number; numberplate.

matrimonio *m* marriage, matrimony.

matriz *f* matrix; womb; mould, form.

maullar *vi* to mew.

mayo *m* May.

mayor *adj* main, chief; (*mus*) major; biggest; eldest; greater, larger; elderly:—*m* chief, boss; adult:—**al por ~** wholesale:—**~es** *mpl* forefathers.

mayoría *f* majority, greater part:—**~ de edad** coming of age.

mayúsculo, la *adj* (*fig*) tremendous: —*f* capital letter.

mazo *m* bunch; club, mallet; bat.

mazorca *f* ear of corn.

me *pn* me; to me.

mear *vi* (*fam*) to pee, piss (*sl*).

mecanógrafo, fa *m/f* typist.

mecer *vt* to rock; to dandle (a child).

mechar *vt* to lard; to stuff.

mechón *m* lock of hair; large bundle of threads or fibres.

media *f* stocking; sock; average.

medianoche *f* midnight.

mediante *prep* by means of.

mediar *vi* to intervene; to mediate.

medicamento *m* medicine.

médico, ca *adj* medical:—*m/f* doctor.

medida *f* measure.

medio, dia *adj* half:—**a medias** partly:—*m* middle; average; way, means; medium.

mediodía *m* noon, midday.

medir *vt* to measure:—**~se** *vr* to be moderate.

medrar *vi* to grow, thrive, prosper; to improve.

médula *f* marrow; essence, substance; pith.

medusa *f* jellyfish.

mejilla *f* cheek.

mejillón *m* mussel.

mejor *adj, adv* better; best.

mejorar *vt* to improve, ameliorate; to enhance:—*vi* to improve; (*med*) to recover, get better:—**~se** *vr* to improve, get better.

melenudo, da *adj* long-haired.

melindroso, sa *adj* prudish, finicky.

mella *f* notch in edged tools; gap.

mellizo, za *adj, m/f* twin.

melocotón *m* peach.

meloso, sa *adj* honeyed; mellow.

membrete *m* letter head.

membrillo *m* quince; quince tree.

memoria *f* memory; report; record:—**~s** *fpl* memoirs *pl.*

mendigar *vt* to beg.

menear *vt* to move from place to place; (*fig*) to handle:—**~se** *vr* to move; to shake; to sway.

menguante *f* waning.

meñique *m* little finger.

menor *m/f* young person, juvenile:—*adj* less; smaller; minor:—**al por ~** retail.

menos *adv* less; least:—**a lo ~** *o* **por lo ~** at least:—*prep* except; minus.

menospreciar *vt* to undervalue; to despise, scorn.

mensaje *m* message.

mensual *adj* monthly.

menta *f* mint.

mente *f* mind; understanding.

mentecato, ta *adj* silly, stupid:—*m/f* idiot.

mentir *vt* to feign; to pretend:—*vi* to lie.

mentira *f* lie, falsehood.

menudo, da *adj* small; minute; petty, insignificant:—**a ~** frequently, often.

mercader *m* dealer, trader.

mercado *m* market; marketplace.

mercancía *f* commodity:—**~s** *fpl* goods *pl*, merchandise.

mercurio *m* mercury.

merecer *vt* to deserve, merit.

meridional *adj* southern.

merienda *f* (light) tea; afternoon snack; picnic.

merluza *f* hake.

mermelada *f* jam.

mero *m* pollack (fish):—**~, ra** *adj* mere, pure.

mes *m* month.

mesa *f* table; desk; plateau:—**~ redonda** round table.

mestizo, za *adj* of mixed race; crossbred:—*m/f* half-caste.

meta *f* goal; finish.

metal *m* metal; (*mus*) brass; timbre (of voice).

meter *vt* to place, put; to insert, put in; to involve; to make, cause:—**~se** *vr* to meddle, interfere.

método *m* method.

metro *m* metre; subway.

mezclar *vt* to mix:—**~se** *vr* to mix; to mingle.

mezquino, na *adj* mean; small-minded, petty; wretched.

mezquita *f* mosque.

mi *adj* my.

mí *pn* me; myself.

miedo *m* fear, dread.

miel *f* honey.

miembro *m* member.

mientras *adv* meanwhile:—*conj* while; as long as.

miércoles *m invar* Wednesday.

mierda *f* (*fam*) shit (*sl*).

miga *f* crumb:—**~s** *fpl* fried bread-crumbs *pl.*

mijo *m* (*bot*) millet.

mil *m* one thousand.

milagro *m* miracle, wonder.

milésimo, ma *adj, m* thousandth.

milímetro *m* millimetre.

milla *f* mile.

millón *m* million.

mimar *vt* to spoil, pamper.

mimbre *m* wicker.

mimo *m* caress; spoiling; mime.

mina *f* mine; underground passage.

minero, ra *m/f* miner.

minifalda *f* miniskirt.

mínimo, ma *adj* minimum.

minoría *f* minority.

minucioso, sa *adj* meticulous; very detailed.

minúsculo, la *adj* minute:—*f* small letter.

minusválido, da *adj* (physically) handicapped:—*m/f* (physically) handicapped person.

minuto *m* minute.

mío, mía *adj* mine.

miope *adj* short-sighted.

mirar *vt* to look at; to observe; to consider:—*vi* to look:—**~se** *vr* to look at oneself; to look at one another.

mirlo *m* blackbird.

misa *f* mass:—**~ del gallo** midnight mass.

miserable *adj* miserable; mean; squalid (place); (*fam*) despicable:—*m/f* rotter.

misericordia *f* mercy.

mismo, ma *adj* same; very.

mitad *f* half; middle.

mitin *m* (political) rally.

mixto, ta *adj* mixed.

mobiliario *m* furniture.

mochila *f* backpack.

mochuelo *m* red owl.

moco *m* snot (*sl*), mucus.

moda *f* fashion, style.

modales *mpl* manners *pl*.

modelo *m* model, pattern.

módico, ca *adj* moderate.

modificar *vt* to modify.

modisto, ta *m/f* dressmaker.

modo *m* mode, method, manner.

modorra *f* drowsiness.

mofarse *vr*:—~ **de** to mock, scoff at.

moflete *m* fat cheek.

moho *m* rust; mould, mildew.

mojar *vt* to wet, moisten:—~se *vr* to get wet.

mojón *m* landmark.

molde *m* mould; pattern; model.

moler *vt* to grind, pound; to tire out; to annoy, bore.

molestar *vt* to annoy, bother; to trouble:—*vi* to be a nuisance.

molino *m* mill.

momentáneo, nea *adj* momentary.

momento *m* moment.

momia *f* mummy.

mondadientes *m* *invar* toothpick.

mondar *vt* to clean; to cleanse; to peel:—~se *vr* ~ **de risa** (*fam*) to split one's sides laughing.

mondo, da *adj* clean; pure:—~ **y lirondo** bare, plain; pure and simple.

moneda *f* money; currency; coin.

monja *f* nun.

mono, na *adj* lovely; pretty; nice:—*m/f* monkey; ape:—*mpl* dungarees *pl*; overalls *pl*.

monstruo *m* monster.

montaje *m* assembly; decor (of theatre); montage.

montaña *f* mountain.

montar *vt* to mount, get on (a bicycle, horse, etc); to assemble, put together; to overlap; to set up (a business); to beat, whip (in cooking):—*vi* to mount; to ride:—~ **a** to amount to.

monte *m* mountain; woodland:—~ **alto** forest:—~ **bajo** scrub.

montón *m* heap, pile; mass:—**a ~ones**, abundantly, by the score.

montura *f* mount; saddle.

monzón *m* monsoon.

mora *f* blackberry.

morado, da *adj* violet, purple.

morcilla *f* black pudding.

mordaz *adj* biting, scathing; pungent.

mordaza *f* gag; clamp.

morder *vt* to bite; to nibble; to corrode, eat away.

moreno, na *adj* brown; swarthy; dark-skinned.

morir *vi* to die; to expire; to die down: —~se *vr* to die; (*fig*) to be dying.

morisco, ca *adj* Moorish.

moroso, sa *adj* slow, sluggish; (*com*) slow to pay up.

morral *m* haversack.

morro *m* snout; nose (of plane, etc).

morsa *f* walrus.

mortal *adj* mortal; fatal, deadly.

mosca *f* fly.

mosquearse *vr* (*fam*) to get cross; (*fam*) to take offence.

mosquitero *m* mosquito net.

mosquito *m* gnat, mosquito.

mostaza *f* mustard.

mosto *m* must, grape juice.

mostrador *m* counter.

mostrar *vt* to show, exhibit; to explain: —~se *vr* to appear, show oneself.

mote *m* nickname.

motivo *m* motive, cause, reason.

moto (*fam*), **motocicleta** *f* motorcycle.

motor *m* engine, motor.

mover *vt* to move; to shake; to drive; (*fig*) to cause:—~se *vr* to move; (*fig*) to get a move on.

móvil *adj* mobile, movable; moving: —*m* motive.

mozo, za *adj* young:—*m/f* youth, young man/girl; waiter/waitress.

muchacho, a *m/f* boy/girl:—*f* maid, maidservant.

mucho, cha *adj* a lot of, much:—*adv* much, a lot; long.

mudar *vt* to change; to shed:—~se *vr* to change one's clothes; to change house:—*vi* to change;

mudo, da *adj* dumb; silent, mute.

mueble *m* piece of furniture:—~s *mpl* furniture.

mueca *f* grimace, funny face.

muela *f* tooth, molar.

muelle *m* spring; regulator; quay.

muérdago *m* (*bot*) mistletoe.

muerte *f* death.

mujer *f* woman.
mulato *adj* mulatto.
muleta *f* crutch.
mullido, da *adj* soft; springy.
mulo, la *m/f* mule.
multa *f* fine, penalty.
mundial *adj* worldwide; world *compd*.
mundo *m* world.
muñeca *f* wrist; child's doll.

municipio *m* town council; municipality.
murciélago *m* bat.
murmullo *m* murmur, mutter.
murmurar *vi* to murmur; to gossip.
muro *m* wall.
músculo *m* muscle.
museo *m* museum.

musgo *m* moss.
música *f* music.
muslo *m* thigh.
mustio, tia *adj* parched, withered; sad, sorrowful.
mutuo, tua *adj* mutual, reciprocal.
muy *adv* very; too; greatly:— ~ **ilustre** most illustrious.

N, Ñ

nabo *m* turnip.

nácar *m* mother-of-pearl, nacre.

nacer *vi* to be born; to bud, shoot (of plants); to rise; to grow.

nacimiento *m* birth; nativity.

nada *f* nothing:—*adv* no way, not at all, by no means.

nadar *vi* to swim.

nadie *pn* nobody, no one.

nafta *f* petrol.

nalgas *fpl* buttocks *pl*.

naranja *f* orange.

nariz *f* nose.

narrar *vt* to narrate, tell.

nata *f* cream.

natillas *fpl* custard.

naturaleza *f* nature.

naufragar *vi* to be shipwrecked; to suffer ruin in one's affairs.

náutica *f* navigation.

navaja *f* penknife; razor.

nave *f* ship; nave; warehouse.

navegar *vt, vi* to navigate; to sail; to fly.

Navidad *f* Christmas.

nebuloso, sa *adj* misty; cloudy; nebulous; foggy; hazy; drizzling:—*f* nebula.

neceser *m* toilet bag; holdall.

necesitar *vt* to need:—*vi* to want, to need.

necio, cia *adj* ignorant; stupid, foolish; imprudent.

nefasto, ta *adj* unlucky.

negado, da *adj* incapable, unfit.

negar *vt* to deny; to refuse:—~**se** *vr* ~ **a hacer** to refuse to do.

negocio *m* business, affair; transaction; firm; place of business.

negro, gra *adj* black:—*m* black:—*m/f* Black.

nene *m*, **nena** *f* baby.

neto, ta *adj* neat, pure; net.

neumático, ca *adj* pneumatic:—*m* tyre.

neutro, tra *adj* neutral; neuter.

nevar *vi* to snow.

nevera *f* icebox.

ni *conj* neither, nor.

nido *m* nest; hiding place.

niebla *f* fog; mist.

nieta *f* granddaughter.

nieto *m* grandson.

nieve *f* snow.

niña *f* little girl; pupil, (of eye).

ningún, ninguno, na *adj* no:—*pn* nobody; none; not one; neither.

niño, ña *adj* childish:—*m/f* child; infant:—**desde** ~ from infancy, from a child:—*m* boy.

nitidez *f* clarity; brightness; sharpness.

nivel *m* level; standard; height:—**a** ~ perfectly level.

no *adv* no; not:—*excl* no!

no obstante *adv* nevertheless, notwithstanding.

noche *f* night; evening; darkness:—~ **buena** Christmas Eve:—~ **vieja** New Year's Eve:—¡**buenas** ~**s**! good night!

noción *f* notion, idea.

nocivo, va *adj* harmful.

nogal *m* walnut tree.

nombrar *vt* to name; to nominate; to appoint.

nombre *m* name; title; reputation.

nómina *f* list; (*com*) payroll.

non *adj* odd, uneven:—*m* odd number.

nor(d)este *adj* northeast, northeastern:—*m* northeast.

nórdico, ca *adj* northern; Nordic.

noria *f* water wheel; big wheel.

noroeste *adj* northwest, northwestern:—*m* northwest.

norte *adj* north, northern:—*m* north; (*fig*) rule, guide.

nos *pn* us; to us; for us; from us; to ourselves.

nosotros, tras *pn* we; us.

nostalgia *f* homesickness.

notar *vt* to note; to mark; to remark:—~**se** *vr* to be obvious.

noticia *f* information; note:—~**s** *fpl* news.

noticiario *m* newsreel; news bulletin.

notificar *vt* to notify, inform.

novato, ta *adj* inexperienced:—*m/f* beginner.

novecientos, tas *adj* nine hundred.

novedad *f* novelty; modernness; newness; piece of news; change.

noveno, na *adj* ninth.

noventa *adj, m* ninety.

novia *f* bride; girlfriend; fiancée.

noviembre *m* November.

novio *m* bridegroom; boyfriend; fiancé.

nube *f* cloud.

nublado, da *adj* cloudy:—*m* storm cloud.

nuca *f* nape (of the neck); scruff of the neck.

nudillo *m* knuckle.

nudo *m* knot.

nuera *f* daughter-in-law.

nuestro, tra *adj* our:—*pn* ours.

nueve *m, adj* nine.

nuevo, va *adj* new; modern; fresh:—*f* piece of news:— **¿que hay de ~?** is there any news?, what's new?

nuez *f* nut; walnut; Adam's apple:—**~ moscada** nutmeg.

número *m* number; cipher.

nunca *adv* never.

nutria *f* otter.

nutrir *vt* to nourish; to feed.

ñaque *m* junk, rubbish.

ñato, ta *adj* snub-nosed.

ñoño, ña *adj* insipid; spineless; silly.

ñoñeria *f* insipidness.

O

o *conj* or; either.

obedecer *vt* to obey.

obeso, sa *adj* obese, fat.

objetar *vi* to object.

objeto *m* object; aim.

obligar *vt* to force:—~**se** *vr* to bind oneself.

obra *f* work; building, construction; play:—**por ~ de** thanks to.

obrero, ra *adj* working; labour *compd*:—*m/f* worker; labourer.

obsequiar *vt* to lavish attention on:— ~ **con** to present with.

observar *vt* to observe; to notice.

obstáculo *m* obstacle, impediment.

obstinarse *vr* to be obstinate:—~ **en** to persist in.

obstruir *vt* to obstruct:—~**se** *vr* to be blocked up, be obstructed.

obtener *vt* to obtain; to gain.

ocasión *f* occasion, opportunity.

ocasionar *vt* to cause, occasion.

occidente *m* occident, west.

océano *m* ocean.

ochenta *m, adj* eighty.

ocho *m, adj* eight.

ochocientos *m, adj* eight hundred.

ocio *m* leisure; pastime.

octavilla *f* pamphlet.

octavo, va *adj* eighth.

octubre *m* October.

ocultar *vt* to hide, conceal.

ocupar *vt* to occupy; to hold (office): —~**se** *vr* ~ **de**, ~ **en** to concern oneself with; to look after.

ocurrencia *f* event; bright idea.

ocurrir *vi* to occur, happen.

odiar *vt* to hate:—~**se** *vr* to hate one another.

oeste *adj* west, western:—*m* west.

ofender *vt* to offend; to injure:—~**se** *vr* to be vexed; to take offence.

oficina *f* office.

oficio *m* employment, occupation; ministry; function; trade, business.

ofrecer *vt* to offer; to present; to exhibit:—~**se** *vr* to offer oneself; to occur, present itself.

oído *m* hearing; ear.

oír *vt, vi* to hear; to listen (to).

ojal *m* buttonhole.

ojalá *conj* if only!, would that!

ojear *vt* to eye, view; to glance.

ojera *f* bag under the eyes.

ojo *m* eye; sight; eye of a needle; arch of a bridge.

ola *f* wave.

oler *vt* to smell, scent:—*vi* to smell:— ~ **a** to smack of.

olfato *m* sense of smell.

olivo *m* olive tree.

olla *f* pan; stew:—~ **exprés,**

~ **a presion** pressure cooker.

olmo *m* elm tree.

olor *m* smell, odour; scent.

olvidar *vt* to forget.

ombligo *m* navel.

once *m, adj* eleven.

onda *f* wave.

opaco, ca *adj* opaque; dark.

opinar *vt* to think:—*vi* to give one's opinion.

oponer *vt* to oppose:—~**se** *vr* to be opposed:—~ **a** to oppose.

oposición *f* opposition: ~**ones** *fpl* public examinations *pl*.

oprimir *vt* to oppress; to crush; to press; to squeeze.

optar *vt* to choose, elect.

optativo, va *adj* optional.

óptimo, ma *adj* best.

opuesto, ta *adj* opposite; contrary; adverse.

orar *vi* to pray.

ordenado, da *adj* methodical; tidy.

ordenador *m* computer.

ordenanza *f* order; statute, ordinance; ordination.

ordenar *vt* to arrange; to order; to ordain:—~**se** *vr* to take holy orders.

ordeñar *vt* to milk.

oreja *f* ear.

orgullo *m* pride, haughtiness.

oriental *adj* oriental, eastern.

orientar *vt* to orient; to point; to direct; to guide:—

~**se** *vr* to get one's bearings; to decide on a course of action.

orificio *m* orifice; mouth; aperture.

orilla *f* limit, border, margin; edge (of cloth); shore.

orín *m* rust.

orina *f* urine.

orinal *m* chamber pot.

oro *m* gold; ~**s** *mpl* diamonds *pl* (cards).

ortiga *f* (*bot*) nettle.

oruga *f* (*bot*) caterpillar.

orzuelo *m* (*med*) stye.

os *pn* you; to you.

osa *f* she-bear:—**O~ Mayor/ Menor** Great/Little Bear.

osar *vi* to dare, venture.

oscuro, ra *adj* obscure; dark.

oso *m* bear:—~ **blanco** polar bear.

ostentar *vt* to show:—*vi* to boast, brag.

ostra *f* oyster.

otoño *m* fall, autumn.

otorgar *vt* to concede; to grant.

otorrino, na, otorrinolaringólogo, ga *m*/*f* ear, nose and throat specialist.

otro, tra *adj* another; other.

oveja *f* sheep.

ovillo *m* ball of wool.

óvulo *m* ovum.

oxidar *vt* to rust:—~**se** *vr* to go rusty.

oyente *m*/*f* listener, hearer.

P

pacificar *vt* to pacify, appease.

pacotilla *f*:—**de** ~ third-rate; cheap.

pactar *vt* to covenant; to contract; to stipulate.

padecer *vt* to suffer; to sustain (an injury); to put up with.

padrastro *m* stepfather.

padre *m* father:—~**s** *mpl* parents *pl*.

pagar *vt* to pay; to pay for; (*fig*) to repay:—*vi* to pay.

página *f* page.

pago *m* payment; reward.

país *m* country; region.

paisaje *m* landscape.

paisano, na *adj* of the same country: —*m/f* fellow countryman/woman.

paja *f* straw; (*fig*) trash.

pájaro *m* bird; sly, acute fellow.

pajita *f* (drinking) straw.

pala *f* spade, shovel.

palabra *f* word:—**de** ~ by word of mouth.

paladar *m* palate; taste, relish.

palanca *f* lever.

palangana *f* basin.

palco *m* box (in a theatre).

paleto, ta *m/f* rustic.

pálido, da *adj* pallid, pale.

palillo *m* small stick; toothpick:—~**s** *mpl* chopsticks *pl*.

paliza *f* beating, thrashing.

palma *f* palm tree; palm of the hand; palm leaf.

palmada *f* slap, clap:—~**s** *fpl* clapping of hands, applause.

palmera *f* palm tree.

palo *m* stick; cudgel; blow given with a stick; post; mast; bat; suit (at cards):— ~**s** *mpl* masting.

paloma *f* pigeon, dove:—~ **torcaz** ring dove:—~ **zorita** wood pigeon.

palomilla *f* moth; wing nut; angle iron.

palpar *vt* to feel, touch.

palta *f* avocado (pear).

pámpano *m* vine branch.

pan *m* bread; loaf; food in general.

pana *f* corduroy.

pañal *m* diaper, nappy.

pandereta *f* tambourine.

pandilla *f* group; gang; clique.

paño *m* cloth; piece of cloth; duster, rag.

pantalla *f* screen; lampshade.

pantalón *m*, **pantalones** *mpl* trousers, pants *pl*.

pantano *m* marsh; reservoir; obstacle, difficulty.

pantorrilla *f* calf (of the leg).

pañuelo *m* handkerchief.

panza *f* belly, paunch.

papá *m* (*fam*) dad, pop.

papada *f* double chin.

papel *m* paper; writing; part, role (in a play):—~ **de estraza** brown paper: —~ **sellado** stamped paper.

papeleo *m* red tape.

paperas *fpl* mumps.

paquete *m* packet; parcel; package tour.

par *adj* equal; alike; even:— *m* pair; couple; peer:—**sin** ~ matchless.

para *prep* for; to, in order to; towards.

parabrisas *m invar* windscreen.

paracaídas *m invar* parachute.

parada *f* halt; suspension; pause; stop; shutdown; stopping place:—~ **de autobús** bus stop.

parado, da *adj* motionless; at a standstill; stopped; standing (up); unemployed.

paraguas *m invar* umbrella.

parar *vi* to stop, halt:—*vt* to stop, detain:—**sin** ~ instantly, without delay: — ~**se** *vr* to stop, halt; to stand up.

parecer *m* opinion, advice, counsel; countenance, air, mien:—*vi* to appear; to seem:—~**se** *vr* ~ **a** to resemble.

parecido, da *adj* resembling, like.

pared *f* wall:—~ **medianera** party wall.

pareja *f* pair, couple, brace.

pariente, ta *m/f* relative, relation.

parir *vt* to give birth to:—*vi* to give birth.

paro *m* strike; unemployment.

párpado *m* eyelid.

parra *f* vine raised on stakes or nailed to a wall.

párrafo *m* paragraph.

parrilla *f* grill; grille.

parte *m* message; report:—*f* part; side; party:—**de ocho dias a esta ~** within these last eight days:—**de ~ a ~** from side to side, through and through.

partera *f* midwife.

particular *adj* particular, special:—*m* private individual; particular matter or subject treated upon.

partida *f* departure; party; item in an account; parcel; game.

partido *m* party; match; team.

partir *vt* to part; to divide, separate; to cut; to break:—*vi* to depart:—**~se** *vr* to break (in two, etc).

parvulario *m* nursery school.

pasa *f* raisin.

pasadizo *m* narrow passage; narrow, covered way.

pasado, da *adj* past; bad; overdone; out of date:—**~ mañana** the day after tomorrow:—**la semana pasada** last week:—*m* past.

pasaje *m* passage; fare; passengers *pl*.

pasajero, ra *adj* transient; transitory; fugitive:—*m/f* traveller; passenger.

pasamanos *m invar* (hand)rail; bannister.

pasar *vt* to pass; to surpass; to suffer; to strain; to dissemble:—*vi* to pass; to

happen:—**~se** *vr* to go over (to another party); to go bad or off.

pasarela *f* footbridge; gangway.

pasatiempo *m* pastime, amusement.

Pascua *f* Passover; Easter.

pasear *vt* to walk:—*vi* **~se** *vr* to walk; to walk about.

pasmar *vt* to amaze; to numb; to chill:—**~se** *vr* to be astonished.

paso *m* pace, step; passage; manner of walking; flight of steps; accident:—*(ferro)* **~ a nivel** level crossing:—**al ~** on the way, in passing.

pasta *f* paste; dough; pastry; *(fam)* dough:—**~s** *fpl* pastries *pl*; pasta:—**~ de dientes** toothpaste.

pastel *m* cake; pie; crayon (for drawing).

pastilla *f* bar (of soap); tablet, pill.

pastor *m* shepherd; pastor.

pata *f* leg (of animal or furniture); foot:—**meter la ~** to put one's foot in it.

patata *f* potato.

patear *vt* to kick; to stamp on.

patillas *fpl* sideburns *pl*.

patín *m* skate; runner.

patinar *vi* to skate; to skid; *(fam)* to blunder.

patio *m* courtyard; playground.

pato *m* duck.

patoso, sa *adj* *(fam)* clumsy.

patraña *f* lie.

patrocinar *vt* to sponsor; to back, support.

patrón, ona *m/f* boss, master/mistress; landlord/lady; patron saint:—*m* pattern.

patronal *adj*:—**la clase ~** management.

patrulla *f* patrol.

paulatino, na *adj* gradual, slow.

pausar *vi* to pause.

pauta *f* guideline.

pavo *m* turkey:—**~ real** peacock.

pavor *m* dread, terror.

payaso, sa *m/f* clown.

payo, ya *m/f* non-gypsy (for a gypsy).

paz *f* peace; tranquillity, ease.

peaje *m* toll.

peana *f* pedestal; footstool.

peatón *m* pedestrian.

peca *f* freckle; spot.

pecado *m* sin.

pecho *m* chest; breast(s) *(pl)*; teat; *(fig)* courage, valour:—**dar el ~ a** to suckle:—**tomar a ~** to take to heart.

pechuga *f* breast of a fowl; *(fam)* bosom.

pedazo *m* piece, bit.

pedernal *m* flint.

pediatra *m/f* pediatrician.

pedicuro, ra *m/f* chiropodist.

pedir *vt* to ask for; to petition; to beg; to order; to need; to solicit:—*vi* to ask.

pedo *m* *(fam)* fart *(sl)*:—**tirarse un ~** to fart *(sl)*.

pegamento *m* glue.

pegar *vt* to cement; to join, unite; to beat:—**~ fuego a** to set fire to:—*vi* to stick; to match:—**~se** *vr* to intrude; to steal in.

pegatina *f* sticker.

peinar *vt* to comb; to style.

peine *m* comb.

pelar *vt* to cut (hair); to strip

off (feathers); to peel:—~se *vr* to peel off; to have one's hair cut.

peldaño *m* step (of a flight of stairs).

pelear *vt* to fight, combat:—~se *vr* to scuffle.

pelele *m* dummy; man of straw.

película *f* film.

peligro *m* danger, peril; risk.

pelirrojo, ja *m/f* redhead:—*adj* red-haired.

pellejo *m* skin; hide, pelt; peel; wine skin; oilskin; drunkard.

pellizcar *vt* to pinch.

pelo *m* hair; pile; flaw (in precious stones).

pelota *f* ball.

peluca *f* wig.

peluquería *f* hairdresser's; barber's (shop).

pelusa *f* bloom (on fruit); fluff.

pena *f* punishment, pain:—**a duras ~s** with great difficulty or trouble.

pendiente *f* slope, declivity:—*m* earring:—*adj* pending; unsettled.

pene *m* penis.

penetrante *adj* deep; sharp; piercing; searching; biting.

penique *m* penny.

penoso, sa *adj* painful.

pensar *vi* to think.

pensativo, va *adj* pensive, thoughtful.

pensión *f* guest-house; pension.

penúltimo, ma *adj* penultimate, last but one.

penumbra *f* half-light.

penuria *f* penury, poverty, neediness, extreme want.

peña *f* rock, large stone.

peón *m* (day) labourer; foot soldier; pawn (at chess).

peor *adj, adv* worse:—~ **que** ~ worse and worse.

pepino *m* cucumber.

pepita *f* kernel; pip.

pequeño, ña *adj* little, small; young.

pera *f* pear.

percatarse *vr*:—~ **de** to notice.

percha *f* coat hook; coat hanger; perch.

percibir *vt* to receive; to perceive, comprehend.

perder *vt* to lose; to waste; to miss:—~se *vr* to go astray; to be lost; to be spoiled.

perdiz *f* partridge.

perdón *m* pardon; mercy:—¡~! sorry!

perdonar *vt* to pardon, forgive; to excuse.

perdurar *vi* to last; to still exist.

perecedero, ra *adj* perishable.

peregrino, na *adj* (*fig*) strange:—*m* pilgrim.

perejil *m* parsley.

pereza *f* laziness, idleness.

perfil *m* profile.

perforar *vt* to perforate; to drill; to punch a hole in:—*vi* to drill.

perfume *m* perfume.

pergamino *m* parchment.

periódico, ca *adj* periodical:—*m* newspaper.

periodista *m/f* journalist.

peripecia *f* vicissitude; sudden change.

periquito *m* budgie.

perito, ta *adj* skilful, experienced:—*m/f* expert; skilled worker; technician.

perjudicar *vt* to prejudice, damage; to injure, hurt.

perjurar *vi* to perjure, swear falsely; to swear.

perla *f* pearl:—**de ~s** fine.

permanecer *vi* to stay; to continue to be.

permiso *m* permission, leave, licence.

permitir *vt* to permit, allow.

permutar *vt* to exchange, permute.

pernera *f* trouser leg.

perno *m* bolt.

pernoctar *vi* to spend the night.

pero *m* kind of apple:—*conj* but, yet.

perogrullada *f* truism, platitude.

perol *m* large metal pan.

perro *m* dog.

perseguir *vt* to pursue; to persecute; to chase after.

perseverar *vi* to persevere, persist.

persiana *f* (Venetian) blind.

persistir *vi* to persist.

persona *f* person:—**de ~ a ~** from person to person.

personaje *m* celebrity; character.

persuadir *vt* to persuade:—~se *vr* to be persuaded.

pertenecer *vi*:—~ **a** to belong to; to appertain, concern.

pértiga *f* long pole or rod.

pertinaz *adj* pertinacious; obstinate.

pertinente *adj* relevant; appropriate.

perturbar *vt* to perturb, disturb.

pervertir *vt* to pervert; to corrupt.

pesa *f* weight.

pesadez *f* heaviness, weight; gravity; slowness; peevishness, fretfulness; trouble; fatigue.

pesadilla *f* nightmare.

pesado, da *adj* peevish; troublesome; cumbersome; tedious; heavy, weighty.

pesar *m* sorrow, grief; repentance:—**a ~ de** in spite of, notwithstanding:—*vi* to weigh; to repent:—*vt* to weigh.

pescado *m* fish (in general).

pescar *vt* to fish for, catch (fish):—*vi* to fish.

pescuezo *m* neck.

pésimo, ma *adj* very bad.

peso *m* weight, heaviness; balance scales *pl*.

pesquisa *f* inquiry, examination.

pestaña *f* eyelash.

pestañear *vi* to blink.

pestillo *m* bolt.

petróleo *m* oil, petroleum.

pez *m* fish:—*f* pitch.

pezón *m* nipple.

pezuña *f* hoof.

piadoso, sa *adj* pious; mild; merciful; moderate.

piar *vi* to squeak; to chirp.

pibe, ba *m/f* boy / girl.

picado, da *adj* pricked; minced, chopped; bad (tooth); cross.

picante *adj* hot, spicy; racy.

picaporte *m* doorhandle; latch.

picar *vt* to prick; to sting; to mince; to nibble:—*vi* to prick; to sting; to itch:—**~se** *vr* to be piqued; to take offence; to be moth-eaten; to begin to rot.

pícaro, ra *adj* roguish; mischievous, malicious; sly:—*m/f* rogue, knave.

pico *m* beak; bill, nib; peak; pick-axe.

pie *m* foot; leg; basis; trunk (of trees); foundation; occasion:—**a ~** on foot.

piedad *f* piety; mercy, pity.

piedra *f* stone.

piel *f* skin; hide; peel.

pienso *m* fodder.

pierna *f* leg (human).

pieza *f* piece; room.

pila *f* battery; trough; font; sink; pile, heap:—**nombre de ~** first name.

píldora *f* pill.

pileta *f* basin; swimming pool.

pimentón *m* paprika.

pimienta *f* pepper.

pimiento *m* pepper, pimiento.

piña *f* pineapple; fir cone; group.

pincel *m* paintbrush.

pinchar *vt* to prick; to puncture.

pincho *m* thorn; snack.

ping-pong *m* table tennis.

pino *m* (*bot*) pine.

piñón *m* pine nut; pinion.

pintar *vt* to paint; to picture; to describe; to exaggerate:—*vi* to paint; (*fam*) to count, to be important:—**~se** *vr* to put on make-up.

pintura *f* painting.

pinza *f* claw; clothes peg; pincers *pl*: —**~s** *fpl* tweezers *pl*.

piojo *m* louse; troublesome hanger-on.

pipa *f* pipe; sunflower seed.

pipí *m* (*fam*):—**hacer ~** to have to go (wee-wee).

piquete *m* prick, jab; hole; (*mil*) squad.

piragua *f* canoe.

piropo *m* compliment; flattery.

pisar *vt* to tread, trample; to stamp on (the ground); to hammer down:—*vi* to tread, walk.

piscina *f* swimming pool.

piso *m* flat, apartment; tread, trampling; floor, pavement; floor, storey.

pisotear *vt* to trample, tread under foot.

pista *f* trace, footprint; clue.

pita *f* (*bot*) agave.

pitar *vt* to blow; to whistle at:—*vi* to whistle; to toot one's horn; to smoke.

pito *m* whistle; horn.

pizarra *f* slate.

pizca *f* mite; pinch.

placa *f* plate; badge.

placer *m* pleasure; delight:—*vt* to please.

plan *m* plan; design; plot; scheme.

plancha *f* plate; iron; gangway.

planear *vt* to plan:—*vi* to glide.

planicie *f* plain.

planificación *f* planning:—**~ familiar** family planning.

plano, na *adj* plain, level, flat:—*m* plan; ground plot:—**~ inclinado** (*ferro*) dead level.

plantación *f* plantation.

plantar *vt* to plant; to fix upright; to strike or hit (a blow); to found; to establish:—**~se** *vr* to stand upright.

plantilla *f* personnel; insole of a shoe.

plata *f* silver; plate (wrought silver); cash:—**en ~** briefly.

plátano *m* banana; plane tree.

plateado, da *adj* silvered; plated.

platicar *vi* to converse.

platillo *m* saucer:—~**s** *mpl* cymbals *pl*: —~ **volador, ~ volante** flying saucer.

platino *m* platinum:—~**s** *mpl* contact points *pl*.

plato *m* dish; plate.

playa *f* beach.

playera *f* T-shirt:—~**s** *fpl* canvas shoes *pl*.

plaza *f* square; place; office, employment; room; seat.

plazo *m* term; instalment; expiry date.

plegar *vt* to fold; to plait.

pleito *m* contract, bargain; dispute, controversy, debate; lawsuit.

plenilunio *m* full moon.

pleno, na *adj* full, complete:—*m* plenum.

pliego *m* sheet of paper.

pliegue *m* fold; plait.

plisado, da *adj* pleated:—*m* pleating.

plomero *m* plumber.

plomo *m* lead:—**a** ~ perpendicularly.

pluma *f* feather, plume.

población *f* population; town.

pobre *adj* poor.

poco, ca *adj* little, scanty; (*pl*) few:—*adv* little:—~ **a** ~ gently; little by little:—*m* small part; little.

podar *vt* to prune.

poder *m* power, authority; command; force:—*vi* to be able to; to possess the power of doing or performing.

podrido, da *adj* rotten, bad; (*fig*) rotten.

poesía *f* poetry.

polea *f* pulley; (*mar*) tackle-block.

polideportivo *m* sports centre.

polilla *f* moth.

pollera *f* skirt.

pollo *m* chicken.

polo *m* pole; ice lolly; polo; polo neck.

polvo *m* powder, dust.

pólvora *f* gunpowder.

pomada *f* cream, ointment.

pomelo *m* grapefruit.

pómez *f*:—**piedra** ~ pumice stone.

pompa *f* pomp; bubble.

pómulo *m* cheekbone.

poner *vt* to put, place; to put on; to impose; to lay (eggs):—~**se** *vr* to oppose; to set (of stars); to become.

poniente *m* west; west wind.

ponzoña *f* poison.

popa *f* (*mar*) poop, stern.

por *prep* for; by; about; by means of; through; on account of.

porción *f* part, portion; lot.

porfiar *vt* to dispute obstinately; to persist in a pursuit.

pormenor *f* detail.

poro *m* pore.

porque *conj* because; since; so that.

porquería *f* nastiness, foulness; brutishness, rudeness; trifle; dirty action.

porrón *m* spouted wine jar.

portada *f* portal, porch; frontispiece.

portaequipajes *m invar* boot (in car); baggage rack.

portarse *vr* to behave.

portátil *adj* portable.

portavoz *m/f* spokesman/woman.

porte *m* transportation (charges *pl*); deportment, demeanour, conduct.

portero *m* porter, gatekeeper.

porvenir *m* future.

posar *vi* to sit, pose:—*vt* to lay down (a burden):—~**se** *vr* to settle; to perch; to land.

posdata *f* postcript.

poseer *vt* to hold, possess.

posesivo, va *adj* possessive.

posibilitar *vt* to make possible; to make feasible.

poso *m* sediment, dregs *pl*.

posponer *vt* to postpone.

postal *adj* postal:—*f* postcard.

poste *m* post, pillar.

postergar *vt* to leave behind; to postpone.

posterioridad *f*:—**con** ~ subsequently, later.

postigo *m* wicket; postern; shutter.

postizo, za *adj* artificial (not natural): —*m* wig.

postrar *vt* to humble, humiliate:—~**se** *vr* to prostrate oneself.

postre *m* dessert.

postura *f* posture, position; attitude; bet, wager; agreement, convention.

potable *adj* drinkable.

potaje *m* pottage; drink made up of several ingredients; medley of various useless things.

potro, ra *m/f* colt; foal.

pozo *m* well.

practicar *vt* to practise.

práctico, ca *adj* practical; skilful, experienced.

prado *m* lawn; meadow.

precaver *vt* to prevent; to guard against.

preceder *vt* to precede, go before.

preciado, da *adj* esteemed, valued.

precinto *m* seal.

precio *m* price; value.

precioso, sa *adj* precious; (*fam*) beautiful.

precisamente *adv* precisely; exactly.

precisar *vt* to compel, oblige; to need.

preciso, sa *adj* necessary, requisite; precise, accurate; abstracted.

precoz *adj* precocious.

precursor, ra *m*/*f* harbinger, forerunner.

predecir *vt* to foretell.

predicar *vt* to preach.

predilecto, ta *adj* darling, favourite.

predisponer *vt* to predispose; to prejudice.

predominar *vi* to predominate, prevail.

preferir *vt* to prefer.

pregón *m* proclamation; hue and cry.

preguntar *vt* to ask; to question; to demand; to inquire.

prejuicio *m* prejudgement; preconception; prejudice.

premiar *vt* to reward, remunerate.

premura *f* pressure, haste, hurry.

preñada *adj* pregnant.

prenda *f* pledge; garment; sweetheart; person or thing dearly loved: —**~s** *fpl* accomplishments, talents *pl*.

prender *vt* to seize, catch, lay hold of; to imprison:—**~se** *vr* to catch fire:—*vi* to take root.

prensar *vt* to press.

preocupar(se) *vt* (*vr*) to worry.

preparar *vt* to prepare:—**~se** *vr* to be prepared.

prepucio *m* foreskin.

presa *f* capture, seizure; dike, dam.

presagio *m* omen.

prescindir *vi*:—**~ de** to do without; to dispense with.

presenciar *vt* to attend; to be present at; to witness.

presentar *vt* to present; to introduce; to offer; to show:—**~se** *vr* to present oneself; to appear; to run (as candidate); to apply.

presentir *vt* to have a premonition of.

preservativo *m* condom, sheath.

presidiario *m* convict.

presilla *f* clip; loop (in clothes).

presión *f* pressure, pressing.

presionar *vt* to press; (*fig*) to put pressure on.

preso, sa *m*/*f* prisoner.

prestar *vt* to lend.

presto, ta *adj* quick; prompt; ready: —*adv* soon; quickly.

presumir *vt* to presume, conjecture: —*vi* to be conceited.

presunto, ta *adj* supposed; so-called.

presupuesto *m* presumed cost; budget.

pretender *vt* to claim; to try, attempt.

pretendiente *m* pretender; suitor.

pretexto *m* pretext; pretence, excuse.

prevalacer *vi* to prevail; to triumph; to take root.

prevenir *vt* to prepare; to

foresee, know in advance; to prevent; to warn:—**~se** *vr* to be prepared; to be predisposed.

prever *vt* to foresee, forecast.

previo, via *adj* previous.

previsión *f* foresight, prevision; forecast.

prima *f* bonus; (female) cousin.

primario, ria *adj* primary.

primavera *f* spring (the season).

primer(o), ra *adj* first; prior; former:—*adv* first; rather, sooner.

primicias *f* first fruits *pl*.

primo, ma *m* cousin.

primogénito, ta *adj*, *m*/*f* first-born.

príncipe *m* prince.

principiante *m* beginner, learner.

principio *m* beginning, commencement; principle.

pringoso, sa *adj* greasy; sticky.

prisa *f* speed; hurry; urgency; promptness.

prismáticos *mpl* binoculars *pl*.

privación *f* deprivation, want.

privado, da *adj* private; particular.

proa *f* (*mar*) prow.

probador *m* fitting room.

probar *vt* to try; to prove; to taste:—*vi* to try.

probeta *f* test tube.

procedente *adj* reasonable; proper:—**~ de** coming from.

procesador *m*:—**~ de textos** word processor.

procesar *vt* to put on trial.

procurar *vt* to try; to obtain; to produce.

prodigar *vt* to waste, lavish.

producir *vt* to produce; (*jur*) to produce as evidence:— ~**se** *vr* to come about; to arise; to be made; to break out.

proeza *f* prowess, valour, bravery.

profanar *vt* to profane, desecrate.

profesor, ra *m/f* teacher.

prófugo *m* fugitive.

profundo, da *adj* profound.

programa *m* program(me).

prohibir *vt* to prohibit, forbid; to hinder.

prójimo *m* fellow creature; neighbour.

prole *f* offspring, progeny; race.

prolijidad *f* prolixity; minute attention to detail.

prólogo *m* prologue.

promedio *m* average; middle.

prometer *vt* to promise; to assure:—~**se** *vr* to become engaged.

promiscuo, cua *adj* promiscuous; confusedly mingled.

promover *vt* to promote, advance; to stir up.

promulgar *vt* to promulgate, publish.

pronosticar *vt* to predict, foretell; to conjecture.

pronto, ta *adj* prompt; ready:—*adv* promptly.

pronunciamiento *m* (*jur*) publication; insurrection, sedition.

pronunciar *vt* to pronounce; to deliver: —~**se** *vr* to rebel.

propaganda *f* propaganda; advertising.

propagar *vt* to propagate.

propasar *vt* to go beyond, exceed.

propenso, sa *adj* prone, inclined.

propiamente *adv* properly; really.

propiciar *vt* to favour; to cause.

propiedad *f* property, possessions *pl*; right of property; propriety.

propina *f* tip.

propio, pia *adj* proper; own; typical; very.

proponer *vt* to propose.

proporcionar *vt* to provide.

propósito *m* aim, purpose:— **a ~** on purpose.

propuesta *f* proposal, offer; representation.

propulsar *vt* to propel; (*fig*) to promote.

prórroga *f* prolongation; extension; extra time.

prorrumpir *vi* to break forth, burst forth.

prosa *f* prose.

proscrito, ta *adj* banned.

proseguir *vt* to continue:—*vi* to continue, go on.

prospección *f* exploration; prospecting.

prosperar *vi* to prosper, thrive.

proteger *vt* protector.

protestar *vt* to protest; to make public declaration (of faith):—*vi* to protest.

provecho *m* profit; advantage.

proveedor, ra *m/f* purveyor, supplier.

provenir *vi* to arise, originate; to issue.

provocar *vt* to provoke; to lead to; to excite.

próximamente *adv* soon.

próximo, ma *adj* next; neighbouring; close, nearby.

proyectar *vt* to throw; to cast; to screen; to plan.

prueba *f* proof; reason; argument; token; experiment; essay; attempt; relish, taste.

púa *f* sharp point, prickle; shoot; pick.

pubertad *f* puberty.

publicar *vt* to publish; to make public.

publicidad *f* publicity; advertising.

público, ca *adj* public:—*m* public; audience; crowd.

puchero *m* pot; stew.

púdico, ca *adj* chaste, pure.

pudiente *adj* rich, opulent.

pudor *m* bashfulness.

pudrir *vt* to rot, putrefy:— ~**se** *vr* to decay, rot.

pueblo *m* people *pl*; town, village; population; populace.

puente *m* bridge.

puerco, ca *adj* nasty; filthy, dirty; rude, coarse:—*m* pig, hog:—~ **espín** porcupine.

pueril *adj* childish; puerile.

puerro *m* leek.

puerta *f* door; doorway; gateway:—~ **trasera** back door.

puerto *m* port, harbour; haven; pass.

pues *adv* then; therefore; well:—¡~! well, then.

puesto *m* place; particular spot; post, employment; barracks *pl*; stand.

púgil *m* boxer.

pujante *adj* powerful, strong; robust; stout, strapping.

pulga *f* flea:—**tener malas ~s** to be easily piqued; to be ill-tempered.

pulgada *f* inch.

pulgar *m* thumb.

pulir *vt* to polish; to put the last touches to.

pulmón *m* lung.

pulpa *f* pulp; soft part (of fruit).

pulpería *f* small grocery store.

pulpo *m* octopus.

pulsar *vt* to touch; to play; to press.

pulsera *f* bracelet.

pulso *m* pulse; wrist; firmness or steadiness of the hand.

pulular *vi* to swarm.

pulverizador *m* spray gun.

puna *f* (*med*) mountain sickness.

puñado *m* handful.

puñal *m* dagger.

puño *m* fist; handful; wristband; cuff; handle.

punta *f* point; end; trace.

puntada *f* stitch.

puntal *m* prop, stay; buttress.

puntapié *m* kick.

puntería *f* aiming.

puntiagudo, da *adj* sharp-pointed.

puntilla *f* narrow lace edging:—**de ~s** on tiptoe.

punto *m* point; end; spot; stitch; full stop.

puntual *adj* punctual; exact; reliable.

punzada *f* prick; sting; pain; compunction.

punzante *adj* sharp.

pupila *f* pupil (of eye).

puro, ra *adj* pure; mere; clear; genuine.

púrpura *f* purple.

purulento, ta *adj* purulent.

puta *f* whore.

Q

que *pn* that; who; which; what:—*conj* that; than.

¿qué? *adj* what?; which?:— *pn* what?; which?.

quebrantar *vt* to break; to crack; to burst; to pound, grind; to violate; to fatigue; to weaken. '

quedar *vi* to stay:—**~se** *vr* to remain.

quedo, da *adj* quiet, still:— *adv* softly, gently.

quejarse *vr* to complain of.

quemar *vt* to burn; to kindle:—**~se** *vr* to be parched with heat; to burn oneself:—*vi* to be too hot.

querella *f* charge; dispute; complaint.

querer *vt* to want; to desire; to will; to love:—*m* will, desire.

querido, da *adj* dear, beloved:—*m/f* darling; lover: —**~ mio, ~da mia** my dear, my love, my darling.

queso *m* cheese.

quicio *m* hook, hinge (of a door).

quien *pn* who; whom.

¿quién? *pn* who?; whom?.

quienquiera *adj* whoever.

quieto, ta *adj* still, peaccable.

quilla *f* keel.

química *f* chemistry.

quina *f* Peruvian bark, quinine.

quince *adj, m* fifteen; fifteenth.

quincena *f* fortnight.

quinientos, tas *adj* five hundred.

quinta *f* country house; levy, drafting of soldiers.

quinto *adj* fifth:—*m* fifth; drafted soldier.

quiosco *m* bandstand; news stand.

quirúrgico, ca *adj* surgical.

quiste *m* cyst.

quitamanchas *m invar* stain remover.

quitanieves *m invar* snow-plough.

quitar *vt* to take away, remove; to take off; to relieve; to annul:—**~se** *vr* to take off (clothes, etc); to withdraw.

quitasol *m* parasol.

quizá, quizás *adv* perhaps.

R

rábano *m* radish.

rabia *f* rage, fury.

rabo *m* tail.

racha *f* gust of wind:—**buena/mala** ~ spell of good/bad luck.

racimo *m* bunch of grapes.

radiografía *f* x-ray.

ráfaga *f* gust; flash; burst.

raído, da *adj* scraped; worn-out; impudent.

raíz *f* root; base, basis; origin:—**bienes raices** *mpl* landed property.

raja *f* splinter, chip (of wood); chink, fissure.

rajatabla *f*:—**a** ~ *adv* strictly.

rallar *vt* to grate.

rama *f* branch (of tree, of family).

ramo *m* branch (of tree).

rampa *f* ramp.

rana *f* frog.

rancho *m* grub; ranch; small farm.

rancio, cia *adj* rank; rancid.

ranura *f* groove; slot.

rapar *vt* to shave; to plunder.

rapaz, za *adj* rapacious:—*m/f* young boy/girl.

rápido, da *adj* quick, rapid, swift.

rapiña *f* robbery.

raptar *vt* to kidnap.

raquítico, ca *adj* stunted; (*fig*) inadequate.

raro, ra *adj* rare, scarce; extraordinary.

ras *m*:—**a** ~ **de** level with:—**a** ~ **de tierra** at ground level.

rascacielos *m invar* sky-scraper.

rascar *vt* to scratch, scrape.

rasgar *vt* to tear, rip.

rasgo *m* dash, stroke; grand or magnanimous action:—~**s** *mpl* features *pl*.

rasguño *m* scratch.

raso *m* satin; glade:—~, **sa** *adj* plain; flat:—**al** ~ in the open air.

raspa *f* beard (of an ear of corn); backbone (of fish); stalk (of grapes); rasp.

raspar *vt* to scrape, rasp.

rastrear *vt* to trace; to inquire into:—*vi* to skim along close to the ground (of birds).

rastrillo *m* rake.

rastro *m* track; rake; trace.

rata *f* rat.

ratificar *vt* to ratify, confirm.

rato *m* moment:—**a** ~**s perdidos** in leisure time.

ratón *m* mouse.

raya *f* stroke; line; part; frontier; ray (fish); roach (fish).

rayar *vt* to draw lines on; to cross out; to underline; to cross; to rifle.

rayo *m* ray, beam (of light).

raza *f* race, lineage; quality; crack, fissure.

razonar *vi* to reason; to discourse, talk.

reaccionar *vi* to react.

real *adj* real, actual; royal:—*m* (*mil*) camp.

realidad *f* reality; sincerity.

realizador, ra *m/f* producer (in TV, etc).

realzar *vt* to raise, elevate; to emboss; to heighten.

reanimar *vt* to cheer, encourage; to reanimate.

reanudar *vt* to resume.

rebaja *f* abatement; deduction:—~**s** *fpl* sale.

rebanada *f* slice.

rebaño *m* flock (of sheep), herd (of cattle).

rebasar *vt* to exceed.

rebatir *vt* to resist; to parry, ward off; to refute; to repress.

rebeca *f* cardigan.

rebelarse *vr* to revolt; to rebel; to resist.

rebosar *vi* to run over, over-flow; to abound.

rebotar *vt* to bounce; to clinch; to repel:—*vi* to rebound.

rebozar *vt* to wrap up; to fry in batter or breadcrumbs.

rebuznar *vi* to bray.

recado *m* message; errand.

recaída *f* relapse.

recalcar *vt* to stress, emphasise.

recalentar *vt* to heat again; to overheat.

recambio *m* spare; refill.

recapacitar *vt* to reflect.

recargar *vt* to overload; to recharge; to charge again.

recatado, da *adj* prudent; circumspect; modest.

recaudar *vt* to gather; to obtain; to recover.

recelo *m* dread; suspicion, mistrust.

receta *f* recipe; prescription.

rechazar *vt* to refuse; to repulse; to contradict.

recibir *vt* to receive, accept; to let in; to go to meet:— **~se** *vr* ~ **de** to qualify as.

recibo *m* receipt.

recién *adv* recently, lately.

reciente *adj* recent; new, fresh; modern.

recio, cia *adj* stout; strong, robust; coarse, thick; rude; arduous, rigid:—*adv* strongly, stoutly:—**hablar** ~ to talk loud.

recipiente *m* container.

reclamación *f* claim; reclamation; protest.

recluir *vt* to shut up.

reclutar *vt* to recruit.

recobrar *vt* to recover:—**~se** *vr* to recover (from sickness).

recodo *m* corner or angle jutting out.

recoger *vt* to collect; to take back; to get; to gather; to shelter; to compile: —**~se** *vr* to take shelter or refuge; to retire; to withdraw from the world.

recompensa *f* compensation; recompense, reward.

reconfortar *vt* to comfort.

reconocer *vt* to recognise; to examine closely; to acknowledge; to consider; (*mil*) to reconnoitre.

reconstituyente *m* tonic.

reconversión *f:*—~ **industrial** industrial rationalisation.

recopilar *vt* to compile.

recordar *vt* to remember; to remind: —*vi* to remember.

recorrer *vt* to run over, peruse; to cover.

recortar *vt* to cut out.

recostar *vt* to lean, recline:— **~se** *vr* to lie down.

recoveco *m* cubby hole; bend.

recreo *m* recreation; playtime (school).

recta *f* straight line.

rectángulo, la *adj* rectangular:—*m* rectangle.

rectitud *f* straightness; rectitude; justness, honesty; exactitude.

recto, ta *adj* straight; right; just, honest:—*m* rectum.

rector, ra *m/f* superior of a community or establishment; rector (of a university); curate, rector:—*adj* governing.

recuadro *m* box; inset.

recuento *m* inventory.

recuerdo *m* souvenir; memory.

recuperar *vt* to recover:—**~se** *vr* to recover (from sickness).

recurrir *vi:*—~ **a** to resort to.

red *f* net; network; snare.

redactar *vt* to draft; to edit.

redada *f:*—~ **policial** police raid.

redimir *vt* to redeem; to ransom.

redoblar *vt* to redouble; to rivet.

redondo, da *adj* round; complete.

reducir *adj* to reduce; to limit:—**~se** *vr* to diminish.

redundancia *f* superfluity, redundancy, excess.

reembolso *m* reimbursement; refund: —**contra ~** C.O.D.

referir *vt* to refer, relate, report:—**~se** *vr* to refer or relate to.

refinado, da *adj* refined; subtle, artful.

reflejar *vt* to reflect.

reflejo *m* reflex; reflection.

reflujo *m* reflux, ebb:—**flujo y ~** the tides *pl*.

reformar *vt* to reform; to correct; to restore:—**~se** *vr* to mend; to have one's manners reformed or corrected.

reforzar *vt* to strengthen, fortify; to encourage.

refrán *m* proverb.

refrescar *vt* to refresh:—**~se** *vr* to get cooler; to go out for a breath of fresh air:—*vi* to cool down.

refriega *f* affray, skirmish, fray.

refrigerador *m*, **refrigeradora** *f* refrigerator, fridge.

refuerzo *m* reinforcement.

refugiar *vt* to shelter:—**~se** *vr* to take refuge.

refunfuñar *vi* to snarl; to growl; to grumble.

regadera *f* watering can.

regalar *vt* to give (as present); to give away; to pamper; to caress.

regaliz *m* licorice.

regalo *m* present, gift; pleasure; comfort.

regañadientes:—**a ~** *adv* reluctantly.

regañar *vt* to scold:—*vi* to growl; to grumble; to quarrel.

regar *vt* to water, irrigate.

regata *f* irrigation ditch; regatta.

regatear *vt* (*com*) to bargain over; to be mean with:—*vi* to haggle; to dribble (in sport).

regazo *m* lap.

regentar *vt* to rule; to govern.

régimen *m* regime, management; diet; (*gr*) rules *pl* of verbs.

registrar *vt* to survey; to inspect, examine; to record, enter in a register: —~**se** *vr* to register; to happen.

regla *f* rule, ruler; period.

reglamentar *vt* to regulate.

regocijar *vt* to gladden:—~**se** *vr* to rejoice.

regordete *adj* chubby, plump.

regresar *vi* to return, go back.

reguero *m* small rivulet; trickle of spilt liquid; drain, gutter.

regular *vt* to regulate, adjust:—*adj* regular; ordinary.

rehén *m* hostage.

rehuir *vt* to avoid.

rehusar *vt* to refuse, decline.

reimpresión *f* reprint.

reina *f* queen.

reincidir *vi*:—~ **en** to relapse into, fall back into.

reino *m* kingdom, reign.

reintegrar *vt* to reintegrate, restore:—~**se** *vr* to be reinstated or restored.

reír(se) *vi* (*vr*) to laugh.

reiterar *vt* to reiterate, repeat.

reivindicar *vt* to claim.

reja *f* ploughshare; lattice, grating.

rejoneador *m* mounted bullfighter.

relación *f* relation; relationship; report; account.

relajar *vt* to relax, slacken:—~**se** *vr* to relax.

relamerse *vr* to lick one's lips; to relish.

relámpago *m* flash of lightning.

relatar *vt* to relate, tell.

relato *m* story; recital.

relegar *vt* to relegate; to banish, exile.

relente *m* evening dew.

relieve *m* relief; (*fig*) prominence.

relinchar *vi* to neigh.

reliquia *f* residue, remains *pl*; (saintly) relic.

rellano *m* landing (of stairs).

rellenar *vt* to fill up; to stuff.

reloj *m* clock; watch.

relucir *vi* to shine, glitter; to excel, be brilliant.

relumbrar *vi* to sparkle, shine.

remachar *vt* to rivet; (*fig*) to drive home.

remache *m* rivet; clinch; obstinacy.

remanente *m* remainder; (*com*) balance; surplus.

remanso *m* stagnant water; quiet place.

remar *vi* to row.

rematar *vt* to terminate, finish; to sell off cheaply:—*vi* to end.

remedar *vt* to copy, imitate; to mimic.

remediar *vt* to remedy; to assist, help; to free from danger; to avoid.

remesa *f* shipment; remittance.

remilgado, da *adj* prim; affected.

remitente *m* sender.

remojar *vt* to steep; to dunk.

remolacha *f* beet.

remolcar *vt* to tow.

remordimiento *m* remorse.

remoto, ta *adj* remote, distant; far.

remover *vt* to stir; to move around.

remozar *vt* to rejuvenate; to renovate.

renacer *vi* to be born again; to revive.

renacuajo *m* tadpole.

rendija *f* crevice, crack, cleft.

rendir *vt* to subject, subdue:—~**se** *vr* to yield; to surrender; to be tired out.

renegar *vt* to deny; to disown; to detest, abhor:—*vi* to apostatise; to blaspheme, curse.

renglón *m* line; item.

reñir *vt, vi* to wrangle, quarrel; to scold, chide.

renombre *m* renown.

renovar *vt* to renew; to renovate; to reform.

renta *f* income; rent; profit.

reo *m* offender, criminal.

reparar *vt* to repair; to consider, observe; to parry:—*vi* ~ **en** to notice; to pass (at cards).

repartir *vt* to distribute; to deliver.

repasar *vt* to revise; to check; to mend.

repente:—**de ~** *adv* suddenly.

repercutir *vi* to reverberate; to rebound.

repetir *vt, vi* to repeat.

repiquetear *vt* to ring merrily.

repisa *f* pedestal, stand; shelf; windowsill.

repleto, ta *adj* replete, very full.

replicar *vi* to reply.

repoblar *vt* to repopulate; to reafforest.

repollo *m* cabbage.

reponer *vt* to replace; to restore:—~**se** *vr* to recover lost health or property.

reportaje *m* report, article.

reposar *vi* to rest, repose.

repostería *f* confectioner's (shop).

reprender *vt* to reprimand.

represa *f* dam; lake.

representar *vt* to represent;

to play on the stage; to look (age).

reprimir *vt* to repress; to check; to contain.

reprobable *adj* reprehensible.

reprochar *vt* to reproach.

repuesto *m* supply; spare part.

repugnancia *f* reluctance; repugnance; disgust.

requerir *vt* to intimate, notify; to request; to require, need; to summon.

requesón *m* cottage cheese.

requiebro *m* endearing expression.

res *f* head of cattle.

resabio *m* (unpleasant) aftertaste; vicious habit, bad custom.

resaca *f* surge, surf; (*fig*) backlash; (*fam*) hangover.

resaltar *vi* to rebound; to jut out; to be evident; to stand out.

resbaladizo, za *adj* slippery.

resbalar(se) *vi* (*vr*) to slip, slide.

rescindir *vt* to rescind, annul.

rescoldo *m* embers *pl*, cinders *pl*.

resecarse *vr* to dry up.

reseña *f* review; account.

resentirse *vr*:—~ **de** to suffer:—~ **con** to resent.

reservar *vt* to keep; to reserve:—~**se** *vr* to preserve oneself; to keep to oneself.

resfriado *m* cold.

resguardar *vt* to preserve, defend:—~**se** *vr* to be on one's guard.

residir *vi* to reside, dwell.

residuo *m* residue, remainder.

resistir *vt* to resist, oppose; to put up with:—*vi* to resist; to hold out.

resol *m* glare (of the sun).

resollar *vi* to wheeze; to take breath.

resolver *vt* to resolve, decide; to analyse:—~**se** *vr* to resolve, determine.

resoplar *vi* to snore; to snort.

resorte *m* spring.

respaldo *m* backing; endorsement; back of a seat.

respetar *vt* to respect; to revere.

respingo *m* start; jump.

respiradero *m* vent, breathing hole; rest, repose.

respirar *vi* to breathe.

resplandecer *vi* to shine; to glisten.

resplandor *m* splendour, brilliance.

responder *vt* to answer:—*vi* to answer; to correspond:—~ **de** to be responsible for.

responso *m* prayer for the dead.

respuesta *f* answer, reply.

resquemor *m* resentment.

restablecer *vt* to re-establish.—~**se** *vr* to recover.

restallar *vi* to crack; to click.

restar *vt* to subtract, take away:—*vi* to be left.

restaurar *vt* to restore.

restituir *vt* to restore; to return.

resto *m* remainder, rest.

restregar *vt* to scrub, rub.

restringir *vt* to restrict, limit; to restrain.

resuelto, ta *adj* resolute, determined; prompt.

resultar *vi* to be; to turn out; to amount to.

resumir *vt* to abridge; to summarise.

retahíla *f* range, series.

retal *m* remnant.

retar *vt* to challenge.

retener *vt* to retain, keep back.

retentiva *f* memory.

retirar *vt* to withdraw, retire; to remove:—~**se** *vr* to retire, retreat; to go to bed.

reto *m* challenge; threat, menace.

retocar *vt* to retouch; to mend; to finish off (work).

retoñar *vi* to sprout.

retorcer *vt* to twist; to wring.

retozar *vi* to frisk, skip.

retraído, da *adj* shy.

retransmitir *vt* to broadcast; to relay; to retransmit.

retraso *m* delay; slowness; backwardness; lateness:— (*ferro*) **el tren ha tenido** ~ the train is overdue or late.

retrato *m* portrait, effigy.

retrete *m* toilet, lavatory.

retribuir *vt* to repay.

retroceder *vi* to go backwards, fly back; to back down.

retrovisor *m* rear-view mirror.

retumbar *vi* to resound, jingle.

reúma *f* rheumatism.

reunir *vt* to reunite; to unite:—~**se** *vr* to gather, meet.

revancha *f* revenge.

revelar *vt* to reveal; to develop (photographs).

reventar *vi* to burst, crack; to explode; to toil, drudge.

reverdecer *vi* to grow green again; to revive.

revés *m* back; wrong side; disappointment, setback.

revisar *vt* to revise, review.

revisor *m* inspector; ticket collector.

revista *f* review, revision; magazine.

revolcarse *vr* to wallow.

revolotear *vi* to flutter.

revoltijo *m* confusion, disorder.

revoltoso, sa *adj* rebellious, unruly.

revolver *vt* to move about; to turn around; to mess up; to revolve; **~se** *vr* to turn round; to change (of the weather).

revuelta *f* turn; disturbance, revolt.

rey *m* king; king (in cards or chess).

rezagar *vt* to leave behind; to defer: **—~se** *vr* to remain behind.

rezar *vi* to pray, say one's prayers.

rezumar *vt* to ooze, leak.

ría *f* estuary.

riada *f* flood.

ribera *f* shore, bank.

rico, ca *adj* rich; delicious; lovely; cute.

riego *m* irrigation.

rienda *f* rein of a bridle:—**dar ~ suelta** to give free rein to.

riesgo *m* risk, danger.

rifa *f* raffle, lottery.

rígido, da *adj* rigid, inflexible; severe.

riguroso, sa *adj* rigorous.

rimar *vi* to rhyme.

rímel, rimmel *m* mascara.

riña *f* quarrel, dispute.

rincón *m* (inside) corner.

rinoceronte *m* rhinoceros.

riñón *m* kidney.

río *m* river, stream.

riqueza *f* riches *pl*, wealth.

risa *f* laugh, laughter.

risco *m* steep rock.

ritmo *m* rhythm.

rizo *m* curl; ripple (on water).

robar *vt* to rob; to steal; to break into.

roble *m* oak tree.

robusto, ta *adj* robust, strong.

roca *f* rock.

rociar *vt* to sprinkle; to spray.

rocío *m* dew.

rodaja *f* slice.

rodaje *m* filming:—**en ~** (*auto*) running in.

rodear *vi* to make a detour:— *vt* to surround, enclose.

rodilla *f* knee:—**de ~s** on one's knees.

rodillo *m* roller; rolling pin.

roer *vt* to gnaw; to corrode.

rogar *vt, vi* to ask for; to beg, entreat; to pray.

rojizo, za *adj* reddish.

rojo, ja *adj* red; ruddy.

rol *m* list, roll, catalogue; role.

rollo *m* roll; coil.

romería *f* pilgrimage.

romero *m* (*bot*) rosemary.

rompecabezas *m invar* riddle; jigsaw.

romper *vt* to break; to tear up; to wear out; to break up (land):—*vi* to break (of waves); to break through.

ron *m* rum.

roña *f* scab, mange; grime; rust.

roncar *vi* to snore; to roar.

ronco, ca *adj* hoarse; husky; raucous.

ronda *f* night patrol; round (of drinks, cards, etc).

ronronear *vi* to purr.

ropa *f* clothes *pl*; clothing; dress.

rosa *f* rose; birthmark.

rosado, da *adj* pink; rosy.

rosca *f* thread (of a screw); coil, spiral.

rosquilla *f* doughnut.

rostro *m* face.

roto, ta *adj* broken, destroyed; debauched.

rótula *f* kneecap; ball-and-socket joint.

rotulador *m* felt-tip pen.

rótulo *m* inscription; label, ticket; placard, poster.

rotundo, da *adj* round; emphatic.

rozar *vt* to rub; to chafe; to nibble (the grass); to scrape; to touch lightly.

rubio, bia *adj* fair-haired, blond(e): —*m/f* blond/blonde.

rudimento *m* principle; beginning:—**~s** *mpl* rudiments *pl*.

rudo, da *adj* rough, coarse; plain, simple; stupid.

rueda *f* wheel; circle; slice, round.

ruedo *m* rotation; border, selvage; arena, bullring.

ruego *m* request, entreaty.

rufián *m* pimp, pander; lout.

rugir *vi* to roar, bellow.

rugoso, sa *adj* wrinkled.

ruido *m* noise, sound; din, row; fuss.

ruin *adj* mean, despicable; stingy.

ruina *f* ruin, collapse; downfall, destruction:—**~s** *fpl* ruins *pl*.

ruiseñor *m* nightingale.

rulo *m* curler.

rumbo *m* (*mar*) course, bearing; road, route, way; course of events, pomp, ostentation.

rumboso, sa *adj* generous, lavish.

rústico, ca *adj* rustic:—*m/f* peasant.

ruta *f* route, itinerary.

rutina *f* routine; habit.

S

sábado *m* Saturday; (Jewish) Sabbath.

sábana *f* sheet; altar cloth.

sabañón *m* chilblain.

sabelotodo *m/f invar* know-all.

saber *vt* to know; to be able to; to find out, learn; to experience:—*vi* ~ **a** to taste of:—*m* learning, knowledge.

sabiduría *f* learning, knowledge; wisdom.

sabio, bia *adj* sage, wise:—*m/f* sage, wise person.

sablazo *m* sword wound; (*fam*) sponging, scrounging.

sabor *m* taste, savour, flavour.

sabroso, sa *adj* tasty, delicious; pleasant; salted.

sabueso *m* bloodhound.

sacacorchos *m invar* corkscrew.

sacapuntas *m invar* pencil sharpener.

sacar *vt* to take out, extract; to get out; to bring out (a book etc); to take off (clothes); to receive, get; (*dep*) to serve.

sacerdote *m* priest.

saco *m* bag, sack; jacket.

sacudir *vt* to shake, jerk; to beat, hit.

sagaz *adj* shrewd, clever, sagacious.

sagrado, da *adj* sacred, holy.

sal *f* salt.

sala *f* large room; (*teat*) house, auditorium; public hall; (*jur*) court; (*med*) ward.

salado, da *adj* salted; witty, amusing.

salario *m* salary.

salchicha *f* sausage.

salchichón *m* (salami-type) sausage.

saldo *m* settlement; balance; remainder:—~**s** *mpl* sale.

salida *f* exit, way out; leaving, departure; production, output; (*com*) sale; sales outlet.

saliente *adj* projecting; rising; (*fig*) outstanding.

salir *vi* to go out, leave; to depart, set out; to appear; to turn out, prove:—~**se** *vr* to escape, leak.

salmo *m* psalm.

salmonete *m* red mullet.

salmuera *f* brine.

salón *m* living room, lounge; public hall.

salpicadero *m* dashboard.

salpicar *vt* to sprinkle, splash, spatter.

salsa *f* sauce.

saltamontes *m invar* grasshopper.

saltar *vt* to jump, leap; to skip, miss out:—*vi* to leap, jump; to bounce; (*fig*) to explode, blow up.

saltimbanqui *m/f* acrobat.

salubre *adj* healthy.

salud *f* health.

saludar *vt* to greet; (*mil*) to salute.

salvado *m* bran.

salvaguardar *vt* to safeguard.

salvaje *adj* savage.

salvar *vt* to save; to rescue; to overcome; to cross, jump across; to cover, travel; to exclude:—~**se** *vr* to escape from danger.

salvavidas *adj invar*:—**bote/ chaleco/cinturón** ~ lifeboat/life jacket/life belt.

salvia *f* (*bot*) sage.

salvo, va *adj* safe:—*adv* save, except (for).

San *adj* Saint (as title).

saña *f* anger, passion.

sanar *vt*, *vi* to heal.

sandalia *f* sandal.

sandez *f* folly, stupidity.

sandía *f* watermelon.

sangre *f* blood:—**a** ~ **fría** in cold blood:—**a** ~ **y fuego** without mercy.

sangriento, ta *adj* bloody, blood-stained, gory; cruel.

sano, na *adj* healthy, fit; intact, sound.

sapo *m* toad.

saquear *vt* to ransack, plunder.

sarampión *m* measles.

sarna *f* itch; mange; (*med*) scabies.

sarpullido *m* (*med*) rash.

sarro *m* (*med*) tartar.

sarta *f* string of beads, etc; string, row.

sartén *f* frying pan.

sastre *m* tailor.

satisfacer *vt* to satisfy; to

pay (a debt):—**~se** *vr* to satisfy oneself; to take revenge.

sauce *m* (*bot*) willow.

saúco *m* (*bot*) elder.

savia *f* sap.

sazonar *vt* to ripen; to season.

se *pn reflexivo* himself; herself; itself; yourself; themselves; yourselves; each other; one another; oneself.

se(p)tiembre *m* September.

sebo *m* fat, grease.

secano *m* dry, arable land which is not irrigated.

secar *vt* to dry:—**~se** *vr* to dry up; to dry oneself.

seco, ca *adj* dry; dried up; skinny; cold (of character); brusque, sharp; bare.

secuestrar *vt* to kidnap; to confiscate.

sed *f* thirst:—**tener ~** to be thirsty.

seda *f* silk.

sedal *m* fishing line.

sede *f* see; seat; headquarters.

sediento, ta *adj* thirsty; eager.

seducir *vt* to seduce; to bribe; to charm, attract.

segar *vt* to reap, harvest; to mow.

seguido, da *adj* continuous; successive; long-lasting:—*adv* straight (on); after; often.

seguir *vt* to follow, pursue; to continue:—*vi* to follow; to carry on:—**~se** *vr* to follow, ensue.

según *prep* according to.

segundo, da *adj* second:—*m* second (of time).

seguro, ra *adj* safe, secure; sure, certain; firm, constant:—*adv* for sure: —*m*

safety device; insurance; safety, certainty.

seis *adj, m* six; sixth.

seiscientos, tas *adj* six hundred.

seísmo *m* earthquake.

sello *m* seal; stamp.

seleccionar *vt* to select, chose, pick.

selectivo *adj* selective.

selva *f* forest.

semáforo *m* traffic lights *pl*; signal.

semana *f* week.

sembrar *vt* to sow; to sprinkle, scatter.

semejante *adj* similar, like:—*m* fellow man.

semestral *adj* half-yearly.

semilla *f* seed.

sémola *f* semolina.

sempiterno, na *adj* everlasting.

seña *f* sign, mark, token; signal; (*mil*) password:—**~s** *fpl* address.

señal *f* sign, token; symptom; signal; landmark; (*com*) deposit.

señalar *vt* to stamp, mark; to signpost; to point out; to fix, settle:—**~se** *vr* to distinguish oneself, excel.

sencillo, lla *adj* simple; natural; unaffected; single.

senda *f*, **sendero** *m* path, footpath.

seno *m* bosom; lap; womb; hole, cavity; sinus:—**~s** *mpl* breasts *pl*.

señor *m* man; gentleman; master; Mr; sir.

señora *f* lady; Mrs; madam; wife.

señorita *f* Miss; young lady.

señorito *m* young gentleman; rich kid.

sensación *f* sensation, feeling; sense.

sensato, ta *adj* sensible.

sensible *adj* sensitive; perceptible, appreciable; regrettable.

sentado, da *adj* sitting, seated; sedate; settled.

sentar *vt* to seat; (*fig*) to establish:—*vi* to suit:—**~se** *vr* to sit down.

sentido *m* sense; feeling; meaning:—**~, da** *adj* regrettable; sensitive.

sentir *vt* to feel; to hear; to perceive; to sense; to suffer from; to regret, be sorry for:—**~se** *vr* to feel; to feel pain; to crack (of walls, etc):—*m* opinion, judgement.

separar *vt* to separate:—**~se** *vr* to separate; to come away, come apart; to withdraw.

septentrional *adj* north, northern.

séptimo, ma *adj* seventh.

sepultar *vt* to bury, inter.

sequía *f* dryness; thirst; drought.

séquito *m* retinue, suite; group of supporters; aftermath.

ser *vi* to be; to exist:—**~ de** to come from; to be made of; to belong to:—*m* being.

serenata *f* (*mus*) serenade.

sereno *m* night watchman:—**~, na** *adj* serene, calm, quiet.

serie *f* series; sequence.

serio, ria *adj* serious; grave; reliable.

serpentear *vi* to wriggle; to wind, snake.

serpiente *f* snake.

serranía *f* range of mountains; mountainous country.

serrar *vt* to saw.

serrín *m* sawdust.

servicial *adj* helpful, obliging.

servilleta *f* napkin, serviette.

servir *vt* to serve; to wait on:—*vi* to serve; to be of use; to be in service: —~**se** *vr* to serve oneself, help oneself; to deign, please; to make use of.

sesenta *m, adj* sixty; sixtieth.

seso *m* brain.

sestear *vi* to take a nap.

seta *f* mushroom.

setecientos, tas *adj* seven hundred.

setenta *adj, m* seventy.

setiembre *m* September.

seto *m* fence; enclosure; hedge.

severo, ra *adj* severe, strict; grave, serious.

sexto, ta *adj, m* sixth.

si *conj* whether; if.

sí *adv* yes; certainly; indeed:—*pn* oneself; himself; herself; itself; yourself; themselves; yourselves; each other; one another.

siderúrgico, ca *adj* iron and steel *compd*:—*f* **la siderúrgica** the iron and steel industry.

sidra *f* cider.

siempre *adv* always; all the time; ever; still:—~ **jamás** for ever and ever.

sien *f* temple (of the head).

sierra *f* saw; range of mountains.

siete *adj, m* seven.

sigilo *m* secrecy.

sigla *f* acronym; abbreviation.

siglo *m* century.

significado *m* significance, meaning.

significativo, va *adj* significant.

signo *m* sign, mark.

siguiente *adj* following, successive, next.

silbar *vt, vi* to hiss; to whistle.

silencio *m* silence:—¡~! silence! quiet!

silla *f* chair; saddle; seat:—~ **de ruedas** wheelchair.

silo *m* silo; underground wheat store.

silueta *f* silhouette; outline; figure.

silvestre *adj* wild, uncultivated; rustic.

símbolo *m* symbol.

simio *m* ape.

simpático, ca *adj* pleasant; kind.

simpatizar *vi*:—~ **con** to get on well with.

simular *vt* to simulate.

sin *prep* without.

sindicato *m* trade(s) union; syndicate.

sinfín *m*:—**un ~ de** a great many.

singular *adj* singular; exceptional; peculiar, odd.

siniestro, tra *adj* left; (*fig*) sinister:—*m* accident.

sino *conj* but; except; save; only:—*m* fate.

sinsabor *m* unpleasantness; disgust.

sinuoso, sa *adj* sinuous; wavy; winding.

sinvergüenza *m/f* rogue.

siquiera *conj* even if, even though:—*adv* at least.

sitio *m* place; spot; site, loca-

tion; room, space; job, post; (*mil*) siege, blockade.

situar *vt* to place, situate; to invest:—~**se** *vr* to be established in place or business.

smoking *m* tuxedo.

sobaco *m* armpit, armhole.

sobar *vt* to handle, soften; to knead; to massage, rub hard; to rumple (clothes); to fondle.

soberbia *f* pride, haughtiness; magnificence.

sobornar *vt* to suborn, bribe.

sobrante *adj* remaining:—*m* surplus, remainder.

sobrar *vt* to exceed, surpass:—*vi* to be more than enough; to remain, be left.

sobre *prep* on; on top of; above, over; more than; besides:—*m* envelope.

sobrecargar *vt* to overload; (*com*) to surcharge.

sobredosis *f* overdose.

sobreentender *vt* to deduce:—~**se** *vr* **se sobreentiende que** . . . it is implied that.

sobrellevar *vt* to carry; to tolerate.

sobremesa *f*:—**de ~** immediately after dinner.

sobrenombre *m* nickname.

sobrepasar *vt* to surpass.

sobresalto *m* start, scare; sudden shock.

sobrevenir *vi* to happen, come unexpectedly; to supervene.

sobrevivir *vi* to survive.

sobrevolar *vt* to fly over.

sobrino, na *m/f* nephew / niece.

sobrio, ria *adj* sober, frugal.

socarrón, ona *adj* sarcastic; ironic(al).

socavar *vt* to undermine.

socio, cia *m/f* associate, member.

socorrista *m/f* first aider; lifeguard.

socorro *m* help, aid, assistance, relief.

soez *adj* dirty, obscene.

sofá *m* sofa.

soga *f* rope.

soja *f* soya.

sol *m* sun; sunshine, sunlight.

solamente *adv* only, solely.

solapa *f* lapel.

solar *m* building site; piece of land; ancestral home of a family:—*adj* solar.

soldado *m/f* soldier:—~ **raso** private.

soldar *vt* to solder; to weld; to unite.

soledad *f* solitude; loneliness.

soler *vi* to be accustomed to, be in the habit of.

solicitar *vt* to ask for, seek; to apply for (a job); to canvass for; to chase after, pursue.

solidario, ria *adj* joint; mutually binding.

soliloquio *m* soliloquy, monologue.

solista *m/f* soloist.

solitario, ria *adj* solitary:—*m* solitaire:—*m/f* hermit.

sollozar *vi* to sob.

solo *m* (*mus*) solo:—~**la** *adj* alone, single:—**a solas** alone, unaided.

sólo *adv* only.

solomillo *m* sirloin.

soltar *vt* to untie, loosen; to set free, let out:—~**se** *vr* to get loose; to come undone.

soltero, ra *m/f* bachelor/

single woman:—*adj* single, unmarried.

soltura *f* looseness, slackness; agility, activity; fluency.

solucionar *vt* to solve; to resolve.

sombra *f* shade; shadow.

sombrero *m* hat.

sombrilla *f* parasol.

sombrío, bría *adj* shady, gloomy; sad.

somero, ra *adj* superficial.

someter *vt* to conquer (a country); to subject to one's will; to submit; to subdue:—~**se** *vr* to give in, submit.

somnífero *m* sleeping pill.

sonar *vt* to ring:—*vi* to sound; to make a noise; to be pronounced; to be talked of; to sound familiar:—~**se** *vr* to blow one's nose.

soñar *vt, vi* to dream.

sondeo *m* sounding; boring; (*fig*) poll.

soneto *m* sonnet.

sonido *m* sound.

sonreír(se) *vi* (*vr*) to smile.

sonrisa *f* smile.

sonrojarse *vr* to blush.

sonsacar *vt* to wheedle; to cajole; to obtain by cunning.

sopa *f* soup; sop.

sopetón *m*:—**de ~** suddenly.

soplar *vt* to blow away, blow off; to blow up, inflate:—*vi* to blow, puff.

soplón, ona *m/f* telltale.

soportal *m* portico.

soportar *vt* to suffer, tolerate; to support.

sorber *vt* to sip; to inhale; to swallow; to absorb.

sorbete *m* sherbet; iced fruit drink.

sordo, da *adj* deaf; silent, quiet:—*m/f* deaf person.

sorprender *vt* to surprise.

sorteo *m* draw; raffle.

sortija *f* ring; ringlet, curl.

sortilegio *m* sorcery.

sosegar *vt* to appease, calm:—*vi* to rest.

soso, sa *adj* insipid, tasteless; dull.

sospechar *vt* to suspect.

sostén *m* support; bra; sustenance.

sostener *vt* to sustain, maintain:—~**se** *vr* to support or maintain oneself; to contrive, remain.

sota *f* knave (at cards).

sótano *m* basement, cellar.

su *pn* his, her, its, one's; their; your.

su(b)stancia *f* substance.

su(b)straer *vt* to remove; (*mat*) to subtract:—~**se** *vr* to avoid; to withdraw.

suave *adj* smooth, soft; delicate; gentle; mild, meek.

subalterno, na *adj* secondary; auxiliary.

subasta *f* auction.

subcampeón, ona *m/f* runner-up.

subestimar *vt* to underestimate.

subir *vt, vi* to raise, lift up; to go up; to climb, ascend, mount; to increase, swell; to get in, get on, board; to rise (in price).

súbito, ta *adj* sudden, hasty; unforeseen.

sublevar *vt* to excite (a rebellion); to incite (a revolt):—~**se** *vr* to revolt.

submarino, na *adj* underwater:—*m* submarine.

subrayar *vt* to underline.

subsanar *vt* to excuse; to mend, repair; to overcome.

subsidio *m* subsidy, aid; benefit, allowance.

subterráneo, nea *adj* subterranean; underground:—*m* underground passage; (*ferro*) underground (railway).

suburbio *m* slum quarter; suburbs *pl*.

subvencionar *vt* to subsidise.

sucedáneo, nea *adj* substitute:—*m* substitute (food).

suceder *vt* to succeed, inherit:—*vi* to happen.

suceso *m* event; incident.

sucesor, ra *m/f* successor; heir.

sucio, cia *adj* dirty, filthy; obscene; dishonest.

sucursal *f* branch (office).

sudar *vt, vi* to sweat.

sudeste *adj* southeast, southeastern: —*m* southeast.

sudoeste *adj* southwest, southwestern:—*m* southwest.

suegra *f* mother-in-law.

suegro *m* father-in-law.

suela *f* sole of the shoe.

sueldo *m* wages *pl*, salary.

suelo *m* ground; floor; soil, surface.

suelto, ta *adj* loose; free; detached; swift:—*m* loose change.

sueño *m* sleep; dream.

suero *m* (*med*) serum; whey.

suerte *f* fate, destiny, chance, lot, fortune, good luck; kind, sort.

sufrir *vt* to suffer; to bear, put up with; to support.

sugerir *vt* to suggest.

sujetador *m* fastener; bra.

sujetar *vt* to fasten, hold down; to subdue; to subject:—**~se** *vr* to subject oneself.

sujeto, ta *adj* fastened, secure; subject, liable:—*m* subject; individual.

sumamente *adv* extremely.

sumar *vt* to add, add up; to collect, gather:—*vi* to add up.

sumergir *vt* to submerge, sink; to immerse.

sumidero *m* sewer, drain.

suministrar *vt* to supply, furnish.

sumiso, sa *adj* submissive, docile.

sumo, ma *adj* great, extreme; highest, greatest:—**a lo ~** at most.

súper *f* four-star (petrol).

superar *vt* to surpass; to overcome; to exceed, go beyond.

superficial *adj* superficial; shallow.

superficie *f* surface; area.

superintendente *m/f* superintendent, supervisor; floorwalker.

superior *adj* superior; upper; higher; better:—*m/f* superior.

supermercado *m* supermarket.

superviviente *m/f* survivor:—*adj* surviving.

suplente *m/f* substitute.

suplicar *vt* to beg (for), plead (for); to beg; to plead with.

suplicio *m* torture.

suplir *vt* to supply; to make good, make up for; to replace.

suponer *vt* to suppose:—*vi* to have authority.

suprimir *vt* to suppress; to abolish; to remove; to delete.

supuesto *m* assumption:—**~, ta** *adj* supposed:—**~ que** *conj* since, granted that.

sur *adj* south, southern:—*m* south; south wind.

surco *m* furrow; groove.

surgir *vi* to emerge; to crop up.

surtido *m* assortment, supply.

surtir *vt* to supply, furnish, provide: —*vi* to spout, spurt.

suscitar *vt* to excite, stir up.

susodicho, cha *adj* above-mentioned.

suspender *vt* to suspend, hang up; to stop; to fail (an exam etc).

suspicaz *adj* suspicious, mistrustful.

suspirar *vi* to sigh.

sustentar *vt* to sustain; to support, nourish.

susto *m* fright, scare.

sustraer *vt* to take away; to subtract.

susurrar *vi* to whisper; to murmur; to rustle:—**~se** *vr* to be whispered about.

sutil *adj* subtle; thin; delicate; very soft; keen, observant.

suyo, ya *adj* his; hers; theirs; one's; his; her; its own; one's own; their own:—**de ~** per se:—**los ~s** *mpl* his own, near friends, relations, family, supporters.

T

tabaco *m* tobacco; (*fam*) cigarettes *pl*.

tabique *m* thin wall; partition wall.

tabla *f* board; shelf; plank; slab; index of a book; bed of earth in a garden.

tablero *m* plank, board; chessboard; dashboard; bulletin board; gambling den.

taburete *m* stool.

tacaño, ña *adj* mean, stingy; crafty.

tachar *vt* to find fault with; to erase.

tachuela *f* tack, nail.

tácito, ta *adj* tacit, silent; implied.

taco *m* stopper, plug; heel (of a shoe); wad; book of coupons; billiard cue.

tacón *m* heel.

tacto *m* touch, feeling; tact.

tahona *f* bakery.

taimado, da *adj* sly, cunning, crafty.

tajo *m* cut, incision; cleft, sheer drop; working area; chopping block.

tal *adj* such:—**con ~ que** provided that:—**no hay ~** no such thing.

taladro *m* drill; borer, gimlet.

talante *m* mood; appearance; aspect; will.

talar *vt* to fell (trees); to desolate.

talega *f*, **talego** *m* bag; bagful.

talla *f* raised work; sculpture; stature, size; measure (of anything); hand, draw, turn (at cards).

tallar *vt* to cut, chop; to carve in wood; to engrave; to measure.

taller *m* workshop, laboratory.

tallo *m* shoot, sprout.

talón *m* heel; receipt; cheque.

tamaño *m* size, shape, bulk.

tambalearse *vr* to stagger, waver.

también *adv* also, as well; likewise; besides.

tambor *m* drum; drummer; eardrum.

tamiz *m* fine sieve.

tampoco *adv* neither, nor.

tan *adv* so.

tanto *m* certain sum or quantity; point; goal:—**~, ta** *adj* so much, as much; very great:—*adv* so much, as much; so long, as long.

tapar *vt* to stop up, cover; to conceal, hide.

tapia *f* wall.

tapicería *f* tapestry; upholstery; upholsterer's shop.

tapiz *m* tapestry; carpet.

tapón *m* cork, plug, bung.

taquigrafía *f* shorthand.

taquilla *f* booking office; takings *pl*.

tardar *vi* to delay; to take a long time; to be late.

tarde *f* afternoon; evening:—*adv* late.

tarea *f* task.

tarima *f* platform; step.

tarjeta *f* card; visiting card:—**~ postal** postcard.

tarro *m* pot.

tarta *f* cake.

tartamudear *vi* to stutter, stammer.

tarugo *m* wooden peg or pin.

tasar *vt* to appraise, value.

tatarabuelo, la *m*/*f* great-great-grandfather/mother.

tataranieto, ta *m*/*f* great-great-grandson/daughter.

tatuaje *m* tattoo; tattooing.

taurino, na *adj* bullfighting *compd*.

taza *f* cup; basin of a fountain.

te *pn* you.

té *m* (*bot*) tea.

teatro *m* theatre, playhouse.

tebeo *m* comic.

techo *m* roof; ceiling.

tecla *f* key (of an organ, piano, etc).

técnico, ca *adj* technical.

tedio *m* boredom; dislike, abhorrence.

tejado *m* roof covered with tiles.

tejer *vt* to weave.

tejo *m* quoit; yew tree.

tejón *m* badger.

tela *f* cloth; material.

telaraña *f* cobweb.

telefax *m invar* fax; fax (machine).

televisor *m* television set.

telón *m* curtain, drape.

tema *m* theme.

temblar *vi* to tremble.

temer *vt* to fear, doubt:—*vi* to be afraid.

temerario, ria *adj* rash.

temible *adj* dreadful, terrible.

témpano *m* ice-floe.

templado, da *adj* temperate, tempered.

templar *vt* to temper, moderate, cool; to tune:—**~se** *vr* to be moderate.

temple *m* temperature; tempera; temperament; tuning:—**al ~** painted in distemper.

temporada *f* time, season; epoch, period.

temprano, na *adj* early, anticipated: —*adv* early; very early, prematurely.

tenaz *adj* tenacious; stubborn.

tenaza(s) *f* (*pl*) tongs *pl*, pincers *pl*.

tender *vt* to stretch out; to expand; to extend; to hang out; to lay:—**~se** *vr* to stretch oneself out.

tendero, ra *m/f* shop-keeper.

tendón *m* tendon, sinew.

tenebroso, sa *adj* dark, obscure.

tenedor *m* holder, keeper, tenant; fork.

tener *vt* to have; to take; to hold; to possess:—**~se** *vr* to stand upright; to stop, halt; to resist; to adhere.

tenia *f* tapeworm.

teñir *vt* to tinge, dye.

tensar *vt* to tauten; to draw.

tentar *vt* to touch; to try; to tempt; to attempt.

tentempié *m* (*fam*) snack.

tenue *adj* thin; tenuous, slender.

terapia *f* therapy.

tercer(o), ra *adj* third:—*m* (*jur*) third party.

tercio, cia *adj* third:—*m* third part.

terciopelo *m* velvet.

terco, ca *adj* obstinate.

tergiversar *vt* to distort.

terminante *adj* decisive; categorical.

terminar *vt* to finish; to end; to terminate:—*vi* to end; to stop.

termo *m* flask.

ternero, ra *m/f* calf; veal; heifer.

ternilla *f* gristle.

ternura *f* tenderness.

terrado *m* terrace.

terrateniente *m/f* landowner.

terraza *f* balcony; (flat) roof; terrace (in fields).

terremoto *m* earthquake.

terreno, na *adj* earthly, terrestrial:—*m* land, ground, field.

terrón *m* clod of earth; lump:—**~ones** *mpl* landed property.

terror *m* terror, dread.

terso, sa *adj* smooth, glossy.

tertulia *f* club, assembly, circle.

tesorero *m* treasurer.

tesoro *m* treasure; exchequer.

testamento *m* will, testament.

testar *vt, vi* to make one's will.

testarudo, da *adj* obstinate.

testificar *vt* to attest, witness.

testigo *m* witness, deponent.

teta *f* breast.

tetera *f* teapot.

tetilla *f* nipple; teat (of a bottle).

tétrico, ca *adj* gloomy, sullen, surly.

tez *f* complexion, hue.

ti *pn* you; yourself.

tía *f* aunt; (*fam*) bird.

tibio, bia *adj* lukewarm.

tiburón *m* shark.

tiempo *m* time; term; weather; (*gr*) tense; occasion, opportunity; season.

tienda *f* tent; awning; tilt; shop.

tierno, na *adj* tender.

tierra *f* earth; land, ground; native country.

tieso, sa *adj* stiff, hard, firm; robust; valiant; stubborn.

tiesto *m* earthen pot.

tigre *m* tiger.

tijeras *fpl* scissors *pl*.

tilde *f* tilde (ñ).

tilo *m* lime tree.

timar *vt* to con; to swindle.

timbre *m* stamp; bell; timbre; stamp duty.

tímido, da *adj* timid; cowardly.

timón *m* helm, rudder.

tímpano *m* ear-drum; small drum.

tina *f* tub; bath (tub).

tinieblas *fpl* darkness; shadows *pl*.

tino *m* skill; judgement, prudence.

tinta *f* ink; tint, dye; colour.

tinte *m* tint, dye; dry cleaner's.

tinto, ta *adj* dyed:—*m* red wine.

tío *m* uncle; (*fam*) guy.

tiovivo *m* merry-go-round.

tipico, ca *adj* typical; characteristic; picturesque; traditional; regional.

tipo *m* type; norm; pattern; guy.

tiquismiquis *m invar* fussy person.

tira *f* abundance; strip.

tirachinas *m invar* catapult.

tirado, da *adj* dirt-cheap; (*fam*) very easy:—*f* cast; distance; series; edition.

tirano, na *m/f* tyrant.

tirante *m* joist; stay; strap; brace:—*adj* taut, extended, drawn.

tirar *vt* to throw; to pull; to draw; to drop; to tend, aim at:—*vi* to shoot; to pull; to go; to tend to.

tirita *f* (sticking) plaster.

tiritar *vi* to shiver.

títere *m* puppet; ridiculous little fellow.

titubear *vi* to stammer; to stagger; to hesitate.

titular *adj* titular:—*m/f* occupant:—*m* headline:—*vt* to title:—~**se** *vr* to obtain a title.

tiza *f* chalk.

tiznar *vt* to stain; to tarnish.

tizón *m* half-burnt wood.

toalla *f* towel.

tobillo *m* ankle.

tobogán *m* toboggan; roller-coaster; slide.

tocadiscos *m invar* record player.

tocado *m* headdress, headgear.

tocar *vt* to touch; to strike; (*mus*) to play; to ring (a bell):—*vi* to belong; to concern; to knock; to call; to be a duty or obligation.

tocino *m* bacon.

todavía *adv* even; yet, still.

todo, da *adj* all, entire; every:—*pn* everything, all:—*m* whole.

todopoderoso, sa *adj* almighty.

toldo *m* awning; parasol.

tomar *vt* to take; to seize, grasp; to understand; to interpret, perceive; to drink; to acquire:—*vi* to drink; to take.

tomavistas *m invar* cine-camera.

tomillo *m* thyme.

tomo *m* bulk; tome; volume.

tonada *f* tune, melody.

tonel *m* cask, barrel.

tonelada *f* ton; (*mar*) tonnage duty.

tónico, ca *adj* tonic, strengthening:—*m* tonic:—*f* tonic (water); (*mus*) tonic; (*fig*) keynote.

tontería *f* foolery, nonsense.

tonto, ta *adj* stupid, foolish.

topar *vt* to run into; to find.

topo *m* mole; stumbler.

toquilla *f* head-scarf; shawl.

tórax *m* thorax.

torbellino *m* whirlwind.

torcer *vt* to twist, curve; to turn; to sprain:—~**se** *vr* to bend; to go wrong:—*vi* to turn off.

torcido, da *adj* oblique; crooked.

tordo *m* thrush:—~, **da** *adj* speckled black and white.

torear *vt* to avoid; to tease:—*vi* to fight bulls.

tormenta *f* storm, tempest.

tornar *vt* to return; to restore:—~**se** *vr* to become:—*vi* to return:—~ **a hacer** to do again.

tornasolado *adj* iridescent; shimmering.

torneo *m* tournament.

tornillo *m* screw.

torno *m* winch; revolution.

toro *m* bull.

toronja *f* grapefruit.

torpe *adj* dull, heavy; stupid.

torre *f* tower; turret; steeple.

torrefacto, ta *adj* roasted.

torta *f* cake; (*fam*) slap.

tortilla *f* omelet; pancake.

tortuga *f* tortoise; turtle.

tos *f* cough.

tosco, ca *adj* coarse, ill-bred, clumsy.

toser *vi* to cough.

tostado, da *adj* parched; sunburnt; light-yellow; light-brown.

tostar *vt* to toast, roast.

total *m* whole, totality:—*adj* total, entire:—*adv* in short.

tóxico, ca *adj* toxic:—*m* poison.

trabajar *vt* to work, labour; to persuade; to push:—*vi* to strive.

trabalenguas *m invar* tongue twister.

trabar *vt* to join, unite; to take hold of; to fetter, shackle.

tracción *f* traction:—~ **delantera/trasera** front-wheel/rear-wheel drive.

traducir *vt* to translate.

traer *vt* to bring, carry; to attract; to persuade; to wear; to cause.

traficar *vi* to trade, do business, deal.

tragaluz *m* skylight.

tragaperras *m* o *f invar* slot machine.

tragar *vt* to swallow; to swallow up.

trago *m* drink; gulp; adversity, misfortune.

traicionar *vt* to betray.

traje *m* suit; dress; costume.

trajinar *vt* to carry:—*vi* to bustle about; to travel around.

trama *f* plot; woof.

tramitar *vt* to transact; to negotiate; to handle.

tramo *m* section; piece of ground; flight of stairs.

tramoya *f* scene, theatrical decoration; trick.

trampa *f* trap, snare; trapdoor; fraud.

trampolín *m* trampoline; diving board.

tramposo, sa *adj* deceitful, swindling.

tranca *f* bar, crossbeam.

trance *m* danger; last stage of life; trance.

tranquilizar *vt* to calm; to reassure.

tranquilo, la *adj* tranquil, calm, quiet.

transbordador *m* ferry.

transbordo *m* transfer: **hacer** ~ to change (trains).

transcurrir *vi* to pass; to turn out.

transeúnte *adj* transitory:— *m* passer-by.

transigir *vi* to compromise.

tránsito *m* passage; transition; road, way; change; removal; death of holy or virtuous persons.

transmitir *vt* to transmit; to broadcast.

transparente *adj* transparent; see-through.

transpirar *vt* to perspire; to transpire.

tranvía *m* tram.

trapo *m* rag, tatter.

tráquea *f* windpipe.

tras *prep* after, behind.

trascender *vi* to smell; to come out: —~ **de** to go beyond.

trasegar *vt* to move about; to decant.

trasero, ra *adj* back:—*m* bottom.

trasfondo *m* background.

trasgredir *vt* to contravene.

trashumante *adj* migrating.

trasladar *vt* to transport; to transfer; to postpone; to transcribe, copy:—~**se** *vr* to move.

trasnochar *vi* to watch, sit up the whole night.

traspasar *vt* to remove, transport; to transfix, pierce; to return; to exceed (the proper bounds); to transfer.

traste *m* fret (of a guitar): **dar al** ~ **con algo** to ruin something.

trastero *m* lumber room.

trastienda *f* back room behind a shop.

trasto *m* piece of junk; useless person.

trastornar *vt* to overthrow, overturn; to confuse:—~**se** *vr* to go crazy.

trastrocar *vt* to invert (the order of).

tratar *vt* to traffic, trade; to use; to treat; to handle; to address; ~**se** *vr* to treat each other.

trato *m* treatment; manner, address; trade, traffic; conversation; (*com*) agreement.

través *m* (*fig*) reverse:—**de** *o* **al** ~ across, crossways:—**a** ~ **de** *prep* across; over; through.

travesía *f* crossing; cross-

street; trajectory; (*mar*) side wind.

travieso, sa *adj* restless, uneasy, fidgety; lively; naughty.

trayecto *m* road; journey, stretch; course.

trazar *vt* to plan out; to project; to trace.

trébedes *fpl* trivet, tripod.

trébol *m* trefoil, clover.

trece *adj, m* thirteen; thirteenth.

trecho *m* space, distance of time or place:—**a** ~**s** at intervals.

tregua *f* truce, cessation of hostilities.

treinta *adj, m* thirty.

tremendo, da *adj* terrible, formidable; awful, grand.

tren *m* train, retinue; show, osten-tation; (*ferro*) train:— ~ **de gran velocidad** fast *or* express train:—~ **de mercancias** freight train.

trenza *f* plait (in hair), plaited silk.

trepar *vi* to climb; to crawl.

tres *adj, m* three.

tresillo *m* three-piece suite; (*mus*) triplet.

tricotar *vi* to knit.

trigésimo, ma *adj, m* thirtieth.

trigo *m* wheat.

trillado, da *adj* beaten; trite, hackneyed:—**camino** ~ common routine.

trinar *vi* to trill, quaver; to be angry.

trinchar *vt* to carve, divide (meat).

trineo *m* sledge.

trino *m* trill.

tripa *f* gut, intestine:—~**s** *fpl* guts; tripe.

tripulación *f* crew.

tripular *vt* to man; to drive.

tris *m* *invar*:—**estar en un ~ de** to be on the point of.

triste *adj* sad, mournful, melancholy.

triturar *vt* to reduce to powder; to grind, pound.

triza *f*:—**hacer ~s** to smash to bits; to tear to shreds.

trocar *vt* to exchange.

trompa *f* trumpet; proboscis; large top.

trompazo *m* heavy blow; accident.

trompeta *f* trumpet:—*m* trumpeter.

tronar *vi* to thunder; to rage.

tronco *m* trunk; log of wood; stock.

tropel *m* confused noise; hurry; bustle, confusion; heap; crowd:—**en ~** in a tumultuous and confused way.

tropezar *vi* to stumble:—*vt* to meet accidentally.

trotamundos *m* *invar* globetrotter.

trotar *vi* to trot.

trozo *m* piece.

trucha *f* trout.

truco *m* knack; trick.

trueno *m* thunderclap.

trueque *m* exchange.

truncar *vt* to truncate, maim.

tu *adj* your.

tú *pn* you.

tubería *f* pipe; pipeline.

tubo *m* tube.

tuerca *f* nut.

tumba *f* tomb.

tumbar *vt* to knock down:—*vi* to fall down:—**~se** *vr* to lie down to sleep.

tumbona *f* easy chair; beach chair.

tunda *f* beating.

tupido, da *adj* dense.

turbar *vt* to disturb, trouble:—**~se** *vr* to be disturbed.

turbio, bia *adj* muddy; troubled.

turno *m* turn; shift; opportunity.

turrón *m* nougat (almond cake).

tutear *vt* to address as 'tu'.

tutor *m* guardian, tutor.

tuyo, ya *adj* yours:—**~s** *pl* friends and relations of the party addressed.

U

u *conj* or (instead of *o* before an *o* or *ho*).

ubicar *vt* to place:—**~se** to be located.

ufanarse *vr* to boast.

últimamente *adv* lately.

ultimar *vt* to finalise; to finish.

último, ma *adj* last; latest; bottom; top.

ultrajar *vt* to outrage; to despise; to abuse.

ultramar *adj, m* overseas.

ultramarinos *mpl* groceries.

umbral *m* threshold.

un, una *art* a, an:—*adj, m* one (for **uno**).

uña *f* nail; hoof; claw, talon.

ungir *vt* to anoint.

ungüento *m* ointment.

únicamente *adv* only, simply.

único, ca *adj* only; singular, unique.

unidad *f* unity; unit; conformity; union.

unificar *vt* to unite.

unir *vt* to join, unite; to mingle; to bind, tie:—**~se** *vr* to associate.

uno *m* one:—**~, una** *adj* one; sole, only:—**~ a otro** one another:—**~ a ~** one by one:—**a una** jointly together.

untar *vt* to anoint; to grease; (*fam*) to bribe.

urbanidad *f* urbanity, politeness.

urbanismo *m* town planning.

urbanización *f* housing estate.

urdir *vt* to warp; to contrive.

urgencia *f* urgency; emergency; need, necessity.

urinario, ria *adj* urinary:—*m* urinal.

urna *f* urn; ballot box.

urraca *f* magpie.

usado, da *adj* used; experienced; worn.

usar *vt* to use, make use of; to wear: —**~se** *vr* to be used.

usted *pn* you.

usuario *m* user.

útero *m* uterus, womb.

util *adj* useful, profitable:—*m* utility.

utilizar *vt* to use; to make useful.

uva *f* grape.

V

vaca *f* cow; beef.

vacaciones *fpl* vacation; holidays *pl*.

vacante *adj* vacant:—*f* vacancy.

vaciar *vt* to empty, clear; to mould:—*vi* to fall, decrease (of waters):—~**se** *vr* to empty.

vacilar *vi* to hesitate; to falter; to fail.

vacío, cía *adj* void, empty; unoccupied; concave; vain; presumptuous: —*m* vacuum; emptiness.

vacuna *f* vaccine.

vacuno, na *adj* bovine, cow *compd*.

vagar *vi* to rove or loiter about; to wander.

vago, ga *adj* vagrant; restless; vague.

vagón *m* (*ferro*) wagon; carriage:—~ **de mercancias** goods wagon.

vaho *m* steam, vapour.

vaina *f* pod, husk.

vaivén *m* fluctuation, instability; giddiness.

vajilla *f* crockery.

vale *m* OK; promissory note, IOU.

valer *vi* to be valuable; to be deserving; to cost; to be valid; to be worth; to produce; to be current:—*vt* to protect, favour; to be worth; to be equivalent to:—~**se** *vr* to employ, make use of; to have recourse to.

valiente *adj* robust, vigorous; valiant, brave; boasting.

valija *f* suitcase.

valioso, sa *adj* valuable.

valla *f* fence; hurdle; barricade.

valle *m* valley.

valor *m* value; price; validity; force; power; courage, valour.

valorar *vt* to value; to evaluate.

vals *m invar* waltz.

valsar *vi* to waltz

válvula *f* valve.

vanidoso, sa *adj* vain, showy; haughty; conceited.

vano, na *adj* vain; useless, frivolous; arrogant; futile:—**en** ~ in vain.

vapor *m* vapour, steam; breath.

vaquero *m* cow-herd:—~, **ra** *adj* belonging to a cowman:—~**s** *mpl* jeans *pl*.

vara *f* rod; pole, staff; stick.

variar *vt* to vary; to modify; to change: —*vi* to vary.

varices *fpl* varicose veins *pl*.

varilla *f* small rod; curtain rod; spindle, pivot.

vario, ria *adj* varied, different; vague; variegated:— ~**s** *pl* some; several.

varón *m* man, male.

vasco, ca *adj*, *m* / *f* Basque.

vasija *f* vessel.

vaso *m* glass; vessel; vase.

vástago *m* bud, shoot; offspring.

vasto, ta *adj* vast, huge.

vaticinar *vt* to divine, foretell.

vatio *m* watt.

vecindad *f* inhabitants of a place; neighbourhood.

vecino, na *adj* neighbouring; near:—*m* neighbour, inhabitant.

veinte *adj*, *m* twenty.

veintena *f* twentieth part; score.

vejar *vt* to vex; to humiliate.

vejez *f* old age.

vejiga *f* bladder.

vela *f* watch; watchfulness; night-guard; candle; sail: —**hacerse a la** ~ to set sail.

velar *vi* to stay awake; to be attentive: —*vt* to guard, watch.

velero, ra *adj* swift-sailing.

veleta *f* weather cock.

vello *m* down; gossamer; short downy hair.

velo *m* veil; pretext.

velocidad *f* speed; velocity.

vena *f* vein.

venado *m* deer; venison.

vencer *vt* to defeat; to conquer, vanquish:—*vi* to win; to expire.

vendaje *m* bandage, dressing for wounds.

vendaval *m* gale.

vender *vt* to sell.

vendimia *f* grape harvest; vintage.

vendimiar *vt* to harvest, gather; to profit from (something).

veneno *m* poison, venom.

venerar *vt* to venerate, worship.

vengar *vt* to revenge, avenge:—~**se** *vr* to take revenge.

venida *f* arrival; return; overflow of a river.

venidero, ra *adj* future:—~**s** *mpl* posterity.

venir *vi* to come, arrive; to follow, succeed; to happen; to spring from: —~**se** *vr* to ferment.

venta *f* sale.

ventaja *f* advantage.

ventana *f* window; window shutter; nostril.

ventilar *vt* to ventilate; to fan; to discuss.

ventisca *f*, **ventisco** *m* snowstorm.

ventosidad *f* flatulence.

ventura *f* happiness; luck, chance, fortune:—**por** ~ by chance.

ver *vt* to see, look at; to observe; to visit:—*vi* to understand; to see:—~**se** *vr* to be seen; to be conspicuous; to find oneself:—~**se con uno** to have a bone to pick with someone: —*m* sense of sight; appearance.

veraneo *m* summer holiday.

verano *m* summer.

veras *fpl* truth, sincerity:—**de** ~ in truth, really.

veraz *adj* truthful.

verbena *f* fair; dance.

verdad *f* truth, veracity; reality; reliability.

verdadero, ra *adj* true; real; sincere.

verde *m, adj* green.

verdura *f* verdure; vegetables *pl*, greens *pl*.

vereda *f* path; pavement, sidewalk.

vergüenza *f* shame; bashfulness; confusion.

verificar *vt* to check, verify:—~**se** *vr* to happen.

verruga *f* wart.

vertedero *m* sewer, drain; tip.

verter *vt* to pour; to spill; to empty:—*vi* to flow.

vértice *m* vertex, zenith; crown (head).

vertiente *f* slope; waterfall, cascade.

vertiginoso, sa *adj* giddy.

vespertino, na *adj* evening *compd*.

vestíbulo *m* vestibule, lobby; foyer.

vestido *m* dress; clothes *pl*.

vestir *vt* to put on; to wear; to dress; to adorn; to cloak, disguise: *vi* to dress:—~**se** to get dressed.

vestuario *m* clothes *pl*; uniform; vestry; changing room.

veta *f* vein (in mines, wood, etc); streak; grain.

veteado, da *adj* veined; striped:—*m* veining; streaks.

veterano, na *adj* experienced, practised:—*m* veteran, old soldier.

veterinaría *f* veterinary medicine.

veterinario, ria *m/f* veterinary surgeon.

vez *f* time; turn; return:—**cada** ~ each time:—**una** ~ once:—**a veces** sometimes, by turns.

veza *f* (*bot*) vetch.

vía *f* way; road, route; mode, manner, method; (*ferro*) railway line.

viajante *m* sales representative.

viajar *vi* to travel.

víbora *f* viper.

vibrar *vt, vi* to vibrate.

vicio *m* vice.

vid *f* (*bot*) vine.

vida *f* life.

vídeo *m* video.

vidriera *f* stained-glass window; shop window.

vidrio *m* glass.

vieira *f* scallop.

viejo, ja *adj* old; ancient, antiquated.

viento *m* wind; air.

vientre *m* belly.

viernes *m invar* Friday:—**V~ Santo** Good Friday.

viga *f* beam; girder.

vigente *adj* in force.

vigésimo, ma *adj, m* twentieth.

vigía *f* (*mar*) lookout:—*m* watchman.

vigilar *vt* to watch over:—*vi* to keep watch.

vil *adj* mean, sordid, low; worthless; infamous; ungrateful.

vilipendiar *vt* to despise, revile.

villancico *m* Christmas carol.

vilo:—**en** ~ *adv* in the air; in suspense.

vinagre *m* vinegar.

vincular *vt* to link.

viñedo *m* vineyard.

vino *m* wine:—~ **tinto** red wine.

violar *vt* to rape; to violate; to profane.

violentar *vt* to force.

violento, ta *adj* violent;

forced; absurd; embarrass-
ing.

violeta *f* violet.

violón *m* double bass.

virar *vi* to swerve.

viril *adj* virile, manly.

virtud *f* virtue.

viruela *f* smallpox.

visa *f*, **visado** *m* visa.

viscoso, sa *adj* viscous, gluti-
nous.

visillos *mpl* net curtains *pl*.

visión *f* sight, vision; fantasy.

visitar *vt* to visit.

vislumbrar *vt* to catch a
glimpse of; to perceive in-
distinctly.

visón *m* mink.

víspera *f* eve; evening before:—~s *pl* vespers.

vista *f* sight, view; vision;
eyesight;   appearance;
looks *pl*; prospect; intention; (*jur*) trial:—*m* customs officer.

vistazo *m* glance.

vistoso, sa *adj* colourful, attractive, lively.

vitalicio, cia *adj* for life.

vitorear *vt* to shout, applaud.

vitrina *f* showcase.

viudo, a *f* widower, widow.

vivaz *adj* lively.

víveres *mpl* provisions.

vivero *m* nursery (for
plants); fish farm.

vivienda *f* housing; flat,
apartment.

viviente *adj* living.

vivir *vt* to live through; to go
through: —*vi* to live; to
last.

vivo, va *adj* alive; lively:—**al**
~ to the life; very realisti-
cally.

vocablo *m* word, term.

vocal *f* vowel:—*m/f* member
(of a committee):—*adj* vocal, oral.

vociferar *vt* to shout; to proclaim in a loud voice:—*vi*
to yell.

volante *adj* flying:—*m* (*auto*)
steering wheel; note; pam-
phlet; shuttlecock.

volar *vi* to fly; to pass swiftly
(of time); to rush, hurry:—
vt to blow up, explode.

volcán *m* volcano.

volcar *vt* to upset, overturn;
to make giddy; to empty
out; to exasperate: —~**se** *vr*
to tip over.

volquete *m* tipcart; dump
truck.

voltear *vt* to turn over; to

overturn:—*vi* to roll over,
tumble.

voltereta *f* tumble; somer-
sault.

voluble *adj* unpredictable;
fickle.

volumen *m* volume; size.

voluntad *f* will, willpower;
wish, desire.

volver *vt* to turn (over); to
turn upside down; to turn
inside out:—*vi* to return,
go back:—~**se** *vr* to turn
around.

vórtice *m* whirlpool.

vos *pn* you.

vosotros, tras *pn pl* you.

votar *vi* to vow; to vote.

voz *f* voice; shout; rumour;
word, term.

vuelo *m* flight; wing; projec-
tion of a building; ruffle,
frill:—**cazar al** ~ to catch in
flight:—~ **chárter** charter
flight.

vuelta *f* turn; circuit; return;
row   of   stitches;   cuff;
change; bend, curve; re-
verse, other side; return
journey.

vuestro, tra *adj* your:—*pn*
yours.

W, X, Y, Z

wagón *m* railway carriage; wagon; van.

wat *m* watt.

wáter *m* toilet, water closet.

whisky *m* whisky.

xenofobia *f* xenophobia.

xilófono *m* xylophone.

y *conj* and.

ya *adv* already; now; immediately; at once; soon:— *conj* ~ **que** since, seeing that:—¡~! of course!, sure!

yacimiento *m* deposit.

yate *m* yacht, sailing boat.

yedra *f* ivy.

yegua *f* mare.

yema *f* bud; leaf; yolk:—~ **del dedo** tip of the finger.

yerno *m* son-in-law.

yeso *m* gypsum; plaster:—~ **mate** plaster of Paris.

yo *pn* I:—~ **mismo** I myself.

yodo *m* iodine.

yogur *m* yogurt.

yunque *m* anvil.

yute *m* jute.

zafiro *m* sapphire.

zaguán *m* porch, hall.

zalamero, ra *adj* flattering:— *m/f* wheedler.

zamarra *f* sheepskin (jacket).

zambullirse *vr* to plunge into water, dive.

zampar *vt* to gobble down; to put away hurriedly:—~**se** *vr* to thrust oneself suddenly into any place; to crash, hurtle.

zanahoria *f* carrot.

zancada *f* stride.

zancudo, da *adj* long legged:—*m* mosquito.

zángano *m* drone; idler, slacker.

zanja *f* ditch, trench.

zapata *f* boot:—~ **de freno** (*auto*) brake shoe.

zapatilla *f* slipper; pump (shoe); (*dep*) trainer, training shoe.

zapato *m* shoe.

zarandear *vt* to shake vigorously.

zarcillo *m* earring; tendril.

zarpar *vi* to weigh anchor.

zarza *f* bramble.

zarzuela *f* Spanish light opera.

zócalo *m* plinth, base; baseboard.

zona *f* zone; area, belt.

zopenco, ca *adj* dull, very stupid.

zoquete *m* block; crust of bread; (*fam*) blockhead.

zorro, a *m* fox; cunning person.

zozobrar *vi* (*mar*) to founder; to capsize; (*fig*) to fail; to be anxious.

zueco *m* wooden shoe; clog.

zumbar *vt* to hit:—~**se** *vr* to hit each other:—*vi* to buzz.

zumo *m* juice.

zurcir *vt* to darn; (*fig*) to join, unite; to hatch (lies).

zurdo, da *adj* left; left-handed.

zurrar *vt* (*fam*) to flog, lay into; (*fig*) to criticise harshly.

English-Spanish Dictionary

A

a *art* un, uno, una:—*prep* a, al, en.

abandon *vt* abandonar, dejar.

abash *vt* avergonzar, causar confusión,

abbey *n* abadía *f*.

abbot *n* abad *m*.

abbreviate *vt* abreviar, acortar.

abbreviation *n* abreviatura *f*.

abdicate *vt* abdicar; renunciar.

abdication *n* abdicación *f*; renuncia *f*.

abdomen *n* abdomen, bajo vientre *m*.

abduct *vt* secuestrar.

aberration *n* error *m*; aberración *f*.

abet *vt*:—**to aid and ~ ser** cómplice de.

abide *vt* soportar, sufrir.

ability *n* habilidad, capacidad.

ablaze *adj* en llamas.

able *adj* capaz, hábil.

able-bodied *adj* robusto/ta, vigoroso/sa.

ably *adv* con habilidad.

abnormal *adj* anormal.

abnormality *n* anormalidad *f*.

aboard *adv* a bordo.

abode *n* domicilio *m*.

abolish *vt* abolir, anular.

abolition *n* abolición, anulación *f*.

abominable *adj* abominable.

abomination *n* abominación *f*.

aboriginal *adj* aborigen.

abort *vi* abortar.

abortion *n* aborto *m*.

abound *vi* abundar.

about *prep* acerca de, acerca.

above *prep* encima.

aboveboard *adj* legitimo/ma.

abrasion *n* abrasión *f*.

abrasive *adj* abrasivo/va.

abroad *adv* en el extranjero.

abrupt *adj* brusco/ca.

abscess *n* absceso *m*.

abscond *vi* esconderse; huirse.

absence *n* ausencia *f*.

absent *adj* ausente.

absentee *n* ausente *m*.

absent-minded *adj* distraído/da.

absolute *adj* absoluto/ta.

absorb *vt* absorber.

abstain *vi* abstenerse.

abstinence *n* abstinencia *f*.

abstinent *adj* abstinente.

abstract *adj* abstracto/ta:—*n* extracto *m*.

abstraction *n* abstracción *f*.

absurd *adj* absurdo/da.

abundance *n* abundancia *f*.

abundant *adj* abundante.

abuse *vt* abusar; maltratar.

abusive *adj* abusivo/va, ofensivo/va.

abysmal *adj* abismal.

abyss *n* abismo *m*.

acacia *n* acacia *f*.

academic *adj* académico/ca.

academy *n* academia *f*.

accede *vi* acceder.

accelerate *vt* acelerar.

accelerator *n* acelerador *m*.

accent *n* acento *m*; tono *m*.

accentuate *vt* acentuar.

accept *vt* aceptar; admitir.

acceptable *adj* aceptable.

acceptance *n* aceptación *f*.

access *n* acceso *m*; entrada *f*.

accessible *adj* accesible.

accession *n* aumento.

accessory *n* accesorio *m*.

accident *n* accidente *m*; casualidad *f*.

acclaim *vt* aclamar, aplaudir.

accommodate *vt* alojar; complacer.

accommodation *n* alojamiento *m*.

accompany *vt* acompañar.

accomplice *n* cómplice *m*.

accomplish *vt* efectuar, completar.

accord *n* acuerdo, convenio *m*.

accordance *n*:—**in ~ with** de acuerdo con.

according *prep* segun, conforme.

accordion *n* (*mus*) acordeón *m*.

account *n* cuenta *f*.

accountability *n* responsabilidad *f*.

accountancy *n* contabilidad *f*.

accountant *n* contable, contador *m*.

accrue *vi* resultar, provenir.

accumulate *vt* acumular; amontonar.

accuracy *n* exactitud *f*.

accurate *adj* exacto/ta.

accursed *adj* maldito/ta.

accuse *vt* acusar; culpar.

accustom *vt* acostumbrar.

ache *n* dolor *m*:—*vi* doler.

achieve *vt* realizar; obtener.

achievement *n* realización *f*.

acid *adj* ácido/da; agrio/ria:—*n* ácido *m*.

acknowledge *vt* reconocer, confesar.

acne *n* acne *m*.

acorn *n* bellota *f*.

acoustics *n* acústica *f*.

acquaint *vt* informar, avisar.

acquaintance *n* conocimiento *m*; conocido *m*.

acquire *vt* adquirir.

acquisition *n* adquisición

acquit *vt* absolver.

acquittal *n* absolución *f*.

acre *n* acre *m*.

acrid *adj* acre.

acrimony *n* acrimonio *m*.

across *adv* de través.

action *n* acción *f*.

activate *vt* activar.

active *adj* activo/va.

activity *n* actividad *f*.

actor *n* actor *m*.

actress *n* actriz *f*.

actual *adj* real; efectivo/va.

actuary *n* actuario de seguros *m*.

acumen *n* agudeza *f*.

acute *adj* agudo/da; ingenioso/sa.

ad *n* aviso *m*.

adage *n* proverbio *m*.

adamant *adj* inflexible.

adapt *vt* adaptar.

adaptor *n* adaptador *m*.

add *vt* añadir, agregar:—**to ~ up** sumar.

adder *n* culebra *f*; víbora *f*.

addict *n* drogadicto *m*.

addiction *n* dependencia *f*.

addition *n* adición *f*.

additional *adj* adicional.

additive *n* aditivo *m*.

address *vt* dirigir:—*n* dirección *f*.

adenoids *npl* vegetaciones adenoideas *fpl*.

adept *adj* hábil.

adequacy *n* suficiencia *f*.

adequate *adj* adecuado/da; suficiente.

adhere *vi* adherir.

adhesion *n* adhesión *f*.

adhesive *adj* pegajoso/sa.

adhesiveness *n* adhesividad *f*.

adieu *adv* adiós:—*n* despedida *f*.

adjacent *adj* adyacente, contiguo/gua.

adjective *n* adjetivo *m*.

adjoining *adj* contiguo/gua.

adjournment *n* prorroga *f*.

adjudicate *vt* adjudicar.

adjust *vt* ajustar, acomodar.

adjustable *adj* ajustable.

adjustment *n* ajustamiento *m*.

ad lib *vt* improvisar.

administer *vt* administrar.

administration *n* administración *f*.

administrative *adj* administrativo/va.

admirable *adj* admirable.

admiral *n* almirante *m*.

admire *vt* admirar.

admirer *n* admira/a *m*/*f*.

admission *adj* entrada *f*.

admit *vt* admitir.

admittance *n* entrada *f*.

admittedly *adj* de acuerdo que.

admonish *vt* amonestar.

ad nauseam *adv* hasta el cansancio.

adolescence *n* adolescencia *f*.

adopt *vt* adoptar.

adorable *adj* adorable.

adore *vt* adorar.

adorn *vt* adornar.

adrift *adv* a la deriva.

adult *adj* adulto/ta.

adulterate *vt* adulterar, corromper.

adulterer *n* adultero *m*.

adultery *n* adulterio *m*.

advance *vt* avanzar; promover.

advantage *n* ventaja *f*.

advantageous *adj* ventajoso/sa.

adventure *n* aventura *f*.

adventurous *adj* intrépido/da.

adverb *n* adverbio *m*.

adversary *n* adversario enemigo *m*.

adversity *n* calamidad *f*; infortunio *m*.

advertise *vt* anunciar.

advertisement *n* aviso *m*.

advice *n* consejo *m*; aviso *m*.

advisability *n* prudencia *f*.

advise *vt* aconsejar; avisar.

advocacy *n* defensa *f*.

advocate *n* abogado *m*; protector *m*.

aerial *n* antena *f*.

aerobics *npl* aerobic *m*.

aerometer *n* areómetro *m*.

aerosol *n* aerosol *m*.

afar *adv* lejos, distante.

affair *n* asunto *m*; negocio *m*.

affect *vt* conmover; afectar.

affection *n* cariño *m*.

affidavit *n* declaración jurada *f*.

affiliate *vt* afiliar.

affiliation *n* afiliación *f*.

affinity *n* afinidad *f*.

affirm *vt* afirmar, declarar.

affirmation *n* afirmación *f*.

affirmative *adj* afirmativo/va.

affix *vt* pegar:—*n* (*gr*) afijo *m*.

afflict *vt* afligir.

affliction *n* aflicción *f*; dolor *m*.

affluence *n* opulencia *f*.

affluent *adj* opulento/ta.

affray *n* asalto *m*; tumulto *m*.

aflame *adv* en llamas.

afloat *adv* flotante, a flote.

afore *prep* antes:—*adv* primero.

afraid *adj* espantado/da.

afresh *adv* de nuevo, otra vez.

after *prep* después.

afterbirth *n* secundinas *fpl*.

after-effects *npl* consecuencias *fpl*.

afterlife *n* vida venidera *f*.

aftermath *n* consecuencias *fpl*.

afternoon *n* tarde *f*.

aftershave *n* aftershave *m*.

aftertaste *n* resabio *m*.

afterwards *adv* después.

again *adv* otra vez.

against *prep* contra.

agate *n* ágata *f*.

age *n* edad *f*; vejez *f*.

agency *n* agencia *f*.

agenda *n* orden del día *m*.

agent *n* agente *m*.

aggrandisement *n* engrandecimiento *m*.

aggravate *vt* agravar, exagerar.

aggregate *n* agregado *m*.

aggregation *n* agregación *f*.

aggression *n* agresión *f*.

aggressor *n* agresor *m*.

aggrieved *adj* ofendido/da.

aghast *adj* horrorizado/da.

agile *adj* ágil; diestro/tra.

agitate *vt* agitar.

ago *adv* pasado.

agonising *adj* atngustioso.

agony *n* agonía *f*.

agree *vt* convenir:—*vi* estar de acuerdo/da.

agreeable *adj* agradable; amable.

agreement *n* acuerdo *m*.

agriculture *n* agricultura *f*.

ah! *excl* ¡ah! ¡ay!

ahead *adv* más allá, delante de otro.

aid *vt* ayudar, socorrer.

AIDS *n* SIDA *m*.

ail *vt* afligir, molestar.

ailment *n* dolencia, indisposición *f*.

aim *vt* apuntar aspirar a; intentar.

air *n* aire *m*:—*vt* airear; ventilar.

air balloon *n* globo aerostático *m*.

airborne *adj* aerotransportado/da.

air-conditioning *n* climatización *f*.

aircraft *n* avión *m*.

air force *n* fuerzas aéreas *fpl*.

airline *n* línea aérea *f*.

airmail *n*:—by ~ por avión,

airplane *n* avión *m*.

airport *n* aeropuerto *m*.

airstrip *n* pista de aterrizaje *f*.

airy *adj* bien ventilado/da.

aisle *n* nave de una iglesia *f*.

akin *adj* parecido/da.

alabaster *n* alabastro *m*.

alarm *n* alarma *f*:—*vt* alarmar; inquietar.

alas *adv* desgraciadamente.

albeit *conj* aunque.

album *n* album *m*.

alchemy *n* alquimia *f*.

alcohol *n* alcohol *m*.

alcoholic *adj* alcohólico/ca:—*n* alcoholizado *m*.

alcove *n* nicho *m*.

alder *n* aliso *m*.

ale *n* cerveza *f*.

alert *adj* vigilante; alerto/ta.

algae *npl* alga *f*.

algebra *n* álgebra *f*.

alias *adj* alias.

alibi *n* (*law*) coartada *f*.

alien *adj* ajeno/na.

alienate *vt* enajenar.

alight *vi* apearse.

align *vt* alinear.

alike *adj* semejante, igual.

alive *adj* vivo/va, viviente; activo/va.

alkali *n* álcali *m*.

alkaline *adj* alcalino/na.

all *adj* todo/da.

allay *vt* aliviar.

allegation *n* alegación *f*.

allege *vt* alegar; declarar.

allegiance *n* lealtad, fidelidad *f*.

allegorical *adj* alegórico/ca.

allegory *n* alegoría *f*.

allergy *n* alergia *f*.

alley *n* callejuela *f*.

alliance *n* alianza *f*.

allied *adj* aliado/da.

alligator *n* caimán *m*.

allocate *vt* repartir.

allot *vt* asignar.

allow *vt* conceder; permitir; dar.

allowance *n* concesión *f*.

alloy *n* liga, mezcla *f*.

allspice *n* pimienta de Jamaica *f*.

allude *vt* aludir.

allure *n* fascinación *f*.

allusion *n* alusión *f*.

allusive *adj* alusivo/va.

alluvial *adj* aluvial.

ally *n* aliado *m*:—*vt* aliar.

almanac *n* almanaque *m*.

almighty *adj* omnipotente, todopoderoso/sa.

almond *n* almendra *f*.

almost *adv* casi; cerca de.

aloft *prep* arriba.

alone *adj* solo.

along *adv* a lo largo.

aloof *adv* lejos.

alphabet *n* alfabeto *m.*

alphabetical *adj* alfabético/ca.

alpine *adj* alpino/na.

already *adv* ya.

also *adv* también, además.

altar *n* altar *m.*

altarpiece *n* retablo *m.*

alter *vt* modificar.

alteration *n* alteración *f.*

alternate *adj* alterno/na:—*vt* alternar, variar.

alternator *n* alternador *m.*

alternative *n* alternativa *f.*

although *conj* aunque, no obstante.

altitude *n* altitud, altura *f.*

altogether *adv* del todo.

aluminium *n* aluminio *m.*

always *adv* siempre, constantemente.

a.m. *adv* de la mañana.

amalgam *n* amalgama *f.*

amalgamate *vt vi* amalgamar(se).

amaryllis *n* (*bot*) amarillas *f.*

amass *vt* acumular, amontonar.

amateur *n* aficionado *m.*

amateurish *adj* torpe.

amaze *vt* asombrar.

amazon *n* amazona *f.*

ambassador *n* embajador *m.*

amber *n* ámbar *m.*

ambidextrous *adj* ambidextro/tra.

ambiguity *n* ambigüedad, duda *f.*

ambiguous *adj* ambiguo:—**~ly** *adv* ambiguamente.

ambition *n* ambición *f.*

amble *vi* andar sin prisa.

ambulance *n* ambulancia *f.*

ambush *n* emboscada *f.*

amenable *adj* sensible.

amend *vt* enmendar.

amendment *n* enmienda *f.*

amends *npl* compensación *f.*

amenities *npl* comodidades *fpl.*

America *n* América *f.*

amethyst *n* amatista *f.*

amiable *adj* amable.

amiableness *n* amabilidad *f.*

amiably *adv* amablemente.

amicable *adj* amigable.

amid(st) *prep* entre, en medio de.

amiss *adv*:—**something's ~** pasa algo malo.

ammonia *n* amoníaco *m.*

ammunition *n* municiones *fpl.*

amnesia *n* amnesia *f.*

amnesty *n* amnistía *f.*

amoral *adv* amoral.

amorous *adj* amoroso/sa.

amount *n* importe *m*; cantidad *f.*

amp(ere) *n* amperio *m.*

amphibian *n* anfibio *m.*

amphibious *adj* anfibio/bia.

amphitheatre *n* anfiteatro *m.*

ample *adj* amplio/lia.

ampleness *n* amplitud, abundancia *f.*

amplifier *n* amplificador *m*

amplify *vt* ampliar, extender.

amplitude *n* amplitud, extensión *f.*

amputate *vt* amputar.

amuse *vt* entretener, divertir.

amusement *n* diversión *f.*

amusing *adj* divertido/da.

an *art* un, uno, una.

anachronism *n* anacronismo *m.*

anaemia *n* anemia *f.*

anaesthetic *n* anestesia *f.*

analogy *n* analogía *f.*

analyse *vt* analizar.

anarchy *n* anarquía *f.*

anatomical *adj* anatómico/ca.

anatomy *n* anatomía *f*

ancestor *n*:—**~s** *pl* antepasados *mpl.*

ancestral *adj* hereditario/ria.

ancestry *n* raza, alcurnia *f.*

anchor *n* ancla *f*:—*vi* anclar.

anchovy *n* anchoa *f.*

ancient *adj* antiguo.

and *conj* y, e.

anecdote *n* anécdota *f*

anemone *n* (*bot*) anémona *f*

angel *n* ángel *m*

anger *n* cólera *f*:—*vt* enojar, irritar.

angle *n* ángulo *m*:—*vt* pescar con cana.

anglicism *n* anglicismo *m.*

angry *adj* enojado/da.

anguish *n* ansia, angustia *f*

angular *adj* angular.

animal *n adj* animal *m.*

animation *n* animación *f*

aniseed *n* anís *m*

ankle *n* tobillo *m.*

annals *n* anales *mpl.*

annex *vt* anejar:—*n* anejo *m.*

annihilate *vt* aniquilar.

annihilation *n* aniquilación *f.*

anniversary *n* aniversario *m.*

annotate *vi* anotar.

announce *vt* anunciar, publicar.

announcement *n* anuncio *m.*

annoy *vt* molestar.

annual *adj* anual.

annunciation *n* anunciación *f*

anoint *vt* untar, ungir.

anomaly *n* anomalía, irregularidad *f.*

anon *adv* más tarde.

anonymity *n* anonimato *m.*

anonymous *adj* anónimo/ma.

anorexia *n* anorexia *f.*

another *adj* otro/tra.

answer *vt* responder.

answering machine *n* contestador automático *m.*

ant *n* hormiga *f.*

antagonise *vt* provocar.

antarctic *adj* antártico/ca.

antelope *n* antílope *m.*

antenna *npl* antena *f.*

anterior *adj* anterior, precedente.

anthem *n* himno *m.*

anthology *n* antología *f.*

anthropology *n* antropología *f*

antibiotic *n* antibiótico *m.*

antibody *n* anticuerpo *m.*

Antichrist *n* Anticristo *m.*

anticipate *vt* anticipar, prevenir.

anticipation *n* anticipación *f.*

antidote *n* antídoto *m.*

antipodes *npl* antipodas *fpl*

antiquarian *n* anticuario *m.*

antiquated *adj* antiguo/gua.

antiquity *n* antigüedad *f.*

antiseptic *adj* antiséptico/ca.

antler *n* cuerna *f.*

anvil *n* yunque *m.*

anxiety *n* ansiedad, ansia *f.*

anxious *adj* ansioso/sa.

any *adj pn* cualquier, cualquiera; alguno, alguna

apart *adv* aparte, separadamente.

apartment *n* departamento *m.*

apathy *n* apatía *f.*

ape *n* mono *m.*

apologise *vt* disculpar.

apology *n* apología, defensa *f.*

apostrophe *n* apóstrofe *m.*

appall *vt* espantar, aterrar.

apparatus *n* aparato *m.*

apparent *adj* evidente, aparente.

apparition *n* aparición, visión *f.*

appeal *vi* apelar.

appear *vi* aparecer.

appease *vt* aplacar.

append *vt* anejar.

appendicitis *n* apendicitis *f.*

appendix *n* apéndice *m.*

appetite *n* apetito *m.*

applaud *vi* aplaudir.

apple *n* manzana *f.*

appliance *n* aparato *m.*

applicable *adj* aplicable.

applicant *n* aspirante, candidato *m.*

application *n* aplicación *f;* solicitud *f.*

applied *adj* aplicado/da.

apply *vt* aplicar.

appoint *vt* nombrar.

appointment *n* cita *f;* nombramiento *m.*

apportion *vt* repartir.

appraisal *n* estimación *f.*

appraise *vt* tasar; estimar.

appreciate *vt* apreciar; agradecer.

apprehend *vt* arrestar.

apprehension *n* aprensión *f.*

apprehensive *adj* aprensivo/va.

apprentice *n* aprendiz *m.*

approach *vt vi* aproximar(se).

appropriate *vt* apropiarse de:—*adj* apropiado/da.

approve (of) *vt* aprobar.

April *n* abril *m.*

apron *n* delantal *m.*

apse *n* ábside *m.*

apt *adj* apto/ta, idóneo/nea.

aptitude *n* aptitud *f.*

aquarium *n* acuario *m.*

Aquarius *n* Acuario *m.*

aqueduct *n* acueducto *m.*

arable *adj* labrantío/tía.

arbitrate *vt* arbitrar.

arcade *n* galería *f.*

arch *n* arco *m.*

archaeology *n* arqueología *f.*

archaic *adj* arcaico/ca.

archbishop *n* arzobispo *m.*

archer *n* arquero *m.*

architect *n* arquitecto/ta *m/f.*

architecture *n* arquitectura *f.*

archives *npl* archivos *mpl.*

arctic *adj* ártico/ca.

area *n* área *f;* espacio *m.*

arena *n* arena *f.*

arguably *adv* posiblemente.

argue *vi* discutir.

argument *n* argumento *m,* controversia *f.*

arid *adj* árido/da, estéril.

aridity *n* sequedad *f.*

Aries *n* Aries *m.*

arise *vi* levantarse.

aristocracy *n* aristocracia *f.*

arithmetic *n* aritmética *f.*

ark *n* arca *f.*

arm *n* brazo *m;* arma *f.*

armament *n* armamento *m.*

armchair *n* sillón *m.*

armour *n* armadura *f.*

armpit *n* sobaco *m.*

army *n* ejercito *m.*

aroma *n* aroma *m.*

around *prep* alrededor de.

arouse *vt* despertar; excitar.

arraign *vt* acusar.

arraignment *n* acusación *f;* proceso criminal *m.*

arrange *vt* organizar.

arrangement *n* colocación *f;* arreglo.

arrant *adj* consumado/da.

array *n* serie *f.*

arrears *npl* resto de una deuda *m;* atraso *m.*

arrest *n* arresto *m:—vt* detener, arrestar.

arrival *n* llegada *f.*

arrive *vi* llegar.

arrogance *n* arrogancia, presunción *f.*

arrogant *adj* arrogante, presuntuoso/sa:—**~ly** *adv* arrogantemente.

arrogate *vt* arrogarse.

arrogation *n* arrogación *f.*

arrow *n* flecha *f.*

arsenal *n* (*mil*) arsenal *m*; (*mar*) atarazana, armería *f.*

arsenic *n* arsénico *m.*

art *n* arte *m.*

arterial *adj* arterial.

artery *n* arteria *f.*

artful *adj* ingenioso/sa.

art gallery *n* pinacoteca *f.*

arthritis *n* artritis *f.*

artichoke *n* alcachofa *f.*

article *n* articulo *m.*

articulate *vt* articular.

artifice *n* artificio *m.*

artillery *n* artillería *f.*

artisan *n* artesano/na *m/f.*

artist *n* artista *m.*

artistry *n* habilidad *f.*

artless *adj* sencillo, simple.

artlessness *n* sencillez *f.*

as *conj* como; mientras.

asbestos *n* asbesto *m.*

ascend *vi* ascender, subir.

ascribe *vt* atribuir.

ash *n* (*bot*) fresno *m*; ceniza *f*

ashamed *adj* avergonzado/da.

ashtray *n* cenicero *m.*

Ash Wednesday *n* miércoles de ceniza *m.*

ask *vt* pedir, rogar, preguntar por.

askew *adv* de lado.

asleep *adj* dormido/da.

asparagus *n* espárrago *m.*

aspect *n* aspecto *m.*

aspen *n* álamo temblón *m.*

asphalt *n* asfalto *m.*

asphyxia *n* (*med*) asfixia *f.*

asphyxiate *vt* asfixiar.

asphyxiation *n* asfixia *f.*

aspiration *n* aspiración *f.*

aspire *vi* aspirar, desear.

aspirin *n* aspirina *f.*

ass *n* asno *m*:—**she ~** burra *f.*

assassin *n* asesino *m.*

assassinate *vt* asesinar.

assault *n* asalto *m.*

assemble *vt* reunir, convocar.

assembly *n* asamblea *f.*

assert *vt* sostener, mantener.

assess *vt* valorar.

assessment *n* valoración *f.*

assets *npl* bienes *mpl.*

assign *vt* asignar.

assimilate *vt* asimilar.

assist *vt* asistir, ayudar.

assistance *n* asistencia *f.*

assistant *n* asistente, ayudante *m.*

associate *vt* asociar.

association *n* asociación, sociedad *f.*

assortment *n* surtido *m.*

assume *vt* asumir; suponer.

assurance *n* seguro *m.*

assure *vt* asegurar.

asterisk *n* asterisco *m.*

asthma *n* asma *f.*

asthmatic *adj* asmático/ca.

astonish *vt* pasmar, sorprender.

astringent *adj* astringente.

astrologer *n* astrólogo/ga *m/f.*

astrology *n* astrología *f.*

astronaut *n* astronauta *m/f.*

astronomer *n* astrónomo *m.*

astronomy *n* astronomía *f.*

astute *adj* astuto/ta.

asylum *n* asilo, refugio *m.*

at *prep* a; en.

atheism *n* ateísmo *m.*

atheist *n* ateo *m*, atea *f.*

athlete *n* atleta *m/f.*

atlas *n* atlas *m.*

atmosphere *n* atmósfera *f.*

atom *n* átomo *m.*

atomic *adj* atómico/ca.

atrocious *adj* atroz.

atrocity *n* atrocidad, enormidad *f.*

attach *vt* adjuntar.

attaché *n* agregado *m.*

attack *vt* atacar; acometer.

attempt *vt* intentar; probar, experimentar.

attend *vt* servir; asistir.

attendant *n* sirviente *m.*

attention *n* atención *f*; cuidado *m.*

attentive *adj* atento/ta; cuidadoso/sa.

attest *vt* atestiguar.

attic *n* desván *m*; guardilla *f.*

attorney *n* abogado *m.*

attract *vt* atraer.

attraction *n* atracción *f*; atractivo *m.*

auburn *adj* moreno/na, castaño/ña.

auction *n* subasta *f.*

auctioneer *n* subastador/a.

audacious *adj* audaz.

audible *adj* perceptible al oído.

audience *n* audiencia *f.*

audit *n* auditoría *f.*

augment *vt* aumentar, acrecentar.

August *n* agosto *m.*

august *adj* augusto/a.

aunt *n* tia *f.*

au pair *n* au pair *f.*

aura *n* aura *f.*

auspicious *adj* propicio/cia.

austere *adj* austero/ra, severo/ra;

authentic *adj* auténtico/ca.

authenticate *vt* autenticar.

authenticity *n* autenticidad *f.*

author *n* autor *m*; escritor *m.*

authorisation *n* autorización *f*.

authorise *vt* autorizar.

authority *n* autoridad *f*.

auto *n* carro, coche *m*.

autograph *n* autógrafo *m*.

automatic *adj* automático/ca.

autonomy *n* autonomía *f*.

autopsy *n* autopsia *f*.

autumn *n* otoño *m*.

auxiliary *adj* auxiliar, asistente.

available *adj* disponible.

avalanche *n* alud *m*.

avarice *n* avaricia *f*.

avenue *n* avenida *f*.

avert *vt* desviar, apartar.

aviary *n* pajarera *f*.

avoid *vt* evitar, escapar.

await *vt* aguardar.

awake *vt* despertar.

award *vt* otorgar:—*n* premio *m*.

aware *adj* consciente; vigilante.

away *adv* ausente, fuera.

awe *n* miedo, temor *m*.

awful *adj* tremendo/da; horroroso/sa.

awhile *adv* un rato, algún tiempo.

awkward *adj* torpe, rudo/da.

awning *n* (*mar*) toldo *m*.

awry *adv* oblicuamente, torcidamente.

axe *n* hacha *f*.

axiom *n* axioma *m*.

axis *n* eje *m*.

axle *n* eje *m*.

B

baboon *n* cinocéfalo *m*.

baby *n* niño pequeño *m*.

bachelor *n* soltero *m*; bachiller *m*.

back *n* dorso *m*.

backbone *n* hueso dorsal, espinazo *m*.

backer *n* partidario/ria *m*.

backgammon *n* juego de chaquete o tablas *m*.

background *n* fondo *m*.

backlash *n* reacción *f*.

backpack *n* mochila *f*.

backside *n* trasero *m*.

backward *adj* tardo/da, lento/ta.

bacon *n* tocino *m*.

bad *adj* mal, malo.

badge *n* señal *f*; símbolo *m*.

badger *n* tejón *m*.

badminton *n* bádminton *m*.

baffle *vt* confundir.

bag *n* saco *m*; bolsa *f*.

baggage *n* bagaje, equipaje *m*.

bail *n* fianza, caución (juratoria) *f*.

bailiff *n* alguacil *m*.

bake *vt* cocer en horno.

bakery *n* panadería *f*.

baking powder *n* levadura *f*.

balance *n* balanza *f*; equilibrio *m*.

balcony *n* balcón *m*.

bald *adj* calvo/va.

ball *n* bola *f*; pelota *f*; baile *m*.

ballad *n* balada *f*.

ballerina *n* bailarina *f*.

ballet *n* ballet *m*.

balloon *n* globo *m*.

ballpoint (pen) *n* bolígrafo *m*.

balm, balsam *n* bálsamo *m*.

balustrade *n* balaustrada *f*.

bamboo *n* bambú *m*.

ban *n* prohibición *f*.

banal *adj* vulgar.

banana *n* plátano *m*.

band *n* faja *f*; cuadrilla *f*.

bandage *n* venda *f*.

bandit *n* bandido/da *m/f*.

bang *n* golpe *m*.

bangle *n* brazalete *m*.

banister(s) *n(pl)* pasamanos *m*.

banjo *n* banjo *m*.

bank *n* orilla (de rió) *f*; montón de tierra *m*; banco *m*.

bank account *n* cuenta de banco *f*.

bankrupt *adj* insolvente.

banner *n* bandera *f*.

banquet *n* banquete *m*.

baptise *vt* bautizar.

bar *n* bar *m*; barra *f*.

barbecue *n* barbacoa *f*.

barber *n* peluquero *m*.

bare *adj* desnudo/da, descubierto/ta.

barely *adv* apenas.

bargain *n* ganga *f*.

barge *n* barcaza *f*.

bark *n* corteza *f*.

barley *n* cebada *f*.

barn *n* granero.

barometer *n* barómetro *m*.

baron *n* barón *m*.

barracks *npl* cuartel *m*.

barrel *n* barril *m*.

barren *adj* estéril, infructuoso/sa.

barrier *n* barrera *f*; obstáculo *m*.

barter *vi* baratar.

base *n* fondo *m*; base *f*; basa *f*.

baseball *n* béisbol *m*.

basement *n* sótano *m*.

basic *adj* básico/ca.

basin *n* jofaina, bacía *f*.

basis *n* base *f*; fundamento *m*.

basket *n* cesta, canasta *f*.

basketball *n* baloncesto *m*.

bastard *n*, *adj* bastardo/da *m/f*.

bat *n* murciélago *m*.

batch *n* serie *f*.

bath *n* baño *m*.

bathe *vt* (*vi*) bañar(se).

bathing suit *n* traje de baño *m*.

bathroom *n* (cuarto de) baño *m*.

baths *npl* piscina *f*.

battery *n* batería *f*.

battle *n* combate *m*.

bawdy *adj* indecente.

bay *n* bahía *f*; laurel.

bazaar *n* bazar *m*.

be *vi* ser; estar.

beach *n* playa, orilla *f*.

beacon *n* almenara *f*.

beagle *n* sabueso *m*.

beak *n* pico *m*.

beam *n* rayo de luz *m*; travesaño *m*.

bean *n* haba *f*.

beansprouts *npl* brotes de soja *mpl*.

bear *vt* llevar alguna cosa como carga; sostener; soportar.

bear *n* oso *m*.

beard *n* barba *f*.

bearer *n* portador/a *m/f*.

beast *n* bestia *f*.

beat *vt* golpear; tocar (un tambor).

beatify *vt* beatificar, santificar.

beautiful *adj* hermoso/sa, bello.

beauty *n* hermosura, belleza *f*.

because *conj* porque, a causa de.

bed *n* cama *f*.

bedroom *n* dormitorio *m*.

bee *n* abeja *f*.

beech *n* haya *f*.

beef *n* carne de vaca *f*.

beefburger *n* hamburguesa *f*.

beefsteak *n* bistec *m*.

beeline *n* línea recta *f*.

beer *n* cerveza *f*.

beetle *n* escarabajo *m*.

befall *vi* suceder, acontecer.

before *adv, prep* antes de; delante.

beg *vt* mendigar.

beggar *n* mendigo/ga *m/f*.

begin *vt vi* comenzar, empezar.

beginning *n* principio *m*.

begrudge *vt* envidiar.

behave *vi* comportarse.

behind *prep* detrás; atrás.

beige *adj* color beige.

belch *vi* eructar.

belief *n* fe, creencia *f*.

believe *vt* creer.

believer *n* creyente, fiel.

bell *n* campana *f*.

bellows *npl* fuelle *m*.

belly *n* vientre *m*; panza *f*.

belong *vi* pertenecer.

beloved *adj* querido/da, amado/da.

below *adv, prep* debajo, inferior; abajo.

belt *n* cinturón, cinto *m*.

bench *n* banco *m*.

bend *vt* encorvar, inclinar, plegar.

beneath *adv, prep* debajo, abajo.

benefit *n* beneficio *m*; utilidad *f*; provecho *m*.

benevolence *n* benevolencia *f*.

benevolent *adj* benévolo.

benign *adj* benigno/na.

bent *n* inclinación *f*.

bereave *vt* privar.

bereavement *n* perdida *f*.

beret *n* boina *f*.

berry *n* baya *f*.

beset *vt* acosar.

beside(s) *prep* al lado de; excepto.

best *adj* mejor.

bestial *adj* bestial, brutal.

bestow *vt* dar, conferir.

bestseller *n* bestseller *m*.

bet *n* apuesta *f*.

betray *vt* traicionar.

betroth *vt* contraer esponsales.

betting *n* juego *m*.

between *prep* entre, en medio de.

beverage *n* bebida *f*.

beware *vi* guardarse.

bewitch *vt* encantar, hechizar.

beyond *prep* más allá.

bias *n* propensión.

bib *n* babador *m*.

Bible *n* Biblia *f*.

bibliography *n* bibliografía *f*.

bicycle *n* bicicleta *f*.

bid *vt* mandar, ordenar; ofrecer.

biennial *adj* bienal.

bifocals *npl* anteojos bifocales *mpl*.

big *adj* grande, lleno/na.

bigamist *n* bígamo/ma *m/f*.

bigamy *n* bigamia *f*.

bigot *n* fanático/ca *m/f*.

bike *n* bici *f*.

bikini *n* bikini *m*.

bile *n* bilis *f*.

bilingual *adj* bilingüe.

bill *n* pico de ave *m*; billete.

billboard *n* cartelera *f*.

billet *n* alojamiento *m*.

billiards *npl* billar *m*.

billion *n* billón *f*.

bin *n* cubo de la basura *m*.

binder *n* encuadernador/a *m/f*.

bingo *n* bingo *m*.

binoculars *npl* prismáticos *mpl*.

biographer *n* biógrafo/fa *m/f*.

biography *n* biografía *f*.

biological *adj* biológico/ca.

biology *n* biología *f*.

birch *n* abedul *m*.

bird *n* ave *f*; pájaro *m*.

birth *n* nacimiento *m*.

birthday *n* cumpleaños *m invar*.

biscuit *n* bizcocho *m*.

bishop *n* obispo *m*.

bit *n* bocado *m*; pedacito *m*.

bitch *n* perra *f*.

bite *vt* morder; picar.

bitter *adj* amargo/ga.

bitumen *n* betún *m*.

bizarre *adj* raro/ra.

blab *vi* chismear.

black *adj* negro/gra, oscuro/ra.

blackberry *n* zarzamora *f*.

blackbird *n* mirlo *m*.

blackboard *n* pizarra *f*.

blackmail *n* chantaje *m*:—*vt* chantajear.

black pudding *n* morcilla *f*.

blacksmith *n* herrero *m*.

bladder *n* vejiga *f*.
blade *n* hoja *f*; filo *m*.
blame *vt* culpar.
blameless *adj* inocente.
blank *adj* blanco/ca.
blanket *n* manta *f*.
blaspheme *vt* blasfemar, jurar.
blasphemy *n* blasfemia *f*.
blatant *adj* obvio.
blaze *n* llama *f*.
bleed *vi*, *vt* sangrar.
blemish *vt* manchar.
bless *vt* bendecir.
blessing *n* bendición *f*.
blight *vt* arruinar.
blind *adj* ciego/ga.
blink *vi* parpadear.
bliss *n* felicidad (eterna) *f*.
blister *n* ampolla *f*.
blitz *n* bombardeo aéreo *m*.
blizzard *n* huracán *m*.
bloated *adj* hinchado/da.
blob *n* gota *f*.
bloc *n* bloque *m*.
block *n* bloque *m*; obstáculo *m*.
blockade *n* bloqueo *m*:—*vt* bloquear.
blond *adj* rubio/bia.
blood *n* sangre *f*.
blood group *n* grupo sanguíneo *m*.
blood poisoning *n* envenenamiento de la sangre. *m*.
blood pressure *n* presión de sangre *f*.
blood test *n* análisis de sangre *m*.
blood transfusion *n* transfusion de sangre *f*.
bloom *n* flor *f*; (*also fig*):—*vi* florecer.
blossom *n* flor *f*.
blot *vt* manchar.
blotchy *adj* muy manchado/da.

blouse *n* blusa *f*.
blow *vi* soplar; sonar.
blubber *n* grasa de ballena *f*.
blue *adj* azul.
bluebell *n* campanilla *f*.
blueprint *n* (*fig*) anteproyecto *m*.
blunder *n* desatino *m*.
blunt *adj* obtuso/sa; grosero/ra.
blush *n* rubor *m*; sonrojo *m*.
boar *n* verraco *m*:—**wild ~** jabalí *m*.
board *n* tabla *f*; mesa *f*.
boarder *n* pensionista *m*.
boarding card *n* tarjeta de embarque *f*.
boast *vi* jactarse.
boat *n* barco *m*.
bobsleigh *n* bob *m*.
bodice *n* corsé *m*.
body *n* cuerpo *m*; individuo *m*; gremio *m*.
body-building *n* culturismo *m*.
bodyguard *n* guardaespaldas *m*.
boil *vi* hervir; bullir.
bold *adj* ardiente, valiente; audaz.
bolt *n* cerrojo *m*.
bomb *n* bomba *f*.
bond *n* ligadura *f*; vinculo *m*.
bondage *n* esclavitud, servidumbre *f*.
bone *n* hueso *m*.
bonfire *n* hoguera *f*.
bonny *adj* bonito/ta.
bonus *n* cuota, prima *f*.
book *n* libro *m*.
bookcase *n* armario para libros *m*.
bookmarker *n* registro *m*.
bookstore *n* librería *f*.
boom *n* trueno *m*.
boon *n* presente, regalo *m*.
booth *n* barraca, cabaña *f*.

booty *n* botín *m*; presa *f*; saqueo *m*.
border *n* orilla *f*; borde *m*.
borderline *n* frontera *f*.
bore *vt* taladrar; barrenar; fastidiar.
boredom *n* aburrimiento *m*.
borrow *vt* pedir prestado/da.
bosom *n* seno, pecho *m*.
boss *n* jefe *m*; patrón/ona *m*/*f*.
botany *n* botánica *f*.
botch *vt* chapuzar.
both *adj* ambos.
bother *vt* preocupar; fastidiar.
bottle *n* botella *f*.
bottom *n* fondo *m*.
bough *n* brazo del árbol *m*; ramo *m*.
boulder *n* canto rodado *m*.
bounce *vi* rebotar.
bound *n* limite *m*; salto *m*.
boundary *n* limite *m*; frontera *f*.
bouquet *n* ramillete de flores *m*.
bourgeois *adj* burgués.
bout *n* ataque *m*.
bow *vt* encorvar, doblar.
bow *n* arco *m*.
bowels *npl* intestinos *mpl*.
bowl *n* taza; bola *f*.
bow tie *n* pajarita *f*.
box *n* caja, cajita *f*.
boxer *n* boxeador *m*.
boxing *n* boxeo *m*.
box office *n* taquilla *f*.
boy *n* muchacho *m*; niño *m*.
boycott *vt* boicotear:—*n* boicot *m*.
boyfriend *n* novio *m*.
bra *n* sujetador *m*.
bracelet *n* brazalete *m*.
bracket *n* puntal *m*; paréntesis *m*.
brag *n* jactancia *f*:—*vi* jactarse.
braid *n* trenza *f*:—*vt* trenzar.

brain *n* cerebro *m*.

brake *n* freno *m*:—*vt vi* frenar.

bran *n* salvado *m*.

branch *n* ramo *m*; rama *f*.

brand *n* marca *f*.

brandy *n* coñac *m*.

brass *n* latón *m*.

brassiere *n* sujetador *m*.

brave *adj* bravo/va, valiente.

bravery *n* valor *m*.

brawl *n* pelea *f*.

brazier *n* brasero *m*.

breach *n* rotura *f*.

bread *n* pan *m*.

breadth *n* anchura *f*.

break *vt* romper; quebrantar.

breakage *n* rotura *f*.

breakfast *n* desayuno *m*:—*vi* desayunar.

breast *n* pecho, seno *m*.

breastbone *n* esternón *m*.

breath *n* aliento *m*, respiración *f*; soplo de aire *m*.

breathe *vt vi* respirar; exhalar.

breathtaking *adj* pasmoso/ sa.

breed *n* casta, raza *f*.

breeze *n* brisa *f*.

brevity *n* brevedad, concisión *f*.

brew *vt* hacer; tramar, mezclar.

bribe *n* cohecho, soborno *m*.

bribery *n* cohecho, soborno *m*.

bric-a-brac *n* baratijas *fpl*.

brick *n* ladrillo *m*.

bricklayer *n* albañil *m*.

bride *n* novia *f*.

bridegroom *n* novio *m*.

bridesmaid *n* madrina de boda *f*.

bridge *n* puente *m/f*.

brief *adj* breve, conciso/sa, sucinto/ta.

briefcase *n* cartera *f*.

brigade *n* (*mil*) brigada *f*.

bright *adj* claro/ra, luciente, brillante.

brighten *vt* pulir, dar lustre.

brilliant *adj* brillante.

bring *vt* llevar, traer.

brisk *adj* vivo/va, alegre, jovial; fresco/ca.

brisket *n* pecho (de un animal) *m*.

briskly *adj* vigorosamente.

bristle *n* cerda, seta *f*:—*vi* erizarse.

bristly *adj* cerdoso/sa, lleno/na de cerdas.

brittle *adj* quebradizo, frágil.

broach *vt* comenzar a hablar de.

broad *adj* ancho.

broad beans *npl* haba gruesa *f*.

broadcast *n* emisión *f*.

broadcasting *n* radiodifusión *f*.

broaden *vt vi* ensanchar(se).

broadly *adv* anchamente.

broad-minded *adj* tolerante.

brocade *n* brocado *m*.

broccoli *n* brécol *m*.

brochure *n* folleto *m*.

broil *vt* asar a la parrilla.

broken *adj* roto/ta.

broker *n* corredor/a *m/f*.

bronchial *adj* bronquial.

bronchitis *n* bronquitis *f*.

bronze *n* bronce *m*.

brooch *n* broche *m*.

brook *n* arroyo *m*.

broom *n* hiniesta *f*; escoba *f*.

broth *n* caldo *m*.

brothel *n* burdel *m*.

brother *n* hermano *m*.

brother-in-law *n* cuñado *m*.

brow *n* caja *f*; frente *f*; cima *f*.

browbeat *vt* intimidar.

brown *adj* moreno/na; castaño/ña.

browse *vt* ramonear.

bruise *vt* magullar.

brunette *n* morena *f*.

brunt *n* choque *m*.

brush *n* cepillo *m*; escobilla *f*.

brusque *adj* brusco/ca.

Brussels sprout *n* col de Bruselas *f*.

brutal *adj* brutal.

brutality *n* brutalidad *f*.

brute *n* bruto *m*.

bubble *n* burbuja *f*.

bubblegum *n* chicle *m*.

bucket *n* cubo, pozal *m*.

buckle *n* hebilla *f*.

bucolic *adj* bucólico/ca.

bud *n* pimpollo, botón *m*:— *vi* brotar.

Buddhism *n* Budismo *m*.

buddy *n* compañero *m*.

budge *vi* moverse.

budgerigar *n* periquito *m*.

budget *n* presupuesto *m*.

buff *n* entusiasta *m*.

buffalo *n* búfalo *m*.

buffet *n* buffet *m*.

buffoon *n* bufón, chocarrero *m*.

bug *n* chinche *m*.

bugle(horn) *n* trompa de caza *f*.

build *vt* edificar; construir.

building *n* edificio *m*; construcción *f*.

bulb *n* bulbo *m*; cebolla *f*.

bulge *vi* combarse:—*n* bombeo *m*.

bulk *n* masa *f*; volumen *m*.

bulky *adj* grueso/sa, grande.

bull *n* toro *m*.

bulldog *n* dogo *m*.

bulldozer *n* aplanadora *f*.

bullet *n* bala *f*.

bullfight *n* corrida de toros *f*.

bullfighter *n* toreo *m*.

bullfighting *n* los toros *mpl*.

bullion *n* oro o plata en barras *m* o *f.*

bullock *n* novillo capado *m.*

bullring *n* plaza de toros *f.*

bully *n* valentón *m:—vt* tiranizar.

bumblebee *n* abejorro *m.*

bump *n* hinchazón *f.*

bun *n* bollo *m*; mono *m.*

bunch *n* ramo *m.*

bundle *n* fardo *m*, haz *m.*

bung *n* tapón *m.*

bungalow *n* bungalow *m.*

bunk *n* litera *f.*

bunker *n* refugio *m*; bunker *m.*

burden *n* carga *f:—vt* cargar.

bureau *n* armario *m*; escritorio *m.*

bureaucracy *n* burocracia *f.*

burglar *n* ladrón *m.*

burial *n* enterramiento *m*; exequias *fpl.*

burial place *n* cementerio *m.*

burly *adj* corpulento/ta, fornido/da.

burn *vt* quemar, abrasar, incendiar:—*vi* arder:—*n* quema dura *f.*

burner *n* quemador *m*; mechero *m.*

burning *adj* ardiente.

burrow *n* conejera *f.*

bursar *n* tesorero *m.*

burse *n* bolsa, lonja *f.*

burst *vi* reventar; abrirse.

bury *vt* enterrar, sepultar; esconder.

bus *n* autobús *m.*

bush *n* arbusto, espinal *m.*

busily *adv* diligentemente, apresuradamente.

business *n* asunto *m*; negocios *mpl.*

businessman *n* hombre de negocios *m.*

bust *n* busto *m.*

bus-stop *n* parada de autobuses *f.*

bustle *vi* hacer ruido.

busy *adj* ocupado/da; entrometido/da.

busybody *n* entrometido *m.*

but *conj* pero; mas.

butcher *n* carnicero *m.*

butcher's (shop) *n* carnicería *f.*

butler *n* mayordomo *m.*

butter *n* mantequilla *f.*

buttercup *n* (*bot*) ranúnculo *m.*

butterfly *n* mariposa *f.*

buttocks *npl* posaderas *fpl.*

button *n* botón *m.*

buttonhole *n* ojal *m.*

buttress *n* estribo *m*; apoyo *m.*

buxom *adj* frescachona.

buy *vt* comprar.

buzz *n* susurro, zumbido *m:—vi* zumbar.

buzzard *n* ratonero común *m.*

buzzer *n* timbre *m.*

by *prep* por; a, en; de; cerca, al lado de.

bypass *n* carretera de circunvalación *f.*

by-product *n* derivado *m.*

bystander *n* mirador *m.*

byte *n* (*comput*) byte *m.*

byword *n* proverbio, refrán *m.*

C

cab *n* taxi *m*.

cabbage *n* berza, col *f*.

cabin *n* cabaña.

cabinet *n* consejo á ministros *m*; gabinete *m*.

cable *n* (*mar*) cable *m*.

cable car *n* teleférico *m*.

cactus *n* cacto *m*.

cadet *n* cadete *m*.

cadge *vt* mangar.

café *n* café *m*.

cage *n* jaula *f*.

cake *n* bollo *m*; tortita *f*.

calculate *vt* calcular.

calculator *n* calculadora *f*.

calendar *n* calendario *m*.

calf *n* ternero *m*.

call *vt* llamar, nombrar.

calligraphy *n* caligrafía *f*.

callous *adj* calloso/sa.

calm *n* calma, tranquilidad.

calorie *n* caloría *f*.

Calvinist *n* calvinista *m*.

camel *n* camello *m*.

cameo *n* camafeo *m*.

camera *n* máquina fotográfica *f*.

camomile *n* manzanilla *f*.

camouflage *n* camuflaje *m*.

camp *n* campo *m*.

campaign *n* campana *f*.

camping *n* camping *m*.

campsite *n* camping *m*.

can *vi* poder:—*n* lata *f*.

canal *n* estanque *m*; canal *m*.

cancel *vt* cancelar; anular.

cancer *n* cáncer *m*.

Cancer *n* Cáncer *m* (signo del zodiaco).

candid *adj* cándido/da, sencillo/lla.

candle *n* candela *f*; vela *f*.

candlestick *n* candelero *m*.

candy *n* caramelo *m*.

cane *n* cana *f*; bastón *m*.

cannabis *n* canabis *f*.

cannibal *n* caníbal *m*.

cannibalism *n* canibalismo *m*.

cannon *n* cañón *m*.

canoe *n* canoa *f*.

canon *n* canon *m*; regla *f*.

can opener *n* abrelatas *m* invar.

canopy *n* dosel, pabellón *m*.

canteen *n* cantina *f*.

canter *n* medio galope *m*.

canvas *n* cañamazo *m*.

canyon *n* cañón *m*.

cap *n* gorra *f*.

capability *n* capacidad *f*.

capable *adj* capaz.

cape *n* cabo, promontorio *m*.

capital *adj* capital; principal.

capitalism *n* capitalismo *m*.

Capitol *n* Capitolio *m*.

capitulate *vi* capitular.

Capricorn *n* Capricornio *m* (signo del zodiaco).

capsule *n* cápsula *f*.

captain *n* capitán *m*.

captivate *vt* cautivar.

capture *n* captura *f*; presa *f*.

car *n* coche, carro *m*; vagón *m*.

carafe *n* garrafa *f*.

caramel *n* caramelo *m*.

carat *n* quilate *m*.

caravan *n* caravana *f*.

carbohydrates *npl* hidratos de carbono *mpl*.

carcass *n* cadáver *m*.

card *n* naipe *m*; carta *f*.

cardboard *n* cartón *m*.

cardinal *adj* cardinal, principal.

care *n* cuidado *m*; solicitud *f*.

career *n* carrera *f*.

caress *n* caricia *f*.

caretaker *n* portero *m*.

cargo *n* cargamento de navío *m*.

caricature *n* caricatura *f*.

carnal *adj* carnal; sensual.

carnation *n* clavel *m*.

carnival *n* carnaval *m*.

carpenter *n* carpintero *m*.

carpentry *n* carpintería *f*.

carpet *n* alfombra *f*.

carrier *n* portador *m*.

carrot *n* zanahoria *f*.

carry *vt* llevar, conducir.

cart *n* carro *m*; carreta *f*.

cartilage *n* cartílago *m*.

carton *n* caja *f*.

cartoon *n* dibujo animado *m*.

carve *vt* cincelar.

carving *n* escultura *f*.

case *n* caja *f*; maleta *f*.

cash *n* dinero contante *m*.

cashier *n* cajero *m*.

cashmere *n* cachemira *f*.

cask *n* barril, tonel *m*.

casserole *n* cazuela *f*.

cassette *n* cassette *m*.

cassock *n* sotana *f*.

castanets *npl* castañetas *fpl*.

castaway *n* réprobo *m*.

caste *n* casta *f*.

castigate *vt* castigar.
castle *n* castillo *m*.
castrate *vt* castrar.
castration *n* capadura *f*.
casual *adj* casual.
cat *n* gato *m*; gata *f*.
catalogue *n* catalogo *m*.
catapult *n* catapulta *f*.
cataract *n* cascada *f*; catarata *f*.
catarrh *n* catarro *m*; reuma *f*.
catastrophe *n* catástrofe *f*.
catch *vt* coger.
catchphrase *n* lema *m*.
catechism *n* catecismo *m*.
categorise *vt* clasificar.
category *n* categoría *f*.
caterpillar *n* oruga *f*.
cathedral *n* catedral *f*.
catholic *adj*, *n* católico *m*.
Catholicism *n* catolicismo *m*.
cattle *n* ganado *m*.
cauliflower *n* coliflor *f*.
cause *n* causa *f*; razón *f*; motivo *m*.
causeway *n* arrecife *m*.
caustic *adj*, *n* cáustico *m*.
cauterise *vt* cauterizar.
caution *n* prudencia.
cavalry *n* caballería *f*.
cave *n* caverna *f*.
caviar *n* caviar *m*.
cease *vt* parar, suspender.
cedar *n* cedro *m*.
cede *vt* ceder.
ceiling *n* techo *m*.
celebrate *vt* celebrar.
celery *n* apio *m*.
celibacy *n* celibato *m*.
cell *n* celdilla *f*; célula *f*; cueva *f*.
cellar *n* sótano *m*.
cellophane *n* celofán *m*.
cement *n* cemento.
cemetery *n* cementerio *m*.
cenotaph *n* cenotafio *m*.

censor *n* censor *m*.
census *n* censo *m*.
cent *n* centavo *m*.
centigrade *n* centígrado *m*.
centilitre *n* centilitro *m*.
centimetre *n* centímetro *m*.
centipede *n* escolopendra *f*.
central *adj* central.
centralise *vt* centralizar.
centre *n* centro *m*.
century *n* siglo *m*.
ceramic *adj* cerámico/ca.
ceremony *n* ceremonia *f*.
certain *adj* cierto/ta, evidente.
certificate *n* certificado, testimonio *m*.
certify *vt* certificar, afirmar.
cervical *adj* cervical.
chaffinch *n* pinzón *m*.
chain *n* cadena *f*.
chair *n* silla *f*.
chamber *n* cámara *f*.
chameleon *n* camaleón *m*.
champagne *n* champaña *m*.
championship *n* campeonato *m*.
chance *n* ventura, suerte *f*; oportunidad *f*.
chancellor *n* canciller *m*.
change *vt* cambiar.
channel *n* canal *m*.
chant *n* canto (llano) *m*.
chaos *n* caos *m*.
chapel *n* capilla *f*.
chaplain *n* capellán *m*.
chapter *n* capitulo *m*.
character *n* carácter *m*.
charcoal *n* carbón de leña *m*.
charge *vt* cargar; acusar, imputar.
charity *n* caridad.
charlatan *n* charlatán/tana *m*/*f*.
charm *n* encanto *m*.
charter flight *n* vuelo charter *m*.
chauffeur *n* chófer *m*.

chauvinist *n* machista *m*.
cheap *adj* barato/ta.
cheat *vt* engañar, defraudar.
checkmate *n* mate *m*.
checkout *n* caja *f*.
cheek *n* mejilla *f*.
cheese *n* queso *m*.
chef *n* jefe de cocina *m*.
chemical *adj* químico/ca.
chemist *n* químico *m*.
cheque *n* cheque *m*.
cheroot *n* puro *m*.
cherry *n* cereza *f*.
cherub *n* querubín *m*.
chess *n* ajedrez *m*.
chest *n* pecho *m*.
chestnut *n* castaña *f*.
chew *vt* mascar, masticar.
chewing gum *n* chicle *m*.
chicken *n* pollo *m*.
chickenpox *n* varicela *f*.
chickpea *n* garbanzo *m*.
chief *adj* principal.
chilblain *n* sabañón *m*.
child *n* niño *m*; niña *f*.
childhood *n* infancia, niñez *f*.
children *npl de* child niños *mpl*.
chimney *n* chimenea *f*.
chimpanzee *n* chimpancé *m*.
chin *n* barbilla *f*.
chiropodist *n* pedicuro *m*.
chirp *vi* chirriar.
chlorine *n* cloro *m*.
chloroform *n* cloroformo *m*.
chocolate *n* chocolate *m*.
choice *n* elección, preferencia *f*.
choir *n* coro *m*.
choke *vt* sofocar.
cholera *n* cólera *m*.
choose *vt* escoger, elegir.
chop *vt* tajar, cortar:—*n* chuleta *f*.
chore *n* faena *f*.
Christ *n* Cristo *m*.

christen *vt* bautizar.

Christianity *n* cristianismo *m*; cristiandad *f*.

Christmas *n* Navidad *f*.

chrome *n* cromo *m*.

chronicle *n* crónica *f*.

chronological *adj* cronológico/ca.

chubby *adj* gordo/da.

chunk *n* trozo *m*.

church *n* iglesia *f*.

churchyard *n* cementerio *m*.

cider *n* sidra *f*.

cigar *n* cigarro *m*.

cigarette *n* cigarrillo *m*.

cinder *n* carbonilla *f*.

cinema *n* cine *m*.

cinnamon *n* canela *f*.

circle *n* circulo *m*.

circumcise *vt* circuncidar.

circumcision *n* circuncisión *f*.

circumference *n* circunferencia *f*; circuito *m*.

circumflex *n* acento circunflejo *m*.

circumstance *n* circunstancia.

circus *n* circo *m*.

cistern *n* cisterna *f*.

cite *vt* citar.

citizen *n* ciudadano *m*.

city *n* ciudad *f*.

civic *adj* cívico/ca.

civil *adj* civil, cortés.

civilisation *n* civilización *f*.

clairvoyant *n* clarividente *m*/*f*.

clam *n* almeja *f*.

clammy *adj* viscoso/sa.

clamour *n* clamor *m*.

clan *n* familia, tribu, raza *f*.

clandestine *adj* clandestino/na.

clap *vt* aplaudir.

claret *n* clarete *m*.

clarify *vt* clarificar, aclarar.

clarinet *n* clarinete *m*.

clarity *n* claridad *f*.

class *n* clase *f*; orden *f*.

classic(al) *adj* clásico/ca:—*n* autor clásico *m*.

classify *vt* clasificar.

classmate *n* compañero de clase *m*.

classroom *n* aula *f*.

clause *n* cláusula *f*.

claw *n* garra *f*.

clay *n* arcilla *f*.

clean *adj* limpio/pia; casto/ta:—*vt* limpiar.

cleanse *vt* limpiar, purificar; purgar.

clear *adj* claro/ra.

clemency *n* clemencia *f*.

clement *adj* clemente, benigno/na.

clergy *n* clero *m*.

clerical *adj* clerical, eclesiástico/ca.

clerk *n* dependiente *m*; oficinista *m*.

clever *adj* listo/ta; hábil.

client *n* cliente *m*/*f*.

cliff *n* acantilado *m*.

climate *n* clima *m*.

climax *n* clímax *m*.

climb *vt* escalar, trepar.

cling *vi* colgar, adherirse.

clinic *n* clínica *f*.

clip *vt* cortar.

clique *n* camarilla *f*.

cloak *n* capa *f*.

cloakroom *n* guardarropa *m*.

clock *n* reloj *m*.

clog *n* zueco *m*.

cloister *n* claustro, monasterio *m*.

close *vt* cerrar; concluir, terminar.

closet *n* armario *m*.

close-up *n* primer plano *m*.

clot *n* grumo *m*; embolia *f*.

cloth *n* paño *m*.

clothe *vt* vestir.

clothes *npl* ropa *f*.

clothespin *n* pinza *f*.

cloud *n* nube *f*.

clout *n* tortazo *m*.

clove *n* clavo *m*.

clover *n* trébol *m*.

clown *n* payaso *m*.

coach *n* autocar, autobús *m*.

coagulate *vt* coagular, cuajar.

coal *n* carbón *m*.

coalition *n* coalición, confederación *f*.

coarse *adj* basto/ta; grosero/ra.

coast *n* costa *f*.

coastguard *n* guardacostas *m invar*.

coat *n* chaqueta *f*; abrigo *m*.

coat hanger *n* percha *f*.

cobbler *n* zapatero *m*.

cobweb *n* telaraña *f*.

cocaine *n* cocaína *f*.

cock *n* gallo *m*; macho *m*.

cockle *n* caracol de mar *m*.

cockpit *n* cabina *f*.

cockroach *n* cucaracha *f*.

cocktail *n* cóctel *m*.

cocoa *n* coco *m*; cacao *m*.

coconut *n* coco *m*.

cod *n* bacalao *m*.

code *n* código *m*.

cod-liver oil *n* aceite de hígado de bacalao *m*.

coffee *n* café *m*.

coffer *n* cofre *m*; caja *f*.

coffin *n* ataúd *m*.

cog *n* diente (de rueda) *m*.

cognac *n* coñac *m*.

cogwheel *n* rueda dentada *f*.

cohabit *vi* cohabitar.

coherence *n* coherencia *f*.

cohesion *n* coherencia *f*.

cohesive *adj* cohesivo.

coil *n* rollo *m*.

coin *n* moneda *f*.

coincide *vi* coincidir.

coke *n* coque *m*.

colander *n* colador, pasador *m*.

cold *adj* frío / ría.

cold sore *n* herpes labial *m*.

coleslaw *n* ensalada de col *f*.

colic *n* cólico *m*.

collaborate *vt* cooperar.

collapse *vi* hundirse.

collapsible *adj* plegable.

collar *n* cuello *m*.

collarbone *n* clavícula *f*.

collate *vt* comparar.

collateral *adj* colateral.

colleague *n* colega *m*.

collect *vt* recoger; coleccionar.

collection *n* colección *f*; compilación *f*.

college *n* colegio *m*.

collide *vi* chocar.

colloquial *adj* familiar.

collusion *n* colusión *f*.

colon *n* dos puntos *mpl*; (*med*) colon *m*.

colonel *n* (*mil*) coronel *m*.

colonial *adj* colonial.

colonise *vt* colonizar.

colony *n* colonia *f*.

colossal *adj* colosal.

colour *n* color *m*.

colt *n* potro *m*.

column *n* columna *f*.

columnist *n* columnista *m*.

coma *n* coma *f*.

comatose *adj* comatoso / sa.

comb *n* peine *m*:—*vt* peinar.

combat *n* combate *m*.

combination *n* combinación *f*.

combine *vt* combinar.

combustion *n* combustión *f*.

come *vi* venir.

comedy *n* comedia *f*.

comet *n* cometa *f*.

comfort *n* confort *m*.

comfortable *adj* cómodo / da.

comma *n* (*gr*) coma *f*.

command *vt* comandar.

commemorate *vt* conmemorar; celebrar.

commence *vt, vi* comenzar.

commencement *n* principio *m*.

commend *vt* encomendar.

commensurate *adj* proporcionado / da.

comment *n* comentario *m*.

commentator *n* comentador *m*.

commerce *n* comercio *m*.

commercial *adj* comercial.

commiserate *vt* compadecer.

commission *n* comisión *f*.

commit *vt* cometer.

committee *n* comité *m*.

commodity *n* comodidad *f*.

common *adj* común.

commotion *n* tumulto *m*.

communicate *vt* comunicar.

communion *n* comunión *f*.

communism *n* comunismo *m*.

community *n* comunidad *f*.

commute *vt* conmutar.

compact *adj* compacto / ta.

compact disc *n* disco compacto *m*.

companion *n* compañero / ra.

company *n* compañía, sociedad *f*.

compare *vt* comparar.

compartment *n* compartimiento *m*.

compass *n* brújula *f*.

compassion *n* compasión *f*.

compatriot *n* compatriota *m*.

compensate *vt* compensar.

compensation *n* compensación *f*.

compère *n* presentador *m*.

compete *vi* concurrir.

competent *adj* competente.

competition *n* competencia *f*.

competitor *n* competidor, rival *m*.

compilation *n* compilación *f*.

complain *vi* quejarse, lamentarse.

complement *n* complemento *m*.

complex *adj* complejo / ja.

complexion *n* tez *f*; aspecto *m*.

complicate *vt* complicar.

component *adj* componente.

compose *vt* componer.

composer *n* autor *m*.

composite *adj* compuesto / ta.

composition *n* composición *f*.

comprehend *vt* comprender, contener; entender.

compress *vt* comprimir.

comprise *vt* comprender.

compromise *n* compromiso *m*.

compulsive *adj* compulsivo / va.

computer *n* ordenador *m*.

comrade *n* camarada.

con *vt* estafar:—*n* estafa *f*.

concave *adj* cóncavo / va.

conceal *vt* ocultar, esconder.

concede *vt* conceder.

conceit *n* concepto *m*, capricho *m*.

conceive *vt* concebir, comprender.

concentrate *vt* concentrar.

concept *n* concepto *m*.

conception *n* concepción *f*.

concern *vt* concernir, importar.

concert *n* concierto *m*.

concession *n* concesión *f*; privilegio *m*.

concise *adj* conciso / sa.

conclude *vt* concluir.

conclusion *n* conclusión.

concord *n* concordia, armonía *f*.

concrete n concreto m.

concussion n concusión f.

condemn vt condenar.

condensation n condensación f.

condiment n condimento m; salsa f.

condition vt condicionar.

conditional adj condicional.

condom n condón m.

conduct n conducta f.

conductor n conductor m.

conduit n conducto m.

cone n cono m.

confection n confitura f.

confectioner's (shop) n pastelería f.

conference n conferencia f.

confess vt, vi confesar(se).

confession n confesión f.

confessional n confesionario m.

confetti n confeti m.

confidant n confidente.

confide vt, vi confiar; fiarse.

confidence n confianza, seguridad f.

confident adj cierto/ta, seguro/ra; confiado/da.

confine vt limitar; aprisionar.

confirm vt confirmar; ratificar.

confiscate vt confiscar.

conflagration n conflagración f.

conflict n conflicto m; combate m; pelea f.

conflicting adj contradictorio/ria.

confluence n confluencia f.

conform vt, vi conformar(se).

conformity n conformidad.

confound vt turbar, confundir.

confront vt afrontar; confrontar.

confrontation n enfrentamiento m.

confuse vt confundir.

congeal vt, vi helar, congelar(se).

congenial adj congenial.

congenital adj congénito/ta.

congested adj atestado/da.

congestion n congestión f; acumulación f.

congratulate vt congratular, felicitar.

congratulations npl felicidades fpl.

congratulatory adj congratulatorio/ria.

congregate vt congregar.

congress n congreso m; conferencia f.

congruity n congruencia f.

coniferous adj (bot) conífero/ra.

conjecture n conjetura.

conjugal adj conyugal.

conjugate vt (gr) conjugar.

conjunction n conjunción f.

conjuncture n coyuntura f.

conjure vi conjurar.

con man n timador m.

connect vt juntar, unir.

connection n conexión f.

connivance n connivencia f.

connive vi tolerar.

connoisseur n conocedor/a m/f.

conquer vt conquistar; vencer.

conqueror n vencedor/a, conquistador/a m/f.

conquest n conquista f.

conscience n conciencia f.

consciousness n conciencia f.

conscript n conscripto m.

conscription n reclutamiento m.

consecrate vt consagrar.

consecration n consagración f.

consecutive adj consecutivo/va.

consensus n consenso m.

consent n consentimiento m; aprobación f.

consequence n consecuencia f.

consequent adj consecutivo/va.

conservation n conservación f.

conservative adj conservativo/va.

conservatory n conservatorio m.

conserve vt conservar.

consider vt considerar.

considerable adj considerable.

considerate adj considerado/da.

consideration n consideración f.

consign vt consignar.

consignment n consignación f.

consist vi consistir.

consistency n consistencia f.

consistent adj consistente.

consolation n consolación f; consuelo m.

console vt consolar.

consolidate vt, vi consolidar(se).

consolidation n consolidación f.

consonant adj consonante.

consort n consorte, socio m.

conspicuous adj conspicuo/cua.

conspiracy n conspiración f.

conspirator n conspirador/a m/f.

conspire vi conspirar.

constancy n constancia.

constant adj constante.

constellation n constelación f.

constipated adj estreñido/da.

constituency *n* junta electoral *f*.

constituent *n* constitutivo *m*.

constitute *vt* constituir.

constitution *n* constitución *f*.

constitutional *adj* constitucional.

constrict *vt* constreñir, estrechar.

construct *vt* construir, edificar.

construction *n* construcción *f*.

consul *n* cónsul *m*.

consulate, consulship *n* consulado *m*.

consult *vt, vi* consultar(se).

consultation *n* consulta *f*.

consume *vt* consumir.

consumer *n* consumidor/a *m/f*.

consumption *n* consumo *m*.

contact *n* contacto *m*.

contact lenses *npl* lentes de contacto *mpl*.

contagious *adj* contagioso/sa.

contain *vt* contener.

container *n* recipiente *m*.

contaminate *vt* contaminar.

contamination *n* contaminación *f*.

contemplate *vt* contemplar.

contemplation *n* contemplación *f*.

contempt *n* desprecio, desdén *m*.

contend *vi* contender.

content *adj* contento/ta, satisfecho/cha.

contention *n* contención, altercación *f*.

contest *vt* contestar, disputar, litigar.

contestant *n* concursante/ta *m/f*.

context *n* contexto *m*.

continent *adj* continente.

contingency *n* contingencia *f*.

contingent *n* contingente *m*; cuota *f*.

continue *vt* continuar.

contort *vt* torcer.

contortion *n* contorsión *f*.

contour *n* contorno *m*.

contraband *n* contrabando *m*.

contraception *n* contracepción *f*.

contraceptive *n* anticonceptivo *m*.

contract *vt* contraer; abreviar; contratar.

contraction *n* contracción *f*; abreviatura *f*.

contradict *vt* contradecir.

contradiction *n* contradicción, oposición *f*.

contraption *n* artilugio *m*.

contrary *adj* contrario/ria, opuesto/ta.

contrast *n* contraste *m*.

contrasting *adj* opuesto/ta.

contributary *adj* contributario/ria.

contribute *vt* contribuir, ayudar.

contrive *vt* inventar, trazar.

control *n* control *m*; inspección *f*:—*vt* controlar; manejar; restringir; gobernar.

controversial *adj* polémico/ca.

controversy *n* controversia *f*.

conurbation *n* urbanización *f*.

convalesce *vi* convalecer.

convalescence *n* convalecencia *f*.

convene *vt* convocar; juntar, unir.

convenient *adj* conveniente.

convent *n* convento *m*.

convention *n* convención *f*.

converge *vi* converger.

conversation *n* conversación *f*.

converse *vi* conversar; platicar.

conversely *adv* mutuamente, recíprocamente.

convert *vt, vi* convertir(se).

convertible *adj* convertible.

convex *adj* convexo/xa.

convey *vt* transportar; transmitir, transferir.

conveyance *n* transporte *m*.

conveyancer *n* notario *m*.

conviction *n* convicción *f*.

convince *vt* convencer.

convivial *adj* sociable; hospitalario/ria.

convoke *vt* convocar, reunir.

convoy *n* convoy *m*.

convulse *vt* conmover, convulsionar.

convulsion *n* convulsión *f*.

convulsive *adj* convulsivo/va.

cook *n* cocinero *m*; cocinera *f*:—*vt* cocinar.

cool *adj* fresco/ca; indiferente.

cooperate *vi* cooperar.

cooperation *n* cooperación *f*.

coordinate *vt* coordinar.

coordination *n* coordinación *f*.

cop *n* (*fam*) poli *m*.

copier *n* copiadora *f*.

copious *adj* copioso/sa, abundante.

copper *n* cobre *m*.

copulate *vi* copularse.

copy *n* copia *f*.

copying machine *n* copiadora *f*.

coral *n* coral *m*.

cord *n* cuerda *f*; cable *m*.

cordial *adj* cordial.

corduroy *n* pana *f*.

core *n* cuesco *m*; interior *m*.

cork n alcornoque m; corcho m.

corkscrew n tirabuzón m.

corn n maíz m; grano m; callo m.

corncob n mazorca f.

cornea n córnea f.

corner n rincón m; esquina f.

cornet n corneta f.

cornflakes npl copos de maíz mpl.

cornice n cornisa f.

coronary n infarto m.

coronation n coronación f.

coroner n oficial que hace la inspección jurídica de los cadáveres m.

corporation n corporación f.

corps n cuerpo (de ejercito) m.

corpse n cadáver m.

correct vt corregir; enmendar.

correctness n exactitud f.

correspond vi corresponder.

correspondence n correspondencia f.

corridor n pasillo m.

corrode vt corroer.

corrosive adj, n corrosivo m.

corrupt vt corromper; sobornar.

corruption n corrupción f; depravación f.

corset n corsé m.

cosily adv cómodamente.

cosmetic adj cosmético/ca.

cosmic adj cósmico/ca.

cosmonaut n cosmonauta m.

cosmopolitan adj cosmopolita.

cosset vt mimar.

cost n coste, precio m:—vi costar.

costume n traje m.

cosy adj cómodo/da.

cottage n casita, casucha f.

cotton n algodón m.

cotton wool n algodón hidrófilo m.

couch n sofá m.

couchette n litera f.

cough n tos f:—vi toser.

council n concilio, consejo m.

counsel n consejo, aviso m.

count vt contar, numerar; calcular.

counter n mostrador m; ficha f.

counterfeit vt contrahacer, imitar, falsear.

counterpart n parte correspondiente f.

countersign vt refrendar.

countess n condesa f.

countless adj innumerable.

countrified adj rústico/ca.

country n país m; campo m; región f; patria f.

county n condado m.

coup n golpe m.

couple n par m.

couplet n copla f; par m.

coupon n cupón m.

courage n coraje, valor f.

courageous adj corajudo/da, valeroso/sa:—~ly adv valerosamente.

courier n correo, mensajero/ra m/f, expreso m.

course n curso m; carrera f; camino m; ruta f.

court n corte f.

courteous adj cortés.

courtesy n cortesía f.

courthouse n palacio de justicia m.

courtyard n patio m.

cousin n primo m; prima f.

cove n (mar) ensenada, caleta f.

covenant n contrato m.

cover n cubierta f; abrigo m.

cover letter n carta de explicación f.

covert adj cubierto/ta; oculto/ta, secreto/ta.

cover-up n encubrimiento m.

covet vt codiciar.

cow n vaca f.

coward n cobarde m/f.

cowardice n cobardía, timidez f.

cowboy n vaquero m.

cower vi agacharse.

cowherd n vaquero m.

crab n cangrejo m.

crab apple n manzana silvestre f.

crack n crujido m; hendedura, quebraja f.

cracker n buscapiés m invar; galleta f.

crackle vi crujir, chillar.

cradle n cuna f.

craft n arte.

craftsman n artífice, artesano m.

craftsmanship n artesanía f.

crafty adj astuto/ta, artificioso/sa.

cramp n calambre m.

cranberry n arandilla f.

crane n grulla f; grua f.

crash vi estallar.

crash helmet n casco m.

crass adj craso/sa.

crater n cráter m; boca de volcán f.

cravat n pañuelo m.

crave vt rogar, suplicar.

craving adj insaciable.

crawl vi arrastrar.

crayfish n cangrejo de río m.

crayon n lápiz m.

craze n manía f.

craziness n locura f.

crazy adj loco/ca.

cream n crema f.

creamy adj cremoso.

crease n pliegue m.

create vt crear; causar.

creation n creación f; elección f.

creator *n* creador/a *m/f.*
creature *n* criatura *f.*
credence *n* creencia, fe *f.*
credibility *n* credibilidad *f.*
credible *adj* creíble.
credit *n* crédito *m.*
creditable *adj* estimable.
credit card *n* tarjeta de crédito *f.*
creed *n* credo *m.*
creek *n* arroyo *m.*
creep *vi* arrastrar, serpear.
creeper *n* (*bot*) enredadera *f.*
cremate *vt* incinerar cadáveres.
cremation *n* cremación *f.*
crematorium *n* crematorio *m.*
crescent *adj* creciente.
cress *n* berro *m.*
crest *n* cresta *f.*
crevasse *n* grieta (de glaciar) *f.*
crevice *n* raja, hendedura *f.*
crew *n* banda, tropa *f.*
crib *n* cuna *f;* pesebre *m.*
cricket *n* grillo *m;* criquet *m.*
crime *n* crimen *m.*
criminal *adj* criminal.
crimson *adj, n* carmesí *m.*
cripple *n, adj* cojo/ja *m/f.*
crisis *n* crisis *f.*
crisp *adj* crujiente.
crispness *n* encrespadura *f.*
criss-cross *adj* entrelazado/da.
criterion *n* criterio *m.*
critic *n* crítico *m;* crítica *f.*
criticise *vt* criticar, censurar.
crochet *n* ganchillo *m.*
crockery *n* loza *fl.*
crocodile *n* cocodrilo *m.*
crook *n* (*fam*) ladrón *m.*
crooked *adj* torcido/da; perverso/sa.
cross *n* cruz *f.*
crossbar *n* travesaño *m.*

crossbreed *n* raza cruzada *f.*
cross-country *n* carrera a campo traviesa *f.*
crossing *n* cruce *m;* paso a nivel *m.*
cross-reference *n* contrarreferencia *f.*
crossroad *n* encrucijada *f.*
crotch *n* entrepierna *f.*
crouch *vi* agacharse, bajarse.
crow *n* cuervo *m.*
crowd *n* publico *m.*
crown *n* corona *f.*
crown prince *n* príncipe real *m.*
crucial *adj* crucial.
crucible *n* crisol *m.*
crucifix *n* crucifijo *m.*
crucifixion *n* crucifixión *f.*
crude *adj* crudo/da, imperfecto/ta.
cruel *adj* cruel.
cruelty *n* crueldad *f.*
cruet *n* vinagrera *f.*
cruiser *n* crucero *m.*
crumb *n* miga *f.*
crumble *vt* desmigajar.
crumple *vt* arrugar.
crunchy *adj* crujiente.
crusade *n* cruzada *f.*
crush *vt* apretar, oprimir.
crust *n* costra *f;* corteza *f.*
crutch *n* muleta *f.*
crux *n* lo esencial.
cry *vt, vi* gritar; exclamar; llorar.
crypt *n* cripta (bóveda subterránea) *f.*
cryptic *adj* enigmático/ca.
crystal *n* cristal *m.*
cub *n* cachorro *m.*
cube *n* cubo *m.*
cuckoo *n* cuclillo, cuco *m.*
cucumber *n* pepino *m.*
cuddle *vt* abrazar.
cudgel *n* garrote, palo *m.*
cue *n* taco (de billar) *m.*

cuff *n* puñada *f;* vuelta *f.*
cull *vt* escoger, elegir.
culminate *vi* culminar.
culpable *adj* culpable.
cult *n* culto *f.*
cultivate *vi* cultivar.
cultivation *n* cultivación *f.*
cultural *adj* cultural.
culture *n* cultura *f.*
cumulative *adj* cumulativo/va.
cunning *adj* astuto/ta; intrigante.
cup *n* taza, jícara *f;* (*bot*) cáliz *m.*
cupboard *n* armario *m.*
curable *adj* curable.
curb *n* freno *m;* bordillo *m.*
curd *n* cuajada *f.*
cure *n* cura *f;* remedio *m.*
curiosity *n* curiosidad *f;* rareza *f.*
curious *adj* curioso/sa:—**~ly** *adv* curiosamente.
curl *n* rizo de pelo *m.*
curly *adj* rizado/da.
currant *n* pasa *f.*
currency *n* moneda *f.*
current *adj* corriente.
current affairs *npl* actualidades *fpl.*
currently *adv* corrientemente; actualmente.
curriculum vitae *n* currículum *m.*
curry *n* curry *m.*
curse *vt* maldecir.
cursor *n* cursor *m.*
curt *adj* sucinto/ta.
curtail *vt* acortar.
curtain *n* cortina *f;* telón (en los teatros) *m.*
curvature *n* curvatura *f.*
curve *vt* encorvar:—*n* curva *f.*
cushion *n* cojín *m;* almohada *f.*

custard *n* natillas *fpl*.

custodian *n* custodio *m*.

custody *n* custodia *f*; prisión *f*.

custom *n* costumbre *f*, uso *m*.

customary *adj* usual, acostumbrado/da, ordinario/ria.

customer *n* cliente *m*/*f*.

customs *npl* aduana *f*.

customs duty *n* derechos de aduana *mpl*.

customs officer *n* aduanero/ra *m*/*f*.

cut *vt* cortar; separar.

cutback *n* reducción *f*.

cute *adj* lindo/da.

cutlery *n* cuchillería *f*.

cutlet *n* chuleta *f*.

cut-rate *adj* a precio reducido.

cut-throat *n* asesino *m*:—*adj* encarnizado/da.

cutting *n* cortadura *f*:—*adj* cortante; mordaz.

cyanide *n* cianuro *m*.

cycle *n* ciclo *m*; bicicleta *f*:—*vi* ir en bicicleta.

cycling *n* ciclismo *m*.

cyclist *n* ciclista *m*/*f*.

cyclone *n* ciclón *m*.

cygnet *n* pollo del cisne *m*.

cylinder *n* cilindro *m*; rollo *m*.

cylindric(al) *adj* cilíndrico/ca.

cymbals *n* címbalo *m*.

cynic(al) *adj* cínico/ca; obsceno/na: —*n* cínico *m* (*filósofo*).

cynicism *n* cinismo *m*.

cypress *n* ciprés *m*.

cyst *n* quiste *m*.

czar *n* zar *m*.

D

dad(dy) *n* papa *m*.
daddy-long-legs *n* típula *m*.
daffodil *n* narciso *m*.
dagger *n* puñal *m*.
daily *adj* diario/ria.
dainty *adj* delicado/da.
dairy *n* lechería *f*.
dairy produce *n* productos lácteos *mpl*.
daisy *n* margarita *f*.
damage *n* daño *m*; perjuicio *m*.
damask *n* damasco *m*.
damn *vt* condenar.
damnation *n* perdición *f*.
damp *adj* húmedo/da..
dampen *vt* mojar.
dampness *n* humedad *f*.
dance *n* danza *f*; baile *m*.
dandelion *n* diente de león *m*.
dandruff *n* caspa *f*.
danger *n* peligro *m*.
dare *vi* atreverse.
daredevil *n* atrevido *m*.
dark *adj* oscuro/ra.
darling *n*, *adj* querido *m*.
darn *vt* zurcir.
dart *n* dardo *m*.
dartboard *n* diana *f*.
dash *vi* irse de prisa.
dashboard *n* tablero de instrumentos *m*.
data *n* datos *mpl*.
database *n* base de datos *f*.
date *n* fecha *f*; cita *f*.
daughter *n* hija *f*:—~ in-law nuera *f*.
dawn *n* alba *f*:—*vi* amanecer.
day *n* día *m*.
dazzle *vt* deslumbrar.
deacon *n* diácono *m*.

dead *adj* muerto/ta.
deadline *n* fecha tope *f*.
deadlock *n* punto muerto *m*.
deaf *adj* sordo/da.
deal *n* convenio *m*; transacción *f*.
dean *n* deán *m*.
dear *adj* querido/da. caro/ra.
dearness *n* carestía *f*.
death *n* muerte *f*.
debacle *n* desastre *m*.
debar *vt* excluir.
debase *vt* degradar.
debate *n* debate *m*; polémica *f*.
debilitate *vt* debilitar.
debt *n* deuda *f*.
decade *n* década *f*.
decadence *n* decadencia *f*.
decaffeinated *adj* descafeinado/da.
decay *vi* decaer; pudrirse.
deceit *n* engaño *m*.
deceive *vt* engañar.
December *n* diciembre *m*.
decent *adj* decente.
decide *vt*, *vi* decidir; resolver.
deciduous *adj* (*bot*) de hoja caduca.
decimal *adj* decimal.
decipher *vt* descifrar.
decision *n* decisión.
declare *vt* declarar.
decline *vt* (*gr*) declinar; evitar.
decompose *vt* descomponer.
decorate *vt* decorar, adornar.
decoration *n* decoración *f*.
decorum *n* decoro *m*.

decrease *vt* disminuir.
decree *n* decreto *m*.
dedicate *vt* dedicar; consagrar.
dedication *n* dedicación *f*.
deduce *vt* deducir.
deep *adj* profundo/da.
deep-freeze *n* congeladora *f*.
deer *n* ciervo *m*.
defamation *n* difamación *f*.
defeat *n* derrota *f*:—*vt* derrotar.
defect *n* defecto *m*.
defend *vt* defender.
defence *n* defensa *f*.
defensive *adj* defensivo/va.
defer *vt* aplazar.
deficient *adj* insuficiente.
deficit *n* déficit *m*.
define *vt* definir.
definition *n* definición *f*.
deflate *vt* desinflar.
deflect *vt* desviar.
deform *vt* desfigurar.
defraud *vt* estafar.
defuse *vt* desactivar.
degenerate *vi* degenerar.
degrade *vt* degradar.
degree *n* grado *m*; titulo *m*.
dehydrated *adj* deshidratado/da.
deity *n* deidad, divinidad *f*.
dejection *n* desaliento *m*.
delay *vt* demorar:—*n* retraso *m*.
delegate *vt* delegar:—*n* delegado *m*.
delete *vt* tachar; borrar.
delicacy *n* delicadeza *f*.
delicate *adj* delicado/da.
delicious *adj* delicioso/sa.
delight *n* delicia *f*.

delinquent *n* delincuente *m*.

delirium *n* delirio *m*.

deliver *vt* entregar.

delivery *n* entrega *f*; parto *m*.

delude *vt* engañar.

deluge *n* diluvio *m*.

demagog(ue) *n* demagogo *m*.

demand *n* demanda *f*.

demean *vi* rebajarse.

demented *adj* demente.

demise *n* desaparición *f*.

democracy *n* democracia *f*.

democrat *n* demócrata *m*/*f*.

demolish *vt* demoler.

demon *n* demonio, diablo *m*.

demonstrate *vt* demostrar.

demoralise *vt* desmoralizar.

demote *vt* degradar.

demure *adj* modesto/ta.

den *n* guarida *f*.

denial *n* negación *f*.

denims *npl* vaqueros *mpl*.

denomination *n* valor *m*.

denote *vt* denotar.

denounce *vt* denunciar.

dense *adj* denso/sa.

density *n* densidad *f*.

dental *adj* dental.

dentist *n* dentista *m*/*f*.

denture *npl* dentadura postiza *f*.

denunciation *n* denuncia *f*.

deny *vt* negar.

deodorant *n* desodorante *m*.

depart *vi* partir(se).

department *n* departamento *m*.

department store *n* gran almacén *m*.

departure lounge *n* sala de embarque *f*.

depend *vi* depender.

depict *vt* pintar, retratar; describir.

deplore *vt* deplorar, lamentar.

deport *vt* deportar.

deposit *vt* depositar.

depositor *n* depositante *m*.

depot *n* depósito *m*.

deprave *vt* depravar.

depravity *n* depravación *f*.

deprecate *vt* lamentar.

depreciate *vi* depreciarse.

depreciation *n* depreciación *f*.

depress *vt* deprimir.

depressed *adj* deprimido/da.

depression *n* depresión *f*.

deprivation *n* privación *f*.

deprive *vt* privar.

depth *n* profundidad *f*.

deputation *n* diputación *f*.

deputise *vi* suplir a.

deputy *n* diputado *m*.

derelict *adj* abandonado/da.

deride *vt* burlar.

derision *n* mofa *f*.

derivative *n* derivado *m*.

derive *vt*, *vi* derivar(se).

derogatory *adj* despectivo/va.

descend *vi* descender.

descendant *n* descendiente *m*.

descent *n* descenso *m*.

describe *vt* describir.

description *n* descripción *f*.

descriptive *adj* descriptivo/va.

desecrate *vt* profanar.

desert *n* desierto *m*.

deserve *vt* merecer.

design *vt* diseñar.

designate *vt* nombrar.

designedly *adv* de propósito.

designer *n* diseñador *m*.

desirable *adj* deseable.

desire *n* deseo *m*.

desk *n* escritorio *m*.

desolate *adj* desierto/ta.

despair *n* desesperación *f*.

desperado *n* bandido *m*.

desperate *adj* desesperado/da.

despise *vt* despreciar.

despite *prep* a pesar de.

despoil *vt* despojar.

despondency *n* abatimiento *m*.

despot *n* déspota *m*/*f*.

dessert *n* postre *m*.

destination *n* destino *m*.

destine *vt* destinar.

destiny *n* destino *m*; suerte *f*.

destitute *adj* indigente.

destroy *vt* destruir.

destruction *n* destrucción.

detach *vt* separar.

detail *n* detalle *m*.

detain *vt* retener; detener.

detect *vt* detectar.

detection *n* descubrimiento *m*.

detective *n* detective *m*/*f*.

deter *vt* disuadir.

detergent *n* detergente *m*.

deteriorate *vt* deteriorar.

determination *n* resolución *f*.

determine *vt* determinar.

deterrent *n* fuerza de disuasión *f*.

detest *vt* detestar.

detonate *vi* detonar.

detonation *n* detonación *f*.

detour *n* desviación *f*.

detriment *n* perjuicio *m*.

devaluation *n* devaluación *f*.

devastate *vt* devastar.

develop *vt* desarrollar.

development *n* desarrollo *m*.

deviate *vi* desviarse.

deviation *n* desviación *f*.

device *n* mecanismo *m*.

devil *n* diablo, demonio *m*.

devious *adj* taimado/da.

devise *vt* inventar.

devote *vt* dedicar.

devour *vt* devorar.

devout *adj* devoto/ta.

dew *n* rocío *m*.

dexterity *n* destreza *f*.

diabetes *n* diabetes *f*.

diabetic *n* diabético *m*.

diadem *n* diadema *f*.

diagnosis n (med) diagnosis f.
diagonal adj, n diagonal (f).
diagram n diagrama m.
dial n cuadrante m.
dialect n dialecto m.
dialogue n dialogo m.
diameter n diámetro m.
diamond n diamante m.
diaper n pañal m.
diaphragm n diafragma m.
diarrhoea n diarrea f.
diary n diario m.
dice npl dados mpl.
dictate vt dictar.
dictation n dictado m.
dictatorship n dictadura f.
diction n dicción f
dictionary n diccionario m.
didactic adj didáctico/ca.
die[1] vi morir.
die[2] n dado m.
diesel n diesel m.
diet n dieta f; régimen m.
differ vi diferenciarse.
difference n diferencia f.
different adj diferente.
difficult adj dificil.
dig vt cavar.
digest vt digerir.
digestion n digestión f.
digger n excavadora f.
digit n dígito m.
digital adj digital.
dignity n dignidad f.
dike n dique m.
dilate vt, vi dilatar(se).
dilemma n dilema m.
dilute vt diluir.
dim adj turbio/bia.
dimension n dimensión, extensión f.
diminish vt, vi disminuir(se).
dimple n hoyuelo m.
din n alboroto m.
dine vi cenar.
diner n restaurante (económico) m.

dinghy n lancha neumática f.
dingy adj sombrío/ria.
dinner n cena f.
dinosaur n dinosaurio m.
diocese n diócesis f.
dip vt mojar.
diphtheria n difteria f.
diploma n diploma m.
diplomacy n diplomacia f.
diplomat n diplomático/ca m/f.
dire adj calamitoso/sa.
direct adj directo/ta. * vt dirigir.
direction n dirección f.
directly adj directamente.
director n director/a m/f.
directory n guía f.
dirt n suciedad f.
disability n incapacidad f.
disabled adj minusválido/da.
disadvantage n desventaja f:—vt perjudicar.
disagree vi no estar de acuerdo.
disappear vi desaparecer.
disappoint vt decepcionar.
disapprove vt desaprobar.
disaster n desastre m.
disbelieve vt desconfiar.
discard vt descartar.
discern vt discernir, percibir.
discharge vt descargar; pagar (una deuda).
disciple n discípulo m.
discipline n disciplina f:—vt disciplinar.
disclose vi revelar.
disco n discoteca f.
discomfort n incomodidad f.
discontent n descontento m:—adj malcontento/ta.
discontinue vi interrumpir.
discord n discordia f.
discount n descuento m; rebaja f.

discover vt descubrir.
discreet adj discreto/ta.
discriminate vt distinguir.
discuss vt discutir.
discussion n discusión f.
disease n enfermedad f.
disembark vt, vi desembarcar.
disentangle vt desenredar.
disfigure vt desfigurar.
disgrace n ignominia f.
disgruntled adj descontento/ta.
disguise vt disfrazar.
disgust n aversión f:—vt repugnar.
dish n fuente f; plato m.
dishevelled adj desarreglado/da.
dishonest adj deshonesto/ta.
dishonesty n falta de honradez f.
dishonour n deshonra, ignominia f.
dishtowel n trapo de fregar m.
dishwasher n lavaplatos m.
disillusion vt desilusionar.
disillusioned adj desilusionado/da.
disincentive n freno m.
disinclination n aversión f.
disinclined adj reacio/cia.
disinfect vt desinfectar.
disinfectant n desinfectante m.
disinherit vt desheredar.
disintegrate vi disgregarse.
disinterested adj desinteresado/da.
disjointed adj inconexo/xa.
disk n disco, disquete m.
diskette n disco, disquete m.
dislike n aversión f.
dislocate vt dislocar.
dislocation n dislocación f.
dislodge vt, vi desalojar.
disloyal adj desleal.

disloyalty *n* deslealtad *f*.
dismal *adj* triste.
dismantle *vt* desmontar.
dismay *n* consternación *f*.
dismember *vt* despedazar.
dismiss *vt* despedir.
dismissal *n* despedida *f*.
disobedience *n* desobediencia *f*.
disobedient *adj* desobediente.
disobey *vt* desobedecer.
disorderly *adj* desarreglado/da.
disorganised *adj* desorganizado/da.
disorientated *adj* desorientado/da.
disown *vt* desconocer.
disparage *vt* despreciar.
disparaging *adj* despreciativo/va.
disparity *n* disparidad *f*.
dispassionate *adj* desapasionado/da.
dispatch *vt* enviar.
dispel *vt* disipar.
dispensary *n* dispensario *m*.
dispense *vt* dispensar; distribuir.
disperse *vt* disipersar.
dispirited *adj* desalentado/da.
displace *vt* desplazar.
display *vt* exponer.
displeased *adj* disgustado/da.
displeasure *n* disgusto *m*.
disposable *adj* desechable.
disposal *n* disposición *f*.
dispose *vt* disponer; arreglar.
disposition *n* disposición *f*.
dispossess *vt* desposeer.
disproportionate *adj* desproporcionado/da.
disprove *vt* refutar.
dispute *n* disputa, controversia *f*.
disqualify *vt* incapacitar.

disregard *vt* desatender:—*n* desdén *m*.
disreputable *adj* de mala fama.
disrespectful *adj* irreverente.
disrobe *vt* desnudar.
disrupt *vt* interrumpir.
disruption *n* interrupción *f*.
dissatisfaction *n* descontento/ta.
dissatisfied *adj* insatisfecho/cha.
dissect *vt* disecar.
dissection *n* disección.
dissent *vi* disentir.
dissertation *n* disertación *f*.
dissident *n* disidente *m*.
dissimilar *adj* distinto.
dissolution *n* disolución *f*.
dissolve *vt* disolver.
dissuade *vt* disuadir.
distance *n* distancia *f*:—**at a ~** de lejos:—*vt* apartar.
distant *adj* distante.
distillery *n* destilería *f*.
distinct *adj* distinto/ta.
distinction *n* distinción *f*.
distinctive *adj* distintivo/va.
distinguish *vt* distinguir.
distort *vt* retorcer.
distorted *adj* distorsionado/da.
distortion *n* distorción *f*.
distract *vt* distraer.
distracted *adj* distraído/da.
distraction *n* distracción *f*; confusión *f*.
distraught *adj* enloquecido/da.
distress *n* angustia *f*.
distribute *vt* distribuir, repartir.
distribution *n* distribución *f*.
district *n* distrito *m*.
disturb *vt* molestar.
disturbance *n* disturbio *m*.
disturbing *adj* inquietante.
disused *adj* abandonado/da.

ditch *n* zanja *f*.
ditto *adv* ídem.
diuretic *adj* (*med*) diurético/ca.
diver *n* buzo *m*.
diverge *vi* divergir.
diverse *adj* diverso/sa, diferente.
diversion *n* diversión *f*.
diversity *n* diversidad *f*.
divert *vt* desviar; divertir.
divide *vt* dividir:—*vi* dividirse.
divine *adj* divino/na.
divinity *n* divinidad *f*.
divorce *n* divorcio *m*.
DJ *n* pinchadiscos *m*.
do *vt* hacer, obrar.
docile *adj* dócil, apacible.
dockyard *n* (*mar*) astillero *m*.
doctor *n* médico/ca *m*/*f*.
doctrine *n* doctrina *f*.
document *n* documento *m*.
documentary *adj* documental.
doe *n* gama *f*:—**~ rabbit** coneja *f*.
dog *n* perro *m*.
do-it-yourself *n* bricolaje *m*.
doll *n* muñeca *f*.
dollar *n* dólar *m*.
dolphin *n* delfín *m*.
dome *n* cúpula *f*.
domestic *adj* doméstico/ca.
domesticity *n* domesticidad *f*.
domicile *n* domicilio *m*.
dominant *adj* dominante.
dominate *vi* dominar.
domineer *vi* dominar.
dominion *n* dominio *m*.
dominoes *npl* domino *m*.
donate *vt* donar.
donation *n* donación *f*.
donkey *n* asno, borrico *m*.
donor *n* donante *m*.
door *n* puerta *f*.
doorbell *n* timbre *m*.
doorman *n* portero *m*.
doormat *n* felpudo *m*.

dormouse n lirón m.

dose n dosis f.

dossier n expediente m.

dot n punto m.

dote vi adorar.

double adj doble.

doubly adj doblemente.

doubt n duda, sospecha f.

doubtful adj dudoso/sa.

doubtless adv sin duda.

dough n masa f.

douse vt apagar.

dove n paloma f.

dovecot n palomar m.

dowdy adj mal vestido/da.

down n plumón m; flojel m:—prep abajo.

downfall n ruina f.

downhearted adj desanimado/da.

downpour n aguacero m.

downtown adv al centro (de la ciudad).

dowry n dote f.

doze vi dormitar.

dozen n docena f.

dozy adj soñoliento/ta.

drab adj gris.

draft n borrador m; quinta f; corriente de aire f.

dragon n dragón m.

dragonfly n libélula f.

drain vt desaguar.

drake n ánade macho m.

drama n drama m.

dramatic adj dramático/ca.

dramatise vt dramatizar.

dramatist n dramaturgo/ga m/f.

drape vt cubrir.

drapes npl cortinas fpl.

drastic adj drástico/ca.

draw vt tirar; dibujar.

drawback n desventaja f.

drawer n cajón m.

drawing n dibujo m.

drawing room n salón m.

dread n terror, espanto m:—vt temer.

dreadful adj espantoso/sa.

dream n sueno m:—vi sonar.

drench vt empapar.

dress vt vestir:—n vestido m.

dresser n aparador m.

dressing gown n bata f.

dressing table n tocador m.

dressmaker n modista f.

dried adj seco/ca.

drill n taladro m.

drink vt, vi beber.

drinkable adj potable.

drip vi gotear.

drive vt manejar.

driver n conductor m.

driveway n entrada f.

drizzle vi lloviznar.

droop vi decaer.

drop n gota f.

drought n seguía f.

drown vt anegar.

drowsiness n somnolencia f.

drowsy adj soñoliento/ta.

drudgery n trabajo monótono m.

drug n droga f:—vt drogar.

drug addict n drogadicto m.

drugstore n farmacia f.

drum n tambor m:—vi tocar el tambor.

drummer n batería m.

drumstick n palillo de tambor m.

drunk adj borracho/cha.

drunkard n borracho m.

drunkenness n borrachera f.

dry adj seco/ca. * vt secar.

dry rot n podredumbre f.

dual adj doble.

dubbed adj doblado/da.

dubious adj dudoso/sa.

duck n pato m.

duckling n patito m.

dud adj estropeado/da.

due adj debido/da.

duel n duelo m.

duet n (mus) duo m.

dull adj lerdo/da. insípido/da.

duly adv debidamente; puntualmente.

dumb adj mudo/da.

dumbbell n pesa f.

dumbfounded adj pasmado/da.

dummy n maniquí m; imbécil m.

dumpling n bola de masa f.

dumpy adj gordito/ta.

dunce n zopenco m.

dune n duna f.

dung n estiércol m.

dungarees npl mono m.

dungeon n calabozo m.

dupe n bobo m.

duplicity n duplicidad f.

durability n durabilidad f.

durable adj duradero/ra.

duration n duración f.

during prep mientras, durante el tiempo que.

dusk n crepúsculo m.

dust n polvo m.

duster n plumero m.

dutch courage n valor fingido m.

duteous adj fiel, leal.

dutiful adj obediente.

duty n deber m; obligación f.

dwarf n enano m; enana f.

dwell vi habitar, morar.

dwelling n habitación f; domicilio m.

dwindle vi mermar, disminuirse.

dye vt teñir:—n tinte m.

dynamic adj dinámico/ca.

dynamite n dinamita f.

dynamo n dinamo f.

dynasty n dinastía f.

dysentery n disenteria f.

dyspepsia n (med) dispepsia f.

E

each *pn* cada uno, cada una.
eager *adj* entusiasmado/da.
eagle *n* águila *f.*
eaglet *n* aguilucho *m.*
ear *n* oreja *f.*
earache *n* dolor de oídos *m.*
eardrum *n* tímpano (del oído) *m.*
early *adj* temprano/na.
earn *vt* ganar; conseguir.
earnest *adj* serio/ria.
earth *n* tierra *f.*
earthenware *n* loza de barro *f.*
earthquake *n* terremoto *m.*
earthworm *n* lombriz *f.*
earthy *adj* sensual.
earwig *n* tijereta *f.*
ease *n* comodidad *f;* facilidad *f.*
easel *n* caballete *m.*
easily *adv* fácilmente.
east *n* este *m;* oriente *m.*
Easter *n* Pascua de Resurrección *f.*
easterly *adj* del este.
eastern *adj* del este, oriental.
easy *adj* fácil; cómodo/da.
easy chair *n* sillón *m.*
eat *vt* comer.
ebb *n* reflujo *m.*
ebony *n* ébano *m.*
eccentric *adj* excéntrico/ca.
echo *n* eco *m.*
eclectic *adj* ecléctico/ca.
eclipse *n* eclipse *m.*
ecology *n* ecología *f.*
economics *npl* economía *f.*
economy *n* economía *f.*
ecstasy *n* éxtasis *m.*

eczema *n* eczema *m.*
eddy *n* reflujo de agua *m.*
edge *n* filo *m.*
edict *n* edicto, mandato *m.*
edit *vt* dirigir; redactar.
edition *n* edición *f.*
editor *n* director *m.*
educate *vt* educar.
education *n* educación *f.*
eel *n* anguila *f.*
effect *n* efecto *m.*
effective *adj* eficaz.
effeminate *adj* afeminado/da.
effervescence *n* efervescencia *f.*
efficacy *n* eficacia *f.*
efficient *adj* eficaz.
effigy *n* efigie, imagen *f.*
effort *n* esfuerzo *m.*
egg *n* huevo *m.*
eggplant *n* berenjena *f.*
ego(t)ist *n* egoísta *m/f.*
eight *num* ocho.
eighteen *num* dieciocho.
eighth *adj* octavo.
eighty *num* ochenta.
either *pn* cualquiera.
eject *vt* expeler, desechar.
elastic *adj* elástico/ca.
elation *n* regocijo *m.*
elbow *n* codo *m.*
elder *n* saúco *m* (árbol):—*adj* mayor.
elect *vt* elegir.
election *n* elección *f.*
electrician *n* electricista *m/f.*
electricity *n* electricidad *f.*
elegance *n* elegancia *f.*
elegant *adj* elegante, delicado/da.

elegy *n* elegía *f.*
element *n* elemento *m.*
elephant *n* elefante *m.*
elevate *vt* elevar, alzar.
elevator *n* ascensor *m.*
eleven *num* once.
eleventh *adj* onceno, undécimo.
elf *n* duende *m.*
elicit *vt* sacar de.
eligible *adj* elegible.
eliminate *vt* eliminar, descartar.
elk *n* alce *m.*
elm *n* olmo *m.*
elocution *n* elocución *f.*
elongate *vt* alargar.
elope *vi* escapar, huir.
elopement *n* fuga *f.*
eloquence *n* elocuencia *f.*
else *pn* otro/ra.
elsewhere *adv* en otra parte.
elude *vt* eludir, evitar.
embargo *n* prohibición *f.*
embark *vt* embarcar.
embarrass *vt* avergonzar.
embarrassment *n* desconcierto *m.*
embassy *n* embajada *f.*
embed *vt* empotrar; clavar.
embellish *vt* hermosear.
embers *npl* rescoldo *m.*
embezzle *vt* desfalcar.
embitter *vt* amargar.
emblem *n* emblema *m.*
embrace *vt* abrazar.
embroider *vt* bordar.
embroil *vt* embrollar; confundir.
embryo *n* embrión *m.*

emerald *n* esmeralda *f*.
emerge *vi* salir, proceder.
emergency *n* emergencia *f*.
emery *n* esmeril *m*.
emigrant *n* emigrante *m*.
emigrate *vi* emigrar.
eminent *adj* eminente.
emission *n* emisión *f*.
emit *vt* emitir.
emotion *n* emoción *f*.
emperor *n* emperador *m*.
emphasis *n* énfasis *m*.
emphasise *vt* hablar con énfasis.
empire *n* imperio *m*.
employ *vt* emplear, ocupar.
employee *n* empleado *m*.
employer *n* patrón *m*; empresario *m*.
empress *n* emperatriz *f*.
empty *adj* vacío/cia.
emulate *vt* emular.
emulsion *n* emulsión *f*.
enable *vt* capacitar.
enact *vt* promulgar.
enamel *n* esmalte *m*.
enchant *vt* encantar.
enchanting *adj* encantador.
encircle *vt* cercar, circundar.
enclose *vt* cercar, circunvalar.
encore *adv* otra vez, de nuevo.
encounter *n* encuentro *m*.
encourage *vt* animar.
encouragement *n* estimulo, patrocinio *m*.
encroach *vt* usurpar.
encumber *vt* embarazar, cargar.
encyclopedia *n* enciclopedia *f*.
end *n* fin *m*.
endanger *vt* peligrar.
endear *vt* encarecer.
endeavour *vi* esforzarse; intentar.
endemic *adj* endémico/ca.
ending *n* conclusión.

endive *n* (*bot*) endibia *f*.
endless *adj* infinito/ta.
endorse *vt* endosar; aprobar.
endow *vt* dotar.
endure *vt* sufrir, soportar.
enemy *n* enemigo/ga.
energetic *adj* enérgico/ca.
energy *n* energía, fuerza *f*.
enforce *vt* hacer cumplir.
engine *n* motor *m*; locomotora *f*.
engineer *n* ingeniero *m*.
engrave *vt* grabar.
enhance *vt* aumentar.
enigma *n* enigma *m*.
enjoy *vt* gozar.
enjoyment *n* disfrute *m*; placer *m*.
enlarge *vt* engrandecer.
enlist *vt* alistar.
enliven *vt* animar.
enmity *n* enemistad *f*; odio *m*.
enormous *adj* enorme.
enough *adv* bastante; basta.
enrage *vt* enfurecer.
enrapture *vt* arrebatar.
enrich *vt* enriquecer.
enrol *vt* registrar.
enrolment *n* inscripción *f*.
ensign *n* (*mil*) bandera *f*.
enslave *vt* esclavizar.
ensue *vi* seguirse.
ensure *vt* asegurar.
entangle *vt* enmarañar.
enter *vt* entrar; admitir.
enterprise *n* empresa *f*.
entertain *vt* divertir; hospedar.
entertainer *n* artista *m*/*f*.
entertainment *n* entretenimiento, pasatiempo *m*.
enthralling *adj* cautivador.
enthusiasm *n* entusiasmo *m*.
entice *vt* tentar; seducir.
entire *adj* entero/ra, completo/ta.
entitle *vt* intitular; conferir algún derecho.

entity *n* entidad *f*.
entrance *n* entrada *f*.
entreat *vt* rogar, suplicar.
entrepreneur *n* empresario *m*.
entrust *vt* confiar.
entry *n* entrada *f*.
entwine *vt* entrelazar.
envelop *n* envolver.
envelope *vt* sobre *m*.
enviable *adj* envidiable.
environment *n* medio ambiente *m*.
environs *npl* vecindad *f*.
envisage *vt* prever; concebir.
envoy *n* enviado *m*.
envy *n* envidia.
ephemeral *adj* efímero/ra.
epic *adj* épico/ca.
epidemic *adj* epidémico/ca.
epilogue *n* epílogo *m*.
Epiphany *n* Epifanía *f*.
episcopacy *n* episcopado *m*.
episcopal *adj* episcopal.
episcopalian *n* anglicano *m*.
episode *n* episodio *m*.
epistle *n* epístola *f*.
epithet *n* epíteto *m*.
epoch *n* época *f*.
equal *adj* igual.
equalise *vt* igualar.
equality *n* igualdad, uniformidad *f*.
equally *adv* igualmente.
equate *vt* equiparar (con).
equation *n* ecuación *f*.
equator *n* ecuador *m*.
equatorial *adj* ecuatorial.
equestrian *adj* ecuestre.
equilibrium *n* equilibrio *m*.
equinox *n* equinoccio *m*.
equip *vt* equipar.
equipment *n* equipaje *m*.
equitable *adj* equitativo/va.
equity *n* equidad *f*.
equivalent *adj*, *n* equivalente *m*.
era *n* era *f*.

eradicate *vt* desarraigar.
eradication *n* extirpación *f*.
erase *vt* borrar.
eraser *n* goma de borrar *f*.
erect *vt* erigir; establecer.
ermine *n* armiño *m*.
erode *vt* erosionar.
erotic *adj* erótico/ca.
err *vi* vagar, errar.
errand *n* recado.
erratic *adj* errático/ca.
erroneous *adj* erróneo/nea.
error *n* error *m*.
erudite *adj* erudito/ta.
erupt *vi* entrar en erupción; hacer erupción.
eruption *n* erupción *f*.
escalate *vi* extenderse.
escalator *n* escalera móvil *f*.
escapade *n* travesura *f*.
escape *vt* evitar; escapar.
escapism *n* escapismo *m*.
escort *n* escolta *f*:—*vt* escoltar.
esoteric *adj* esotérico/ca.
especial *adj* especial.
essay *n* ensayo *m*.
essence *n* esencia *f*.
essential *n* esencia *f*:—*adj* esencial.
establish *vt* establecer.
establishment *n* establecimiento *m*.
estate *n* estado *m*.
esteem *vt* estimar, apreciar.
estimate *vt* estimar, apreciar.
estuary *n* estuario.
etch *vt* grabar al aguafuerte.
eternal *adj* eterno/na.
eternity *n* eternidad *f*.
ether *n* éter *m*.
ethical *adj* ético/ca.
ethics *npl* ética *f*.
ethnic *adj* étnico/ca.
ethos *n* genio *m*.
etiquette *n* etiqueta *f*.
etymology *n* etimología *f*.
Eucharist *n* Eucaristía *f*.

eulogy *n* elogio.
eunuch *n* eunuco *m*.
euphemism *n* eufemismo *m*.
evacuate *vt* evacuar.
evacuation *n* evacuación *f*.
evade *vt* evadir.
evaluate *vt* evaluar.
evangelical *adj* evangélico/ca.
evaporate *vt* evaporar.
evasion *n* evasión *f*.
evasive *adj* evasivo/va.
eve *n* víspera *f*.
even *adj* llano/na, igual; par, semejante:—*adv* aun; aun cuando, supuesto que; no obstante.
evening *n* tarde *f*.
event *n* acontecimiento, evento *m*.
eventuality *n* eventualidad *f*.
ever *adv* siempre.
every *adj* cada uno o cada una.
evict *vt* desahuciar.
eviction *n* desahucio *m*.
evidence *n* evidencia *f*.
evil *adj* malo/la, depravado/da.
evocative *adj* sugestivo/va.
evoke *vt* evocar.
evolution *n* evolución *f*.
evolve *vt*, *vi* evolucionar.
ewe *n* oveja *f*.
exacerbate *vt* exacerbar.
exact *adj* exacto/ta.
exacting *adj* exigente.
exaggerate *vt* exagerar.
exaggeration *n* exageración *f*.
exalt *vt* exaltar.
exaltation *n* exaltación.
examination *n* examen *m*.
examine *vt* examinar.
examiner *n* inspector/a *m/f*.
example *n* ejemplar *m*; ejemplo *m*.
excavate *vt* excavar.
excavation *n* excavación *f*.

exceed *vt* exceder.
exceedingly *adv* extremamente, en sumo grado.
excel *vt* sobresalir.
excellence *n* excelencia *f*.
excellent *adj* excelente.
except *vt* exceptuar, excluir:— **~(ing)** *prep* excepto, a excepción de.
exception *n* excepción, exclusión *f*.
exceptional *adj* excepcional.
excerpt *n* extracto *m*.
excess *n* exceso *m*.
excessive *adj* excesivo/va.
exchange *vt* cambiar; trocar.
exchange rate *n* tipo de cambio *m*.
excitability *n* excitabilidad *f*.
excitable *adj* excitable.
excite *vt* excitar; estimular.
excited *adj* emocionado/da.
excitement *n* estímulo *m*, excitación *f*.
exclaim *vi* exclamar.
exclamation *n* exclamación *f*.
exclamation mark *n* punto de admiración *m*.
exclamatory *adj* exclamatorio/ria.
exclude *vt* excluir; exceptuar.
exclusion *n* exclusión,*f*.
exclusive *adj* exclusivo/va.
excommunicate *vt* excomulgar.
excommunication *n* excomunión *f*.
excrement *n* excremento *m*.
excruciating *adj* atroz.
excursion *n* excursión *f*.
excusable *adj* excusable.
excuse *vt* disculpar.
execute *vt* ejecutar.
execution *n* ejecución *f*.
executioner *n* ejecutor/a.
executive *adj* ejecutivo/va.
executor *n* testamentario/ria, albacea *m/f*.

exemplary *adj* ejemplar.
exemplify *vt* ejemplificar.
exempt *adj* exento/ta.
exemption *n* exención *f.*
exercise *n* ejercicio *m.*
exercise book *n* cuaderno *m.*
exertion *n* esfuerzo *m.*
exhale *vt* exhalar.
exhaust *n* escape *m.*
exhausted *adj* agotado/da.
exhaustion *n* agotamiento *m.*
exhaustive *adj* comprensivo/
va.
exhibit *vt* exhibir; mostrar.
exhibition *n* exposición *f.*
exhilarating *adj* estimulante.
exhort *vt* exhortar, excitar.
exhume *vt* exhumar.
exile *n* destierro *m.*
exist *vi* existir.
existence *n* existencia *f.*
exit *n* salida *f.*—*vi* hacer mutis.
exit ramp *n* vía de acceso *f.*
exodus *n* éxodo *m.*
exonerate *vt* exonerar.
exhorbitant *adj* exorbitante.
exorcise *vt* exorcizar, conjurar.
exorcism *n* exorcismo *m.*
exotic *adj* exótico/ca.
expand *vt* extender, dilatar.
expatriate *vt* expatriar.
expect *vt* esperar.
expectant mother *n* mujer
encinta *f.*
expediency *n* conveniencia *f.*
expedition *n* expedición *f.*
expel *vt* expeler, desterrar.
expend *vt* expender.
expendable *adj* prescindible.
expenditure *n* gasto, desem-
bolso *m.*
expense *n* gasto *m*; coste *m.*
experience *n* experiencia *f*;
practica *f.*
experienced *adj* experimen-
tado/da.

experiment *n* experimento *m.*
expert *adj* experto/ta.
expertise *n* pericia *f.*
expiration *n* expiración *f.*
expire *vi* expirar.
explain *vt* explanar, explicar.
explanation *n* explanación,
explicación *f.*
expletive *adj* expletivo/va.
explicit *adj* explícito/ta.
explode *vt, vi* estallar, explotar.
exploit *vt* explotar.
exploitation *n* explotación *f.*
exploration *n* exploración *f.*
exploratory *adj* exploratorio/
ria.
explore *vt* explorar.
explorer *n* explorador *m.*
explosion *n* explosión *f.*
explosive *adj, n* explosivo *m.*
exponent *n* (*math*) exponente
m.
export *vt* exportar.
expose *vt* exponer; mostrar.
exposed *adj* expuesto/ta.
exposition *n* exposición *f.*
expostulate *vi* debatir, contender.
exposure *n* exposición *f.*
expound *vt* exponer.
express *vt* exprimir; representar.
expression *n* expresión *f.*
expressionless *adj* sin expresión (cara).
expressway *n* autopista *f.*
expulsion *n* explosión *f.*
expurgate *vt* expurgar.
exquisite *adj* exquisito/ta.
extend *vt* extender.
extension *n* extensión *f.*
extensive *adj* extenso/sa.
extent *n* extensión *f.*
extenuate *vt* extenuar.
exterior *adj, n* exterior *m.*
exterminate *vt* exterminar.

extermination *n* extermin-
ación *f.*
external *adj* externo/na.
extinct *adj* extinto/ta.
extinction *n* extinción *f.*
extinguish *vt* extinguir.
extinguisher *n* extintor *m.*
extol *vt* alabar, magnificar.
extort *vt* sacar por fuerza.
extortion *n* extorsión *f.*
extortionate *adj* excesivo/va.
extra *adv* extra.
extract *vt* extraer.
extracurricular *adj* extraescolar.
extradition *n* (*law*) extra-
dición *f.*
extramarital *adj* extra-
matrimonial.
extraneous *adj* extraño/ña.
extraordinary *adj* extraordina-
rio/ria.
extravagance *n* extravagancia *f.*
extravagant *adj* extravagante.
extreme *adj* extremo/ma.
extremist *adj, n* extremista
m/f.
extremity *n* extremidad *f.*
extrovert *adj, n* extrovertido
m.
exuberance *n* exuberancia *f.*
exuberant *adj* exuberante.
exult *vt* exultar.
exultation *n* exultación *f*; regocijo *m.*
eye *n* ojo *m*:—*vt* ojear, contemplar, observar.
eyeball *n* globo del ojo *m.*
eyebrow *n* ceja *f.*
eyelash *n* pestaña *f.*
eyelid *n* párpado *m.*
eyesight *n* vista *f.*
eyewitness *n* testigo ocular
m.
eyrie *n* aguilera *f.*

F

fabric *n* tejido *m*.
fabricate *vt* fabricar.
fabulous *adj* fabuloso/sa.
facade *n* fachada *f*.
face *n* cara, faz *f*; superficie *f*.
facet *n* faceta *f*.
facetious *adj* chistoso/sa.
facile *adj* fácil.
facilitate *vt* facilitar.
facility *n* facilidad *f*.
facsimile *n* facsímile *m*; telefax *m*.
fact *n* hecho *m*.
faction *n* facción *f*.
factor *n* factor *m*.
factory *n* fabrica *f*.
faculty *n* facultad *f*.
fad *n* moda , manía *f*.
fade *vi* decaer.
fail *vt* suspender, reprobar; fallar a.
failure *n* falta *f*; culpa *f*.
faint *vi* desmayarse, debilitarse.
faint-hearted *adj* cobarde.
fair *adj* hermoso/sa, bello/la; blanco/ca; rubio/bia; claro/ra, sereno/na; favorable; recto/ta, justo/ta; franco/ca: —*adv* limpio: —*n* feria *f*.
fairly *adv* justamente.
fairy *n* hada *f*.
faith *n* fe *f*; dogma de fe *m*.
faithfulness *n* fidelidad *f*.
fake *n* falsificación *f*.
falcon *n* halcón *m*.
fall *vi* caer(se).
fallacy *n* falacia.
fallible *adj* falible.
false *adj* falso/sa.
falsify *vt* falsificar.

fame *n* fama *f*.
famed *adj* celebrado/da, famoso/sa.
familiar *adj* familiar.
family *n* familia *f*.
famine *n* hambre *f*; carestía *f*.
famous *adj* famoso/sa.
fan *n* abanico *m*; aficionado *m*.
fanatic *adj*, *n* fanático *m*.
fanciful *adj* imaginativo/va.
fancy *n* fantasía, imaginación *f*.
fanfare *n* (*mus*) fanfarria *f*.
fang *n* colmillo *m*.
fantastic *adj* fantástico/ca.
fantasy *n* fantasía *f*.
far *adv* lejos.
faraway *adj* remoto/ta.
farce *n* farsa *f*.
fare *n* precio *m*; tarifa *f*.
farm *n* finca *f*, granja *f*.
farmer *n* estanciero *m*; granjero *m*.
fascinate *vt* fascinar, encantar.
fascism *n* fascismo.
fashion *n* moda *f*; forma.
fashionable *adj* a la moda.
fashion show *n* desfile de modelos *m*.
fast *vi* ayunar; *adv* rápidamente.
fasten *vt* abrochar.
fastidious *adj* fastidioso/sa.
fat *adj* gordo/da.
fatal *adj* fatal.
fate *n* hado, destino *m*.
fateful *adj* fatídico/ca.
father *n* padre *m*.
father-in-law *n* suegro *m*.

fatherland *n* patria *f*.
fathom *n* braza (medida) *f*.
fatigue *n* fatiga *f*.
fatty *adj* graso/sa.
fault *n* falta, culpa *f*.
fauna *n* fauna *f*.
faux pas *n* plancha *f*.
favour *n* favor.
favourite *n* favorito *m*.
fawn *n* cervato *m*.
fax *n* facsímil(e) *m*; telefax *m*.
fear *vi* temer:—*n* miedo *m*.
fearful *adj* medroso/sa, temeroso/sa.
feasible *adj* factible.
feast *n* banquete.
feat *n* hecho *m*.
feather *n* pluma *f*.
feature *n* característica *f*; rasgo *m*.
February *n* febrero *m*.
federal *adj* federal.
federalist *n* federalista *m*/*f*.
federation *n* federación *f*.
fed-up *adj* harto/ta.
fee *n* honorarios *mpl*.
feeble *adj* flaco/ca, débil.
feed *vt* nutrir; alimentar.
feedback *n* reacción *f*.
feel *vt* sentir; tocar.
feign *vt* inventar, fingir.
feline *adj* gatuno/na.
fellowship *n* compañerismo *m*.
felon *n* criminal *m*/*f*.
felony *n* crimen *m*.
felt *n* fieltro *m*.
female *n* hembra *f*:—*adj* femenino/na.
feminine *adj* femenino/na.

feminist *n* feminista *m*/*f*.
fence *n* cerca *f*; defensa *f*.
fennel *n* (*bot*) hinojo *m*.
fern *n* (*bot*) helecho *m*.
ferocious *adj* feroz.
ferret *n* hurón *m*.
ferry *n* barca de pasaje *f*.
fertile *adj* fértil, fecundo/da.
fester *vi* enconarse.
festival *n* fiesta *f*; festival *m*.
fetch *vt* ir a buscar.
fete *n* fiesta *f*.
fetus *n* feto *m*.
feud *n* riña, contienda *f*.
feudal *adj* feudal.
fever *n* fiebre *f*.
feverish *adj* febril.
few *adj* poco/ca.
fewer *adj* menor.
fewest *adj* los menos.
fiancé *n* novio *m*.
fiancée *n* novia *f*.
fib *n* mentira *f*.
fibre *n* fibra, hebra *f*.
fickle *adj* voluble.
fiction *n* ficción *f*.
fiddle *n* violín *m*; trampa *f*.
fidelity *n* fidelidad *f*.
field *n* campo *m*.
fieldmouse *n* ratón de campo *m*.
fierce *adj* fiero/ra, feroz.
fierceness *n* fiereza, ferocidad *f*.
fiery *adj* ardiente; apasionado/da.
fifteen *adj, n* quince.
fifteenth *adj, n* decimoquinto/ta.
fifth *adj, n* quinto/ta.
fiftieth *adj, n* quincuagésimo/ma.
fifty *adj, n* cincuenta.
fig *n* higo *m*.
fight *vt, vi* reñir; batallar; combatir.
fig-leaf *n* hoja de higuera *f*.

figurative *adj* figurativo/va.
figure *n* figura.
filament *n* filamento *m*.
fill *vt* llenar; hartar.
fillet *n* filete *m*.
filling station *n* estación de servicio *f*.
fillip *n* (*fig*) estimulo *m*.
filly *n* potra *f*.
film *n* película *f*; film *m*.
filter *n* filtro *m*.
filth(iness) *n* inmundicia, porquería *f*.
fin *n* aleta *f*.
final *adj* final, último/ma.
finalise *vt* concluir.
finance *n* fondos *mpl*.
financier *n* financiero *m*.
find *vt* hallar, descubrir.
finesse *n* sutileza *f*.
finger *n* dedo *m*.
fingernail *n* uña *f*.
finish *vt* acabar, terminar, concluir.
finite *adj* finito/ta.
fir *n* abeto *m*.
fire *n* fuego *m*; incendio *m*.
firearm *n* arma de fuego *f*.
firefly *n* luciérnaga *f*.
firewood *n* leña *f*.
fireworks *npl* fuegos artificiales *mpl*.
firm *adj* firme, estable.
firmament *n* firmamento *m*.
firmness *n* firmeza *f*.
first *adj* primero/ra.
fiscal *adj* fiscal.
fish *n* pez *m*.
fishbone *n* espina *f*.
fisherman *n* pescador *m*.
fishy *adj* (*fig*) sospechoso/sa.
fist *n* puño *m*.
fitness *n* salud *f*.
five *adj, n* cinco.
fix *vt* fijar.
fixation *n* obsesión *f*.

fizzy *adj* gaseoso/sa.
flabbergasted *adj* pasmado/da.
flabby *adj* blando/da.
flaccid *adj* flojo/ja.
flag *n* bandera *f*.
flagpole *n* asta de bandera *f*.
flagrant *adj* flagrante; notorio/ria.
flagship *n* navío almirante *m*.
flair *n* aptitud especial *f*.
flake *n* copo *m*.
flamboyant *adj* vistoso/sa.
flame *n* llama *f*.
flamingo *n* flamenco *m*.
flammable *adj* inflamable.
flank *n* ijada *f*.
flannel *n* franela *f*.
flare *vi* lucir, brillar.
flash *n* flash *m*.
flask *n* frasco *m*.
flat *adj* llano/na, plano/na.
flatness *n* llanura *f*.
flatten *vt* allanar.
flatter *vt* adular.
flattery *n* adulación *f*.
flatulence *n* (*med*) flatulencia *f*.
flaunt *vt* ostentar.
flavour *n* sabor *m*.
flavourless *adj* soso/sa.
flaw *n* falta *m*.
flawless *adj* sin defecto.
flax *n* lino *m*.
flea *n* pulga *f*.
fleck *n* mota *f*.
flee *vt* huir de.
fleece *n* vellón *m*.
fleet *n* flota *f*.
flesh *n* carne *f*.
flex *n* cordón *m*.
flexibility *n* flexibilidad *f*.
flexible *adj* flexible.
flight *n* vuelo *m*.
flight attendant *n* tripulante auxiliar *m*.

flimsy *adj* débil; fútil.

flinch *vi* encogerse.

fling *vt* lanzar.

flint *n* pedernal *m*.

flip *vt* arrojar.

flippant *adj* petulante.

flipper *n* aleta *f*.

flirt *vi* coquetear:—*n* coqueta *f*.

flirtation *n* coquetería *f*.

flock *n* manada *f*.

flog *vt* azotar.

flogging *n* tunda, zurra *f*.

flood *n* diluvio *m*; inundación *f*.

flooding *n* inundación *f*.

floodlight *n* foco *m*.

floor *n* suelo, piso *m*.

floorboard *n* tabla *f*.

flop *n* fracaso *m*.

floppy *adj* flojo/ja.

flora *n* flora *f*.

floral *adj* floral.

florescence *n* florescencia *f*.

florid *adj* florido/da.

florist *n* florista *m*/*f*.

florist's (shop) *n* florería *f*.

flotilla *n* (*mar*) flotilla *f*.

flounder *n* platija (pez de mar) *f*.

flour *n* harina *f*.

flourish *vi* florecer.

flout *vt* burlarse de.

flow *vi* fluir.

flower *n* flor *f*.

flowerbed *n* cuadro (en un jardín) *m*.

flowerpot *n* tiesto de flores *m*.

flowery *adj* florido/da.

fluctuate *vi* fluctuar.

fluctuation *n* fluctuación *f*.

fluency *n* fluidez *f*.

fluent *adj* fluido/da.

fluff *n* pelusa *f*.

fluid *adj*, *n* fluido/da *m*.

fluidity *n* fluidez *f*.

fluke *n* (*sl*) chiripa *f*.

fluoride *n* fluoruro *m*.

flurry *n* ráfaga *f*; agitación *f*.

flute *n* flauta *f*.

flutter *vi* revolotear; estar en agitación.

flux *n* flujo *m*.

fly *vt* pilotar; transportar:—*vi* volar.

flying saucer *n* platillo volante *m*.

foal *n* potro *m*.

foam *n* espuma *f*.

foamy *adj* espumoso/sa.

focus *n* foco.

fodder *n* forraje *m*.

foe *n* adversario/ria *m*/*f*, enemigo *m*.

fog *n* niebla *f*.

foggy *adj* nebuloso/sa.

fold *n* redil *m*; pliegue *m*.

folder *n* carpeta *f*.

folding *adj* plegable.

foliage *n* follaje *m*.

folio *n* folio *m*.

folk *n* gente *f*.

folklore *n* folklore *m*.

folk song *n* canción folklórica *f*.

follow *vt* seguir; acompañar.

follower *n* seguidor/a *m*/*f*.

following *adj* siguiente.

folly *n* extravagancia *f*.

foment *vt* fomentar.

fond *adj* cariñoso/sa.

fondle *vt* acariciar.

fondness *n* gusto *m*; cariño *m*.

font *n* pila bautismal *f*.

food *n* comida *f*.

food mixer *n* batidora *f*.

food poisoning *n* botulismo *m*.

fool *n* loco/ca, tonto/ta *m*/*f*.

foolish *adj* bobo/ba, tonto/ta.

foolscap *n* papel tamaño folio *m*.

foot *n* pie *m*; pata *f*.

footage *n* imágenes *fpl*.

football *n* balón *m*; fútbol *m*.

footballer *n* futbolista *m*/*f*.

footnote *n* nota de pie *f*.

footpath *n* senda *f*.

footprint *n* huella *f*.

for *prep* por, a causa de; para.

forbid *vt* prohibir.

force *n* fuerza *f*; poder, vigor *m*.

forced *adj* forzado/da.

forceful *adj* enérgico/ca.

forceps *n* fórceps *m*.

ford *n* vado *m*.

fore *n*:—**to the ~** en evidencia.

forearm *n* antebrazo *m*.

foreboding *n* presentimiento *m*.

forecast *vt* pronosticar.

forecourt *n* patio *m*.

forefather *n* abuelo, antecesor *m*.

forefinger *n* índice *m*.

forefront *n*:—**in the ~ of** en la vanguardia de.

forego *vt* ceder.

foreground *n* delantera *f*.

forehead *n* frente *f*.

foreign *adj* extranjero/ra; extraño/ña.

foreigner *n* extranjero/ra, forastero/ra *m*/*f*.

foreign exchange *n* divisas *fpl*.

foreleg *n* pata delantera *f*.

foreman *n* capataz *m*.

foremost *adj* principal.

forensic *adj* forense.

forerunner *n* precursor/a *m*/*f*.

foresee *vt* prever.

foresight *n* previsión *f*.

forest *n* bosque *m*; selva *f*.

forester *n* guardabosque *m*.

forestry *n* silvicultura *f*.

foretaste *n* muestra *f*.

foretell *vt* predecir, profetizar.

forethought *n* providencia *f*.

forever *adv* para siempre.

foreword *n* prefacio *m*.

forfeit *n* confiscación *f*.

forge *n* fragua *f*; fabrica de metales *f*.

forger *n* falsificador/a *m*/*f*.

forgery *n* falsificación *f*.

forget *vt* olvidar.

forgetful *adj* olvidadizo/za.

forget-me-not *n* (*bot*) no-meolvides *m*.

forgive *vt* perdonar.

forgiveness *n* perdón *m*.

fork *n* tenedor *m*.

form *n* forma *f*; modelo *m*; modo *m*.

formal *adj* formal.

formality *n* formalidad *f*.

format *n* formato *m*.

formation *n* formación *f*.

formative *adj* formativo/va.

former *adj* precedente; anterior.

formidable *adj* formidable.

formula *n* fórmula *f*.

formulate *vt* formular.

forsake *vt* dejar.

fort *n* castillo *m*.

forthright *adj* franco/ca.

forthwith *adj* inmediata-mente.

fortieth *adj*, *n* cuadragésimo *m*.

fortification *n* fortificación *f*.

fortify *vt* fortificar.

fortitude *n* fortaleza *f*.

fortnight *n* quince días *mpl*.

fortress *n* (*mil*) fortaleza *f*.

fortuitous *adj* impensado/da.

fortunate *adj* afortunado/da.

fortune *n* fortuna, suerte *f*.

fortune-teller *n* sortílego/ga.

forty *adj*, *n* cuarenta.

forum *n* foro *m*.

forward *adj* avanzado/da; delantero/ra.

forwardness *n* precocidad *f*; audacia *f*.

fossil *adj*, *n* fósil *m*.

foster *vt* criar.

foul *adj* sucio/cia, puerco/ca; impuro/ra.

found *vt* fundar, establecer.

foundation *n* fundación *f*.

founder *n* fundador/a *m*/*f*.

foundling *n* niño expósito *m*, niña expósita *f*.

foundry *n* fundería *f*.

fount, fountain *n* fuente *f*.

fountainhead *n* origen de fuente *m*.

four *adj*, *n* cuatro.

fourfold *adj* cuádruple.

fourteen *adj*, *n* catorce.

fourteenth *adj*, *n* decimo-cuarto/ta.

fourth *adj*, *n* cuarto/ta:—*n* cuarto *m*: —**~ly** *adv* en cuarto lugar.

fowl *n* ave *f*.

fox *n* zorra *f*.

foyer *n* vestíbulo *m*.

fracas *n* riña *f*.

fraction *n* fracción *f*.

fracture *n* fractura *f*.

fragile *adj* frágil; débil.

fragility *n* fragilidad *f*.

fragment *n* fragmento *m*.

fragrance *n* fragancia *f*.

fragrant *adj* fragante, oloroso/sa.

frail *adj* frágil, débil.

frailty *n* fragilidad *f*; debilidad *f*.

frame *n* armazón *m*; marco, cerco *m*.

franchise *n* sufragio *m*.

frank *adj* franco/ca, liberal.

frankly *adv* francamente.

frantic *adj* frenético/ca.

fraternise *vi* hermanarse.

fraternity *n* fraternidad *f*.

fraud *n* fraude *m*.

fraudulent *adj* fraudulento/ta.

fraught *adj* cargado/da, lleno/na.

freak *n* fenómeno *m*.

freckle *n* peca *f*.

freckled *adj* pecoso/sa.

free *adj* libre; liberal; suelto/ta.

freedom *n* libertad *f*.

freehold *n* propiedad vitalicia *f*.

free-for-all *n* riña general *f*.

freelance *adj*, *adv* por cuenta propia.

freemason *n* francmasón *m*.

freemasonry *n* francmason-ería *f*.

freeway *n* autopista *f*.

freewheel *vi* ir en punto muerto.

freeze *vi* helar(se).

freezer *n* congeladora *f*.

freight *n* carga *f*; flete *m*.

freighter *n* fletador *m*.

frenzy *n* frenesí *m*; locura *f*.

frequency *n* frecuencia *f*.

fresco *n* fresco *m*.

fresh *adj* fresco/ca; nuevo/va.

freshly *adv* nuevamente.

freshman *n* novicio *m*.

freshwater *adj* de agua dulce.

fret *vi* agitarse.

friar *n* fraile *m*.

friction *n* fricción *f*.

Friday *n* viernes *m*:—**Good ~** Viernes Santo *m*.

friend *n* amigo *m*; amiga *f*.

friendship *n* amistad *f*.

frieze *n* friso *m*.

frigate *n* (*mar*) fragata *f*.

fright *n* espanto, terror *m*.

frighten *vt* espantar.

frigid *adj* frío/ría, frígido/da.

fringe *n* franja *f*.

frisk *vt* cachear.

frivolity *n* frivolidad *f*.

frock *n* vestido *m*.

frog *n* rana *f*.

frolic *vi* juguetear.

from *prep* de; después; desde.

front *n* parte delantera *f*; fachada *f*; paseo marítimo *m*; frente *m*.

frontal *adj* de frente.

frontier *n* frontera *f*.

frost *n* helada *f*; hielo *m*.

froth *n* espuma (de algún líquido) *f*.

frown *vt* mirar con ceño.

frozen *adj* helado/da.

fruit *n* fruta *f*; fruto *m*.

fruiterer *n* frutero *m*.

fruiterer's (shop) *n* frutería *f*.

fruit juice *n* jugo de fruta *m*.

fruitless *adj* estéril; inútil.

fruit salad *n* ensalada de frutas *f*.

fruit tree *n* frutal *m*.

frustrate *vt* frustrar; anular.

fry *vt* freír.

frying pan *n* sartén *f*.

fuchsia *n* (*bot*) fucsia *f*.

fuel *n* combustible *m*.

fuel tank *n* deposito *m*.

fugitive *adj*, *n* fugitivo *m*.

fulcrum *n* fulcro *m*.

fulfil *vt* cumplir; realizar.

fulfilment *n* cumplimiento *m*.

full *adj* lleno/na.

full moon *n* plenilunio *m*; luna llena *f*.

fulsome *adj* exagerado/da.

fumble *vi* manejar torpemente.

fume *vi* humear; encolerizarse.

fun *n* diversión *f*; alegría *f*.

function *n* función *f*.

functional *adj* funcional.

fund *n* fondo *m*.

fundamental *adj* fundamental.

funeral *n* funerales *mpl*.

fungus *n* hongo *m*; seta *f*.

funnel *n* embudo *m*.

funny *adj* divertido/da; curioso/sa.

fur *n* piel *f*.

furious *adj* furioso/sa.

furnace *n* horno *m*; hornaza *f*.

furnish *vt* amueblar.

furnishings *npl* muebles *mpl*.

furniture *n* muebles *mpl*.

furrow *n* surco *m*.

furry *adj* peludo/da.

furthermore *adv* además.

fury *n* furor *m*; furia *f*; ira *f*.

fuse *vt*, *vi* fundir; derretirse.

fuse box *n* caja de fusibles *f*.

fusion *n* fusión *f*.

fuss *n* lío *m*; alboroto *m*.

fussy *adj* jactancioso/sa.

futile *adj* fútil, frívolo/la.

futility *n* futilidad *f*.

future *adj* futuro/ra.

fuzzy *adj* borroso/sa; muy rizado/da.

G

gable *n* aguilón *m*.
gag *n* mordaza *f*; chiste *m*.
gaiety *n* alegría *f*.
gain *n* ganancia *f*.
gala *n* fiesta *f*.
galaxy *n* galaxia *f*.
gale *n* vendaval *m*.
gallant *adj* galante.
gallery *n* galería *f*.
gallon *n* galón *m* (medida).
gallop *n* galope *m*.
gallows *n* horca *f*.
galore *adv* en abundancia.
gambit *n* estrategia *f*.
gamble *vi* jugar; especular *f*.
gambler *n* jugador *m*.
game *n* juego *m*; pasatiempo *m*.
gamekeeper *n* guardabosques *m*.
gaming *n* juego *m*.
gammon *n* jamón *m*.
gander *n* ganso *m*.
gang *n* pandilla, banda *f*.
gangrene *n* gangrena *f*.
gangster *n* gangster *m*.
gangway *n* pasarela *f*.
gap *n* hueco *m*; claro *m*; intervalo *m*.
garage *n* garaje *m*.
garbage *n* basura *f*.
garden *n* jardín *m*.
gargoyle *n* gárgola *f*.
garish *adj* ostentoso/sa.
garland *n* guirnalda *f*.
garlic *n* ajo *m*.
garment *n* prenda *f*.
garnish *vt* guarnecer *m*.
garter *n* liga *f*.
gas *n* gas *m*; gasolina *f*.

gash *n* cuchillada *f*.
gasoline *n* gasolina *f*.
gasp *vi* jadear.
gastric *adj* gástrico/ca.
gastronomic *adj* gastronómico/ca.
gate *n* puerta *f*.
gateway *n* puerta *f*.
gather *vt* recoger.
gathering *n* reunión *f*.
gaudy *adj* chillón/ona.
gauge *n* calibre *m*.
gauze *n* gasa *f*.
gay *adj* alegre; vivo/va; gay.
gazelle *n* gacela *f*.
gazette *n* gaceta *f*.
gazetteer *n* gacetero *m*.
gear *n* atavío *m*; vestido *m*.
gearbox *n* caja de cambios *f*.
gel *n* gel *m*.
gelatin(e) *n* jaletina, jalea *f*.
gelignite *n* gelignita *f*.
gem *n* joya *f*.
Gemini *n* Géminis *m* (signo del zodiaco).
gender *n* género *m*.
gene *n* gen *m*.
genealogy *n* genealogía *f*.
general *adj* general, común.
generalise *vt* generalizar.
generation *n* generación *f*.
generic *adj* genérico/ca.
generosity *n* generosidad.
generous *adj* generoso/sa.
genetics *npl* genética *f*.
genial *adj* genial.
genitals *npl* genitales *mpl*.
genius *n* genio *m*.
genteel *adj* refinado, elegante.
gentile *n* gentil.

gentle *adj* suave.
gentleman *n* caballero *m*.
gentry *n* alta burguesía *f*.
gents *n* aseos *mpl*.
genuine *adj* genuino/na.
genus *n* genero *m*.
geographer *n* geógrafo/fa *m/f*.
geography *n* geografía *f*.
geology *n* geología *f*.
geometry *n* geometría *f*.
geranium *n* (*bot*) geranio *m*.
germ *n* (*bot*) germen *m*.
germinate *vi* brotar.
gesticulate *vi* gesticular.
gesture *n* gesto *m*.
get *vt* ganar; conseguir, obtener.
geyser *n* géiser *m m*.
ghastly *adj* espantoso/sa.
gherkin *n* pepinillo *m*.
ghost *n* fantasma *m*.
ghostly *adj* fantasmal.
giant *n* gigante *m*.
giddy *adj* vertiginoso/sa.
gift *n* regalo *m*.
giggle *vi* reírse tontamente.
gin *n* ginebra *f*.
ginger *n* jengibre *m*.
ginger-haired *adj* pelirrojo/ja.
giraffe *n* jirafa *f*.
girl *n* muchacha, chica *f*.
girlfriend *n* amiga *f*; novia *f*.
giro *n* giro postal *m*.
girth *n* cincha *f*; circunferencia *f*.
give *vt*, *vi* dar.
glacier *n* glaciar *m*.
glad *adj* alegre, contento/ta.

gladiator *n* gladiator *m*.

glamour *n* encanto*m*.

gland *n* glándula *f*.

glare *n* deslumbramiento *m*.

glass *n* vidrio.

glean *vt* espigar; recoger.

glee *n* alegría *f*; gozo *m*.

glib *adj* con poca sinceridad, elocuente pero falso.

glide *vi* resbalar.

glimmer *n* vislumbre *f*.

glimpse *n* vislumbre *f*.

glint *vi* centellear.

glisten, glitter *vi* relucir, brillar.

gloat *vi* ojear con admiración.

global *adj* mundial.

globe *n* globo *m*; esfera *f*.

gloom, gloominess *n* oscuridad *f*; melancolía.

glorify *vt* glorificar, celebrar.

glory *n* gloria, fama, celebridad *f*.

gloss *n* glosa *f*; lustre *m*.

glossary *n* glosario *m*.

glove *n* guante *m*.

glow *vi* arder; inflamarse; relucir.

glower *vi* mirar con ceño.

glue *n* cola *f*.

glum *adj* abatido/da, triste.

glut *n* hartura, abundancia *f*.

gluttony *n* glotonería *f*.

glycerine *n* glicerina *f*.

gnarled *adj* nudoso/sa.

gnash *vt, vi* rechinar; crujir los dientes.

gnat *n* mosquito *m*.

gnaw *vt* roer.

gnome *n* gnomo *m*.

go *vi* ir, irse.

goal *n* meta *f*; fin *m*.

goalkeeper *n* portero *m*.

gobble *vt* engullir, tragar.

go-between *n* mediador/a *m*/*f*.

goblet *n* copa *f*.

goblin *n* espíritu ambulante, duende *m*.

God *n* Dios *m*.

godchild *n* ahijado, hijo de pila *m*.

goddaughter *n* ahijada, hija de pila *f*.

goddess *n* diosa *f*.

godfather *n* padrino *m*.

godmother *n* madrina *f*.

godsend *n* don del cielo *m*.

godson *n* ahijado *m*.

goggle-eyed *adj* bizco/ca.

goggles *npl* anteojos *mpl*.

gold *n* oro *m*.

goldfish *n* pez de colores *m*.

gold-plated *adj* chapado/da en oro.

golf *n* golf *m*.

golf course *n* campo de golf *m*.

golfer *n* golfista *m*/*f*.

gondolier *n* gondolero/ra *m*/*f*.

gone *adj* ido/da; perdido/da; pasado/da; gastado/da; muerto/ta.

gong *n* atabal chino *m*.

good *adj* bueno/na.

goodbye ! *excl* ¿adiós!

Good Friday *n* Viernes Santo *m*.

good-looking *adj* guapo/pa.

goodness *n* bondad *f*.

goodwill *n* benevolencia, bondad *f*.

goose *n* ganso *m*; oca *f*.

gooseberry *n* grosella espinosa *f*.

gorge *n* barranco *m*.

gorgeous *adj* maravilloso/sa.

gorilla *n* gorila *m*.

gorse *n* aulaga *f*.

gory *adj* sangriento/ta.

goshawk *n* azor *m*.

gospel *n* evangelio *m*.

gossamer *n* vello *m*.

gossip *n* charla *f*.

gothic *adj* gótico/ca.

gout *n* gota *f* (enfermedad).

govern *vt* gobernar, dirigir.

governess *n* gobernadora *f*.

government *n* gobierno *m*.

governor *n* gobernador *m*.

gown *n* toga *f*.

grab *vt* agarrar.

grace *n* gracia.

graceful *adj* gracioso/sa.

gracious *adj* gracioso/sa.

gradation *n* gradación *f*.

grade *n* grado *m*.

gradient *n* (*rail*) pendiente.

gradual *adj* gradual.

graduate *vi* graduarse.

graduation *n* graduación *f*.

graffiti *n* pintadas *fpl*.

graft *n* injerto *m*.

grain *n* grano *m*.

gram *n* gramo *m* (peso).

grammar *n* gramática *f*.

granary *n* granero *m*.

grand *adj* grande, ilustre.

grandchild *n* nieto *m*; nieta *f*.

grandad *n* abuelo *m*.

granddaughter *n* nieta *f*.

grandeur *n* grandeza *f*.

grandfather *n* abuelo *m*.

grandiose *adj* grandioso/sa.

grandma *n* abuelita *f*.

grandmother *n* abuela *f*.

grandparents *npl* abuelos *mpl*.

grand piano *n* piano de cola *m*.

grandson *n* nieto *m*..

grandstand *n* tribuna *f*.

granite *n* granito *m*.

granny *n* abuelita *f*.

grant *vt* conceder.

granule *n* gránulo *m*.

grape *n* uva *f*:—**bunch of ~s** racimo de uvas *m*.

grapefruit *n* toronja *f*.

graph *n* gráfica *f*.

graphics *n* artes gráficas *fpl*; gráficos *mpl*.

grasp *vt* empuñar.

grass *n* hierba *f*.

grasshopper *n* saltamontes *m*.

grassland *n* pampa , pradera *f*.

grass snake *n* culebra *f*.

gratify *vt* contentar; gratificar.

gratifying *adj* grato/ta.

grating *n* rejado *m*.

gratis *adv* gratis.

gratitude *n* gratitud *f*.

grave *n* sepultura *f*.

gravel *n* cascajo *m*.

gravestone *n* piedra sepulcra *f*.

graveyard *n* cementerio *m*.

gravity *n* gravedad *f*.

gravy *n* jugo de la carne *f*; salsa *f*.

graze *vt* pastorear.

grease *n* grasa *f*:—*vt* untar.

greasy *adj* grasiento/ta.

great *adj* gran, grande.

greatcoat *n* sobretodo *m*.

greatness *n* grandeza *f*.

greedily *adv* vorazmente.

greediness, greed *n* gula *f*; codicia *f*.

Greek *n* griego (idioma) *m*.

green *adj* verde.

greengrocer *n* verdulero *m*.

greenhouse *n* invernadero *m*.

greet *vt* saludar, congratular.

greeting *n* saludo *m*.

greeting(s) card *n* tarjeta de felicitaciones *f*.

grenade *n* (*mil*) granada *f*.

grenadier *n* granadero *m*.

grey *adj* gris.

greyhound *n* galgo *m*.

greyish *adj* pardusco/ca.

grid *n* reja *f*; red *f*.

grief *n* dolor *m*.

grieve *vt* agraviar.

grievous *adj* doloroso/sa.

griffin *n* grifo *m*.

grill *n* parrilla *f*.

grim *adj* feo, fea.

grimace *n* visaje *m*.

grime *n* porquería *f*.

grin *n* mueca *f*.

grind *vt* moler.

grinder *n* molinero *m*.

grip *n* asimiento *m*.

grisly *adj* horroroso/sa.

gristle *n* tendón, nervio *m*.

grit *n* gravilla *f*; valor *m*.

groan *vi* gemir, suspirar.

grocer *n* tendero/ra, abarrotero/ra *m*/*f*.

groceries *npl* comestibles *mpl*.

groin *n* ingle *f*.

groom *n* establero *m*.

groove *n* ranura *f*.

gross *adj* grueso/sa.

grotesque *adj* grotesco/ca.

grotto *n* gruta *f*.

ground *n* tierra *f*.

ground floor *n* planta baja *f*.

group *n* grupo *m*..

grouse *n* urogallo *m*:—*vi* quejarse.

grove *n* arboleda *f*.

grovel *vi* arrastrarse.

grow *vt* cultivar:—*vi* crecer, aumentarse.

growl *vi* regañar, gruñir.

grown-up *n* adulto *m*.

grub *n* gusano *m*.

grubby *adj* sucio/cia.

grudge *n* rencor, odio *m*; envidia *f*:—*vt*, *vi* envidiar.

gruesome *adj* horrible.

gruff *adj* brusco/ca.

grumble *vi* gruñir; murmurar.

grunt *vi* gruñir.

G-string *n* taparrabo *m*.

guarantee *n* garantía *f*.

guard *n* guardia *f*.

guardianship *n* tutela *f*.

guerrilla *n* guerrillero *m*.

guess *vt*, *vi* conjeturar; adivinar; suponer.

guest *n* huésped/a.

guffaw *n* carcajada *f*.

guide *vt* guiar, dirigir:—*n* guía *m*.

guidebook *n* guía *f*.

guild *n* gremio *m*.

guile *n* astucia *f*.

guilt *n* culpabilidad *f*.

guilty *adj* reo, rea, culpable.

guinea pig *n* cobayo *m*.

guise *n* manera *f*.

guitar *n* guitarra *f*.

gulf *n* golfo *m*.

gull *n* gaviota *f*.

gullet *n* esófago *m*.

gullible *adj* crédulo/la.

gully *n* barranco *m*.

gulp *n* trago *m*.

gum *n* goma *f*.

gum tree *n* árbol gomero *m*.

gun *n* pistola *f*; escopeta *f*.

gunboat *n* cañonera *f*.

gunpowder *n* pólvora *f*.

gunshot *n* escopetazo *m*.

gurgle *vi* gorgotear.

guru *n* gurú *m*.

gush *vi* brotar.

gusset *n* escudete *m*.

gut *n* intestino *m*.

gutter *n* canalón *m*; arroyo *m*.

guy *n* tío *m*; tipo *m*.

gym(nasium) *n* gimnasio *m*.

gymnast *n* gimnasta *m*/*f*.

gynaecologist *n* ginecólogo/ga *m*/*f*.

gypsy *n* gitano/na *m*/*f*.

gyrate *vi* girar.

H

haberdasher *n* camisero/ra *m*/*f*.

habit *n* costumbre *f*.

habitable *adj* habitable.

habitat *n* hábitat *m*.

habitual *adj* habitual.

haddock *n* merlango *m*.

haemorrhage *n* hemorragia *f*.

haemorrhoids *npl* hemorroides *mpl*.

hag *n* bruja *f*.

hail *n* granizo *m*.

hair *n* pelo; cabello *m*.

hairbrush *n* cepillo *m*.

haircut *n* corte de pelo *m*.

hairdresser *n* peluquero *m*.

hairdryer *n* secador de pelo *m*.

hairspray *n* laca *f*.

hairstyle *n* peinado *m*.

half *n* mitad *f*.

half-caste *adj* mestizo/za.

hall *n* vestíbulo *m*.

hallow *vt* consagrar, santificar.

hallucination *n* alucinación *f*.

halo *n* halo *m*.

halt *vi* parar.

halve *vt* partir por mitad.

ham *n* jamón *m*.

hamburger *n* hamburguesa *f*.

hamlet *n* aldea *f*.

hammer *n* martillo *m*.

hammock *n* hamaca *f*.

hamper *n* cesto *f*.

hamstring *vt* desjarretar.

hand *n* mano *f*.

handbag *n* cartera *f*.

handful *n* puñado *m*.

handicap *n* desventaja *f*.

handicraft *n* artesanía *f*.

handkerchief *n* pañuelo *m*.

handle *n* mango, puño *m*; asa; manija *f*.

handshake *n* apretón de manos *m*.

handsome *adj* guapo/pa.

handwriting *n* letra *f*.

handy *adj* practico/ca.

hang *vt* colgar.

hanger *n* percha *f*.

hangover *n* resaca *f*.

happen *vi* pasar; acontecer.

happiness *n* felicidad *f*.

happy *adj* feliz.

harass *vt* cansar, fatigar.

harbinger *n* precursor *m*.

harbour *n* puerto *m*.

hard *adj* duro/ra, firme.

harden *vt, vi* endurecer(se).

hardiness *n* robustez *f*.

hardly *adv* apenas.

hardship *n* penas *fpl*.

hard-up *adj* sin plata.

hardy *adj* fuerte.

hare *n* liebre *f*.

hare-lipped *adj* labihendido/da.

haricot *n* alubia *f*.

harlequin *n* arlequín *m*.

harm *n* mal, daño *m*.

harmful *adj* perjudicial.

harmless *adj* inocuo/cua.

harmonic *adj* armónico/ca.

harmonious *adj* armonioso/sa.

harmonise *vt* armonizar.

harmony *n* armonía *f*.

harp *n* arpa *f*.

harpoon *n* arpón *m*.

harsh *adj* duro/ra; austero/ra.

harvest *n* cosecha *f*.

harvester *n* cosechadora *f*.

hash *n* hachís *m*.

hassock *n* cojín de paja *m*.

haste *n* apuro *m*.

hasten *vt* acelerar.

hasty *adj* apresurado/da.

hat *n* sombrero *m*.

hatch *vt* incubar; tramar*f*.

hatchet *n* hacha *f*.

hatchway *n* (*mar*) escotilla *f*.

hate *n* odio.

hateful *adj* odioso/sa.

hatred *n* odio, aborrecimiento *m*.

haughty *adj* altanero/ra, orgulloso/sa.

haul *vt* tirar:—*n* botín *m*.

hauler *n* transportista *m*/*f*.

haunch *n* anca *f*.

haunt *vt* frecuentar, rondar.

have *vt* haber; tener, poseer.

haven *n* asilo *m*.

havoc *n* estrago *m*.

hawk *n* halcón *m*.

hawthorn *n* espino blanco *m*.

hay *n* heno *m*.

hazard *n* riesgo *m*.

haze *n* niebla *f*.

hazel *n* avellano *m*.

hazelnut *n* avellana *f*.

hazy *adj* oscuro/ra.

he *pn* el.

head *n* cabeza *f*.

headache *n* dolor de cabeza *m*.

headlight *n* faro *m*.

headline *n* titular *m*.

headmaster *n* director *m*.

headphones *npl* auriculares *mpl*.

heal *vt, vi* curar.

health *n* salud *f*
healthy *adj* sano/na.
heap *n* montón *m*.
hear *vt* oír; escuchar.
hearing *n* oído *m*.
hearing aid *n* audífono *m*.
hearse *n* coche fúnebre *m*.
heart *n* corazón *m*.
heart attack *n* infarto *m*.
heartburn *n* acedia *f*.
hearth *n* hogar *m*.
heartily *adv* sinceramente.
heartless *adj* cruel.
hearty *adj* cordial.
heat *n* calor *m*.
heater *n* calentador *m*.
heathen *n* pagano *m*.
heating *n* calefacción *f*.
heatwave *n* ola de calor *f*.
heaven *n* cielo *m*.
heavily *adv* pesadamente.
heavy *adj* pesado/da.
Hebrew *n* hebreo *m*.
heckle *vt* interrumpir.
hectic *adj* agitado/da.
hedge *n* seto *m*.
hedgehog *n* erizo *m*.
heed *vt* hacer caso de.
heedless *adj* descuidado/da.
heel *n* talón *m*.
hefty *adj* grande.
heifer *n* ternera *f*.
height *n* altura *f*; altitud *f*.
heinous *adj* atroz.
heir *n* heredero/ra *m/f*.
heirloom *n* reliquia de familia *f*.
helicopter *n* helicóptero *m*.
hell *n* infierno *m*.
helm *n* (*mar*) timón *m*.
helmet *n* casco *m*.
help *vt, vi* ayudar, socorrer.
helper *n* ayudante *m*.
helpful *adj* útil.
helping *n* ración *f*.
helpless *adj* indefenso/sa.
hem *n* ribete *m*.

he-man *n* macho *m*.
hemisphere *n* hemisferio *m*.
hemp *n* cáñamo *m*.
hen *n* gallina *f*.
henchman *n* secuaz *m*.
henceforth, henceforward *adv* de aquí en adelante.
hepatitis *n* hepatitis *f*.
her *pn* su; ella; de ella; a ella.
herald *n* heraldo *m*.
heraldry *n* heráldica *f*.
herb *n* hierba *fl*.
herbaceous *adj* herbáceo/cea.
herbalist *n* herbolario *m*.
herbivorous *adj* herbívoro/ra.
herd *n* rebaño *m*.
here *adv* aquí, acá.
hereabout(s) *adv* aquí alrededor.
hereafter *adv* en el futuro.
hereby *adv* por esto.
hereditary *adj* hereditario/ria.
heresy *n* herejía *f*.
heretic *n* hereje *m/f*.
heritage *n* patrimonio *m*.
hermetic *adj* hermético/ca.
hermit *n* ermitaño/ña *m/f*.
hermitage *n* ermita *f*.
hernia *n* hernia *f*.
hero *n* héroe *m*.
heroic *adj* heroico/ca.
heroine *n* heroína *f*.
heroism *n* heroísmo *m*.
heron *n* garza *f*.
herring *n* arenque *m*.
herself *pn* ella misma.
hesitant *adj* vacilante.
hesitate *vt* dudar; tardar.
heterosexual *adj, n* heterosexual *m*.
hew *vt* tajar; cortar.
heyday *n* apogeo *m*.
hi *excl* ¿hola!
hiatus *n* (*gr*) hiato *m*.
hibernate *vi* invernar.
hiccup *n* hipo *m*.
hickory *n* noguera americana *f*.

hide *vt* esconder *f*.
hideaway *n* escondite *m*.
hideous *adj* horrible.
hierarchy *n* jerarquía *f*.
hieroglyphic *adj* jeroglífico/ca.
hi-fi *n* estéreo, hi-fi *m*.
high *adj* alto/ta; elevado/da.
highlight *n* punto culminante *m*.
highway *n* carretera *f*.
hike *vi* ir de excursión.
hijack *vt* secuestrar.
hilarious *adj* alegre.
hill, hillock *n* colina *f*.
him *pn* le, lo, el.
himself *pn* el mismo, se, si mismo.
hinder *vt* impedir.
hindrance *n* impedimento, obstáculo *m*.
hinge *n* bisagra *f*.
hip *n* cadera *f*.
hippopotamus *n* hipopótamo *m*.
hire *vt* alquilar.
his *pn* su, suyo, de el.
Hispanic *adj* hispano/na; hispánico/ca.
hiss *vt, vi* silbar.
historian *n* historiador *m*.
history *n* historia *f*.
hit *vt* golpear.
hitch *vt* atar.
hitch-hike *vi* hacer autostop.
hive *n* colmena *f*.
hoax *n* trampa *f*.
hobble *vi* cojear.
hobby *n* pasatiempo *m*.
hockey *n* hockey *m*.
hodge-podge *n* mezcolanza *f*.
hoe *n* azadón *m*.
hog *n* cerdo, puerco *m*.
hoist *vt* alzar.
hold *vt* tener; detener; contener.
hole *n* agujero *m*.
holiday *n* día de fiesta *m*:—
~**s** *pl* vacaciones *fpl*.

hollow *adj* hueco/ca.
holly *n* (*bot*) acebo *m.*
hollyhock *n* malva hortense *f.*
holocaust *n* holocausto *m.*
holster *n* pistolera *f.*
holy *adj* santo/ta.
holy week *n* semana santa *f.*
homage *n* homenaje *m.*
home *n* casa *f.*
home address *n* domicilio *m.*
homely *adj* casero/ra.
homoeopathist *n* homeopatista *m/f.*
homoeopathy *n* homeopatía *f.*
homesick *adj* nostálgico/ca.
homework *n* deberes *mpl.*
homicide *n* homicidio *m*; homicida *m.*
homosexual *adj, n* homosexual *m.*
honest *adj* honrado/da.
honesty *n* honradez *f.*
honey *n* miel *f.*
honeycomb *n* panal *m.*
honeymoon *n* luna de miel *f.*
honeysuckle *n* (*bot*) madreselva *f.*
honorary *adj* honorario/ria.
honour *n* honra *f*; honor *m*:— *vt* honrar.
hood *n* capo *m*; capucha *f.*
hoof *n* pezuña *f.*
hook *n* gancho *m.*
hooligan *n* gamberro *m.*
hoop *n* aro *m.*
hooter *n* sirena *f.*
hop *n* (*bot*) lúpulo.
hope *n* esperanza *f.*
horde *n* horda *f.*
horizon *n* horizonte *m.*
horizontal *adj* horizontal.
hormone *n* hormona *f.*
horn *n* cuerno *m.*
hornet *n* avispón *m.*
horny *adj* calloso/sa.

horoscope *n* horóscopo *m.*
horrendous *adj* horrendo/da.
horrible *adj* horrible.
horrid *adj* horrible.
horrific *adj* horroroso/sa.
horrify *vt* horrorizar.
horror *n* horror, terror *m.*
hors d'oeuvre *n* entremeses *mpl.*
horse *n* caballo *m*
horse chestnut *n* castaño de Indias *m.*
horsefly *n* moscarda *f.*
horseradish *n* rábano silvestre *m.*
horticulture *n* horticultura, jardinería *f.*
horticulturist *n* jardinero/ra *m/f.*
hosepipe *n* manga *f.*
hosiery *n* calcetería *f.*
hospital *n* hospital *m.*
hospitality *n* hospitalidad *f.*
host *n* anfitrión *m*; hostia *f.*
hostage *n* rehén *m.*
hostess *n* anfitriona *f.*
hostile *adj* hostil.
hot *adj* caliente; cálido/da.
hotbed *n* semillero *m.*
hotel *n* hotel *m.*
hotelier *n* hotelero/ra *m/f.*
hour *n* hora *f.*
hour-glass *n* reloj de arena *m.*
house *n* casa *f.*
household *n* familia *f.*
houseless *adv* sin casa.
housewife *n* ama de casa *f.*
hovel *n* choza, cabaña *f.*
hover *vi* flotar.
how *adv* cómo.
howl *vi* aullar.
hub *n* centro *m.*
hue *n* color *m.*
hug *vt* abrazar:—*n* abrazo *m.*
huge *adj* vasto/ta, enorme.
hum *vi* canturrear.

human *adv* humano/na.
humane *adv* humano/na.
humanist *n* humanista *m/f.*
humanitarian *adj* humanitario/ria.
humanity *n* humanidad *f.*
humble *adj* humilde.
humid *adj* húmedo/da.
humidity *n* humedad *f.*
humiliate *vt* humillar.
humming-bird *n* colibrí *m.*
humorist *n* humorista *m./f*
humorous *adj* gracioso/sa.
humour *n* sentido del humor *m.*
hundred *adj* ciento.
hundredth *adj* centésimo.
hundredweight *n* quintal *m.*
hunger *n* hambre *f.*
hunt *vt* cazar; perseguir.
hunter *n* cazador/a *m/f.*
hurdle *n* valla *f.*
hurricane *n* huracán *m.*
hurt *vt* hacer daño, ofender
hurtful *adj* dañoso/sa:—~ly *adv* dañosamente.
husband *n* marido *m.*
hush! *excl* ¡chitón!, ¡silencio!.
husk *n* cáscara *f.*
hut *n* cabaña *f.*
hutch *n* conejera *f.*
hyacinth *n* jacinto *m.*
hydraulic *adj* hidráulico/ca.
hydrofoil *n* aerodeslizador *m.*
hydrogen *n* hidroala *f.*
hyena *n* hiena *f.*
hygiene *n* higiene *f.*
hymn *n* himno *m.*
hypermarket *n* hipermercado *m.*
hyphen *n* (*gr*) guión *m.*
hypocrisy *n* hipocresía *f.*
hypocrite *n* hipócrita *m/f.*
hysterical *adj* histérico/ca.
hysterics *npl* histeria *f.*

I

I *pn* yo.
ice *n* hielo *m:*—*vt* helar.
ice cream *n* helado *m.*
ice rink *n* pista de hielo *f.*
icicle *n* carámbano *m.*
idea *n* idea *f.*
ideal *adj* ideal.
identical *adj* idéntico/ca.
identification *n* identificación *f.*
identify *vt* identificar.
identity *n* identidad *f.*
ideology *n* ideología *f.*
idiom *n* idioma *m.*
idiosyncrasy *n* idiosincrasia *f.*
idiot *n* idiota, necio *m.*
idiotic *adj* tonto/ta, bobo/ba.
idle *adj* desocupado/da.
idol *n* ídolo *m.*
idolatry *n* idolatría *f.*
idyllic *adj* idílico/ca.
i.e. *adv* esto es.
if *conj* si, aunque.
ignite *vt* encender.
ignoble *adj* innoble.
ignorance *n* ignorancia *f.*
ignorant *adj* ignorante.
ignore *vt* no hacer caso de.
ill *adj* malo/la, enfermo/ma.
ill-advised *adj* imprudente.
illegal *adj* ~ly *adv* ilegal-(mente).
illegible *adj* ilegible.
illegitimate *adj* ilegítimo/ma.
ill feeling *n* rencor *m.*
illiterate *adj* analfabeto/ta.

illness *n* enfermedad *f.*
illogical *adj* ilógico/ca.
illuminate *vt* iluminar.
illusion *n* ilusión *f.*
illustrate *vt* ilustrar.
illustration *n* ilustración *f.*
image *n* imagen *f.*
imagination *n* imaginación *f.*
imagine *vt* imaginarse.
imbalance *n* desequilibrio *m.*
imbecile *adj* imbécil.
imitate *vt* imitar, copiar.
imitation *n* imitación, copia *f.*
immaculate *adj* inmaculado/da.
immature *adj* inmaduro/ra.
immediate *adj* inmediato/ta.
immense *adj* inmenso/sa.
immigrant *n* inmigrante *m.*
immigration *n* inmigración *f.*
imminent *adj* inminente.
immodest *adj* inmodesto/ta.
immoral *adj* inmoral.
immortal *adj* inmortal.
immune *adj* inmune.
imp *n* diablillo, duende *m.*
impact *n* impacto *m.*
impair *vt* disminuir.
impartial *adj* ~ly *adv* imparcial(mente).
impatience *n* impaciencia *f.*
impede *vt* estorbar.
impel *vt* impeler.
impending *adj* inminente.

imperative *adj* imperativo/va.
imperfect *adj* imperfecto/ta
imperial *adj* imperial.
impersonal *adj,* ~ly *adv* impersonal-(mente).
impetus *n* ímpetu *m.*
impiety *n* irmpiedad *f.*
implant *vt* implantar.
implement *n* herramienta.
implore *vt* suplicar.
imply *vt* suponer.
impolite *adj* maleducado/da.
import *vt* importar.
importance *n* importancia *f.*
important *adj* importante.
impose *vt* imponer.
impostor *n* impostor *m.*
impotence *n* impotencia *f.*
impotent *adj* impotente.
impound *vt* embargar.
impoverish *vt* empobrecer.
impractical *adj* poco práctico/ca.
imprecise *adj* impreciso/sa.
impress *vt* impresionar.
impression *n* impresión *f;* edición *f.*
impressive *adj* impresionante.
imprint *n* sello *m:*—*vt* imprimir; estampar.
improbable *adj* improbable.
improper *adj* impropio/pia.
improve *vt, vi* mejorar.
improvise *vt* improvisar.
impulse *n* impulso *m.*
impure *adj* impuro/ra.
impurity *n* impureza *f.*
in *prep* en.
inability *n* incapacidad *f.*

inaccessible *adj* inaccesible.

inaccurate *adj* inexacto/ta.

inadequate *adj* inadecuado/da, defectuoso/sa.

inadmissible *adj* inadmisible.

inadvertently *adv* sin querer.

inappropriate *adj* impropio/pia.

inaudible *adj* inaudible.

inaugurate *vt* inaugurar.

in-between *adj* intermedio/dia.

inborn, inbred *adj* innato/ta.

incapable *adj* incapaz.

incarcerate *vt* encarcelar.

incarnation *n* encarnación *f*.

incendiary *n* bomba incendiaria *f*.

incense *n* incienso *m*.

incentive *n* incentivo *m*.

incessant *adj* incesante.

incest *n* incesto *m*.

inch *n* pulgada *f*.

incident *n* incidente *m*.

incinerator *n* incinerador *m*.

inclination *n* inclinación.

incline *vt, vi* inclinar(se).

include *vt* incluir.

inclusive *adj* inclusivo/va.

incognito *adv* de incógnito.

incoherent *adj* incoherente.

income *n* renta *f*

incompatible *adj* incompatible.

incompetence *n* incompetencia *f*.

incomplete *adj* incompleto/ta.

incomprehensible *adj* incomprensible.

inconceivable *adj* inconcebible.

incontinence *n* incontinencia *f*.

inconvenience *n* incomodidad *f*.

incorrect *adj* incorrecto/ta.

increase *vt* acrecentar, aumentar

incredible *adj* increíble.

incubate *vi* incubar.

incubator *n* incubadora *f*.

incurable *adj* incurable.

indecency *n* indecencia *f*.

indecent *adj* indecente:— ~ly *adv* indecentemente.

indecisive *adj* indeciso/sa.

indeed *adv* verdaderamente, de veras.

independence *n* independencia *f*.

independent *adj* independiente.

indescribable *adj* indescriptible.

index *n* índice *m*.

indicate *vt* indicar.

indifference *n* indiferencia *f*.

indigenous *adj* indígena.

indigestion *n* indigestión *f*.

indignation *n* indignación *f*.

indigo *n* añil *m*.

indirect *adj* indirecto/ta.

indiscreet *adj* indiscreto/ta.

indispensable *adj* indispensable.

indistinguishable *adj* indistinguible.

individual *adj* individual *m*.

indoors *adv* dentro.

indulge *vt, vi* conceder; ser indulgente.

industrialist *n* industrial *m*.

industry *n* industria *f*.

inedible *adj* no comestible.

ineffective, ineffectual *adj* ineficaz.

inefficiency *n* ineficacia *f*.

ineligible *adj* inelegible.

inept *adj* incompetente.

inequality *n* desigualdad *f*.

inevitable *adj* inevitable.

inexpensive *adj* económico/ca.

inexperience *n* inexperiencia *f*.

inexpert *adj* inexperto/ta.

inexplicable *adj* inexplicable.

infallible *adj* infalible.

infamy *n* infamia *f*.

infancy *n* infancia *f*.

infant *n* niño/ña *m/f*.

infantile *adj* infantil.

infantry *n* infantería *f*.

infatuation *n* infatuación *f*.

infect *vt* infectar.

infection *n* infección *f*.

inferior *adj* inferior.

infernal *adj* infernal.

inferno *n* infierno *m*.

infest *vt* infestar.

infidelity *n* infidelidad *f*.

infinite *adj* infinito/ta.

infinitive *n* infinitivo *m*.

infinity *n* infinito *m*; infinidad *f*.

infirm *adj* enfermo/ma.

infirmary *n* enfermería *f*.

infirmity *n* fragilidad, enfermedad *f*.

inflammation *n* inflamación *f*.

inflatable *adj* inflable.

inflate *vt* inflar, hinchar.

inflation *n* inflación *f*.

inflict *vt* imponer.

influence *n* influencia *f*.

influenza *n* gripe *f*.

inform *vt* informar.

informal *adj* informal.

information *n* información *f*.

infrastructure *n* infraestructura *f*.

infuriate *vt* enfurecer.

infusion *n* infusión *f*.

ingenious *adj* ingenioso/sa.

ingenuity *n* ingeniosidad *f*.

ingot *n* barra de metal *f*.

ingrained *adj* inveterado/da.

ingratitude *n* ingratitud *f*.

ingredient *n* ingrediente *m*.

inhabit *vt, vi* habitar.
inhabitant *n* habitante *m*.
inhale *vt* inhalar.
inherent *adj* inherente.
inherit *vt* heredar.
inheritance *n* herencia *f*.
inhibit *vt* inhibir.
inhospitable *adj* inhospitalario/ria.
inhuman *adj* inhumano/na.
inhumanity *n* inhumanidad, crueldad *f*.
initial *adj* inicial.
initiate *vt* iniciar.
initiative *n* iniciativa *f*.
inject *vt* inyectar.
injection *n* inyección *f*.
injure *vt* herir.
injury *n* daño *m*.
injustice *n* injusticia *f*.
ink *n* tinta *f*.
inkling *n* sospecha *f*.
inlaid *adj* taraceado/da.
in-laws *npl* suegros *mpl*.
inlay *vt* taracear.
inlet *n* entsenada *f*.
inmate *n* preso *m*.
inn *n* posada *f*; mesón *m*.
innkeeper *n* posadero/ra, mesonero/ra *m/f*.
innocence *n* inocencia *f*.
innocent *adj* inocente.
innovate *vt* innovar.
innovation *n* innovación *f*.
innuendo *n* indirecta, insinuación *f*.
inoffensive *adj* inofensivo/va.
inorganic *adj* inorgánico/ca.
inpatient *n* paciente interno *m*.
input *n* entrada *f*.
inquest *n* encuesta judicial *f*.
inquire *vt, vi* preguntar.
inquiry *n* pesquisa *f*.

inquisition *n* inquisición *f*.
inquisitive *adj* curioso/sa.
insane *adj* loco/ca, demente.
insanity *n* locura *f*.
inscription *n* inscripción *f*.
inscrutable *adj* inescrutable.
insect *n* insecto *m*.
insecticide *n* insecticida *m*.
insecure *adj* inseguro/ra.
insensitive *adj* insensible.
inseparable *adj* inseparable.
insert *vt* introducir.
insertion *n* inserción *f*.
inside *n* interior *m*:—*adv* dentro.
inside out *adv* al revés; a fondo.
insignia *npl* insignias *fpl*.
insignificant *adj* insignificante.
insincere *adj* poco sincero/ra.
insipid *adj* insípido/da.
insist *vi* insistir.
insole *n* plantilla *f*.
insolence *n* insolencia *f*.
insoluble *adj* insoluble.
insomnia *n* insomnio *m*.
insomuch *conj* puesto que.
inspect *vt* examinar, inspeccionar.
inspection *n* inspección *f*.
inspire *vt* inspirar.
instability *n* inestabilidad *f*.
instance *n* ejemplo *m*.
instant *adj* inmediato/ta.
instead (of) *pr* por, en lugar de, en vez de.
instil *vt* inculcar.
instinct *n* instinto *m*.
instinctive *adj* instintivo/va.
institute *vt* establecer:—*n* instituto *m*.
institution *n* institución *f*.
instruct *vt* instruir, enseñar.
instruction *n* instrucción *f*.
instrument *n* instrumento *m*.

instrumental *adj* instrumental.
insufferable *adj* insoportable.
insufficient *adj* insuficiente.
insulate *vt* aislar.
insulin *n* insulina *f*.
insult *vt* insultar:—*n* insulto *m*.
insurance *n* (*com*) seguro *m*.
insure *vt* asegurar.
intact *adj* intacto/ta.
integral *adj* íntegro/gra.
integrate *vt* integrar.
integrity *n* integridad *f*.
intellect *n* intelecto *m*.
intelligence *n* inteligencia *f*.
intend *vi* tener intención.
intense *adj* intenso/sa.
intensity *n* intensidad *f*.
intention *n* intención *f*.
inter *vt* enterrar.
interaction *n* interacción *f*.
intercourse *n* relaciones sexuales *fpl*.
interest *vt* interesar.
interesting *adj* interesante.
interest rate *n* tipo de interés *m*.
interfere *vi* entrometerse.
interference *n* interferencia *f*.
interior *adj* interior.
interlude *n* intermedio *m*.
intermediate *adj* intermedio/dia.
interment *n* entierro *m*; sepultura *f*.
intermission *n* descanso *m*.
intermittent *adj* intermitente.
internal *adj* interno/na.
international *adj* internacional.
interpret *vt* interpretar.
interpretation *n* interpretación *f*.
interpreter *n* intérprete *m/f*.
interregnum *n* interregno *m*.

interrelated *adj* interrelacionado/da.

interrogate *vt* interrogar.

interrogation *n* interrogatorio *m*.

interrogative *adj* interrogativo/va.

interrupt *vt* interrumpir.

interruption *n* interrupción *f*.

intersect *vi* cruzarse.

intersection *n* cruce *m*.

intersperse *vt* esparcir.

intertwine *vt* entretejer.

interval *n* intervalo *m*.

intervene *vi* intervenir.

intervention *n* intervención *f*.

interview *n* entrevista *f*.

interviewer *n* entrevistador/a *m*/*f*.

intestine *n* intestino *m*.

intimacy *n* intimidad *f*.

intimate *n* amigo/ga íntimo/ma.

intimidate *vt* intimidar.

into *prep* en, dentro, adentro.

intolerable *adj* intolerable.

intolerance *n* intolerancia *f*.

intoxicate *vt* embriagar.

intravenous *adj* intravenoso/sa.

intrepid *adj* intrépido/da.

intricate *adj* intricado/da.

intrigue *n* intriga *f*:—*vi* intrigar.

intriguing *adj* fascinante.

intrinsic *adj* intrínseco/ca.

introduce *vt* introducir.

introduction *n* introducción *f*.

introvert *n* introvertido *m*.

intrude *vi* entrometerse.

intruder *n* intruso/sa *m*/*f*.

intuition *n* intuición *f*.

intuitive *adj* intuitivo/va.

inundate *vt* inundar.

inundation *n* inundación *f*.

invade *vt* invadir.

invalid *adj* inválido/da.

invalidate *vt* invalidar, anular.

invaluable *adj* inapreciable.

invariable *adj* invariable.

invariably *adv* invariablemente.

invasion *n* invasión *f*.

invent *vt* inventar.

invention *n* invento *m*.

inventor *n* inventor *m*.

inventory *n* inventario *m*.

inversion *n* inversión *f*.

invert *vt* invertir.

invest *vt* invertir.

investigate *vt* investigar.

investment *n* inversión *f*.

invigilate *vt* vigilar.

invigorating *adj* vigorizante.

invincible *adj* invencible.

invisible *adj* invisible.

invitation *n* invitación *f*.

invite *vt* invitar.

invoice *n* (*com*) factura *f*.

involuntarily *adv* involuntariamente.

involve *vt* implicar.

involvement *n* compromiso *m*.

iodine *n* (*chem*) yodo *m*.

IOU (I owe you) *n* vale *m*.

irate, ireful *adj* enojado/da.

iris *n* iris *m*.

irksome *adj* fastidioso/sa.

iron *n* hierro *m*:—*adj* férreo/rea:—*vt* planchar.

ironic *adj* irónico/ca:—**~ly** *adv* con ironía.

ironwork *n* herraje *m*:—**~s** *pl* herrería *f*.

irony *n* ironía *f*.

irradiate *vt* irradiar.

irrational *adj* irracional.

irreconcilable *adj* irreconciliable.

irregular *adj* **~ly** *adv* irregular(mente).

irrelevant *adj* impertinente.

irreparable *adj* irreparable.

irresistible *adj* irresistible.

irresponsible *adj* irresponsable.

irrigate *vt* regar.

irrigation *n* riego *m*.

irritable *adj* irritable.

irritant *n* (*med*) irritante *m*.

irritate *vt* irritar.

island *n* isla *f*.

isle *n* isla *f*.

isolate *vt* aislar.

issue *n* asunto *m*.

it *pn* el, ella, ello, lo, la, le.

italic *n* cursiva *f*.

itch *n* picazón *f*:—*vi* picar.

item *n* artículo *m*.

itemise *vt* detallar.

itinerary *n* itinerario *m*.

its *pn* su, suyo.

itself *pn* el mismo, la misma, lo mismo.

ivory *n* marfil *m*.

ivy *n* hiedra *f*.

J, K

jab *vt* clavar.
jabber *vi* farfullar.
jack *n* gato *m*; sota *f*.
jackal *n* chacal *m*.
jackboots *npl* botas militares *fpl*.
jackdaw *n* grajo *m*.
jacket *n* chaqueta*f*.
jack-knife *vi* colear.
jackpot *n* premio gordo *m*.
jade *n* jade *m*.
jagged *adj* dentado/da.
jaguar *n* jaguar *m*.
jail *n* cárcel *f*.
jailer *n* carcelero/ra *m/f*.
jam *n* conserva *f*; mermelada de frutas *f*.
jangle *vi* sonar.
January *n* enero *m*.
jargon *n* jerigonza *f*.
jasmine *n* jazmín *m*.
jaundice *n* ictericia *f*.
jaunt *n* excursión *f*.
jaunty *adj* alegre.
javelin *n* jabalina *f*.
jaw *n* mandíbula *f*.
jay *n* arrendajo *m*.
jazz *n* jazz *m*.
jealous *adj* celoso/sa.
jealousy *n* celos *mpl*; envidia *f*.
jeans *npl* vaqueros *mpl*.
jeep *n* jeep *m*.
jeer *vi* befar.
jelly *n* jalea, gelatina *f*.
jellyfish *n* aguamar *m*; medusa *f*.
jeopardise *vt* arriesgar.
jersey *n* jersey *m*.
jest *n* broma *f*.

jester *n* bufón/ona *m/f*.
Jesuit *n* jesuita *m*.
Jesus *n* Jesús *m*.
jet *n* avión a reacción *m*
jettison *vt* desechar.
jetty *n* muelle *m*.
Jew *n* judío/día *m/f*.
jewel *n* joya *f*.
jewellery *n* joyería *f*.
Jewish *adj* judío/día.
jib *n* (*mar*) foque *m*.
jibe *n* mofa *f*.
jig *n* giga *f*.
jigsaw *n* rompecabezas *m*.
jilt *vt* dejar.
job *n* trabajo *m*.
jockey *n* jinete *m/f*.
jocular *adj* jocoso/sa, alegre.
jog *vi* hacer footing.
jogging *n* footing *m*.
join *vt* juntar, unir.
joiner *n* carpintero/ra *m/f*.
joinery *n* carpintería *f*.
joint *n* articulación *f*.
jointly *adv* conjuntamente.
joke *n* broma *f*:—*vi* bromear.
joker *n* comodín *m*.
jollity *n* alegría *f*.
jolly *adj* alegre.
jolt *vt* sacudir:—*n* sacudida *f*.
jostle *vt* codear.
journal *n* revista *f*.
journalism *n* periodismo *m*.
journalist *n* periodista *m/f*.
journey *n* viaje *m*:—*vt* viajar.
jovial *adj* jovial.
joy *n* alegría *f*; jubilo *m*.
jubilant *adj* jubiloso/sa.
jubilation *n* jubilo/la, regocijo *m*.

jubilee *n* jubileo *m*.
Judaism *n* judaísmo *m*.
judge *n* juez/a *m/f*:—*vt* juzgar.
judgment *n* juicio *m*.
judicial *adj* ~ly *adv* judicial-(mente).
judiciary *n* judicatura *m*.
judicious *adj* prudente.
judo *n* judo *m*.
jug *n* jarro *m*.
juggle *vi* hacer juegos malabares.
juggler *n* malabarista *m/f*.
juice *n* jugo *m*; suco *m*.
juicy *adj* jugoso/sa.
jukebox *n* gramola *f*.
July *n* julio *m*.
jumble *vt* mezclar.
jump *vi* saltar
jumper *n* suéter *m*.
jumpy *adj* nervioso/sa.
juncture *n* coyuntura *f*.
June *n* junio *m*.
jungle *n* selva *f*.
junior *adj* más joven.
juniper *n* (*bot*) enebro *m*.
junk *n* basura *f*; baratijas *fpl*.
junta *n* junta *f*.
jurisdiction *n* jurisdicción *f*.
jurisprudence *n* jurisprudencia *f*.
jurist *n* jurista *m/f*.
jury *n* jurado *m*.
just *adj* justo/ta.
justice *n* justicia *f*.
justification *n* justificación *f*.
justify *vt* justificar.
justly *adv* justamente.
justness *n* justicia *f*.
jut *vi*:—**to ~ out** sobresalir.

jute *n* yute *m*.

juvenile *adj* juvenil.

juxtaposition *n* yuxtaposición *f*.

kaleidoscope *n* calidoscopio *m*.

kangaroo *n* canguro *m*.

karate *n* karate *m*.

kebab *n* pincho *m*.

keel *n* (*mar*) quilla *f*.

keen *adj* agudo/da; vivo/va.

keep *vt* mantener; guardar; conservar.

keeper *n* guardián/ana *m*/*f*.

keepsake *n* recuerdo *m*.

keg *n* barril *m*.

kennel *n* perrera *f*.

kernel *n* fruta *f*; meollo *m*.

kerosene *n* kerosene *m*.

ketchup *n* catsup *m*.

kettle *n* hervidor *m*.

key *n* llave *f*; (*mus*) clave *f*; tecla *f*.

keyboard *n* teclado *m*.

keyhole *n* ojo de la cerradura *m*.

key ring *n* llavero *m*.

khaki *n* caqui *m*.

kick *vt*, *vi* patear.

kid *n* chico *m*.

kidnap *vt* secuestrar.

kidnapper *n* secuestrador/a *m*/*f*.

kidney *n* riñón *m*.

killer *n* asesino/na *m*/*f*.

killing *n* asesinato *m*.

kiln *n* horno *m*.

kilo *n* kilo *m*.

kilobyte *n* kiloocteto *m*.

kilogram *n* kilo *m*.

kilometre *n* kilómetro *m*.

kilt *n* falda escocesa *f*.

kin *n* parientes *mpl*.

kind *adj* cariñoso/sa:—*n* genero *m*.

kind-hearted *adj* bondadoso/sa.

kindle *vt*, *vi* encender.

kindly *adj* bondadoso/sa.

kindness *n* bondad *f*.

kindred *adj* emparentado/da.

kinetic *adj* cinético/ca.

king *n* rey *m*.

kingdom *n* reino *m*.

kingfisher *n* martín pescador *m*.

kiosk *n* quiosco *m*.

kiss *n* beso *m*:—*vt* besar.

kit *n* equipo *m*.

kitchen *n* cocina *f*.

kite *n* cometa *f*.

kitten *n* gatillo *m*.

knack *n* don *m*.

knapsack *n* mochila *f*.

knave *n* bribón

knead *vt* amasar.

knee *n* rodilla *f*.

kneel *vi* arrodillarse.

knell *n* toque de difuntos *m*.

knife *n* cuchillo *m*.

knight *n* caballero *m*.

knit *vt*, *vi* tejer.

knitting needle *n* aguja de tejer *f*.

knitwear *n* prendas de punto *fpl*.

knob *n* bulto *m*.

knock *vt*, *vi* golpear.

knocker *n* aldaba *f*.

knock-kneed *adj* patizambo/ba.

knock-out *n* K.O. *m*.

knoll *n* cima de una colina *f*.

knot *n* nudo *m*; lazo *m*:—*vt* anudar.

knotty *adj* escabroso/sa.

know *vt*, *vi* conocer; saber.

know-all *n* sabelotodo *m*/*f*.

know-how *n* conocimientos *mpl*.

knowing *adj* entendido/da:—~ly *adv* a sabiendas.

knowledge *n* conocimiento *m*.

knowledgeable *adj* bien informado/da.

knuckle *n* nudillo *m*.

L

label *n* etiqueta *f.*
laboratory *n* laboratorio *m.*
laborious *adj* laborioso/sa.
labour *n* trabajo *m.*
labourer *n* peón *m.*
labyrinth *n* laberinto *m.*
lace *n* cordón.
lacerate *vt* lacerar.
lack *vt, vi* faltar.
lacquer *n* laca *f.*
lad *n* muchacho *m.*
ladder *n* escalera *f.*
ladle *n* cucharón *m.*
lady *n* señora *f.*
lag *vi* quedarse atrás.
lager *n* cerveza (rubia) *f.*
lagoon *n* laguna *f.*
lake *n* lago *m.*
lamb *n* cordero *m*:—*vi* parir.
lame *adj* cojo/ja.
lament *vt, vi* lamentar(se).
lamp *n* lámpara *f.*
lampoon *n* sátira *f.*
lampshade *n* pantalla *f.*
lance *n* lanza *f.*
lancet *n* lanceta *f.*
land *n* país *m*; tierra *f.*
landing *n* desembarco *m.*
landmark *n* lugar conocido *m.*
landscape *n* paisaje *m.*
lane *n* callejuela *f.*
language *n* lengua *f*; lenguaje *m.*
lank *adj* lacio/cia.
lanky *adj* larguirucho.
lantern *n* linterna *f*; farol *m.*
lap *n* regazo *m.*
lapel *n* solapa *f.*
lapse *n* lapso *m.*

larceny *n* latrocinio *m.*
larch *n* alerce *m.*
lard *n* manteca de cerdo *f.*
larder *n* despensa *f.*
large *adj* grande.
lark *n* alondra *f.*
larva *n* larva, oruga *f.*
laryngitis *n* laringitis *f.*
larynx *n* laringe *f.*
lascivious *adj* lascivo/va.
laser *n* láser *m.*
lash *n* latigazo *m.*
lasso *n* lazo *m.*
last *adj* último/ma.
lasting *adj* duradero/ra, permanente.
latch *n* picaporte *m.*
late *adj* tarde; difunto/ta.
latent *adj* latente.
lathe *n* torno *m.*
lather *n* espuma *f.*
latitude *n* latitud *f.*
latter *adj* último/ma.
lattice *n* celosía *f.*
laugh *vi* reir.
laughter *n* risa *f.*
launch *vt, vi* lanzar(se):—*n* (*mar*) lancha *f.*
launching *n* lanzamiento *m.*
launder *vt* lavar.
laundry *n* lavandería *f.*
laurel *n* laurel *m.*
lava *n* lava *f.*
lavatory *n* water *m.*
lavender *n* (*bot*) espliego *m*, lavándula *f.*
lavish *adj* pródigo/ga:—~ly *adv* pródigamente:—*vt* disipar.
law *n* ley *f*; derecho *m.*

law court *n* tribunal *m.*
lawn *n* pasto *m.*
lawnmower *n* cortacésped *m.*
law suit *n* proceso *m.*
lawyer *n* abogado/da *m/f.*
laxative *n* laxante *m.*
lay *vt* poner.
layabout *n* vago/ga *m/f.*
layer *n* capa *f.*
layout *n* composición *f.*
laze *vi* holgazanear.
laziness *n* pereza *f.*
lazy *adj* perezoso/sa.
lead *n* plomo *m.*
leader *n* jefe/fa *m/f.*
leaf *n* hoja *f.*
leaflet *n* folleto *m.*
league *n* liga, alianza *f.*
leak *n* escape *m.*
lean *vt, vi* apoyar(se).
leap *vi* saltar
leap year *n* año bisiesto *m.*
learn *vt, vi* aprender.
lease *n* arriendo *m*:—*vt* arrendar.
leash *n* correa *f.*
least *adj* mínimo/ma.
leather *n* cuero *m.*
leave *n* licencia *f*; permiso *m.*
lecherous *adj* lascivo/va.
lecture *n* conferencia *f.*
ledge *n* reborde *m.*
ledger *n* (*com*) libro mayor *m.*
leech *n* sanguijuela *f.*
leek *n* (*bot*) puerro *m.*
left *adj* izquierdo/da.
left-handed *adj* zurdo/da.

leftovers *npl* sobras *fpl*.

leg *n* pierna *f*

legacy *n* herencia *f*.

legal *adj* legal.

legalise *vt* legalizar.

legend *n* leyenda *f*.

legendary *adj* legendario/ria.

legible *adj* legible.

legion *n* legión *f*.

legislate *vt* legislar.

legislation *n* legislación *f*.

leisure *n* ocio *m*:—**~ly** *adj* sin prisa: —**at ~** desocupado/da.

lemon *n* limón *m*.

lemonade *n* limonada *f*.

lend *vt* prestar.

length *n* largo *m*; duración *f*.

lenient *adj* indulgente.

lens *n* lente *f*.

Lent *n* Cuaresma *f*.

lentil *n* lenteja *f*.

leopard *n* leopardo *m*.

leotard *n* leotardo *m*.

leper *n* leproso/sa *m/f*.

leprosy *n* lepra *f*.

lesbian *n* lesbiana *f*.

less *adj* menor.

lesson *n* lección *f*.

let *vt* dejar, permitir.

lethal *adj* mortal.

lethargy *n* letargo *m*.

letter *n* letra *f*; carta *f*.

lettuce *n* lechuga *f*.

leukaemia *n* leucemia *f*.

level *adj* llano/na, igual.

lever *n* palanca *f*.

leverage *n* influencia *f*.

levy *n* leva (de tropas) *f*.

lexicon *n* léxico *m*.

liability *n* responsabilidad *f*.

liable *adj* sujeto/ta; responsable.

liaise *vi* enlazar.

liaison *n* enlace *m*.

liar *n* embustero *m*.

libel *n* difamación *f*:—*vt* difamar.

liberal *adj* liberal.

liberate *vt* libertar.

liberation *n* liberación *f*.

liberty *n* libertad *f*.

Libra *n* Libra *f*.

librarian *n* bibliotecario *m*.

library *n* biblioteca *f*.

licence *n* licencia *f*.

lick *vt* lamer.

lid *n* tapa *f*.

lie *n* mentira *f*.

life *n* vida *f*.

life jacket *n* chaleco salvavidas *m*.

lifelike *adj* natural.

lift *vt* levantar.

ligament *n* ligamento *m*.

light *n* luz *f*.

light bulb *n* foco *m*; bombilla *f*.

lighter *n* encendedor *m*.

lighthouse *n* (*mar*) faro *m*.

lightning *n* relámpago *m*.

like *adj* semejante; igual.

likeness *n* semejanza *f*.

lilac *n* lila *f*.

lily *n* lirio *m*.

limb *n* miembro *m*.

lime *n* cal *f*; lima *f*.

limestone *n* piedra caliza *f*.

limit *n* limite *m*.

line *n* línea *f*.

linen *n* lino *m*.

liner *n* transatlántico *m*.

linger *vi* persistir.

lingerie *n* ropa interior *f*.

linguist *n* lingüista *m*.

lining *n* forro *m*.

link *n* eslabón *m*.

linoleum *n* linóleo *m*.

lintel *n* dintel *m*.

lion *n* león *m*.

lip *n* labio *m*.

liqueur *n* licor *m*.

liquid *adj* líquido/da

liquor *n* licor *m*.

liquorice *n* orozuz *m*; regalicia *f*.

lisp *vi* cecear.

list *n* lista *f*.

listen *vi* escuchar.

literature *n* literatura *f*.

lithe *adj* ágil.

lithograph *n* litografía *f*.

litigation *n* litigio *m*.

litre *n* litro *m*.

litter *n* litera *f*.

little *adj* pequeño/ña, poco/ca

live *vi* vivir; habitar.

liver *n* hígado *m*.

livestock *n* ganado *m*.

living *n* vida *f*:—*adj* vivo/va.

living room *n* sala de estar *f*.

lizard *n* lagarto *m*.

load *vt* cargar

loaf *n* pan *m*.

loam *n* marga *f*.

loan *n* préstamo *m*.

loathe *vt* aborrecer.

loathing *n* aversión *f*.

lobby *n* vestíbulo *m*.

lobe *n* lóbulo *m*.

lobster *n* langosta *f*.

local *adj* local.

locality *n* localidad *f*.

locate *vt* localizar.

location *n* situación *f*.

loch *n* lago *m*.

lock *n* cerradura *f*.

locker *n* vestuario *m*.

locket *n* medallón *m*.

locomotive *n* locomotora *f*.

locust *n* langosta *f*.

loft *n* desván *m*.

lofty *adj* alto/ta.

log *n* leño *m*.

logic *n* lógica *f*.

logo *n* logotipo *m*.

loiter *vi* merodear.

lollipop *n* pirulí *m*.
loneliness *n* soledad *f*.
long *adj* largo/ga.
longitude *n* longitud *f*.
look *vi* mirar *f*.
looking glass *n* espejo *m*.
loop *n* lazo *m*.
loose *adj* suelto/ta.
loot *vt* saquear:—*n* botín *m*.
lop *vt* desmochar.
lord *n* señor *m*.
lose *vt* perder.
loss *n* perdida *f*.
lotion *n* loción *f*.
lottery *n* lotería *f*.
loud *adj* fuerte:—**~ly** *adv* fuerte.
loudspeaker *n* altavoz *m*.
lounge *n* salón *m*.

louse *n* piojo (*pl* **lice**) *m*.
lout *n* gamberro *m*.
love *n* amor, cariño *m*.
lovely *adj* hermoso/sa.
lover *n* amante *m*.
low *adj* bajo/ja.
loyal *adj* leal; fiel.
lozenge *n* pastilla *f*.
lubricant *n* lubricante *m*.
lubricate *vt* lubricar.
luck *n* suerte *f*; fortuna *f*.
lucrative *adj* lucrativo/va.
ludricrous *adj* absurdo/da.
lug *vt* arrastrar.
luggage *n* equipaje *m*.
lull *vt* acunar:—*n* tregua *f*.
lullaby *n* nana *f*.
lumbago *n* lumbago *m*.

luminous *adj* luminoso/sa.
lump *n* terrón *m*.
lunacy *n* locura *f*.
lunar *adj* lunar.
lunatic *adj* loco/ca.
lunch, luncheon *n* merienda *f*.
lungs *npl* pulmones *mpl*.
luscious *adj* delicioso/sa.
lush *adj* exuberante.
lust *n* lujuria, sensualidad *f*.
lustre *n* lustre *m*.
luxurious *adj* lujoso/sa.
luxury *n* lujo *m*.
lymph *n* linfa *f*.
lynx *n* lince *m*.
lyrical *adj* lírico/ca.
lyrics *npl* letra *f*.

M

macaroni n macarrones mpl.

macaroon n almendrado m.

mace n maza f; macis f.

machine n maquina f.

machinery n maquinaria, mecanica f.

mackerel n escombro m.

mad adj loco, furioso, rabioso.

madam n madama, senora f.

madhouse n casa de locos f.

madness n locura f.

magazine n revista f.

maggot n gusano m.

magic n magia f.

magician n mago m

magistrate n magistrado m.

magnet n iman m.

magnetic adj magnetico.

magnificent adj magnifico.

magnify vt aumentar.

magnifying glass n lupa f.

magnitude n magnitud f.

magpie n urraca f.

mahogany n caoba f.

mail n correo m.

maim vt mutilar.

main adj principal.

maintain vt mantener.

maintenance n mantenimiento m.

maize n maiz m.

majesty n majestad f.

major adj principal

make vt hacer, crear.

make-up n maquillaje m.

malaria n malaria f.

male adj masculino:—n macho m.

malice n malicia f.

malicious adj malicioso.

mall n centro comercial m.

malleable adj maleable.

mallet n mazo m.

mallows n (bot) malva f.

malnutrition n desnutricion f.

malpractice n negligencia f.

malt n malta f.

maltreat vt maltratar.

mammal n mamifero m.

mammoth adj gigantesco.

man n hombre m.

manage vt, vi manejar, dirigir.

management n direccion f.

manager n director m.

mandate n mandato m.

mane n crines del caballo fpl.

manoeuvre n maniobra f.

mangle n rodillo m.

mangy adj sarnoso.

manhood n edad viril f.

mania n mania f.

maniac n maniaco m.

manipulate vt manejar.

mankind n genero humano m.

man-made n artificial.

manner n manera f; modo m

mansion n palacio m.

mantelpiece n repisa de chimenea f.

manual adj, n manual m.

manufacture n fabricacion f.

manufacturer n fabricante m.

manuscript n manuscrito m.

many adj muchos, muchas.

map n mapa m.

maple n arce m.

mar vt estropear.

marathon n maraton m.

marble n marmol m.

March n marzo m.

mare n yegua f.

margarine n margarina f.

margin n margen m; borde m.

marigold n (bot) calendula f.

marijuana n marijuana f.

marine adj marinom.

marital adj marital.

mark n marca f.

market n mercado m.

marmalade n mermelada de naranja f.

maroon adj marron.

marquee n entoldado m.

marriage n matrimonio m

marrow n medula f.

marry vi casar(se).

marsh n pantano m.

marshy adj pantanoso.

martyr n martir m.

marvel n maravilla f.

marvellous adj maravilloso.

marzipan n mazapan m.

mascara n rimel m.

masculine adj masculino.

mask n mascara f.

masochist n masoquista m.

mason n albanil m.

mass n masa f; misa f;

massacre n carniceria, matanza f.

massage n masaje m.

massive adj enorme.

mast n mastil m.

masterpiece n obra maestra f.

masticate vt masticar.

mat n estera f.

match n fosforo m, cerilla f.

mate n companero m:—vt acoplar.

mathematics npl matematicas fpl.

matinee n funcion de la tarde f.

mating n aparejamiento m.

matriculate vt matricular.

matriculation n matriculacion f.

matt adj mate.

matter n materia, substancia f.

mattress n colchon m.

mature adj maduro.

mauve adj de color malva.

maximum n maximo m.

May n mayo m.

mayonnaise n mayonesa f.

mayor n alcalde m.

maze n laberinto m.

me pn me; mi.

meal n comida f; harina f.

mean adj tacano.

meander vi serpentear.

meaning n sentido, significado m.

meantime, meanwhile adv mientras tanto.

measles npl sarampion m.

measurement n medida f.

meat n carne f.

mechanic n mecanico m.

mechanism n mecanismo m.

medal n medalla f.

media npl medios de comunicacion mpl.

medical adj medico.

medicate vt medicinar.

medicine n medicina f.

medieval adj medieval.

mediocre adj mediocre.

meditate vi meditar.

meditation n meditacion f.

Mediterranean adj mediterraneo.

medium n medio m.

meet vt encontrar.

meeting n reunion f.

megaphone n megafono m.

melancholy n melancolia f.

mellow adj maduro.

mellowness n madurez f.

melody n melodia f.

melon n melon m.

melt vt derretir.

member n miembro m.

membrane n membrana f.

memento n memento m.

memoir n memoria f.

memorandum n memorandum m.

memorial n monumento conmemorativo m.

memory n memoria f; recuerdo m.

menace n amenaza f.

menagerie n casa de fieras f.

mend vt reparar.

menial adj domestico.

meningitis n meningitis f.

menopause n menopausia f.

menstruation n menstruacion f.

mental adj mental.

mention n mencion f.

mentor n mentor m.

menu n menu m; carta f.

merchandise n mercancia f.

merchant n comerciante m.

mercury n mercurio m.

mercy n compasion f.

mere adj mero.

meridian n meridiano m.

merit n merito m.

mermaid n sirena f.

merry adj alegre.

merry-go-round n tiovivo m.

mesh n malla f.

mesmerise vt hipnotizar.

mess n lio m.

message n mensaje m.

metabolism n metabolismo n.

metal n metal m.

metallic adj metalico.

metamorphosis n metamorfosis f.

metaphor n metafora f.

meteor n meteoro m.

meteorological adj meteorologico.

meteorology n meteorologia f.

meter n medidor m.

method n metodo m.

methodical adj metodico.

Methodist n metodista m.

metre n metro m.

metric adj metrico.

metropolis n metropoli f.

metropolitan adj metropolitano.

mettle n valor m.

mew vi maullar.

mezzanine n entresuelo m.

microbe n microbio m.

microphone n microfono m.

microchip n microplaqueta f.

microscope n microscopio m.

microwave n horno microondas m.

mid adj medio.

midday n mediodia m.

middle adj mediom.

midge n mosca f.

midget n enano m.

midnight n medianoche f.

midst n medio, centro m.

midsummer n pleno verano m.

midwife n partera f.

might n poder m; fuerza f.

mighty adj fuerte.

migraine n jaqueca f.

migrate vi emigrar.

migration n emigracion f.

mike n microfono m.

mild adj apacible; suave.

mildew n moho m.

mileage n kilometraje m.

milieu n ambiente m.

militant adj militante.

military adj militar.

milk n leche f.

milkshake n batido m

milky adj lechoso:—**M~ Way** n Via Lactea f.

mill n molino m.

millennium n milenio m.

miller n molinero m.

milligram n miligramo m.

milliliter n mililitro m.

millimeter n milimetro m.

milliner n sombrerero.

million n millon m.

millionaire n millonario m.

millionth adj n millonésimo.

mime n mimo m.

mimic vt imitar.

mince vt picar.

mind n mente f.

mine pn mio, mia, mi.—n mina:—vi minar.

miner n minero m.

mineral adj, n mineral m.

mineral water n agua mineral f.

mingle vt mezclar.

miniature n miniatura f.

minimal adj minimo.

minimum n minimum m.

mining n explotacion minera f.

minister n ministro m.

mink n vison m.

minnow n pecicillo m (pez).

minor adj menor

mint n (bot) menta f.

minus adv menos.

minute adj diminuto.

minute n minuto m.

miracle n milagro m.

mirage n espejismo m.

mire n fango m.

mirror n espejo m.

mirth n alegria f.

misbehave vi portarse mal.

miscarry vi abortar.

miscellaneous adj varios, varias.

miser n avaro m.

miserable adj miserable.

miserly adj mezquino, tacano.

misery n miseria f.

mislay vt extraviar.

mislead vt enganar.

misogynist n misogino m.

Miss n senorita f.

miss vt perder; echar de menos.

missile n misil m.

mission n mision f.

missionary n misionero m.

mist n niebla f.

mistake vt entender mal

Mister n Senor m.

mistletoe n (bot) muerdago m.

mistress n amante f.

mistrust vt desconfiar.

mitigate vt mitigar.

mitigation n mitigacion f.

mitre n mitra f.

mittens npl manoplas fpl.

mix vt mezclar.

mixer n licuadora f.

mixture n mezcla f.

moan n gemido m.

moat n foso m.

mob n multitud f.

mobile adj movil.

mode n modo m.

model n modelo m.

moderate adj moderado.

moderation n moderacion f.

modern adj moderno.

modernise vt modernizar.

modest adj modesto.

modesty n modestia f.

modify vt modificar.

module n modulo m.

mogul n magnate m.

mohair n mohair m.

moist adj humedo.

moisture n humedad f.

mold n molde m.

mole n topo m.

molecule n molecula f.

molest vt importunar.

mom n mama f.

moment n momento m.

momentum n impetu m.

mommy n mama f.

monarch n monarca m.

monarchy n monarquia f.

monastery n monasterio m.

Monday n lunes m.

monetary adj monetario.

money n moneda f; dinero m.

mongol n mongolico m.

mongrel adj, n mestizo m.

monk n monje m.

monkey n mono m.

monopoly n monopolio m.

monotonous adj monotono.

monsoon n (mar) monzon m.

monster n monstruo m.

month n mes m.

monthly adj, adv mensual-(mente).

monument n monumento m.

mood n humor m.

moody adj malhumorado.

moon n luna f.

moor n paramo.

moorland n paramo m.

moose n alce m.

mop n fregona f.

mope vi estar triste.

moped n ciclomotor m.

morality n etica, moralidad f.

morbid adj morboso.

more adj, adv mas.

moreover adv ademas.

morgue n deposito de cadaveres m.

morning n manana f:—**good ~** buenos dias mpl.

moron *n* imbecil *m*.

morphine *n* morfina *f*.

morse *n* morse *m*.

morsel *n* bocado *m*.

mortal *adj* mortal

mortality *n* mortalidad *f*.

mortar *n* mortero *m*.

mortgage *n* hipoteca *f*.

mortify *vt* mortificar.

mortuary *n* deposito de cadaveres *m*.

mosaic *n* mosaico *m*.

mosque *n* mezquita *f*.

mosquito *n* mosquito *m*.

moss *n* (*bot*) musgo *m*.

most *adj* la mayoria de.

motel *n* motel *m*.

moth *n* polilla *f*.

mother *n* madre *f*.

mother-in-law *n* suegra *f*.

mother-of-pearl *n* nacar *m*.

motif *n* tema *m*.

motion *n* movimiento *m*.

motive *n* motivo *m*.

motor *n* motor *m*.

motorbike *n* moto *f*.

motorcycle *n* motocicleta *f*.

motor vehicle *n* automovil *m*.

motto *n* lema *m*.

mount *n* monte *m*.

mountain *n* montana *f*.

mountaineering *n* montañismo *m*.

mourn *vt* lamentar.

mourner *n* doliente *m*.

mourning *n* luto *m*.

mouse *n* (*pl* mice) raton *m*.

mousse *n* mousse *f*.

moustache *n* bigote *m*.

mouth *n* boca *f*;

mouthful *n* bocado *m*.

mouthwash *n* enjuague *m*.

mouthwatering *adj* apetitoso.

move *vt* mover.

movement *n* movimiento *m*.

movie *n* pelicula *f*.

moving *adj* conmovedor.

mow *vt* segar.

mower *n* cortacesped *m*; mocion *f*.

Mrs *n* senora *f*.

much *adj, adv* mucho.

muck *n* suciedad *f*.

mucous *adj* mocoso.

mud *n* barro *m*.

muddle *vt* confundir *m*; confusion *f*.

muffle *vt* embozar.

mug *n* jarra *f*.

mulberry *n* mora *f*.

mule *n* mulo *m*, mula *f*.

multiple *adj* multiplo *m*.

multiplication *n* multiplicacion *f*.

multiply *vt* multiplicar.

multitude *n* multitud *f*.

mumble *vt, vi* refunfunar.

mummy *n* momia *f*.

mumps *npl* paperas *fpl*.

munch *vt* mascar.

mundane *adj* trivial.

municipal *adj* municipal.

municipality *n* municipalidad *f*.

mural *n* mural *m*.

murder *n* asesinato *m*; homicidio *m*.

murky *adj* sombrio.

murmur *n* murmullo.

muscle *n* musculo *m*.

muse *vi* meditar.

museum *n* museo *m*.

mushroom *n* (*bot*) seta *f*; champinon *m*.

music *n* musica *f*.

musician *n* musico *m*.

musk *n* musco *m*.

muslin *n* muselina *f*.

mussel *n* marisco *m*.

must *v aux* estar obligado.

mustard *n* mostaza *f*.

mute *adj* mudo, silencioso.

mutilate *vt* mutilar.

mutter *vt, vi* murmurar.

mutton *n* carnero *m*.

mutual *adj* mutuo, mutual.

muzzle *n* bozal *m*.

my *pn* mi, mis; mio, mia; mios, mias.

myriad *n* miriada *f*.

myrrh *n* mirra *f*.

myrtle *n* mirto, arrayan *m*.

myself *pn* yo mismo.

mysterious *adj* misterioso.

mystery *n* misterio *m*.

mystic(al) *adj* mistico.

mystify *vt* dejar perplejo.

mystique *n* misterio *m*.

myth *n* mito *m*.

mythology *n* mitologia *f*.

N

nag *n* jaca *f*:—*vt* reganar.
nagging *adj* persistente.
nail *n* una *f*; garra *f*; clavo *m*.
naive *adj* ingenuo.
naked *adj* desnudo.
name *n* nombre *m*.
nameless *adj* anonimo.
namely *adv* a saber.
namesake *n* tocayo *m*.
nanny *n* ninera *f*.
nap *n* sueno ligero *m*.
nape *n* nuca *f*.
napkin *n* servilleta *f*.
narcissus *n* (*bot*) narciso *m*.
narcotic *adj, n* narcotico *m*.
narrate *vt* narrar.
narrative *adj* narrativo.
narrow *adj* angosto, estrecho.
nasal *adj* nasal.
nasty *adj* sucio, puerco.
natal *adj* nativo; natal.
nation *n* nacion *f*.
nationalise *vt* nacionalizar.
nationalism *n* nacionalismo *m*.
nationalist *adj, n* nacionalista *m*.
nationality *n* nacionalidad *f*.
native *adj* nativo *m*.
native language *n* lengua materna *f*.
Nativity *n* Navidad *f*.
natural *adj* natural.
naturalise *vt* naturalizar.
naturalist *n* naturalista *m*.
nature *n* naturaleza *f*.
naught *n* cero *m*.
naughty *adj* malo.
nausea *n* nausea.

nauseous *adj* fastidioso.
nautic(al), naval *adj* nautico, naval.
nave *n* nave (de la iglesia) *f*.
navel *n* ombligo *m*.
navigate *vi* navegar.
navigation *n* navegacion *f*.
navy *n* marina *f*.
Nazi *n* nazi *m*.
near *prep* cerca de.
nearby *adj* cercano.
nearly *adv* casi.
near-sighted *adj* miope.
nebulous *adj* nebuloso.
necessarily *adv* necesariamente.
necessary *adj* necesario.
necessity *n* necesidad *f*.
neck *n* cuello *m*.
necklace *n* collar *m*.
necktie *n* corbata *f*.
nectar *n* nectar *m*.
need *n* necesidad *f*.
needle *n* aguja *f*.
needless *adj* superfluo.
needlework *n* costura *f*
needy *adj* necesitado, pobre.
negation *n* negacion *f*.
negative *adj* negativo.
neglect *vt* descuidar.
negligee *n* salto de cama *m*.
negligence *n* negligencia *f*
negligible *adj* insignificante.
negotiate *vt, vi* negociar (con).
negotiation *n* negociacion *f*; negocio *m*.
Negress *n* negra *f*.
Negro *adj, n* negro *m*.
neighbour *n* vecino *m*.

neighbourhood *n* vecindad *f*; vecindario *m*.
neither *conj* ni:—*pn* ninguno.
neon *n* neon *m*.
neon light *n* luz de neon *f*.
nephew *n* sobrino *m*.
nepotism *n* nepotismo *m*.
nerve *n* nervio *m*; valor *m*.
nerve-racking *adj* espantoso.
nervous *adj* nervioso; nervudo.
nervous breakdown *n* crisis nerviosa *f*.
nest *n* nido *m*.
nest egg *n* (*fig*) ahorros *mpl*.
nestle *vt* anidarse.
net *n* red *f*.
netball *n* basquet *m*.
nettle *n* ortiga *f*.
network *n* red *f*.
neurosis *n* neurosis *f* invar.
neurotic *adj, n* neurotico *m*.
neuter *adj* (*gr*) neutro.
neutral *adj* neutral.
neutrality *n* neutralidad *f*.
neutron *n* neutron *m*.
never *adv* nunca, jamas.
nevertheless *adv* no obstante.
new *adj* nuevo.
news *npl* novedad, noticias *fpl*.
newscaster *n* presentador *m*.
newspaper *n* periodico *m*.
next *adj* proximo.
nib *n* pico *m*.
nibble *vt* picar.
nice *adj* simpatico.
niche *n* nicho *m*.
nickel *n* niquel *m*

nickname *n* mote.

nicotine *n* nicotina *f.*

niece *n* sobrina *f.*

niggling *adj* insignificante.

night *n* noche *f.*

nightclub *n* cabaret *m.*

nightfall *n* anochecer *m.*

nightingale *n* ruisenor *m.*

nightmare *n* pesadilla *f.*

nihilist *n* nihilista *m.*

nimble *adj* ligero, activo, listo, agil.

nine *adj, n* nueve.

nineteen *adj, n* diecinueve.

nineteenth *adj, n* decimonono.

ninetieth *adj, n* nonagesimo.

ninety *adj, n* noventa.

ninth *adj, n* nono, noveno.

nip *vt* pellizcar; morder.

nipple *n* pezon *m;* tetilla *f.*

nit *n* liendre *f.*

nitrogen *n* nitrogeno *m.*

no *adv* no.

nobility *n* nobleza *f.*

noble *adj* noble.

nobleman *n* noble *m.*

nobody *n* nadie, ninguna persona *f.*

nocturnal *adj* nocturnal.

noise *n* ruido *m.*

noisy *adj* ruidoso, turbulento.

nominate *vt* nombrar.

nomination *n* nominacion *f.*

nominee *n* candidato *m.*

non-alcoholic *adj* no alcoholico.

nonchalant *adj* indiferente.

nondescript *adj* no descrito.

none *adj* nadie, ninguno.

nonentity *n* nulidad *f.*

nonetheless *adv* sin embargo.

nonsense *n* disparate *m.*

noodles *npl* fideos *mpl.*

noon *n* mediodia *m.*

noose *n* lazo corredizo *m.*

nor *conj* ni.

normal *adj* normal.

north *n* norte *m.*

North America *n* America del Norte *f.*

northeast *n* nor(d)este *m.*

northerly, northern *adj* norteno.

North Pole *n* polo artico *m.*

northwest *n* nor(d)oeste *m.*

nose *n* nariz *f*

nosebleed *n* hemorragia nasal *f.*

nostalgia *n* nostalgia *f.*

nostril *n* ventana de la nariz *f.*

not *adv* no.

notable *adj* notable.

notably *adv* especialmente.

notary *n* notario *m.*

notch *n* muesca *f.*

note *n* nota, marca *f.*

notebook *n* librito de apuntes *m.*

noted *adj* afamado, celebre.

nothing *n* nada *f.*

notice *n* noticia *f;* aviso *m.*

notification *n* notificacion *f.*

notify *vt* notificar.

notion *n* nocion *f.*

notoriety *n* notoriedad *f.*

notwithstanding *conj* no obstante, aunque.

nougat *n* turron *m.*

nought *n* cero *m.*

noun *n* (*gr*) sustantivo *m.*

nourish *vt* nutrir, alimentar.

novel *n* novela *f.*

novelist *n* novelista *m.*

novelty *n* novedad *f.*

November *n* noviembre *m.*

novice *n* novicio *m.*

now *adv* ahora.

nowadays *adv* hoy (en) dia.

nowhere *adv* en ninguna parte.

noxious *adj* nocivo, danoso.

nozzle *n* boquilla *f.*

nuance *n* matiz *m.*

nuclear *adj* nuclear.

nucleus *n* nucleo *m.*

nude *adj* desnudo.

nudge *vt* dar un codazo a.

nudist *n* nudista *m.*

nudity *n* desnudez *f.*

null *adj* nulo.

nullify *vt* anular.

numb *adj* entorpecido.

number *n* numero *m.*

numerous *adj* numeroso.

nun *n* monja *f.*

nunnery *n* convento de monjas *m.*

nuptial *adj* nupcial *fpl.*

nurse *n* enfermera *f.*

nursery *n* guarderia infantil *f*

nursery rhyme *n* cancion infantil *f.*

nursery school *n* parvulario *m.*

nursing home *n* clinica de reposo *f.*

nurture *vt* criar.

nut *n* nuez *f.*

nutcrackers *npl* cascanueces *m.*

nutmeg *n* nuez moscada *f.*

nutritious *adj* nutritivo.

nut shell *n* cascara de nuez *f.*

nylon *n* nilon *m.*

O

oak *n* roble *m*.

oar *n* remo *m*.

oasis *n* oasis *f*.

oat *n* avena *f*.

oath *n* juramento *m*.

obedience *n* obediencia *f*.

obese *adj* obeso, gordo.

obey *vt* obedecer.

obituary *n* necrologia *f*.

object *n* objeto *m*:—*vt* objetar.

objective *adj, n* objetivo *m*.

oblige *vt* obligar.

obliterate *vt* borrar.

oblivion *n* olvido *m*.

oblong *adj* oblongo.

obnoxious *adj* odioso.

oboe *n* oboe *m*.

obscene *adj* obsceno.

obscenity *n* obscenidad *f*.

obscure *adj* oscuro.

observatory *n* observatorio *m*.

observe *vt* observar, mirar.

obsess *vt* obsesionar.

obsolete *adj* en desuso.

obstacle *n* obstaculo *m*.

obstinate *adj* obstinado.

obstruct *vt* obstruir; impedir.

obtain *vt* obtener, adquirir.

obvious *adj* obvio, evidente.

occasion *n* ocasion *f*.

occupant, occupier *n* ocupador *m*

occupation *n* ocupacion *f*; empleo *m*.

occupy *vt* ocupar.

occur *vi* pasar.

ocean *n* oceano *m*; alta mar *f*.

ocher *n* ocre *m*.

octave *n* octava *f*.

October *n* octubre *m*.

octopus *n* pulpo *m*.

odd *adj* impar.

oddity *n* singularidad.

odious *adj* odioso.

odour *n* olor *m*.

of *prep* de.

off *adv* desconectado; apagado

offence *n* ofensa *f*.

offend *vt* ofender.

offensive *adj* ofensivo.

offer *vt* ofrecer.

offering *n* sacrificio *m*.

office *n* oficina *f*.

officer *n* oficial, empleado *m*.

official *adj* oficial.

offspring *n* prole *f*.

ogle *vt* comerse con los ojos.

oil *n* aceite *m*.

oil painting *n* pintura al oleo *f*.

oil rig *n* torre de perforacion *f*.

oil tanker *n* petrolero *m*.

ointment *n* unguento *m*.

OK, okay *excl* vale.

old *adj* viejo; antiguo.

old age *n* vejez *f*.

olive *n* olivo *m*.

omelette *n* tortilla de huevos *f*.

omen *n* agüero.

ominous *adj* ominoso.

omission *n* omisión *f*.

omit *vt* omitir.

omnipotence *n* omnipotencia *f*.

on *prep* sobre, encima, en; de; a.

one *adj* un, uno.

oneself *pn* si mismo; si misma.

ongoing *adj* continuo.

onion *n* cebolla *f*.

onlooker *n* espectador *m*.

only *adj* unico, solo.

onus *n* responsabilidad *f*.

onwards *adv* adelante.

opaque *adj* opaco.

open *adj* abierto; *vi* abrirse.

open-minded *adj* imparcial.

opera *n* opera *f*.

operate *vi* obrar.

operation *n* operacion *f*.

operational *adj* operacional.

operative *adj* operativo.

operator *n* operario *m*; operador *m*.

ophthalmic *adj* oftálmico.

opinion *n* opinion *f*.

opinion poll *n* sondeo *m*.

opponent *n* antagonista *m*.

opportune *adj* oportuno.

opportunity *n* oportunidad *f*.

oppose *vt* oponerse.

opposite *adj* opuesto; contrario.

opposition *n* oposicion *f*.

oppress *vt* oprimir.

oppression *n* opresion *f*.

optic(al) *adj* optico *f*.

optician *n* optico *m*.

optimist *n* optimista *m*.

optimum *adj* optimum.

option *n* opcion *f*; deseo *m*.

opulent *adj* opulento.

or *conj* o; u.

oracle *n* oraculo *m*.

oral *adj* oral.

orange *n* naranja *f*.

orbit *n* orbita *f*.

orchard *n* huerto *m.*

orchestra *n* orquesta *f.*

orchid *n* orquidea *f.*

order *n* orden *mf;* regla *f;* mandar.

ordinary *adj* ordinario.

ore *n* mineral *m.*

organ *n* organo *m.*

organic *adj* organico.

organisation *n* organizacion *f.*

organise *vt* organizar.

organism *n* organismo *m.*

organist *n* organista *m.*

orgasm *n* orgasmo *m.*

orgy *n* orgia *f.*

oriental *adj* oriental.

orifice *n* orificio *m.*

origin *n* origen *m.*

original *adj* original.

originate *vi* originar.

ornament *n* ornamento *m.*

ornate *adj* adornado.

orphan *adj, n* huerfano *m.*

orphanage *n* orfanato *m.*

orthodox *adj* ortodoxo.

orthopaedic *adj* ortopedico.

oscillate *vi* oscilar.

osprey *n* aguila marina *f.*

ostensibly *adv* aparentemente.

ostentatious *adj* ostentoso.

osteopath *n* osteopata *m.*

ostrich *n* avestruz *m.*

other *pn* otro.

otter *n* nutria *f.*

ouch *excl* ¡ay!

ought *v aux* deber, ser menester.

ounce *n* onza *f.*

our, ours *pn* nuestro, nuestra, nuestros, nuestras.

ourselves *pn pl* nosotros mismos.

out *adv* fuera.

outbreak *n* erupcion *f.*

outcast *n* paria *m.*

outcome *n* resultado *m.*

outcry *n* clamor *m.*

outdo *vt* exceder a otro, sobrepujar.

outer *adj* exterior.

outermost *adj* extremo; lo mas exterior.

outfit *n* vestidos *mpl;* ropa *f.*

outline *n* contorno *m*

outlook *n* perspectiva *f.*

out-of-date *adj* caducado; pasado de moda.

outpatient *n* paciente externo *m.*

output *n* rendimiento *m.*

outrage *n* ultraje *m.*

outrageous *adj* ultrajoso.

outside *n* superficie *f;* exterior *m.*

outsider *n* forastero *m.*

outskirts *npl* alrededores *mpl.*

outstanding *adj* excepcional.

outwit *vt* enganar a uno a fuerza de tretas.

oval *n* ovalo *m:—adj* oval.

ovary *n* ovario *m.*

oven *n* horno *m.*

ovenproof *adj* resistente al horno.

over *prep* sobre, encima.

overbearing *adj* despotico.

overcharge *vt* sobrecargar.

overcoat *n* abrigo *m.*

overdose *n* sobredosis *f.*

overdue *adj* retrasado.

overeat *vi* atracarse.

overflow *vt, vi* inundar.

overhaul *vt* revisar.

overkill *n* exceso de medios *m.*

overlap *vi* traslaparse.

overleaf *adv* al dorso.

overload *vt* sobrecargar.

overpower *vt* predominar, oprimir.

overseas *adv* en ultramar:— *adj* extranjero.

oversee *vt* inspeccionar.

overshadow *vt* eclipsar.

overstate *vi* exagerar.

overstep *vt* exceder, pasar de.

overtake *vt* sobrepasar.

overtime *n* horas extra *fpl.*

overtone *n* tono *m.*

owe *vt* deber.

owl *n* buho *m.*

own *adj* propio.

owner *n* dueno, propietario *m.*

ownership *n* posesion *f.*

ox *n* buey *m.*

oxidise *vt* oxidar.

oxygen *n* oxigeno *m.*

oyster *n* ostra *f.*

ozone *n* ozono *m.*

P

pa *n* papa *m.*
pace *n* paso *m.*
pacemaker *n* marcapasos *m.*
pacific(al) *adj* pacifico.
pacify *vt* pacificar.
package *n* paquete *m*
packet *n* paquete *m.*
packing *n* embalaje *m.*
pact *n* pacto *m.*
pad *n* bloc *m.*
paddle *vi* remar
paddock *n* corral *m.*
paddy *n* arrozal *m.*
pagan *adj, n* pagano *m.*
page *n* pagina *f.*
pain *n* pena *f;* castigo *m;* dolor *m.*
painkiller *n* analgesico *m.*
paint *vt* pintar.
paintbrush *n* pincel *m.*
painter *n* pintor *m.*
painting *n* pintura *f.*
pair *n* par *m.*
pajamas *npl* pijama *m.*
palatial *adj* palatino.
pale *adj* palido; claro.
pallet *n* pallet *m.*
palliative *adj, n* paliativo *m.*
pallid *adj* palido.
pallor *n* palidez *f.*
palm *n* (*bot*) palma *f.*
Palm Sunday *n* Domingo de Ramos *m.*
palpable *adj* palpable.
paltry *adj* irrisorio; mezquino.
pamphlet *n* folleto *m.*
pan *n* cazuela *f.*
pancake *n* bunuelo *m.*
pandemonium *n* jaleo *m.*
pane *n* cristal *m.*

panel *n* panel *m*
pang *n* angustia *f.*
panic *adj, n* panico *m.*
pansy *n* (*bot*) pensamiento *m.*
pant *vi* jadear.
panther *n* pantera *f.*
pantry *n* despensa *f.*
papacy *n* papado *m.*
papal *adj* papal.
paper *n* papel *m.*
paperback *n* libro de bolsillo *m.*
paper clip *n* clip *m.*
paperweight *n* sujetapapeles *m.*
paprika *n* pimienta hungara *f.*
parachute *n* paracaidas *m.*
paradise *n* paraiso *m.*
paradox *n* paradoja *f.*
paragon *n* modelo perfecto *m.*
paragraph *n* parrafo *m.*
parallel *adj* paralelo.
paralysis *n* paralisis *f.*
paralytic(al) *adj* paralitico.
paralyze *vt* paralizar.
paramedic *n* ambulanciero *m.*
paramount *adj* supremo.
paranoid *adj* paranoico.
parasite *n* parásito *m.*
parasol *n* parasol *m.*
parcel *n* paquete *m.*
parch *vt* resecar.
pardon *n* perdon *m.*
parent *n* padre *m;* madre *f.*
parentage *n* parentela *f.*
parental *adj* paternal.
parenthesis *n* parentesis *m.*

parish *n* parroquia *f.*
parity *n* paridad *f.*
park *n* parque *m.*
parliament *n* parlamento *m.*
parlour *n* sala de recibimiento *f.*
parody *n* parodia *f.*
parrot *n* papagayo *m.*
parsley *n* (*bot*) perejil *m.*
parsnip *n* (*bot*) chirivia *f.*
part *n* parte *f.*
participate *vi* participar (en).
particle *n* particula *f.*
particular *adj* particular.
parting *n* separacion *f.*
partition *n* particion.
partner *n* socio, companero *m.*
partridge *n* perdiz *f.*
party *n* partido *m;* fiesta *f.*
pass *vt* pasar.
passage *n* pasaje *m*
passbook *n* libreta de depositos *f.*
passenger *n* pasajero *m.*
passion *n* pasion *f*
passionate *adj* apasionado.
passive *adj* pasivo.
Passover *n* Pascua *f.*
passport *n* pasaporte *m.*
password *n* contrasena *f.*
past *adj* pasado.
pasta *n* pasta *f.*
paste *n* pasta *f.*
pastime *n* pasatiempo *m f.*
pastor *n* pastor *m.*
pastry *n* pasteleria *f.*
pasture *n* pasto *m.*
patch *n* remiendo *m;* parche *m.*

patent *adj* patente.
path *n* senda *f*.
pathetic *adj* patetico.
patience *n* paciencia *f*.
patient *adj* paciente.
patio *n* patio *m*.
patriot *n* patriota *m*.
patriotism *n* patriotismo *m*.
patrol *n* patrulla *f*.
patron *n* patron *m*.
patronise *vt* patrocinar.
pattern *n* patron *m*; dibujo *m*.
pauper *n* pobre *m*.
pause *n* pausa *f*.
pave *vt* empedrar.
pavement *n* calzada *f*.
pavilion *n* pabellon *m*.
paw *n* pata *f*.
pay *vt* pagar.
pea *n* guisante *m*.
peace *n* paz *f*.
peach *n* melocoton *m*.
peacock *n* pavon, pavo real *m*.
peak *n* cima *f*.
peanut *n* cacahuete *m*.
pear *n* pera *f*.
pearl *n* perla *f*.
peasant *n* campesino *m*.
pebble *n* guija *f*.
peculiar *adj* peculiar.
pedal *n* pedal *m*.
pedestal *n* pedestal *m*.
pedestrian *n* peaton *m*.
pedigree *n* genealogia *f*.
peel *vt* pelar.
peg *n* clavija *f*.
pelican *n* pelicano *m*.
pen *n* boligrafo *m*; pluma *f*
penal *adj* penal.
pence *n* d *pl* of penny.
pencil *n* lapiz *m*.
pendulum *n* pendulo *m*.
penetrate *vt* penetrar.
penguin *n* pinguino *m*.
penicillin *n* penicilina *f*.
peninsula *n* peninsula *f*.

penis *n* pene *m*.
penitence *n* penitencia *f*.
penknife *n* navaja *f*.
penny *n* penique *m*.
pension *n* pension *f*.
pensive *adj* pensativo.
Pentecost *n* Pentecostes *m*.
penthouse *n* atico *m*.
people *n* pueblo *m*; nacion *f*; gente *f*.
pepper *n* pimienta *f*.
peppermint *n* menta *f*.
perceive *vt* percibir.
percentage *n* porcentaje *m*.
perception *n* percepcion*f*.
percolator *n* cafetera de filtro *f*.
percussion *n* percusion *f*; golpe *m*.
perennial *adj* perenne; perpetuo.
perfect *adj* perfecto.
perform *vt* ejecutar.
performance *n* ejecucion *f*.
perfume *n* perfume *m*; fragancia *f*:—*vt* perfumar.
perhaps *adv* quiza, quizas.
peril *n* peligro *m*.
period *n* periodo *m*.
periodical *n* jornal, periodico *m*.
perk *n* extra *m*.
perm *n* permanente *f*.
permanent *adj*, **~ly** *adv* permanente(mente).
permissible *adj* licito.
permission *n* permiso *m*.
permit *vt* permitir.
perplex *vt* confundir.
persecute *vt* perseguir.
persevere *vi* perseverar.
persist *vi* persistir.
person *n* persona *f*.
personality *n* personalidad *f*.
personnel *n* personal *m*.
perspective *n* perspectiva *f*.

perspiration *n* transpiracion *f*.
perspire *vi* transpirar.
persuade *vt* persuadir.
perturb *vt* perturbar.
peruse *vt* leer.
perverse *adj* perverso.
pessimist *n* pesimista *m*.
pester *vt* molestar.
pet *n* animal domestico *m*.
petal *n* (*bot*) petalo *m*.
petition *n* presentacion, peticion *f*.
petroleum *n* petroleo *m*.
petticoat *n* enaguas *fpl*.
petty *adj* mezquino.
pewter *n* peltre *m*.
phantom *n* fantasma *m*.
pharmacist *n* farmacéutico *m*.
pharmacy *n* farmacia *f*.
phase *n* fase *f*.
pheasant *n* faisan *m*.
phenomenon *n* fenomeno *m*.
phial *n* redomilla *f*.
philosopher *n* filosofo *m*.
philosophy *n* filosofia *f*.
phlegm *n* flema *f*.
phobia *n* fobia *f*.
phone *n* telefono *m*.
photocopier *n* fotocopiadora *f*.
photocopy *n* fotocopia *f*.
photograph *n* fotografia *f*:— *vt* fotografiar.
photographic *adj* fotografico.
photography *n* fotografia *f*.
phrase *n* frase *f*.
physical *adj* fisico.
physician *n* medico *m*.
physicist *n* fisico *m*.
physiotherapy *n* fisioterapia *f*.
physique *n* fisico *m*.
pianist *n* pianista *m*, *f*.
piano *n* piano *m*.
piccolo *n* flautin *m*.

pick *vt* escoger, elegir.

pickle *n* escabeche *m*.

picnic *n* comida, merienda *f*.

picture *n* pintura *f*.

picturesque *adj* pintoresco.

pie *n* pastel *m*; tarta *f*.

piece *n* pedazo *m*; pieza *f*.

pierce *vt* penetrar, agujerear.

pig *n* cerdo *m*.

pigeon *n* paloma *f*.

pigtail *n* trenza *f*.

pike *n* lucio *m*; pica *f*.

pile *n* estaca *f*; pila *f*; monton *m*.

pilgrim *n* peregrino *m*.

pill *n* pildora *f*.

pillar *n* pilar *m*.

pillow *n* almohada *f*.

pilot *n* piloto *m*.

pimple *n* grano *m*.

pin *n* alfiler *m*.

pinball *n* fliper *m*.

pincers *n* pinzas *fpl*.

pinch *vt* pellizcar.

pine *n* (*bot*) pino *m*.

pineapple *n* pina *f*, ananas *m*.

pink *n* rosa *f*.

pinnacle *n* cumbre *f*.

pint *n* pinta *f*.

pioneer *n* pionero *m*.

pious *adj* pio.

pip *n* pepita *f*.

pipe *n* tubo.

pirate *n* pirata *m*.

pirouette *n* pirueta *f*.

Pisces *n* Piscis *m* (signo del zodiaco).

piss *n* (*sl*) meados *mpl*.

pistol *n* pistola *f*.

piston *n* embolo *m*.

pit *n* hoyo *m*; mina *f*.

pitcher *n* cantaro *m*.

pitchfork *n* horca *f*.

pity *n* piedad, compasion *f*.

pivot *n* eje *m*.

pizza *n* pizza *f*.

placard *n* pancarta *f*.

placate *vt* apaciguar.

place *n* lugar, sitio *m*.

placid *adj* placido.

plagiarism *n* plagio *m*.

plague *n* peste, plaga *f*.

plaice *n* platija *f* (pez).

plaid *n* tartan *m*.

plain *adj* liso, llano

plaintiff *n* (*law*) demandador *m*.

plait *n* pliegue *m*; trenza *f*.

plan *n* plano *m*.

plane *n* avion *m*; plano *m*.

planet *n* planeta *m*.

plank *n* tabla *f*.

plant *n* planta *f*.

plantation *n* plantacion *f*.

plaque *n* placa *f*.

plaster *n* yeso *m*.

plastic *adj* plastico.

plate *n* plato *m*.

plateau *n* meseta *f*.

platform *n* plataforma *f*.

platinum *n* platino *m*.

platoon *n* (*mil*) peloton *m*.

play *n* juego *m*.

playboy *n* playboy *m*.

player *n* jugador *m*

plea *n* defensa *f*.

pleasant *adj* agradable.

please *vt* agradar.

pleasure *n* gusto, placer *m*.

pleat *n* pliegue *m*.

plentiful *adj* copioso.

plethora *n* pletora, replecion *f*.

pleurisy *n* pleuresia *f*.

pliers *npl* alicates *mpl*.

plinth *n* plinto *m*.

plough *n* arado *m*.

ploy *n* truco *m*.

plug *n* tapon *m*.

plum *n* ciruela *f*.

plumage *n* plumaje *m*.

plumb *n* plomada *f*.

plumber *n* plomero *m*.

plume *n* pluma *f*.

plump *adj* gordo.

plunder *vt* saquear.

plunge *vi* sumergir(se), precipitarse.

pluperfect *n* (*gr*) pluscuamperfecto *m*.

plural *adj*, *n* plural *m*.

plus *n* signo de mas *m*.

plush *adj* de felpa.

plutonium *n* plutonio *m*.

plywood *n* madera contrachapada *f*.

pneumatic *adj* neumatico.

pneumonia *n* pulmonia *f*.

poach *vt* escalfar.

pocket *n* bolsillo *m*.

pod *n* vaina *f*.

poem *n* poema *m*.

poet *n* poeta *m*.

poetry *n* poesia *f*.

poignant *adj* punzante.

point *n* punta *f*; punto *m*.

point-blank *adv* directamente.

poise *n* peso *m*; equilibrio *m*.

poison *n* veneno *m*.

poker *n* atizador *m*; poker *m*.

polar *adj* polar.

pole *n* polo *m*.

police *n* policia *f*.

policy *n* politica *f*.

polio *n* polio *f*.

polish *vt* pulir, alisar.

polite *adj* pulido, cortes.

politician *n* politico *m*.

politics *npl* politica *f*.

polka *n* polca *f*

pollen *n* (*bot*) polen *m*.

pollute *vt* ensuciar.

pollution *n* polucion, contaminacion *f*.

polo *n* polo *m*.

polyester *n* poliester *m*.

polytechnic *n* politecnico *m*.

pomegranate *n* granada *f*.

pomp *n* pompa *f*; esplendor *m*.

pompom *n* borla *f*.

pompous *adj* pomposo.

pond *n* estanque *m*.

ponder *vt* ponderar, considerar.

ponderous *adj* ponderoso, pesado.

pontoon *n* ponton *m*.

pony *n* jaca *f*.

pool *n* charca *f*; piscina.

poor *adj* pobre

pop *n* papá *m*.

popcorn *n* palomitas *fpl*.

Pope *n* papa *m*.

poplar *n* alamo *m*.

poppy *n* (*bot*) amapola *f*.

popular *adj*, **~ly** *adv* popular-(mente).

populate *vi* poblar.

population *n* poblacion *f*.

porcelain *n* porcelana *f*.

porch *n* portico *m*.

porcupine *n* puerco espin *m*.

pore *n* poro *m*.

pork *n* carne de puerco *f*.

pornography *n* pornografia *f*.

porous *adj* poroso.

porpoise *n* marsopa *f*.

porridge *n* gachas de avena *fpl*.

port *n* puerto *m* *m*.

portable *adj* portatil.

portal *n* portal *m* *f*.

porter *n* portero *m*.

portfolio *n* cartera *f*.

porthole *n* portilla *f*.

portico *n* portico *m*.

portion *n* porcion*f*.

portly *adj* rollizo.

portrait *n* retrato *m*.

portray *vt* retratar.

pose *n* postura *f*; pose *f*.

posh *adj* elegante.

position *n* posicion *f*.

positive *adj* positivo.

posse *n* peloton *m*.

possess *vt* poseer.

possession *n* posesion *f*.

possibility *n* posibilidad *f*.

possible *adj* posible.

post *n* correo *m*; puesto *m*.

postage stamp *n* sello *m*.

postcard *n* tarjeta postal *f*.

poster *n* cartel *m*.

posterior *n* trasero *m*.

posterity *n* posteridad *f*.

postgraduate *n* posgraduado *m*.

posthumous *adj* postumo.

postman *n* cartero *m*.

post office *n* correos *m*.

postpone *vt* diferir.

posture *n* postura *f*.

posy *n* ramillete de flores *m*.

pot *n* marmita *f*.

potato *n* patata *f*; papa *f*.

potent *adj* potente.

potential *adj* potencial.

pothole *n* bache *m*.

potion *n* pocion *f*.

potter *n* alfarero *m*.

pottery *n* cerámica *f*.

pouch *n* bolsa *f*.

poultice *n* cataplasma *f*.

poultry *n* aves caseras *fpl*.

pound *n* libra *f*; libra esterlina *f*.

pour *vt* echar; servir.

pout *vi* ponerse cenudo.

poverty *n* pobreza *f*.

powder *n* polvo *m*.

power *n* poder *m*.

practicable *adj* practicable; hacedero.

practical *adj* práctico:—**~ly** *adv* prácticamente.

practicality *n* factibilidad *f*.

practice *n* practica *f*.

pragmatic *adj* pragmático.

prairie *n* pampa *f*.

praise *n* renombre *m*.

prattle *vi* charlar:—*n* charla *f*.

prawn *n* gamba *f*.

pray *vi* rezar.

prayer *n* oracion *f*.

preach *vi* predicar.

preacher *n* pastor *m*.

precaution *n* precaucion *f*.

precede *vt* anteceder.

precious *adj* precioso.

precise *n* preciso.

precision *n* precision *f*.

preconception *n* preocupacion *f*.

predator *n* animal de rapina *m*.

predict *vt* predecir.

prediction *n* prediccion *f*.

predominant *adj* predominante.

predominate *vt* predominar.

preface *n* prefacio *m*.

prefer *vt* preferir.

preference *n* preferencia *f*.

prefix *vt* prefijar.

pregnancy *n* embarazo *m*.

pregnant *adj* embarazada.

prehistoric *adj* prehistorico.

prejudice *n* perjuicio *m*.

preliminary *adj* preliminar.

prelude *n* preludio *m*.

premature *adj* prematuro.

premier *n* primer ministro *m*.

premises *npl* establecimiento *m*.

premium *n* premio *m*.

premonition *n* presentimiento *m*.

prepare *vt* preparar(se).

preposition *n* preposicion *f*.

preposterous *adj* prepostero; absurdo.

prerequisite *n* requisito *m*.

prerogative *n* prerrogativa *f*.

prescribe *vi* prescribir; recetar.

prescription *n* prescripcion *f*.

present *n* regalo *m*.

presentation *n* presentacion *f*.

preservation *n* preservacion *f*.

preservative *n* preservativo *m*.

preserve *vt* preservar.

preside *vi* presidir.

presidency *n* presidencia *f*.

president *n* presidente *m*.

press *vt* empujar *n* prensa.

pressure *n* presion *f*.

prestige *n* prestigio *m*.

presume *vt* presumir, suponer.

pretence *n* pretexto *m*; pretension *f*.

pretend *vi* pretender.

preterite *n* preterito *m*.

pretext *n* pretexto *m*.

pretty *adj* lindo.

prevent *vt* prevenir.

preview *n* preestreno *m*.

previous *adj* previo.

prey *n* presa *f*.

price *n* precio *m*; premio *m*.

prick *vt* punzar, picar.

pride *n* orgullo *m*.

priest *n* sacerdote *m*.

priggish *adj* afectado.

prim *adj* peripuesto.

primary *adj* primario.

primate *n* primado *m*.

primeval *adj* primitivo.

primitive *adj* primitivo.

primrose *n* (*bot*) primula *f*.

prince *n* principe *m*.

princess *n* princesa *f*.

principle *n* principio *m*.

printer *n* impresor *m*.

prior *adj* anterior.

priority *n* prioridad *f*.

priory *n* priorato *m*.

prism *n* prisma *m*.

prison *n* prision, carcel *f*.

prisoner *n* prisionero *m*.

pristine *adj* pristino.

privacy *n* soledad *f*.

private *adj* secreto, privado; particular.

private eye *n* detective privado *m*.

privet *n* alhena *f*.

privilege *n* privilegio *m*.

prize *n* premio *m*.

probability *n* probabilidad *f*.

probable *adj* probable.

probation *n* prueba *f*.

problem *n* problema *m*.

procedure *n* procedimiento

proceed *vi* proceder.

process *n* proceso *m*.

procession *n* procesion *f*.

proclaim *vt* proclamar.

proclamation *n* proclamacion *f*.

procure *vt* procurar.

prod *vt* empujar.

prodigal *adj* prodigo.

prodigious *adj* prodigioso.

prodigy *n* prodigio *m*.

produce *vt* producir

product *n* producto *m*; obra *f*; efecto *m*.

production *n* produccion *f*.

profane *adj* profano.

profess *vt* profesar.

profession *n* profesion *f*.

professor *n* profesor, catedrático *m*.

proficient *adj* proficiente.

profile *n* perfil *m*.

profit *n* ganancia *f*.

profound *adj* profundo.

profuse *adj* profuso.

program *n* programa *m*.

progress *n* progreso *m*.

prohibit *vt* prohibir.

project *vt* proyectar

prominent *adj* prominente, saledizo.

promiscuous *adj* promiscuo.

promise *n* promesa *f*.

promontory *n* promontorio *m*.

promote *vt* promover.

promotion *n* promocion *f*.

prone *adj* inclinado.

prong *n* diente *m*.

pronoun *n* pronombre *m*.

pronounce *vt* pronunciar.

proof *n* prueba *f*.

propaganda *n* propaganda *f*.

propel *vt* impeler.

propeller *n* helice *f*.

propensity *n* propension *f*.

proper *adj* propio.

property *n* propiedad *f*.

prophecy *n* profecia *f*.

prophesy *vt* profetizar.

prophet *n* profeta *m*.

prophetic *adj* profetico.

proportion *n* proporcion *f*.

proportional *adj* proporcional.

proposal *n* propuesta *f*.

propose *vt* proponer.

proposition *n* proposicion *f*.

proprietor *n* propietario *m*.

propriety *n* propiedad *f*.

pro rata *adv* a prorrateo.

prosaic *adj* prosaico.

prose *n* prosa *f*.

prosecute *vt* proseguir.

prosecution *n* prosecucion *f*.

prosecutor *n* acusador *m*.

prospect *n* perspectiva *f*.

prospectus *n* prospecto *m*.

prosper *vi* prosperar.

prosperity *n* prosperidad *f*.

prostitute *n* prostituta *f*.

prostitution *n* prostitucion *f*.

prostrate *adj* postrado.

protagonist *n* protagonista *m*.

protect *vt* proteger.

protection *n* proteccion *f*.

protective *adj* protectorio.

protector *n* protector, patrono *m*.

protege *n* protegido *m*.

protein *n* proteina *f*.

protest *vi* protestar.

Protestant *n* protestante *m*.

protester *n* manifestante *m*.

protocol n protocolo m.

prototype n prototipo m.

protracted adj prolongado.

protrude vi sobresalir.

proud adj soberbio, orgulloso.

prove vt probar.

proverb n proverbio m.

provide vt proveer.

provided conj:—~ **that** con tal que.

providence n providencia f.

province n provincia f

provincial adj, n provincial m.

provision n provision f.

proviso n estipulacion f.

provocation n provocacion f.

provocative adj provocativo.

provoke vt provocar.

prowess n proeza f.

prowl vi rondar.

proximity n proximidad f.

proxy n poder m; apoderado m.

prudence n prudencia f.

prudent adj prudente.

prudish adj gazmono.

prussic acid n acido prúsico m.

pry vi espiar, acechar.

psalm n salmo m.

pseudonym n seudonimo m.

psyche n psique f.

psychiatrist n psiquiatra m.

psychiatry n psiquiatria f.

psychic adj psiquico.

psychoanalysis n psicoanalisis m.

psychoanalyst n psicoanalista m.

psychological adj psicologico.

psychologist n psicologo m.

psychology n psicologia f.

puberty n pubertad f.

public adj publico

publicise vt publicitar.

publicity n publicidad f.

publish vt publicar.

publisher n publicador m.

pucker vt arrugar, hacer pliegues.

pudding n pudin m

puddle n charco m.

puff n soplo m.

pull vt tirar.

pulley n polea f.

pullover n jersey m.

pulp n pulpa f.

pulpit n pulpito m.

pulsate vi pulsar.

pulse n pulso m; legumbres fpl.

pumice n piedra pomez f.

pummel vt aporrear.

pump n bomba f.

pumpkin n calabaza f.

pun n equivoco, chiste m.

punch n punetazo m.

punctual adj puntual.

punctuate vi puntuar.

punctuation n puntuacion f.

pungent adj picante.

punish vt castigar.

punishment n castigo m.

punk n punki m.

punt n barco llano m.

pup n cachorro m.

pupil n alumno m.

puppet n titere m.

puppy n perrito m.

purchase vt comprar.

pure adj puro.

puree n pure m.

purification n purificacion f.

purify vt purificar.

puritan n puritano m.

purity n pureza f.

purple adj purpureo.

purpose n intencion f.

purr vi ronronear.

purse n bolsa f; cartera f.

pursue vi perseguir.

pursuit n perseguimiento m.

purveyor n abastecedor m.

push vt empujar

pusher n traficante de drogas m.

push-up n plancha f.

put vt poner, colocar.

putrid adj podrido.

putty n masilla f.

puzzle n acertijo m.

puzzling adj extrano.

pylon n torre de conduccion electrica f.

pyramid n piramide f.

python n piton atigrado m.

Q

quack *vi* graznar.

quadrangle *n* cuadrangulo *m*.

quadrant *n* cuadrante *m*.

quadrilateral *adj* cuadrilatero.

quadruped *n* cuadrupedo *m*.

quadruple *adj* cuadruplo.

quadruplet *n* cuatrillizo *m*.

quagmire *n* tremedal *m*.

quail *n* codorniz *f*.

quaint *adj* pulido; exquisito.

quake *vi* temblar; tiritar.

qualification *n* calificacion *f*.

qualify *vt* calificar.

quality *n* calidad *f*.

qualm *n* escrupulo *m*.

quandary *n* incertidumbre *f*.

quantitative *adj* cuantitativo.

quantity *n* cantidad *f*.

quarantine *n* cuarentena *f*.

quarrel *n* rina, contienda *f*.

quarrelsome *adj* pendenciero.

quarry *n* cantera *f*.

quarter *n* cuarto *m*r.

quarterly *adj* trimestral.

quartermaster *n* (*mil*) comisario *m*.

quartet *n* (*mus*) cuarteto *m*.

quartz *n* (*min*) cuarzo *m*.

quash *vt* fracasar; anular.

quay *n* muelle *m*.

queasy *adj* nauseabundo.

queen *n* reina *f*.

queer *adj* extrano.

quell *vt* calmar.

quench *vt* apagar.

query *n* cuestion.

quest *n* pesquisa *f*.

question *n* pregunta *f*; cuestion *f*.

questionable *adj* cuestionable.

question mark *n* punto de interrogación *m*.

questionnaire *n* cuestionario *m*.

quibble *vi* buscar evasivas.

quick *adj* rapido.

quicken *vt* apresurar.

quicksand *n* arena movediza *f*.

quicksilver *n* azogue, mercurio *m*.

quick-witted *adj* agudo, perspicaz.

quiet *adj* callado.

quinine *n* quinina *f*.

quintet *n* (*mus*) quinteto *m*.

quintuple *adj* quintuplo.

quintuplet *n* quintillizo *m*.

quip *n* indirecta *f*:—*vt* echar pullas.

quirk *n* peculiaridad *f*.

quit *vt* dejar.

quite *adv* bastante.

quits *adv* ¡en paz!.

quiver *vi* temblar.

quixotic *adj* quijotesco.

quiz *n* concurso *m*.

quizzical *adj* burlon.

quota *n* cuota *f*.

quotation *n* citacion, cita *f*.

quotation marks *npl* comillas *fpl*.

quote *vt* citar.

quotient *n* cociente *m*.

R

rabbi *n* rabi *m*.
rabbit *n* conejo *m*.
rabble *n* gentuza *f*.
rabid *adj* rabioso.
rabies *n* rabia *f*.
race *n* raza.
rack *n* rejilla *f*.
racket *n* ruido *m*; raqueta *f*.
racy *adj* picante.
radiance *n* brillantez *f*.
radiant *adj* radiante.
radiate *vt*, *vi* radiar.
radiation *n* radiacion *f*.
radiator *n* radiador *m*.
radical *adj*, **~ly** *adv* radical-(mente).
radio *n* radio *f*.
radioactive *adj* radioactivo.
radish *n* rabano *m*.
radius *n* radio *f*.
raffle *n* rifa *f*.
raft *n* balsa *f*.
rafter *n* par *m*; viga *f*.
rag *n* trapo *m*.
rage *n* rabia *f*.
raid *n* incursion *f*.
rail *n* baranda, barandilla *f*.
railroad, railway *n* ferrocarril *m*.
rain *n* lluvia *f*.
rainbow *n* arco iris *m*.
raise *vt* levantar, alzar.
raisin *n* pasa *f*.
rake *n* rastro *m*.
ram *n* carnero *m*.
ramble *vi* divagar.
ramification *n* ramificacion *f*.
ramp *n* rampa *f*.
rampant *adj* exuberante.

ramshackle *adj* en ruina.
ranch *n* hacienda *f*.
rancid *adj* rancio.
rancor *n* rencor *m*.
random *adj* fortuito, sin orden.
range *vt* colocar, ordenar.
ransack *vt* saquear.
ransom *n* rescate *m*.
rape *n* violacion *f*.
rapid *adj* rapido.
rapist *n* violador *m*.
rapture *n* rapto *m*.
rare *adj* raro.
rascal *n* picaro *m*.
rash *adj* precipitado *m*; erupción (cutánea) *f*.
raspberry *n* frambuesa *f*.
rat *n* rata *f*.
rate *n* tasa *f*, precio, valor *m*.
rather *adv* mas bien; antes.
ratification *n* ratificacion *f*.
ratify *vt* ratificar.
ratio *n* razon *f*.
ration *n* racion *f*.
rational *adj* racional.
ravage *vt* saquear.
rave *vi* delirar.
raven *n* cuervo *m*.
ravine *n* barranco *m*.
ravish *vt* encantar.
ravishing *adj* encantador.
raw *adj* crudo.
ray *n* rayo de luz *m*; raya *f* (pez).
raze *vt* arrasar.
razor *n* navaja.
reach *vt* alcanzar.
react *vi* reaccionar.
reaction *n* reaccion *f*.

read *vt* leer.
readable *adj* legible.
reader *n* lector *m*.
readjust *vt* reajustar.
ready *adj* listo, pronto.
real *adj* real.
realisation *n* realizacion *f*.
realise *adv* darse cuenta de; realizar.
reality *n* realidad *f*.
realm *n* reino *m*.
ream *n* resma *f*.
reap *vt* segar.
reappear *vi* reaparecer.
rear *n* parte trasera *fr*.
rearmament *n* rearme *m*.
reason *n* razon *f*; causa *f*:— *vt*, *vi* razonar.
reassure *vt* tranquilizar, alentar; (*com*) asegurar.
rebel *n* rebelde *m/f*.
rebellion *n* rebelion *f*.
rebound *vi* rebotar.
rebuke *vt* reprender.
rebut *vi* repercutir.
recede *vi* retroceder.
receipt *n* recibo *m*
receive *vt* recibir.
recent *adj* reciente.
reception *n* recepcion *f*.
recess *n* descanso *m*.
recession *n* retirada *f*; (*com*) recesion *f*.
recipe *n* receta *f*.
recipient *n* recipiente *m*.
recital *n* recital *m*.
recite *vt* recitar.
reckless *adj* temerario.
reckon *vt* contar.
recline *vt*, *vi* reclinar(se).

recluse *n* recluso/a *m*/*f*.
recognise *vt* reconocer.
recommend *vt* recomendar.
recommendation *n* recomendacion *f*.
recompense *n* recompensa *f*.
reconcile *vt* reconciliar.
reconsider *vt* considerar de nuevo.
record *vt* registrar; grabar.
recourse *n* recurso *m*.
recover *vt* recobrar; recuperar.
recovery *n* convalecencia *f*; recobro *m*.
recreation *n* recreacion *f*; recreo *m*.
recruit *vt* reclutar.
rectangle *n* rectangulo *m*.
rectify *vt* rectificar.
rectilinear *adj* rectilineo.
rector *n* rector *m*.
recur *vi* repetirse.
red *adj* rojo; tinto:—*n* rojo *m*.
redeem *vt* redimir.
redemption *n* redencion *f*.
redhot *adj* candente, ardiente.
redress *vt* corregir.
reduce *vt* reducir.
reduction *n* reduccion *f*.
reed *n* cana *f*.
reek *n* mal olor.
refectory *n* refectorio *m*.
refer *vt*, *vi* referir.
referee *n* arbitro *m*.
reference *n* referencia.
refine *vt* refinar.
refit *vt* reparar.
reflect *vt*, *vi* reflejar.
reflection *n* reflexion *f*.
reflex *adj* reflejo.
reform *vt*, *vi* reformar(se).
refresh *vt* refrescar.
refreshment *n* refresco.
refrigerator *n* nevera *f*.
refuge *n* refugio, asilo *m*.
refugee *n* refugiado *m*/*f*.

refund *vt* devolver.
refurbish *vt* restaurar.
refusal *n* negativa *f*.
refuse *vt* rehusar.
refute *vt* refutar.
regal *adj* real.
regard *vt* estimar.
regardless *adv* a pesar de todo.
regatta *n* regata *f*.
regime *n* regimen *m*.
region *n* region *f*.
register *n* registro *m*.
registrar *n* registrador *m*.
registration *n* registro *m*.
registry *n* registro *m*.
regular *adj* regular.
regulation *n* regulacion *f*.
reign *n* reinado, reino *m*.
reinforce *vt* reforzar.
reinstate *vt* reintegrar.
reject *vt* rechazar.
rejection *n* rechazo *m*.
rejoice *vt*, *vi* regocijar(se).
relapse *vi* recaer.
relate *vt*, *vi* relatar.
relation *n* relacion *f*.
relationship *n* parentesco *m*; relacion *f*.
relative *adj* relativo.
relax *vt*, *vi* relajar.
release *vt* soltar, libertar.
relic *n* reliquia *f*.
relief *n* relieve *m*.
relieve *vt* aliviar.
religion *n* religion *f*.
rely *vi* confiar en; contar con.
remain *vi* quedar.
remains *npl* restos *mpl*.
remark *n* observacion, nota *f*.
remedial *adv* curativo.
remedy *n* remedio *m*.
remember *vt* acordarse de; recordar.
remind *vt* recordar.
remit *vt*, *vi* remitir.

remorse *n* remordimiento *m*.
remote *adj* remoto.
remove *vt* quitar.
renew *vt* renovar.
renovate *vt* renovar.
rent *n* renta *f*.
rental *n* alquiler *m*.
repair *vt* reparar.
repeat *vt* repetir.
repel *vt* repeler.
repetition *n* repeticion *f*.
replace *vt* reemplazar.
reply *n* respuesta *f*.
repose *vt*, *vi* reposar.
represent *vt* representar.
reproduce *vt* reproducir.
reproduction *n* reproduccion *f*.
reptile *n* reptil *m*.
republic *n* republica *f*.
repugnance *n* repugnancia *f*.
repulse *vt* repulsar.
request *n* peticion.
require *vt* requerir.
rescue *vt* librar.
research *vt* investigar.
resemble *vt* asemejarse.
resent *vt* resentirse.
reserve *vt* reservar.
residence *n* residencia *f*.
resign *vt*, *vi* resignar.
resin *n* resina *f*.
resist *vt* resistir, oponerse.
resolve *vt*, *vr* resolver(se).
resort *vi* recurrir.
resource *n* recurso *m*.
respect *n* respecto *m*.
respite *n* suspension *f*.
respond *vt* responder.
rest *n* reposo *m*.
restless *adj* insomne.
restore *vt* restaurar.
restrict *vt* restringir.
result *vi* resultar.
resume *vt* resumir.
resurrection *n* resurreccion *f*.

resuscitate *vt* resucitar.
retail *vt* revender *f*.
retain *vt* retener.
reticence *n* reticencia *f*.
retina *n* retina *f*.
retire *vt*, *vi* retirar(se).
retreat *n* retirada *f*.
return *vt* retribuir; restituir; devolver.
reveal *vt* revelar.
revenge *vt* vengar:—*n* venganza *f*.
revenue *n* renta *f*
revere *vt* reverenciar.
reverse *vt* trastrocar.
review *vt* rever.
revise *vt* rever; repasar.
revival *n* restauracion *f*.
revolt *vi* rebelarse.
revolution *n* revolucion *f*.
revolve *vt* revolver.
revue *n* revista *f*.
reward *n* recompensa *f*.
rheumatism *n* reumatismo *m*.
rhinoceros *n* rinoceronte *m*.
rhombus *n* rombo *m*.
rhubarb *n* ruibarbo *m*.
rhyme *n* rima *f*.
rhythm *n* ritmo *m*.
rib *n* costilla *f*.
ribbon *n* liston *m*.
rice *n* arroz *m*.
rich *adj* rico.
riches *npl* riqueza *f*.
rickets *n* raquitis *f*.
rid *vt* librar.
riddle *n* enigma *m*.
ride *vi* cabalgar.
ridge *n* espinazo.
ridiculous *adj* ridiculoso.
rifle *n* rifle *m*.
right *adj* derecho, recto; justo.—*n* derecho *m*; título *m*; privilegio *m*.
rigid *adj* rigido.
rigor *n* rigor *m*.

rind *n* corteza *f*.
rinse *vt* lavar, limpiar.
rise *vi* levantarse.
risk *n* riesgo, peligro *m*.
rite *n* rito *m*.
ritual *adj*, *n* ritual *m*.
rival *adj* emulo.
river *n* rio *m*.
road *n* camino *m*.
roadsign *n* senal de trafico *f*.
roar *vi* rugir.
roast *vt* asar.
rob *vt* robar.
robber *n* robador, ladron *m*.
robbery *n* robo *m*.
robust *adj* robusto.
rock *n* roca *f*.
rocket *n* cohete *m*.
rodent *n* roedor *m*.
rogue *n* bribon *m*.
roll *vt* rodar.
Roman Catholic *adj*, *n* catolico/a *m/f* (romano/a).
romance *n* romance *m*.
roof *n* tejado *m*.
room *n* habitacion, sala *f*.
roomy *adj* espacioso.
root *n* raiz *f*.
rope *n* cuerda *f*.
rosary *n* rosario *m*.
rose *n* rosa *f*.
rosebed *n* campo de rosales *m*.
rosebud *n* capullo de rosa *m*.
rosemary *n* (*bot*) romero *m*.
rosette *n* roseta *f*.
rot *vi* pudrirse.
rotten *adj* podrido.
rouble *n* rublo *m*.
rouge *n* arrebol *m*.
rough *adj* aspero.
roulette *n* ruleta *f*.
round *adj* redondo.
rouse *vt* despertar.
route *n* ruta *f*.
routine *adj* rutinario.
row *n* camorra *f*.

row *n* (line) hilera, fila *f*:—*vt* (*mar*) remar, bogar.
royal *adj* real.
royalty *n* realeza, dignidad real *f*.
rub *vt* estregar, fregar, frotar.
rubber *n* caucho *m*, goma *f*.
rubber-band *n* goma, gomita *f*.
rubbish *n* basura *f*.
rubric *n* rubrica *f*.
ruby *n* rubi *m*.
rucksack *n* mochila *f*.
rudder *n* timon *m*.
rude *adj* rudo, brutal.
rudiment *n* rudimentos *mpl*.
rue *vi* compadecerse.
rug *n* alfombra *f*.
rugby *n* rugby *m*.
ruin *n* ruina *f*.
ruinous *adj* ruinoso.
rule *n* mando *m*; regla *f*.
ruler *n* gobernador *m*; regla *f*.
rum *n* ron *m*.
rumour *n* rumor *m*.
run *vt* dirigir; organizar, *vi* correr.
runaway *n* fugitivo.
rung *n* escalon.
runway *n* pista de aterrizaje *f*.
rupture *n* rotura *f*.
rural *adj* rural.
ruse *n* astucia *f*.
rush *n* junco *m*; rafaga *f*.
rusk *n* galleta *f*.
russet *adj* bermejo.
rust *n* herrumbre *f*.
rustic *adj* rustico.
rustle *vi* crujir.
rut *n* celo *m*.
ruthless *adj* cruel.
rye *n* (*bot*) centeno *m*.

S

Sabbath *n* sabado *m*.
sabotage *n* sabotaje *m*.
saccharin *n* sacarina *f*.
sachet *n* sobrecito *m*.
sack *n* saco *m*:—*vt* despedir.
sacrament *n* sacramento *m*.
sacred *adj* sagrado.
sacredness *n* santidad *f*.
sacrifice *n* sacrificio *m*.
sacrilege *n* sacrilegio *m*.
sad *adj* triste.
saddle *n* silla *f*.
sadness *n* tristeza *f*.
safari *n* safari *m*.
safe *adj* seguro; *n* caja fuerte *f*.
safety *n* seguridad *f*
saffron *n* azafran *m*.
sage *n* (*bot*) salvia *f*.
Sagittarius *n* Sagitario *m* (signo del zodiaco).
sago *n* (*bot*) zagu *m*.
sail *n* vela *f*.
sailor *n* marinero *m*.
saint *n* santo *m*; santa *f*.
sake *n* causa, razon *f*.
salad *n* ensalada *f*.
salamander *n* salamandra *f*.
salary *n* sueldo *m*.
sale *n* venta *f*.
salient *adj* saliente.
saline *adj* salino.
saliva *n* saliva *f*.
salmon *n* salmon *m*.
salmon trout *n* trucha salmonada *f*.
saloon *n* bar *m*.
salt *n* sal *f*.
salubrious *adj* salubre.
salutation *n* salutacion *f*.
salute *vt* saludar.

same *adj* mismo, idéntico/a
sample *n* muestra *f*; ejemplo *m*.
sanctify *vt* santificar.
sanctuary *n* santuario *m*.
sand *n* arena *f*.
sandal *n* sandalia *f*.
sandstone *n* piedra arenisca *f*.
sandwich *n* bocadillo *m*.
sane *adj* sapo.
sanitarium *n* sanatorio *m*.
sanity *n* juicio sano *m*.
sap *n* savia *f*.
sapling *n* arbolito *m*.
sapphire *n* zafir *m*.
sarcasm *n* sarcasmo *m*.
sarcophagus *n* sarcofago.
sardine *n* sardina *f*.
Satan *n* Satanas *m*.
satchel *n* mochila *f*.
satellite *n* satelite *m*.
satin *n* raso *m*.
satire *n* satira *f*.
satisfaction *n* satisfaccion *f*.
satisfy *vt* satisfacer.
Saturday *n* sabado *m*.
satyr *n* satiro *m*.
sauce *n* salsa *f*.
saucepan *n* cazo *m*.
saucer *n* platillo *m*.
sausage *n* salchicha *f*.
savage *adj* salvaje
savagery *n* crueldad *f*.
savannah *n* sabana *f*.
save *vt* salvar.
saveloy *n* chorizo *m*.
Saviour *n* Salvador *m*.
savoury *adj* sabroso.
saw *n* sierra *f*.
saxophone *n* saxofono *m*.
say *vt* decir.

saying *n* dicho *m*.
scab *n* rona *f*.
scald *vt* escaldar.
scale *n* balanza *f*.
scalp *n* cabellera *f*.
scamp *n* bribon.
scampi *npl* gambas *fpl*.
scan *vt* escudrinar.
scandal *n* escandalo *m*.
scandalise *vt* escandalizar.
scar *n* cicatriz *f*.
scarce *adj* raro.
scare *vt* espantar.
scarf *n* bufanda *f*.
scarlet *n* escarlata *f*.
scarp *n* escarpa *f*.
scene *n* escena *f*.
scenery *n* vista *f*.
schedule *n* horario *m*.
scheme *n* proyecto, plan *m*.
schism *n* cisma *m*.
scholar *n* estudiante *m*
school *n* escuela *f*.
schoolteacher *n* maestro, tra *m*/*f*; profesor, ra *m*/*f*.
science *n* ciencia *f*.
scientist *n* cientifico, ca *m*/*f*.
scissors *npl* tijeras *fpl*.
scooter *n* moto *f*
scorch *vt* quemar.
scorn *vt*, *vi* despreciar
Scorpio *n* Escorpion *m* (signo del zodiaco).
scorpion *n* escorpion *m*.
Scotch *n* whisky escoces *m*.
scoundrel *n* picaro *m*.
scramble *vi* arrapar.
scrap *n* migaja *f*; sobras *fpl*.
scrape *vt*, *vi* raer, raspar.
scraper *n* rascador *m*.

scratch *vt* rascar

scrawl *vt, vi* garrapatear.

scream, screech *vi* chillar.

screen *n* pantalla *f.*

screenplay *n* guion *m.*

screw *n* tornillo *m.*

screwdriver *n* destornillador *m.*

scribble *vt* escarabajear.

scribe *n* escritor *m.*

script *n* guion *m;* letra *f.*

Scripture *n* Escritura sagrada *f.*

scruffy *adj* desalinado.

scruple *n* escrupulo *m.*

scullery *n* fregadero *m.*

sculptor *n* escultor, ra *m/f.*

sculpture *n* escultura *f.*

scum *n* espuma *f;* escoria *f.*

scurvy *n* escorbuto *m.*

scythe *n* guadana *f.*

sea *n* mar *m/f.—adj* de *mar.*

sea breeze *n* viento de *mar m.*

seafood *n* mariscos *mpl.*

sea front *n* paseo maritimo *m.*

seagull *n* gaviota *f.*

sea horse *n* hipocampo *m.*

seal *n* sello *m;* foca *f.*

seam *n* costura *f.*

seaman *n* marinero *m.*

sea plane *n* hidroavion *m.*

sear *vt* cauterizar.

search *vt* examinar, buscar.

seashore *n* ribera *f,* litoral *m.*

seasick *adj* mareado.

season *n* estacion *f.*

seasoning *n* condimento *m.*

seat *n* asiento *m;* silla *f.*

seat belt *n* cinturon de seguridad *m.*

seaweed *n* alga marina *f.*

seclude *vt* apartar.

seclusion *n* separacion *f.*

second *adj* segundo.

secondary *adj* secundario.

secondhand *n* segunda mano *f.*

secret *adj, n* secreto *m.*

secretary *n* secretario, ria *m/f.*

sect *n* secta *f.*

section *n* seccion *f.*

sector *n* sector *m.*

secular *adj* secular.

secure *adj* seguro.

security *n* seguridad *f.*

sedate *adj* sosegado.

sedative *n* sedativo *m.*

sedge *n* (*bot*) junco *m.*

sediment *n* sedimento *m*

sedition *n* sedicion *f.*

seduce *vt* seducir.

seducer *n* seductor *m.*

seduction *n* seduccion *f.*

seductive *adj* seductivo.

see *vt, vi* ver

seed *n* semilla.

seedy *adj* desaseado.

seek *vt, vi* buscar.

seem *vi* parecer.

seemliness *n* decensia *f.*

seesaw *n* vaiven *m.*

seethe *vi* hervir.

segment *n* segmento *m.*

seize *vt* asir.

seizure *n* captura *f.*

seldom *adv* raramente.

select *vt* elegir.

selection *n* seleccion *f.*

self *n* uno mismo.

selfish *adj* egoista.

self-portrait *n* autorretrato *m.*

selfsame *adj* identico.

sell *vt, vi* vender.

semen *n* semen *m.*

semester *n* semestre *m.*

semicircle *n* semicirculo *m.*

semicircular *adj* semicircular.

semicolon *n* punto y coma *m.*

seminary *n* seminario *m.*

senate *n* senado *m.*

senator *n* senador, ra *m/f.*

send *vt* enviar.

sender *n* remitente *m.*

senile *adj* senil.

senior *n* mayor *m.*

senna *n* (*bot*) sena *f.*

sensation *n* sensacion *f.*

sense *n* sentido *m.*

sensibility *n* sensibilidad *f.*

sensible *adj* sensato/a, juicioso/a.

sensitive *adj* sensitivo.

sensual, sensuous *adj* sensual.

sensuality *n* sensualidad *f.*

sentence *n* oracion *f;* sentencia *f.*

sentiment *n* sentimiento *m.*

sentinel, sentry *n* centinela *m.*

separate *vt* (*vi*) separar(se).

separation *n* separacion *f.*

September *n* se(p)tiembre *m.*

sepulcher *n* sepulcro *m.*

sequel *n* continuacion *f.*

sequence *n* serie *f.*

seraph *n* serafin *m.*

serenade *n* serenata *f.*

serene *adj* seneno.

serenity *n* serenidad *f.*

serf *n* siervo *m.*

sergeant *n* sargento *m.*

serial *adj* consecutivo.

series *n* serie *f.*

serious *adj* serio, grave.

sermon *n* sermon *f.*

serious *adj* seroso.

serpent *n* serpiente *f.*

serpentine *adj* serpentino.

serrated *adj* serrado.

serum *n* suero *m.*

servant *n* criado *m;* criada *f.*

serve *vt, vi* servir.

service *n* servicio *m.*

servile *adj* servil.

session *n* junta *f;* sesion *f.*

set *vt* poner, colocar, fijar.

settee *n* sofa *m.*

setter *n* perro de muestra *m.*

seven *adj, n* siete.

seventeen *adj, n* diez y siete, diecisiete.

seventeenth *adj, n* decimoseptimo.

seventh *adj, n* septimo.
seventieth *adj, n* septuagesimo.
seventy *adj, n* setenta.
sever *vt, vi* separar.
several *adj, pn* varios.
severance *n* separacion *f.*
severe *adj* severo.
severity *n* severidad *f.*
sew *vt, vi* coser.
sewer *n* albanal *m.*
sex *n* sexo *m.*
sexist *adj n* sexista *m/f.*
sexual *adj* sexual.
sexy *adj* sexy.
shade *n* sombra.
shadow *n* sombra *f.*
shaft *n* flecha, saeta *f.*
shake *vt* sacudir; agitar.
shallow *adj* somero.
sham *vt* enganar.
shame *n* verguenza *f.*
shamefaced *adj* vergonzoso.
shampoo champu *m.*
shamrock *n* trebol *m.*
shank *n* pierna *f.*
shanty *n* chabola *f.*
shantytown *n* barrio de chabolas *m.*
shape *vt, vi* formar; *n* forma *m.*
shapeless *adj* informe.
shapely *adj* bien hecho.
share *n* parte, porcion *f;* compartir.
shark *n* tiburon *m.*
sharp *adj* agudo.
shatter *vt* destrozar.
shave *vt* afeitar.
shaver *n* maquina de afeitar *f.*
shawl *n* chal *m.*
she *pn* ella.
sheaf *n* gavilla *f*
shear *vt* atusar.
sheath *n* vaina *f.*
shed *vt* verter; cabana *f.*
sheen *n* resplandor *m.*
sheep *n* oveja *f.*
sheer *adj* puro, claro.

sheet *n* sabana *f.*
sheet lightning *n* relampagueamiento *m.*
shelf *n* anaquel *m.*
shell *n* cascara *f;* concha *f.*
shelter *n* guardia *f;* amparo *m.*
shepherd *n* pastor *m.*
sherbet *n* sorbete *m.*
sheriff *n* sherif *m.*
sherry *n* jerez *m.*
shield *n* escudo *m.*
shift *vi* cambiarse.
shinbone *n* espinilla *f.*
shine *vi* lucir, brillar.
shiny *adj* brillante.
ship *n* nave *f;* barco *m.*
shipwreck *n* naufragio *m.*
shirt *n* camisa *f.*
shit *excl* (*sl*) ¡mierda!
shiver *vi* tiritar de frio.
shoal *n* banco *m.*
shock *n* choque *m.*
shock absorber *n* amortiguador *m.*
shoddy *adj* de pacotilla.
shoe *n* zapato *m.*
shoelace *n* correa de zapato *f.*
shoemaker *n* zapatero *m.*
shoot *vt* tirar.
shop *n* tienda *f.*
shopper *n* comprador, ra *m/f.*
shopping *n* compras *fpl.*
shopping centre *n* centro comercial *m.*
shore *n* costa, ribera *f.*
short *adj* corto breve.
short-sighted *adj* corto de vista.
shot *n* tiro *m.*
shotgun *n* escopeta *f.*
shoulder *n* hombro *m.*
shout *vi* gritar, aclamar.
shove *vt, vi* empujar.
shovel *n* pala *f.*
show *vt* mostrar.
shower *n* nubada *f;* llovizna *f;* ducha *f.*

showy *adj* ostentoso.
shred *n* cacho, pedazo.
shrewd *adj* astuto.
shriek *vt, vi* chillar
shrimp *n* camaron *m.*
shrine *n* relicario *m.*
shrink *vi* encogerse.
shroud *n* cubierta *f.*
Shrove Tuesday *n* martes de carnaval *m.*
shrub *n* arbusto *m,*
shrug *vt* encogerse de hombros.
shun *vt* huir, evitar.
shut *vt* cerrar.
shutter *n* contraventana *f.*
shuttle *n* lanzadera *f.*
shuttlecock *n* volante *m.*
shy *adj* timido.
shyness *n* timidez *f.*
sick *adj* malo, enfermo.
sickle *n* hoz *f.*
sickness *n* enfermedad *f.*
side *n* lado *m.*
sideboard *n* aparador *m;* alacena *f.*
siege *n* (*mil*) sitio *m.*
sieve *n* tamiz *m.*
sift *vt* cerner.
sigh *vi* suspirar.
sight *n* vista *f.*
sightseeing *n* excursionismo, turismo *m.*
sign *n* senal *f.*
signal *n* senal *f.*
signature *n* firma *f.*
significance *n* importancia *f.*
signify *vt* significar.
signpost *n* indicador *m.*
silence *n* silencio *m.*
silk *n* seda *f.*
silky *adj* hecho de seda; sedeno.
sill *n* repisa *f.*
silly *adj* tonto.
silver *n* plata *f.*
similar *adj* similar; semejante.

similarity *n* semejanza *f*.
simile *n* simil *m*.
simmer *vi* hervir a fuego lento.
simple *adj* simple.
simplicity *n* sencillez *ff*.
simulate *vt* simular.
simulation *n* simulacion *f*.
sin *n* pecado *m*.
since *adv* desde.
sincerity *n* sinceridad *f*.
sinew *n* tendon *m*; nervio *m*.
sing *vi, vt* cantar.
singe *vt* chamuscar.
singer *n* cantor *m*; cantora *f*.
single *adj* solo; soltero, soltera.
singly *adv* separadamente.
singular *adj* singular.
sinister *adj* siniestro.
sink *vi* hundirse.
sinner *n* pecador *m*; pecadora *f*.
sinus *n* seno *m*.
sip *vt* sorber:—*n* sorbo *m*.
siphon *n* sifon *m*.
sir *n* senor *m*.
siren *n* sirena *f*.
sister *n* hermana *f*.
sister-in-law *n* cunada *f*.
sisterly *adj* con hermandad.
sit *vi* sentarse.
site *n* sitio *m*; situacion *f*.
sit-in *n* ocupacion *f*.
sitting room *n* sala de estar *f*.
situation *n* situacion *f*.
six *adj, n* seis.
sixteen *adj, n* diez y seis, dieciseis.
sixteenth *adj, n* decimosexto.
sixth *adj, n* sexto.
sixtieth *adj, n* sexagesimo.
sixty *adj, n* sesenta.
size *n* tamano *m*.
skate *n* patin *m*:—*vi* patinar.
skeleton *n* esqueleto *m*.
skeptic *n* esceptico.
skepticism *n* escepticismo *m*.

sketch *n* esbozo *m*.
ski *n* esqui *m*:—*vi* esquiar.
skid *n* patinazo *m*.
skill *n* destreza *f*.
skim *vt* espumar.
skin *n* piel *f*; cutis *m*/*f*.
skip *vi* saltar, brincar.
skirt *n* falda.
skittle *n* bolo *m*.
skulk *vi* escuchar, acechar.
skull *n* craneo *m*.
sky *n* cielo *m*.
skyscraper *n* rascacielos *m* invar.
slab *n* losa *f*.
slack *adj* flojo.
slag *n* escoria *f*.
slander *vt* calumniar *f*.
slang *n* argot *m f*.
slap *n* manotada *f*.
slate *n* pizarra *f*.
slave *n* esclavo *m*.
slaver *n* baba *f*:—*vi* babosear.
slay *vt* matar.
sled, sleigh *n* trineo *m*.
sleek *adj* liso.
sleep *vi* dormir.
sleeping bag *n* saco de dormir *m*.
sleeping pill *n* somnifero *m*.
sleepwalking *n* sonambulismo *m*.
sleet *n* aguanieve *f*.
sleeve *n* manga *f*.
slender *adj* delgado.
slice *n* rebanada *f*.
slide *vi* resbalar, deslizarse.
slight *adj* ligero.
slim *adj* delgado.
slime *n* lodo *m f*.
slimy *adj* viscoso, pegajoso.
sling *n* honda *f*; cabestrillo *m*.
slip *vi* resbalar; escapar.
slipper *n* zapatilla *f*.
slogan *n* eslogan, lema *m*.
slope *n* cuesta *f*.
slow *adj* tardio, lento, torpe.

slum *n* tugurio *m*.
slump *n* depresion *f*.
slur *vt* ensuciar; calumniar.
slut *n* marrana *f*.
sly *adj* astuto.
smack *n* sabor, gusto *m*; chasquido de latigo *m*.
small *adj* pequeno.
smallpox *n* viruelas *fpl*.
smalltalk *n* charla, prosa *f*.
smart *adj* elegante; listo.
smash *vt* romper, quebrantar
smell *vt, vi* oler.
smile *vi* sonreirse:—*n* sonrisa *f*.
smoke *n* humo *m*; fumar.
smoker *n* fumador, ra *m*/*f*.
smooth *adj* liso.
smug *adj* presumido.
smut *n* tiznon *m*.
snack *n* bocadom.
snag *n* problema *m*.
snail *n* caracol *m*.
snake *n* culebra *f*.
snap *vt, vi* romper.
snapdragon *n* (*bot*) antirrino *m*.
snatch *vt* arrebatar.
sneeze *vi* estornudar.
sniff *vt* oler:—*vi* resollar con fuerza.
snob *n* (e)snob *m*/*f*.
snore *vi* roncar.
snow *n* nieve *f*.
snowdrop *n* (*bot*) campanilla blanca *f*.
snowman *n* figura de nieve *f*.
snub *vt* reprender.
snuff *n* rape *m*.
so *adv* asi; de este modo; tan.
soap *n* jabon *m*.
soap opera *n* telenovela *f*.
soar *vi* remontarse.
sob *n* sollozo *m*:—*vi* sollozar.
soccer *n* futbol *m*.
sociable *adj* sociable.
social *adj* social.
socialism *n* socialismo *m*.

society *n* sociedad *f*.

sociologist *n* sociologo, ga *m/f*.

sociology *n* sociologia *f*.

sock *n* calcetin *m*.

socket *n* enchufe *m*.

sod *n* cesped *m*.

soda *n* sosa *f*.

sofa *n* sofa *m*.

soft *adj* blando.

soil *vt* ensuciar, tierra *f*.

solar *adj* solar.

soldier *n* soldado *m*.

sole *n* planta del pie *f*.

solemn *adj*, **~ly** *adv* solemne-(mente).

solicitor *n* representante, agente *m/f*.

solid *adj* solido.

solitaire *n* solitario *m*; grueso diamante *m*.

solitude *n* soledad *f*.

solo *n* (*mus*) solo *m*.

solstice *n* solsticio *m*.

soluble *adj* soluble.

solution *n* solucion *f*.

solve *vt* resolver.

some *adj* algo de, un poco, algun, alguno, alguna, unos, pocos, ciertos.

somebody *n* alguien *m*.

something *n* alguna cosa, algo.

sometimes *adv* a veces.

somnambulism *n* somnambulismo *m*.

somnambulist *n* somnambulo *m*.

somnolence *n* somnolencia *f*.

son *n* hijo *m*.

sonata *n* (*mus*) sonata *f*.

song *n* cancion.

son-in-law *n* yerno *m*.

sonnet *n* soneto *m*.

soon *adv* pronto.

soot *n* hollin *m*.

soothe *vt* adular; calmar.

sop *n* sopa *f*.

sophisticate *vt* sofisticar.

sophisticated *adj* sofisticado.

sorcerer *n* hechicero *m*.

sorcery *n* hechizo*m*.

sordid *adj* sordido.

sore *n* llaga, ulcera *f*.

sorrow *n* pesar *m*; tristeza *f*.

sorry *adj* triste.

soul *n* alma *f*.

sound *adj* sano; sonido,*vi* sonar.

soup *n* sopa *f*.

sour *adj* agrio.

souvenir *n* recuerdo *m*.

south *n* sur *m*.

sovereign *adj*, *n* soberano, na (*m/f*).

sovereignty *n* soberania *f*.

sow *n* puerca *f*.

sow *vt* sembrar.

space *n* espacio *m*.

spacious *adj* espacioso.

spade *n* laya.

spaghetti *n* espaguetis *mpl*.

span *n* palmo *m*.

spangle *n* lentejuela *f*.

spaniel *n* perro de aguas *m*.

Spanish *adj* espanol(a)

spar *n* palo *m*.

spark *n* chispa *f*.

sparkle *n* centella.

sparrow *n* gorrion *m*.

sparse *adj* delgado.

spasm *n* espasmo *m*.

spatula *n* espatula *f*.

spawn *n* freza *f*.

speak *vt*, *vi* hablar.

spear *n* lanza *f*.

special *adj* especial.

species *n* especie *f*.

specific *adj* especifico *m*.

specimen *n* muestra *f*.

spectacle *n* espectaculo *m*.

spectator *n* espectador, ra *m/f*.

spectre *n* espectro *m*.

speculate *vi* especular.

speculation *n* especulacion *f*.

speed *n* prisa *f*; velocidad *f*.

spell *n* hechizo*m*.

spelling *n* ortografia *f*.

spend *vt* gastar.

sperm *n* esperma *f*.

spew *vi* (*sl*) vomitar.

sphere *n* esfera *f*.

spherical *adj* esferico.

spice *n* especia *f*.

spicy *adj* aromatico.

spider *n* arana *f*.

spike *n* espigon *m*.

spill *vt* derramar.

spin *vt* hilar.

spinach *n* espinaca *f*.

spinal *adj* espinal.

spine *n* espinazo *m*.

spinster *n* soltera *f*.

spiral *adj* espiral.

spire *n* espira *f*.

spirit *n* aliento *m*; espiritu *m*.

spiritual *adj*, **~ly** *adv* espiritual-(mente).

spiritualist *n* espiritualista *m*.

spit *n* asador *m*; saliva *f*.

spite *n* rencor *m*.

splash *vt* salpicar.

spleen *n* bazo *m*.

splendid *adj* esplendido.

splendor *n* esplendor *m*.

splint *n* tablilla *f*.

splinter *n* cacho *m*.

split *n* hendedura *f*.

spoil *vt* despojar.

spoke *n* rayo de la rueda *m*.

spokesman *n* portavoz *m*.

sponge *n* esponja *f*.

sponsor *n* fiador *m*.

spontaneity *n* espontaneidad *f*.

spool *n* carrete *m*.

spoon *n* cuchara *f*.

spoonful *n* cucharada *f*.

sport *n* deporte *m*

spot *n* mancha *f*.

spouse *n* esposo *m*; esposa *f*.

sprain *adj* descoyuntar.
sprat *n* meleta, nuesa *f* (pez).
sprawl *vi* revolcarse.
spray *n* rociada *f*; espray *m*.
spread *vt* extender
spree *n* fiesta *f*; juerga *f*.
sprig *n* ramito *m*.
sprinkle *vt* rociar.
spur *n* espuela *f*.
spurn *vt* despreciar.
spy *n* espia *m*.
squad *n* escuadra *f*.
squadron *n* (*mil*) escuadron *m*.
squalid *adj* sucio.
squall *n* rafaga *f*.
squalor *n* porqueria *f*.
squander *vt* malgastar.
square *adj* cuadrado *m*; plaza *f*.
squash *vt* aplastar
squaw *n* hembra de un indiano *f*.
squeak *vi* planir
squeamish *adj* fastidioso.
squeeze *vt* apretar.
squid *n* calamar *m*.
squint *adj* bizco.
squirrel *n* ardilla *f*.
stable *n* establo *m*.
stack *n* pila *f*.
staff *n* personal *m*.
stag *n* ciervo *m*.
stage *n* etapa *f*; escena *f*
stagnate *vi* estancarse.
stain *vt* manchar.
stair *n* escalon *m*.
staircase *n* escalera *f*.
stale *adj* anejo.
stalk , tronco *m*.
stall *n* pesebre *m*; tienda portatil *f*.
stallion *n* semental *m*.
stamina *n* resistencia *f*.
stammer *vi* tartamudear
stamp estampar, imprimir; sello *m*.
stampede *n* estampida *f*.

stand *vi* estar de pie o derecho; stand *m*.
standard *n* estandarte *m*.
staple *n* grapa *f*.
star *n* estrella *f*.
starch *n* almidon *m*.
stark *adj* fuerte, aspero.
starling *n* estornino *m*.
start *vi* empezar.
startle *vt* sobresaltar.
starvation *n* hambre *f*.
state *n* estado *m*; condicion *f*.
statement *n* afirmacion *f*.
static *adj* estatico.
station *n* estacion *f*.
stationary *adj* estacionario, fijo.
stationery *n* papeleria *f*.
statistics *npl* estadistica *f*.
statuary *n* estatuario *m*.
statue *n* estatua *f*.
stature *n* estatura *f*.
statute *n* estatuto *m*.
stay *n* estancia *f*.
steak *n* filete *m*; bistec *m*.
steal *vt, vi* robar.
stealth *n* hurto *m*.
steam *n* vapor *m*.
steel *n* acero *m*.
steep *adj* escarpado.
steeple *n* torre *f*; campanario *m*.
steer *n* novillo *m*:—*vt* manejar, conducir.
steering wheel *n* volante *m*.
stem *n* vastago.
stench *n* hedor *m*.
stencil *n* cliche *m*.
stenographer *n* taquigrafo, fa *m/f*.
stenography *n* taquigrafia *f*.
step *n* paso, escalon *m*.
stepbrother *n* hermanastro *m*.
stepdaughter *n* hijastra *f*.
stepfather *n* padrastro *m*.
stepmother *n* madrastra *f*.
stepsister *n* hermanastra *f*.

stepson *n* hijastro *m*.
stereo *n* estereo *m*.
stereotype *n* estereotipo *m*.
sterile *adj* esteril.
sterling *n* libras esterlinas *fpl*.
stethoscope *n* (*med*) estetoscopio *m*.
stew *vt* estofar *f*.
steward *n* mayordomo *m*
stick *n* palo, pegarse.
stiff *adj* tieso.
stifle *vt* sufocar.
stigma *n* estigma *m*.
stigmatise *vt* infamar.
stiletto *n* estilete *m*
still tranquilo; *adv* todavia.
still-born *adj* nacido muerto.
stilts *npl* zancos *mpl*.
stimulant *n* estimulante *m*.
stimulate *vt* estimular.
stimulus *n* estimulo *m*.
sting *vt* picar o morder (un insecto).
stingy *adj* mezquino.
stink *vi* heder.
stint *n* tarea *f*.
stipulate *vt* estipular.
stipulation *n* estipulacion *f*
stir *vt* agitar.
stirrup *n* estribo *m*.
stitch *vt* coser.
stoat *n* comadreja *f*.
stock *n* ganado *m*; caldo *m*.
stockbroker *n* agente de bolsa *m/f*.
stock exchange *n* bolsa *f*.
stocking *n* media *f*.
stock market *n* bolsa *f*.
stoic *n* estoico *m*.
stoical *adj* estoico.
stole *n* estola *f*.
stomach *n* estomago *m*.
stone *n* piedra *f*.
stop *vt* detener, parar.
stopwatch *n* cronometro *m*.
store *n* provision *f*; almacen *m*.

stork *n* ciguena *f*.
storm *n* tempestad.
story *n* historia *f*.
stout *adj* robusto.
stove *n* estufa *f*.
straight *adj* derecho.
strain *vt* colar, filtrar; *n* tension *f*.
strainer *n* colador *m*.
strange *adj* raro/a, extranjero.
stranger *n* desconocido *m*; extranjero, ra *m/f*.
strangle *vt* ahogar.
strap *n* correa.
strapping *adj* abultado.
stratagem *n* estratagema *f*; astucia *f*.
strategic *adj* estrategico *m*.
strategy *n* estrategia *f*.
stratum *n* estrato *m*.
straw *n* paja *m*; pajita *f*.
strawberry *n* fresa *f*.
stray *vi* extraviarse.
streak *n* raya.
stream *n* arroyo, rio.
street *n* calle *f*.
streetcar *n* tranvia *f*.
strength *n* fuerza.
strenuous *adj* arduo.
stress *n* presion *f*; estres *m*.
stretch *vt, vi* extender.
stretcher *n* camilla *f*.
strew *vt* esparcir.
strict *adj* estricto.
stride *n* tranco *m*.
string *n* cordon *m*.
stringent *adj* astringente.
strip *vt* desnudar.
stripe *n* raya.
strive *vi* esforzarse.
stroll *n* paseo.
strong *adj* fuerte.
strongbox *n* cofre fuerte *m*.
structure *n* estructura *f*.
struggle *vi* esforzarse.
strum *vt* (*mus*) rasguear.
strut *vi* pavonearse.

stubborn *adj* obstinado.
stucco *n* estuco *m*.
stud *n* corchete *m*.
student *n* estudiante *m/f*.
studio *n* estudio de un artista *m*.
studious *adj* estudioso.
study *n* estudio *m*.
stuff *n* materia *f*.
stuffing *n* relleno *m*.
stumble *vi* tropezar
stump *n* tronco *m*.
stun *vt* aturdir.
stunt *n* vuelo acrobático *m*; truco publicitario *m*.
stuntman *n* especialista *m*.
stupid *adj* estupido.
sturdy *adj* fuerte.
sturgeon *n* esturion *m*.
stutter *vi* tartamudear.
sty *n* zahurda *f*.
stye *n* orzuelo *m*.
style *n* estilo *m*.
stylish *adj* elegante.
suave *adj* afable.
subdivide *vt* subdividir.
subdue *vt* sojuzgar, sujetar.
subject *adj* sujeto.
subjunctive *n* subjuntivo *m*.
sublime *adj* sublime
submarine *adj* submarino.
submerge *vt* sumergir.
submit *vt*, (*vi*) someter(se).
subordinate *adj* subordinado, inferior:—*vt* subordinar.
subscribe *vt, vi* suscribir.
subsequent *adj*, ~**ly** *adv* subsiguien-te(mente).
subservient *adj* subordinado.
subside *vi* sumergirse.
subsidence *n* derrumbamiento *m*.
subsidiary *adj* subsidiario.
subsidise *vt* subvencionar.
subsidy *n* subvencion *f*.
substance *n* substancia *f*.
substitute *vt* sustituir.

substratum *n* lecho *m*.
subterranean *adj* subterraneo.
subtitle *n* subtitulo *m*.
subtle *adj* sutil.
suburb *n* suburbio *m*.
subversion *n* subversion *f*.
subway *n* metro *m*.
succeed *vt, vi* seguir; conseguir, lograr, tener exito.
success *n* exito *m*.
succumb *vi* sucumbir.
such *adj* tal.
suck *vt, vi* chupar.
sudden *adj* repentino, no previsto.
sue *vt* poner por justicia; suplicar.
suede *n* ante *m*.
suffer *vt, vi* sufrir, padecer.
sufficient *adj* suficiente.
suffocate *vt* sufocar.
suffrage *n* sufragio.
sugar *n* azucar *m*.
sugar cane *n* cana de azucar *f*.
suggest *vt* sugerir.
suggestion *n* sugestion *f*.
suicide *n* suicidio *m*.
suit *n* conjunto *m*; traje *m*.
suitcase *n* maleta *f*.
suitor *n* suplicante *m*.
sultan *n* sultan *m*.
sultana *n* sultana *f*.
sum *n* suma *f*.
summary *adj, n* sumario (*m*).
summer *n* verano *m*.
summit *n* apice *m*.
summon *vt* citar.
summons *n* citacion *f*.
sumptuous *adj* suntuoso.
sun *n* sol *m*.
sunbathe *vi* tomar el sol.
Sunday *n* domingo *m*.
sundial *n* reloj de sol *m*.
sundry *adj* varios.
sunflower *n* girasol *m*.
sunglasses *npl* gafas o antojos de sol *mpl*.

sunlight *n* luz del sol *f*.

sunrise *n* salida del sol *f*.

sunset *n* puesta del sol *f*.

sunshade *n* quitasol *m*.

sunstroke *n* insolacion *f*.

suntan *n* bronceado *m*.

suntan oil *n* aceite bronceador *m*.

superb *adj* magnifico.

superficial *adj* superficial.

superfluity *n* superfluidad *f*.

superior *adj, n* superior (*m*).

supermarket *n* supermercado *m*.

supernatural *n* sobrenatural.

superpower *n* superpotencia *f*.

superstition *n* supersticion *f*.

supertanker *n* superpetrolero *m*.

supervise *vt* inspeccionar.

supper *n* cena *f*.

supple *adj* flexible.

supplement *n* suplemento *m*.

supplementary *adj* adicional.

suppleness *n* flexibilidad *f*.

suppli(c)ant *n* suplicante *m*.

supplicate *vt* suplicar.

supplication *n* suplica, suplicacion *f*.

supplier *n* distribuidor, ra *m / f*.

supply *vt* suministrar; suplir, completar; surtir:—*n* provision *f*; suministro *m*.

support *vt* sostener; soportar, asistir: —*n* apoyo *m*.

supportable *adj* soportable.

supporter *n* partidario, ria; aficionado, da *m / f*.

suppose *vt, vi* suponer.

supposition *n* suposicion *f*.

suppress *vt* suprimir.

suppression *n* supresion *f*.

supremacy *n* supremacia *f*.

supreme *adj* supremo:—**~ly** *adv* supremamente.

surcharge *vt* sobrecargar:—*n* sobretasa *f*.

sure *adj* seguro, cierto; firme; estable:—**to be ~** sin duda; ya se ve:—**~ly** *adv* ciertamente, seguramente, sin duda.

sureness *n* certeza, seguridad *f*.

surety *n* seguridad *f*; fiador *m*.

surf *n* (*mar*) resaca *f*.

surface *n* superficie *f*:—*vt* revestir:—*vi* salir a la superficie.

surfboard *n* plancha (de surf) *f*.

surfeit *n* exceso *m*.

surge *n* ola, onda *f*:—*vi* avanzar en tropel.

surgeon *n* cirujano, na *m / f*.

surgery *n* cirujia *m*.

surgical *adj* quirurgico.

surliness *n* mal humor *m*.

surly *adj* aspero de genio.

surmise *vt* sospechar:—*n* sospecha *f*.

surmount *vt* sobrepujar.

surmountable *adj* superable.

surname *n* apellido, sobrenombre *m*.

surpass *vt* sobresalir, sobrepujar, exceder, aventajar.

surpassing *adj* sobresaliente.

surplice *n* sobrepelliz *f*.

surplus *n* excedente *m*; sobrante *m*:—*adj* sobrante.

surprise *vt* sorprender:—*n* sorpresa *f*.

surprising *adj* sorprendente.

surrender *vt, vi* rendir; ceder; rendirse:—*n* rendicion *f*.

surreptitious *adj* subrepticio:—**~ly** *adv* subrepticiamente.

surrogate *vt* subrogar:—*n* subrogado *m*.

surrogate mother *n* madre portadora *f*.

surround *vt* circundar, cercar, rodear.

survey *vt* inspeccionar, examinar; apear: —*n* inspeccion *f*; apeo (de tierras) *m*.

survive *vi* sobrevivir:—*vt* sobrevivir a.

survivor *n* sobreviviente *m / f*.

susceptibility *n* susceptibilidad *f*.

susceptible *adj* susceptible.

suspect *vt, vi* sospechar:—*n* sospechoso, sa *m / f*.

suspend *vt* suspender.

suspense *n* suspense *m*; detencion *f*; incertidumbre *f*.

suspension *n* suspension *f*.

suspension bridge *n* puente colgante o colgado *m*.

suspicion *n* sospecha *f*.

suspicious *adj* suspicaz:—**~ly** *adv* sospechosamente.

suspiciousness *n* suspicacia *f*.

sustain *vt* sostener, sustentar, mantener; apoyar; sufrir.

sustenance *n* sostenimiento, sustento *m*.

suture *n* sutura, costura *f*.

swab *n* algodon *m*; frotis *m* invar.

swaddle *vt* fajar.

swaddling-clothes *npl* panales *mpl*.

swagger *vi* baladronear.

swallow *n* golondrina *f*:—*vt* tragar, engullir.

swamp *n* pantano *m*.

swampy *adj* pantanoso.

swan *n* cisne *m*.

swap *vt* canjear:—*n* intercambio *m*.

swarm *n* enjambre *m*; gentio *m*; hormiguero *m*:—*vi* enjam brar; hormiguear de gente; abundar.

swarthy *adj* atezado.

swarthiness *n* tez morena *f.*

swashbuckling *adj* fanfarron.

swath *n* tranco *m.*

swathe *vt* fajar:—*n* faja *f.*

sway *vt* mover:—*vi* ladearse, inclinarse:—*n* balanceo *m;* poder, imperio, influjo *m.*

swear *vt, vi* jurar; hacer jurar; juramentar.

sweat *n* sudor *m:*—*vi* sudar; trabajar con fatiga.

sweater, sweatshirt *n* sueter *m.*

sweep *vt, vi* barrer; arrebatar; deshollinar; pasar o tocar liger amente; oscilar:—*n* barredura *f;* vuelta *f;* giro *m.*

sweeping *adj* rapido:—**~s** *pl* barreduras *fpl.*

sweepstake *n* loteria *f.*

sweet *adj* dulce, grato, gustoso; suave; oloroso; melodioso; hermoso; amable: —*adv* dulcemente, suavemente:—*n* dulce, caramelo *m.*

sweetbread *n* mellejas de ternera *fpl.*

sweeten *vt* endulzar; suavizar; aplacar; perfumar.

sweetener *n* edulcorante *m.*

sweetheart *n* novio, via *m/f;* querida *f.*

sweetmeats *npl* dulces secos *mpl.*

sweetness *n* dulzura, suavidad *f.*

swell *vi* hincharse; ensoberbecerse; embravecerse:—*vt* hin char, inflar, agravar:—*n* marejada *f:*—*adj* (*fam*) estupendo, fenomenal.

swelling *n* hinchazon *f;* tumor *m.*

swelter *vi* ahogarse de calor.

swerve *vi* vagar; desviarse.

swift *adj* veloz, ligero, rapido:—*n* vencejo, *m.*

swiftly *adv* velozmente.

swiftness *n* velocidad, rapidez *f.*

swill *vt* beber con exceso:—*n* bazofia *f.*

swim *vi* nadar; abundar en:—*vt* pasar a nado:—*n* nadada *f.*

swimming *n* natacion *f;* vertigo *m.*

swimming pool *n* piscina *f.*

swimsuit *n* traje de bano *m.*

swindle *vt* estafar.

swindler *n* trampista *m.*

swine *n* puerco, cochino *m.*

swing *vi* balancear, columpiarse; vibrar; agitarse:—*vt* colum piar; balancear; girar:—*n* vibracion *f;* balanceo *m.*

swinging *adj* (*fam*) alegre.

swinging door *n* puerta giratoria *f.*

swirl *n* hacer remolinos (en el agua).

switch *n* varilla *f;* interruptor *m;* (*rail*) aguja *f:*—*vt* cambiar de:—**to ~ off** apagar; parar:—**to ~ on** encender, prender.

switchboard *n* centralita (de teléfonos) *f.*

swivel *vt* girar.

swoon *vi* desmayarse:—*n* desmayo, deliquio, pasmo *m.*

swoop *vi* calarse:—*n* calada; redada *f:* —**in one ~** de un golpe.

sword *n* espada *f.*

swordfish *n* pez espada *f.*

swordsman *n* guerrero *m.*

sycamore *n* sicomoro *m* (arbol).

sycophant *n* sicofante *m.*

syllabic *adj* silabico.

syllable *n* silaba *f.*

syllabus *n* programa de estudios *m.*

syllogism *n* silogismo *m.*

sylph *n* silfio *m;* silfida *f.*

symbol *n* simbolo *m.*

symbolic(al) *adj* simbolico.

symbolise *vt* simbolizar.

symmetrical *adj* simetrico:— **~ly** *adv* con simetria.

symmetry *n* simetria *f.*

sympathetic *adj* simpatico:— **~ally** *adv* simpaticamente.

sympathise *vi* compadecerse.

sympathy *n* simpatia *f.*

symphony *n* sinfonia *f.*

symposium *n* simposio *m.*

symptom *n* sintoma *m.*

synagogue *n* sinagoga *f.*

synchronism *n* sincronismo *m.*

syndicate *n* sindicato *m.*

syndrome *n* sindrome *m.*

synod *n* sinodo *m.*

synonym *n* sinonimo *m.*

synonymous *adj* sinonimo:— **~ly** *adv* con sinonimia.

synopsis *n* sinopsis *f;* sumario *m.*

synoptical *adj* sinoptico.

syntax *n* sintaxis *f.*

synthesis *n* sintesis *f.*

syringe *n* jeringa, lavativa *f:*—*vt* jeringar.

system *n* sistema *m.*

systematic *adj* sistematico:— **~ally** *adv* sistematicamente.

systems analyst *n* analista de sistemas *m/f.*

T

table *n* mesa *f m*.
tablecloth *n* mantel *m*.
tablespoon *n* cuchara para comer *f*.
tablet *n* tableta *f m*.
table tennis *n* ping-pong *m*.
taboo *adj* tabu.
tacit *adj* tacito.
taciturn *adj* taciturno.
tack *n* tachuela *f*.
tact *n* tacto *m*.
tactician *n* tactico *m*.
tactics *npl* tactica *f*.
tadpole *n* ranilla *f*.
taffeta *n* tafetan *m*.
tag *n* herrete *m*.
tail *n* cola *f*.
tailor *n* sastre *m*.
tailor-made *adj* hecho a la medida.
taint *vt* tachar.
take *vt* tomar, coger.
takeoff *n* despegue *m*.
takings *npl* ingresos *mpl*.
talc *n* talco *m*.
talent *n* talento *m*.
talisman *n* talisman *m*.
talk *vi* hablar.
talkative *adj* locuaz.
tall *adj* alto.
talon *n* garra de ave de rapina *f*.
tambourine *n* pandereta *f*.
tame *adj* amansado.
tamper *vi* tocar.
tampon *n* tampon *m*.
tan *vt* broncear.
tang *n* sabor fuerte *m*.
tangerine *n* mandarina *f*.
tangle *vt* enredar.

tank *n* cisterna *f*; aljibe *m*.
tanned *adj* bronceado.
tantrum *n* rabieta *f*.
tap espita *f*.
tape *n* cinta *f*.
tape measure *n* metro *m*.
tapestry *n* tapiz *mf*.
tar *n* brea *f*.
target *n* blanco *m* (para tirar).
tariff *n* tarifa *f*.
tarmac *n* pista *f*.
tarnish *vt* deslustrar.
tarpaulin *n* alquitranado *m*.
tarragon *n* (*bot*) estragon *m*.
tartan *n* tela escocesa *f*.
tartar *n* tartaro *m*.
task *n* tarea *f*.
tassel *n* borlita *f*.
taste *n* gusto *m*; sabor *m*.
tasty *adj* sabroso.
tattoo *n* tatuaje *m*.
taunt *vt* mofar
Taurus *n* Tauro *m*.
tax *n* impuesto *m*.
taxi *n* taxi *m*.
tea *n* te *m*.
teach *vt* ensenar.
teacher *n* profesor, ra *m/f*.
teak *n* teca *f* (arbol).
team *n* equipo *m*.
teamster *n* camionero *m*.
teapot *n* tetera *f*.
tear *vt* despedazar, rasgar.
tear *n* lagrima *f*.
tease *vt* tomar el pelo.
teaspoon *n* cucharita *f*.
teat *n* ubre, teta *f*.
technical *adj* tecnico.
technician *n* tecnico *m*.

technique *n* tecnica *f*.
technology *n* tecnologia *f*.
teddy (bear) *n* osito de felpa *m*.
tedious *adj* tedioso.
tedium *n* tediom.
tee-shirt *n* camiseta *f*.
teeth *npl* de tooth.
telegram *n* telegrama *m*.
telegraph *n* telegrafo *m*.
telegraphic *adj* telegrafico.
telepathy *n* telepatia *f*.
telephone *n* telefono *m*.
telescope *n* telescopio *m*.
telescopic *adj* telescopico.
television *n* television *f*.
tell *vi* decir.
temper *vt* templar:—*n* mal genio *m*.
temperament *n* temperamento *m*.
temperate *adj* templado.
temperature *n* temperatura *f*.
template *n* plantilla *f*.
temple *n* templo *m*.
temporary *adj* temporal.
tempt *vt* tentar.
temptation *n* tentacion *f*.
ten *adj*, *n* diez.
tenacity *n* tenacidad *f*.
tenancy *n* tenencia *f*.
tenant *n* arrendador *m*.
tend *vt* guardar.
tendency *n* tendencia *f*.
tender *adj* tierno, estimar.
tendon *n* tendon *m*.
tennis *n* tenis *m*.
tense *adj* tieso, tenso
tension *n* tension *f*.

tent *n* tienda de campana *f*.

tentacle *n* tentaculo *m*.

tenth *adj*, *n* decimo.

tenure *n* tenencia *f*.

tepid *adj* tibio.

term *n* termino *m*.

terminal *adj* mortal.

termination *n* terminacion *f*.

terminus *n* terminal *f*.

terrace *n* terraza *f*.

terrain *n* terreno *m*.

terrestrial *adj* terrestre.

terrible *adj* terrible.

terrier *n* terrier *m*.

terrific *adj* fantastico.

terrify *vt* aterrar.

territorial *adj* territorial.

territory *n* territorio, distrito *m*.

terror *n* terror *m*.

terrorism *n* terrorismo *m*.

test *n* examen *m*.

testament *n* testamento *m*.

testicles *npl* testiculos *mpl*.

testify *vt* testificar.

testimony *n* testimonio *m*.

tetanus *n* tetano *m*.

tether *vt* atar.

text *n* texto *m*.

textiles *npl* textiles *mpl*.

texture *n* textura *f*.

than *adv* que, de.

thank *vt* agradecer.

thanks *npl* gracias *fpl*.

that *pn* aquel, aquello, aquella; que; este.

thaw *n* deshielo *m*.

the *art* el, la, lo; los, las.

theater *n* teatro *m*.

theft *n* robo *m*.

their *pn* su, suyo, suya; de ellos, de ellas:—~s el suyo, la suya, los suyos, las suyas; de ellos, de ellas.

them *pn* los, las, les; ellos, ellas.

theme *n* tema *m*.

themselves *pn* *pl* ellos mismos, ellas mismas; si mismos; se.

then *adv* entonces, despues.

theology *n* teologia *f*.

theory *n* teoria *f*.

therapist *n* terapeuta *m*.

therapy *n* terapia *f*.

there *adv* alli, alla.

thermal *adj* termal.

thermometer *n* termometro *m*.

thesaurus *n* tesoro *m*.

these *pn* *pl* estos, estas.

thesis *n* tesis *f*.

they *pn* *pl* ellos, ellas.

thick *adj* espeso.

thicken *vi* espesar.

thief *n* ladron *m*.

thigh *n* muslo *m*.

thimble *n* dedal *m*.

thin *adj* delgado.

thing *n* cosa *f*.

think *vi* pensar.

third *adj* tercero.

thirst *n* sed *f*.

thirteen *adj*, *n* trece.

thirteenth *adj*, *n* decimotercio.

thirtieth *adj*, *n* trigesimo.

thirty *adj*, *n* treinta.

this *adj* este, esta, esto:—*pn* este, esta, esto.

thorn *n* espino *m*; espina *f*.

those *pn* *pl* esos, esas; aquellos, aquellas:—*adj* esos, esas; aquellos, aquellas.

thought *n* pensamiento *m*.

thousand *adj*, *n* mil.

thousandth *adj*, *n* milesimo.

thrash *vt* golpear.

thread *n* hilo *m*.

threat *n* amenaza *f*.

threaten *vt* amenazar.

three *adj*, *n* tres.

threshold *n* umbral *m*.

thrifty *adj* economico.

thrill *vt* emocionar.

thrive *vi* prosperar.

throat *n* garganta *f*.

throb *vi* palpitar.

throne *n* trono *m*.

through *prep* por; durante; mediante.

throw *vt* echar.

thrush *n* tordo *m* (ave).

thrust *vt* empujar.

thug *n* gamberro *m*.

thumb *n* pulgar *m*.

thump *n* golpe *m*.

thunder *n* trueno *m*.

Thursday *n* jueves *m*.

thus *adv* asi, de este modo.

thyme *n* (*bot*) tomillo *m*.

thyroid *n* tiroides *m*.

tiara *n* tiara *f*.

tic *n* tic *m*.

ticket *n* billete *m*

tickle *vt* hacer cosquillas.

tidal *adj* (*mar*) de marea.

tide *n* marea *f*.

tidy *adj* ordenado.

tie *vt* anudar, atar

tiger *n* tigre *m*.

tight *adj* tirante, apretado/a.

tile *n* azulejo *m*.

till *n* caja *f*:—*vt* cultivar.

timber *n* madera de construccion *f*

time *n* tiempo; epoca *f*.

timer *n* interruptor *m*.

timid *adj* timido.

timidity *n* timidez *f*.

tin *n* estano *m*.

tinfoil *n* papel de estano *m*.

tinsel *n* oropel *m*.

tint *n* tinte *m*.

tiny *adj* pequeno, chico.

tip *n* punta, extremidad *f*; propina *f*.

tire *vt* cansar, fatigar.

tissue *n* tejido *m*.

title *n* titulo *m*.

titular *adj* titular.

to *prep* a; para; por; de; hasta; en; con; que.

toad n sapo m.

toadstool n (bot) hongovejin m.

toast vt tostar; brindar.

toaster n tostadora f.

tobacco n tabaco m.

tobacco shop n tabaqueria f.

today adv hoy.

toe n dedo del pie m.

together adv juntamente.

toilet n servicios mpl.

toilet paper n papel higienico m.

token n senal f.

tolerate vt tolerar.

tomato n tomate m.

tomb n tumba f.

tomboy n muchachota f.

tombstone n piedra sepulcral f.

tomcat n gato m.

tomorrow adv, n manana f.

ton n tonelada f.

tongs npl tenacillas fpl.

tongue n lengua f.

tonic n (med) tonico.

tonight adv, n esta tarde (f).

tonsil n amigdala f.

too adv demasiado; tambien.

tool n herramienta f.

tooth n diente m.

toothache n dolor de muelas m.

top n cima.

topaz n topacio m.

topic n tema m.

topless adj topless.

topographic(al) adj topografico.

topography n topografia f.

torch n antorcha f.

torment vt atormentar.

tornado n tornado m.

torrent n torrente m.

torrid adj apasionado.

tortoise n tortuga f.

tortoiseshell adj de carey.

tortuous adj tortuoso.

torture n tortura f.

toss vt tirar, lanzar.

total adj total.

totalitarian adj totalitario.

totality n totalidad f.

totter vi vacilar.

touch vt tocar.

touchdown n aterrizaje m.

touching adj patetico, conmovedor.

tough adj duro

toupee n tupe m.

tour n viaje m.

touring n viajes turisticos mpl.

tourism n turismo m.

tourist n turista m/f.

tourist office n oficina de turismo f.

tournament n torneo m.

tow n remolque m.

toward(s) prep, adv hacia.

towel n toalla f.

tower n torre m.

town n ciudad f.

town hall n ayuntamiento m.

toy n juguete m.

toyshop n jugueteria f.

trace n huellaf:—vt trazar.

trade n comercio m; ocupacion f.

trade(s) union n sindicato m.

tradition n tradicion f

traditional adj tradicional.

traffic n trafico m.

traffic lights npl semaforo m.

tragedy n tragedia f.

tragic adj tragico.

trail vt, vi rastrear.

train vt entrenar * n tren m.

trainee n aprendiz m.

trainer n entrenador m.

trait n rasgo m.

traitor n traidor m.

tramp n vagabundo m.

trample vt pisotear.

trampoline n trampolin m.

trance n rapto m.

tranquil adj tranquilo.

tranquilliser n tranquilizante m.

transact vt negociar.

transaction n transaccion f.

transatlantic adj transatlántico.

transcription n traslado m.

transfer vt transferir.

transform vt transformar.

transformation n transformacion f.

transfusion n transfusion f.

transit n transito m.

transition n transito m; transicion f.

translate vt traducir.

translation n traduccion f.

translator n traductor, ra m/f.

transmit vt transmitir.

transparent adj transparente.

transpire vi resultar.

transplant vt trasplantar.

transport vt transportar.

trap n trampa f.

trapeze n trapecio m.

trappings npl adornos mpl.

trash n pacotilla f.

travel vi viajar.

trawler n pesquero de arrastre m.

tray n bandeja f

treachery n traicion f.

tread vi pisar.

treason n traicion n.

treasure n tesoro m.

treasurer n tesorero m.

treat vt tratar.

treatise n tratado m.

treatment n trato m.

treaty n tratado m.

treble adj triple.

treble clef n clave de sol f.

tree n arbol m.

trellis n enrejado m.

tremble vi temblar.

tremendous adj tremendo.

tremor *n* temblor *m*.

trench *n* foso *m*.

trend *n* tendencia *f*.

trendy *adj* de moda.

trespass *vt* transpasar.

tress *n* trenza *f*.

trestle *n* caballete de serrador *m*.

trial *n* proceso *m*.

triangle *n* triangulo *m*.

triangular *adj* triangular.

tribal *adj* tribal.

tribe *n* tribu *f*.

tribunal *n* tribunal *m*.

tributary *adj*, *n* tributario *m*.

tribute *n* tributo *m*.

trice *n* momento, tris *m*.

trick *n* engano.

trickle *vi* gotear.

tricky *adj* dificil.

tricycle *n* triciclo *m*.

trifle *n* bagatela.

trigger *n* gatillo *m*.

trigonometry *n* trigonometria *f*.

trim *adj* aseado.

Trinity *n* Trinidad *f*.

trinket *n* joya.

trio *n* (*mus*) trio *m*.

trip *vt* hacer caer; viaje corto *m*.

tripe *n* callos *mpl*.

triple *adj* triple.

triplets *npl* trillizos *mpl*.

triplicate *n* triplicado *m*.

tripod *n* tripode *m*.

triumph *n* triunfo *m*.

triumphal *adj* triunfal.

triumphant *adj* triunfante.

trivia *npl* trivialidades *fpl*.

trivial *adj* trivial.

trolley *n* carrito *m*.

trombone *n* trombon *m*.

trophy *n* trofeo *m*.

tropical *adj* tropico.

trot *n* trote *m*.

trouble *vt* afligir.

trough *n* abrevadero *m*.

trousers *npl* pantalones *mpl*.

trout *n* trucha *f*.

trowel *n* paleta *f*.

truce *n* tregua *f*.

truck *n* camion *m*

true *adj* verdadero.

truffle *n* trufa *f*.

truly *adv* en verdad.

trumpet *n* trompeta *f*.

trunk *n* baul, cofre *m*; trompa *f*.

trust *n* confianza *f*.

truth *n* verdad *f*.

try *vt* examinar, tentar.

tub *n* balde, cubo *m*.

tuba *n* tuba *f*.

tube *n* tubo *m*.

tuberculosis *n* tuberculosis *f*.

Tuesday *n* martes *m*.

tuition *n* enseñanza. *f*.

tulip *n* tulipan *m*.

tumble *vi* caer.

tumbler *n* vaso *m*.

tummy *n* barriga *f*.

tumor *n* tumor *m*.

tumultuous *adj* tumultuoso.

tuna *n* atun *m*.

tune *n* tono *m*.

tunic *n* tunica *f*.

tunnel *n* tunel *m*.

turban *n* turbante *m*.

turbine *n* turbina *f*.

turbulence *n* turbulencia *f*.

tureen *n* sopera *f*.

turf *n* cesped *m*.

turgid *adj* pesado.

turkey *n* pavo *m*.

turmoil *n* disturbio *m*.

turn *vi* volver.

turncoat *n* desertor *m*.

turnip *n* nabo *m*.

turnover *n* facturacion *f*.

turnstile *n* torniquete *m*.

turpentine *n* trementina *f*.

turquoise *n* turquesa *f*.

turret *n* torrecilla *f*.

turtle *n* galapago *m*.

turtledove *n* tortola *f*.

tusk *n* colmillo *m*.

tussle *n* pelea *f*.

tutor *n* tutor *m*.

tuxedo *n* smoking *m*.

twang *n* gangueo *m*.

tweezers *npl* tenacillas *fpl*.

twelfth *adj*, *n* duodecimo.

twelve *adj*, *n* doce.

twentieth *adj*, *n* vigesimo.

twenty *adj*, *n* veinte.

twice *adv* dos veces.

twig *n* ramita *f*:—*vi* caer en la cuenta.

twilight *n* crepusculo *m*.

twin *n* gemelo *m*.

twist *vt* torcer.

twit *n* (*col*) tonto *m*.

twitch *vi* moverse nerviosamente.

two *adj*, *n* dos.

two-faced *adj* falso.

tycoon *n* magnate *m*.

type *n* tipo *m*; letra *f*; modelo *m*:—*vt* escribir a maquina.

typewriter *n* maquina de escribir *f*.

typical *adj* tipico.

tyrannical *adj* tiranico.

tyranny *n* tirania *f*.

tyrant *n* tirano *m*.

U

ubiquitous *adj* ubicuo.
udder *n* ubre *f*.
ugh *excl* ¡uf!
ugliness *n* fealdad *f*.
ugly *adj* feo; peligroso.
ulcer *n* ulcera *f*.
ulterior *adj* ulterior.
ultimate *adj* ultimo.
ultimatum *n* ultimatum *m*.
umbrella *n* paraguas *m invar*.
umpire *n* arbitro *m*.
unable *adj* incapaz.
unaccompanied *adj* solo.
unaccustomed *adj* desacostumbrado.
unanimity *n* unanimidad *f*.
unanimous *adj* unanime.
unanswerable *adj* incontrovertible.
unapproachable *adj* inaccesible.
unbearable *adj* intolerable.
unbecoming *adj* indecente.
unbutton *vt* desabotonar.
uncanny *adj* extraordinario.
unchanged *adj* no alterado.
uncharitable *adj* nada caritativo.
uncle *n* tio.
uncomfortable *adj* incomodo.
uncommon *adj* raro.
uncompromising *adj* irreconciliable.
unconscious *adj* inconsciente.
unconventional *adj* poco convencional.
uncork *vt* destapar.
uncouth *adj* grosero.
uncover *vt* descubrir.
undaunted *adj* intrepido.

under *prep* debajo de.
under-age *adj* menor de edad.
underclothing *n* ropa intima *f*.
underdeveloped *adj* subdesarrollado.
underdog *n* desvalido *m*.
underestimate *vt* subestimar.
undergo *vt* sufrir.
undergraduate *n* estudiante *m*.
underground *n* movimiento clandestino *m*.
underline *vt* subrayar.
underpaid *adj* mal pagado.
undershirt *n* camiseta *f*.
understand *vt* entender, comprender.
understatement *n* subestimacion *f*.
underwear *n* ropa intima *f*.
underworld *n* hampa *f*.
undetermined *adj* indeterminado, indeciso.
undigested *adj* indigesto.
undisciplined *adj* indisciplinado.
undismayed *adj* intrepido.
undisputed *adj* incontestable.
undisturbed *adj* quieto, tranquilo.
undivided *adj* indiviso, entero.
undo *vt* deshacer, destar.
undoubted *adj* indudable.
undress *vi* desnudarse.
undue *adj* indebido.
undulating *adj* ondulante.
unduly *adv* indebidamente.
undying *adj* inmortal.
unearth *vt* desenterrar.

uneasy *adj* inquieto.
uneducated *adj* ignorante.
unemployed *adj* parado.
unemployment *n* paro *m*.
unenlightened *adj* no iluminado.
unenviable *adj* poco enviiable.
unequal *adj* desigual.
unequaled *adj* incomparable.
uneven *adj* desigual.
unexpected *adj* inesperado.
unexplored *adj* inexplorado.
unfair *adj* injusto.
unfaithful *adj* infiel.
unfamiliar *adj* desacostumbrado.
unfashionable *adj* pasado de moda.
unfasten *vt* desatar.
unfavorable *adj* desfavorable.
unfeeling *adj* insensible.
unfit *adj* indispuesto.
unfold *vt* desplegar.
unforeseen *adj* imprevisto.
unforgettable *adj* inolvidable.
unforgivable *adj* imperdonable.
unforgiving *adj* implacable.
unfortunate *adj* desafortunado.
unfounded *adj* sin fundamento.
unfriendly *adj* antipatico.
unfruitful *adj* esteril; infructuoso.
unfurnished *adj* sin muebles.
ungrateful *adj* ingrato.
unhappily *adv* infelizmente.
unhappy *adj* infeliz.

unhealthy *adj* malsano.

unhook *vt* desenganchar; descolgar; desabrochar.

unhoped(-for) *adj* inesperado.

unhurt *adj* ileso.

unicorn *n* unicornio *m*.

uniform *adj* uniforme:—*n* uniforme *m*.

uniformity *adj* uniformidad *f*.

unify *vt* unificar.

unimaginable *adj* inimaginable.

unimportant *adj* nada importante.

uninformed *adj* ignorante.

uninhabitable *adj* inhabitable.

uninhabited *adj* inhabitado, desierto.

uninjured *adj* ileso, no danado.

unintelligible *adj* ininteligible.

unintentional *adj* involuntario.

uninterested *adj* desinteresado.

uninteresting *adj* poco interesante.

uninvited *adj* no convidado.

union *n* union *f*; sindicato *m*.

unionist *n* unitario *m*.

unique *adj* unico, uno, singular.

unit *n* unidad *f*.

unite *vt vi* unir(se), juntarse.

United States (of America) *npl* Estados Unidos (de América) *mpl*.

unity *n* unidad *f*.

universal *adj* universal.

universe *n* universo *m*.

university *n* universidad *f*.

unjust *adj* injusto.

unkind *adj* poco amable.

unknown *adj* incognito.

unlawful *adj* ilícito/a.

unless *conj* a menos que, si no.

unload *vt* descargar.

unluckily *adv* desafortunadamente.

unlucky *adj* desafortunado.

unmarried *adj* soltero; soltera.

unmerited *adj* desmerecido.

unmistakable *adj* evidente.

unmoved *adj* inmoto, firme.

unnatural *adj* antinatural.

unnecessary *adj* inutil, innecesario.

unnoticed *adj* no observado.

unobserved *adj* invertido/a.

unobtainable *adj* inconseguible.

unobtrusive *adj* modesto.

unoccupied *adj* desocupado.

unofficial *adj* no oficial.

unpack *vt* desempacar; desenvolver.

unpaid *adj* no pagado.

unpleasant *adj* desagradable.

unpopular *adj* no popular.

unpracticed *adj* inexperto.

unprecedented *adj* sin ejemplo.

unpredictable *adj* imprevisible.

unprepared *adj* no preparado.

unprofitable *adj* inútil, vano; poco lucrativo.

unpunished *adj* impune.

unqualified *adj* sin titulos; total.

unquestionable *adj* indubitable.

unravel *vt* desenredar.

unrealistic *adj* poco realista.

unreasonable *adv* irracionalmente.

unrelated *adj* sin relacion; inconexo.

unrelenting *adj* incompasivo, inflexible.

unreliable *adj* poco fiable.

unrestrained *adj* desenfrenado; ilimitado.

unripe *adj* inmaduro.

unrivaled *adj* sin rival.

unroll *vt* desenrollar.

unsafe *adj* inseguro.

unsatisfactory *adj* insatisfactorio.

unscrew *vt* destornillar.

unscrupulous *adj* sin escrupulos.

unseemly *adj* indecente.

unseen *adj* invisible.

unselfish *adj* desinteresado.

unsettle *vt* perturbar.

unshaken *adj* firme, estable.

unskilled *adj* inhabil.

unsociable *adj* insociable.

unspeakable *adj* inefable.

unstable *adj* instable, inconstante.

unsteady *adj* inestable.

unsuccessful *adj* infeliz, desafortunado.

unsuitable *adj* inapropiado; inoportuno.

unsure *adj* inseguro.

unsympathetic *adj* inompasivo.

untapped *adj* sin explotar.

untenable *adj* insostenible.

unthinkable *adj* inconcebible.

unthinking *adj* desatento, irreflexivo.

untidiness *n* desalino *m*.

untidy *adj* desordenado; sucio.

untie *vt* desatar, deshacer, soltar.

until *prep* hasta:—*conj* hasta que.

untimely *adj* intempestivo.

untiring *adj* incansable.

untold *adj* nunca dicho; indecible; incalculable.

untouched *adj* intacto.

untoward *adj* impropio; adverso.

untried *adj* no ensayado o probado.

untroubled *adj* no perturbado, tranquilo.

untrue *adj* falso.

untrustworthy *adj* indigno de confianza.

untruth *n* falsedad, mentira *f.*

unused *adj* isin usar, no usado.

unusual *adj* inusitado, raro:—**~ly** *adv* inusitadamente, raramente.

unveil *vt* quitar el velo, descubrir.

unwavering *adj* inquebrantable.

unwelcome *adj* desagradable, inoportuno.

unwell *adj* enfermizo, malo.

unwieldy *adj* pesado.

unwilling *adj* desinclinado:— **~ly** *adv* de mala gana.

unwillingness *n* mala gana, repugnancia *f.*

unwind *vt* desenredar, desenmaranar: —*vi* relajarse.

unwise *adj* imprudente.

unwitting *adj* inconsciente.

unworkable *adj* poco practico.

unworthy *adj* indigno.

unwrap *vt* desenvolver.

unwritten *adj* no escrito.

up *adv* arriba, en lo alto; levantado:—*prep* hacia; hasta.

upbringing *n* educacion *f.*

update *vt* poner al dia.

upheaval *n* agitacion *f.*

uphill *adj* dificil, penoso:— *adv* cuesta arriba.

uphold *vt* sos tener, apoyar.

upholstery *n* tapiceria *f.*

upkeep *n* manteniniento *m.*

uplift *vt* levantar.

upon *prep* sobre, encima.

upper *adj* superior; mas elevado.

upper-class *adj* de la clase alta.

upper-hand *n* (*fig*) superioridad *f.*

uppermost *adj* mas alto, supremo:—**to be ~** predominar.

upright *adj* derecho, perpendicular, recto; puesto en pie; hon rado.

uprising *n* sublevacion *f.*

uproar *n* tumulto, alboroto *m.*

uproot *vt* desarraigar.

upset *vt* trastornar; derramar, volcar:—*n* reves *m*; trastorno *m*:—*adj* molesto; revuelto.

upshot *n* remate *m*; fin *m*; conclusion *f.*

upside-down *adv* de arriba abajo.

upstairs *adv* de arriba.

upstart *n* advenedizo *m.*

uptight *adj* nervioso.

up-to-date *adj* al dia.

upturn *n* mejora *f.*

upward *adj* ascendente:—**~s** *adv* hacia arriba.

urban *adj* urbano.

urbane *adj* cortes.

urchin *n* golfillo *m.*

urge *vt* animar:—*n* impulso *m*; deseo *m.*

urgency *n* urgencia *f.*

urgent *adj* urgente.

urinal *n* orinal *m.*

urinate *vi* orinar.

urine *n* orina *f.*

urn *n* urna *f.*

us *pn* nos; nosotros.

usage *n* tratamiento *m*; uso *m.*

use *n* uso *m*; utilidad, practica *f*:—*vt* usar, emplear.

used *adj* usado.

useful *adj* , **~ly** *adv* util- (mente).

usefulness *n* utilidad *f.*

useless *adj* inútil:—**~ly** *adv* inútilmente.

uselessness *n* inutilidad *f.*

user-friendly *adj* amistoso.

usher *n* ujier *m*; acomodador *m.*

usherette *n* acomodadora *f.*

usual *adj* usual, comun, normal:—**~ly** *adv* normalmente.

usurer *n* usurero *m.*

usurp *vt* usurpar.

usury *n* usura *f.*

utensil *n* utensilio *m.*

uterus *n* utero *m.*

utilise *vt* utilizar.

utility *n* utilidad *f.*

utmost *adj* extremo, sumo; ultimo.

utter *adj* total; todo; entero:—*vt* proferir; expresar; publicar.

utterance *n* expresion *f.*

utterly *adv* enteramente, del todo.

V

vacancy *n* cuarto libre *m*.
vacant *adj* vacio; desocupado.
vacate *vt* desocupar.
vacation *n* vacaciones *fpl*.
vaccinate *vt* vacunar.
vaccination *n* vacunacion *f*.
vaccine *n* vacuna *f*.
vacuous *adj* necio/a, bobo/a.
vacuum *n* vacio *m*.
vagina *n* vagina *f*.
vagrant *n* vagabundo.
vague *adj* vago.
vain *adj* vano.
valet *n* criado *m*.
valiant *adj* valiente.
valid *adj* valido.
valley *n* valle *m*.
valor *n* valor*m*.
valuable *adj* precioso.
valuation *n* tasa, valuacion *f*.
value *n* valor.
valued *adj* apreciado.
valve *n* valvula *f*.
vampire *n* vampiro *m*.
van *n* camioneta *f*.
vandal *n* gamberro *m*.
vandalise *vt* danar.
vandalism *n* vandalismo *m*.
vanguard *n* vanguardia *f*.
vanilla *n* vainilla *f*.
vanish *vi* desvanecerse.
vanity *n* vanidad *f*.
vanquish *vt* vencer.
vantage point *n* punto panoramico *m*.
vapor *n* vapor *m*.
variable *adj* variable.
variance *n* discordia *f*.
variation *n* variacion *f*.

varicose vein *n* variz *f*.
varied *adj* variado.
variety *n* variedad *f*.
various *adj* vario.
varnish *n* barniz *m*.
vary *vt, vi* variar.
vase *n* florero *m*.
vast *adj* vasto.
vat *n* tina *f*.
vault *n* boveda *f*.
veal *n* ternera *f*.
veer *vi* (*mar*) virar.
vegetable *adj* vegetal, *n* ~s *pl* legumbres *fpl*.
vegetable garden *n* huerta *f*.
vegetarian *n* vegetariano, na *m/f*.
vegetate *vi* vegetar.
vegetation *n* vegetacion *f*.
vehemence *n* vehemencia *f*.
vehement *adj* vehemente.
vehicle *n* vehiculo *m*.
veil *n* velo *m*.
vein *n* vena *f*.
velocity *n* velocidad *f*.
velvet *n* terciopelo *m*.
vendor *n* vendedor *m*.
veneer *n* chapa *f*.
venerable *adj* venerable.
venerate *vt* venerar.
veneration *n* veneracion *f*.
venereal *adj* venereo.
vengeance *n* venganza *f*.
venial *adj* venial.
venison *n* (carne de) venado *f*.
venom *n* veneno *m*.
venomous *adj* venenoso.
vent *n* respiradero *m*; salida *f*.

ventilate *vt* ventilar.
ventilation *n* ventilacion *f*.
ventilator *n* ventilador *m*.
ventriloquist *n* ventrilocuo *m*.
venture *n* empresa *f*:—*vi* aventurarse.
venue *n* lugar de reunion *m*.
veranda(h) *n* terraza *f*.
verb *n* (*gr*) verbo *m*.
verbal *adj* verbal.
verdict *n* (law) veredicto *m*.
verification *n* verificacion *f*.
verify *vt* verificar.
veritable *adj* verdadero.
vermin *n* bichos *mpl*.
vermouth *n* vermut *m*.
versatile *adj* versatil.
verse *n* verso *m*.
versed *adj* versado.
version *n* version *f*.
versus *prep* contra.
vertebra *n* vertebra *f*.
vertebral, vertebrate *adj* vertebral.
vertical *adj* , ~**ly** *adv* vertical(mente).
vertigo *n* vertigo *m*.
very *adj adv* muy, mucho.
vessel *n* vasija *f*.
vest *n* chaleco *m*.
vestibule *n* vestibulo *m*.
vestige *n* vestigio *m*.
vestry *n* sacristia *f*.
veteran *adj, n* veterano (*m*).
veterinary *adj* veterinario.
veto *n* veto *m*.
vex *vt* molestar.
via *prep* por.
viaduct *n* viaducto *m*.

vial *n* redoma *f*.
vibrate *vi* vibrar.
vibration *n* vibracion *f*.
vicarious *adj* sustituto.
vice *n* vicio *m*
vice versa *adv* viceversa.
vicinity *n* vecindad *f*.
vicious *adj* vicioso.
victim *n* victima *f*.
victimise *vt* victimizar.
victor *n* vencedor *m*.
victorious *adj* victorioso.
victory *n* victoria *f*.
video *n* videofilm *m*; video cassette *f*; videograbadora *f*.
video tape *n* cinta de video *f*.
vie *vi* competir.
view *n* vista *f*.
viewpoint *n* punto de vista *m*.
vigilance *n* vigilancia *f*.
vigilant *adj* vigilante.
vigorous *adj* vigoroso.
vigour *n* vigor *m*.
vile *adj* vil.
vilify *vt* envilecer.
villa *n* chalet *m*.
village *n* aldea *f*.
villain *n* malvado *m*.
vindicate *vt* vindicar.
vindication *n* vindicacion *f*.
vindictive *adj* vengativo.
vine *n* vid *f*.
vinegar *n* vinagre *m*.
vineyard *n* vina *f*.
vintage *n* vendimia *f*.
vinyl *n* vinilo *m*.

viola *n* (*mus*) viola *f*.
violate *vt* violar.
violation *n* violacion *f*.
violence *n* violencia *f*.
violent *adj* violento.
violet *n* (*bot*) violeta *f*.
violin *n* (*mus*) violin *m*.
viper *n* vibora *f*.
virgin *n* virgen *f*.
virginity *n* virginidad *f*.
Virgo *n* Virgo *f* (signo del zodiaco).
virile *adj* viril.
virility *n* virilidad *f*.
virtual *adj* , **~ly** *adv* virtual-(mente).
virtue *n* virtud *f*.
virtuous *adj* virtuoso.
virulent *adj* virulento.
virus *n* virus *m*.
visa *n* visado *m*, visa *f*.
vis-a-vis *prep* con respecto a.
visibility *n* visibilidad *f*.
visible *adj* visible.
vision *n* vista *f*.
visit *vt* visitar:—*n* visita *f*.
visitor *n* visitante *m* / *f*.
visor *n* visera *f*.
vista *n* vista, perspectiva *f*.
visual *adj* visual.
visualise *vt* imaginarse.
vital *adj* vital.
vitality *n* vitalidad *f*.
vitamin *n* vitamina *f*.
vitiate *vt* viciar.
vivacious *adj* vivaz.
vivid *adj* vivo.
vivisection *n* viviseccion *f*.

vocabulary *n* vocabulario *m*.
vocal *adj* vocal.
vocation *n* vocacion *f*.
vociferous *adj* vocinglero.
vodka *n* vodka *m*.
vogue *n* moda *f*; boga *f*.
voice *n* voz *f*:—*vt* expresar.
void *adj* nulo:—*n* vacio *m*.
volatile *adj* volatil; voluble.
volcanic *adj* volcanico.
volcano *n* volcan *m*.
volition *n* voluntad *f*.
volley *n* descarga *f*; salva *f*; rociada *f*; volea *f*.
volleyball *n* voleibol *m*.
volt *n* voltio *m*.
voltage *n* voltaje *m*.
voluble *adj* locuaz.
volume *n* volumen *m*.
voluntarily *adv* voluntaria-mente.
voluntary *adj* voluntario.
volunteer *n* voluntario *m*.
voluptuous *adj* voluptuoso.
vomit *vt*, *vi* vomitar.
vortex *n* remolino *m*.
vote *n* voto.
voter *n* votante *m* / *f*.
voting *n* votacion *f*.
voucher *n* vale *m*.
vow *n* voto *m*.
vowel *n* vocal *f*.
voyage *n* viaje *m*.
vulgar *adj* ordinario.
vulgarity *n* groseria.
vulnerable *adj* vulnerable.
vulture *n* buitre *m*.

W

wad *n* fajo *m*.
waddle *vi* anadear.
wade *vi* vadear.
wafer *n* galleta *f*.
waffle *n* gofre *m*.
wag *vt* menear.
wage *n* salario *m*.
waggon *n* carro *m*
wail *n* lamento *m*.
waist *n* cintura *f*.
wait *vi* esperar.
waiter *n* camarero *m*.
waiting list *n* lista de espera *f*.
waiting room *n* sala de espera *f*.
waive *vt* suspender.
wake *vi* despertarse.
waken *vt*, (*vi*) despertar(se).
walk *vt*, *vi* pasear; andar.
walking stick *n* baston *m*.
wall *n* pared *f*; muralla *f*; muro *m*.
wallet *n* cartera.
wallflower *n* (*bot*) aleli *m*.
wallpaper *n* papel pintado *m*.
walnut *n* nogal *m*; nuez *f*.
walrus *n* morsa *f*.
waltz *n* vals *m* (baile).
wan *adj* palido.
wand *n* varita magica *f*.
wane *vi* menguar.
want *vt* querer.
wanton *adj* lascivo.
war *n* guerra *f*.
ward *n* sala *f*
wardrobe *n* guardarropa *f*.
warehouse *n* almacen *m*.
warm *adj* calido; caliente.

warm-hearted *adj* afectuoso.
warmth *n* calor *m*.
warn *vt* avisar.
warning *n* aviso *m*.
warp *vi* torcerse.
warrant *n* orden judicial *f*.
warranty *n* garantia *f*.
warren *n* conejero *m*.
warrior *n* guerrero *m*.
wart *n* verruga *f*.
wary *adj* cauto.
wash *vt* lavar.
washbowl *n* lavabo *m*.
washing machine *n* lavadora *f*.
washing-up *n* fregado *m*.
wasp *n* avispa *f*.
waste *vt* malgastar.
watch *n* reloj *m*; vigilar.
watchdog *n* perro guardian *m*.
water *n* agua *f*.
watercolor *n* acuarela *f*.
waterfall *n* cascada *f*.
watering-can *n* regadera *f*.
waterlily *n* ninfea *f*.
water melon *n* sandia *f*.
watertight *adj* impermeable.
watt *n* vatio *m*.
wave *n* ola, onda *f*.
waver *vi* vacilar.
wax *n* cera *f*.
way *n* camino *m*; via *f*.
we *pn* nosotros, nosotras.
weak *adj* , ~ly *adv* debil-(mente).
wealth *n* riqueza *f*.
wealthy *adj* rico.
weapon *n* arma *f*.
wear *vt* gastar, consumir; usar, llevar.

weary *adj* cansado.
weasel *n* comadreja *f*.
weather *n* tiempo *m*.
weave *vt* tejer; trenzar.
weaving *n* tejido *m*.
web *n* telarana *f*.
wed *vt*, *vi* casar(se).
wedge *n* cuna *f*.
Wednesday *n* miercoles *m*.
wee *adj* pequenito.
weed *n* mala hierba *f*.
week *n* semana *f*.
weekend *n* fin de semana *m*.
weekly *adj* semanal.
weep *vt*, *vi* llorar.
weeping willow *n* sauce lloron *m*.
weigh *vt*, *vi* pesar.
weight *n* peso *m*.
welcome *adj* recibido con agrado:—~! ¡bienvenido!.
weld *vt* soldar.
welfare *n* prosperidad *f*
well *n* fuente *f adv* bien.
wench *n* mozuela *f*.
west *n* oeste, occidente *m*.
wet *adj* humedo, mojado.
whale *n* ballena *f*.
wharf *n* muelle *m*.
what *pn* que, qué?, el que, la que, lo que.
whatever *pn* cualquier o cualquiera cosa que.
wheat *n* trigo *m*.
wheel *n* rueda *f*.
wheelbarrow *n* carretilla *f*.
wheelchair *n* sillita de ruedas *f*.
wheeze *vi* jadear.
when *adv* cuando.

whenever *adv* cuando; cada vez que.

where *adv* dónde? *conj* donde.

whether *conj* si.

which *pn* que; lo que; el que, el cual; cual:—*adj* qué?; cuyo.

while *n* rato *m*; vez *f*:—*conj* durante; mientras; aunque.

whim *n* antojo *m*.

whine *vi* llorar, lamentar

whinny *vi* relinchar.

whip *n* azote *m*; latigo *m*.

whirlpool *n* vortice *m*.

whirlwind *n* torbellino *m*.

whiskey *n* whisky *m*.

whisper *vi* cuchichear.

whistle *vi* silbar

white *adj* blanco.

who *pn* quién?, que.

whoever *pn* quienquiera, cualquiera.

whole *adj* todo

wholemeal *adj* integral.

wholly *adv* enteramente.

whom *pn* quién? que.

whooping cough *n* tos ferina *f*.

whore *n* puta *f*.

why *n* por qué?

wick *n* mecha *f*.

wicked *adj* malvado.

wide *adj* ancho.

widen *vt* ensanchar.

widow *n* viuda *f*.

widower *n* viudo *m*.

width *n* anchura *f*.

wield *vt* manejar.

wife *n* esposa *f*.

wig *n* peluca *f*.

wild *adj* silvestre.

wilderness *n* desierto *m*.

wild life *n* fauna *f*.

will *n* voluntad *f*.

willful *adj* deliberado; testarudo.

willow *n* sauce *m* (arbol).

willpower *n* fuerza de voluntad *f*.

wilt *vi* marchitarse.

wily *adj* astuto.

win *vt* ganar.

wince *vi* encogerse, estremecerse.

winch *n* torno *m*.

wind *n* viento *m*

wind *vt* enrollar.

windfall *n* golpe de suerte *m*.

winding *adj* tortuoso.

windmill *n* molino de viento *m*.

window *n* ventana *f*.

window box *n* jardinera de ventana *f*.

window ledge *n* repisa *f*.

window pane *n* cristal *m*.

window sill *n* repisa *f*.

windpipe *n* traquea *f*.

windshield *n* parabrisas *m* invar.

windy *adj* de mucho viento.

wine *n* vino *m*.

wine cellar *n* bodega *f*.

wine glass *n* copa *f*.

wing *n* ala *f*.

winged *adj* alado.

wink *vi* guinar

winner *n* ganador.

winter *n* invierno *m*.

wintry *adj* invernal.

wipe *vt* limpiar.

wisdom *n* sabiduria *f*.

wisdom teeth *npl* muelas de juicio *fpl*.

wise *adj* sabio.

wisecrack *n* broma *f*.

wish *vt* querer

wishful *adj* deseoso.

wit *n* entendimiento *m*.

witch *n* bruja *f*.

witchcraft *n* brujeria *f*.

with *prep* con; por, de, a.

withdraw *vt* quitar.

withdrawal *n* retirada *f*.

withdrawn *adj* reservado.

withhold *vt* detener.

within *prep* dentro de.

without *prep* sin.

withstand *vt* resistir.

witless *adj* necio.

witness *n* testigo *m*.

witticism *n* ocurrencia *f*.

wittily *adv* ingeniosamente.

witty *adj* ingenioso.

wizard *n* brujo *m*.

woe *n* dolor *m*; miseria *f*.

woeful *adj* triste.

wolf *n* lobo *m*.

woman *n* mujer *f*.

womb *n* utero *m*.

wonder *n* milagro *m*.

wonderful *adj* maravilloso.

won't *abrev* de will not.

woo *vt* cortejar.

wood *n* bosque *m*; selva *f*; madera *f*; lena *f*.

woodland *n* arbolado *m*.

woodlouse *n* cochinilla *f*.

woodpecker *n* picamaderos *m* invar.

woodworm *n* carcoma *f*.

wool *n* lana *f*.

woolen *adj* de lana.

word *n* palabra *f*.

wordy *adj* verboso.

work *vi* trabajar; obrar.

world *n* mundo *m*.

worm *n* gusano *m*.

worn-out *adj* gastado.

worried *adj* preocupado.

worry *vt* preocupar.

worse *adj*, *adv* peor.

worship *n* culto *m*; adoracion *f*.

worst *adj* el/la peor

worth *n* valor *m*.

worthwhile *adj* que vale la pena; valioso.

worthy *adj* digno.

wound *n* herida *f*.

wrangle *vi* renir *f*.

wrap *vt* envolver.

wrath *n* ira *f*.

wreath *n* corona *f*.

wreck *n* naufragio *m*; ruina *f*.

wreckage *n* restos *mpl*.

wren *n* reyezuelo *m* (avecilla).

wrestle *vi* luchar; disputar.

wrestling *n* lucha *f*.

wretched *adj* infeliz, miserable.

wring *vt* torcer.

wrinkle *n* arruga *f*.

wrist *n* muneca *f*.

wristband *n* puno de camisa *m*.

wristwatch *n* reloj de pulsera *m*.

writ *n* escrito *m*; escritura *f*.

write *vt* escribir.

write-off *n* perdida total *f*.

writer *n* escritor, ra, *m/f*; autor, ra *m/f*.

writhe *vi* retorcerse.

writing *n* escritura *f*

writing desk *n* escritorio *m*.

writing paper *n* papel para escribir *m*.

wrong *n* injuria *f*; injusticia *f*.

wrongful *adj* injusto.

wrongly *adv* injustamente.

wry *adj* ironico.

X, Y, Z

Xmas *n* Navidad *f*.
X-ray *n* radiografia *f*.
xylophone *n* xilofano *m*.
yacht *n* yate *m*.
yachting *n* balandrismo *m*.
Yankee *n* yanqui *m*.
yard *n* corral *m*; yarda *f*.
yardstick *n* criterio *m*.
yarn *n* estambre *m*; hilo de lino *m*.
yawn *vi* bostezar
yeah *adv* si.
year *n* ano *m*.
yearling *n* primal *m*, ala *f*.
yearly *adj* anual.
yearn *vi* anorar.
yearning *n* anoranza *f*.
yeast *n* levadura *f*.
yell *vi* aullar
yellow *adj* amarillo.
yelp *vi* latir, ganir.
yes *adv, n* si (*m*).

yesterday *adv, n* ayer (*m*).
yet *conj* sin embargo; pero:— *adv* todavia.
yew *n* tejo *m*.
yield *vt* dar, producir.
yoga *n* yoga *m*.
yog(h)urt *n* yogur *m*.
yoke *n* yugo *m*.
yolk *n* yema de huevo *f*.
yonder *adv* alla.
you *pn* vosotros, tu, usted, ustedes.
young *adj* joven.
youngster *n* jovencito, ta *m*/*f*.
your(s) *pn* tuyo, vuestro, suyo:—**sincerely ~s** su seguro ser vidor.
yourself *pn* tu mismo, usted mismo, vosotros mismos, ustedes mismos.
youth *n* juventud *f*.

youthful *adj* juvenil.
youthfulness *n* juventud *f*.
yuppie *adj, n* yuppie *m*/*f*.
zany *adj* estrafalario.
zap *vt* borrar.
zeal *n* celo *m*; ardor *m*.
zealous *adj* celoso.
zebra *n* cebra *f*.
zenith *n* cenit *m*.
zero *n* zero, cero *m*.
zest *n* animo *m*.
zigzag *n* zigzag *m*.
zinc *n* zinc *m*.
zip, zipper *n* cremallera *f*.
zodiac *n* zodiaco *m*.
zone *n* banda, faja *f*; zona *f*.
zoo *n* zoo *m*.
zoological *adj* zoologico.
zoologist *n* zoologo, ga *m*/*f*.
zoology *n* zoologia *f*.
zoom *vi* zumbar.
zoom lens *n* zoom *m*.

Spanish Verbs

Verb Forms

Auxiliary: auxiliary verbs are used to form compound tenses of verbs, eg *have* in *I have seen*. The auxiliary verb in Spanish is *haber*.

Compound: compound tenses are verb tenses consisting of more than one element. In Spanish, compound tenses are formed by the auxiliary verb and the *past participle*, eg *ha escrito – he has written*.

Conditional: the *conditional* is introduced in English by the auxiliary *would*, eg *I would come if I had the time*. In Spanish, this is rendered by a single verb form, eg *vendría*.

Imperative: the *imperative* is used for giving orders, eg *estáte formal – be good*, or making suggestions, eg *vámonos – let's go*.

Imperfect indicative: in Spanish this tense describes habitual or continuous action in the past, eg *hablábamos*.

Indicative: the normal form of a verb, as in *hablo – I speak*, *ha venido – he has come*, *estoy probando – I am trying*.

Perfect indicative: this is one of the two tenses (the other is the *preterite*) used to describe completed past action in Spanish. It comprises the *auxiliary haber* and the *past participle*, eg *he visto – I have seen*.

Pluperfect indicative: in Spanish and English, this tense is used to describe an action occurring in the past before another past action, eg *había ido antes de que llegué – he had gone before I arrived*. In Spanish the *pluperfect indicative* is formed by the *imperfect indicative* of *haber* and the *past participle*, eg *habían comenzado – they had started*.

Preterite: this tense is used to describe completed past action, eg *llegó ayer – he arrived yesterday*.

Past participle: this is the form used after the auxiliary *have* in English and after *haber* in Spanish, eg *comido – eaten* in *he comido I have eaten*.

Present participle: this is the form which ends in *-ing* in English, eg *singing – cantando*.

Subjunctive: the subjunctive exists in English but goes almost unnoticed as it almost always takes the same form as the indicative. One exception is *if I were you*. It is however widely used in Spanish.

abrir *to open*

Gerund *abriendo*
Past participle *abierto*

Present indicative	Present subjunctive
abro	abra
abres	abras
abre	abra
abrimos	abramos
abrís	abráis
abren	abran

Imperfect indicative	Imperfect subjunctive
abría	abriera
abrías	abrieras
abría	abriera
abríamos	abriéramos
abríais	abrierais
abrían	abrieran

Preterite	Future
abrí	abriré
abriste	abrirás
abrió	abrirá
abrimos	abriremos
abristeis	abriréis
abrieron	abrirán

Perfect indicative	Conditional
he abierto	abriría
has abierto	abrirías
ha abierto	abriría
hemos abierto	abriríamos
habéis abierto	abriríais
han abierto	abrirían

Pluperfect indicative	Imperative
había abierto	–
habías abierto	abre
había abierto	abra
habíamos abierto	abramos
habíais abierto	abrid
habían abierto	abran

aburrir *to bore, annoy*

Gerund *aburriendo*
Past participle *aburrido*

Present indicative	Present subjunctive
aburro	aburra
aburres	aburras
aburre	aburra
aburrimos	aburramos
aburrís	aburráis
aburren	aburran

Imperfect indicative	Imperfect subjunctive
aburría	aburriera
aburrías	aburrieras
aburría	aburriera
aburríamos	aburriéramos
aburríais	aburrierais
aburrían	aburrieran

Preterite	Future
aburrí	aburriré
aburriste	aburrirás
aburrió	aburrirá
aburrimos	aburriremos
aburristeis	aburriréis
aburrieron	aburrirán

Perfect indicative	Conditional
he aburrido	aburriría
has aburrido	aburrirías
ha aburrido	aburriría
hemos aburrido	aburriríamos
habéis aburrido	aburriríais
han aburrido	aburrirían

Pluperfect indicative	Imperative
había aburrido	–
habías aburrido	aburre
había aburrido	aburra
habíamos aburrido	aburramos
habíais aburrido	aburrid
habían aburrido	aburran

acabar *to finish*

Gerund *acabando*
Past participle *acabado*

Present indicative	Present subjunctive
acabo	acabe
acabas	acabes
acaba	acabe
acabamos	acabemos
acabáis	acabéis
acaban	acaben

Imperfect indicative	Imperfect subjunctive
acababa	acabara
acababas	acabaras
acababa	acabara
acabábamos	acabáramos
acababais	acabarais
acababan	acabaran

Preterite	Future
acabé	acabaré
acabaste	acabarás
acabó	acabará
acabamos	acabaremos
acabasteis	acabaréis
acabaron	acabarán

Perfect indicative	Conditional
he acabado	acabaría
has acabado	acabarías
ha acabado	acabaría
hemos acabado	acabaríamos
habéis acabado	acabaríais
han acabado	acabarían

Pluperfect indicative	Imperative
había acabado	–
habías acabado	acaba
había acabado	acabe
habíamos acabado	acabemos
habíais acabado	acabad
habían acabado	acaben

aceptar *to accept*

Gerund *aceptando*
Past participle *aceptado*

Present indicative	Present subjunctive
acepto	acepte
aceptas	aceptes
acepta	acepte
aceptamos	aceptemos
aceptáis	aceptéis
aceptan	acepten

Imperfect indicative	Imperfect subjunctive
aceptaba	aceptara
aceptabas	aceptaras
aceptaba	aceptara
aceptábamos	aceptáramos
aceptabais	aceptarais
aceptaban	aceptaran

Preterite	Future
acepté	aceptaré
aceptaste	aceptarás
aceptó	aceptará
aceptamos	aceptaremos
aceptasteis	aceptaréis
aceptaron	aceptarán

Perfect indicative	Conditional
he aceptado	aceptaría
has aceptado	aceptarías
ha aceptado	aceptaría
hemos aceptado	aceptaríamos
habéis aceptado	aceptaríais
han aceptado	aceptarían

Pluperfect indicative	Imperative
había aceptado	–
habías aceptado	acepta
había aceptado	acepte
habíamos aceptado	aceptemos
habíais aceptado	aceptad
habían aceptado	acepten

aconsejar *to advise*

Gerund *aconsejando*
Past participle *aconsejado*

Present indicative	Present subjunctive
aconsejo	aconseje
aconsejas	aconsejes
aconseja	aconseje
aconsejamos	aconsejemos
aconsejáis	aconsejéis
aconsejan	aconsejen

Imperfect indicative	Imperfect subjunctive
aconsejaba	aconsejara
aconsejabas	aconsejaras
aconsejaba	aconsejara
aconsejábamos	aconsejáramos
aconsejabais	aconsejarais
aconsejaban	aconsejaran

Preterite	Future
aconsejé	aconsejaré
aconsejaste	aconsejarás
aconsejó	aconsejará
aconsejamos	aconsejaremos
aconsejasteis	aconsejaréis
aconsejaron	aconsejarán

Perfect indicative	Conditional
he aconsejado	aconsejaría
has aconsejado	aconsejarías
ha aconsejado	aconsejaría
hemos aconsejado	aconsejaríamos
habéis aconsejado	aconsejaríais
han aconsejado	aconsejarían

Pluperfect indicative	Imperative
había aconsejado	–
habías aconsejado	aconseja
había aconsejado	aconseje
habíamos aconsejado	aconsejemos
habíais aconsejado	aconsejad
habían aconsejado	aconsejen

acordarse *to remember*

Gerund *acordándose*
Past participle *acordado*

Present indicative	Present subjunctive
me acuerdo	me acuerde
te acuerdas	te acuerdes
se acuerda	se acuerde
nos acordamos	nos acordemos
os acordáis	os acordéis
se acuerdan	se acuerden

Imperfect indicative	Imperfect subjunctive
me acordaba	me acordara
te acordabas	te acordaras
se acordaba	se acordara
nos acordábamos	nos acordáramos
os acordabais	os acordarais
se acordaban	se acordaran

Preterite	Future
me acordé	me acordaré
te acordaste	te acordarás
se acordó	se acordará
nos acordamos	nos acordaremos
os acordasteis	os acordaréis
se acordaron	se acordarán

Perfect indicative	Conditional
me he acordado	me acordaría
te has acordado	te acordarías
se ha acordado	se acordaría
nos hemos acordado	nos acordaríamos
os habéis acordado	os acordaríais
se han acordado	se acordarían

Pluperfect indicative	Imperative
me había acordado	–
te habías acordado	acuérdate
se había acordado	acuérdese
nos habíamos acordado	acordémonos
os habíais acordado	acordaos
se habían acordado	acuérdense

acostarse *to go to bed*

Gerund *acostándose*
Past participle *acostado*

Present indicative	**Present subjunctive**
me acuesto	me acueste
te acuestas	te acuestes
se acuesta	se acueste
nos acostamos	nos acostemos
os acostáis	os acostéis
se acuestan	se acuesten

Imperfect indicative	**Imperfect subjunctive**
me acostaba	me acostara
te acostabas	te acostaras
se acostaba	se acostara
nos acostábamos	nos acostáramos
os acostabais	os acostarais
se acostaban	se acostaran

Preterite	**Future**
me acosté	me acostaré
te acostaste	te acostarás
se acostó	se acostará
nos acostamos	nos acostaremos
os acostasteis	os acostaréis
se acostaron	se acostarán

Perfect indicative	**Conditional**
me he acostado	me acostaría
te has acostado	te acostarías
se ha acostado	se acostaría
nos hemos acostado	nos acostaríamos
os habéis acostado	os acostaríais
se han acostado	se acostarían

Pluperfect indicative	**Imperative**
me había acostado	–
te habías acostado	acuéstate
se había acostado	acuéstese
nos habíamos acostado	acostémonos
os habíais acostado	acostaos
se habían acostado	acuéstense

agradecer *to thank*

Gerund *agradeciendo*
Past participle *agradecido*

Present indicative	**Present subjunctive**
agradezco	agradezca
agradeces	agradezcas
agradece	agradezca
agradecemos	agradezcamos
agradecéis	agradezcáis
agradecen	agradezcan

Imperfect indicative	**Imperfect subjunctive**
agradecía	agradeciera
agradecías	agradecieras
agradecía	agradeciera
agradecíamos	agradeciéramos
agradecíais	agradecierais
agradecían	agradecieran

Preterite	**Future**
agradecí	agradeceré
agradeciste	agradecerás
agradeció	agradecerá
agradecimos	agradeceremos
agradecisteis	agradeceréis
agradecieron	agradecerán

Perfect indicative	**Conditional**
he agradecido	agradecería
has agradecido	agradecerías
ha agradecido	agradecería
hemos agradecido	agradeceríamos
habéis agradecido	agradeceríais
han agradecido	agradecerían

Pluperfect indicative	**Imperative**
había agradecido	–
habías agradecido	agradece
había agradecido	agradezca
habíamos agradecido	agradezcamos
habíais agradecido	agradeced
habían agradecido	agradezcan

alcanzar *to reach*

Gerund *alcanzando*
Past participle *alcanzado*

Present indicative	Present subjunctive
alcanzo	alcance
alcanzas	alcances
alcanza	alcance
alcanzamos	alcancemos
alcanzáis	alcancéis
alcanzan	alcancen

Imperfect indicative	Imperfect subjunctive
alcanzaba	alcanzara
alcanzabas	alcanzaras
alcanzaba	alcanzara
alcanzábamos	alcanzáramos
alcanzabais	alcanzarais
alcanzaban	alcanzaran

Preterite	Future
alcancé	alcanzaré
alcanzaste	alcanzarás
alcanzó	alcanzará
alcanzamos	alcanzaremos
alcanzasteis	alcanzaréis
alcanzaron	alcanzarán

Perfect indicative	Conditional
he alcanzado	alcanzaría
has alcanzado	alcanzarías
ha alcanzado	alcanzaría
hemos alcanzado	alcanzaríamos
habéis alcanzado	alcanzaríais
han alcanzado	alcanzarían

Pluperfect indicative	Imperative
había alcanzado	–
habías alcanzado	alcanza
había alcanzado	alcance
habíamos alcanzado	alcancemos
habíais alcanzado	alcanzad
habían alcanzado	alcancen

almorzar *to have lunch*

Gerund *almorzando*
Past participle *almorzado*

Present indicative	Present subjunctive
almuerzo	almuerce
almuerzas	almuerces
almuerza	almuerce
almorzamos	almorcemos
almorzáis	almorcéis
almuerzan	almuercen

Imperfect indicative	Imperfect subjunctive
almorzaba	almorzara
almorzabas	almorzaras
almorzaba	almorzara
almorzábamos	almorzáramos
almorzabais	almorzarais
almorzaban	almorzaran

Preterite	Future
almorcé	almorzaré
almorzaste	almorzarás
almorzó	almorzará
almorzamos	almorzaremos
almorzasteis	almorzaréis
almorzaron	almorzarán

Perfect indicative	Conditional
he almorzado	almorzaría
has almorzado	almorzarías
ha almorzado	almorzaría
hemos almorzado	almorzaríamos
habéis almorzado	almorzaríais
han almorzado	almorzarían

Pluperfect indicative	Imperative
había almorzado	–
habías almorzado	almuerza
había almorzado	almuerce
habíamos almorzado	almorcemos
habíais almorzado	almorzad
habían almorzado	almuercen

amar *to love*

Gerund *amando*
 Past participle *amado*

Present indicative	Present subjunctive	Imperfect indicative	Imperfect subjunctive
Present indicative	**Present subjunctive**		
amo	ame		
amas	ames		
ama	ame		
amamos	amemos		
amáis	améis		
aman	amen		

Imperfect indicative	**Imperfect subjunctive**
amaba	amara
amabas	amaras
amaba	amara
amábamos	amáramos
amabais	amarais
amaban	amaran

Preterite	**Future**
amé	amaré
amaste	amarás
amó	amará
amamos	amaremos
amasteis	amaréis
amaron	amarán

Perfect indicative	**Conditional**
he amado	
has amado	amaría
ha amado	amarías
hemos amado	amaría
habéis amado	amaríamos
han amado	amaríais
	amarían

Pluperfect indicative	**Imperative**
había amado	–
habías amado	ama
había amado	ame
habíamos amado	amemos
habíais amado	amad
habían amado	amen

andar *to walk*

Gerund *andando*
 Past participle *andado*

Present indicative	Present subjunctive
ando	ande
andas	andes
anda	ande
andamos	andemos
andáis	andéis
andan	anden

Imperfect indicative	**Imperfect subjunctive**
andaba	anduviera
andabas	anduvieras
andaba	anduviera
andábamos	anduviéramos
andabais	anduvierais
andaban	anduvieran

Preterite	**Future**
anduve	andaré
anduviste	andarás
anduvo	andará
anduvimos	andaremos
anduvisteis	andaréis
anduvieron	andarán

Perfect indicative	**Conditional**
he andado	
has andado	andaría
ha andado	andarías
hemos andado	andaría
habéis andado	andaríamos
han andado	andaríais
	andarían

Pluperfect indicative	**Imperative**
había andado	–
habías andado	anda
había andado	ande
habíamos andado	andemos
habíais andado	andad
habían andado	anden

aparecer *to appear*

Gerund *apareciendo*
Past participle *aparecido*

Present indicative	**Present subjunctive**
aparezco	aparezca
apareces	aparezcas
aparece	aparezca
aparecemos	aparezcamos
aparecéis	aparezcáis
aparecen	aparezcan

Imperfect indicative	**Imperfect subjunctive**
aparecía	apareciera
aparecías	aparecieras
aparecía	apareciera
aparecíamos	apareciéramos
aparecíais	aparecierais
aparecían	aparecieran

Preterite	**Future**
aparecí	apareceré
apareciste	aparecerás
apareció	aparecerá
aparecimos	apareceremos
aparecisteis	apareceréis
aparecieron	aparecerán

Perfect indicative	**Conditional**
he aparecido	aparecería
has aparecido	aparecerías
ha aparecido	aparecería
hemos aparecido	apareceríamos
habéis aparecido	apareceríais
han aparecido	aparecerían

Pluperfect indicative	**Imperative**
había aparecido	–
habías aparecido	aparece
había aparecido	aparezca
habíamos aparecido	aparezcamos
habíais aparecido	apareced
habían aparecido	aparezcan

aprender *to learn*

Gerund *aprendiendo*
Past participle *aprendido*

Present indicative	**Present subjunctive**
aprendo	aprenda
aprendes	aprendas
aprende	aprenda
aprendemos	aprendamos
aprendéis	aprendáis
aprenden	aprendan

Imperfect indicative	**Imperfect subjunctive**
aprendía	aprendiera
aprendías	aprendieras
aprendía	aprendiera
aprendíamos	aprendiéramos
aprendíais	aprendierais
aprendían	aprendieran

Preterite	**Future**
aprendí	aprenderé
aprendiste	aprenderás
aprendió	aprenderá
aprendimos	aprenderemos
aprendisteis	aprenderéis
aprendieron	aprenderán

Perfect indicative	**Conditional**
he aprendido	aprendería
has aprendido	aprenderías
ha aprendido	aprendería
hemos aprendido	aprenderíamos
habéis aprendido	aprenderíais
han aprendido	aprenderían

Pluperfect indicative	**Imperative**
había aprendido	–
habías aprendido	aprende
había aprendido	aprenda
habíamos aprendido	aprendamos
habíais aprendido	aprended
habían aprendido	aprendan

aprobar *to approve*

Gerund *aprobando*
Past participle *aprobado*

Present indicative	Present subjunctive
apruebo	apruebe
apruebas	apruebes
aprueba	apruebe
aprobamos	aprobemos
aprobáis	aprobéis
aprueban	aprueben

Imperfect indicative	Imperfect subjunctive
aprobaba	aprobara
aprobabas	aprobaras
aprobaba	aprobara
aprobábamos	aprobáramos
aprobabais	aprobarais
aprobaban	aprobaran

Preterite	Future
aprobé	aprobaré
aprobaste	aprobarás
aprobó	aprobará
aprobamos	aprobaremos
aprobasteis	aprobaréis
aprobaron	aprobarán

Perfect indicative	Conditional
he aprobado	aprobaría
has aprobado	aprobarías
ha aprobado	aprobaría
hemos aprobado	aprobaríamos
habéis aprobado	aprobaríais
han aprobado	aprobarían

Pluperfect indicative	Imperative
había aprobado	–
habías aprobado	aprueba
había aprobado	apruebe
habíamos aprobado	aprobemos
habíais aprobado	aprobad
habían aprobado	aprueben

argüir *to argue*

Gerund *arguyendo*
Past participle *argüido*

Present indicative	Present subjunctive
arguyo	arguya
arguyes	arguyas
arguye	arguya
argüimos	arguyamos
argüís	arguyáis
arguyen	arguyan

Imperfect indicative	Imperfect subjunctive
argüía	arguyera
argüías	arguyeras
argüía	arguyera
argüíamos	arguyéramos
argüíais	arguyerais
argüían	arguyeran

Preterite	Future
argüí	argüiré
argüiste	argüirás
arguyó	argüirá
argüimos	argüiremos
argüisteis	argüiréis
arguyeron	argüirán

Perfect indicative	Conditional
he argüido	argüiría
has argüido	argüirías
ha argüido	argüiría
hemos argüido	argüiríamos
habéis argüido	argüiríais
han argüido	argüirían

Pluperfect indicative	Imperative
había argüido	–
habías argüido	arguye
había argüido	arguya
habíamos argüido	arguyamos
habíais argüido	argüid
habían argüido	arguyan

arreglar *to arrange*

Gerund *arreglando*
Past participle *arreglado*

Present indicative	Present subjunctive
arreglo	arregle
arreglas	arregles
arregla	arregle
arreglamos	arreglemos
arregláis	arregléis
arreglan	arreglen

Imperfect indicative	Imperfect subjunctive
arreglaba	arreglara
arreglabas	arreglaras
arreglaba	arreglara
arreglábamos	arregláramos
arreglabais	arreglarais
arreglaban	arreglaran

Preterite	Future
arreglé	arreglaré
arreglaste	arreglarás
arregló	arreglará
arreglamos	arreglaremos
arreglasteis	arreglaréis
arreglaron	arreglarán

Perfect indicative	Conditional
he arreglado	arreglaría
has arreglado	arreglarías
ha arreglado	arreglaría
hemos arreglado	arreglaríamos
habéis arreglado	arreglaríais
han arreglado	arreglarían

Pluperfect indicative	Imperative
había arreglado	–
habías arreglado	arregla
había arreglado	arregle
habíamos arreglado	arreglemos
habíais arreglado	arreglad
habían arreglado	arreglen

atravesar *to cross*

Gerund *atravesando*
Past participle *atravesado*

Present indicative	Present subjunctive
atravieso	atraviese
atraviesas	atravieses
atraviesa	atraviese
atravesamos	atravesemos
atravesáis	atraveséis
atraviesan	atraviesen

Imperfect indicative	Imperfect subjunctive
atravesaba	atravesara
atravesabas	atravesaras
atravesaba	atravesara
atravesábamos	atravesáramos
atravesabais	atravesarais
atravesaban	atravesaran

Preterite	Future
atravesé	atravesaré
atravesaste	atravesarás
atravesó	atravesará
atravesamos	atravesaremos
atravesasteis	atravesaréis
atravesaron	atravesarán

Perfect indicative	Conditional
he atravesado	atravesaría
has atravesado	atravesarías
ha atravesado	atravesaría
hemos atravesado	atravesaríamos
habéis atravesado	atravesaríais
han atravesado	atravesarían

Pluperfect indicative	Imperative
había atravesado	–
habías atravesado	atraviesa
había atravesado	atraviese
habíamos atravesado	atravesemos
habíais atravesado	atravesad
habían atravesado	atraviesen

avergonzarse *to be ashamed*

Gerund *avergonzándose*
Past participle *avergonzado*

Present indicative	Present subjunctive
me avergüenzo	me avergüence
te avergüenzas	te avergüences
se avergüenza	se avergüence
nos avergonzamos	nos avergoncemos
os avergonzáis	os avergoncéis
se avergüenzan	se avergüencen

Imperfect indicative	Imperfect subjunctive
me avergonzaba	me avergonzara
te avergonzabas	te avergonzaras
se avergonzaba	se avergonzara
nos avergonzábamos	nos avergonzáramos
os avergonzabais	os avergonzarais
se avergonzaban	se avergonzaran

Preterite	Future
me avergoncé	me avergonzaré
te avergonzaste	te avergonzarás
se avergonzó	se avergonzará
nos avergonzamos	nos avergonzaremos
os avergonzasteis	os avergonzaréis
se avergonzaron	se avergonzarán

Perfect indicative	Conditional
me he avergonzado	me avergonzaría
te has avergonzado	te avergonzarías
se ha avergonzado	se avergonzaría
nos hemos avergonzado	nos avergonzaríamos
os habéis avergonzado	os avergonzaríais
se han avergonzado	se avergonzarían

Pluperfect indicative	Imperative
me había avergonzado	–
te habías avergonzado	avergüénzate
se había avergonzado	avergüéncese
nos habíamos avergonzado	avergoncémonos
os habíais avergonzado	avergonzaos
se habían avergonzado	avergüéncense

averiguar *to find out, verify*

Gerund *averiguando*
Past participle *averiguado*

Present indicative	Present subjunctive
averiguo	averigüe
averiguas	averigües
averigua	averigüe
averiguamos	averigüemos
averiguáis	averigüéis
averiguan	averigüen

Imperfect indicative	Imperfect subjunctive
averiguaba	averiguara
averiguabas	averiguaras
averiguaba	averiguara
averiguábamos	averiguáramos
averiguabais	averiguarais
averiguaban	averiguaran

Preterite	Future
averigüé	averiguaré
averiguaste	averiguarás
averiguó	averiguará
averiguamos	averiguaremos
averiguasteis	averiguaréis
averiguaron	averiguarán

Perfect indicative	Conditional
he averiguado	averiguaría
has averiguado	averiguarías
ha averiguado	averiguaría
hemos averiguado	averiguaríamos
habéis averiguado	averiguaríais
han averiguado	averiguarían

Pluperfect indicative	Imperative
había averiguado	–
habías averiguado	averigua
había averiguado	averigüe
habíamos averiguado	averigüemos
habíais averiguado	averiguad
habían averiguado	averigüen

bajar *to go down*

Gerund *bajando*
Past participle *bajado*

Present indicative	Present subjunctive
bajo	baje
bajas	bajes
baja	baje
bajamos	bajemos
bajáis	bajéis
bajan	bajen

Imperfect indicative	Imperfect subjunctive
bajaba	bajara
bajabas	bajaras
bajaba	bajara
bajábamos	bajáramos
bajabais	bajarais
bajaban	bajaran

Preterite	Future
bajé	bajaré
bajaste	bajarás
bajó	bajará
bajamos	bajaremos
bajasteis	bajaréis
bajaron	bajarán

Perfect indicative	Conditional
he bajado	bajaría
has bajado	bajarías
ha bajado	bajaría
hemos bajado	bajaríamos
habéis bajado	bajaríais
han bajado	bajarían

Pluperfect indicative	Imperative
había bajado	–
habías bajado	baja
había bajado	baje
habíamos bajado	bajemos
habíais bajado	bajad
habían bajado	bajen

bañarse *to bathe, have a bath*

Gerund *bañándose*
Past participle *bañado*

Present indicative	Present subjunctive
me baño	me bañe
te bañas	te bañes
se baña	se bañe
nos bañamos	nos bañemos
os bañáis	os bañéis
se bañan	se bañen

Imperfect indicative	Imperfect subjunctive
me bañaba	me bañara
te bañabas	te bañaras
se bañaba	se bañara
nos bañábamos	nos bañáramos
os bañabais	os bañarais
se bañaban	se bañaran

Preterite	Future
me bañé	me bañaré
te bañaste	te bañarás
se bañó	se bañará
nos bañamos	nos bañaremos
os bañasteis	os bañaréis
se bañaron	se bañarán

Perfect indicative	Conditional
me he bañado	me bañaría
te has bañado	te bañarías
se ha bañado	se bañaría
nos hemos bañado	nos bañaríamos
os habéis bañado	os bañaríais
se han bañado	se bañarían

Pluperfect indicative	Imperative
me había bañado	–
te habías bañado	báñate
se había bañado	báñese
nos habíamos bañado	bañémonos
os habíais bañado	bañaos
se habían bañado	báñense

beber *to drink*
Gerund *bebiendo*
Past participle *bebido*

Present indicative	Present subjunctive
bebo	beba
bebes	bebas
bebe	beba
bebemos	bebamos
bebéis	bebáis
beben	beban

Imperfect indicative	Imperfect subjunctive
bebía	bebiera
bebías	bebieras
bebía	bebiera
bebíamos	bebiéramos
bebíais	bebierais
bebían	bebieran

Preterite	Future
bebí	beberé
bebiste	beberás
bebió	beberá
bebimos	beberemos
bebisteis	beberéis
bebieron	beberán

Perfect indicative	Conditional
he bebido	bebería
has bebido	beberías
ha bebido	bebería
hemos bebido	beberíamos
habéis bebido	beberíais
han bebido	beberían

Pluperfect indicative	Imperative
había bebido	–
habías bebido	bebe
había bebido	beba
habíamos bebido	bebamos
habíais bebido	bebed
habían bebido	beban

buscar *to look for*
Gerund *buscando*
Past participle *buscado*

Present indicative	Present subjunctive
busco	busque
buscas	busques
busca	busque
buscamos	busquemos
buscáis	busquéis
buscan	busquen

Imperfect indicative	Imperfect subjunctive
buscaba	buscara
buscabas	buscaras
buscaba	buscara
buscábamos	buscáramos
buscabais	buscarais
buscaban	buscaran

Preterite	Future
busqué	buscaré
buscaste	buscarás
buscó	buscará
buscamos	buscaremos
buscasteis	buscaréis
buscaron	buscarán

Perfect indicative	Conditional
he buscado	buscaría
has buscado	buscarías
ha buscado	buscaría
hemos buscado	buscaríamos
habéis buscado	buscaríais
han buscado	buscarían

Pluperfect indicative	Imperative
había buscado	–
habías buscado	busca
había buscado	busque
habíamos buscado	busquemos
habíais buscado	buscad
habían buscado	busquen

caber *to fit*

Gerund *cabiendo*
Past participle *cabido*

Present indicative	Present subjunctive
quepo	quepa
cabes	quepas
cabe	quepa
cabemos	quepamos
cabéis	quepáis
caben	quepan

Imperfect indicative	Imperfect subjunctive
cabía	cupiera
cabías	cupieras
cabía	cupiera
cabíamos	cupiéramos
cabíais	cupierais
cabían	cupieran

Preterite	Future
cupe	cabré
cupiste	cabrás
cupo	cabrá
cupimos	cabremos
cupisteis	cabréis
cupieron	cabrán

Perfect indicative	Conditional
he cabido	cabría
has cabido	cabrías
ha cabido	cabría
hemos cabido	cabríamos
habéis cabido	cabríais
han cabido	cabrían

Pluperfect indicative	Imperative
había cabido	–
habías cabido	cabe
había cabido	quepa
habíamos cabido	quepamos
habíais cabido	cabed
habían cabido	quepan

caer *to fall*

Gerund *cayendo*
Past participle *caído*

Present indicative	Present subjunctive
caigo	caiga
caes	caigas
cae	caiga
caemos	caigamos
caéis	caigáis
caen	caigan

Imperfect indicative	Imperfect subjunctive
caía	cayera
caías	cayeras
caía	cayera
caíamos	cayéramos
caíais	cayerais
caían	cayeran

Preterite	Future
caí	caeré
caíste	caerás
cayó	caerá
caímos	caeremos
caísteis	caeréis
cayeron	caerán

Perfect indicative	Conditional
he caído	caería
has caído	caerías
ha caído	caería
hemos caído	caeríamos
habéis caído	caeríais
han caído	caerían

Pluperfect indicative	Imperative
había caído	–
habías caído	cae
había caído	caiga
habíamos caído	caigamos
habíais caído	caed
habían caído	caigan

cambiar *to change*

Gerund *cambiando*
Past participle *cambiado*

Present indicative	Present subjunctive
cambio	cambie
cambias	cambies
cambia	cambie
cambiamos	cambiemos
cambiáis	cambiéis
cambian	cambien

Imperfect indicative	Imperfect subjunctive
cambiaba	cambiara
cambiabas	cambiaras
cambiaba	cambiara
cambiábamos	cambiáramos
cambiabais	cambiarais
cambiaban	cambiaran

Preterite	Future
cambié	cambiaré
cambiaste	cambiarás
cambió	cambiará
cambiamos	cambiaremos
cambiasteis	cambiaréis
cambiaron	cambiarán

Perfect indicative	Conditional
he cambiado	cambiaría
has cambiado	cambiarías
ha cambiado	cambiaría
hemos cambiado	cambiaríamos
habéis cambiado	cambiaríais
han cambiado	cambiarían

Pluperfect indicative	Imperative
había cambiado	–
habías cambiado	cambia
había cambiado	cambie
habíamos cambiado	cambiemos
habíais cambiado	cambiad
habían cambiado	cambien

cantar *to sing*

Gerund *cantando*
Past participle *cantado*

Present indicative	Present subjunctive
canto	cante
cantas	cantes
canta	cante
cantamos	cantemos
cantáis	cantéis
cantan	canten

Imperfect indicative	Imperfect subjunctive
cantaba	cantara
cantabas	cantaras
cantaba	cantara
cantábamos	cantáramos
cantabais	cantarais
cantaban	cantaran

Preterite	Future
canté	cantaré
cantaste	cantarás
cantó	cantará
cantamos	cantaremos
cantasteis	cantaréis
cantaron	cantarán

Perfect indicative	Conditional
he cantado	cantaría
has cantado	cantarías
ha cantado	cantaría
hemos cantado	cantaríamos
habéis cantado	cantaríais
han cantado	cantarían

Pluperfect indicative	Imperative
había cantado	–
habías cantado	canta
había cantado	cante
habíamos cantado	cantemos
habíais cantado	cantad
habían cantado	canten

cargar *to load*

Gerund *cargando*
Past participle *cargado*

Present indicative	**Present subjunctive**
cargo	cargue
cargas	cargues
carga	cargue
cargamos	carguemos
cargáis	carguéis
cargan	carguen

Imperfect indicative	**Imperfect subjunctive**
cargaba	cargara
cargabas	cargaras
cargaba	cargara
cargábamos	cargáramos
cargabais	cargarais
cargaban	cargaran

Preterite	**Future**
cargué	cargaré
cargaste	cargarás
cargó	cargará
cargamos	cargaremos
cargasteis	cargaréis
cargaron	cargarán

Perfect indicative	**Conditional**
he cargado	cargaría
has cargado	cargarías
ha cargado	cargaría
hemos cargado	cargaríamos
habéis cargado	cargaríais
han cargado	cargarían

Pluperfect indicative	**Imperative**
había cargado	–
habías cargado	carga
había cargado	cargue
habíamos cargado	carguemos
habíais cargado	cargad
habían cargado	carguen

casarse *to get married*

Gerund *casándose*
Past participle *casado*

Present indicative	**Present subjunctive**
me caso	me case
te casas	te cases
se casa	se case
nos casamos	nos casemos
os casáis	os caséis
se casan	se casen

Imperfect indicative	**Imperfect subjunctive**
me casaba	me casara
te casabas	te casaras
se casaba	se casara
nos casábamos	nos casáramos
os casabais	os casarais
se casaban	se casaran

Preterite	**Future**
me casé	me casaré
te casaste	te casarás
se casó	se casará
nos casamos	nos casaremos
os casasteis	os casaréis
se casaron	se casarán

Perfect indicative	**Conditional**
me he casado	me casaría
te has casado	te casarías
se ha casado	se casaría
nos hemos casado	nos casaríamos
os habéis casado	os casaríais
se han casado	se casarían

Pluperfect indicative	**Imperative**
me había casado	–
te habías casado	cásate
se había casado	cásese
nos habíamos casado	casémonos
os habíais casado	casaos
se habían casado	cásense

cenar *to have supper*

Gerund *cenando*
Past participle *cenado*

Present indicative	Present subjunctive
ceno	cene
cenas	cenes
cena	cene
cenamos	cenemos
cenáis	cenéis
cenan	cenen

Imperfect indicative	Imperfect subjunctive
cenaba	cenara
cenabas	cenaras
cenaba	cenara
cenábamos	cenáramos
cenabais	cenarais
cenaban	cenaran

Preterite	Future
cené	cenaré
cenaste	cenarás
cenó	cenará
cenamos	cenaremos
cenasteis	cenaréis
cenaron	cenarán

Perfect indicative	Conditional
he cenado	cenaría
has cenado	cenarías
ha cenado	cenaría
hemos cenado	cenaríamos
habéis cenado	cenaríais
han cenado	cenarían

Pluperfect indicative	Imperative
había cenado	–
habías cenado	cena
había cenado	cene
habíamos cenado	cenemos
habíais cenado	cenad
habían cenado	cenen

cerrar *to close*

Gerund *cerrando*
Past participle *cerrado*

Present indicative	Present subjunctive
cierro	cierre
cierras	cierres
cierra	cierre
cerramos	cerremos
cerráis	cerréis
cierran	cierren

Imperfect indicative	Imperfect subjunctive
cerraba	cerrara
cerrabas	cerraras
cerraba	cerrara
cerrábamos	cerráramos
cerrabais	cerrarais
cerraban	cerraran

Preterite	Future
cerré	cerraré
cerraste	cerrarás
cerró	cerrará
cerramos	cerraremos
cerrasteis	cerraréis
cerraron	cerrarán

Perfect indicative	Conditional
he cerrado	cerraría
has cerrado	cerrarías
ha cerrado	cerraría
hemos cerrado	cerraríamos
habéis cerrado	cerraríais
han cerrado	cerrarían

Pluperfect indicative	Imperative
había cerrado	–
habías cerrado	cierra
había cerrado	cierre
habíamos cerrado	cerremos
habíais cerrado	cerrad
habían cerrado	cierren

cocer *to boil*

Gerund *cociendo*
Past participle *cocido*

Present indicative	**Present subjunctive**
cuezo	cueza
cueces	cuezas
cuece	cueza
cocemos	cozamos
cocéis	cozáis
cuecen	cuezan

Imperfect indicative	**Imperfect subjunctive**
cocía	cociera
cocías	cocieras
cocía	cociera
cocíamos	cociéramos
cocíais	cocierais
cocían	cocieran

Preterite	**Future**
cocí	coceré
cociste	cocerás
coció	cocerá
cocimos	coceremos
cocisteis	coceréis
cocieron	cocerán

Perfect indicative	**Conditional**
he cocido	cocería
has cocido	cocerías
ha cocido	cocería
hemos cocido	coceríamos
habéis cocido	coceríais
han cocido	cocerían

Pluperfect indicative	**Imperative**
había cocido	–
habías cocido	cuece
había cocido	cueza
habíamos cocido	cozamos
habíais cocido	coced
habían cocido	cuezan

coger *to catch*

Gerund *cogiendo*
Past participle *cogido*

Present indicative	**Present subjunctive**
cojo	coja
coges	cojas
coge	coja
cogemos	cojamos
cogéis	cojáis
cogen	cojan

Imperfect indicative	**Imperfect subjunctive**
cogía	cogiera
cogías	cogieras
cogía	cogiera
cogíamos	cogiéramos
cogíais	cogierais
cogían	cogieran

Preterite	**Future**
cogí	cogeré
cogiste	cogerás
cogió	cogerá
cogimos	cogeremos
cogisteis	cogeréis
cogieron	cogerán

Perfect indicative	**Conditional**
he cogido	cogería
has cogido	cogerías
ha cogido	cogería
hemos cogido	cogeríamos
habéis cogido	cogeríais
han cogido	cogerían

Pluperfect indicative	**Imperative**
había cogido	–
habías cogido	coge
había cogido	coja
habíamos cogido	cojamos
habíais cogido	coged
habían cogido	cojan

colgar *to hang*

Gerund *colgando*
Past participle *colgado*

Present indicative	Present subjunctive
cuelgo	cuelgue
cuelgas	cuelgues
cuelga	cuelgue
colgamos	colguemos
colgáis	colguéis
cuelgan	cuelguen

Imperfect indicative	Imperfect subjunctive
colgaba	colgara
colgabas	colgaras
colgaba	colgara
colgábamos	colgáramos
colgabais	colgarais
colgaban	colgaran

Preterite	Future
colgué	colgaré
colgaste	colgarás
colgó	colgará
colgamos	colgaremos
colgasteis	colgaréis
colgaron	colgarán

Perfect indicative	Conditional
he colgado	colgaría
has colgado	colgarías
ha colgado	colgaría
hemos colgado	colgaríamos
habéis colgado	colgaríais
han colgado	colgarían

Pluperfect indicative	Imperative
había colgado	–
habías colgado	cuelga
había colgado	cuelgue
habíamos colgado	colguemos
habíais colgado	colgad
habían colgado	cuelguen

comenzar *to start*

Gerund *comenzando*
Past participle *comenzado*

Present indicative	Present subjunctive
comienzo	comience
comienzas	comiences
comienza	comience
comenzamos	comencemos
comenzáis	comencéis
comienzan	comiencen

Imperfect indicative	Imperfect subjunctive
comenzaba	comenzara
comenzabas	comenzaras
comenzaba	comenzara
comenzábamos	comenzáramos
comenzabais	comenzarais
comenzaban	comenzaran

Preterite	Future
comencé	comenzaré
comenzaste	comenzarás
comenzó	comenzará
comenzamos	comenzaremos
comenzasteis	comenzaréis
comenzaron	comenzarán

Perfect indicative	Conditional
he comenzado	comenzaría
has comenzado	comenzarías
ha comenzado	comenzaría
hemos comenzado	comenzaríamos
habéis comenzado	comenzaríais
han comenzado	comenzarían

Pluperfect indicative	Imperative
había comenzado	–
habías comenzado	comienza
había comenzado	comience
habíamos comenzado	comencemos
habíais comenzado	comenzad
habían comenzado	comiencen

comer *to eat*

Gerund *comiendo*
Past participle *comido*

Present indicative	Present subjunctive
como	coma
comes	comas
come	coma
comemos	comamos
coméis	comáis
comen	coman

Imperfect indicative	Imperfect subjunctive
comía	comiera
comías	comieras
comía	comiera
comíamos	comiéramos
comíais	comierais
comían	comieran

Preterite	Future
comí	comeré
comiste	comerás
comió	comerá
comimos	comeremos
comisteis	comeréis
comieron	comerán

Perfect indicative	Conditional
he comido	comería
has comido	comerías
ha comido	comería
hemos comido	comeríamos
habéis comido	comeríais
han comido	comerían

Pluperfect indicative	Imperative
había comido	–
habías comido	come
había comido	coma
habíamos comido	comamos
habíais comido	comed
habían comido	coman

comprar *to buy*

Gerund *comprando*
Past participle *comprado*

Present indicative	Present subjunctive
compro	compre
compras	compres
compra	compre
compramos	compremos
compráis	compréis
compran	compren

Imperfect indicative	Imperfect subjunctive
compraba	comprara
comprabas	compraras
compraba	comprara
comprábamos	compráramos
comprabais	comprarais
compraban	compraran

Preterite	Future
compré	compraré
compraste	comprarás
compró	comprará
compramos	compraremos
comprasteis	compraréis
compraron	comprarán

Perfect indicative	Conditional
he comprado	compraría
has comprado	comprarías
ha comprado	compraría
hemos comprado	compraríamos
habéis comprado	compraríais
han comprado	comprarían

Pluperfect indicative	Imperative
había comprado	–
habías comprado	compra
había comprado	compre
habíamos comprado	compremos
habíais comprado	comprad
habían comprado	compren

conducir *to drive, to lead*

Gerund *conduciendo*
Past participle *conducido*

Present indicative	**Present subjunctive**
conduzco	conduzca
conduces	conduzcas
conduce	conduzca
conducimos	conduzcamos
conducís	conduzcáis
conducen	conduzcan

Imperfect indicative	**Imperfect subjunctive**
conducía	condujera
conducías	condujeras
conducía	condujera
conducíamos	condujéramos
conducíais	condujerais
conducían	condujeran

Preterite	**Future**
conduje	conduciré
condujiste	conducirás
condujo	conducirá
condujimos	conduciremos
condujisteis	conduciréis
condujeron	conducirán

Perfect indicative	**Conditional**
he conducido	conduciría
has conducido	conducirías
ha conducido	conduciría
hemos conducido	conduciríamos
habéis conducido	conduciríais
han conducido	conducirían

Pluperfect indicative	**Imperative**
había conducido	–
habías conducido	conduce
había conducido	conduzca
habíamos conducido	conduzcamos
habíais conducido	conducid
habían conducido	conduzcan

conocer *to know*

Gerund *conociendo*
Past participle *conocido*

Present indicative	**Present subjunctive**
conozco	conozca
conoces	conozcas
conoce	conozca
conocemos	conozcamos
conocéis	conozcáis
conocen	conozcan

Imperfect indicative	**Imperfect subjunctive**
conocía	conociera
conocías	conocieras
conocía	conociera
conocíamos	conociéramos
conocíais	conocierais
conocían	conocieran

Preterite	**Future**
conocí	conoceré
conociste	conocerás
conoció	conocerá
conocimos	conoceremos
conocisteis	conoceréis
conocieron	conocerán

Perfect indicative	**Conditional**
he conocido	conocería
has conocido	conocerías
ha conocido	conocería
hemos conocido	conoceríamos
habéis conocido	conoceríais
han conocido	conocerían

Pluperfect indicative	**Imperative**
había conocido	–
habías conocido	conoce
había conocido	conozca
habíamos conocido	conozcamos
habíais conocido	conoced
habían conocido	conozcan

conseguir *to succeed, manage*

Gerund *consiguiendo*
Past participle *conseguido*

Present indicative	Present subjunctive
consigo	consiga
consigues	consigas
consigue	consiga
conseguimos	consigamos
conseguís	consigáis
consiguen	consigan

Imperfect indicative	Imperfect subjunctive
conseguía	consiguiera
conseguías	consiguieras
conseguía	consiguiera
conseguíamos	consiguiéramos
conseguíais	consiguierais
conseguían	consiguieran

Preterite	Future
conseguí	conseguiré
conseguiste	conseguirás
consiguió	conseguirá
conseguimos	conseguiremos
conseguisteis	conseguiréis
consiguieron	conseguirán

Perfect indicative	Conditional
he conseguido	conseguiría
has conseguido	conseguirías
ha conseguido	conseguiría
hemos conseguido	conseguiríamos
habéis conseguido	conseguiríais
han conseguido	conseguirían

Pluperfect indicative	Imperative
había conseguido	–
habías conseguido	consigue
había conseguido	consiga
habíamos conseguido	consigamos
habíais conseguido	conseguid
habían conseguido	consigan

construir *to build*

Gerund *construyendo*
Past participle *construido*

Present indicative	Present subjunctive
construyo	construya
construyes	construyas
construye	construya
construimos	construyamos
construís	construyáis
construyen	construyan

Imperfect indicative	Imperfect subjunctive
construía	construyera
construías	construyeras
construía	construyera
construíamos	construyéramos
construíais	construyerais
construían	construyeran

Preterite	Future
construí	construiré
construiste	construirás
construyó	construirá
construimos	construiremos
construisteis	construiréis
construyeron	construirán

Perfect indicative	Conditional
he construido	construiría
has construido	construirías
ha construido	construiría
hemos construido	construiríamos
habéis construido	construiríais
han construido	construirían

Pluperfect indicative	Imperative
había construido	–
habías construido	construye
había construido	construya
habíamos construido	construyamos
habíais construido	construid
habían construido	construyan

contar *to tell, to count*

Gerund *contando*
Past participle *contado*

Present indicative	Present subjunctive
cuento	cuente
cuentas	cuentes
cuenta	cuente
contamos	contemos
contáis	contéis
cuentan	cuenten

Imperfect indicative	Imperfect subjunctive
contaba	contara
contabas	contaras
contaba	contara
contábamos	contáramos
contabais	contarais
contaban	contaran

Preterite	Future
conté	contaré
contaste	contarás
contó	contará
contamos	contaremos
contasteis	contaréis
contaron	contarán

Perfect indicative	Conditional
he contado	contaría
has contado	contarías
ha contado	contaría
hemos contado	contaríamos
habéis contado	contaríais
han contado	contarían

Pluperfect indicative	Imperative
había contado	–
habías contado	cuenta
había contado	cuente
habíamos contado	contemos
habíais contado	contad
habían contado	cuenten

contestar *to answer*

Gerund *contestando*
Past participle *contestado*

Present indicative	Present subjunctive
contesto	conteste
contestas	contestes
contesta	conteste
contestamos	contestemos
contestáis	contestéis
contestan	contesten

Imperfect indicative	Imperfect subjunctive
contestaba	contestara
contestabas	contestaras
contestaba	contestara
contestábamos	contestáramos
contestabais	contestarais
contestaban	contestaran

Preterite	Future
contesté	contestaré
contestaste	contestarás
contestó	contestará
contestamos	contestaremos
contestasteis	contestaréis
contestaron	contestarán

Perfect indicative	Conditional
he contestado	contestaría
has contestado	contestarías
ha contestado	contestaría
hemos contestado	contestaríamos
habéis contestado	contestaríais
han contestado	contestarían

Pluperfect indicative	Imperative
había contestado	–
habías contestado	contesta
había contestado	conteste
habíamos contestado	contestemos
habíais contestado	contestad
habían contestado	contesten

continuar *to continue*

Gerund *continuando*
Past participle *continuado*

Present indicative	Present subjunctive
continúo	continúe
continúas	continúes
continúa	continúe
continuamos	continuemos
continuáis	continuéis
continúan	continúen

Imperfect indicative	Imperfect subjunctive
continuaba	continuara
continuabas	continuaras
continuaba	continuara
continuábamos	continuáramos
continuabais	continuarais
continuaban	continuaran

Preterite	Future
continué	continuaré
continuaste	continuarás
continuó	continuará
continuamos	continuaremos
continuastcis	continuaréis
continuaron	continuarán

Perfect indicative	Conditional
he continuado	continuaría
has continuado	continuarías
ha continuado	continuaría
hemos continuado	continuaríamos
habéis continuado	continuaríais
han continuado	continuarían

Pluperfect indicative	Imperative
había continuado	–
habías continuado	continúa
había continuado	continúe
habíamos continuado	.continuemos
habíais continuado	continuad
habían continuado	continúen

correr *to run*

Gerund *corriendo*
Past participle *corrido*

Present indicative	Present subjunctive
corro	corra
corres	corras
corre	corra
corremos	corramos
corréis	corráis
corren	corran

Imperfect indicative	Imperfect subjunctive
corría	corriera
corrías	corrieras
corría	corriera
corríamos	corriéramos
corríais	corrierais
corrían	corrieran

Preterite	Future
corrí	correré
corriste	correrás
corrió	correrá
corrimos	correremos
corristeis	correréis
corrieron	correrán

Perfect indicative	Conditional
he corrido	correría
has corrido	correrías
ha corrido	correría
hemos corrido	correríamos
habéis corrido	correríais
han corrido	correrían

Pluperfect indicative	Imperative
había corrido	–
habías corrido	corre
había corrido	corra
habíamos corrido	corramos
habíais corrido	corred
habían corrido	corran

cortar *to cut*

Gerund *cortando*
Past participle *cortado*

Present indicative	**Present subjunctive**
corto	corte
cortas	cortes
corta	corte
cortamos	cortemos
cortáis	cortéis
cortan	corten

Imperfect indicative	**Imperfect subjunctive**
cortaba	cortara
cortabas	cortaras
cortaba	cortara
cortábamos	cortáramos
cortabais	cortarais
cortaban	cortaran

Preterite	**Future**
corté	cortaré
cortaste	cortarás
cortó	cortará
cortamos	cortaremos
cortasteis	cortaréis
cortaron	cortarán

Perfect indicative	**Conditional**
he cortado	cortaría
has cortado	cortarías
ha cortado	cortaría
hemos cortado	cortaríamos
habéis cortado	cortaríais
han cortado	cortarían

Pluperfect indicative	**Imperative**
había cortado	–
habías cortado	corta
había cortado	corte
habíamos cortado	cortemos
habíais cortado	cortad
habían cortado	corten

costar *to cost*

Gerund *costando*
Past participle *costado*

Present indicative	**Present subjunctive**
cuesto	cueste
cuestas	cuestes
cuesta	cueste
costamos	costemos
costáis	costéis
cuestan	cuesten

Imperfect indicative	**Imperfect subjunctive**
costaba	costara
costabas	costaras
costaba	costara
costábamos	costáramos
costabais	costarais
costaban	costaran

Preterite	**Future**
costé	costaré
costaste	costarás
costó	costará
costamos	costaremos
costasteis	costaréis
costaron	costarán

Perfect indicative	**Conditional**
he costado	costaría
has costado	costarías
ha costado	costaría
hemos costado	costaríamos
habéis costado	costaríais
han costado	costarían

Pluperfect indicative	**Imperative**
había costado	–
habías costado	cuesta
había costado	cueste
habíamos costado	costemos
habíais costado	costad
habían costado	cuesten

crecer *to grow, increase*

Gerund *creciendo*
Past participle *crecido*

Present indicative	Present subjunctive
crezco	crezca
creces	crezcas
crece	crezca
crecemos	crezcamos
crecéis	crezcáis
crecen	crezcan

Imperfect indicative	Imperfect subjunctive
crecía	creciera
crecías	crecieras
crecía	creciera
crecíamos	creciéramos
crecíais	crecierais
crecían	crecieran

Preterite	Future
crecí	creceré
creciste	crecerás
creció	crecerá
crecimos	creceremos
crecisteis	creceréis
crecieron	crecerán

Perfect indicative	Conditional
he crecido	crecería
has crecido	crecerías
ha crecido	crecería
hemos crecido	creceríamos
habéis crecido	creceríais
han crecido	crecerían

Pluperfect indicative	Imperative
había crecido	–
habías crecido	crece
había crecido	crezca
habíamos crecido	crezcamos
habíais crecido	creced
habían crecido	crezcan

creer *to believe*

Gerund *creyendo*
Past participle *creído*

Present indicative	Present subjunctive
creo	crea
crees	creas
cree	crea
creemos	creamos
creéis	creáis
creen	crean

Imperfect indicative	Imperfect subjunctive
creía	creyera
creías	creyeras
creía	creyera
creíamos	creyéramos
creíais	creyerais
creían	creyeran

Preterite	Future
creí	creeré
creíste	creerás
creyó	creerá
creímos	creeremos
creísteis	creeréis
creyeron	creerán

Perfect indicative	Conditional
he creído	creería
has creído	creerías
ha creído	creería
hemos creído	creeríamos
habéis creído	creeríais
han creído	creerían

Pluperfect indicative	Imperative
había creído	–
habías creído	cree
había creído	crea
habíamos creído	creamos
habíais creído	creed
habían creído	crean

cubrir *to cover*

Gerund *cubriendo*
Past participle *cubierto*

Present indicative	Present subjunctive
cubro	cubra
cubres	cubras
cubre	cubra
cubrimos	cubramos
cubrís	cubráis
cubren	cubran

Imperfect indicative	Imperfect subjunctive
cubría	cubriera
cubrías	cubrieras
cubría	cubriera
cubríamos	cubriéramos
cubríais	cubrierais
cubrían	cubrieran

Preterite	Future
cubrí	cubriré
cubriste	cubrirás
cubrió	cubrirá
cubrimos	cubriremos
cubristeis	cubriréis
cubrieron	cubrirán

Perfect indicative	Conditional
he cubierto	cubriría
has cubierto	cubrirías
ha cubierto	cubriría
hemos cubierto	cubriríamos
habéis cubierto	cubriríais
han cubierto	cubrirían

Pluperfect indicative	Imperative
había cubierto	–
habías cubierto	cubre
había cubierto	cubra
habíamos cubierto	cubramos
habíais cubierto	cubrid
habían cubierto	cubran

dar *to give*

Gerund *dando*
Past participle *dado*

Present indicative	Present subjunctive
doy	dé
das	des
da	dé
damos	demos
dais	deis
dan	den

Imperfect indicative	Imperfect subjunctive
daba	diera
dabas	dieras
daba	diera
dábamos	diéramos
dabais	dierais
daban	dieran

Preterite	Future
di	daré
diste	darás
dio	dará
dimos	daremos
disteis	daréis
dieron	darán

Perfect indicative	Conditional
he dado	daría
has dado	darías
ha dado	daría
hemos dado	daríamos
habéis dado	daríais
han dado	darían

Pluperfect indicative	Imperative
había dado	–
habías dado	da
había dado	dé
habíamos dado	demos
habíais dado	dad
habían dado	den

deber *to have to, owe*

Gerund *debiendo*
Past participle *debido*

Present indicative	Present subjunctive
debo	deba
debes	debas
debe	deba
debemos	debamos
debéis	debáis
deben	deban

Imperfect indicative	Imperfect subjunctive
debía	debiera
debías	debieras
debía	debiera
debíamos	debiéramos
debíais	debierais
debían	debieran

Preterite	Future
debí	deberé
debiste	deberás
debió	deberá
debimos	deberemos
debisteis	deberéis
debieron	deberán

Perfect indicative	Conditional
he debido	debería
has debido	deberías
ha debido	debería
hemos debido	deberíamos
habéis debido	deberíais
han debido	deberían

Pluperfect indicative	Imperative
había debido	–
habías debido	debe
había debido	deba
habíamos debido	debamos
habíais debido	debed
habían debido	deban

decidir *to decide*

Gerund *decidiendo*
Past participle *decidido*

Present indicative	Present subjunctive
decido	decida
decides	decidas
decide	decida
decidimos	decidamos
decidís	decidáis
deciden	decidan

Imperfect indicative	Imperfect subjunctive
decidía	decidiera
decidías	decidieras
decidía	decidiera
decidíamos	decidiéramos
decidíais	decidierais
decidían	decidieran

Preterite	Future
decidí	decidiré
decidiste	decidirás
decidió	decidirá
decidimos	decidiremos
decidisteis	decidiréis
decidieron	decidirán

Perfect indicative	Conditional
he decidido	decidiría
has decidido	decidirías
ha decidido	decidiría
hemos decidido	decidiríamos
habéis decidido	decidiríais
han decidido	decidirían

Pluperfect indicative	Imperative
había decidido	–
habías decidido	decide
había decidido	decida
habíamos decidido	decidamos
habíais decidido	decidid
habían decidido	decidan

decir *to say*

Gerund *diciendo*
Past participle *dicho*

Present indicative	Present subjunctive
digo	diga
dices	digas
dice	diga
decimos	digamos
decís	digáis
dicen	digan

Imperfect indicative	Imperfect subjunctive
decía	dijera
decías	dijeras
decía	dijera
decíamos	dijéramos
decíais	dijerais
decían	dijeran

Preterite	Future
dije	diré
dijiste	dirás
dijo	dirá
dijimos	diremos
dijisteis	diréis
dijeron	dirán

Perfect indicative	Conditional
he dicho	diría
has dicho	dirías
ha dicho	diría
hemos dicho	diríamos
habéis dicho	diríais
han dicho	dirían

Pluperfect indicative	Imperative
había dicho	–
habías dicho	di
había dicho	diga
habíamos dicho	digamos
habíais dicho	decid
habían dicho	digan

dejar *to leave, let*

Gerund *dejando*
Past participle *dejado*

Present indicative	Present subjunctive
dejo	deje
dejas	dejes
deja	deje
dejamos	dejemos
dejáis	dejéis
dejan	dejen

Imperfect indicative	Imperfect subjunctive
dejaba	dejara
dejabas	dejaras
dejaba	dejara
dejábamos	dejáramos
dejabais	dejarais
dejaban	dejaran

Preterite	Future
dejé	dejaré
dejaste	dejarás
dejó	dejará
dejamos	dejaremos
dejasteis	dejaréis
dejaron	dejarán

Perfect indicative	Conditional
he dejado	dejaría
has dejado	dejarías
ha dejado	dejaría
hemos dejado	dejaríamos
habéis dejado	dejaríais
han dejado	dejarían

Pluperfect indicative	Imperative
había dejado	–
habías dejado	deja
había dejado	deje
habíamos dejado	dejemos
habíais dejado	dejad
habían dejado	dejen

descender *to go down*

Gerund *descendiendo*
Past participle *descendido*

Present indicative	Present subjunctive
desciendo	descienda
desciendes	desciendas
desciende	descienda
descendemos	descendamos
descendéis	descendáis
descienden	desciendan

Imperfect indicative	Imperfect subjunctive
descendía	descendiera
descendías	descendieras
descendía	descendiera
descendíamos	descendiéramos
descendíais	descendierais
descendían	descendieran

Preterite	Future
descendí	descenderé
descendiste	descenderás
descendió	descenderá
descendimos	descenderemos
descendisteis	descenderéis
descendieron	descenderán

Perfect indicative	Conditional
he descendido	descendería
has descendido	descenderías
ha descendido	descendería
hemos descendido	descenderíamos
habéis descendido	descenderíais
han descendido	descenderían

Pluperfect indicative	Imperative
había descendido	–
habías descendido	desciende
había descendido	descienda
habíamos descendido	descendamos
habíais descendido	descended
habían descendido	desciendan

describir *to describe*

Gerund *describiendo*
Past participle *descrito*

Present indicative	Present subjunctive
describo	describa
describes	describas
describe	describa
describimos	describamos
describís	describáis
describen	describan

Imperfect indicative	Imperfect subjunctive
describía	describiera
describías	describieras
describía	describiera
describíamos	describiéramos
describíais	describierais
describían	describieran

Preterite	Future
describí	describiré
describiste	describirás
describió	describirá
describimos	describiremos
describisteis	describiréis
describieron	describirán

Perfect indicative	Conditional
he descrito	describiría
has descrito	describirías
ha descrito	describiría
hemos descrito	describiríamos
habéis descrito	describiríais
han descrito	describirían

Pluperfect indicative	Imperative
había descrito	–
habías descrito	describe
había descrito	describa
habíamos descrito	describamos
habíais descrito	describid
habían descrito	describan

descubrir *to discover*

Gerund *descubriendo*
Past participle *descubierto*

Present indicative	Present subjunctive
descubro	descubra
descubres	descubras
descubre	descubra
descubrimos	descubramos
descubrís	descubráis
descubren	descubran

Imperfect indicative	Imperfect subjunctive
descubría	descubriera
descubrías	descubrieras
descubría	descubriera
descubríamos	descubriéramos
descubríais	descubrierais
descubrían	descubrieran

Preterite	Future
descubrí	descubriré
descubriste	descubrirás
descubrió	descubrirá
descubrimos	descubriremos
descubristeis	descubriréis
descubrieron	descubrirán

Perfect indicative	Conditional
he descubierto	descubriría
has descubierto	descubrirías
ha descubierto	descubriría
hemos descubierto	descubriríamos
habéis descubierto	descubriríais
han descubierto	descubrirían

Pluperfect indicative	Imperative
había descubierto	–
habías descubierto	descubre
había descubierto	descubra
habíamos descubierto	descubramos
habíais descubierto	descubrid
habían descubierto	descubran

despertarse *to wake up*

Gerund *despertándose*
Past participle *despertado*

Present indicative	Present subjunctive
me despierto	me despierte
te despiertas	te despiertes
se despierta	se despierte
nos despertamos	nos despertemos
os despertáis	os despertéis
se despiertan	se despierten

Imperfect indicative	Imperfect subjunctive
me despertaba	me despertara
te despertabas	te despertaras
se despertaba	se despertara
nos despertábamos	nos despertáramos
os despertabais	os despertarais
se despertaban	se despertaran

Preterite	Future
me desperté	me despertaré
te despertaste	te despertarás
se despertó	se despertará
nos despertamos	nos despertaremos
os despertasteis	os despertaréis
se despertaron	se despertarán

Perfect indicative	Conditional
me he despertado	me despertaría
te has despertado	te despertarías
se ha despertado	se despertaría
nos hemos despertado	nos despertaríamos
os habéis despertado	os despertaríais
se han despertado	se despertarían

Pluperfect indicative	Imperative
me había despertado	–
te habías despertado	despiértate
se había despertado	despiértese
nos habíamos despertado	despertémonos
os habíais despertado	despertaos
se habían despertado	despiértense

destruir *to destroy*

Gerund *destruyendo*
Past participle *destruido*

Present indicative	Present subjunctive
destruyo	destruya
destruyes	destruyas
destruye	destruya
destruimos	destruyamos
destruís	destruyáis
destruyen	destruyan

Imperfect indicative	Imperfect subjunctive
destruía	destruyera
destruías	destruyeras
destruía	destruyera
destruíamos	destruyéramos
destruíais	destruyerais
destruían	destruyeran

Preterite	Future
destruí	destruiré
destruiste	destruirás
destruyó	destruirá
destruimos	destruiremos
destruisteis	destruiréis
destruyeron	destruirán

Perfect indicative	Conditional
he destruido	destruiría
has destruido	destruirías
ha destruido	destruiría
hemos destruido	destruiríamos
habéis destruido	destruiríais
han destruido	destruirían

Pluperfect indicative	Imperative
había destruido	–
habías destruido	destruye
había destruido	destruya
habíamos destruido	destruyamos
habíais destruido	destruid
habían destruido	destruyan

dirigir *to direct*

Gerund *dirigiendo*
Past participle *dirigido*

Present indicative	Present subjunctive
dirijo	dirija
diriges	dirijas
dirige	dirija
dirigimos	dirijamos
dirigís	dirijáis
dirigen	dirijan

Imperfect indicative	Imperfect subjunctive
dirigía	dirigiera
dirigías	dirigieras
dirigía	dirigiera
dirigíamos	dirigiéramos
dirigíais	dirigierais
dirigían	dirigieran

Preterite	Future
dirigí	dirigiré
dirigiste	dirigirás
dirigió	dirigirá
dirigimos	dirigiremos
dirigisteis	dirigiréis
dirigieron	dirigirán

Perfect indicative	Conditional
he dirigido	dirigiría
has dirigido	dirigirías
ha dirigido	dirigiría
hemos dirigido	dirigiríamos
habéis dirigido	dirigiríais
han dirigido	dirigirían

Pluperfect indicative	Imperative
había dirigido	–
habías dirigido	dirige
había dirigido	dirija
habíamos dirigido	dirijamos
habíais dirigido	dirigid
habían dirigido	dirijan

distinguir *to distinguish*

Gerund *distinguiendo*
Past participle *distinguido*

Present indicative	Present subjunctive
distingo	distinga
distingues	distingas
distingue	distinga
distinguimos	distingamos
distinguís	distingáis
distinguen	distingan

Imperfect indicative	Imperfect subjunctive
distinguía	distinguiera
distinguías	distinguieras
distinguía	distinguiera
distinguíamos	distinguiéramos
distinguíais	distinguierais
distinguían	distinguieran

Preterite	Future
distinguí	distinguiré
distinguiste	distinguirás
distinguió	distinguirá
distinguimos	distinguiremos
distinguisteis	distinguiréis
distinguieron	distinguirán

Perfect indicative	Conditional
he distinguido	distinguiría
has distinguido	distinguirías
ha distinguido	distinguiría
hemos distinguido	distinguiríamos
habéis distinguido	distinguiríais
han distinguido	distinguirían

Pluperfect indicative	Imperative
había distinguido	–
habías distinguido	distingue
había distinguido	distinga
habíamos distinguido	distingamos
habíais distinguido	distinguid
habían distinguido	distingan

divertirse *to enjoy oneself*

Gerund *divertiéndose*
Past participle *divertido*

Present indicative	Present subjunctive
me divierto	me divierta
te diviertes	te diviertas
se divierte	se divierta
nos divertimos	nos divirtamos
os divertís	os divirtáis
se divierten	se diviertan

Imperfect indicative	Imperfect subjunctive
me divertía	me divirtiera
te divertías	te divirtieras
se divertía	se divirtiera
nos divertíamos	nos divirtiéramos
os divertíais	os divirtierais
se divertían	se divirtieran

Preterite	Future
me divertí	me divertiré
te divertiste	te divertirás
se divirtió	se divertirá
nos divertimos	nos divertiremos
os divertisteis	os divertiréis
se divirtieron	se divertirán

Perfect indicative	Conditional
me he divertido	me divertiría
te has divertido	te divertirías
se ha divertido	se divertiría
nos hemos divertido	nos divertiríamos
os habéis divertido	os divertiríais
se han divertido	se divertirían

Pluperfect indicative	Imperative
me había divertido	–
te habías divertido	diviértete
se había divertido	diviértase
nos habíamos divertido	divirtámonos
os habíais divertido	divertíos
se habían divertido	diviértanse

dormir *to sleep*

Gerund *durmiendo*
Past participle *dormido*

Present indicative	Present subjunctive
duermo	duerma
duermes	duermas
duerme	duerma
dormimos	durmamos
dormís	durmáis
duermen	duerman

Imperfect indicative	Imperfect subjunctive
dormía	durmiera
dormías	durmieras
dormía	durmiera
dormíamos	durmiéramos
dormíais	durmierais
dormían	durmieran

Preterite	Future
dormí	dormiré
dormiste	dormirás
durmió	dormirá
dormimos	dormiremos
dormisteis	dormiréis
durmieron	dormirán

Perfect indicative	Conditional
he dormido	dormiría
has dormido	dormirías
ha dormido	dormiría
hemos dormido	dormiríamos
habéis dormido	dormiríais
han dormido	dormirían

Pluperfect indicative	Imperative
había dormido	–
habías dormido	duerme
había dormido	duerma
habíamos dormido	durmamos
habíais dormido	dormid
habían dormido	duerman

embarcar *to embark*

Gerund *embarcando*
Past participle *embarcado*

Present indicative	Present subjunctive
embarco	embarque
embarcas	embarques
embarca	embarque
embarcamos	embarquemos
embarcáis	embarquéis
embarcan	embarquen

Imperfect indicative	Imperfect subjunctive
embarcaba	embarcara
embarcabas	embarcaras
embarcaba	embarcara
embarcábamos	embarcáramos
embarcabais	embarcarais
embarcaban	embarcaran

Preterite	Future
embarqué	embarcaré
embarcaste	embarcarás
embarcó	embarcará
embarcamos	embarcaremos
embarcasteis	embarcaréis
embarcaron	embarcarán

Perfect indicative	Conditional
he embarcado	embarcaría
has embarcado	embarcarías
ha embarcado	embarcaría
hemos embarcado	embarcaríamos
habéis embarcado	embarcaríais
han embarcado	embarcarían

Pluperfect indicative	Imperative
había embarcado	–
habías embarcado	embarca
había embarcado	embarque
habíamos embarcado	embarquemos
habíais embarcado	embarcad
habían embarcado	embarquen

empezar *to begin*

Gerund *empezando*
Past participle *empezado*

Present indicative	Present subjunctive
empiezo	empiece
empiezas	empieces
empieza	empiece
empezamos	empecemos
empezáis	empecéis
empiezan	empiecen

Imperfect indicative	Imperfect subjunctive
empezaba	empezara
empezabas	empezaras
empezaba	empezara
empezábamos	empezáramos
empezabais	empezarais
empezaban	empezaran

Preterite	Future
empecé	empezaré
empezaste	empezarás
empezó	empezará
empezamos	empezaremos
empezasteis	empezaréis
empezaron	empezarán

Perfect indicative	Conditional
he empezado	empezaría
has empezado	empezarías
ha empezado	empezaría
hemos empezado	empezaríamos
habéis empezado	empezaríais
han empezado	empezarían

Pluperfect indicative	Imperative
había empezado	–
habías empezado	empieza
había empezado	empiece
habíamos empezado	empecemos
habíais empezado	empezad
habían empezado	empiecen

empujar *to push*

Gerund *empujando*
Past participle *empujado*

Present indicative	Present subjunctive
empujo	empuje
empujas	empujes
empuja	empuje
empujamos	empujemos
empujáis	empujéis
empujan	empujen

Imperfect indicative	Imperfect subjunctive
empujaba	empujara
empujabas	empujaras
empujaba	empujara
empujábamos	empujáramos
empujabais	empujarais
empujaban	empujaran

Preterite	Future
empujé	empujaré
empujaste	empujarás
empujó	empujará
empujamos	empujaremos
empujasteis	empujaréis
empujaron	empujarán

Perfect indicative	Conditional
he empujado	empujaría
has empujado	empujarías
ha empujado	empujaría
hemos empujado	empujaríamos
habéis empujado	empujaríais
han empujado	empujarían

Pluperfect indicative	Imperative
había empujado	–
habías empujado	empuja
había empujado	empuje
habíamos empujado	empujemos
habíais empujado	empujad
habían empujado	empujen

encender *to light, to turn on*

Gerund *encendiendo*
Past participle *encendido*

Present indicative	Present subjunctive
enciendo	encienda
enciendes	enciendas
enciende	encienda
encendemos	encendamos
encendéis	encendáis
encienden	enciendan

Imperfect indicative	Imperfect subjunctive
encendía	encendiera
encendías	encendieras
encendía	encendiera
encendíamos	encendiéramos
encendíais	encendierais
encendían	encendieran

Preterite	Future
encendí	encenderé
encendiste	encenderás
encendió	encenderá
encendimos	encenderemos
encendisteis	encenderéis
encendieron	encenderán

Perfect indicative	Conditional
he encendido	encendería
has encendido	encenderías
ha encendido	encendería
hemos encendido	encenderíamos
habéis encendido	encenderíais
han encendido	encenderían

Pluperfect indicative	Imperative
había encendido	–
habías encendido	enciende
había encendido	encienda
habíamos encendido	encendamos
habíais encendido	encended
habían encendido	enciendan

encontrar *to find*

Gerund *encontrando*
Past participle *encontrado*

Present indicative	Present subjunctive
encuentro	encuentre
encuentras	encuentres
encuentra	encuentre
encontramos	encontremos
encontráis	encontréis
encuentran	encuentren

Imperfect indicative	Imperfect subjunctive
encontraba	encontrara
encontrabas	encontraras
encontraba	encontrara
encontrábamos	encontráramos
encontrabais	encontrarais
encontraban	encontraran

Preterite	Future
encontré	encontraré
encontraste	encontrarás
encontró	encontrará
encontramos	encontraremos
encontrasteis	encontraréis
encontraron	encontrarán

Perfect indicative	Conditional
he encontrado	encontraría
has encontrado	encontrarías
ha encontrado	encontraría
hemos encontrado	encontraríamos
habéis encontrado	encontraríais
han encontrado	encontrarían

Pluperfect indicative	Imperative
había encontrado	–
habías encontrado	encuentra
había encontrado	encuentre
habíamos encontrado	encontremos
habíais encontrado	encontrad
habían encontrado	encuentren

entender *to understand*

Gerund *entendiendo*
Past participle *entendido*

Present indicative	Present subjunctive
entiendo	entienda
entiendes	entiendas
entiende	entienda
entendemos	entendamos
entendéis	entendáis
entienden	entiendan

Imperfect indicative	Imperfect subjunctive
entendía	entendiera
entendías	entendieras
entendía	entendiera
entendíamos	entendiéramos
entendíais	entendierais
entendían	entendieran

Preterite	Future
entendí	entenderé
entendiste	entenderás
entendió	entenderá
entendimos	entenderemos
entendisteis	entenderéis
entendieron	entenderán

Perfect indicative	Conditional
he entendido	entendería
has entendido	entenderías
ha entendido	entendería
hemos entendido	entenderíamos
habéis entendido	entenderíais
han entendido	entenderían

Pluperfect indicative	Imperative
había entendido	–
habías entendido	entiende
había entendido	entienda
habíamos entendido	entendamos
habíais entendido	entended
habían entendido	entiendan

entrar *to enter, go in*

Gerund *entrando*
Past participle *entrado*

Present indicative	Present subjunctive
entro	entre
entras	entres
entra	entre
entramos	entremos
entráis	entréis
entran	entren

Imperfect indicative	Imperfect subjunctive
entraba	entrara
entrabas	entraras
entraba	entrara
entrábamos	entráramos
entrabais	entrarais
entraban	entraran

Preterite	Future
entré	entraré
entraste	entrarás
entró	entrará
entramos	entraremos
entrasteis	entraréis
entraron	entrarán

Perfect indicative	Conditional
he entrado	entraría
has entrado	entrarías
ha entrado	entraría
hemos entrado	entraríamos
habéis entrado	entraríais
han entrado	entrarían

Pluperfect indicative	Imperative
había entrado	–
habías entrado	entra
había entrado	entre
habíamos entrado	entremos
habíais entrado	entrad
habían entrado	entren

enviar *to send*

Gerund *enviando*
Past participle *enviado*

Present indicative	Present subjunctive
envío	envíe
envías	envíes
envía	envíe
enviamos	enviemos
enviáis	enviéis
envían	envíen

Imperfect indicative	Imperfect subjunctive
enviaba	enviara
enviabas	enviaras
enviaba	enviara
enviábamos	enviáramos
enviabais	enviarais
enviaban	enviaran

Preterite	Future
envié	enviaré
enviaste	enviarás
envió	enviará
enviamos	enviaremos
enviasteis	enviaréis
enviaron	enviarán

Perfect indicative	Conditional
he enviado	enviaría
has enviado	enviarías
ha enviado	enviaría
hemos enviado	enviaríamos
habéis enviado	enviaríais
han enviado	enviarían

Pluperfect indicative	Imperative
había enviado	–
habías enviado	envía
había enviado	envíe
habíamos enviado	enviemos
habíais enviado	enviad
habían enviado	envíen

equivocarse *to make a mistake*

Gerund *equivocándose*
Past participle *equivocado*

Present indicative	Present subjunctive
me equivoco	me equivoque
te equivocas	te equivoques
se equivoca	se equivoque
nos equivocamos	nos equivoquemos
os equivocáis	os equivoquéis
se equivocan	se equivoquen

Imperfect indicative	Imperfect subjunctive
me equivocaba	me equivocara
te equivocabas	te equivocaras
se equivocaba	se equivocara
nos equivocábamos	nos equivocáramos
os equivocabais	os equivocarais
se equivocaban	se equivocaran

Preterite	Future
me equivoqué	me equivocaré
te equivocaste	te equivocarás
se equivocó	se equivocará
nos equivocamos	nos equivocaremos
os equivocasteis	os equivocaréis
se equivocaron	se equivocarán

Perfect indicative	Conditional
me he equivocado	me equivocaría
te has equivocado	te equivocarías
se ha equivocado	se equivocaría
nos hemos equivocado	nos equivocaríamos
os habéis equivocado	os equivocaríais
se han equivocado	se equivocarían

Pluperfect indicative	Imperative
me había equivocado	–
te habías equivocado	equivócate
se había equivocado	equivóquese
nos habíamos equivocado	equivoquémonos
os habíais equivocado	equivocaos
se habían equivocado	equivóquense

errar *to err, wander*

Gerund *errando*
Past participle *errado*

Present indicative	Present subjunctive
yerro	yerre
yerras	yerres
yerra	yerre
erramos	erremos
erráis	erréis
yerran	yerren

Imperfect indicative	Imperfect subjunctive
erraba	errara
errabas	erraras
erraba	errara
errábamos	erráramos
errabais	errarais
erraban	erraran

Preterite	Future
erré	erraré
erraste	errarás
erró	errará
erramos	erraremos
errasteis	erraréis
erraron	errarán

Perfect indicative	Conditional
he errado	
has errado	erraría
ha errado	errarías
hemos errado	erraría
habéis errado	erraríamos
han errado	erraríais
	errarían

Pluperfect indicative	Imperative
había errado	
habías errado	–
había errado	yerra
habíamos errado	yerre
habíais errado	erremos
habían errado	errad
	yerren

escoger *to choose*

Gerund *escogiendo*
Past participle *escogido*

Present indicative	Present subjunctive
escojo	escoja
escoges	escojas
escoge	escoja
escogemos	escojamos
escogéis	escojáis
escogen	escojan

Imperfect indicative	Imperfect subjunctive
escogía	escogiera
escogías	escogieras
escogía	escogiera
escogíamos	escogiéramos
escogíais	escogierais
escogían	escogieran

Preterite	Future
escogí	escogeré
escogiste	escogerás
escogió	escogerá
escogimos	escogeremos
escogisteis	escogeréis
escogieron	escogerán

Perfect indicative	Conditional
he escogido	
has escogido	escogería
ha escogido	escogerías
hemos escogido	escogería
habéis escogido	escogeríamos
han escogido	escogeríais
	escogerían

Pluperfect indicative	Imperative
había escogido	
habías escogido	–
había escogido	escoge
habíamos escogido	escoja
habíais escogido	escojamos
habían escogido	escoged
	escojan

escribir *to write*

Gerund *escribiendo*
Past participle *escrito*

Present indicative	**Present subjunctive**
escribo	escriba
escribes	escribas
escribe	escriba
escribimos	escribamos
escribís	escribáis
escriben	escriban

Imperfect indicative	**Imperfect subjunctive**
escribía	escribiera
escribías	escribieras
escribía	escribiera
escribíamos	escribiéramos
escribíais	escribierais
escribían	escribieran

Preterite	**Future**
escribí	escribiré
escribiste	escribirás
escribió	escribirá
escribimos	escribiremos
escribisteis	escribiréis
escribieron	escribirán

Perfect indicative	**Conditional**
he escrito	escribiría
has escrito	escribirías
ha escrito	escribiría
hemos escrito	escribiríamos
habéis escrito	escribiríais
han escrito	escribirían

Pluperfect indicative	**Imperative**
había escrito	–
habías escrito	escribe
había escrito	escriba
habíamos escrito	escribamos
habíais escrito	escribid
habían escrito	escriban

escuchar *to listen*

Gerund *escuchando*
Past participle *escuchado*

Present indicative	**Present subjunctive**
escucho	escuche
escuchas	escuches
escucha	escuche
escuchamos	escuchemos
escucháis	escuchéis
escuchan	escuchen

Imperfect indicative	**Imperfect subjunctive**
escuchaba	escuchara
escuchabas	escucharas
escuchaba	escuchara
escuchábamos	escucháramos
escuchabais	escucharais
escuchaban	escucharan

Preterite	**Future**
escuché	escucharé
escuchaste	escucharás
escuchó	escuchará
escuchamos	escucharemos
escuchasteis	escucharéis
escucharon	escucharán

Perfect indicative	**Conditional**
he escuchado	escucharía
has escuchado	escucharías
ha escuchado	escucharía
hemos escuchado	escucharíamos
habéis escuchado	escucharíais
han escuchado	escucharían

Pluperfect indicative	**Imperative**
había escuchado	–
habías escuchado	escucha
había escuchado	escuche
habíamos escuchado	escuchemos
habíais escuchado	escuchad
habían escuchado	escuchen

esforzarse *to make an effort*

Gerund *esforzándose*
Past participle *esforzado*

Present indicative	Present subjunctive
me esfuerzo	me esfuerce
te esfuerzas	te esfuerces
se esfuerza	se esfuerce
nos esforzamos	nos esforcemos
os esforzáis	os esforcéis
se esfuerzan	se esfuercen

Imperfect indicative	Imperfect subjunctive
me esforzaba	me esforzara
te esforzabas	te esforzaras
se esforzaba	se esforzara
nos esforzábamos	nos esforzáramos
os esforzabais	os esforzarais
se esforzaban	se esforzaran

Preterite	Future
me esforcé	me esforzaré
te esforzaste	te esforzarás
se esforzó	se esforzará
nos esforzamos	nos esforzaremos
os esforzasteis	os esforzaréis
se esforzaron	se esforzarán

Perfect indicative	Conditional
me he esforzado	me esforzaría
te has esforzado	te esforzarías
se ha esforzado	se esforzaría
nos hemos esforzado	nos esforzaríamos
os habéis esforzado	os esforzaríais
se han esforzado	se esforzarían

Pluperfect indicative	Imperative
me había esforzado	–
te habías esforzado	esfuérzate
se había esforzado	esfuércese
nos habíamos esforzado	esforcémonos
os habíais esforzado	esforzaos
se habían esforzado	esfuércense

esperar *to hope; to wait*

Gerund *esperando*
Past participle *esperado*

Present indicative	Present subjunctive
espero	espere
esperas	esperes
espera	espere
esperamos	esperemos
esperáis	esperéis
esperan	esperen

Imperfect indicative	Imperfect subjunctive
esperaba	esperara
esperabas	esperaras
esperaba	esperara
esperábamos	esperáramos
esperabais	esperarais
esperaban	esperaran

Preterite	Future
esperé	esperaré
esperaste	esperarás
esperó	esperará
esperamos	esperaremos
esperasteis	esperaréis
esperaron	esperarán

Perfect indicative	Conditional
he esperado	esperaría
has esperado	esperarías
ha esperado	esperaría
hemos esperado	esperaríamos
habéis esperado	esperaríais
han esperado	esperarían

Pluperfect indicative	Imperative
había esperado	–
habías esperado	espera
había esperado	espere
habíamos esperado	esperemos
habíais esperado	esperad
habían esperado	esperen

estar *to be*

Gerund *estando*
Past participle *estado*

Present indicative	Present subjunctive
estoy	esté
estás	estés
está	esté
estamos	estemos
estáis	estéis
están	estén

Imperfect indicative	Imperfect subjunctive
estaba	estuviera
estabas	estuvieras
estaba	estuviera
estábamos	estuviéramos
estabais	estuvierais
estaban	estuvieran

Preterite	Future
estuve	estaré
estuviste	estarás
estuvo	estará
estuvimos	estaremos
estuvisteis	estaréis
estuvieron	estarán

Perfect indicative	Conditional
he estado	estaría
has estado	estarías
ha estado	estaría
hemos estado	estaríamos
habéis estado	estaríais
han estado	estarían

Pluperfect indicative	Imperative
había estado	–
habías estado	está
había estado	esté
habíamos estado	estemos
habíais estado	estad
habían estado	estén

estudiar *to study*

Gerund *estudiando*
Past participle *estudiado*

Present indicative	Present subjunctive
estudio	estudie
estudias	estudies
estudia	estudie
estudiamos	estudiemos
estudiáis	estudiéis
estudian	estudien

Imperfect indicative	Imperfect subjunctive
estudiaba	estudiara
estudiabas	estudiaras
estudiaba	estudiara
estudiábamos	estudiáramos
estudiabais	estudiarais
estudiaban	estudiaran

Preterite	Future
estudié	estudiaré
estudiaste	estudiarás
estudió	estudiará
estudiamos	estudiaremos
estudiasteis	estudiaréis
estudiaron	estudiarán

Perfect indicative	Conditional
he estudiado	estudiaría
has estudiado	estudiarías
ha estudiado	estudiaría
hemos estudiado	estudiaríamos
habéis estudiado	estudiaríais
han estudiado	estudiarían

Pluperfect indicative	Imperative
había estudiado	–
habías estudiado	estudia
había estudiado	estudie
habíamos estudiado	estudiemos
habíais estudiado	estudiad
habían estudiado	estudien

exigir *to demand*

Gerund *exigiendo*
Past participle *exigido*

Present indicative	Present subjunctive
exijo	exija
exiges	exijas
exige	exija
exigimos	exijamos
exigís	exijáis
exigen	exijan

Imperfect indicative	Imperfect subjunctive
exigía	exigiera
exigías	exigieras
exigía	exigiera
exigíamos	exigiéramos
exigíais	exigierais
exigían	exigieran

Preterite	Future
exigí	exigiré
exigiste	exigirás
exigió	exigirá
exigimos	exigiremos
exigisteis	exigiréis
exigieron	exigirán

Perfect indicative	Conditional
he exigido	exigiría
has exigido	exigirías
ha exigido	exigiría
hemos exigido	exigiríamos
habéis exigido	exigiríais
han exigido	exigirían

Pluperfect indicative	Imperative
había exigido	–
habías exigido	exige
había exigido	exija
habíamos exigido	exijamos
habíais exigido	exigid
habían exigido	exijan

explicar *to explain*

Gerund *explicando*
Past participle *explicado*

Present indicative	Present subjunctive
explico	explique
explicas	expliques
explica	explique
explicamos	expliquemos
explicáis	expliquéis
explican	expliquen

Imperfect indicative	Imperfect subjunctive
explicaba	explicara
explicabas	explicaras
explicaba	explicara
explicábamos	explicáramos
explicabais	explicarais
explicaban	explicaran

Preterite	Future
expliqué	explicaré
explicaste	explicarás
explicó	explicará
explicamos	explicaremos
explicasteis	explicaréis
explicaron	explicarán

Perfect indicative	Conditional
he explicado	explicaría
has explicado	explicarías
ha explicado	explicaría
hemos explicado	explicaríamos
habéis explicado	explicaríais
han explicado	explicarían

Pluperfect indicative	Imperative
había explicado	–
habías explicado	explica
había explicado	explique
habíamos explicado	expliquemos
habíais explicado	explicad
habían explicado	expliquen

fregar *to wash up*

Gerund *fregando*
Past participle *fregado*

Present indicative	Present subjunctive
friego	friegue
friegas	friegues
friega	friegue
fregamos	freguemos
fregáis	freguéis
friegan	frieguen

Imperfect indicative	Imperfect subjunctive
fregaba	fregara
fregabas	fregaras
fregaba	fregara
fregábamos	fregáramos
fregabais	fregarais
fregaban	fregaran

Preterite	Future
fregué	fregaré
fregaste	fregarás
fregó	fregará
fregamos	fregaremos
fregasteis	fregaréis
fregaron	fregarán

Perfect indicative	Conditional
he fregado	fregaría
has fregado	fregarías
ha fregado	fregaría
hemos fregado	fregaríamos
habéis fregado	fregaríais
han fregado	fregarían

Pluperfect indicative	Imperative
había fregado	–
habías fregado	friega
había fregado	friegue
habíamos fregado	freguemos
habíais fregado	fregad
habían fregado	frieguen

freír *to fry*

Gerund *friendo*
Past participle *frito*

Present indicative	Present subjunctive
frío	fría
fríes	frías
fríe	fría
freímos	friamos
freís	friáis
fríen	frían

Imperfect indicative	Imperfect subjunctive
freía	friera
freías	frieras
freía	friera
freíamos	friéramos
freíais	frierais
freían	frieran

Preterite	Future
freí	freiré
freíste	freirás
frió	freirá
freímos	freiremos
freísteis	freiréis
frieron	freirán

Perfect indicative	Conditional
he frito	freiría
has frito	freirías
ha frito	freiría
hemos frito	freiríamos
habéis frito	freiríais
han frito	freirían

Pluperfect indicative	Imperative
había frito	–
habías frito	fríe
había frito	fría
habíamos frito	friamos
habíais frito	freíd
habían frito	frían

gemir *to groan; to roar*

Gerund *gimiendo*
Past participle *gemido*

Present indicative	Present subjunctive
gimo	gima
gimes	gimas
gime	gima
gemimos	gimamos
gemís	gimáis
gimen	giman

Imperfect indicative	Imperfect subjunctive
gemía	gimiera
gemías	gimieras
gemía	gimiera
gemíamos	gimiéramos
gemíais	gimierais
gemían	gimieran

Preterite	Future
gemí	gemiré
gemiste	gemirás
gimió	gemirá
gemimos	gemiremos
gemisteis	gemiréis
gimieron	gemirán

Perfect indicative	Conditional
he gemido	gemiría
has gemido	gemirías
ha gemido	gemiría
hemos gemido	gemiríamos
habéis gemido	gemiríais
han gemido	gemirían

Pluperfect indicative	Imperative
había gemido	–
habías gemido	gime
había gemido	gima
habíamos gemido	gimamos
habíais gemido	gemid
habían gemido	giman

guiar *to guide*

Gerund *guiando*
Past participle *guiado*

Present indicative	Present subjunctive
guío	guíe
guías	guíes
guía	guíe
guiamos	guiemos
guiáis	guiéis
guían	guíen

Imperfect indicative	Imperfect subjunctive
guiaba	guiara
guiabas	guiaras
guiaba	guiara
guiábamos	guiáramos
guiabais	guiarais
guiaban	guiaran

Preterite	Future
guié	guiaré
guiaste	guiarás
guió	guiará
guiamos	guiaremos
guiasteis	guiaréis
guiaron	guiarán

Perfect indicative	Conditional
he guiado	guiaría
has guiado	guiarías
ha guiado	guiaría
hemos guiado	guiaríamos
habéis guiado	guiaríais
han guiado	guiarían

Pluperfect indicative	Imperative
había guiado	–
habías guiado	guía
había guiado	guíe
habíamos guiado	guiemos
habíais guiado	guiad
habían guiado	guíen

gustar *to please*

Gerund *gustando*
Past participle *gustado*

Present indicative	Present subjunctive
gusto	guste
gustas	gustes
gusta	guste
gustamos	gustemos
gustáis	gustéis
gustan	gusten

Imperfect indicative	Imperfect subjunctive
gustaba	gustara
gustabas	gustaras
gustaba	gustara
gustábamos	gustáramos
gustabais	gustarais
gustaban	gustaran

Preterite	Future
gusté	gustaré
gustaste	gustarás
gustó	gustará
gustamos	gustaremos
gustasteis	gustaréis
gustaron	gustarán

Perfect indicative	Conditional
he gustado	gustaría
has gustado	gustarías
ha gustado	gustaría
hemos gustado	gustaríamos
habéis gustado	gustaríais
han gustado	gustarían

Pluperfect indicative	Imperative
había gustado	–
habías gustado	gusta
había gustado	guste
habíamos gustado	gustemos
habíais gustado	gustad
habían gustado	gusten

haber *to have*

Gerund *habiendo*
Past participle *habido*

Present indicative	Present subjunctive
he	haya
has	hayas
ha	haya
hemos	hayamos
habéis	hayáis
han	hayan

Imperfect indicative	Imperfect subjunctive
había	hubiera
habías	hubieras
había	hubiera
habíamos	hubiéramos
habíais	hubierais
habían	hubieran

Preterite	Future
hube	habré
hubiste	habrás
hubo	habrá
hubimos	habremos
hubisteis	habréis
hubieron	habrán

Perfect indicative	Conditional
he habido	habría
has habido	habrías
ha habido	habría
hemos habido	habríamos
habéis habido	habríais
han habido	habrían

Pluperfect indicative	Imperative
había habido	–
habías habido	he
había habido	haya
habíamos habido	hayamos
habíais habido	habed
habían habido	hayan

hablar *to talk, speak*

Gerund *hablando*
Past participle *hablado*

Present indicative	Present subjunctive
hablo	hable
hablas	hables
habla	hable
hablamos	hablemos
habláis	habléis
hablan	hablen

Imperfect indicative	Imperfect subjunctive
hablaba	hablara
hablabas	hablaras
hablaba	hablara
hablábamos	habláramos
hablabais	hablarais
hablaban	hablaran

Preterite	Future
hablé	hablaré
hablaste	hablarás
habló	hablará
hablamos	hablaremos
hablasteis	hablaréis
hablaron	hablarán

Perfect indicative	Conditional
he hablado	hablaría
has hablado	hablarías
ha hablado	hablaría
hemos hablado	hablaríamos
habéis hablado	hablaríais
han hablado	hablarían

Pluperfect indicative	Imperative
había hablado	–
habías hablado	habla
había hablado	hable
habíamos hablado	hablemos
habíais hablado	hablad
habían hablado	hablen

hacer *to do, to make*

Gerund *haciendo*
Past participle *hecho*

Present indicative	Present subjunctive
hago	haga
haces	hagas
hace	haga
hacemos	hagamos
hacéis	hagáis
hacen	hagan

Imperfect indicative	Imperfect subjunctive
hacía	hiciera
hacías	hicieras
hacía	hiciera
hacíamos	hiciéramos
hacíais	hicierais
hacían	hicieran

Preterite	Future
hice	haré
hiciste	harás
hizo	hará
hicimos	haremos
hicisteis	haréis
hicieron	harán

Perfect indicative	Conditional
he hecho	haría
has hecho	harías
ha hecho	haría
hemos hecho	haríamos
habéis hecho	haríais
han hecho	harían

Pluperfect indicative	Imperative
había hecho	–
habías hecho	haz
había hecho	haga
habíamos hecho	hagamos
habíais hecho	haced
habían hecho	hagan

herir *to hurt*

Gerund *hiriendo*
Past participle *herido*

Present indicative	Present subjunctive
hiero	hiera
hieres	hieras
hiere	hiera
herimos	hiramos
herís	hiráis
hieren	hieran

Imperfect indicative	Imperfect subjunctive
hería	hiriera
herías	hirieras
hería	hiriera
heríamos	hiriéramos
heríais	hiricrais
herían	hirieran

Preterite	Future
herí	heriré
heriste	herirás
hirió	herirá
herimos	heriremos
heristeis	heriréis
hirieron	herirán

Perfect indicative	Conditional
he herido	heriría
has herido	herirías
ha herido	heriría
hemos herido	heriríamos
habéis herido	heriríais
han herido	herirían

Pluperfect indicative	Imperative
había herido	–
habías herido	hiere
había herido	hiera
habíamos herido	hiramos
habíais herido	herid
habían herido	hieran

huir *to run away*

Gerund *huyendo*
Past participle *huido*

Present indicative	Present subjunctive
huyo	huya
huyes	huyas
huye	huya
huimos	huyamos
huís	huyáis
huyen	huyan

Imperfect indicative	Imperfect subjunctive
huía	huyera
huías	huyeras
huía	huyera
huíamos	huyéramos
huíais	huyerais
huían	huyeran

Preterite	Future
huí	huiré
huiste	huirás
huyó	huirá
huimos	huiremos
huisteis	huiréis
huyeron	huirán

Perfect indicative	Conditional
he huido	huiría
has huido	huirías
ha huido	huiría
hemos huido	huiríamos
habéis huido	huiríais
han huido	huirían

Pluperfect indicative	Imperative
había huido	–
habías huido	huye
había huido	huya
habíamos huido	huyamos
habíais huido	huid
habían huido	huyan

intentar *to try*

Gerund *intentando*
Past participle *intentado*

Present indicative	Present subjunctive
intento	intente
intentas	intentes
intenta	intente
intentamos	intentemos
intentáis	intentéis
intentan	intenten

Imperfect indicative	Imperfect subjunctive
intentaba	intentara
intentabas	intentaras
intentaba	intentara
intentábamos	intentáramos
intentabais	intentarais
intentaban	intentaran

Preterite	Future
intenté	intentaré
intentaste	intentarás
intentó	intentará
intentamos	intentaremos
intentasteis	intentaréis
intentaron	intentarán

Perfect indicative	Conditional
he intentado	intentaría
has intentado	intentarías
ha intentado	intentaría
hemos intentado	intentaríamos
habéis intentado	intentaríais
han intentado	intentarían

Pluperfect indicative	Imperative
había intentado	–
habías intentado	intenta
había intentado	intente
habíamos intentado	intentemos
habíais intentado	intentad
habían intentado	intenten

introducir *to introduce*

Gerund *introduciendo*
Past participle *introducido*

Present indicative	Present subjunctive
introduzco	introduzca
introduces	introduzcas
introduce	introduzca
introducimos	introduzcamos
introducís	introduzcáis
introducen	introduzcan

Imperfect indicative	Imperfect subjunctive
introducía	introdujera
introducías	introdujeras
introducía	introdujera
introducíamos	introdujéramos
introducíais	introdujerais
introducían	introdujeran

Preterite	Future
introduje	introduciré
introdujiste	introducirás
introdujo	introducirá
introdujimos	introduciremos
introdujisteis	introduciréis
introdujeron	introducirán

Perfect indicative	Conditional
he introducido	introduciría
has introducido	introducirías
ha introducido	introduciría
hemos introducido	introduciríamos
habéis introducido	introduciríais
han introducido	introducirían

Pluperfect indicative	Imperative
había introducido	–
habías introducido	introduce
había introducido	introduzca
habíamos introducido	introduzcamos
habíais introducido	introducid
habían introducido	introduzcan

ir *to go*

Gerund *yendo*
Past participle *ido*

Present indicative	Present subjunctive
voy	vaya
vas	vayas
va	vaya
vamos	vayamos
vais	vayáis
van	vayan

Imperfect indicative	Imperfect subjunctive
iba	fuera
ibas	fueras
iba	fuera
íbamos	fuéramos
ibais	fuerais
iban	fueran

Preterite	Future
fui	iré
fuiste	irás
fue	irá
fuimos	iremos
fuisteis	iréis
fueron	irán

Perfect indicative	Conditional
he ido	iría
has ido	irías
ha ido	iría
hemos ido	iríamos
habéis ido	iríais
han ido	irían

Pluperfect indicative	Imperative
había ido	–
habías ido	ve
había ido	vaya
habíamos ido	vayamos
habíais ido	id
habían ido	vayan

jugar *to play*

Gerund *jugando*
Past participle *jugado*

Present indicative	Present subjunctive
juego	juegue
juegas	juegues
juega	juegue
jugamos	juguemos
jugáis	juguéis
juegan	jueguen

Imperfect indicative	Imperfect subjunctive
jugaba	jugara
jugabas	jugaras
jugaba	jugara
jugábamos	jugáramos
jugabais	jugarais
jugaban	jugaran

Preterite	Future
jugué	jugaré
jugaste	jugarás
jugó	jugará
jugamos	jugaremos
jugasteis	jugaréis
jugaron	jugarán

Perfect indicative	Conditional
he jugado	jugaría
has jugado	jugarías
ha jugado	jugaría
hemos jugado	jugaríamos
habéis jugado	jugaríais
han jugado	jugarían

Pluperfect indicative	Imperative
había jugado	–
habías jugado	juega
había jugado	juegue
habíamos jugado	juguemos
habíais jugado	jugad
habían jugado	jueguen

juzgar *to judge*

Gerund *juzgando*
Past participle *juzgado*

Present indicative	Present subjunctive
juzgo	juzgue
juzgas	juzgues
juzga	juzgue
juzgamos	juzguemos
juzgáis	juzguéis
juzgan	juzguen

Imperfect indicative	Imperfect subjunctive
juzgaba	juzgara
juzgabas	juzgaras
juzgaba	juzgara
juzgábamos	juzgáramos
juzgabais	juzgarais
juzgaban	juzgaran

Preterite	Future
juzgué	juzgaré
juzgaste	juzgarás
juzgó	juzgará
juzgamos	juzgaremos
juzgasteis	juzgaréis
juzgaron	juzgarán

Perfect indicative	Conditional
he juzgado	juzgaría
has juzgado	juzgarías
ha juzgado	juzgaría
hemos juzgado	juzgaríamos
habéis juzgado	juzgaríais
han juzgado	juzgarían

Pluperfect indicative	Imperative
había juzgado	–
habías juzgado	juzga
había juzgado	juzgue
habíamos juzgado	juzguemos
habíais juzgado	juzgad
habían juzgado	juzguen

lavar *to wash*

Gerund *lavando*
Past participle *lavado*

Present indicative	Present subjunctive
lavo	lave
lavas	laves
lava	lave
lavamos	lavemos
laváis	lavéis
lavan	laven

Imperfect indicative	Imperfect subjunctive
lavaba	lavara
lavabas	lavaras
lavaba	lavara
lavábamos	laváramos
lavabais	lavarais
lavaban	lavaran

Preterite	Future
lavé	lavaré
lavaste	lavarás
lavó	lavará
lavamos	lavaremos
lavasteis	lavaréis
lavaron	lavarán

Perfect indicative	Conditional
he lavado	lavaría
has lavado	lavarías
ha lavado	lavaría
hemos lavado	lavaríamos
habéis lavado	lavaríais
han lavado	lavarían

Pluperfect indicative	Imperative
había lavado	–
habías lavado	lava
había lavado	lave
habíamos lavado	lavemos
habíais lavado	lavad
habían lavado	laven

leer *to read*

Gerund *leyendo*
Past participle *leído*

Present indicative	Present subjunctive
leo	lea
lees	leas
lee	lea
leemos	leamos
leéis	leáis
leen	lean

Imperfect indicative	Imperfect subjunctive
leía	leyera
leías	leyeras
leía	leyera
leíamos	leyéramos
leíais	leyerais
leían	leyeran

Preterite	Future
leí	leeré
leíste	leerás
leyó	leerá
leímos	leeremos
leísteis	leeréis
leyeron	leerán

Perfect indicative	Conditional
he leído	leería
has leído	leerías
ha leído	leería
hemos leído	leeríamos
habéis leído	leeríais
han leído	leerían

Pluperfect indicative	Imperative
había leído	–
habías leído	lee
había leído	lea
habíamos leído	leamos
habíais leído	leed
habían leído	lean

levantarse *to get up*

Gerund *levantándose*
Past participle *levantado*

Present indicative	Present subjunctive
me levanto	me levante
te levantas	te levantes
se levanta	se levante
nos levantamos	nos levantemos
os levantáis	os levantéis
se levantan	se levanten

Imperfect indicative	Imperfect subjunctive
me levantaba	me levantara
te levantabas	te levantaras
se levantaba	se levantara
nos levantábamos	nos levantáramos
os levantabais	os levantarais
se levantaban	se levantaran

Preterite	Future
me levanté	me levantaré
te levantaste	te levantarás
se levantó	se levantará
nos levantamos	nos levantaremos
os levantasteis	os levantaréis
se levantaron	se levantarán

Perfect indicative	Conditional
me he levantado	me levantaría
te has levantado	te levantarías
se ha levantado	se levantaría
nos hemos levantado	nos levantaríamos
os habéis levantado	os levantaríais
se han levantado	se levantarían

Pluperfect indicative	Imperative
me había levantado	–
te habías levantado	levántate
se había levantado	levántese
nos habíamos levantado	levantémonos
os habíais levantado	levantaos
se habían levantado	levántense

llamar *to call*

Gerund *llamando*
Past participle *llamado*

Present indicative	**Present subjunctive**
llamo	llame
llamas	llames
llama	llame
llamamos	llamemos
llamáis	llaméis
llaman	llamen

Imperfect indicative	**Imperfect subjunctive**
llamaba	llamara
llamabas	llamaras
llamaba	llamara
llamábamos	llamáramos
llamabais	llamarais
llamaban	llamaran

Preterite	**Future**
llamé	llamaré
llamaste	llamarás
llamó	llamará
llamamos	llamaremos
llamasteis	llamaréis
llamaron	llamarán

Perfect indicative	**Conditional**
he llamado	llamaría
has llamado	llamarías
ha llamado	llamaría
hemos llamado	llamaríamos
habéis llamado	llamaríais
han llamado	llamarían

Pluperfect indicative	**Imperative**
había llamado	–
habías llamado	llama
había llamado	llame
habíamos llamado	llamemos
habíais llamado	llamad
habían llamado	llamen

llegar *to arrive*

Gerund *llegando*
Past participle *llegado*

Present indicative	**Present subjunctive**
llego	llegue
llegas	llegues
llega	llegue
llegamos	lleguemos
llegáis	lleguéis
llegan	lleguen

Imperfect indicative	**Imperfect subjunctive**
llegaba	llegara
llegabas	llegaras
llegaba	llegara
llegábamos	llegáramos
llegabais	llegarais
llegaban	llegaran

Preterite	**Future**
llegué	llegaré
llegaste	llegarás
llegó	llegará
llegamos	llegaremos
llegasteis	llegaréis
llegaron	llegarán

Perfect indicative	**Conditional**
he llegado	llegaría
has llegado	llegarías
ha llegado	llegaría
hemos llegado	llegaríamos
habéis llegado	llegaríais
han llegado	llegarían

Pluperfect indicative	**Imperative**
había llegado	–
habías llegado	llega
había llegado	llegue
habíamos llegado	lleguemos
habíais llegado	llegad
habían llegado	lleguen

llenar *to fill*

Gerund *llenando*
Past participle *llenado*

Present indicative	Present subjunctive
lleno	llene
llenas	llenes
llena	llene
llenamos	llenemos
llenáis	llenéis
llenan	llenen

Imperfect indicative	Imperfect subjunctive
llenaba	llenara
llenabas	llenaras
llenaba	llenara
llenábamos	llenáramos
llenabais	llenarais
llenaban	llenaran

Preterite	Future
llené	llenaré
llenaste	llenarás
llenó	llenará
llenamos	llenaremos
llenasteis	llenaréis
llenaron	llenarán

Perfect indicative	Conditional
he llenado	llenaría
has llenado	llenarías
ha llenado	llenaría
hemos llenado	llenaríamos
habéis llenado	llenaríais
han llenado	llenarían

Pluperfect indicative	Imperative
había llenado	–
habías llenado	llena
había llenado	llene
habíamos llenado	llenemos
habíais llenado	llenad
habían llenado	llenen

matar *to kill*

Gerund *matando*
Past participle *matado*

Present indicative	Present subjunctive
mato	mate
matas	mates
mata	mate
matamos	matemos
matáis	matéis
matan	maten

Imperfect indicative	Imperfect subjunctive
mataba	matara
matabas	mataras
mataba	matara
matábamos	matáramos
matabais	matarais
mataban	mataran

Preterite	Future
maté	mataré
mataste	matarás
mató	matará
matamos	mataremos
matasteis	mataréis
mataron	matarán

Perfect indicative	Conditional
he matado	mataría
has matado	matarías
ha matado	mataría
hemos matado	mataríamos
habéis matado	mataríais
han matado	matarían

Pluperfect indicative	Imperative
había matado	–
habías matado	mata
había matado	mate
habíamos matado	matemos
habíais matado	matad
habían matado	maten

mentir *to (tell a) lie*

Gerund *mintiendo*
Past participle *mentido*

Present indicative	**Present subjunctive**
miento	mienta
mientes	mientas
miente	mienta
mentimos	mintamos
mentís	mintáis
mienten	mientan

Imperfect indicative	**Imperfect subjunctive**
mentía	mintiera
mentías	mintieras
mentía	mintiera
mentíamos	mintiéramos
mentíais	mintierais
mentían	mintieran

Preterite	**Future**
mentí	mentiré
mentiste	mentirás
mintió	mentirá
mentimos	mentiremos
mentisteis	mentiréis
mintieron	mentirán

Perfect indicative	**Conditional**
he mentido	mentiría
has mentido	mentirías
ha mentido	mentiría
hemos mentido	mentiríamos
habéis mentido	mentiríais
han mentido	mentirían

Pluperfect indicative	**Imperative**
había mentido	–
habías mentido	miente
había mentido	mienta
habíamos mentido	mintamos
habíais mentido	mentid
habían mentido	mientan

merecer *to deserve*

Gerund *mereciendo*
Past participle *merecido*

Present indicative	**Present subjunctive**
merezco	merezca
mereces	merezcas
merece	merezca
merecemos	merezcamos
merecéis	merezcáis
merecen	merezcan

Imperfect indicative	**Imperfect subjunctive**
merecía	mereciera
merecías	merecieras
merecía	mereciera
merecíamos	mereciéramos
merecíais	merecierais
merecían	merecieran

Preterite	**Future**
merecí	mereceré
mereciste	merecerás
mereció	merecerá
merecimos	mereceremos
merecisteis	mereceréis
merecieron	merecerán

Perfect indicative	**Conditional**
he merecido	merecería
has merecido	merecerías
ha merecido	merecería
hemos merecido	mereceríamos
habéis merecido	mereceríais
han merecido	merecerían

Pluperfect indicative	**Imperative**
había merecido	–
habías merecido	merece
había merecido	merezca
habíamos merecido	merezcamos
habíais merecido	mereced
habían merecido	merezcan

morder *to bite*

Gerund *mordiendo*
Past participle *mordido*

Present indicative	**Present subjunctive**
muerdo	muerda
muerdes	muerdas
muerde	muerda
mordemos	mordamos
mordéis	mordáis
muerden	muerdan

Imperfect indicative	**Imperfect subjunctive**
mordía	mordiera
mordías	mordieras
mordía	mordiera
mordíamos	mordiéramos
mordíais	mordierais
mordían	mordieran

Preterite	**Future**
mordí	morderé
mordiste	morderás
mordió	morderá
mordimos	morderemos
mordisteis	morderéis
mordieron	morderán

Perfect indicative	**Conditional**
he mordido	mordería
has mordido	morderías
ha mordido	mordería
hemos mordido	morderíamos
habéis mordido	morderíais
han mordido	morderían

Pluperfect indicative	**Imperative**
había mordido	–
habías mordido	muerde
había mordido	muerda
habíamos mordido	mordamos
habíais mordido	morded
habían mordido	muerdan

morir *to die*

Gerund *muriendo*
Past participle *muerto*

Present indicative	**Present subjunctive**
muero	muera
mueres	mueras
muere	muera
morimos	muramos
morís	muráis
mueren	mueran

Imperfect indicative	**Imperfect subjunctive**
moría	muriera
morías	murieras
moría	muriera
moríamos	muriéramos
moríais	murierais
morían	murieran

Preterite	**Future**
morí	moriré
moriste	morirás
murió	morirá
morimos	moriremos
moristeis	moriréis
murieron	morirán

Perfect indicative	**Conditional**
he muerto	moriría
has muerto	morirías
ha muerto	moriría
hemos muerto	moriríamos
habéis muerto	moriríais
han muerto	morirían

Pluperfect indicative	**Imperative**
había muerto	–
habías muerto	muere
había muerto	muera
habíamos muerto	muramos
habíais muerto	morid
habían muerto	mueran

mover *to move*

Gerund *moviendo*
Past participle *movido*

Present indicative	Present subjunctive
muevo	mueva
mueves	muevas
mueve	mueva
movemos	movamos
movéis	mováis
mueven	muevan

Imperfect indicative	Imperfect subjunctive
movía	moviera
movías	movieras
movía	moviera
movíamos	moviéramos
movíais	movierais
movían	movieran

Preterite	Future
moví	moveré
moviste	moverás
movió	moverá
movimos	moveremos
movisteis	moveréis
movieron	moverán

Perfect indicative	Conditional
he movido	movería
has movido	moverías
ha movido	movería
hemos movido	moveríamos
habéis movido	moveríais
han movido	moverían

Pluperfect indicative	Imperative
había movido	–
habías movido	mueve
había movido	mueva
habíamos movido	movamos
habíais movido	moved
habían movido	muevan

nacer *to be born*

Gerund *naciendo*
Past participle *nacido*

Present indicative	Present subjunctive
nazco	nazca
naces	nazcas
nace	nazca
nacemos	nazcamos
nacéis	nazcáis
nacen	nazcan

Imperfect indicative	Imperfect subjunctive
nacía	naciera
nacías	nacieras
nacía	naciera
nacíamos	naciéramos
nacíais	nacierais
nacían	nacieran

Preterite	Future
nací	naceré
naciste	nacerás
nació	nacerá
nacimos	naceremos
nacisteis	naceréis
nacieron	nacerán

Perfect indicative	Conditional
he nacido	nacería
has nacido	nacerías
ha nacido	nacería
hemos nacido	naceríamos
habéis nacido	naceríais
han nacido	nacerían

Pluperfect indicative	Imperative
había nacido	-
habías nacido	nace
había nacido	nazca
habíamos nacido	nazcamos
habíais nacido	naced
habían nacido	nazcan

nadar *to swim*

Gerund *nadando*
Past participle *nadado*

Present indicative	Present subjunctive
nado	nade
nadas	nades
nada	nade
nadamos	nademos
nadáis	nadéis
nadan	naden

Imperfect indicative	Imperfect subjunctive
nadaba	nadara
nadabas	nadaras
nadaba	nadara
nadábamos	nadáramos
nadabais	nadarais
nadaban	nadaran

Preterite	Future
nadé	nadaré
nadaste	nadarás
nadó	nadará
nadamos	nadaremos
nadasteis	nadaréis
nadaron	nadarán

Perfect indicative	Conditional
he nadado	nadaría
has nadado	nadarías
ha nadado	nadaría
hemos nadado	nadaríamos
habéis nadado	nadaríais
han nadado	nadarían

Pluperfect indicative	Imperative
había nadado	–
habías nadado	nada
había nadado	nade
habíamos nadado	nademos
habíais nadado	nadad
habían nadado	naden

necesitar *to need*

Gerund *necesitando*
Past participle *necesitado*

Present indicative	Present subjunctive
necesito	necesite
necesitas	necesites
necesita	necesite
necesitamos	necesitemos
necesitáis	necesitéis
necesitan	necesiten

Imperfect indicative	Imperfect subjunctive
necesitaba	necesitara
necesitabas	necesitaras
necesitaba	necesitara
necesitábamos	necesitáramos
necesitabais	necesitarais
necesitaban	necesitaran

Preterite	Future
necesité	necesitaré
necesitaste	necesitarás
necesitó	necesitará
necesitamos	necesitaremos
necesitasteis	necesitaréis
necesitaron	necesitarán

Perfect indicative	Conditional
he necesitado	necesitaría
has necesitado	necesitarías
ha necesitado	necesitaría
hemos necesitado	necesitaríamos
habéis necesitado	necesitaríais
han necesitado	necesitarían

Pluperfect indicative	Imperative
había necesitado	–
habías necesitado	necesita
había necesitado	necesite
habíamos necesitado	necesitemos
habíais necesitado	necesitad
habían necesitado	necesiten

negar *to deny*

Gerund *negando*
Past participle *negado*

Present indicative	Present subjunctive
niego	niegue
niegas	niegues
niega	niegue
negamos	neguemos
negáis	neguéis
niegan	nieguen

Imperfect indicative	Imperfect subjunctive
negaba	negara
negabas	negaras
negaba	negara
negábamos	negáramos
negabais	negarais
negaban	negaran

Preterite	Future
negué	negaré
negaste	negarás
negó	negará
negamos	negaremos
negasteis	negaréis
negaron	negarán

Perfect indicative	Conditional
he negado	negaría
has negado	negarías
ha negado	negaría
hemos negado	negaríamos
habéis negado	negaríais
han negado	negarían

Pluperfect indicative	Imperative
había negado	–
habías negado	niega
había negado	niegue
habíamos negado	neguemos
habíais negado	negad
habían negado	nieguen

obedecer *to obey*

Gerund *obedeciendo*
Past participle *obedecido*

Present indicative	Present subjunctive
obedezco	obedezca
obedeces	obedezcas
obedece	obedezca
obedecemos	obedezcamos
obedecéis	obedezcáis
obedecen	obedezcan

Imperfect indicative	Imperfect subjunctive
obedecía	obedeciera
obedecías	obedecieras
obedecía	obedeciera
obedecíamos	obedeciéramos
obedecíais	obedecierais
obedecían	obedecieran

Preterite	Future
obedecí	obedeceré
obedeciste	obedecerás
obedeció	obedecerá
obedecimos	obedeceremos
obedecisteis	obedeceréis
obedecieron	obedecerán

Perfect indicative	Conditional
he obedecido	obedecería
has obedecido	obedecerías
ha obedecido	obedecería
hemos obedecido	obedeceríamos
habéis obedecido	obedeceríais
han obedecido	obedecerían

Pluperfect indicative	Imperative
había obedecido	–
habías obedecido	obedece
había obedecido	obedezca
habíamos obedecido	obedezcamos
habíais obedecido	obedeced
habían obedecido	obedezcan

obligar *to oblige, to compel*

Gerund *obligando*
Past participle *obligado*

Present indicative	**Present subjunctive**
obligo	obligue
obligas	obligues
obliga	obligue
obligamos	obliguemos
obligáis	obliguéis
obligan	obliguen

Imperfect indicative	**Imperfect subjunctive**
obligaba	obligara
obligabas	obligaras
obligaba	obligara
obligábamos	obligáramos
obligabais	obligarais
obligaban	obligaran

Preterite	**Future**
obligué	obligaré
obligaste	obligarás
obligó	obligará
obligamos	obligaremos
obligasteis	obligaréis
obligaron	obligarán

Perfect indicative	**Conditional**
he obligado	obligaría
has obligado	obligarías
ha obligado	obligaría
hemos obligado	obligaríamos
habéis obligado	obligaríais
han obligado	obligarían

Pluperfect indicative	**Imperative**
había obligado	–
habías obligado	obliga
había obligado	obligue
habíamos obligado	obliguemos
habíais obligado	obligad
habían obligado	obliguen

ofrecer *to offer*

Gerund *ofreciendo*
Past participle *ofrecido*

Present indicative	**Present subjunctive**
ofrezco	ofrezca
ofreces	ofrezcas
ofrece	ofrezca
ofrecemos	ofrezcamos
ofrecéis	ofrezcáis
ofrecen	ofrezcan

Imperfect indicative	**Imperfect subjunctive**
ofrecía	ofreciera
ofrecías	ofrecieras
ofrecía	ofreciera
ofrecíamos	ofreciéramos
ofrecíais	ofrecierais
ofrecían	ofrecieran

Preterite	**Future**
ofrecí	ofreceré
ofreciste	ofrecerás
ofreció	ofrecerá
ofrecimos	ofreceremos
ofrecisteis	ofreceréis
ofrecieron	ofrecerán

Perfect indicative	**Conditional**
he ofrecido	ofrecería
has ofrecido	ofrecerías
ha ofrecido	ofrecería
hemos ofrecido	ofreceríamos
habéis ofrecido	ofreceríais
han ofrecido	ofrecerían

Pluperfect indicative	**Imperative**
había ofrecido	Present indicative–
habías ofrecido	ofrece
había ofrecido	ofrezca
habíamos ofrecido	ofrezcamos
habíais ofrecido	ofreced
habían ofrecido	ofrezcan

oír *to hear*

Gerund *oyendo*
Past participle *oído*

Present indicative	Present subjunctive
oigo	oiga
oyes	oigas
oye	oiga
oímos	oigamos
oís	oigáis
oyen	oigan

Imperfect indicative	Imperfect subjunctive
oía	oyera
oías	oyeras
oía	oyera
oíamos	oyéramos
oíais	oyerais
oían	oyeran

Preterite	Future
oí	oiré
oíste	oirás
oyó	oirá
oímos	oiremos
oísteis	oiréis
oyeron	oirán

Perfect indicative	Conditional
he oído	oiría
has oído	oirías
ha oído	oiría
hemos oído	oiríamos
habéis oído	oiríais
han oído	oirían

Pluperfect indicative	Imperative
había oído	–
habías oído	oye
había oído	oiga
habíamos oído	oigamos
habíais oído	oíd
habían oído	oigan

oler *to smell*

Gerund *oliendo*
Past participle *olido*

Present indicative	Present subjunctive
huelo	huela
hueles	huelas
huele	huela
olemos	olamos
oléis	oláis
huelen	huelan

Imperfect indicative	Imperfect subjunctive
olía	oliera
olías	olieras
olía	oliera
olíamos	oliéramos
olíais	olierais
olían	olieran

Preterite	Future
olí	oleré
oliste	olerás
olió	olerá
olimos	oleremos
olisteis	oleréis
olieron	olerán

Perfect indicative	Conditional
he olido	olería
has olido	olerías
ha olido	olería
hemos olido	oleríamos
habéis olido	oleríais
han olido	olerían

Pluperfect indicative	Imperative
había olido	–
habías olido	huele
había olido	huela
habíamos olido	olamos
habíais olido	oled
habían olido	huelan

pagar *to pay*

Gerund *pagando*
Past participle *pagado*

Present indicative	Present subjunctive
pago	pague
pagas	pagues
paga	pague
pagamos	paguemos
pagáis	paguéis
pagan	paguen

Imperfect indicative	Imperfect subjunctive
pagaba	pagara
pagabas	pagaras
pagaba	pagara
pagábamos	pagáramos
pagabais	pagarais
pagaban	pagaran

Preterite	Future
pagué	pagaré
pagaste	pagarás
pagó	pagará
pagamos	pagaremos
pagasteis	pagaréis
pagaron	pagarán

Perfect indicative	Conditional
he pagado	pagaría
has pagado	pagarías
ha pagado	pagaría
hemos pagado	pagaríamos
habéis pagado	pagaríais
han pagado	pagarían

Pluperfect indicative	Imperative
había pagado	–
habías pagado	paga
había pagado	pague
habíamos pagado	paguemos
habíais pagado	pagad
habían pagado	paguen

parecer *to seem*

Gerund *pareciendo*
Past participle *parecido*

Present indicative	Present subjunctive
parezco	parezca
pareces	parezcas
parece	parezca
parecemos	parezcamos
parecéis	parezcáis
parecen	parezcan

Imperfect indicative	Imperfect subjunctive
parecía	pareciera
parecías	parecieras
parecía	pareciera
parecíamos	pareciéramos
parecíais	parecierais
parecían	parecieran

Preterite	Future
parecí	pareceré
pareciste	parecerás
pareció	parecerá
parecimos	pareceremos
parecisteis	pareceréis
parecieron	parecerán

Perfect indicative	Conditional
he parecido	parecería
has parecido	parecerías
ha parecido	parecería
hemos parecido	pareceríamos
habéis parecido	pareceríais
han parecido	parecerían

Pluperfect indicative	Imperative
había parecido	–
habías parecido	parece
había parecido	parezca
habíamos parecido	parezcamos
habíais parecido	pareced
habían parecido	parezcan

pasear *to walk*

Gerund *paseando*
Past participle *paseado*

Present indicative	Present subjunctive
paseo	pasee
paseas	pasees
pasea	pasee
paseamos	paseemos
paseáis	paseéis
pasean	paseen

Imperfect indicative	Imperfect subjunctive
paseaba	paseara
paseabas	pasearas
paseaba	paseara
paseábamos	paseáramos
paseabais	pasearais
paseaban	pasearan

Preterite	Future
paseé	pasearé
paseaste	pasearás
paseó	paseará
paseamos	pasearemos
paseasteis	pasearéis
pasearon	pasearán

Perfect indicative	Conditional
he paseado	pasearía
has paseado	pasearías
ha paseado	pasearía
hemos paseado	pasearíamos
habéis paseado	pasearíais
han paseado	pasearían

Pluperfect indicative	Imperative
había paseado	–
habías paseado	pasea
había paseado	pasee
habíamos paseado	paseemos
habíais paseado	pasead
habían paseado	paseen

pedir *to ask for*

Gerund *pidiendo*
Past participle *pedido*

Present indicative	Present subjunctive
pido	pida
pides	pidas
pide	pida
pedimos	pidamos
pedís	pidáis
piden	pidan

Imperfect indicative	Imperfect subjunctive
pedía	pidiera
pedías	pidieras
pedía	pidiera
pedíamos	pidiéramos
pedíais	pidierais
pedían	pidieran

Preterite	Future
pedí	pediré
pediste	pedirás
pidió	pedirá
pedimos	pediremos
pedisteis	pediréis
pidieron	pedirán

Perfect indicative	Conditional
he pedido	pediría
has pedido	pedirías
ha pedido	pediría
hemos pedido	pediríamos
habéis pedido	pediríais
han pedido	pedirían

Pluperfect indicative	Imperative
había pedido	–
habías pedido	pide
había pedido	pida
habíamos pedido	pidamos
habíais pedido	pedid
habían pedido	pidan

pensar *to think*

Gerund *pensando*
Past participle *pensado*

Present indicative	**Present subjunctive**
pienso	piense
piensas	pienses
piensa	piense
pensamos	pensemos
pensáis	penséis
piensan	piensen

Imperfect indicative	**Imperfect subjunctive**
pensaba	pensara
pensabas	pensaras
pensaba	pensara
pensábamos	pensáramos
pensabais	pensarais
pensaban	pensaran

Preterite	**Future**
pensé	pensaré
pensaste	pensarás
pensó	pensará
pensamos	pensaremos
pensasteis	pensaréis
pensaron	pensarán

Perfect indicative	**Conditional**
he pensado	pensaría
has pensado	pensarías
ha pensado	pensaría
hemos pensado	pensaríamos
habéis pensado	pensaríais
han pensado	pensarían

Pluperfect indicative	**Imperative**
había pensado	–
habías pensado	piensa
había pensado	piense
habíamos pensado	pensemos
habíais pensado	pensad
habían pensado	piensen

perder *to lose*

Gerund *perdiendo*
Past participle *perdido*

Present indicative	**Present subjunctive**
pierdo	pierda
pierdes	pierdas
pierde	pierda
perdemos	perdamos
perdéis	perdáis
pierden	pierdan

Imperfect indicative	**Imperfect subjunctive**
perdía	perdiera
perdías	perdieras
perdía	perdiera
perdíamos	perdiéramos
perdíais	perdierais
perdían	perdieran

Preterite	**Future**
perdí	perderé
perdiste	perderás
perdió	perderá
perdimos	perderemos
perdisteis	perderéis
perdieron	perderán

Perfect indicative	**Conditional**
he perdido	perdería
has perdido	perderías
ha perdido	perdería
hemos perdido	perderíamos
habéis perdido	perderíais
han perdido	perderían

Pluperfect indicative	**Imperative**
había perdido	–
habías perdido	pierde
había perdido	pierda
habíamos perdido	perdamos
habíais perdido	perded
habían perdido	pierdan

pertenecer *to belong*

Gerund *perteneciendo*
Past participle *pertenecido*

Present indicative	Present subjunctive
pertenezco	pertenezca
perteneces	pertenezcas
pertenece	pertenezca
pertenecemos	pertenezcamos
pertenecéis	pertenezcáis
pertenecen	pertenezcan

Imperfect indicative	Imperfect subjunctive
pertenecía	perteneciera
pertenecías	pertenecieras
pertenecía	perteneciera
pertenecíamos	perteneciéramos
pertenecíais	pertenecierais
pertenecían	pertenecieran

Preterite	Future
pertenecí	perteneceré
perteneciste	pertenecerás
perteneció	pertenecerá
pertenecimos	perteneceremos
pertenecisteis	perteneceréis
pertenecieron	pertenecerán

Perfect indicative	Conditional
he pertenecido	pertenecería
has pertenecido	pertenecerías
ha pertenecido	pertenecería
hemos pertenecido	perteneceríamos
habéis pertenecido	perteneceríais
han pertenecido	pertenecerían

Pluperfect indicative	Imperative
había pertenecido	–
habías pertenecido	pertenece
había pertenecido	pertenezca
habíamos pertenecido	pertenezcamos
habíais pertenecido	perteneced
habían pertenecido	pertenezcan

poder *to be able to, can*

Gerund *pudiendo*
Past participle *podido*

Present indicative	Present subjunctive
puedo	pueda
puedes	puedas
puede	pueda
podemos	podamos
podéis	podáis
pueden	puedan

Imperfect indicative	Imperfect subjunctive
podía	pudiera
podías	pudieras
podía	pudiera
podíamos	pudiéramos
podíais	pudierais
podían	pudieran

Preterite	Future
pude	podré
pudiste	podrás
pudo	podrá
pudimos	podremos
pudisteis	podréis
pudieron	podrán

Perfect indicative	Conditional
he podido	podría
has podido	podrías
ha podido	podría
hemos podido	podríamos
habéis podido	podríais
han podido	podrían

Pluperfect indicative	Imperative
había podido	–
habías podido	puede
había podido	pueda
habíamos podido	podamos
habíais podido	poded
habían podido	puedan

poner *to put*

Gerund *poniendo*
Past participle *puesto*

Present indicative	Present subjunctive
pongo	ponga
pones	pongas
pone	ponga
ponemos	pongamos
ponéis	pongáis
ponen	pongan

Imperfect indicative	Imperfect subjunctive
ponía	pusiera
ponías	pusieras
ponía	pusicra
poníamos	pusiéramos
poníais	pusierais
ponían	pusieran

Preterite	Future
puse	pondré
pusiste	pondrás
puso	pondrá
pusimos	pondremos
pusisteis	pondréis
pusieron	pondrán

Perfect indicative	Conditional
he puesto	pondría
has puesto	pondrías
ha puesto	pondría
hemos puesto	pondríamos
habéis puesto	pondríais
han puesto	pondrían

Pluperfect indicative	Imperative
había puesto	–
habías puesto	pon
había puesto	ponga
habíamos puesto	pongamos
habíais puesto	poned
habían puesto	pongan

preferir *to prefer*

Gerund *prefiriendo*
Past participle *preferido*

Present indicative	Preprefect subjunctive
prefiero	prefiera
prefieres	prefieras
prefiere	prefiera
preferimos	prefiramos
preferís	prefiráis
prefieren	prefieran

Imperfect indicative	Imperfect subjunctive
prefería	prefiriera
preferías	prefirieras
prefería	prefiriera
preferíamos	prefiriéramos
preferíais	prefirierais
preferían	prefirieran

Preterite	Future
preferí	preferiré
preferiste	preferirás
prefirió	preferirá
preferimos	preferiremos
preferisteis	preferiréis
prefirieron	preferirán

Perfect indicative	Conditional
he preferido	preferiría
has preferido	preferirías
ha preferido	preferiría
hemos preferido	preferiríamos
habéis preferido	preferiríais
han preferido	preferirían

Pluperfect indicative	Imperative
había preferido	–
habías preferido	prefiere
había preferido	prefiera
habíamos preferido	prefiramos
habíais preferido	preferid
habían preferido	prefieran

probar *to taste, try*

Gerund *probando*
Past participle *probado*

Present indicative	Present subjunctive
pruebo	pruebe
pruebas	pruebes
prueba	pruebe
probamos	probemos
probáis	probéis
prueban	prueben

Imperfect indicative	Imperfect subjunctive
probaba	probara
probabas	probaras
probaba	probara
probábamos	probáramos
probabais	probarais
probaban	probaran

Preterite	Future
probé	probaré
probaste	probarás
probó	probará
probamos	probaremos
probasteis	probaréis
probaron	probarán

Perfect indicative	Conditional
he probado	probaría
has probado	probarías
ha probado	probaría
hemos probado	probaríamos
habéis probado	probaríais
han probado	probarían

Pluperfect indicative	Imperative
había probado	–
habías probado	prueba
había probado	pruebe
habíamos probado	probemos
habíais probado	probad
habían probado	prueben

prohibir *to forbid*

Gerund *prohibiendo*
Past participle *prohibido*

Present indicative	Present subjunctive
prohíbo	prohíba
prohíbes	prohíbas
prohíbe	prohíba
prohibimos	prohibamos
prohibís	prohibáis
prohíben	prohíban

Imperfect indicative	Imperfect subjunctive
prohibía	prohibiera
prohibías	prohibieras
prohibía	prohibiera
prohibíamos	prohibiéramos
prohibíais	prohibierais
prohibían	prohibieran

Preterite	Future
prohibí	prohibiré
prohibiste	prohibirás
prohibió	prohibirá
prohibimos	prohibiremos
prohibisteis	prohibiréis
prohibieron	prohibirán

Perfect indicative	Conditional
he prohibido	prohibiría
has prohibido	prohibirías
ha prohibido	prohibiría
hemos prohibido	prohibiríamos
habéis prohibido	prohibiríais
han prohibido	prohibirían

Pluperfect indicative	Imperative
había prohibido	–
habías prohibido	prohíbe
había prohibido	prohíba
habíamos prohibido	prohibamos
habíais prohibido	prohibid
habían prohibido	prohíban

querer *to want, to love*

Gerund *queriendo*
Past participle *querido*

Present indicative	Present subjunctive
quiero	quiera
quieres	quieras
quiere	quiera
queremos	queramos
queréis	queráis
quieren	quieran

Imperfect indicative	Imperfect subjunctive
quería	quisiera
querías	quisieras
quería	quisiera
queríamos	quisiéramos
queríais	quisierais
querían	quisieran

Preterite	Future
quise	querré
quisiste	querrás
quiso	querrá
quisimos	querremos
quisisteis	querréis
quisieron	querrán

Perfect indicative	Conditional
he querido	querría
has querido	querrías
ha querido	querría
hemos querido	querríamos
habéis querido	querríais
han querido	querrían

Pluperfect indicative	Imperative
había querido	–
habías querido	quiere
había querido	quiera
habíamos querido	queramos
habíais querido	quered
habían querido	quieran

recibir *to receive*

Gerund *recibiendo*
Past participle *recibido*

Present indicative	Present subjunctive
recibo	reciba
recibes	recibas
recibe	reciba
recibimos	recibamos
recibís	recibáis
reciben	reciban

Imperfect indicative	Imperfect subjunctive
recibía	recibiera
recibías	recibieras
recibía	recibiera
recibíamos	recibiéramos
recibíais	recibierais
recibían	recibieran

Preterite	Future
recibí	recibiré
recibiste	recibirás
recibió	recibirá
recibimos	recibiremos
recibisteis	recibiréis
recibieron	recibirán

Perfect indicative	Conditional
he recibido	recibiría
has recibido	recibirías
ha recibido	recibiría
hemos recibido	recibiríamos
habéis recibido	recibiríais
han recibido	recibirían

Pluperfect indicative	Imperative
había recibido	–
habías recibido	recibe
había recibido	reciba
habíamos recibido	recibamos
habíais recibido	recibid
habían recibido	reciban

recordar *to remember*

Gerund *recordando*
Past participle *recordado*

Present indicative	**Present subjunctive**
recuerdo	recuerde
recuerdas	recuerdes
recuerda	recuerde
recordamos	recordemos
recordáis	recordéis
recuerdan	recuerden

Imperfect indicative	**Imperfect subjunctive**
recordaba	recordara
recordabas	recordaras
recordaba	recordara
recordábamos	recordáramos
recordabais	recordarais
recordaban	recordaran

Preterite	**Future**
recordé	recordaré
recordaste	recordarás
recordó	recordará
recordamos	recordaremos
recordasteis	recordaréis
recordaron	recordarán

Perfect indicative	**Conditional**
he recordado	recordaría
has recordado	recordarías
ha recordado	recordaría
hemos recordado	recordaríamos
habéis recordado	recordaríais
han recordado	recordarían

Pluperfect indicative	**Imperative**
había recordado	–
habías recordado	recuerda
había recordado	recuerde
habíamos recordado	recordemos
habíais recordado	recordad
habían recordado	recuerden

reducir *to reduce*

Gerund *reduciendo*
Past participle *reducido*

Present indicative	**Present subjunctive**
reduzco	reduzca
reduces	reduzcas
reduce	reduzca
reducimos	reduzcamos
reducís	reduzcáis
reducen	reduzcan

Imperfect indicative	**Imperfect subjunctive**
reducía	redujera
reducías	redujeras
reducía	redujera
reducíamos	redujéramos
reducíais	redujerais
reducían	redujeran

Preterite	**Future**
reduje	reduciré
redujiste	reducirás
redujo	reducirá
redujimos	reduciremos
redujisteis	reduciréis
redujeron	reducirán

Perfect indicative	**Conditional**
he reducido	reduciría
has reducido	reducirías
ha reducido	reduciría
hemos reducido	reduciríamos
habéis reducido	reduciríais
han reducido	reducirían

Pluperfect indicative	**Imperative**
había reducido	–
habías reducido	reduce
había reducido	reduzca
habíamos reducido	reduzcamos
habíais reducido	reducid
habían reducido	reduzcan

rehusar *to refuse*

Gerund *rehusando*
Past participle *rehusado*

Present indicative	**Present subjunctive**
rehúso	rehúse
rehúsas	rehúses
rehúsa	rehúse
rehusamos	rehusemos
rehusáis	rehuséis
rehúsan	rehúsen

Imperfect indicative	**Imperfect subjunctive**
rehusaba	rehusara
rehusabas	rehusaras
rehusaba	rehusara
rehusábamos	rehusáramos
rehusabais	rehusarais
rehusaban	rehusaran

Preterite	**Future**
rehusé	rehusaré
rehusaste	rehusarás
rehusó	rehusará
rehusamos	rehusaremos
rehusasteis	rehusaréis
rehusaron	rehusarán

Perfect indicative	**Conditional**
he rehusado	rehusaría
has rehusado	rehusarías
ha rehusado	rehusaría
hemos rehusado	rehusaríamos
habéis rehusado	rehusaríais
han rehusado	rehusarían

Pluperfect indicative	**Imperative**
había rehusado	–
habías rehusado	rehúsa
había rehusado	rehúse
habíamos rehusado	rehusemos
habíais rehusado	rehusad
habían rehusado	rehúsen

reír *to laugh*

Gerund *riendo*
Past participle *reído*

Present indicative	**Present subjunctive**
río	ría
ríes	rías
ríe	ría
reímos	riamos
reís	riáis
ríen	rían

Imperfect indicative	**Imperfect subjunctive**
reía	riera
reías	rieras
reía	riera
reíamos	riéramos
reíais	rierais
reían	rieran

Preterite	**Future**
reí	reiré
reíste	reirás
rió	reirá
reímos	reiremos
reísteis	reiréis
rieron	reirán

Perfect indicative	**Conditional**
he reído	reiría
has reído	reirías
ha reído	reiría
hemos reído	reiríamos
habéis reído	reiríais
han reído	reirían

Pluperfect indicative	**Imperative**
había reído	–
habías reído	ríe
había reído	ría
habíamos reído	riamos
habíais reído	reíd
habían reído	rían

reñir *to quarrel*

Gerund *riñendo*
Past participle *reñido*

Present indicative	Present subjunctive
riño	riña
riñes	riñas
riñe	riña
reñimos	riñamos
reñís	riñáis
riñen	riñan

Imperfect indicative	Imperfect subjunctive
reñía	riñera
reñías	riñeras
reñía	riñera
reñíamos	riñéramos
reñíais	riñerais
reñían	riñeran

Preterite	Future
reñí	reñiré
reñiste	reñirás
riñó	reñirá
reñimos	reñiremos
reñisteis	reñiréis
riñeron	reñirán

Perfect indicative	Conditional
he reñido	reñiría
has reñido	reñirías
ha reñido	reñiría
hemos reñido	reñiríamos
habéis reñido	reñiríais
han reñido	reñirían

Pluperfect indicative	Imperative
había reñido	–
habías reñido	riñe
había reñido	riña
habíamos reñido	riñamos
habíais reñido	reñid
habían reñido	riñan

repetir *to repeat*

Gerund *repitiendo*
Past participle *repetido*

Present indicative	Present subjunctive
repito	repita
repites	repitas
repite	repita
repetimos	repitamos
repetís	repitáis
repiten	repitan

Imperfect indicative	Imperfect subjunctive
repetía	repitiera
repetías	repitieras
repetía	repitiera
repetíamos	repitiéramos
repetíais	repitierais
repetían	repitieran

Preterite	Future
repetí	repetiré
repetiste	repetirás
repitió	repetirá
repetimos	repetiremos
repetisteis	repetiréis
repitieron	repetirán

Perfect indicative	Conditional
he repetido	repetiría
has repetido	repetirías
ha repetido	repetiría
hemos repetido	repetiríamos
habéis repetido	repetiríais
han repetido	repetirían

Pluperfect indicative	Imperative
había repetido	–
habías repetido	repite
había repetido	repita
habíamos repetido	repitamos
habíais repetido	repetid
habían repetido	repitan

rogar *to plead, to beg*

Gerund *rogando*
Past participle *rogado*

Present indicative	Present subjunctive
ruego	ruegue
ruegas	ruegues
ruega	ruegue
rogamos	roguemos
rogáis	roguéis
ruegan	rueguen

Imperfect indicative	Imperfect subjunctive
rogaba	rogara
rogabas	rogaras
rogaba	rogara
rogábamos	rogáramos
rogabais	rogarais
rogaban	rogaran

Preterite	Future
rogué	rogaré
rogaste	rogarás
rogó	rogará
rogamos	rogaremos
rogasteis	rogaréis
rogaron	rogarán

Perfect indicative	Conditional
he rogado	rogaría
has rogado	rogarías
ha rogado	rogaría
hemos rogado	rogaríamos
habéis rogado	rogaríais
han rogado	rogarían

Pluperfect indicative	Imperative
había rogado	–
habías rogado	ruega
había rogado	ruegue
habíamos rogado	roguemos
habíais rogado	rogad
habían rogado	rueguen

romper *to break*

Gerund *rompiendo*
Past participle *roto*

Present indicative	Present subjunctive
rompo	rompa
rompes	rompas
rompe	rompa
rompemos	rompamos
rompéis	rompáis
rompen	rompan

Imperfect indicative	Imperfect subjunctive
rompía	rompiera
rompías	rompieras
rompía	rompiera
rompíamos	rompiéramos
rompíais	rompierais
rompían	rompieran

Preterite	Future
rompí	romperé
rompiste	romperás
rompió	romperá
rompimos	romperemos
rompisteis	romperéis
rompieron	romperán

Perfect indicative	Conditional
he roto	rompería
has roto	romperías
ha roto	rompería
hemos roto	romperíamos
habéis roto	romperíais
han roto	romperían

Pluperfect indicative	Imperative
había roto	–
habías roto	rompe
había roto	rompa
habíamos roto	rompamos
habíais roto	romped
habían roto	rompan

saber *to know*

Gerund *sabiendo*
Past participle *sabido*

Present indicative	Present subjunctive
sé	sepa
sabes	sepas
sabe	sepa
sabemos	sepamos
sabéis	sepáis
saben	sepan

Imperfect indicative	Imperfect subjunctive
sabía	supiera
sabías	supieras
sabía	supiera
sabíamos	supiéramos
sabíais	supierais
sabían	supieran

Preterite	Future
supe	sabré
supiste	sabrás
supo	sabrá
supimos	sabremos
supisteis	sabréis
supieron	sabrán

Perfect indicative	Conditional
he sabido	sabría
has sabido	sabrías
ha sabido	sabría
hemos sabido	sabríamos
habéis sabido	sabríais
han sabido	sabrían

Pluperfect indicative	Imperative
había sabido	–
habías sabido	sabe
había sabido	sepa
habíamos sabido	sepamos
habíais sabido	sabed
habían sabido	sepan

sacar *to take out*

Gerund *sacando*
Past participle *sacado*

Present indicative	Present subjunctive
saco	saque
sacas	saques
saca	saque
sacamos	saquemos
sacáis	saquéis
sacan	saquen

Imperfect indicative	Imperfect subjunctive
sacaba	sacara
sacabas	sacaras
sacaba	sacara
sacábamos	sacáramos
sacabais	sacarais
sacaban	sacaran

Preterite	Future
saqué	sacaré
sacaste	sacarás
sacó	sacará
sacamos	sacaremos
sacasteis	sacaréis
sacaron	sacarán

Perfect indicative	Conditional
he sacado	sacaría
has sacado	sacarías
ha sacado	sacaría
hemos sacado	sacaríamos
habéis sacado	sacaríais
han sacado	sacarían

Pluperfect indicative	Imperative
había sacado	–
habías sacado	saca
había sacado	saque
habíamos sacado	saquemos
habíais sacado	sacad
habían sacado	saquen

salir *to go out*

Gerund *saliendo*
Past participle *salido*

Present indicative	**Present subjunctive**
salgo	salga
sales	salgas
sale	salga
salimos	salgamos
salís	salgáis
salen	salgan

Imperfect indicative	**Imperfect subjunctive**
salía	saliera
salías	salieras
salía	saliera
salíamos	saliéramos
salíais	salierais
salían	salieran

Preterite	**Future**
salí	saldré
saliste	saldrás
salió	saldrá
salimos	saldremos
salisteis	saldréis
salieron	saldrán

Perfect indicative	**Conditional**
he salido	saldría
has salido	saldrías
ha salido	saldría
hemos salido	saldríamos
habéis salido	saldríais
han salido	saldrían

Pluperfect indicative	**Imperative**
había salido	–
habías salido	sal
había salido	salga
habíamos salido	salgamos
habíais salido	salid
habían salido	salgan

satisfacer *to satisfy*

Gerund *satisfaciendo*
Past participle *satisfecho*

Present indicative	**Present subjunctive**
satisfago	satisfaga
satisfaces	satisfagas
satisface	satisfaga
satisfacemos	satisfagamos
satisfacéis	satisfagáis
satisfacen	satisfagan

Imperfect indicative	**Imperfect subjunctive**
satisfacía	satisficiera
satisfacías	satisficieras
satisfacía	satisficiera
satisfacíamos	satisficiéramos
satisfacíais	satisficierais
satisfacían	satisficieran

Preterite	**Future**
satisfice	satisfaré
satisficiste	satisfarás
satisfizo	satisfará
satisficimos	satisfaremos
satisficisteis	satisfaréis
satisficieron	satisfarán

Perfect indicative	**Conditional**
he satisfecho	satisfaría
has satisfecho	satisfarías
ha satisfecho	satisfaría
hemos satisfecho	satisfaríamos
habéis satisfecho	satisfaríais
han satisfecho	satisfarían

Pluperfect indicative	**Imperative**
había satisfecho	–
habías satisfecho	satisfaz; satisface
había satisfecho	satisfaga
habíamos satisfecho	satisfagamos
habíais satisfecho	satisfaced
habían satisfecho	satisfagan

secar *to dry*

Gerund *secando*
Past participle *secado*

Present indicative	Present subjunctive
seco	seque
secas	seques
seca	seque
secamos	sequemos
secáis	sequéis
secan	sequen

Imperfect indicative	Imperfect subjunctive
secaba	secara
secabas	secaras
secaba	secara
secábamos	secáramos
secabais	secarais
secaban	secaran

Preterite	Future
sequé	secaré
secaste	secarás
secó	secará
secamos	secaremos
secasteis	secaréis
secaron	secarán

Perfect indicative	Conditional
he secado	secaría
has secado	secarías
ha secado	secaría
hemos secado	secaríamos
habéis secado	secaríais
han secado	secarían

Pluperfect indicative	Imperative
había secado	–
habías secado	seca
había secado	seque
habíamos secado	sequemos
habíais secado	secad
habían secado	sequen

seguir *to follow*

Gerund *siguiendo*
Past participle *seguido*

Present indicative	Present subjunctive
sigo	siga
sigues	sigas
sigue	siga
seguimos	sigamos
seguís	sigáis
siguen	sigan

Imperfect indicative	Imperfect subjunctive
seguía	siguiera
seguías	siguieras
seguía	siguiera
seguíamos	siguiéramos
seguíais	siguierais
seguían	siguieran

Preterite	Future
seguí	seguiré
seguiste	seguirás
siguió	seguirá
seguimos	seguiremos
seguisteis	seguiréis
siguieron	seguirán

Perfect indicative	Conditional
he seguido	seguiría
has seguido	seguirías
ha seguido	seguiría
hemos seguido	seguiríamos
habéis seguido	seguiríais
han seguido	seguirían

Pluperfect indicative	Imperative
había seguido	–
habías seguido	sigue
había seguido	siga
habíamos seguido	sigamos
habíais seguido	seguid
habían seguido	sigan

sentarse *to sit down*

Gerund *sentándose*
Past participle *sentado*

Present indicative	Present subjunctive
me siento	me siente
te sientas	te sientes
se sienta	se siente
nos sentamos	nos sentemos
os sentáis	os sentéis
se sientan	se sienten

Imperfect indicative	Imperfect subjunctive
me sentaba	me sentara
te sentabas	te sentaras
se sentaba	se sentara
nos sentábamos	nos sentáramos
os sentabais	os sentarais
se sentaban	se sentaran

Preterite	Future
me senté	me sentaré
te sentaste	te sentarás
se sentó	se sentará
nos sentamos	nos sentaremos
os sentasteis	os sentaréis
se sentaron	se sentarán

Perfect indicative	Conditional
me he sentado	me sentaría
te has sentado	te sentarías
se ha sentado	se sentaría
nos hemos sentado	nos sentaríamos
os habéis sentado	os sentaríais
se han sentado	se sentarían

Pluperfect indicative	Imperative
me había sentado	–
te habías sentado	siéntate
se había sentado	siéntese
nos habíamos sentado	sentémonos
os habíais sentado	sentaos
se habían sentado	siéntense

sentir *to feel*

Gerund *sintiendo*
Past participle *sentido*

Present indicative	Present subjunctive
siento	sienta
sientes	sientas
siente	sienta
sentimos	sintamos
sentís	sintáis
sienten	sientan

Imperfect indicative	Imperfect subjunctive
sentía	sintiera
sentías	sintieras
sentía	sintiera
sentíamos	sintiéramos
sentíais	sintierais
sentían	sintieran

Preterite	Future
sentí	sentiré
sentiste	sentirás
sintió	sentirá
sentimos	sentiremos
sentisteis	sentiréis
sintieron	sentirán

Perfect indicative	Conditional
he sentido	sentiría
has sentido	sentirías
ha sentido	sentiría
hemos sentido	sentiríamos
habéis sentido	sentiríais
han sentido	sentirían

Pluperfect indicative	Imperative
había sentido	–
habías sentido	siente
había sentido	sienta
habíamos sentido	sintamos
habíais sentido	sentid
habían sentido	sientan

ser *to be*

Gerund *siendo*
Past participle *sido*

Present indicative	Present subjunctive
soy	sea
eres	seas
es	sea
somos	seamos
sois	seáis
son	sean

Imperfect indicative	Imperfect subjunctive
era	fuera
eras	fueras
era	fuera
éramos	fuéramos
erais	fuerais
eran	fueran

Preterite	Future
fui	seré
fuiste	serás
fue	será
fuimos	seremos
fuisteis	seréis
fueron	serán

Perfect indicative	Conditional
he sido	sería
has sido	serías
ha sido	sería
hemos sido	seríamos
habéis sido	seríais
han sido	serían

Pluperfect indicative	Imperative
había sido	–
habías sido	sé
había sido	sea
habíamos sido	seamos
habíais sido	sed
habían sido	sean

servir *to serve*

Gerund *sirviendo*
Past participle *servido*

Present indicative	Present subjunctive
sirvo	sirva
sirves	sirvas
sirve	sirva
servimos	sirvamos
servís	sirváis
sirven	sirvan

Imperfect indicative	Imperfect subjunctive
servía	sirviera
servías	sirvieras
servía	sirviera
servíamos	sirviéramos
servíais	sirvierais
servían	sirvieran

Preterite	Future
serví	serviré
serviste	servirás
sirvió	servirá
servimos	serviremos
servisteis	serviréis
sirvieron	servirán

Perfect indicative	Conditional
he servido	serviría
has servido	servirías
ha servido	serviría
hemos servido	serviríamos
habéis servido	serviríais
han servido	servirían

Pluperfect indicative	Imperative
había servido	–
habías servido	sirve
había servido	sirva
habíamos servido	sirvamos
habíais servido	servid
habían servido	sirvan

situar *to situate*

Gerund *situando*
Past participle *situado*

Present indicative	Present subjunctive
sitúo	sitúe
sitúas	sitúes
sitúa	sitúe
situamos	situemos
situáis	situéis
sitúan	sitúen

Imperfect indicative	Imperfect subjunctive
situaba	situara
situabas	situaras
situaba	situara
situábamos	situáramos
situabais	situarais
situaban	situaran

Preterite	Future
situé	situaré
situaste	situarás
situó	situará
situamos	situaremos
situasteis	situaréis
situaron	situarán

Perfect indicative	Conditional
he situado	situaría
has situado	situarías
ha situado	situaría
hemos situado	situaríamos
habéis situado	situaríais
han situado	situarían

Pluperfect indicative	Imperative
había situado	–
habías situado	sitúa
había situado	sitúe
habíamos situado	situemos
habíais situado	situad
habían situado	sitúen

soler *to be accustomed to*

Gerund *soliendo*
Past participle *solido*

Present indicative	Present subjunctive
suelo	suela
sueles	suelas
suele	suela
solemos	solamos
soléis	soláis
suelen	suelan

Imperfect indicative	Imperfect subjunctive
solía	soliera
solías	solieras
solía	soliera
solíamos	soliéramos
solíais	solierais
solían	solieran

Preterite	Future
solí	–
soliste	–
solió	–
solimos	–
solisteis	–
solieron	–

Perfect indicative	Conditional
–	–
–	–
–	–
–	–
–	–
–	–

Pluperfect indicative	Imperative
–	—

soñar *to dream*

Gerund *soñando*
Past participle *soñado*

Present indicative	Present subjunctive
sueño	sueñe
sueñas	sueñes
sueña	sueñe
soñamos	soñemos
soñáis	soñéis
sueñan	sueñen

Imperfect indicative	Imperfect subjunctive
soñaba	soñara
soñabas	soñaras
soñaba	soñara
soñábamos	soñáramos
soñabais	soñarais
soñaban	soñaran

Preterite	Future
soñé	soñaré
soñaste	soñarás
soñó	soñará
soñamos	soñaremos
soñasteis	soñaréis
soñaron	soñarán

Perfect indicative	Conditional
he soñado	soñaría
has soñado	soñarías
ha soñado	soñaría
hemos soñado	soñaríamos
habéis soñado	soñaríais
han soñado	soñarían

Pluperfect indicative	Imperative
había soñado	–
habías soñado	sueña
había soñado	sueñe
habíamos soñado	soñemos
habíais soñado	soñad
habían soñado	sueñen

sonreír *to smile*

Gerund *sonriendo*
Past participle *sonreído*

Present indicative	Present subjunctive
sonrío	sonría
sonríes	sonrías
sonríe	sonría
sonreímos	sonriamos
sonreís	sonriáis
sonríen	sonrían

Imperfect indicative	Imperfect subjunctive
sonreía	sonriera
sonreías	sonrieras
sonreía	sonriera
sonreíamos	sonriéramos
sonreíais	sonrierais
sonreían	sonrieran

Preterite	Future
sonreí	sonreiré
sonreíste	sonreirás
sonrió	sonreirá
sonreímos	sonreiremos
sonreísteis	sonreiréis
sonrieron	sonreirán

Perfect indicative	Conditional
he sonreído	sonreiría
has sonreído	sonreirías
ha sonreído	sonreiría
hemos sonreído	sonreiríamos
habéis sonreído	sonreiríais
han sonreído	sonreirían

Pluperfect indicative	Imperative
había sonreído	–
habías sonreído	sonríe
había sonreído	sonría
habíamos sonreído	sonriamos
habíais sonreído	sonreíd
habían sonreído	sonrían

subir *to go up*

Gerund *subiendo*
Past participle *subido*

Present indicative	**Present subjunctive**
subo	suba
subes	subas
sube	suba
subimos	subamos
subís	subáis
suben	suban

Imperfect indicative	**Imperfect subjunctive**
subía	subiera
subías	subieras
subía	subiera
subíamos	subiéramos
subíais	subierais
subían	subieran

Preterite	**Future**
subí	subiré
subiste	subirás
subió	subirá
subimos	subiremos
subisteis	subiréis
subieron	subirán

Perfect indicative	**Conditional**
he subido	subiría
has subido	subirías
ha subido	subiría
hemos subido	subiríamos
habéis subido	subiríais
han subido	subirían

Pluperfect indicative	**Imperative**
había subido	–
habías subido	sube
había subido	suba
habíamos subido	subamos
habíais subido	subid
habían subido	suban

sugerir *to suggest*

Gerund *sugiriendo*
Past participle *sugerido*

Present indicative	**Present subjunctive**
sugiero	sugiera
sugieres	sugieras
sugiere	sugiera
sugerimos	sugiramos
sugerís	sugiráis
sugieren	sugieran

Imperfect indicative	**Imperfect subjunctive**
sugería	sugiriera
sugerías	sugirieras
sugería	sugiriera
sugeríamos	sugiriéramos
sugeríais	sugirierais
sugerían	sugirieran

Preterite	**Future**
sugerí	sugeriré
sugeriste	sugerirás
sugirió	sugerirá
sugerimos	sugeriremos
sugeristeis	sugeriréis
sugirieron	sugerirán

Perfect indicative	**Conditional**
he sugerido	sugeriría
has sugerido	sugerirías
ha sugerido	sugeriría
hemos sugerido	sugeriríamos
habéis sugerido	sugeriríais
han sugerido	sugerirían

Pluperfect indicative	**Imperative**
había sugerido	–
habías sugerido	sugiere
había sugerido	sugiera
habíamos sugerido	sugiramos
habíais sugerido	sugerid
habían sugerido	sugieran

tener *to have*

Gerund *teniendo*
Past participle *tenido*

Present indicative	Present subjunctive
tengo	tenga
tienes	tengas
tiene	tenga
tenemos	tengamos
tenéis	tengáis
tienen	tengan

Imperfect indicative	Imperfect subjunctive
tenía	tuviera
tenías	tuvieras
tenía	tuviera
teníamos	tuviéramos
teníais	tuvierais
tenían	tuvieran

Preterite	Future
tuve	tendré
tuviste	tendrás
tuvo	tendrá
tuvimos	tendremos
tuvisteis	tendréis
tuvieron	tendrán

Perfect indicative	Conditional
he tenido	tendría
has tenido	tendrías
ha tenido	tendría
hemos tenido	tendríamos
habéis tenido	tendríais
han tenido	tendrían

Pluperfect indicative	Imperative
había tenido	–
habías tenido	ten
había tenido	tenga
habíamos tenido	tengamos
habíais tenido	tened
habían tenido	tengan

terminar *to finish*

Gerund *terminando*
Past participle *terminado*

Present indicative	Present subjunctive
termino	termine
terminas	termines
termina	termine
terminamos	terminemos
termináis	terminéis
terminan	terminen

Imperfect indicative	Imperfect subjunctive
terminaba	terminara
terminabas	terminaras
terminaba	terminara
terminábamos	termináramos
terminabais	terminarais
terminaban	terminaran

Preterite	Future
terminé	terminaré
terminaste	terminarás
terminó	terminará
terminamos	terminaremos
terminasteis	terminaréis
terminaron	terminarán

Perfect indicative	Conditional
he terminado	terminaría
has terminado	terminarías
ha terminado	terminaría
hemos terminado	terminaríamos
habéis terminado	terminaríais
han terminado	terminarían

Pluperfect indicative	Imperative
había terminado	–
habías terminado	termina
había terminado	termine
habíamos terminado	terminemos
habíais terminado	terminad
habían terminado	terminen

tocar *to touch*

Gerund *tocando*
Past participle *tocado*

Present indicative	**Present subjunctive**
toco	toque
tocas	toques
toca	toque
tocamos	toquemos
tocáis	toquéis
tocan	toquen

Imperfect indicative	**Imperfect subjunctive**
tocaba	tocara
tocabas	tocaras
tocaba	tocara
tocábamos	tocáramos
tocabais	tocarais
tocaban	tocaran

Preterite	**Future**
toqué	tocaré
tocaste	tocarás
tocó	tocará
tocamos	tocaremos
tocasteis	tocaréis
tocaron	tocarán

Perfect indicative	**Conditional**
he tocado	tocaría
has tocado	tocarías
ha tocado	tocaría
hemos tocado	tocaríamos
habéis tocado	tocaríais
han tocado	tocarían

Pluperfect indicative	**Imperative**
había tocado	–
habías tocado	toca
había tocado	toque
habíamos tocado	toquemos
habíais tocado	tocad
habían tocado	toquen

tomar *to take*

Gerund *tomando*
Past participle *tomado*

Present indicative	**Present subjunctive**
tomo	tome
tomas	tomes
toma	tome
tomamos	tomemos
tomáis	toméis
toman	tomen

Imperfect indicative	**Imperfect subjunctive**
tomaba	tomara
tomabas	tomaras
tomaba	tomara
tomábamos	tomáramos
tomabais	tomarais
tomaban	tomaran

Preterite	**Future**
tomé	tomaré
tomaste	tomarás
tomó	tomará
tomamos	tomaremos
tomasteis	tomaréis
tomaron	tomarán

Perfect indicative	**Conditional**
he tomado	tomaría
has tomado	tomarías
ha tomado	tomaría
hemos tomado	tomaríamos
habéis tomado	tomaríais
han tomado	tomarían

Pluperfect indicative	**Imperative**
había tomado	–
habías tomado	toma
había tomado	tome
habíamos tomado	tomemos
habíais tomado	tomad
habían tomado	tomen

torcer *to twist*

Gerund *torciendo*
Past participle *torcido*

Present indicative	Present subjunctive
tuerzo	tuerza
tuerces	tuerzas
tuerce	tuerza
torcemos	torzamos
torcéis	torzáis
tuercen	tuerzan

Imperfect indicative	Imperfect subjunctive
torcía	torciera
torcías	torcieras
torcía	torciera
torcíamos	torciéramos
torcíais	torcierais
torcían	torcieran

Preterite	Future
torcí	torceré
torciste	torcerás
torció	torcerá
torcimos	torceremos
torcisteis	torceréis
torcieron	torcerán

Perfect indicative	Conditional
he torcido	torcería
has torcido	torcerías
ha torcido	torcería
hemos torcido	torceríamos
habéis torcido	torceríais
han torcido	torcerían

Pluperfect indicative	Imperative
había torcido	–
habías torcido	tuerce
había torcido	tuerza
habíamos torcido	torzamos
habíais torcido	torced
habían torcido	tuerzan

toser *to cough*

Gerund *tosiendo*
Past participle *tosido*

Present indicative	Present subjunctive
toso	tosa
toses	tosas
tose	tosa
tosemos	tosamos
toséis	tosáis
tosen	tosan

Imperfect indicative	Imperfect subjunctive
tosía	tosiera
tosías	tosieras
tosía	tosiera
tosíamos	tosiéramos
tosíais	tosierais
tosían	tosieran

Preterite	Future
tosí	toseré
tosiste	toserás
tosió	toserá
tosimos	toseremos
tosisteis	toseréis
tosieron	toserán

Perfect indicative	Conditional
he tosido	tosería
has tosido	toserías
ha tosido	tosería
hemos tosido	toseríamos
habéis tosido	toseríais
han tosido	toserían

Pluperfect indicative	Imperative
había tosido	–
habías tosido	tose
había tosido	tosa
habíamos tosido	tosamos
habíais tosido	tosed
habían tosido	tosan

trabajar *to work*

Gerund *trabajando*
Past participle *trabajado*

Present indicative	Present subjunctive
trabajo	trabaje
trabajas	trabajes
trabaja	trabaje
trabajamos	trabajemos
trabajáis	trabajéis
trabajan	trabajen

Imperfect indicative	Imperfect subjunctive
trabajaba	trabajara
trabajabas	trabajaras
trabajaba	trabajara
trabajábamos	trabajáramos
trabajabais	trabajarais
trabajaban	trabajaran

Preterite	Future
trabajé	trabajaré
trabajaste	trabajarás
trabajó	trabajará
trabajamos	trabajaremos
trabajasteis	trabajaréis
trabajaron	trabajarán

Perfect indicative	Conditional
he trabajado	trabajaría
has trabajado	trabajarías
ha trabajado	trabajaría
hemos trabajado	trabajaríamos
habéis trabajado	trabajaríais
han trabajado	trabajarían

Pluperfect indicative	Imperative
había trabajado	–
habías trabajado	trabaja
había trabajado	trabaje
habíamos trabajado	trabajemos
habíais trabajado	trabajad
habían trabajado	trabajen

traducir *to translate*

Gerund *traduciendo*
Past participle *traducido*

Present indicative	Present subjunctive
traduzco	traduzca
traduces	traduzcas
traduce	traduzca
traducimos	traduzcamos
traducís	traduzcáis
traducen	traduzcan

Imperfect indicative	Imperfect subjunctive
traducía	tradujera
traducías	tradujeras
traducía	tradujera
traducíamos	tradujéramos
traducíais	tradujerais
traducían	tradujeran

Preterite	Future
traduje	traduciré
tradujiste	traducirás
tradujo	traducirá
tradujimos	traduciremos
tradujisteis	traduciréis
tradujeron	traducirán

Perfect indicative	Conditional
he traducido	traduciría
has traducido	traducirías
ha traducido	traduciría
hemos traducido	traduciríamos
habéis traducido	traduciríais
han traducido	traducirían

Pluperfect indicative	Imperative
había traducido	–
habías traducido	traduce
había traducido	traduzca
habíamos traducido	traduzcamos
habíais traducido	traducid
habían traducido	traduzcan

traer *to bring*

Gerund *trayendo*
Past participle *traído*

Present inditrative	Present subjunctive
traigo	traiga
traes	traigas
trae	traiga
traemos	traigamos
traéis	traigáis
traen	traigan

Imperfect inditrative	Imperfect subjunctive
traía	trajera
traías	trajeras
traía	trajera
traíamos	trajéramos
traíais	trajerais
traían	trajeran

Preterite	Future
traje	traeré
trajiste	traerás
trajo	traerá
trajimos	traeremos
trajisteis	traeréis
trajeron	traerán

Perfect inditrative	Conditional
he traído	traería
has traído	traerías
ha traído	traería
hemos traído	traeríamos
habéis traído	traeríais
han traído	traerían

Pluperfect inditrative	Imperative
había traído	–
habías traído	trae
había traído	traiga
habíamos traído	traigamos
habíais traído	traed
habían traído	traigan

tropezar *to stumble*

Gerund *tropezando*
Past participle *tropezado*

Present indicative	Present subjunctive
tropiezo	tropiece
tropiezas	tropieces
tropieza	tropiece
tropezamos	tropecemos
tropezáis	tropecéis
tropiezan	tropiecen

Imperfect indicative	Imperfect subjunctive
tropezaba	tropezara
tropezabas	tropezaras
tropezaba	tropezara
tropezábamos	tropezáramos
tropezabais	tropezarais
tropezaban	tropezaran

Preterite	Future
tropecé	tropezaré
tropezaste	tropezarás
tropezó	tropezará
tropezamos	tropezaremos
tropezasteis	tropezaréis
tropezaron	tropezarán

Perfect indicative	Conditional
he tropezado	tropezaría
has tropezado	tropezarías
ha tropezado	tropezaría
hemos tropezado	tropezaríamos
habéis tropezado	tropezaríais
han tropezado	tropezarían

Pluperfect indicative	Imperative
había tropezado	–
habías tropezado	tropieza
había tropezado	tropiece
habíamos tropezado	tropecemos
habíais tropezado	tropezad
habían tropezado	tropiecen

vaciar *to empty*

Gerund *vaciando*
Past participle *vaciado*

Present indicative	Present subjunctive
vacío	vacíe
vacías	vacíes
vacía	vacíe
vaciamos	vaciemos
vaciáis	vaciéis
vacían	vacíen

Imperfect indicative	Imperfect subjunctive
vaciaba	vaciara
vaciabas	vaciaras
vaciaba	vaciara
vaciábamos	vaciáramos
vaciabais	vaciarais
vaciaban	vaciaran

Preterite	Future
vacié	vaciaré
vaciaste	vaciarás
vació	vaciará
vaciamos	vaciaremos
vaciasteis	vaciaréis
vaciaron	vaciarán

Perfect indicative	Conditional
he vaciado	vaciaría
has vaciado	vaciarías
ha vaciado	vaciaría
hemos vaciado	vaciaríamos
habéis vaciado	vaciaríais
han vaciado	vaciarían

Pluperfect indicative	Imperative
había vaciado	–
habías vaciado	vacía
había vaciado	vacíe
habíamos vaciado	vaciemos
habíais vaciado	vaciad
habían vaciado	vacíen

valer *to be worth*

Gerund *valiendo*
Past participle *valido*

Present indicative	Present subjunctive
valgo	valga
vales	valgas
vale	valga
valemos	valgamos
valéis	valgáis
valen	valgan

Imperfect indicative	Imperfect subjunctive
valía	valiera
valías	valieras
valía	valiera
valíamos	valiéramos
valíais	valierais
valían	valieran

Preterite	Future
valí	valdré
valiste	valdrás
valió	valdrá
valimos	valdremos
valisteis	valdréis
valieron	valdrán

Perfect indicative	Conditional
he valido	valdría
has valido	valdrías
ha valido	valdría
hemos valido	valdríamos
habéis valido	valdríais
han valido	valdrían

Pluperfect indicative	Imperative
había valido	–
habías valido	vale
había valido	valga
habíamos valido	valgamos
habíais valido	valed
habían valido	valgan

vencer *to win*

Gerund *venciendo*
Past participle *vencido*

Present indicative	Present subjunctive
venzo	venza
vences	venzas
vence	venza
vencemos	venzamos
vencéis	venzáis
vencen	venzan

Imperfect indicative	Imperfect subjunctive
vencía	venciera
vencías	vencieras
vencía	venciera
vencíamos	venciéramos
vencíais	vencierais
vencían	vencieran

Preterite	Future
vencí	venceré
venciste	vencerás
venció	vencerá
vencimos	venceremos
vencisteis	venceréis
vencieron	vencerán

Perfect indicative	Conditional
he vencido	vencería
has vencido	vencerías
ha vencido	vencería
hemos vencido	venceríamos
habéis vencido	venceríais
han vencido	vencerían

Pluperfect indicative	Imperative
había vencido	–
habías vencido	vence
había vencido	venza
habíamos vencido	venzamos
habíais vencido	venced
habían vencido	venzan

vender *to sell*

Gerund *vendiendo*
Past participle *vendido*

Present indicative	Present subjunctive
vendo	venda
vendes	vendas
vende	venda
vendemos	vendamos
vendéis	vendáis
venden	vendan

Imperfect indicative	Imperfect subjunctive
vendía	vendiera
vendías	vendieras
vendía	vendiera
vendíamos	vendiéramos
vendíais	vendierais
vendían	vendieran

Preterite	Future
vendí	venderé
vendiste	venderás
vendió	venderá
vendimos	venderemos
vendisteis	venderéis
vendieron	venderán

Perfect indicative	Conditional
he vendido	vendería
has vendido	venderías
ha vendido	vendería
hemos vendido	venderíamos
habéis vendido	venderíais
han vendido	venderían

Pluperfect indicative	Imperative
había vendido	–
habías vendido	vende
había vendido	venda
habíamos vendido	vendamos
habíais vendido	vended
habían vendido	vendan

venir *to come*

Gerund *viniendo*
Past participle *venido*

Present indicative	Present subjunctive
vengo	venga
vienes	vengas
viene	venga
venimos	vengamos
venís	vengáis
vienen	vengan

Imperfect indicative	Imperfect subjunctive
venía	viniera
venías	vinieras
venía	viniera
veníamos	viniéramos
veníais	vinierais
venían	vinieran

Preterite	Future
vine	vendré
viniste	vendrás
vino	vendrá
vinimos	vendremos
vinisteis	vendréis
vinieron	vendrán

Perfect indicative	Conditional
he venido	vendría
has venido	vendrías
ha venido	vendría
hemos venido	vendríamos
habéis venido	vendríais
han venido	vendrían

Pluperfect indicative	Imperative
había venido	–
habías venido	ven
había venido	venga
habíamos venido	vengamos
habíais venido	venid
habían venido	vengan

ver *to see*

Gerund *viendo*
Past participle *visto*

Present indicative	Present subjunctive
veo	vea
ves	veas
ve	vea
vemos	veamos
veis	veáis
ven	vean

Imperfect indicative	Imperfect subjunctive
veía	viera
veías	vieras
veía	viera
veíamos	viéramos
veíais	vierais
veían	vieran

Preterite	Future
vi	veré
viste	verás
vio	verá
vimos	veremos
visteis	veréis
vieron	verán

Perfect indicative	Conditional
he visto	vería
has visto	verías
ha visto	vería
hemos visto	veríamos
habéis visto	veríais
han visto	verían

Pluperfect indicative	Imperative
había visto	–
habías visto	ve
había visto	vea
habíamos visto	veamos
habíais visto	ved
habían visto	vean

vestirse *to get dressed*

Gerund *vistiéndose*
Past participle *vestido*

Present indicative	Present subjunctive
me visto	me vista
te vistes	te vistas
se viste	se vista
nos vestimos	nos vistamos
os vestís	os vistáis
se visten	se vistan

Imperfect indicative	Imperfect subjunctive
me vestía	me vistiera
te vestías	te vistieras
se vestía	se vistiera
nos vestíamos	nos vistiéramos
os vestíais	os vistierais
se vestían	se vistieran

Preterite	Future
me vestí	me vestiré
te vestiste	te vestirás
se vistió	se vestirá
nos vestimos	nos vestiremos
os vestisteis	os vestiréis
se vistieron	se vestirán

Perfect indicative	Conditional
me he vestido	me vestiría
te has vestido	te vestirías
se ha vestido	se vestiría
nos hemos vestido	nos vestiríamos
os habéis vestido	os vestiríais
se han vestido	se vestirían

Pluperfect indicative	Imperative
me había vestido	–
te habías vestido	vístete
se había vestido	vístase
nos habíamos vestido	vistámonos
os habíais vestido	vestíos
se habían vestido	vístanse

viajar *to travel*

Gerund *viajando*
Past participle *viajado*

Present indicative	Present subjunctive
viajo	viaje
viajas	viajes
viaja	viaje
viajamos	viajemos
viajáis	viajéis
viajan	viajen

Imperfect indicative	Imperfect subjunctive
viajaba	viajara
viajabas	viajaras
viajaba	viajara
viajábamos	viajáramos
viajabais	viajarais
viajaban	viajaran

Preterite	Future
viajé	viajaré
viajaste	viajarás
viajó	viajará
viajamos	viajaremos
viajasteis	viajaréis
viajaron	viajarán

Perfect indicative	Conditional
he viajado	viajaría
has viajado	viajarías
ha viajado	viajaría
hemos viajado	viajaríamos
habéis viajado	viajaríais
han viajado	viajarían

Pluperfect indicative	Imperative
había viajado	–
habías viajado	viaja
había viajado	viaje
habíamos viajado	viajemos
habíais viajado	viajad
habían viajado	viajen

vivir *to live*

Gerund *viviendo*
Past participle *vivido*

Present indicative	Present subjunctive
vivo	viva
vives	vivas
vive	viva
vivimos	vivamos
vivís	viváis
viven	vivan

Imperfect indicative	Imperfect subjunctive
vivía	viviera
vivías	vivieras
vivía	viviera
vivíamos	viviéramos
vivíais	vivierais
vivían	vivieran

Preterite	Future
viví	viviré
viviste	vivirás
vivió	vivirá
vivimos	viviremos
vivisteis	viviréis
vivieron	vivirán

Perfect indicative	Conditional
he vivido	viviría
has vivido	vivirías
ha vivido	viviría
hemos vivido	viviríamos
habéis vivido	viviríais
han vivido	vivirían

Pluperfect indicative	Imperative
había vivido	–
habías vivido	vive
había vivido	viva
habíamos vivido	vivamos
habíais vivido	vivid
habían vivido	vivan

volar *to fly*

Gerund *volando*
Past participle *volado*

Present indicative	Present subjunctive
vuelo	vuele
vuelas	vueles
vuela	vuele
volamos	volemos
voláis	voléis
vuelan	vuelen

Imperfect indicative	Imperfect subjunctive
volaba	volara
volabas	volaras
volaba	volara
volábamos	voláramos
volabais	volarais
volaban	volaran

Preterite	Future
volé	volaré
volaste	volarás
voló	volará
volamos	volaremos
volasteis	volaréis
volaron	volarán

Perfect indicative	Conditional
he volado	volaría
has volado	volarías
ha volado	volaría
hemos volado	volaríamos
habéis volado	volaríais
han volado	volarían

Pluperfect indicative	Imperative
había volado	–
habías volado	vuela
había volado	vuele
habíamos volado	volemos
habíais volado	volad
habían volado	vuelen

volver *to return*

Gerund *volviendo*
Past participle *vuelto*

Present indicative	Present subjunctive
vuelvo	vuelva
vuelves	vuelvas
vuelve	vuelva
volvemos	volvamos
volvéis	volváis
vuelven	vuelvan

Imperfect indicative	Imperfect subjunctive
volvía	volviera
volvías	volvieras
volvía	volviera
volvíamos	volviéramos
volvíais	volvierais
volvían	volvieran

Preterite	Future
volví	volveré
volviste	volverás
volvió	volverá
volvimos	volveremos
volvisteis	volveréis
volvieron	volverán

Perfect indicative	Conditional
he vuelto	volvería
has vuelto	volverías
ha vuelto	volvería
hemos vuelto	volveríamos
habéis vuelto	volveríais
han vuelto	volverían

Pluperfect indicative	Imperative
había vuelto	–
habías vuelto	vuelve
había vuelto	vuelva
habíamos vuelto	volvamos
habíais vuelto	volved
habían vuelto	vuelvan

yacer *to lie*

Gerund *yaciendo*
Past participle *yacido*

Present indicative	Present subjunctive
yaczco; yazgo; yago	yazca; yazga yaga
yaces	yazcas; yazgas; yagas
yace	yazca; yazga; yaga
yacemos	yazcamos; yazgamos; yagamos
yacéis	yazcáis; yazgáis; yagáis
yacen	yazcan; yazgan; yagan

Imperfect indicative	Imperfect subjunctive
yacía	yaciera
yacías	yacieras
yacía	yaciera
yacíamos	yaciéramos
yacíais	yacierais
yacían	yacieran

Preterite	Future
yací	yaceré
yaciste	yacerás
yació	yacerá
yacimos	yaceremos
yacisteis	yaceréis
yacieron	yacerán

Perfect indicative	Conditional
he yacido	yacería
has yacido	yacerías
ha yacido	yacería
hemos yacido	yaceríamos
habéis yacido	yaceríais
han yacido	yacerían

Pluperfect indicative	Imperative
había yacido	–
habías yacido	yace; yaz
había yacido	yazca; yazga yaga
habíamos yacido	yazcamos; yazgamos; yagamos
habíais yacido	yaced
habían yacido	yazcan; yazgan; yagan

Irregular English Verbs

Present tense	Past tense	Past participle	Present tense	Past tense	Past participle
arise	arose	arisen	creep	crept	crept
awake	awoke	awaked, awoke	cut	cut	cut
be [I am, you/			deal	dealt	dealt
we/they are,			dig	dug	dug
he/she/it is,			do [he/she/		
gérondif being]	was, were	been	it does]	did	done
bear	bore	borne	draw	drew	drawn
beat	beat	beaten	dream	dreamed,	dreamed,
become	became	become		dreamt	dreamt
begin	began	begun	drink	drank	drunk
behold	beheld	beheld	drive	drove	driven
bend	bent	bent	dwell	dwelt,	dwelt, dwelled
beseech	besought,	besought,		dwelled	
	beseeched	beseeched	eat	ate	eaten
beset	beset	beset	fall	fell	fallen
bet	bet, betted	bet, betted	feed	fed	fed
bid	bade, bid	bid, bidden	feel	felt	felt
bite	bit	bitten	fight	fought	fought
bleed	bled	bled	find	found	found
bless	blessed, blest	blessed, blest	flee	fled	fled
blow	blew	blown	fling	flung	flung
break	broke	broken	fly [he/she/		
breed	bred	bred	it flies]	flew	flown
bring	brought	brought	forbid	forbade	forbidden
build	built	built	forecast	forecast	forecast
burn	burnt,	burnt, burned	forget	forgot	forgotten
	burned		forgive	forgave	forgiven
burst	burst	burst	forsake	forsook	forsaken
buy	bought	bought	forsee	foresaw	foreseen
can	could	(been able)	freeze	froze	frozen
cast	cast	cast	get	got	got, (US) gotten
catch	caught	caught	give	gave	given
choose	chose	chosen	go [he/she/		
cling	clung	clung	it goes]	went	gone
come	came	come	grind	ground	ground
cost	cost	cost	grow	grew	grown

Present tense	Past tense	Past participle	Present tense	Past tense	Past participle
hang	hung, hanged	hung, hanged	sell	sold	sold
have [I/you/			send	sent	sent
we/they have,			set	set	set
he/she/it has,			sew	sewed	sewn, sewed
gérondif having]	had	had	shake	shook	shaken
hear	heard	heard	shall	should	—
hide	hid	hidden	shear	sheared	sheared, shorn
hit	hit	hit	shed	shed	shed
hold	held	held	shine	shone	shone
hurt	hurt	hurt	shoot	shot	shot
keep	kept	kept	show	showed	shown, showed
kneel	knelt	knelt	shrink	shrank	shrunk
know	knew	known	shut	shut	shut
lay	laid	laid	sing	sang	sung
lead	led	led	sink	sank	sunk
lean	leant, leaned	leant, leaned	sit	sat	sat
leap	leapt, leaped	leapt, leaped	slay	slew	slain
learn	learnt, learned	learnt, learned	sleep	slept	slept
leave	left	left	slide	slid	slid
lend	lent	lent	sling	slung	slung
let	let	let	smell	smelt, smelled	smelt, smelled
lie [*gérondif* lying]	lay	lain	sow	sowed	sown, sowed
light	lighted, lit	lighted, lit	speak	spoke	spoken
lose	lost	lost	speed	sped, speeded	sped, speeded
make	made	made	spell	spelt, spelled	spelt, spelled
may	might	—	spend	spent	spent
mean	meant	meant	spill	spilt, spilled	spilt, spilled
meet	met	met	spin	spun	spun
mistake	mistook	mistaken	spit	spat	spat
mow	mowed	mowed, mown	split	split	split
must	(had to)	(had to)	spoil	spoilt	spoilt
overcome	overcame	overcome	spread	spread	spread
pay	paid	paid	spring	sprang	sprung
put	put	put	stand	stood	stood
quit	quit, quitted	quit, quitted	steal	stole	stolen
read	read	read	stick	stuck	stuck
rid	rid	rid	sting	stung	stung
ride	rode	ridden	stink	stank	stunk
ring	rang	rung	stride	strode	stridden
rise	rose	risen	strike	struck	struck
run	ran	run	strive	strove	striven
saw	sawed	sawn, sawed	swear	swore	sworn
say	said	said	sweep	swept	swept
see	saw	seen	swell	swelled	swelled, swollen
seek	sought	sought	swim	swam	swum

Present tense	Past tense	Past participle	Present tense	Past tense	Past participle
swing	swung	swung	wear	wore	worn
take	took	taken	weave	wove,	wove, woven
teach	taught	taught	wed	wedded	wed, wedded
tear	tore	torn	weep	wept	wept
tell	told	told	win	won	won
think	thought	thought	wind	wound	wound
throw	threw	thrown	withdraw	withdrew	withdrawn
thrust	thrust	thrust	withhold	withheld	withheld
tread	trod	trodden, trod	withstand	withstood	withstood
understand	understood	understood	wring	wrung	wrung
upset	upset	upset	write	wrote	written
wake	woke	woken			

Spanish Vocabulary

The Body   El Cuerpo

1

head	la cabeza
hair	los cabellos, el pelo
dark	moreno
fair	rubio
bald	calvo
brown (hair)	castaño
smooth	liso
curly	rizado
grey hair	las cana
scalp	el cuero cabelludo

2

face	la cara
features	los rasgos
forehead	la frente
cheek	la mejilla
wrinkle	la arruga
dimple	el hoyuelo
chin	la barbilla
beautiful	hermoso
handsome	guapo
pretty	bonito

3

ugly	feo
ugliness	la fealdad
beauty	la hermosura
beauty spot	el lunar
freckle	la peca
freckled	pecoso
ear	la oreja
hearing	el oído
to hear	oír
to listen	escuchar

4

listener	el oyente
earlobe	el lóbulo de la oreja
deaf	sordo
mute	mudo
deaf-mute	el sordomudo *m*, la sordomuda *f*
deafness	la sordera
to deafen	ensordecer

deafening	ensordecedor
eardrum	el tímpano
sound	el sonido

5

noise	el ruido
eye	el ojo
sense	el sentido
eyesight	la vista
tear	la lágrima
eyebrow	la ceja
to frown	fruncir las cejas
eyelid	el párpado
eyelash	la pestaña
pupil	la pupila

6

retina	la retina
iris	el iris
glance	la vislumbre
to see	ver
to look	mirar
look	la mirada
visible	visible
invisible	invisible
blind	ciego
blindness	la ceguera

7

to blind	cegar
blind spot	el punto ciego
one-eyed	tuerto
cross-eyed	bizco
to observe	observar
to notice	reparar
expression	la expresión
to smile	sonreír
smile	la sonrisa
to laugh	reír

8

laugh	la risa
laughing *adj*	risueño
mouth	la boca
tongue	la lengua
lip	el labio
tooth	el diente

eyetooth	el colmillo
gum	la encía
palate	el paladar
to say	decir

9

saying	el dicho
to speak	hablar
to shout	gritar
to be quiet	callarse
touch	el tacto
to touch	tocar
to feel	sentir
tactile	táctil
nose	la nariz
nostril	la ventana de la nariz

10

bridge (nose)	el caballete
smell (sense)	el olfato
smell	el olor
to smell (of)	oler (a)
to taste (of)	saber (a)
to taste	probar
taste (sense)	el gusto
taste bud	la papila gustativa
tasty	sabroso
tasting	la degustación

11

moustache	el bigote
beard	la barba
facial hair	el vello facial
sideburns	las patillas
dandruff	la caspa
plait	la trenza
curl	el rizo
to shave	afeitarse
to grow a beard	dejar crecer la barba
bearded	barbudo

12

clean-shaven	rasurado
jaw	la mandíbula
throat	la garganta
neck	el cuello
shoulder	el hombro

back	la espalda
chest	el pecho
breast	el seno
to breathe	respirar
breath	el aliento

13

breathing	la respiración
lung	el pulmón
windpipe	la tráquea
heart	el corazón
heartbeat	el latido (del corazón)
rib	la costilla
side	el costado
limb	el miembro
leg	la pierna
lame	cojo

14

to limp	cojear
thigh	el muslo
calf	la pantorrilla
tendon	el tendón
groin	el ingle
muscle	el músculo
knee	la rodilla
kneecap	la rótula
to kneel	arrodillarse
foot	el pie

15

heel	el talón
toe	el dedo del pie
sole	la planta del pie
ankle	el tobillo
instep	el empeine
arm	el brazo
forearm	el antebrazo
right-handed	diestro
left-handed	zurdo
right	la derecha

16

left	la izquierda
hand	la mano
to handle	manejar
handshake	el apretón (de manos)

handful	el puñado	tall	alto
finger	el dedo	short	bajo, corto
index finger	el (dedo) índice	fat	gordo
thumb	el pulgar	thin	delgado
palm	la palma	strong	fuerte
nail	la uña	strength	la fuerza
		weak	débil

17

wrist	la muñeca	
elbow	el codo	**21**
fist	el puño	

wrist	la muñeca		
elbow	el codo	knock-kneed	patizambo
fist	el puño	bow-legged	estevado
knuckle	el nudillo	to stand	estar de pie
bone	el hueso	to stand up	levantarse
spine	la espina dorsal	to raise	levantar
skeleton	el esqueleto	to lie down	acostarse
skull	el cráneo	to sleep	dormir
blood	la sangre	sleep	el sueño
vein	la vena	to be sleepy	tener sueño
		to dream	soñar

18

artery	la arteria	**22**	
capillary	el capilar	to doze	dormitar
liver	el hígado	to fall asleep	dormirse
skin	la piel	asleep	dormido
pore	el poro	to be awake	estar despierto
sweat	el sudor	to wake up	despertarse
to sweat	sudar	drowsy	somnoliento
scar	la cicatriz	dream	el sueño
wart	la verruga	nightmare	la pesadilla
complexion	la tez	conscious	consciente
		unconscious	inconsciente

19

brain	el cerebro	
kidney	el riñon	
bladder	la vejiga	
spleen	el bazo	

Clothes   La Ropa

brain	el cerebro		
kidney	el riñon	**23**	
bladder	la vejiga	jacket	la chaqueta
spleen	el bazo	trousers	el pantalón
gland	la glándula	jeans	los vaqueros
larynx	la laringe	dungarees	el peto
ligament	el ligamento	overalls	el mono
cartilage	el cartílago	braces	los tirantes
womb	la matriz, el útero	sweater	el suéter
ovary	el ovario	sock	el calcetín
		to darn	remendar
20		raincoat	el impermeable
height	la talla		
big	grande		
small	pequeño		

24

overcoat	el abrigo
to shelter	abrigar
to protect	proteger
hat	el sombrero
shadow	la sombra
brim	las alas
cap	la gorra
glasses	las gafas
earmuffs	las orejeras
walking stick	el bastón

25

umbrella	la paraguas
cloth	la tela, el paño
fine	fino
thick	espeso
coarse	basto
shirt	la camisa
T-shirt	la camiseta
tie	la corbata
handkerchief	el pañuelo
suit	el traje

26

waistcoat	el chaleco
skirt	la falda
miniskirt	la minifalda
blouse	la blusa
stockings	las medias
veil	el velo
beret	la boina
collar	el cuello
gloves	las guantes
belt	el cinturón

27

scarf	la bufanda
handkerchief	el pañuelo
button	el botón
to button	abrochar
to unbutton	desabrochar
new	nuevo
second-hand	de segunda mano
graceful	gracioso
narrow	estrecho
broad	ancho

28

ready-made	hecho
to make	hacer
to get made	mandar hacer
to wear	llevar
to use	usar
worn out	usado
useful	útil
useless	inútil
practical	práctico

29

housecoat	la bata
nightdress	el camisón
pyjamas	el pijama
underpants	los calzoncillos
knickers	las bragas
petticoat	la enagua
slip	la combinación
bra	el sostén, el sujetador
leotard	la malla

30

coat hanger	la percha
zip	la cremallera
wristband	la muñequera
sweatshirt	la sudadera
shorts	el pantalón corto
tracksuit	el chándal
dress	el vestido
to dress	vestir
to dress oneself	vestirse
to take off	quitarse

31

to remove	quitar
to undress	desnudarse
naked	desnudo
to put	poner
to put on	ponerse
sash	la faja
apron	el delantal
shawl	la manta
sleeve	la manga
to sew	coser

32

seam	la costura

seamstress	la costurera
thread	el hilo
needle	la aguja
hole	el agujero
scissors	las tijeras
ribbon	la cinta
linen	el lino
lace	el encaje
velcro	el velcro

33

fur	la piel
furry	afelpado
silk	la seda
silky	sedoso
velvet	el terciopelo
cotton	el algodón
nylon	el nailón
fan	el abanico
in fashion	de moda
out of fashion	pasado de moda

34

dressmaker	la modista
pocket	el bolsillo
bag	la bolsa
pin	el alfiler
to tie	atar
to untie	desatar
to loosen	soltar
sandal	la sandalia
slipper	la pantufla, la zapatilla
pair	el par

35

lace	el lazo
shoe	el zapato
sole	la suela
heel	el tacón
to polish	pulir
shoe polish	el betún
shoehorn	el calzador
boot	la bota
leather	el cuero
rubber	el caucho

36

suede	el ante
barefoot	descalzado
to put on one´s shoes	calzarse
to take off one´s shoes	descalzarse
footwear	el calzado
shoemaker	el zapatero
ring	el anillo
diamond	el diamante
necklace	el collar
bracelet	el brazalete

Family and Relationships   La Familia y Las Relaciones

37

father	el padre
mother	la madre
parents	los padres
son	el hijo
daughter	la hija
children	los hijos
brother	el hermano
sister	la hermana
brotherhood	la hermandad
brotherly	fraternal

38

elder	mayor
younger	menor
husband	el marido
wife	la esposa
uncle	el tío
aunt	la tía
nephew	el sobrino
niece	la sobrina
grandfather	el abuelo
grandmother	la abuela

39

grandparents	los abuelos
grandson	el nieto
granddaughter	la nieta
boy	el chico, el muchacho
girl	la chica, la muchacha
cousin	el primo *m*, la prima *f*

twin	el gemelo		couple	la pareja
baby	el bebé		love	el amor
child	el niño *m*, la niña *f*		to fall in love	enamorarse
to be born	nacer		to marry	casarse con
			wedding	la boda
40			honeymoon	la luna de miel
to grow up	crecer			
name	el nombre		**44**	
surname	el apellido		maternity	la maternidad
birthday	el cumpleaños		paternity	la paternidad
age	la edad		to be pregnant	estar embarazada
old	viejo		to give birth	parir
to get old	envejecer		childbirth	el parto
old man	el viejo		nurse	la nodriza
old woman	la vieja		child minder	la niñera
youth	la juventud		to baby-sit	hacer de canguro
			baby-sitter	el canguro *m*, la
41				canguro *f*
young	joven		godmother	la madrina
young man	el joven			
young woman	la joven		**45**	
father-in-law	el suegro		godfather	el padrino
mother-in-law	la suegra		baptism	el bautismo
son-in-law	el yerno		to baptise	bautizar
daughter-in-law	la nuera		crèche	la guardería
brother-in-law	el cuñado		to breast-feed	dar de pecho
sister-in-law	la cuñada		infancy	la primera infancia
orphan	el huérfano *m*, la		to spoil (child)	mimar
	huérfana *f*		spoiled	mimado
			divorce	el divorcio
42			separation	la separación
stepfather	el padrastro			
stepmother	la madrastra		**46**	
stepson	el hijastro		family planning	la planificación
stepdaughter	la hijastra			familiar
stepbrother	el hermanastro		contraception	la contracepción
stepsister	la hermanastra		contraceptive	el contraconceptivo
bachelor	el soltero		contraceptive pill	la píldora
spinster	la soltera			anticonceptivo
widower	el viudo		condom	el preservativo
widow	la viuda		abortion	el aborto
			to have an abortion	abortar
43			period	la regla, el período
ancestor	el antepasado		to menstruate	menstruar
descendant	el descendiente		to conceive	concebir
boyfriend	el novio			
girlfriend	la novia		**47**	
			middle-aged	de mediana edad

menopause	la menopausia
to retire	jubilarse
pensioner	el pensionista *m*, la pensionista *f*
the aging process	el envejecimiento
old age	la vejez
death	la muerte
to die	morir
dying	moribundo
deathbed	el lecho de muerte

48

dead man	el muerto
dead woman	la muerta
death certificate	el certificado de defunción
mourning	el duelo
burial	el entierro
to bury	enterrar
grave	la tumba, la sepultura
cemetery	el cementerio, el campo santo
wake	el velorio
coffin	el ataúd

49

deceased, late	difunto
to console	consolar
to weep	llorar
to wear mourning	llevar luto
to survive	sobrevivir
survivor	el sobreviviente
crematorium	el crematorio
cremation	la cremación
to cremate	cremar
ashes	las cenizas

Health   La Salud

50

sickness	la enfermedad
nurse	el enfermero *m*, la enfermera *f*
infirmary	la enfermería
sick	enfermo
hospital	el hospital

patient	el paciente
cough	la tos
to cough	toser
to injure	herir
injury	la herida

51

cramp	el calambre
to cut oneself	cortarse
to dislocate	dislocarse
to faint	desmayarse
to be ill	estar enfermo, estar malo
to become ill	ponerse enfermo
to look after	cuidar
care	el cuidado
careful	cuidadoso

52

carelessness	el descuido
careless	descuidado
negligent	negligente
doctor	el médico *m*, la médica *f*
medicine	la medicina
prescription	la receta
pharmacist	el farmacéutico *m*, la farmacéutica *f*
pharmacy	la farmacia
cure	la cura
curable	curable

53

incurable	incurable
to cure	curar
healer	el curador *m*, la curadora *f*
to get well	sanar
healthy	sano
unhealthy	malsano
to recover	restablecerse
pain	el dolor
painful	doloroso
to suffer	padecer

54

| diet | el régimen |
| obesity | la obesidad |

obese	obeso		swollen	hinchado
anorexic	anoréxico		boil	el divieso
anorexia	la anorexia		to bleed	sangrar
obsession	la obsesión		to clot	coagularse
to get fat	engordar		blood cell	la célula sanguínea
headache	el dolor de cabeza		blood group	el grupo sanguíneo
aspirin	la aspirina		blood pressure	la presión sanguínea
migraine	la jaqueca		blood test	el análisis de sangre
			check up	el chequeo

55

toothache	el dolor de muelas
stomach upset	el trastorno estomacal
indigestion	la indigestión
food poisoning	la intoxicación alimenticia
sore throat	el dolor de garganta
hoarse	ronco
pale	pálido
to turn pale	palidecer
to faint	desmayarse
cold (*illness*)	el catarro, el resfriado

59

epidemic	la epidemia
plague	la plaga
allergy	la alergía
allergic	alérgico
angina	la angina
tonsillitis	la amigdalitis
fracture	la fractura
cast	la escayola
crutch	la muleta
wheelchair	la silla de ruedas

56

to catch a cold	resfriarse
wound	la herida
surgeon	el cirujano
to heat	calentar
hot	caliente
temperature	la calentura
perspiration	la transpiración
sweaty	sudoroso
fever	la fiebre
germ	el germen

60

haemophiliac	el hemofílico *m*, la hemofílica
haemophilia	la hemofilia
cholesterol	el colesterol
vitamin	la vitamina
calorie	la caloría
handicapped person	el minusválido
handicap	la minusvalía
pneumonia	la pulmonia
heart attack	el infarto
bypass operation	la operación de bypass

57

microbe	el microbio
contagious	contagioso
vaccine	la vacuna
to shiver	temblar
madness	la locura
mad	loco
drug	la droga
pill	la píldora
to scar	cicatrizarse
stitches	los puntos

61

heart surgery	la cirugía cardíaca
microsurgery	la microcirugía
pacemaker	el marcapasos
heart transplant	el trasplante del corazón
smallpox	la viruela
stroke	la apoplejía
tumour	el tumor
HIV positive	VIH positivo

58

to relieve	aliviar

Health

AIDS	el SIDA
cancer	el cáncer

62

breast cancer	el cáncer de mama
chemotherapy	la quimioterapia
screening	la exploración
diagnosis	el diagnóstico
antibody	el anticuerpo
antibiotic	el antibiótico
depression	la depresión
depressed	deprimido
to depress	deprimir
to undergo	operarse
an operation	

63

painkiller	el analgésico
treatment	el tratamiento
anaesthetic	la anestesia
anaesthetist	el anestesista *m*,
	la anestesista *f*
donor	el donante *m*, la donante *f*
genetic engineering	la ingeniera genética
test-tube baby	el bebé probeta
infertile	estéril
hormone	la hormona

64

psychologist	el psicólogo *m*,
	la psicóloga *f*
psychology	la psicología
psychoanalyst	el psicoanalista *m*,
	la psicoanalista *f*
psychoanalysis	el psicoanálisis
psychosomatic	psicosomático
hypochondriac	hipocondríaco
plastic surgery	la cirugía estética
face-lift	el estiramiento facial
implant	el implante
self-esteem	la autoestima

65

to smoke	fumar
passive smoking	el fumar pasivo
to inhale	inhalar
withdrawal syndrome	el síndrome de
	abstinencia

alcohol	el alcohol
hangover	la resaca
alcoholic	el alcohólico *m*, la
	alcohólica
drug addict	el toxicómano
drug addiction	la toxicomanía
drugs traffic	el narcotráfico

66

heroin	la heroína
cocaine	la cocaína
drugs trafficker	el narcotraficante
to launder money	blanquear el dinero
syringe	la jeringuilla
to inject	inyectar
to take drugs	drogarse
clinic	la clínica
outpatient	el paciente externo
therapy	la terapia

Nature — La Naturaleza

67

world	el mundo
natural	natural
creation	la creación
the Big Bang theory	la teoría de la gran
	explosión
supernatural	sobrenatural
to create	crear
sky	el cielo
galaxy	la galaxia
the Milky Way	la Vía Láctea
the Plough	el carro, la Osa Mayor

68

astronomer	el astrónomo *m*, la
	astrónoma
astronomy	la astronomía
telescope	el telescopio
UFO	OVNI (objeto volante
	no identificado)
light year	el año luz
asteroid	el asteroide
meteor	el meteorito

comet	el cometa		eruption	la erupción
star	la estrella		deserted	desierto
starry	estrellado		desert	el desierto
			plain	la llanura

69

to twinkle	centellear		**73**	
to shine	resplandecer		flat	llano, plano
planet	el planeta		level	el nivel
earth	la Tierra		valley	el valle
Mercury	el Mercurio		hill	la colina
Venus	el Venus		mountain	el monte, la montaña
Mars	el Marte		mountainous	montañoso
Jupiter	el Júpiter		peak	el pico
Saturn	el Saturno		summit	la cumbre, la cima
Neptune	el Neptuno		range of mountains	la cordillera
			crag	el peñasco

70

Uranus	el Urano		**74**	
Pluto	el Plutón		rock	la roca
orbit	la órbita		steep	empinado
to orbit	orbitar		slope	la cuesta
gravity	la gravedad		coast	la costa
satellite	el satélite		coastal	costero
moon	la luna		shore	la orilla
eclipse	el eclipse		beach	la playa
sun	el sol		cliff	el acantilado
sunspot	la mancha solar		sea	el *or* la mar
			tide	la marea

71

ray	el rayo		**75**	
to radiate	radiar		high tide	la pleamar
radiant	radioso		low tide	la bajamar
to shine	brillar		ebb tide	el reflujo
shining	brillante		flood tide	el flujo
brilliancy	el brillo		wave	la ola
sunrise	la salida del sol		foam	la espuma
to rise	salir		tempest	la tempestad
sunset	la puesta del sol		hurricane	el huracán
to set (*sun*)	ponerse		gulf	el golfo
			bay	la bahía

72

dawn	el amanecer		**76**	
to dawn	amanecer		cape	el cabo
dusk	el crepúsculo		straits	el estrecho
to grow dark	anochecer		island	la isla
earthquake	el terremoto		spring,	la fuente
volcano	el volcán		fountain	el surtidor

waterfall	la cascada	rain	la lluvia
stream	el arroyo	rainy	lluvioso
river	el río	to rain	llover
current	la corriente	drop	la gota
draught	la corriente de aire	shower	el chaparrón, el aguacero
		cloud	la nube
77		cloudy	nublado
glacier	el glaciar		
iceberg	el iceberg		
ice cap	el casquete de hielo	**81**	
icefloe	el témpano de hielo	to cloud over	nublarse
to flood	inundar	to clear up	despejar
flood	la inundación	lightning	el relámpago
border	el borde	lightning conductor	el pararrayos
lake	el lago	to flash (*lightning*)	relampaguear
pond	el estanque	sheet lightning	el relámpago fucilazo
marsh	el pantano	fork lightning	el relámpago en zigzag
78		harmful	dañoso
deep	hondo, profundo	to harm	hacer daño
depth	la profundidad	thunder	el trueno
weather	el tiempo		
fine, fair	ameno	**82**	
climate	el clima	to thunder	tronar
barometer	el barómetro	fog	la bruma
thermometer	el termómetro	mist	la niebla
degree	el grado	foggy	brumoso
air	el aire	misty	nebuloso
breeze	la brisa	snow	la nieve
		to snow	nevar
79		snowstorm	la ventisca
cool, fresh	fresco	snowfall	la nevada
wind	el viento	hailstone	el granizo
windy	ventoso		
dampness	la humedad	**83**	
damp	húmedo	to hail	granizar
to wet	mojar	to freeze	helar
wet	mojado	frozen	helado
storm	la tormenta, la borrasca	icicle	el carámbano
		frost	la escarcha
stormy	borrascoso	to thaw	deshelarse
dry	seco	ice	el hielo
		thaw	el deshielo
80		heatwave	la ola de calor
drought	la sequía	sultry	bochornoso
to dry	secar		
rainbow	el arco iris		

Minerals

Los Minerales

84

metal	el metal
mine	la mina
mineral	el mineral
forge	la fragua
to forge	fraguar, forjar
steel	el acero
iron	el hierro
iron *adj*	ferreo
bronze	el bronze
brass	el latón

85

copper	el cobre
tin	el estaño
lead	el plomo
zinc	el zinc
nickel	el níquel
aluminium	el aluminio
silver	el plato
gold	el oro
platinum	el platino
mould	el molde

86

to extract	extraer
to exploit	explotar
miner	el minero
to melt, smelt	fundir
to mould	moldar
rust	la herrumbre
rusty	herrumbroso
to solder	soldar
to alloy	alear
alloy	la aleación

87

stone	la piedra
stony	pedregoso
quarry	la cantera
granite	el granito
to polish	pulir
polished	pulido
smooth	liso
marble	el mármol

lime	la cal
chalk	la creta

88

clay	la arcilla
sulphur	el azufre
jewel	la joya
pearl	la perla
diamond	el diamante
ruby	el rubí
emerald	la esmeralda
mother-of-pearl	el nácar
enamel	el esmalte
sapphire	el zafiro

89

agate	el ágata
opal	el ópalo
lapis-lazuli	el lapislázuli
obsidian	la obsidiana
garnet	el granate
alkali	el álcali
acid	el ácido
acidity	la acidez
plutonium	el plutonio
radium	el radio

Animals

Los Animales

90

domestic	doméstico
tame	manso
cat	el gato
kitten	el gatito
to mew	maullar
feline	felino
claw	la garra
dog	el perro
bitch	la perra
puppy	el cachorro

91

to bark	ladrar
canine	canino
watchful	vigilante
watchdog	el perro guardián

Animals   **Animals**

pet	el animal doméstico	wild, savage	salvaje
breed	la raza	carnivorous	carnicero, carnívoro
greyhound	el galgo	herbivorous	herbívoro
alsatian	el pastor alemán	omnivorous	omnívoro
terrapin	la tortuga de agua dulce	quadruped	el cuádrupedo
		biped	el bípedo
hamster	el hámster	mammal	el mamífero
		warm-blooded	de sangre caliente

92

aquarium	el acuario	**96**	
aquatic	acuático	predator	el depredador
horse	el caballo	prey	la presa
to neigh	relinchar	lion	el león
stallion	el semental	lioness	la leona
mare	la yegua	lion cub	el cachorro de león
colt	el potro	to roar	bramar, rugir
donkey	el asno, el burro	mane	la melena
to bray	rebuznar	tiger	el tigre
mule	el mulo	tigress	la tigresa
		cheetah	el leopardo cazador

93

male	el macho	**97**	
female	la hembra	leopard	el leopardo
livestock	el ganado	lynx	el lince
horn	el cuerno, el asta	mountain lion	la puma
paw	la pata	panther	la pantera
hoof	la pezuña	wolverine	el carcayú
tail	el rabo, la cola	hyaena	la hiena
flock	el rebaño	jackal	el chacal
cow	la vaca	carrion	la carroña
ox	el buey	jaguar	el jaguar
		tapir	el tapir

94

to low	mugir	**98**	
bull	el toro	buffalo	el búfalo
calf	el ternero	mongoose	la mangosta
heifer	la novilla	porcupine	el puerco espín
lamb	el cordero	armadillo	el armadillo
sheep	la oveja	skunk	la mofeta
ram	el carnero	sloth	el perezoso
ewe	la oveja	rhinoceros	el rinoceronte
goat	la cabra	hippopotamus	el hipopótamo
pig	el cerdo, el puerco	wolf	el lobo
		pack	la manada

95

| to grunt | gruñir | **99** | |
| to fatten | cebar | bear | el oso |

319

to hibernate	invernar	hutch	la conejera
zebra	la cebra	rat	la rata
bison	el bisonte	bat	el murciélago
to graze	apacentar	nocturnal	nocturno
pasture	el pasto	primate	el primate
wild boar	el jabalí	gorilla	el gorila
ferocious	feroz	monkey	el mono
bristle	la cerda	orang-utan	el orangután
elephant	el elefante	baboon	el mandril
		chimpanzee	el chimpancé

100

tusk	el comillo	**104**	
trunk	la trompa	gibbon	el gibón
camel	el camello	marsupial	el marsupial
hump	la giba	kangaroo	el canguro
dromedary	el dromedario	koala	la coala
llama	la llama	giant panda	el panda gigante
deer	el ciervo	invertebrate	el invertebrado
doe	la gama	exoskeleton	el dermatoesqueleto
stag	el ciervo	insect	el insecto
elk	el alce	to hum	zumbar
		humming	el zumbido

101

moose	el alce de América	**105**	
antler	la cuerna	antenna	la antena
fox	el zorro	worm	el gusano
cunning	astuto	to worm	serpentear
craft, cunning	la astucia	earthworm	la lombriz
hare	la liebre	tapeworm	la lombriz intestinal
badger	el tejón	parasite	el parásito
otter	la nutria	beetle	el escarabajo
dormouse	el lirón	stag beetle	el ciervo volante
shrew	la musaraña	silkworm	el gusano de seda
		caterpillar	la oruga

102

hedgehog	el erizo	**106**	
weasel	la comadreja	chrysalis	la crisálida
mink	el visón	metamorphosis	la metamorfosis
beaver	el castor	to metamorphose	metamorfosear
dam	la presa	butterfly	la mariposa
mole	el topo	moth	la mariposa nocturna
molehill	la topera	fly	la mosca
mouse	el ratón	bluebottle	la moscarda
mousetrap	la ratonera	spider	la araña
		web	la telaraña

103

rabbit	el conejo	to spin	devanar

VOCABULARY

107
wasp	la avispa
hornet	el avispón
to sting	picar
sting	la picadura
bee	la abeja
worker (*bee, ant*)	la obrera
bumblebee	el abejorro
queen bee	la abeja madre
beehive	la colmena
apiary	el abejar

108
apiarist	el apicultor
drone	el zángano
honey	la miel
honeycomb	el panal
grasshopper	el saltamontes
locust	la langosta
to infest	infestar
cricket	el grillo
glow-worm	la luciérnaga
ant	la hormiga

109
anthill	el hormiguero
colony	la colonia
to itch	hormiguear
itch	el hormigueo
termite	la termita
troublesome	molesto
to molest	molestar
mosquito	el mosquito
mosquito net	el mosquitero
malaria	la malaria

110
flea	la pulga
earwig	la tijereta
praying mantis	la mantis religiosa
scorpion	el escorpión
snail	el caracol
slug	el limaco
louse	el piojo
lousy	piojoso
centipede	el ciempiés
millipede	el milpiés

111
reptile	el reptil
cold-blooded	de sangre fría
tortoise	la tortuga
turtle	la tortuga marina
crocodile	el cocodrilo
alligator	el caimán
serpent	la serpiente
snake	la culebra
slowworm	el lución
harmless	inofensivo

112
crawl	arrastrarse
viper	la víbora
fang	el colmillo
python	el pitón
anaconda	la anaconda
rattlesnake	la serpiente de cascabel
cobra	la cobra
poison	el veneno
antidote	el antídoto
poisonous	venenoso

113
bird	el pájaro
aviary	la avería
ostrich	el avestruz
beak, bill	el pico
wing	el ala
to fly	volar
flight	el vuelo
flightless	incapaz de volar
to lay (eggs)	poner (huevos)
to nest	anidar

114
canary	el canario
robin redbreast	el pitirrojo
chaffinch	el pinzón
nightingale	el ruiseñor
sparrow	el gorrión
swallow	la golondrina
lark	la alondra
cuckoo	el cuclillo
magpie	la urraca

115

blackbird	el mirlo
crow	el cuervo
to caw	graznar
seagull	la gaviota
albatross	el albatros
cormorant	el cormorán
partridge	la perdiz
pheasant	el faisán
stork	la cigüeña
owl	el buho

116

rooster	el gallo
cockcrow	el canto del gallo
to crow	cacarear
cock-a-doodle-do	quiquiriquí
hen	la gallina
feather	la pluma
to pluck	desplumar
chicken	el pollo
to brood	empollar
to breed	criar

117

pigeon	la paloma
duck	el pato
goose	el ganso
swan	el cisne
parrot	el loro
toucan	el tucán
turkey	el pavo
peacock	el pavo real
hummingbird	el colibrí
bird of paradise	la ave del paraíso

118

rapacious	rapaz
bird of prey	el ave de rapiña
eagle	el águila *f*
vulture	el buitre
peregrine falcon	el halcón peregrino
to swoop	abatirse
falcon	el halcón
falconer	el halconero
falconry	la halconería
condor	el cóndor

hawk	el halcón
to hover (*hawk*)	cernerse

119

amphibious	anfibio
amphibian	el anfibio
frog	la rana
bullfrog	la rana toro
tadpole	el renacuajo
toad	el sapo
salamander	la salamandra
crustacean	el crustácep
crab	el cangrejo
prawn	la gamba

120

fish	el pez
goldfish	el pez de colores
piranha	la piraña
voracious	voraz
carp	la carpa
sturgeon	el esturión
caviar	el caviar
trout	la trucha
hake	la merluza
herring	el arenque

121

sardine	la sardina
skate	la raya
cod	el bacalao
eel	la anguila
electric eel	la anguila eléctrica
elver	la angula
salmon	el salmón
school (*fish*)	el cardumen, el banco
coral	el coral
coral reef	el arrecife de coral

122

flipper	la aleta
fin	la aleta
gills	las agallas
shell	la concha
scale	la escama
squid	el calamar
octopus	el pulpo

tentacle	el tentáculo	root	la raíz
cuttlefish	la sepia	to root (*pig etc*)	hozar
crayfish	el ástaco	to take root	arraigar
		to uproot	desarraigar
123		radical	radical
lobster	la langosta	tendril	el zarcillo
sea urchin	el erizo de mar	stalk	el tallo
sea horse	el caballito de mar	sap	la savia
starfish	la estrella de mar		
shellfish	el molusco	**127**	
oyster	la ostra	foliage	el follaje
shark	el tiburón	leaf	la hoja
whale	la ballena	leafy	frondoso
killer whale	la orca	to shed leaves	deshojarse
dolphin	el delfín	deciduous	de hoja caduca
		evergreen	de hoja perenne
124		perennial	perenne
seal	la foca	thorn	la espina
sea lion	el león marino	thorn tree	el espino
walrus	la morsa	thorny	espinoso
natural selection	la selección natural		
survival of the fittest	la supervivencia de los más aptos	**128**	
		weed	la mala hierba
evolution	la evolución	to weed	desherbar
to evolve	evolucionar	to thin	entresacar
zoology	la zoología	thistle	el cardo
zoologist	el zoólogo *m*, la zoóloga *f*	nettle	la ortiga
zoo	el zoo	briar	la zarza
		hemlock	la cicuta
125		deadly nightshade	la belladona
habitat	el habitat	Venus flytrap	la atrapamoscas
extinct	extinto	rush	el junco
dinosaur	el dinosaurio		
mammoth	el mamut	**129**	
dodo	el dodó	reed	la caña
yeti	el yeti	epiphyte	el epifito
mythical	mitíco	moss	el musgo
myth	el mito	spider plant	la malambre
unicorn	el unicornio	bud	el brote, el capullo
dragon	el dragón	to bud	brotar
		flower	la flor
		to flower	florecer
Plants	**Las Plantas**	blooming	florido
		petal	el pétalo
126			
to plant	plantar	**130**	
to transplant	trasplantar	to wither	marchitarse

withered	marchito	crocus	el azafrán
garland	la guirnalda	carnation	el clavel
scent	la fragancia	bluebell	la campanula
garden	el jardín	poppy	la amapola
gardener	el jardinero	cornflower	el alciano
landscape gardener	el jardinero paisajista	buttercup	el botón de oro
to water	regar	daffodil	el narciso
watering can	la regadera	forget-me-not	la no me olvides
irrigation	el riego		

131

herb	la hierba (fina)
thyme	el tomillo
rosemary	el romero
sage	la salivia
parsley	el perejil
mint	la menta
tarragon	el dragoncillo
coriander	el culantro
dill	el eneldo
watercress	el berro

135

foxglove	la dedalera
sunflower	el girasol
dandelion	el diente de león
snapdragon	la boca de dragón
marigold	la caléndula
orchid	la orquídea
bush	el arbusto
magnolia	la magnolia
fuchsia	la fucsia
rhododendron	el rododendro

132

balsam	el bálsamo
chicory	la escarola
chive	el cebollino
mustard	la mostaza
basil	la albahaca
clover	el trébol
grass	la hierba
shrub	el arbusto
myrtle	el mirto
gorse	la aulaga

136

rock plant	la planta rupestre
heather	el brezo
undergrowth	la maleza
scrub	el monte bajo
broom	la hiniesta
mallow	la malva
laurel	el laurel
privet	el ligustro
hedge	el seto
to enclose	cercar

133

flowerbed	el arriate
pansy	el pensamiento
primrose	la prímula
daisy	la margarita
anemone	la anemona
tulip	el tulipán
hyacinth	el jacinto
lily	el lirio
lily of the valley	el muguete
mignonette	la reseda

137

vegetables	las hortalizas
kitchen garden	el huerto
mushroom	la seta
fungus	el hongo
harmful	nocivo
leek	el puerro
radish	el rábano
lettuce	la lechuga
celery	el apio
rhubarb	el ruibarbo

134

snowdrop	la campanilla blanca

138

chard	la acelga

spinach	la espinaca
turnip	el nabo
potato	la patata
to peel	pelar
to scrape	raspar
husk	la vaina
to husk	desvainar
cabbage	la berza, la col
hedge	el seto

139

fruit	la fruta
fruit tree	el árbol frutal
to graft	injertar
graft	el injerto
to shake	sacudir
to prune	podar
pear tree	el peral
pear	la pera
apple tree	el manzano
cherry tree	el cerezo

140

cherry	la cereza
plum	la ciruela
plum tree	el ciruelo
prune	la ciruela seca
stone	el hueso
to stone	deshuesar
almond	la almendra
almond tree	el almendro
peach	el melocotón
peach tree	el melocotonero

141

apricot	el albaricoque
apricot tree	el albaricoquero
walnut	la nuez
walnut tree	el nogal
chestnut	la castaña
chestnut tree	el castaño
hazelnut	la avellana
hazelnut tree	el avellano
lemon	el limón
lemon tree	el limonero

142

orange	la naranja
orange tree	el naranjo
olive	la aceituna
olive tree	el olivo
date	el dátil
palm tree	la palmera, la palma
pomegranate	la granada
pomegranate tree	el granado
banana tree	el plátano
pineapple	el ananá

143

coconut	el coco
coconut tree	el cocotero
sugar cane	la caña de azúcar
yam	la batata
lychee	el lychee
kiwi	el kiwi
ripe	maduro
to ripen	madurar
juicy	suculento
strawberry	la fresa

144

strawberry plant	el fresal
medlar	la níspola
medlar tree	el níspero
raspberry	la frambuesa
raspberry bush	el frambueso
blackcurrant	la grosella
currant bush	el grosellero
gooseberry	la uva espina
grape	la uva
raisin	la pasa

145

vine	la vid
vineyard	la viña, el viñedo
vintner	el viñero
grape harvest	la vendimia
to gather grapes	vendimiar
press	la prensa
to press	prensar
forest trees	los árboles de bosque
wood	el bosque
jungle	la selva

146

woody	silvoso
wild, uncultivated	silvestre
ivy	la hiedra
to climb	trepar
creeping	trepador
wisteria	la glicina
mistletoe	el muérdago
berry	la baya
rosewood	el palosanto
juniper	el enebro
fern	el helecho

147

tree	el árbol
bark	la corteza
branch	la rama
twig	la ramita
knot	el nudo
tree ring	el anillo de árbol
trunk	el tronco
oak	el roble
acorn	la bellota
holm oak	la encina

148

beech	el haya
ash	el fresno
elm	el olmo
poplar	el álamo
aspen	el álamo temblón
lime	el tilo
birch	el abedul
fir	el abeto
conifer	la conífera
coniferous	conífero

149

cone	el cono
pine	el pino
hop	el lúpulo
monkey puzzle	la araucaria
sycamore	el sicomoro
maple	el arce
holly	el acebo
alder	el aliso
bamboo	el bambú
eucalyptus	el eucalipto

150

acacia	la acacia
rubber tree	el caucho
mahogany	la caoba
ebony	el ébano
cedar	el cedro
cactus	el cactus
cacao tree	el cacao
giant sequoia	la secuoya gigante
bonsai	el bonsai
yew	el tejo

151

weeping willow	el sauce llorón
azalea	la azalea
catkin	el amento
spore	la espora
pollination	la polinización
to pollinate	polinizar
pollen	el polen
to fertilise	fecundar
stock (*species*)	el alhelí
hybrid	el híbrido

The Environment   El Medio Ambiente

152

environmental	medioambiental
environmentalist	el ambientalista *m*, la ambientalista *f*
environmentalism	el ambientalismo
pollution	la contaminación
conserve	conservar
conservation	la conservación
waste	el despilfarro
to waste	despilfarrar
rubbish	la basura
rubbish tip	el vertedero

153

sewage	las aguas residuales
spill	el vertido
poisonous	venenoso
to poison	envenenar
industrial waste	los residuos industriales

toxic	tóxico
pollutant	el contaminante
to pollute	contaminar
consumerism	el consumismo
consumerist	consumista

154

to consume	consumir
solar panel	el placa solar
windmill	el molino
wind energy	la energía eólica
wave energy	la energía de las ondas
wildlife	la fauna
harmful	nocivo
atmosphere	la atmósfera
smog	la niebla tóxica
unleaded petrol	la gasolina sin plomo

155

ecosystem	el ecosistema
ecology	la ecología
ecologist	el ecologista
acid rain	la lluvia ácida
deforestation	la deforestación
to deforest	deforestar
rainforest	la selva
underdeveloped	subdesarrollado
industrialised	industrializado
ozone layer	la capa de ozono

156

oil slick	la marea negra
oil spill	la fuga de petróleo
greenhouse effect	el efecto invernadero
to recycle	reciclar
recycling	el reciclaje
renewable	renovable
fossil fuels	los combustibles fósiles
resource	el recurso
landfill	el vertedero de basuras
to waste	despilfarrar

157

decibel	el decibel
to soundproof	insonorizar
radiation	la radiación

radioactive	radioactivo
nuclear energy	la energía nuclear
fallout	el polvillo radiactivo
reactor	el reactor
fission	la fisión
fusion	la fusión
leak	la fuga

The Home   La Casa

158

house	la casa
apartment block	el edificio de pisos
to let	alquilar
tenant	el inquilino
housing	el alojamiento
to change	mudar
to move house	mudarse
landlord, owner	el dueño, el propietario
own	propio
ownership	la propiedad

159

country house	la casa de campo
farmhouse	el caserío, la quinta
villa	el chalet
cottage	la casita, la choza
chalet	el chalet
terraced house	la casa adosada
semi-detached house	la casa pareada
country house	la casa solariega
mansion	la mansión
palace	el palacio

160

castle	el castillo
igloo	el iglú
teepee	el tipi
log cabin	la cabina de troncos
houseboat	el bote-vivienda
hut	la casilla
house trailer	la casa rodante
penthouse	la casa de azotea
lighthouse	el faro
shack	la casucha

161

building	el edificio, la construcción
to build	edificar, construir
building site	la obra
building contractor	el contratista
repair	reparar
solid	sólido
to destroy	destruir
to demolish	derribar
garage	el garaje
shed	el cobertizo

162

door	la puerta
doorknocker	la aldaba
to knock at the door	llamar a la puerta
doormat	el felpudo
doorbell	el timbre
threshold	el umbral
bolt	el cerrojo
plan	el plan
foundations	las fundaciones
to found	fundar

163

cement	el cemento
concrete	el hormigón
stone	la piedra
cornerstone	la piedra angular
antiquated	antiguo
modern	moderno
luxurious	lujoso
roomy	espacioso
whitewashed	blanqueado
neglected	descuidado

164

worm-eaten	carcomido
moth-eaten	apollillado
shanty	la chabola
shantytown	la barriada
brick	el ladrillo
sand	la arena
slate	la pizarra
gutter	la canaleta
drainpipe	el caño de desagüe
step	el peldaño

165

plaster	el yeso
skirting	el zócalo
floor	el suelo
wall	el muro
partition wall	la pared
wood	la madera
board	la tabla
beam	la viga
to sustain	sostener
to contain	contener

166

facade	la fachada
outside	el exterior
inside	el interior
window	la ventana
windowsill	el alféizar
venetian blind	la celosía
shutter	la persiana
balcony	el balcón
windowpanes	los cristales
glass	el vidrio

167

porch	el pórtico
door	la puerta
hinge	el gozne
front door	el portal
doorkeeper	el portero
to open	abrir
opening	la abertura
entrance	la entrada
to enter	entrar (en)
to go out	salir

168

way out	la salida
lock	la cerradura
to shut	cerrar
key	la llave
to lock	cerrar con llave
padlock	el candado
staircase	la escalera
upstairs	escalera arriba
downstairs	escalera abajo
landing	el rellano

169

ladder	la escala
banisters	la barandilla
lift	el ascensor
to go up	subir
to ascend	ascender
ascent	la subida
to go down	bajar
descent	la bajada
low	bajo
storeys	los pisos

170

ground floor	el piso bajo
first floor	el piso principal
cellar	la bodega
tile	la teja
roof	el tejado, el techo
ceiling	el techo
floor	el suelo
to turn	girar
to return	volver
return	la vuelta

171

to give back	devolver
chimney	la chimenea
hearth	el hogar
fire	el fuego
spark	la chispa
to sparkle	chispear
flame	la llama
ashes	las cenizas
stove	la estufa
smoke	el humo

172

to smoke (*of fire*)	humear
to burn	quemar
to blaze	arder
ardent	ardiente
coal	el carbón
charcoal	el carbón de leña
embers	el rescoldo
to scorch	abrasar
to glow	resplandecer
firewood	la leña

173

woodcutter	el leñador
shovel	la pala
poker	el hurgón
to poke	atizar
matches	los fósforos, las cerillas
wax	la cera
to light	encender
box	la caja
drawer	el cajón
chest of drawers	la cómoda

174

comfortable	cómodo
uncomfortable	incómodo
lighting	el alumbrado
dazzle, splendour	la lumbre
to light up	alumbrar
to put out, extinguish	apagar
light	la luz
lamp	la lámpara
lampshade	la pantalla
wick	la torcida, la mecha

175

candle	la candela
candlestick	el candelero
room	el cuarto, la habitación
to inhabit	habitar
inhabitant	el habitante
to reside	morar
residence	la morada
hall (*large room*)	la sala
furniture	los muebles
a piece of furniture	un mueble

176

furnished	amueblado
corridor	el pasillo
hall, lobby	el vestíbulo
hall stand	el perchero
sitting room	la sala de estar
lounge	el salón
to serve	servir
guest	el invitado, el convidado

to invite	invitar	floor tile	la baldosa
table	la mesa	tiling	el embaldosado
		picture	el cuadro

177

seat	el asiento	**181**	
to sit down	sentarse	frame	el marco
to be sitting	estar sentado	portrait	el retrato
cushion	el cojín	photograph	la fotografía
stool	el taburete	photograph album	el álbum fotográfico
chair	la silla	dining room	el comedor
armchair	el sillón, la butaca	to eat, dine	comer
rocking chair	la mecedora	meals	las comidas
sofa	el sofá	breakfast	el desayuno
couch	el canapé	to breakfast	desayunar
bench	el banco	lunch	el almuerzo

178

bookcase	la estantería	**182**	
bookshelf	el estante	dinner	la comida
bookrest	el atril	to lunch	almorzar
library	la biblioteca	supper	la cena
office, study	el despacho	to have supper	cenar
writing desk	el escritorio, el bufete	sideboard	el aparador
to write	escribir	larder	la alacena
handwriting	la escritura	pantry	la despensa
paper	el papel	shelf	el anaquel, la balda
		cup	la taza
		draining board	el escurridero

179

record-player	el tocadiscos	**183**	
LP	el elepé	sugarbowl	el azucarero
hi-fi	la alta fidelidad	coffeepot	la cafetera
television	la televisión	teapot	la tetera
video recorder	el aparato de video	tray	la bandeja
radiator	el radiador	table service	el servicio de mesa
radio	la radio	tablecloth	el mantel
ornament	un adorno	napkin	la servilleta
clock	el reloj	plate	el plato
grandfather clock	el reloj de pie	saucer	el platillo
		serving dish	la fuente

180

tapestry	la tapicería	**184**	
a tapestry	un tapiz	microwave	el microondas
to hang	colgar	to microwave	calentar en
to take down	descolgar		microondas
wallpaper	el papel pintado	food mixer	el robot de cocina
to wallpaper	empapelar	refrigerator	el refrigerador
tile (*decorative*)	el azulejo	grater	el rallador

flower-pot	el florero
(drinking) glass	el vaso, la copa
glassware	la cristalería
to cook	cocinar
to boil	cocer

185

gas cooker	la cocina de gas
electric cooker	la cocina éléctrica
grill	el grill
barbecue grill	la parrilla
saucepan	la cacerola
refuse, rubbish	la basura
washing machine	la lavadora
sewing machine	la máquina de coser
washing powder	el detergente
vacuum cleaner	la aspiradora

186

electricity	la electricidad
fusebox	la caja de fusibles
central heating	la calefacción central
light bulb	la bombilla
switch	el interruptor
to switch on	encender
to switch off	apagar
plug	el enchufe
socket	la toma de corriente
air conditioning	el aire acondicionado

187

lid, cover	la tapa
to cover	tapar
to uncover	destapar
to uncork	descorchar
crockery	la vajilla
to cover	cubrir
discover	descubrir
spoon	la cuchara
teaspoon	la cucharita
spoonful	la cucharada

188

fork	el tenedor
cutlery	la cuchillería
set of cutlery	los cubiertos
knife	el cuchillo

to carve (meat)	trinchar
to cut	cortar
sharp	cortante
bottle	la botella
cork	el corcho
corkscrew	el sacacorchos

189

to pull out	sacar
to drink	beber
beverage, drink	la bebida
to toast (*health*)	brindar
oven	el horno
utensils	los utensilios
saucepan	la cacerola
frying pan	la sartén
pot	el puchero, la olla
pitcher	el cántaro

190

bucket	el cubo
to pour out	verter
basket	el cesto
to fill	llenar
full	lleno
empty	vacío
to empty	vaciar
broom	la escoba
to sweep	barrer
to rub, scrub	frotar

191

to wash (*dishes*)	fregar
bedroom	el dormitorio, la alcoba
to go to bed	acostarse
bed	la cama
bedspread	la cubrecama
bunk bed	la litera
cot	la cuna
mattress	el colchón
sheets	las sábanas
electric blanket	la manta eléctrica

192

bolster	el cabezal
pillow	la almohada
carpet	la alfombra

rug, mat	el tapete
to wake	despertar
to awake	despertarse
to get up early	madrugar
the early hours	la madrugada
curtain	la cortina
attic	la buhardilla

193

alarm clock	el despertador
hot-water bottle	la bolsa de agua caliente
nightcap	el gorro de dormir
to sleepwalk	pasearse dormido
sleepwalker	el sonámbulo *m*, la sonámbua *f*
sleepwalking	el sonambulismo
wardrobe	el guardaropa
to keep, preserve	guardar
dressing table	el tocador
screen	el biombo

194

bathroom	el cuarto de baño
bath	el baño
bathtub	la bañera
to bathe	bañarse
to wash	lavar
to wash oneself	lavarse
towel	la toalla
washbasin	el lavabo
shower	la ducha
to take a share	ducharse

195

tap	el grifo
to turn on (tap)	abrir (el grifo)
to turn off (tap)	cerrar (el grifo)
sponge	la esponja
facecloth	el paño
toothbrush	el cepillo de dientes
toothpaste	el dentífrico
toothpick	el palillo
toilet paper	el papel higiénico
toilet bowl	el inodoro

196

soap	el jabón

shampoo	el champú
makeup	el maquillaje
face cream	la crema de belleza
face pack	la mascarilla
compact	la polvera
lipstick	la barra de labios
nail file	la lima de uñas
nail clippers	el cortauñas
nail varnish	el esmalte de uñas

197

hairpin	la horquilla
hairdryer	el secador
hairspray	el fijador
hairslide	el pasador
hairpiece	el postizo
hairnet	la redecilla
to wipe	enjugar
to clean	limpiar
clean	limpio
dirty	sucio

198

mirror	el espejo
basin	la palangana, la jofaina
jug	el jarro
razor (cutthroat)	la navaja
smoke detector	el detector de humo
razorblade	la hoja de afeitar
electric razor	la máquina de afeitar
shaving foam	la espuma de afeitar
comb	el peine
to comb (oneself)	peinarse

199

tools	las herramientas
saw	la sierra
to saw	aserrar
drill	el taladro
drill bit	la broca
sawdust	el serrín
hammer	el martillo
nail	el clavo
to nail	clavar
spade	la pala
pickaxe	el pico

200

screw	el tornillo
screwdriver	el destornillador
axe	la hacha
paint	la pintura
paintbrush	la brocha
to paint	pintar
glue	la cola
to glue, stick	pegar
sander	el lijadora
sandpaper	el papel de lija

Society   La Sociedad

201

street	la calle
walk, promenade	el paseo
to go for a walk	pasear
passer-by	el transeúnte
avenue	la avenida
kiosk	el quiosco
native of	natural de, oriundo de
compatriot	el compatriota
pavement	la acera
gutter	la cuneta

202

road	el camino
high road	la carretera
street lamp	el farol
traffic	la circulación
frequented	frecuentado
to frequent	frecuentar
pedestrian	el peatón
pedestrian area	la zona peatonal
square	la plaza
park	el parque

203

crossroads	el cruce
corner	la esquina, el rincón
alley	el callejón
quarter (of town)	el barrio
slum	el barrio bajo
outskirts	los alrededores
around	alrededor de

dormitory town	la ciudad dormitoria
premises	el local
warehouse	el almacén

204

cul-de-sac	el callejón sin salida
one-way	único sentido
traffic jam	el embotellamiento
rush hour	la hora punta
zebra crossing	el paso de cebra
shop window	el escaparate
poster	el cartel
bus stop	la parada de autobús
to queue	hacer cola
routine	la rutina

205

shop	la tienda
shopkeeper	el tendero
counter	el mostrador
to show	mostrar
inn	la posada, la fonda
innkeeper	el posadero
to stay	quedarse
lodging house	la pensión
guest	el huésped
board and lodgings	comida y alojamiento

206

profession	la profesión
trade	el oficio
mechanic	el mecánico
engineer	el ingeniero
spinner	el hilandero
workman	el obrero
operative	el operario
apprentice	el aprendiz
apprenticeship	el aprendizaje
day labourer	el jornalero

207

fireman	el bombero
fire station	la estación de bomberos
fire hydrant	la boca de riego
shop assistant	el dependiente
fishmonger	el pescadero

fishmonger's	la pescadería	blacksmith	el herrero
street sweeper	el barrendero	horseshoe	la herradura
library	la biblioteca	to shoe (horses)	herrar
librarian	el bibliotecario	shepherd	el pastor
notary	el notario	cowboy	el vaquero

208

policeman	el policía
police (force)	la policía
police station	la comisaría
secretary	el secretario
plumber	el plomero
jeweller	el joyero
stonecutter	el picapedrero
hatter	el sombrerero
hatter's shop	la sombrerería

209

carpenter	el carpintero
ironmonger	el quincallero
miller	el molinero
mill	el molino
to grind	moler
baker	el panadero
to knead	amasar
bakery	la panadería
barber	el peluquero
barbershop	la peluquería

210

tobacconist	el estanquero
tobacconist's	el estanco
rag-and-bone-man	el trapero
tailor	el sastre
tailor's	la sastrería
butcher	el carnicero
butcher's	la carnicería
milkman	el lechero
dairy	la lechería
glazier	el vidriero

211

bricklayer	el albañil
stationer	el papelero
stationer's shop	la papelería
upholsterer	el tapicero
photographer	el fotógrafo

212

farm	la finca, la granja
to lease	arrendar
country estate	la hacienda
courtyard	el patio
well	el pozo
stable	la cuadra, el establo
hayfork	la horca
straw	la paja
hay	el heno
grain	el grano

213

agriculture	la agricultura
agricultural	agrícola
rustic	campestre
countryside	el campo
peasant	el campesino
farmer	el agricultor, el granjero
to cultivate	cultivar
cultivation	el cultivo
tillage	la labranza
to plough	arar

214

plough	el arado
furrow	el surco
fertiliser	el abono
to fertilise (crop)	abonar
fertile	fértil
barren	estéril
dry	arido
to sow	sembrar
seed	la semilla, la simiente
sowing	la siembra

215

to scatter	esparcir
to germinate	germinar
to mow	segar

reaper	el segador		comercio
reaping machine	la segadora	branch	la sucursal
combine harvester	la cosechadora	export	la exportación
sickle	la hoz	import	la importación
scythe	la guadaña	company	la sociedad, la
to harvest	cosechar		compañia
harvest	la cosecha	partner	el socio
		to associate	asociar
216		businessman	el comerciante, el
rake	el rastrillo		negociante
to rake	rastrillar	business	el negocio
spade	la pala		
to dig	cavar	**220**	
hoe	la azada	subject	el asunto
meadow	el prado	to offer	ofrecer
silage	el ensilaje	offer	la oferta
wheat	el trigo	demand	la demanda
oats	la avena	account	la cuenta
barley	la cebada	current account	la cuenta corriente
ear (of wheat)	la espiga	to settle	arreglar
		order	el pedido
217		to cancel	anular
maize	la maíz	on credit	a crédito
rice	el arroz		
alfalfa	la alfalfa	**221**	
pile	el montón	by instalments	a plazos
to pile up	amontonar	for cash	al contado
tractor	el tractor	market	el mercado
harrow	la rastra	deposit	el depósito
baler	la empacadora	goods	la mercancía, los
rotovator	el motocultor		géneros
milking machine	la ordeñadora	bargain	la ganga
		second-hand	de ocasión
218		cheap	barato
to milk	ordeñar	expensive	caro
stockbreeder	el ganadero	to bargain, haggle	regatear
stockbreeding	la ganadería		
fodder, feed	el pienso	**222**	
to irrigate	regar	packaging	el embalaje
greenhouse	el invernadero	to pack up	embalar
subsidy	el subsidio	to unpack	desembalar
grape harvest	la vendimia	to wrap	envolver
grape picker	el vendimiador	to unwrap	desenvolver
		transport	el transporte
219		to transport	transportar
commerce	el comercio	carriage	el porte
firm	la firma, la casa de	portable	portátil
		delivery	la entrega

223

to deliver	entregar
to dispatch	despachar
office	la oficina
manager	el gerente *m*, la gerente *f*
accountant	el contable
clerk	el dependiente
to employ	emplear
employee	el empleado
employment	el empleo

224

employer	el empleador
unemployment	el desempleo, el paro
unemployed	desempleado, parado
chief	el jefe
typewriter	la máquina de escribir
typist	el mecanógrafo *m*, la mecanógrafa *f*
typing	la mecanografía
shorthand	la taquigrafía
shorthand typist	el taquimecanógrafo *m*, la taquimecanó-grafa *f*
audiotypist	el audiomecanógrafo *m*, la audiomecanó-grafa *f*

225

director	el director, la director
managing director	el director gerente
board of directors	la junta directiva
shareholder	el accionista
dividend	el dividendo
takeover	la adquisición
to list (*shares*)	cotizar
asset	el activo
liability	el pasivo
contract	el contrato

226

purchase	la compra
to buy	comprar
to sell	vender
sale	la venta
buyer	el comprador
seller	el vendedor
wholesale	(al) por mayor
retail	(al) por menor
auction	la subasta
to bid	pujar

227

to auction	subastar
client	el cliente
clientele	la clientela
catalogue	el catálogo
price	el precio
quantity	la cantidad
gross	bruto
net	neto
to cost	costar
cost	el coste, el costo

228

free of charge	gratuito
to pay	pagar
wages	el sueldo, la paga
salary	el salario
payment	el pago
in advance	adelantado
invoice	la factura
checkout	la caja
cashier	el cajero *m*, la cajera *f*
accounts	la contabilidad

229

balance sheet	el balance general
income	los ingresos
expenditure	los gastos
to spend	gastar
to acknowledge receipt	acusar recibo
to receive	recibir
reception	el recibimiento
profit	la ganancia, el beneficio
loss	la pérdida
loan	el préstamo

230

to borrow	pedir prestado
to lend	prestar
to prepare	preparar, aprestar

to obtain	lograr
creditor	el acreedor
debt	la deuda
debtor	el deudor
to get into debt	endeudarse
to be in debt	estar en deuda
bankruptcy	la quiebra

231

to go bankrupt	quebrar
bankruptcy	la quiebra
banking	la banca
bank	el banco
banknote	el billete de banco
banker	el banquero
bankbook	la libreta de ahorros
bankcard	la tarjeta de crédito
bank account	la cuenta bancaria
savings bank	la caja de ahorros

232

to save (*money*)	economizar, ahorrar
capital	el capital
interest	el interés
income	la renta
stock exchange	la bolsa
share	la acción
shareholder	el accionista
exchange	el cambio
rate	el tipo
to exchange	cambiar

233

to be worth	valer
value	el valor
to value	valuar
discount	el descuento
to deduct	rebajar
to cash a cheque	cobrar un cheque
payable on sight	pagadero a la vista
signature	la firma
to sign	firmar
draft	el giro

234

postal order	el giro postal
to fall due	vencer

due	vencido
date	la fecha
to date	fechar
to inform	avisar
warning	el aviso
coin	la moneda
money	el dinero
mint	la casa de la moneda

235

post office	el correos
mail	el correo
by return of post	a vuelta de correo
postcard	la tarjeta (postal)
letter	la carta
postman	el cartero
letterbox	el buzón
collection	la recogida
to collect	recoger
delivery	el reparto

236

to distribute	distribuir
envelope	el sobre
postage	el franqueo
to frank	franquear
to seal	sellar
stamp	el sello
postmark	el matasellos
to stamp	timbrar
to pack	empaquetar
to unpack	desempaquetar

237

to register	certificar
to forward	expedir
sender	el remitente
addressee	el destinario
unknown	desconocido
to send	enviar
price list	la tarifa
courier	el mensajero
air mail	el correo aéreo
by airmail	por avión

238

pound sterling	la libra esterlina

franc	el franco
mark	el marco
dollar	el dólar
penny	el penique
shilling	el chelín
ingot	el lingote
foreign currencies	las divisas
speculation	la especulación
speculator	el especulador

239

wealthy	adinerado
wealth	la riqueza, el caudal
rich	rico
to get rich	enriquecerse
to acquire	adquirir
to possess	poseer
fortune	la fortuna
fortunate	afortunado
poverty	la pobreza
poor	pobre
necessity	la necesidad, el menester

240

to need	necesitar
misery	la miseria
miserable	miserable
beggar	el mendigo
to beg	mendigar
homeless	sin techo
squatter	el ocupa *m*, la ocupa *f*
eviction	el desalojo
malnourished	desnutrido
disadvantaged	desfavorecido

241

industry	la industria
industrialist	el industrial
manufacture	la manufactura, la fabricación
to manufacture	fabricar
factory	la fábrica
manufacturer	el fabricante
trademark	la marca (de fábrica)
machine	la máquina
machinery	la maquinaria
to undertake	emprender

242

enterprise	la empresa
expert	el perito
skill	la pericia
skilful	diestro, hábil
ability	la habilidad
clumsy	torpe
to keep busy	occuparse
busy	ocupado
lazy	perezoso
strike	la huelga

243

striker	el huelgista
lock-out	el cierre patronal
blackleg	el rompehuelgas
picket	el piquete
to go on strike	hacer huelga
trade union	el sindicato
trade unionist	el sindicalista *m*, la sindicalista *f*
trade unionism	el sindicalismo
minimum wage	el salario mínimo
market economy	la economía de mercado

244

government	el gobierno
to govern	gobernar
politics	la política
political	político
politician	el político
socialist	socialista
conservative	conservador
fascist	fascista
communist	comunista

245

monarchy	la monarquía
monarch	el monarca
king	el rey
queen	la reina
viceroy	el virrey
to reign	reinar
royal	real
crown	la corona

to crown	coronar
throne	el trono

246

court	la corte
courtier	el cortesano
chancellor	el canciller
rank	el rango
prince	el príncipe
princess	la princesa
title	el título
subject	el súbdito
emperor	el emperador
empress	la emperatriz

247

revolution	la revolución
guillotine	la guillotina
to guillotine	guillotinar
counterrevolution	la contrarrevolución
aristocracy	la aristocracia
aristocrat	el aristócrata *m*, la aristócrata
confiscate	confiscar
confiscation	la confiscación
secular	secular
secularisation	la secularización

248

republic	la república
republican	republicano
president	el presidente
embassy	la embajada
ambassador	el embajador
consul	el cónsul
consulate	el consulado
state	el estado
city state	la ciudad estado
councillor	el consejero

249

council	el consejo
to advise	aconsejar
to administer	administrar
minister	el ministro
ministry	el ministerio
cabinet	el gabinete

deputy	el diputado
parliament	el parlamento, las cortes (*Spain*)
senate	el senado
senator	el senador

250

session	la sesión
to deliberate	deliberar
dialogue	el dialógo
discuss	discutir
adopt	adoptar
decree	el decreto
to decree	decretar
to proclaim	proclamar
election	la elección
referendum	el referéndum

251

to elect	elegir
to vote	votar
vote	el voto
town council	el ayuntamiento
mayor	el alcalde
bailiff	el alguacil
justice	la justicia
just	justo
unjust	injusto
judge	el juez

252

to judge	juzgar
court	el juzgado
judgment	el juicio
injury	el perjuicio
to protect	proteger
law	la ley
legal	legal
illegal	ilegal
to bequeath	legar
beneficiary	el beneficiario

253

to make a will	testar
will	el testamento
heir	el heredero
heiress	la heredera

to inherit	heredar	traitor	el traidor
inheritance	la herencia	treason	la traición
tribunal	el tribunal	fraud	el fraude
to summons	citar, emplazar	bigamy	la bigamía
summons	la citación	bigamist	el bígamo
appointment	la cita	assault	la agresión, el asalto
		blackmail	el chantaje
254		to blackmail	chantajear
trial	el proceso		
lawsuit	el pleito	**258**	
lawyer	el abogado	rape	la violación
to advocate	abogar	rapist	el violador
to swear	jurar	guilty	culpable
oath	el juramento	innocent	inocente
witness	un testigo	defence	la defensa
to bear witness	atestiguar	to defend	defender
testimony	el testimonio	to prohibit	prohibir
evidence	las pruebas	acquittal	la absolución
		to acquit	absolver
255			
to infringe	infringir, transgredir	**259**	
indictment	la acusación	sentence	el dictamen, la sentencia
to plead	alegar		
to accuse	acusar	to sentence	sentenciar, fallar
accused	el acusado, el reo	verdict	el fallo
plaintiff	el demandante	fine	la multa
defendant	el demandado	conviction	la condena
to sue	demandar	to condemn	condenar
fault	la culpa	prison	la cárcel, la prisión
jury	el jurado	to imprison	encarcelar
		prisoner	el preso, el prisionero
256		to arrest	detener
crime	el crimen		
murderer	el asesino	**260**	
to murder	asesinar	capital punishment	la pena de muerte
murder	el asesinato	executioner	el verdugo
to kill	matar	gallows	la horca
suicide	el suicidio (*act*), el suicida (*person*)	firing squad	el pelotón de fusilamiento
to commit	cometer	electric chair	la silla eléctrica
offence	el delito	pardon	el indulto
thief	el ladrón	remission	la remisión
bandit	el bandido	parole	la libertad condicional
		false imprisonment	la detención ilegal
257		self-defence	la defensa propia
theft	el robo		
to steal	robar	**261**	
		army	el ejército

to drill	ejercitar
military	militar
soldier	el soldado
conscription	la conscripción
conscript	el quinto
conscientious objector	el objetor de conciencia
recruit	el recluta
flag	la bandera
troops	la tropa

262

officer	el oficial
sergeant	el sargento
corporal	el cabo
rank	el grado
general	el general
colonel	el coronel
captain	el capitán
lieutenant	el teniente
discipline	la disciplina
order	la orden

263

disorder	el desorden
infantry	la infantería
cavalry	la caballería
artillery	la artillería
cannon	el cañón
grenade	la granada
to explode	estallar
gunpowder	la pólvora
ammunition	las municiones
bomb	la bomba

264

to shell	bombardear
bombardment	el bombardeo
guard, watch	la guardia
sentry	el centinela
garrison	la guarnición
barracks	el cuartel
regiment	el regimiento
detachment	el destacamento
reinforcement	el refuerzo
battalion	el batallón

265

to equip	equipar
equipment	el equipaje
uniform	el uniforme
flak jacket	el chaleco antibala
firearm	el arma f de fuego
to arm	armar
to disarm	desarmar
to load	cargar
to unload	descargar
to shoot	fusilar

266

shot	el disparo
bullet	la bala
bulletproof	antibalas
cartridge	el cartucho
revolver	el revólver
bayonet	la bayoneta
dagger	el puñal
tank	el tanque
armoured car	el coche blindado
barbed wire	el alambre de púas

267

cold war	la guerra fría
superpower	la superpotencia
rocket	el cohete
nuclear warhead	la ojiva nuclear
blockade	el bloqueo
holocaust	el holocausto
friendly fire	el fuego amigo
ceasefire	el alto el fuego
disarmament	el desarme
pacifism	el pacifismo

268

war	la guerra
warlike	guerrero
warrior	el guerrero
guerrilla	el guerrillero
guerrilla warfare	la guerrilla
campaign	la campaña
siege	el sitio
to besiege	sitiar
fort	el fuerte
spy	un espía

269

attack	el ataque
to attack	atacar
assault	asaltar
ambush	la emboscada
to surrender	rendirse
surrender	la rendición
encounter	el encuentro
to meet	encontrar
fight	el combate
to fight	combatir, pelear

270

combatant	el combatiente
exploit	la hazaña
battlefield	el campo de batalla
trench	la trinchera
to repel	rechazar
retreat	la retirada
flight	la fuga, la huida
to flee	huir
defeat	la derrota
to defeat	derrotar

271

to pursue	perseguir
pursuit	el perseguimiento
to conquer	vencer
victor	el vencedor
vanquished	el vencido
armistice	el armisticio
treaty	el tratado
peace	la paz
captivity	el cautiverio
to escape	escaparse

272

to encamp	acampar
encampment	el campamento
to manoeuvre	maniobrar
manoeuvre	la maniobra
wounded	herido
hero	el héroe
heroine	la heroína
medal	la medalla
pension	la pensión
war memorial	el monumento a los caídos

273

navy	la marina
sailor	el marino, el marinero
admiral	el almirante
squadron	la escuadra
fleet	la flota, la armada
to float	flotar
to sail	navegar
navigator	el navegante
warship	el buque de guerra
battleship	el acorazado

274

aircraft carrier	el portaaviones
fighter plane	el avión de caza
destroyer	el destructor
minesweeper	el dragaminas
submarine	el submarino
aerodrome	el aeródromo
spotter plane	el avión observador
air raid	el ataque aéreo
to bomb	bombardear
parachute	el paracaídas

275

parachutist	el paracaidista
surface to air missile	el misil tierra-aire
helicopter	el helicóptero
to bring down	derribar
anti-aircraft gun	el cañón antiaéreo
bomb shelter	el refugio antiaéreo
bomb disposal	la neutralización de bombas
bomber (*plane*)	el bombardero
to explode	explotar
explosion	la explosión

276

religion	la religión
religious	religioso
God	Dios
god	el dios
goddess	la diosa
monk	el fraile
nun	la monja
divine	divino
omnipotent	omnipotente
saviour	el salvador

277

safe	salvo
pagan	pagano
Christianity	el cristianismo
Christian	cristiano
catholic	católico
Catholicism	el catolicismo
Protestantism	el protestantismo
protestant	protestante
Calvinism	el calvinismo
Calvinist	calvinista

278

Presbyterian	presbiteriano
Mormonism	el mormonismo
Mormon	mormón
Bible	la biblia
Koran	el Corán
Islam	el Islam
Muslim	mahometano
Hindu	hindú
Hinduism	el hinduismo
Buddhist	budista

279

Buddhism	el budismo
Jewish	judío
Judaism	el judaísmo
Rastafarian	rastafariano
scientology	la cientología
scientologist	cientólogo
to convert	convertir
sect	la secta
animism	el animismo
voodoo	el vudú

280

witch doctor	el hechicero
atheist	ateo
atheism	el ateísmo
agnostic	agnóstico
agnosticism	el agnosticismo
heretic	el hereje
heresy	la herejía
fundamentalist	fundamentalista
fundamentalism	el fundamentalismo
to believe	creer

281

believer	el creyente
belief	la creencia
faith	la fe
church	la iglesia
chapel	la capilla
chalice	el cáliz
altar	el altar
mass	la misa
blessing	la bendición
to bless	bendecir

282

to curse	maldecir
clergy	el clero
clergyman	el clérigo
to preach	predicar
preacher	el predicador
sermon	el sermón
apostle	el apóstol
angel	el ángel
holy	santo
saint	el santo *m*, la santa *f*

283

blessed	beato
sacred	sagrado
devil	el diablo
devilish	diabólico
cult	el culto
solemn	solemne
prayer	el rezo
to pray	rezar
devout	devoto
fervent	fervoroso

284

sin	el pecado
to sin	pecar
sinner	el pecador
repentant	penitente
to baptise	bautizar
pope	el papa
cardinal	el cardenal
bishop	el obispo
archbishop	el arzobispo
priest	el cura, el sacerdote

285

parish	la parroquia
abbot	el abad
abbess	la abadesa
abbey	la abadía
convent	el convento
monastery	el monasterio
minister	el pastor
pilgrim	el peregrino
pilgrimage	la peregrinación
to celebrate	celebrar

The Intellect and Emotions / El Intelecto y Las Emociones

286

mind	la mente, el ánimo
thought	el pensamiento
to think of	pensar en
to meditate	meditar
to remember	acordarse de
to agree with	acordarse con
agreement	el acuerdo
soul	el alma *f*
to occur, come to mind	ocurrirse
recollection	el recuerdo

287

renown	la buena fama
to perceive	percibir
to understand	entender
understanding	el entendimiento
intelligence	la inteligencia
intelligent	inteligente
clever	listo
stupid	estúpido
stupidity	la estúpidez
worthy	digno

288

unworthy	indigno
reason	la razón
reasonable	razonable
unreasonable	desrazonable
to reason	razonar

to discuss	discutir
to convince	convencer
opinion	la opinión
to affirm	afirmar
to deny	negar

289

certainty	la certeza, la certidumbre
certain	cierto
uncertain	incierto
sure	seguro
unsure	inseguro
security	la seguridad
to risk	arriesgar
doubt	la duda
doubtful	dudoso
mistake	la equivocación

290

to make a mistake	equivocarse
suspicion	la sospecha
to suspect	sospechar
suspicious	sospechoso
desire	el deseo
to desire	desear
to grant	conceder
will	la voluntad
to decide	decidir
undecided	indeciso

291

to hesitate	vacilar
capable	capaz
incapable	incapaz
capability	la capacidad
talent	el talento
disposition, temper	el genio
character	el carácter
to rejoice	alegrarse
cheerfulness	la alegría
happiness	la felicidad

292

cheerful	alegre
sad	triste
sadness	la tristeza

The Intellect and Emotions		The Intellect and Emotions	
to grieve	afligir	frightful	espantoso
enjoyment	el goce	to astonish	asombrar
happy	feliz, dichoso	astonishment	el asombro
unhappy	infeliz	to encourage	animar
unfortunate	desdichado	to discourage	desanimar
contented	contento	conscience	la conciencia
discontented	descontento	scruple	el escrúpulo
		remorse	el remordimiento

293

		297	
discontent	el disgusto	repentance	el arrepentimiento
displeased	disgustado	to repent	arrepentirse
pleasure	el placer	to regret, feel	sentir
to please	agradar	sentiment	el sentimiento
to displease	desagradar	consent	el consentimiento
pain	la pena	to consent	consentir
painful	penoso	mercy	la misericordia
sigh	el suspiro	charitable	caritativo
to sigh	suspirar	pity	la lástima
to complain	quejarse	piety	la piedad

294

		298	
complaint	la queja	impiety	la impiedad
to protest	protestar	friendly	simpático
depressed	abatido	unfriendly	antipático
to despair	desesperar	favour	el favor
despair	la desesperación	to favour	favorecer
hope	la esperanza	favourable	favorable
to hope	esperar, aguardar	unfavourable	desfavorable
expectation	la espera	confidence	la confianza
consolation	el consuelo	trustful	confiado
to comfort	confortar	mistrustful	desconfiado

295

		299	
consoling	consolador	to trust	confiar (en)
calm	la calma	friendship	la amistad
calm	calmoso	friendly	amistoso
restless	inquieto	kind	amable
anxiety	la inquietud	friend	el amigo
fear	el miedo	enemy	el enemigo
to fear	temer	hatred	el odio
to be afraid	tener miedo	to hate	odiar
to frighten	asustar	hateful	odioso
to be frightened	asustarse	contempt	el desdén, el desprecio

296

		300	
terror	el terror	to despise	despreciar
to terrify	aterrar, aterrorizar		

to get angry	enfadarse
quarrel	la riña
to quarrel	reñir
to reconcile	reconciliar
quality	la cualidad
virtue	la virtud
virtuous	virtuoso
vice	el vicio
vicious	vicioso

301

addicted	adicto
defect	el defecto
fault	la falta
to lack; to fail	faltar
custom	la costumbre
to be necessary	hacer falta
to become accustomed	acostumbrarse
habit	el hábito
to boast about	jactarse de
moderate	moderado

302

goodness	la bondad
kind	bondadoso
wickedness	la maldad
gratitude	el agradecimiento
ungrateful	ingrato
ingratitude	la ingratitud
grateful	agradecido
ungrateful	desagradecido
to thank	agradecer
thanks, thank you	gracias

303

honesty	la honradez
honourable	honrado, honorable
to honour	honrar
to dishonour	deshonrar
honour	la honra, el honor
dishonour	la deshonra, el deshonor
honest	honesto
dishonest	deshonesto

304

| modesty | el pudor |

shame	la vergüenza
shameful	vergonzoso
to be ashamed	avergonzarse
audacity	la audacia
audacious	audaz
daring	atrevido
boldness	el atrevimiento
fearless	intrépido
to dare	osar

305

reckless	temerario
timid	tímido
timidity	la timidez
rude	grosero
rudeness	la grosería
courtesy	la cortesía
polite	cortés
impolite	descortés
villain	el pícaro
envy	la envidia

306

loyal	leal
disloyal	desleal
generous	generoso
generosity	la generosidad
selfishness	el egoísmo
selfish	egoísta
egoist	el egoísta
greed	la avaricia
stingy	avaro
miser	el avaro

307

truth	la verdad
true	verdadero
to lie	mentir
liar	el mentiroso
lie	la mentira, el embuste
hypocritical	hipócrita
hypocrite	el hipócrita
frank	franco
frankness	la franqueza
accuracy	la exactitud

308

| inaccuracy | la inexactitud |

punctuality	la puntualidad
faithfulness	la fidelidad
unfaithfulness	la infidelidad
faithful	fiel
unfaithful	infiel
coward	el cobarde
cowardice	la cobardía
anger	la ira, la cólera
offence	la ofensa

309

to offend	ofender, agraviar
to insult	insultar, injuriar
excuse	la excusa
to excuse	excusar
humble	humilde
humility	la humildad
pride	el orgullo
proud	orgulloso
vain	vanidoso
to be obstinate	obstinarse

310

obstinaçy	la obstinación
whim	el capricho
sober	sobrio
sobriety	la sobriedad
sensual	sensual
sensuality	la sensualidad
hedonistic	hedonista
lust	la lujuria
revenge	la venganza
to revenge	vengar

311

vindictive	vengativo
jealous	celoso
temperamental	temperamental
affectionate	cariñoso
imaginative	imaginativo
extrovert	extrovertido
introvert	introvertido
demanding	exigente
sincere	sincero
sincerity	la sinceridad

312

optimistic	optimista

optimist	el optimista
pessimistic	pesimista
pessimist	el pesimista
perceptive	perceptivo
cautious	cauteloso
sensitive	sensible
sensitivity	la sensibilidad
sensible	sensato
common sense	el sentido común

Education and Learning

La Educación y Los Conocimientos

313

to educate	educar
educational	educacional
educationalist	el educationalista *m*, la educationalista *f*
adult education	la educación de adultos
mixed education	la educación mixta
primary school	la escuela primaria
to teach	enseñar
teacher	el profesor
tutor	el preceptor
college	el instituto, el colegio

314

university	la universidad
class	la clase
pupil	el alumno
boarder	el interno
day pupil	el externo
to study	estudiar
student	el estudiante
grant	la beca
scholarship holder	el becario
desk	el pupitre

315

blackboard	la pizarra
chalk	la tiza
pencil	el lápiz
ink	la tinta
pen	el bolígrafo, la pluma
ruler	la regla

line	la línea
exercise book	el cuaderno
to bind (*books*)	encuadernar
page	la página

316

to fold	plegar, doblar
sheet of paper	la hoja de papel
cover (*book*)	la cubierta
work	el trabajo
to work	trabajar
hard-working	trabajador
studious	aplicado
lesson	la lección
to learn	aprender
to forget	olvidar

317

forgetful	olvidadizo
forgetfulness	el olvido
absentminded	distraído
course	el curso
attention	la atención
to be attentive	atender
attentive	atento
inattentive	desatento
to explain	explicar
explanation	la explicación

318

task	la tarea
theme	el tema
thematic	temático
exercise	el ejercicio
to exercise	ejercer
practice	la práctica
to practise	practicar
easy	fácil
easiness	la facilidad
difficult	difícil

319

difficulty	la dificultad
progress	el progreso
homework	los deberes
must	deber
to owe	deber

examination	el examen
to sit an examination	presentarse a un examen
to pass an examination	aprobar un examen
to copy	copiar
to swot	empollar

320

to examine	examinar
examiner	el examinador
proof	la prueba
to try	probar
to blame	reprobar
blame	la reprobación
approve	aprobar
disapprove	desaprobar
mark	la nota
to note	anotar

321

annotation	la anotación
remarkable	notable
prize	el premio
to reward	premiar
to praise	elogiar
praise	el elogio, la alabanza
holidays	las vacaciones
vacancy	la vacante
conduct	la conducta
to behave	comportarse

322

effort	el esfuerzo
to endeavour	esforzarse
to try	procurar, intentar
obedience	la obediencia
disobedience	la desobediencia
obedient	obediente
disobedient	desobediente
to obey	obedecer
to disobey	desobedecer
laziness	la pereza

323

strict	severo
severity	la severidad
threat	la amenaza

to threaten	amenazar
punishment	el castigo
to punish	castigar
to deserve	merecer
grammar	la gramática
to indicate	indicar
indication	la indicación

324

to point out	señalar
spelling	la ortografía
to spell	deletrear
full stop	el punto
colon	los dos puntos
semicolon	el punto y coma
comma	la coma
question mark	el signo de interrogación
exclamation mark	el signo de admiración
to note down	apuntar

325

to ask (*question*)	preguntar
to ask for	pedir
to answer	contestar
answer	la contestación
to admire	admirar
admiration	la admiración
to exclaim	exclamar
article	el artículo
noun	el sustantivo
to name	nombrar

326

appointment	el nombramiento
to call	llamar
to be called	llamarse
reference	la referencia
to relate to	referirse a
fixed	fijo
to fix	fijar
to join	juntar
together	junto con
join	la juntura

327

to correspond	corresponder

correspondence	la correspondencia
sentence	la frase
language	el idioma
idiomatic	idiomático
idiom	el modismo
speech	el habla
talkative	hablador
voice	la voz
word	la palabra

328

to express	exprimir
expressive	expresivo
vocabulary	el vocabulario
dictionary	el diccionario
letter	la letra
speech	el discurso
lecture	la conferencia
lecturer	el conferenciante
orator	el orador
eloquence	la elocuencia

329

eloquent	elocuente
elocution	la elocución
to converse	conversar
conversation	la conversación
to understand	comprender
to pronounce	pronunciar
to correct	corregir
example	el ejemplo
meaning	la significación
to mean	significar, querer decir

330

translation	la traducción
to translate	traducir
translator	el traductor
interpreter	el intérprete
to interpret	interpretar
interpretative	interpretativo
interpretation	la interpretación
to imagine	imaginar
imagination	la imaginación

331

idea	la idea

essay	el ensayo, la composición
essayist	el ensayista
thesis	la tesis
doctorate	el doctorado
to develop	desarrollar
to roll up	arrollar
roll	el rollo
object	el objeto
describe	describir

332

description	la descripción
fable	la fábula
drama	el drama
comedy	la comedia
comical	cómico
chapter	el capítulo
to interest	interesar
interesting	interesante
attractive	atractivo
to attract	atraer

333

to publish	publicar, editar
to print	imprimir
printer	el impresor
printing	la impresión
newspaper	el periódico, el diario
journalist	el periodista
magazine	la revista
news	las noticias
to announce	anunciar
advertisement	el anuncio

334

history	la historia
historian	el historiador
the Stone Age	la Edad de Piedra
the Bronze Age	la Edad de Bronce
the Iron Age	la Edad de Hierro
the Dark Ages	las Edades bárbaras
the Middle Ages	la Edad Media
archaeology	la arqueología
archaeologist	el arqueólogo
to excavate	excavar

335

carbon dating	la datación por la carbono catorce
event	el suceso
to happen	suceder, acontecer
to civilise	civilizar
civilisation	la civilización
knight	el caballero
chivalry	la caballerosidad
explorer	el explorador
to explore	explorar
discovery	el descubrimiento

336

to discover	descubrir
pirate	el pirata
piracy	la piratería
treasure	el tesoro
conquest	la conquista
conqueror	el conquistador
to conquer	conquistar
empire	el imperio
imperial	imperial
slave	el esclavo

337

emancipation	la emancipación
to emancipate	emancipar
destiny	el destino
to destine	destinar
power	el poder, la potencia
powerful	poderoso
to be able, can	poder
slavery	la esclavitud
to free	liberar
reformation	la reforma

338

liberator	el libertador
nationalism	el nacionalismo
nationalist	el nacionalista
alliance	la alianza
to ally	aliar
ally	el aliado
to enlarge	ampliar
increase	el aumento
to increase	aumentar
to diminish	disminuir

339

decline	la decadencia
to decay	to decline
renowned	célebre
to disturb	turbar
to emigrate	emigrar
emigrant	el emigrante
rebel	el rebelde
rebellion	la rebelión
rising	la sublevación
independence	la independencia

340

geography	la geografía
map	el mapa
North Pole	el Polo Norte
South Pole	el Polo Sur
north	el norte
south	el sur
east	el este
west	el oeste
compass	la brújula
magnetic north	el polo magnético

341

distant	lejano
distance	la distancia
near	cercano
to approach	acercarse
neighbour	el vecino
to determine	determinar
limit	el límite
region	la región, la comarca
country	el país
compatriot	el paisano

342

citizen	el ciudadano
city	la ciudad
population	la población
to people	poblar
populous	poblado
village	el pueblo, la aldea
people	la gente; el pueblo
province	la provincia
provincial	provincial, provinciano
place	el lugar

Places — Los Lugares

343

Africa	el África
African	africano
North America	la América del Norte
North American	norteamericano
South America	Sudamérica, la América del Sur
South American	sudamericano
Central America	Centroamérica, la América Central
Central American	centroamericano
Australia	Australia
Australian	australiano

344

Europe	Europa
European	europeo
Arctic	el Ártico
Antarctica	la Antártida
Oceania	la Oceanía
Oceanian	oceánico
Asia	Asia
Asian	asiáticio
New Zealand	Nueva Zelanda
New Zealander	neozelandés

345

Spain	España
Spanish	español
Germany	Alemania
German	alemán
Italy	Italia
Italian	italiano
Greece	Grecia
Greek	griego
Russia	Rusia
Russian	ruso

346

Switzerland	Suiza
Swiss	suizo
Holland	Holanda
Dutch	holandés
Portugal	Portugal
Portuguese	portugués

Belgium	Bélgica		Alsatian	alsaciano
Belgian	belga		Lorraine	Lorena
Great Britain	La Gran Bretaña		Dordogne	Dordoña
British Isles	las Islas Británicas		Auvergne	Auvernia
			Provence	Provenza

347

United Kingdom	el Reino Unido
British	británico
England	Inglaterra
English	inglés
Scotland	Escocia
Scottish	Escocés
Wales	Gales
Welsh	galés
Northern Ireland	Irlanda del Norte
Northern Irish	norirlandés

348

Ireland	Irlanda
Irish	irlandés
France	Francia
French	francés
Austria	Austria
Austrian	austriaco
Scandinavia	Escandinavia
Scandinavian	escandinavo
Iceland	Islandia
Icelandic	islandés

349

Greenland	Groenlandia
Greenlander	groenlandés
Sweden	Suecia
Swedish	sueco
Norway	Noruega
Norwegian	noruego
Finland	Finlandia
Finnish	finlandés
Denmark	Dinamarca
Danish	danés

350

Bavaria	Baviera
Bavarian	bávaro
Saxony	Sajonia
Saxon	sajón
Alsace	Alsacia

351

(adjectival forms given with the city names below describe both the city and its inhabitants, eg el londinense: the Londoner)

London	Londres
London *adj*	londinense
Paris	París
Parisian	parisiense
Madrid	Madrid
Madrid *adj*	madrileño
Edinburgh	Edinburgo
The Hague	La Haya

352

Toulouse	Tolosa
Milan	Milano
Lisbon	Lisboa
Lisbon *adj*	lisbonense
Bordeaux	Burdeos
Bordeaux *adj*	bordelés
Lyons	Lión
Lyons *adj*	lionés
Marseilles	Marsella
Marseilles *adj*	marsellés

353

Rome	Roma
Roman	romano
Venice	Venecia
Venetian	veneciano
Naples	Nápoles
Neapolitan	napolitano
Florence	Florencia
Florentine	florentino
Turin	Turín
Cologne	Colonia

354

Hamburg	Hamburgo
Hanover	Hanovre
Basle	Basilea

Vienna	Viena	Bosnia	Bosnia
Viennese	vienés	Bosnian	bosnio
Antwerp	Amberes	Serbia	Serbia
Berlin	Berlín	Serbian	serbio
Berlin *adj*	berlinés	Albania	Albania
Geneva	Ginebra	Albanian	albanés
Geneva *adj*	ginebrino	Romania	Rumania
		Romanian	rumano

355

Athens	Atenas	**359**	
Brussels	Bruselas	Bulgaria	Bulgaria
Strasbourg	Estrasburgo	Bulgarian	búlgaro
Bruges	Brujas	Macedonia	Macedonia
Moscow	Moscú	Macedonian	macedónico
Muscovite	moscovita	Moldova	Moldavia
St Petersburg	San Petersburgo	Moldovan	moldavo
Warsaw	Varsovia	Belarus	Bielorrusia
Prague	Praga	Belorussian	bielorruso
Budapest	Budapest	Ukraine	Ucrania
		Ukrainian	ucranio

356

Stockholm	Estocolmo	**360**	
Oslo	Oslo	Estonia	Estonia
Copenhagen	Copenhague	Estonian	estonio
New York	Nueva York	Latvia	Latvia
New York *adj*	neoyorquino	Latvian	latvio
Havana	La Habana	Lithuania	Lituania
Cairo	el Cairo	Lithuanian	lituano
Capetown	Ciudad del Cabo	Armenia	Armenia
Beijing	Pekín	Armenian	armenio
Mexico City	Ciudad de México	Azerbaijan	Azerbaiyán
		Azerbaijani	Azerbaiyaní

357

Poland	Polonia	**361**	
Polish	polaco	Georgia	Georgia
Czech Republic	la República Checa	Georgian	georgiano
Czech	checo	Siberia	Siberia
Slovakia	Eslovaquia	Siberian	siberiano
Slovak	eslovaco	Turkey	Turquía
Slovenia	Eslovenia	Turkish	turco
Slovene	esloveno	Arabia	Arabia
Croatia	Croacia	Arab	árabe
Croatian	croata	Morocco	Marruecos
		Moroccan	marroquí

358

Hungary	Hungría	**362**	
Hungarian	húngaro	Egypt	Egipto

Egyptian	egipcio	Brazilian	brasileño
China	China	Chile	Chile
Chinese	chino	Chilean	chileno
India	La India	Argentina	Argentina
Indian	indio	Argentinian	argentino
Japan	El Japón	Uruguay	El Uruguay
Japanese	japonés	Uruguayan	uruguayo
Ghana	Ghana	Bolivia	Bolivia
Ghanaian	ghaneano	Bolivian	boliviano

363

Algeria	Argelia	**367**	
Algerian	argelino	Pyrenees	Los Pirineos
Tunisia	Túnez	Alps	Los Alpes
Tunisian	tunecino	Atlas Mountains	los Atlas
South Africa	Sudáfrica	Dolomites	las Dolomitas
South African	sudafricano	Carpathians	los Montes Cárpatos
Israel	Israel	Andes	Los Andes
Israeli	israelí	Himalayas	el Himalaya
Palestine	Palestina	Mont Blanc	el Monte Blanco
Palestinian	palestino	Table Mountain	El Monte de la Mesa
		Everest	el Everest

364

Castile	Castilla	**368**	
Castilian	castellano	Amazon	el Amazonas
Andalusia	Andalucía	Nile	el Nilo
Andalusian	andaluz	Rhine	el Rin
Catalonia	Cataluña	Rhône	el Ródano
Catalan	catalán	Tagus	el Tajo
Galicia	Galicia	Danube	el Danubio
Galician	gallego	Thames	el Támesis
Basque Country	El País Vasco	Seine	el Sena
Basque	vasco	Loire	el Loira
		Ebro	el Ebro

365

United States	Los Estados Unidos	**369**	
North American	estadounidense	Atlantic	el Atlántico
Canada	El Canadá	Pacific	el Pacífico
Canadian	canadiense	Arctic Ocean	el Océano Glacial Ártico
Mexico	México		
Mexican	mexicano	Indian Ocean	el Océano Índico
Colombia	Colombia	Antarctic Ocean	el Océano Antártico
Colombian	colombiano	Mediterranean	el Mediterráneo
Peru	El Perú	North Sea	el Mar del Norte
Peruvian	peruano	Black Sea	el Mar Negro
		Red Sea	el Mar Rojo
		Caribbean	el Mar Caribe

366

Brazil	El Brasil

370

Baltic Sea	el Mar Báltico
English Channel	La Mancha
Bay of Biscay	el Golfo de Vizcaya
West Indies	las Antillas
Canaries	Las Canarias
The Philippines	las Filipinas
Balearic Islands	las Islas Baleares
Sicily	Sicilia
Sardinia	Cerdeña
Corsica	Córcega

371

Corsican	corso
Rhodes	Rodas
Crete	Creta
Cretan	cretense
Cyprus	Chipre
Cypriot	chipriota
Dardanelles	los Dardanelos
Bosphorus	el Bósforo
Scilly Isles	las Sorlingas
Falkland Islands	las Malvinas

Science   La Ciencia

372

weights	las pesas
weight	el peso
to weigh	pesar
heavy	pesado
light	ligero
scales	la balanza
to measure	medir
measure	la medida
to compare	comparar
comparison	la comparación

373

to contain	contener
contents	el contenido
metric system	el sistema métrico
metre	el metro
centimetre	el centímetro
millimetre	el milímetro
gram	el gramo
kilogram	el kilogramo
litre	el litro
hectare	la hectárea

374

kilometre	el kilómetro
ton	la tonelada
inch	la pulgada
foot	el pie
mile	la milla
arithmetic	la aritmética
mathematics	la matemática
to calculate	calcular
to count	contar
number	el número

375

figure	la cifra
zero	el cero
addition	la adición
to add	adicionar, sumar
subtraction	la sustracción
remainder	la resta
equal	igual
equality	la igualdad
to multiply	multiplicar
product	el producto

376

to produce	producir
producer	el productor
to divide	dividir, partir
part	la parte
fraction	la fracción
half	la mitad
third	el tercio
quarter	el cuarto
dozen	la docena
double	doble

377

triple	triple
geometry	la geometría
algebra	el álgebra
space	el espacio
spacious	espacioso
parallel	paralelo
perpendicular	perpendicular
horizontal	horizontal
horizon	el horizonte
right angle	el ángulo recto

378

triangle	el triángulo
square	el cuadrado
curved	curvo
straight	recto
circumference	la circunferencia
circle	el círculo
centre	el centro
diameter	el diámetro
problem	el problema
correct	correcto

379

incorrect	incorrecto
wrong	falso
simple	sencillo
to complicate	complicar
to demonstrate	demostrar
to solve	resolver
result	el resultado
to result	resultar
physics	la físcia
physical	físico

380

matter	la materia
pressure	la presión
phenomenon	el fenómeno
strange	extraño
movement	el movimiento
to move	moverse
mobile	móvil
immobile	inmóvil
electric	eléctrico
electricity	la electricidad

381

mechanics	la mecánica
invent	inventar
optics	la óptica
optical	óptico
microscope	el microscopio
lens	el lente
to reflect	reflejar
reflection	la reflexión
chemistry	la química
chemical	químico

382

biology	la biología
biological	biológico
biologist	el biólogo
to research	investigar
researcher	el investigador
element	el elemento
oxygen	el oxígeno
hydrogen	el hidrógeno
atom	el átomo
nucleus	el núcleo

383

laboratory	el laboratorio
experiment	el experimento
mixture	la mezcla
mixed	mixto
to decompose	descomponer
to compose	componer
compound	compuesto
rare	raro
science	la ciencia
scientific	científico

384

scientist	el científico *m*, la científica *f*
knowledge	el conocimiento, el saber
to know (*something*)	saber
to know (*person*)	conocer
wisdom	la sabiduría
wise	sabio
sage	el sabio
to be ignorant of	ignorar
experience	la experiencia
inexperience	la inexperiencia

Communications Las Communicaciones

385

telegraph	el telégrafo
telegram	el telegrama
to telegraph	telegrafiar
telex	el télex

telephone	el teléfono	computerese	la jerga infórmatica
to telephone	telefonear	to computerise	computerizar, informatizar
telephonist	el telefonista *m*, la telefonista *f*	computerisation	la computerización
call	la llamada		
receiver	el auricular	**389**	
mouthpiece	el micrófono	to program	programar
		programmer	el programador
386		systems analyst	el analista de sistemas
telephone booth	la cabina telefónica	wordprocessor	el procesador de textos
telephone exchange	la central telefónica		
telephone directory	la guía telefónica	memory	la memoria
telephone subscriber	el abonado	disk drive	la unidad de disco
answerphone	el contestador (automático)	software	el software
		hardware	el hardware
to hang up	colgar	disk drive	la disquetera
engaged	comunicando	cursor	el cursor
to dial	marcar		
radiotelephone	el radioteléfono	**390**	
videophone	el videófono	menu	el menú
		to store	almacenar
387		file	el archivo
fax	el fax, el telefax	to file	archivar
to fax	faxear, mandar por fax	data	los datos
		database	la base de datos
modem	el módem	desktop publishing	la edición electrónica
electronic mail	el correo electrónico	to lay out	componer
information technology	la informática	silicon	el silicio
microelectronics	la microelectrónica	silicon chip	la pastilla de silicio
screen	la pantalla		
keyboard	el teclado	**391**	
key	la tecla	user-friendly	fácil de usar
mouse	el ratón	laser printer	la impresora láser
		ink jet printer	la impresora de chorro de tinta
388			
computer	la computadora, el ordenador	scanner	el analizador de léxico
computer language	el lenguaje de ordenador	circuit	el circuito
		fibreoptics	la transmisión por fibra óptica
computer literate	competente en la informática		
		machine translation	la traducción automática
computer scientist	el informático *m*, la informática *f*	to network	interconectar
computer game	el vídeojuego	networking	la interconexión
computer animation	la animación por ordenador	information superhighway	la autopista informática
computer-aided design	el diseño asistido por ordenador		

The Arts and Entertainment

Las Artes y La Diversión

392

painting	la pintura
painter	el pintor
to paint	pintar
picturesque	pintoresco
artist	el artista
museum	el museo
engraving	el grabado
to engrave	grabar
print	la estampa
background	el fondo

393

foreground	el primer plano
still life	el bodegón
drawing	el dibujo
to draw	dibujar
draughtsman	el dibujante
outline	el contorno
to imitate	imitar
imitation	la imitación
abstract	abstracto
innovative	innovativo

394

innovation	la innovación
resemblance	la semejanza
similar	semejante, parecido
forgery	la falsificación
forger	el falsificador *m*, la falsificadora *f*
auction	la subasta
to bid	pujar
lot	el lote
reserve price	el precio mínimo
exhibition	la exposición

395

antique	la antigüedad
antique dealer	el anticuario
art dealer	un marchante de arte
palette	la paleta
brush	el pincel
easel	el caballete

colour	el color
to colour	colorear
coloured	colorado
dull	mate

396

multicoloured	multicolor
contrast	el contraste
to contrast	contrastar
white	blanco
black	negro
light blue	azul claro
dark green	verde oscuro
yellow	amarillo
brown	moreno
chestnut	castaño

397

pink	rosado
red	rojo
violet	violeta
mauve	morado
purple	purpúreo
gilt	dorado
to gild	dorar
grey	gris
patron	el mecenas
patronage	el mecenazgo

398

patronise	fomentar
oils	el óleo
watercolour	la acuarela
fresco	el fresco
triptych	el tríptico
cartoon	el cartón
the Renaissance	el Renacimiento
Renaissance art	el arte renacentista
crayon	el creyón
canvas	el lienzo

399

gallery	la galería
tone	el matiz
landscape	el paisaje
portrait	el retrato
portraitist	el retratista

miniature	la miniatura	stained glass	el cristal de colores
miniaturist	el miniaturista	transept	el crucero
landscape painter	el paisajista	flying buttress	el arbotante
impressionism	el impresionismo	font	la pila
impressionist	el impresionista	crypt	la cripta
		basilica	la basílica

400

surrealism	el surrealismo	**404**	
surrealist	surrealista	Gothic	gótico
cubism	el cubismo	Romanesque	románico
cubist	cubista	Baroque	barroco
symbol	el símbolo	mosque	la mezquita
to symbolise	simbolizar	minaret	el alminar
symbolic	simbólico	synagogue	la sinagoga
sculpture	la escultura	pagoda	la pagoda
sculptor	el escultor	mausoleum	el mausoleo
workshop	el taller	pyramid	la pirámide
		Sphinx	la esfinge

401

to carve	tallar	**405**	
model	el modelo	temple	el templo
statue	la estatua	Corinthian	corintio
bust	el busto	Ionian	jónico
group	el grupo	Doric	dórico
chisel	el cincel	forum	el foro
cast	el vaciado	amphitheatre	el anfiteatro
shape	la forma	aqueduct	el acueducto
to shape	formar	dolmen	el dolmen
architecture	la arquitectura	menhir	el menhir
		cave painting	la pintura rupestre

402

architect	el arquitecto	**406**	
vault	la bóveda	illiterate	analfabeto
dome	la cúpula	literate	alfabetizado
pillar	el pilar	oral culture	la cultura oral
arch	el arco	ballad	el romance
tower	la torre	saga	la saga
scaffolding	el andamio	tradition	la tradición
arch	el arco	story	la historia
column	la columna	storyteller	el cuentista
plinth	el zócalo	narrative	la narración
		to learn by heart	aprender de memoria

403

nave	la nave	**407**	
cathedral	la catedral	literature	la literatura
cathedral city	la ciudad catedralicio	papyrus	el papiro
apse	el ábside	parchment	el pergamino

alphabet	el alfabeto
character	el carácter
author	el autor
writer	el escritor
editor	el editor
edition	la edición
copyright	los derechos de reproducción

408

style	el estilo
reader	el lector *m*, la lectora *f*
biography	la biografía
biographer	el biógrafo *m*, la biógrafa
biographical	biográfico
autobiography	la autobiografía
autobiographical	autobiográfico
fiction	la ficción
fictional	ficticio
science fiction	la ciencia-ficción

409

novel	la novela
novelist	el novelista
publisher	la editorial
royalties	los derechos del autor
bookshop	la librería
bookseller	el librero
encyclopaedia	la enciclopedia
encyclopaedic	enciclopédico
paperback	el libro de bolsillo
poetry	la poesía

410

poet	el poeta *m*, la poeta *f*
poetic	poético
rhyme	la rima
to rhyme	rimar
metre	el metro
stanza	la estrofa
sonnet	el soneto
assonance	la asonancia
syllable	la sílaba
nursery rhyme	la canción infantil

411

fairy tale	el cuento de hada

Cinderella	Cenicienta
Red Riding Hood	Caperucita Roja
Snow White	Blancanieves
dwarf	el enano
goblin	el duende
gnome	el gnomo
elf	el geniecillo, el elfo
Sleeping Beauty	la Bella Durmiente
Snow Queen	Reina de las nieves

412

Puss in Boots	el gato con botas
Bluebeard	Barba Azul
witch	la bruja
wizard	el brujo
spell	el hechizo
to cast a spell	hechizar
magician	el mago
magic	la magia
magical	mágico
mermaid	la sirena

413

mythology	la mitologia
Homer	Homero
Homeric	homérico
Iliad	la Ilíada
Odyssey	la Odisea
Odysseus	Odiseo
Trojan	troyano
Trojan horse	el caballo de Troya
Achilles	Aquiles
Achilles' heel	el talón de Aquiles

414

Cyclops	el cíclope
Atlantis	la Atlántida
Romulus	Rómulo
Hercules	Hércules
Herculean	hercúleo
The Arabian Nights	Las mil y una noches
Armageddon	el Armagedón
Valhalla	el Valhala
Thor	Tor
rune	la runa

415

masterpiece	la obra maestra

music	la música
musician	el músico
to play (an instrument)	tocar
composer	el compositor
orchestra	la orquesta
symphony	la sinfonía
aria	la aria
overture	la obertura
march	la marcha

416

soft	suave
stringed instrument	el instrumento de cuerda
wind instrument	el instrumento de viento
brass instrument	el instrumento de metal
piano	el piano
pianist	el pianista
organ	el órgano
organist	el organista
harmony	la harmonía
flute	la flauta

417

to blow	soplar
bagpipes	la gaita
cornet	la corneta
violin	el violín
auditorium	el auditorio
score	la partitura
opera	la ópera
tenor	el tenor
soprano	el soprano m, la soprano f
baritone	el barítono

418

bass	bajo
conductor	el director
instrumentalist	el instrumentalista m, la instrumentalista f
rehearsal	el ensayo
violin	el violín
viola	la viola
violinist	el violinista

cello	el violonchelo
bow	el arco
guitar	la guitarra

419

to strum	tañer
harp	el harpa
flute	la flauta
oboe	el oboe
clarinet	el clarinete
bassoon	el fagot
trumpet	la trompeta
trombone	el trombón
French horn	la trompa de llaves
tuba	la tuba

420

songbook	el cancionero
singing	el canto
to sing	cantar
to enchant	encantar
enchanting, delightful	encantador
spell, charm	el encanto
singer	el cantante m, la cantante f
choir	el coro
to accompany	acompañar
accompaniment	el acompañamiento

421

song	la canción, la copla
refrain	el estribillo
concert	el concierto
to syncopate	sincopar
jazz	el jazz
beat	el ritmo
saxophone	el saxofón
rock music	la música rock
rock star	la estrella de rock
drums	la batería

422

synthesiser	el sinetizador
folk music	la música folklórica
mandolin	la mandolina
ocarina	la ocarina
drum	el tambor

accordion	el acordeón
xylophone	el xilófono
tambourine	la pandereta
zither	la cítara
concertina	la concertina

423

dance, dancing	la danza
to dance	danzar, bailar
ball, dance	el baile
dancer	el bailarín *m*, la bailarina
theatre	el teatro
theatrical	teatral
mask	la máscara
box office	la taquilla
seat, place	la localidad
stalls	las butacas
box (*theatre*)	el palco

424

pit	el patio, la platea
stage	el escenario
scene	la escena
act	el acto
interval	el entreacto
scenery	las decoraciones, la escenografía
curtain	el telón
play	la obra (de teatro)
playwright	el dramaturgo
character	el personaje

425

tragedy	la tragedia
comedy	la comedia
actor	el actor
actress	la actriz
to play a role	desempeñar un papel
to be word-perfect	saber perfectamente su papel
costume	el vestuario
lighting	la iluminación
dénouement	el desenlace
to stage, represent	representar

426

performance	la función, la representación
flop	el fracaso
to flop	fracasar
debut	el estreno
trapdoor	el escotillón
to be a success	tener éxito
audience	el auditorio
spectator	el espectador
applause	los aplausos
whistling, hissing	el silbo

427

cinema	el cine
screen	la pantalla
to dub	doblar
to subtitle	subtitular
subtitle	el subtítulo
sequel	la continuación
director	el director
producer	el productor
to censor	censurar
censorship	la censura

428

to whistle, hiss	silbar
amusements	los recreos
playground	el patio de recreo
to enjoy oneself	divertirse, recrearse
entertaining	divertido
amusing	ameno
pastime	el pasatiempo
rest	el descanso
to rest	descansar
weariness	el cansancio

429

to get tired	cansarse
tired	cansado
to get bored	aburrirse
boring	aburrido
fair	la feria
festival	la verbena, la fiesta
crowd	la muchedumbre
to assemble	concurrir
circus	el circo
trapeze	el trapecio

430

trapeze	el trapecista *m*, la trapecista *f*
tightrope	la cuerda floja
tightrope walker	el funámbulo *m*, la funámbula
acrobat	el acróbata *m*, la acróbata *f*
acrobatic	acrobático
acrobatics	la acrobacia
clown	el payaso
joke	la broma
lottery	la lotería
to be lucky	tener suerte

431

luck	la suerte
swing	el columpio
to swing (oneself)	columpiarse
seesaw	el balancín
roundabout	el tiovivo
game	el juego
to play	jugar
player	el jugador
toy	el juguete
match	el partido

432

to win	ganar
to lose	perder
to draw	empatar
to cheat	engañar
deceit	el engaño
deceitful	engañoso
meeting	la reunión
to meet	reunirse
to join	unirse
party	la tertulia, el guateque

433

to visit	visitar
visit	la visita
playing cards	los naipes
to deal	repartir
to shuffle	barajar
suit	el palo
billiards	el billar

cue	el taco
cannon	la carambola
spin	el efecto

434

chess	el ajedrez
piece	la pieza
pawn	el peón
rook	la torre
bishop	el alfil
knight	el caballo
chessboard	el tablero (de ajedrez)
draughts	las damas
dice	los dados
jigsaw	el rompecabezas, el puzzle

Sport   El Deporte

435

sport	el deporte
swimming	la natación
to swim	nadar
swimmer	el nadador *m*, la nadadora *f*
breaststroke	la braza de pecho
crawl	el crol
backstroke	la braza de espalda
butterfly	la braza de mariposa
lifeguard	el salvavidas
to dive	zambullirse

436

high diving	el salto de palanca
to row	remar
rower	el remador
oar	el remo
canoe	la piragua
canoeing	el piragüismo
canoeist	el piragüista
paddle	el canalete
skate	el patín
to skate	patinar

437

figure skating	el patinaje artístico

rollerskates	los patines de ruedas
skateboard	el monopatín
amateur	el aficionado
fan	el hincha
bet	la apuesta
to bet	apostar
odds	las ventajas
ball	la pelota
football (*sport*)	el fútbol

438

football	el balón
footballer	el futbolista
football pools	las quinelas
referee	el arbitro
penalty	el penálty
corner	el córner, el saque de esquina
offside	fuera de juego
forward	el delantero
defender	el defensa
midfielder	el centrocampista

439

winger	el ala
to score	marcar
to shoot	chutar, tirar
to dribble	regatear
goal (*objective*)	la meta, la portería
goal (*score*)	el gol
goalkeeper	el portero, el guardameta
goalscorer	el goleador
goal-kick	el saque de portería
team	el equipo

440

league	la liga
trophy	el trofeo
knockout competition	el concurso eliminatorio
rugby	el rugby
to tackle	placar
scrum	la melé
scrum-half	el medio de melé
fly-half	el apertura
prop	el pilar
fullback	el zaguero

441

American football	el fútbol americano
tennis	el tenis
lawn tennis	el tenis sobre hierba
tennis player	el tenista *m*, la tenista *f*
set	el set
volley	el voleo
to serve	sacar
table tennis	el tenis de mesa, el ping-pong
racket	la raqueta
boxing	el boxeo

442

boxer	el boxeador
wrestling	la lucha
champion	el campeón
fencing	la esgrima
fencer	el esgrimidor
foil	el florete
gymnast	el gimnasta
gymnastics	la gimnasia
somersault	el salto mortal
cycling	el ciclismo

443

cyclist	el ciclista
mountain bicycle	la bicicleta de montaña
time trial	la cronometrada
stage	la etapa
yellow jersey	el maillot amarillo
horseriding	la equitación
showjumping	el concurso de saltos
dressage	la doma clásica
polo	el polo
horseman	el jinete

444

grandstand	la tribuna
racecourse	la pista
race	la carrera
to run	correr
bullfight	la corrida (de toros)
bull fighter	el torero
motor racing	el automovilismo deportivo
scrambling	el motocross

hockey	el hockey
bowls	el juego de las bochas

445

stadium	el estadio
high jump	el salto de altura
record	el récord
long jump	el salto de longitud
triple jump	el triple salto
pole vault	el salto con pértiga
long distance runner	el corredor de fondo
lap	la vuelta
marathon	el maratón
training	el entrenamiento

446

athletics	el atletismo
athlete	el atleta *m*, la atleta *f*
sprinter	el esprínter
sprint	el esprint
to sprint	esprintar
track	la pista
starting blocks	los tacos de salida
hurdle	la valla
javelin	la jabalina
shotput	el lanzamiento de
peso	

447

discus	el disco
hammer	el martillo
relay race	la carrera de relevos
baton	el testigo
Olympic Games	los Juegos Olímpicos
triathlon	el triatlón
triathlete	el triatleta
decathlon	el decatlón
decathlete	el decatleta
pentathlon	el pentatlón

448

pentathlete	el pentatleta
mountaineering	el montanismo
mountaineer	el montanista, el alpinista
rock climbing	la escalada en rocas
rock climber	el escalador (de rocas)

ice-axe	el piolet
skiing	el esquí
to ski	esquiar
ski	el esquí
cross-country skiing	el esquí nórdico

449

ski-lift	el telesquí
skier	el esquiador
ski-stick	el bastón de esquiar
ski-jumping	el salto de esquí
snowshoe	la raqueta (de nieve)
sledge	el trineo
ice hockey	el hockey sobre hielo
puck	el puck
water skiing	el esquí acuático
outboard motor	el motor fuera-bordo

450

slalom	el slalom
to abseil	descender en rappel
to fish	pescar
angling	la pesca (con caña)
fishing rod	la caña
reel	el carrete
bait	el cebo
to bait	cebar
hook	el anzuelo
fly fishing	la pesca a mosca

Food and Drink   La Comida y La Bebida

451

food	el alimento
provisions	las provisiones
to nourish	alimentar
appetite	el apetito
snack	la merienda
to have a snack	merendar
hunger	el hambre
hungry	hambriento
thirst	la sed
thirsty	sediento

452

to be hungry	tener hambre

to be thirsty	tener sed	**456**	
sweet	dulce	fast food	el fast-food
to have a sweet tooth	ser goloso	hamburger	la hamburguesa
sugar	el azúcar	hot dog	el perrito caliente
sugary	azucarado	pizza	la pizza
tasteless	soso	fat	la grasa
bitter	amargo	fatty food	la comida grasosa
milk	la leche	frozen food	el alimento congelado
to pasteurise	pasteurizar	french fries	las patatas fritas
		crisps	las papas fritas
453		confectionery	las golosinas
skimmed milk	la leche desnatada		
whole milk	la leche sin desnatar	**457**	
cream	la nata, la crema	vegetable	el legumbre, la verdura
butter	la mantequilla		
buttermilk	el suero de leche	carrot	la zanahoria
cheese	el queso	broccoli	el bróculi
egg	el huevo	onion	la cebolla
yolk	la yema (de huevo)	celery	el apio
egg white	la clara (de huevo)	radish	el rábano
shell	la cáscara	spinach	la espinaca
		asparagus	el espárrago
454		cucumber	el pepino
soft boiled egg	el huevo pasado por agua	gherkin	el pepinillo
scrambled eggs	los huevos revueltos	**458**	
omelette	la tortilla	lettuce	la lechuga
bread	el pan	tomato	el tomate
brown bread	el pan moreno	pea	el guisante
sliced bread	el pan de molde	chickpea	el garbanzo
loaf	el pan	bean	el haba
roll	el panecillo, el bollo	French bean	la judía
crumb	la miga	haricot bean	la judía blanca
crust	la corteza	cauliflower	la coliflor
		Brussels sprout	la col de Bruselas
455		aubergine	la berenjena
health foods	los alimentos naturales		
organically grown	cultivado biológicamente	**459**	
		salad	la ensalada
vegetarian	el vegeteriano *m*, la vegeteriana *f*	corn	el maíz
		beetroot	la remolacha
fibre	la fibra	green pepper	el pimiento verde
wholemeal bread	el pan integral	mashed potato	el puré de patatas
rye bread	el pan de centeno	garlic	el ajo
to slim	adelgazar	courgette	la calabacita
lentil	la lenteja	marrow	el calabacín
margarine	la margarina		
polyunsaturated	poliinsaturado		

460

tomato	el tomate
mushroom	el champiñon
condiment	el condimento
spice	la especia
ginger	el jengibre
mustard	la mostaza
nutmeg	la nuez moscada
cinnamon	la canela
turmeric	la cúrcuma
saffron	el azafrán

461

soup	la sopa
soup tureen	la sopera
broth	el caldo
beef	la carne de vaca
veal	la ternera
steak	el filete
rare	poco hecho
well done	bien hecho
sauce	la salsa
gravy	el jugo de carne

462

cutlet	la chuleta
ham	el jamón
bacon	el tocino
sausage	la salchicha
pepperoni	el salchichón
blood sausage	la morcilla
raw	crudo
soft	tierno, blando
hard	duro
stew	el cocido

463

tripe	los callos
cooking	la cocina
cook	el cocinero
to cook	cocer
to roast	asar
roast	el asado
to stew	guisar
to slice	tajar
slice	la tajada
to fry	freír

464

fried	frito
chicken	el pollo
breast	la pechuga
leg	la pata
ham	el jamón
to cure	curar
to smoke (food)	ahumar
lamb	el cordero
pork	el cerdo
veal	la ternera

465

to grill	hacer al grill
to barbecue	asar a la parrilla
barbecue	la parrillada
to bake	hornear
breaded	empanado
scampi	los langostinos rebozados
to stuff	estofar
spit	el espetón
suckling pig	el lechón
shank (lamb)	la pierna (de cordero)

466

fish	el pescado
haddock	el abadejo
mussel	los mejillón
mullet	el salmonete
mackerel	la caballa
clam	la almeja
sole	el lenguado
tuna	el atún
salad	la ensalada
oil	el aceite

467

vinegar	el vinagre
sour	agrio
cruet-stand	las vinagreras
salt	la sal
saltcellar	el salero
to salt	salar
pepper	la pimienta
pepperpot	el pimentero
mustard	la mostaza
mayonnaise	la mayonesa

468

jam	la confitura, la mermelada
marmalade	la mermelada de naranjas
cake	el pastel
pastry-cook	el pastelero
dough	la pasta
dessert	el postre
pancake	la torta
rice pudding	el arroz con leche
custard	las natillas
roast apple	la manzana asada

469

caramel cream	el flan
ice cream	el helado
chocolate	el chocolate
chocolate mousse	el mousse de chocolate
fritters	los churros
sponge cake	el bizcocho
fruit salad	la macedonia de frutas
whipped cream	la nata montada
cheese cake	la tarta de queso
lemon meringue	el merengue de limón

470

pudding	el budín
biscuit	el bizcocho, la galleta
baby food	la comida para bebés
flour	la harina
self-raising flour	la harina de fuerza
yeast	la levadura
baking soda	el bicarbonato de sosa
lard	la manteca
oil	el aceite
sunflower oil	el aceite de girasol

471

olive oil	el aceite de oliva
rice	el arroz
yoghurt	el yogur
doughnut	el buñuelo
apple compote	la compota de manzana
sandwich	el sandwich, el bocadillo

spaghetti	los espaguetis
cake	la tarta
noodle	el tallarín
frog legs	las patas de rana

472

restaurant	el restaurante
menu	el menú
starter	el entremés
first course	el primer plato
waitress	la camarera
waiter	el camarero
drink	la bebida
to drink	beber
to sip	sorber
to gulp	tragar

473

to empty	vaciar
empty	vacío
nonalcoholic drink	la bebida sin alcohol
wine	el vino
red wine	el vino tinto
rosé wine	el vino rosado
vintage	añejo
beer	la cerveza
water	el agua
drinkable	potable

474

milkshake	el batido
tonic	la tónica
juice	el jugo
soft drink	el refresco
sherry	el jerez
dry	seco
sherbet	el sorbete
lemonade	la limonada
fizzy	gaseoso
to uncork	descorchar

475

corkscrew	el sacacorchos
liqueur	el licor
spirits	los licores
cognac	el coñac

tonic water	la tónica	hotel	el hotel
orange drink	la naranjada	hotelier	el hotelero
mineral water	el agua mineral	reception	la recepción
cappuccino	el capuchino		
tea	el té	**479**	
camomile tea	la manzanilla	information desk	la conserjería
		lobby	el vestíbulo
476		service	el servicio
lemon tea	el té con limón	to book in advance	reservar por
coffee	el café		adelantado
coffee with milk	el café con leche	vacant	libre
decaffeinated coffee	el descafeinado	bill	la cuenta
iced coffee	el cafe con hielo	tip	la propina
instant coffee	el cafe instantáneo	hostel	el albergue
soda	la soda	youth hostel	el albergue de
whisky	el whisky		juventud
canned beer	la cerveza enlatada	boarding house	la pensión
bottled beer	la cerveza		
	embotellada	**480**	
		camping	el cámping
		campsite	el campamento
477		to go camping	hacer cámping
cider	la sidra	camp-chair	la silla plegadiza
champagne	el champán	camping-van	la camioneta-casa
vermouth	el vermut	air mattress	la colchoneta
vodka	el vodka		hinchable
rum	el ron	bottle opener	el abrebotellas
Irish coffee	el cafe irlandés	camp bed	la cama plegable
anise	el anís	tin opener	el abrelatas
brandy	el aguardiente		
cherry brandy	el aguardiente de	**481**	
	cerezas	campfire	la hoguera (de
applejack	el aguardiente de		campamento)
	manzanas	flashlight	la linterna
		fly sheet	el toldo impermeable
		ground	el suelo
Travel and	**Los Viajes y**	ground sheet	el suelo impermeable
Tourism	**El Turismo**	guy line	el viento
		mallet	el mazo
478		shelter	el abrigo
to travel	viajar	to take shelter	abrigarse
traveller	el viajero	to get wet	mojarse
travel agency	la agencia de viajes		
travel agent	el agente de viajes	**482**	
package holiday	las vacaciones todo	sleeping bag	el saco de dormir
	pagado	to sleep out	dormir al aire libre
tourist	el turista	tent	la tienda
tourist season	la temporada turística		

tent peg	la clavija	railhead	la estación terminal
tent pole	el mástil de tienda	railtrack	la vía férrea
thermos flask	el termo	railworker	el ferroviario
caravan	la caravana	stationmaster	el jefe de la estación
to go caravaning	viajar en caravana	waiting room	la sala de espera
to live rough	vivir sin comodidades	single ticket	el billete sencillo
tramp	el vagabundo	return ticket	el billete de ida y vuelta

483

self-catering apartment	el piso sin pensión	to examine	revisar
day-tripper	el excursionista	ticket inspector	el revisador
trip	la excursión		

487

railway	el ferrocarril	guard	el jefe de tren
platform	el andén	engine driver	el maquinista
to derail	descarrillar	signalman	el guardavía
derailment	el descarrillamiento	locomotive	la locomotora
to collide	chocar	carriage	el vagón
collision	el choque	sleeping car	el coche cama
accident	el accidente	dining car	el vagón restaurante
		luggage	el equipaje
		to check in	facturar

484

timetable	el horario	left-luggage	la consigna
guidebook	la guía		

488

train	el tren	trunk	el baúl
express train	el expreso	case	la maleta
through train	el tren directo	rucksack	la mochila
to arrive	llegar	stop	la parada
arrival	llegada	to stop	pararse
to leave	salir	stay	la estancia
departure	la salida	customs	la aduana
departure board	el tablón de salidas	customs officer	el aduanero
		examination	el registro
		to examine	registrar

485

underground railway	el metro		

489

diesel	el diesel	duty	el derecho
steam	el vapor	tax	el impuesto
corridor	el pasillo	to tax	tasar
to alight	apearse	to declare	declarar
halt	el apeadero	duty-free	libre de impuestos
compartment	el departamento	passport	el pasaporte
tunnel	el túnel	identity card	el carné, la cédula de identidad
viaduct	el viaducto		
cutting	el desmonte	bus	el autobús

486

		taxi	el taxi
railway network	la red ferroviaria	taxi driver	el taxista

490

driving licence	el permiso de conducir
to drive	conducir, manejar
motor car	el coche, el automóvil
motoring	el automovilismo
motorist	el automovilista
to hire	alquilar
trailer	el remolque
to give someone a lift	llevar a alguien
hitchhiker	el autostopista
to hitchhike	hacer autostop, hacer dedo

491

hitchhiking	el autostopismo
sharp bend	la curva cerrada
to skid	resbalar
door (*vehicle*)	la portezuela
window (*vehicle*)	la ventanilla
to park	aparcar
to slow down	moderar la marcha
to accelerate	acelerar
to start up	arrancar
to overtake	adelantar

492

aerial	la antena
air filter	el filtro de aire
alternator	el alternador
antifreeze	el anti-congelante
gearbox	la caja de cambios
axle	el eje
battery	la batería
flat	descargado
bonnet	el capó
boot	el maletero

493

brake fluid	el líquido de frenos
brake	el freno
to brake	frenar
bumper	parachoques
carburettor	carburador
child seat	la silla de niño
choke	el estárter
clutch	el embrague

cylinder	el cilindro
horsepower	el caballo (de fuerza)

494

disc brake	el freno de disco
distributor	el distribuidor
dynamo	el dinamo
dynamic	dinámico
engine	el motor
exhaust	el tubo de escape
fan belt	la correa de ventilador
fuel gauge	el indicador de carburante
fuel pump	la bomba de carburante
fuse	el fusible

495

gear lever	la palanca de cambios
generator	el generador
to generate	generar
alternating current	la corriente alterna
hand brake	el freno de mano
hazard lights	las luces de emergencia
horn	la bocina
ignition	el contacto
ignition key	la llave de contacto
indicator	el intermitente

496

jack	el gato
silencer	el silenciador
number plate	la matrícula
oil filter	el filtro de aceite
points	los platinos
rear view mirror	el espejo retrovisor
reflector	el reflectante
reverse light	la luz de marcha atrás
roof-rack	el portaequipajes
seat	el asiento

497

seat belt	el cinturón de seguridad
shock absorber	el amortiguador
socket set	el juego de llaves de tubo

spanner	la llave inglesa	passage	el pasaje
spare part	el repuesto	passenger	el pasajero
spark plug	la bujía	cabin	el camarote
speedometer	el velocímetro	deck	el puente
starter motor	el motor de arranque	mast	el mástil
steering wheel	el volante	pilot	el piloto
sun roof	el techo solar	rudder	el timón
		crew	la tripulación
498		anchor	el ancla, *f*
suspension	la suspensión		
towbar	la barra de remolque	**502**	
transmission	la transmisión	to cast anchor	fondear
tyre	el neumático	anchorage	el ancladero
wheel	la rueda	cargo	la carga, el
windscreen	el parabrisas		cargamento
wipers	las limpiaparabrisas	to sink	hundirse
wrench	arranque	sinking	el hundimiento
air bag	la bolsa de aire	shipwreck	el naufragio
four-wheel drive	la tracción de cuatro	signal	la señal
	por cuatro	to signal	señalar
		lighthouse	el faro
499		port	el puerto
motorbike	la motocicleta		
helmet	el casco	**503**	
bicycle	la bicicleta	quay	el muelle
racing cycle	la bicicleta de carreras	oil tanker	el petrolero
pedal	el pedal	to launch	arriar al agua
to pedal	pedalear	salvage	el salvamento
tube	la cámara	to salvage	salvar
to puncture	pincharse	free on board	franco a bordo
chain	la cadena	waybill	la carta de porte
pannier bag	la cartera	hovercraft	el hidrodeslizador
500		**504**	
ship	el buque	stern	la popa
boat	el barco, la barca	prow	la proa
sail	la vela	starboard	el estribor
to embark	embarcarse	port	el babor
to disembark	desembarcar	keel	la quila
on board	a bordo	hold	la bodega
disembarkment	el desembarco	figurehead	el figurón de proa
to tow	remolcar	funnel	la chimenea
tug	el remolcador	rigging	la jarcia
crossing	la travesía	sail	la vela
501		**505**	
to cross	atravesar	raft	el embalse

galley	la galera
clinker-built	de tingladillo
galleon	el galeón
clipper	el clíper
schooner	la goleta
whaler	el ballenero
trawler	el arrastrero
to trawl	rastrear
factory ship	el buque factoría

506

hydrofoil	la hidroala
powerboat	el motorbote
rubber dinghy	la lancha neumática
pontoon	el pontón
life raft	la balsa salvavidas
aqualung	la escafandra autónoma
diver	el buceador
navigation	la navegación
to navigate	navegar
to weigh anchor	zarpar

507

balloon	el globo
airship	el dirigible
aviation	la aviación
airplane	el avión
flying boat	el hidroavión
airport	el aeropuerto
air terminal	la terminal aérea
passenger	el pasajero
business class	la clase de negociante
tourist class	la clase turística

508

farewell	la despedida
air hostess	la azafata
to land	aterrizar
forced landing	el aterrizaje forzoso
to take off	despegar
take-off	el despegue
seatbelt	el cinturón
to fly	volar
propeller	la hélice
pilot	el piloto

509

autopilot	el piloto automático
black box	la caja negra
runway	la pista de aterrizaje
undercarriage	el tren de aterizaje
sound barrier	la barrera sonora
to crash	estrellarse
glider	el planeador
to glide	planear
hang-glider	el ala delta
autogyro	el autogiro

Numbers — Los números

1	uno, una
2	dos
3	tres
4	cuatro
5	cinco
6	seis
7	siete
8	ocho
9	nueve
10	diez
11	once
12	doce
13	trece
14	catorce
15	quince
16	dieciséis
17	diecisiete
18	dieciocho
19	diecinueve
20	veinte
21	veintiuno
22	veintidós
23	veintitrés
24	veinticuatro
25	veinticinco
26	veintiséis
27	veintisiete
28	veintiocho
29	veintinueve
30	treinta
40	cuarenta
50	cincuenta
60	sesenta

70	setenta	300th	trecentésimo
80	ochenta	400th	quadringentésimo
90	noventa	500th	quingentésimo
100	ciento or cien (*before a noun*)	600th	sexcentésimo
		700th	septingentésimo
200	doscientos	800th	octingentésimo
300	trescientos	900th	noningentésimo
400	cuatrocientos	1000th	milésimo
500	quinientos	2000th	dos milésimo
600	seiscientos	millionth	millonésimo
700	setecientos	two millionth	dos millonésimo
800	ochocientos		
900	novecientos		
1000	mil		
2000	dos mil		
1000000	un millón		
1st	primero		
2nd	segundo		
3rd	tercero		

Proverbs and idioms
Los proverbios y los modismos

to be homesick
tener morriña

to have pins and needles
tener hormigueo

don't mention it
no hay de qué

it's none of your business
no tiene nada que ver contigo

it's all the same
me da igual

as deaf as a post
sordo como una tapia

to sleep like a log
dormir como un lirón

as drunk as a lord
más borracho que una cuba

a bird in the hand is worth two in the bush
más vale pájaro en mano que ciento volando

to kill two birds with one stone
matar dos pájaros de un tiro

4th	cuarto
5th	quinto
6th	sexto
7th	séptimo
8th	octavo
9th	noveno
10th	décimo
11th	undécimo
12th	duodécimo
13th	decimotercero
14th	decimocuarto
15th	decimoquinto
16th	decimosexto
17th	decimoséptimo
18th	decimoctavo
19th	decimonoveno
20th	vigésimo
21st	vigésimo primero
30th	trigésimo
31st	trigésimo primero
40th	cuadragésimo
50th	quincuagésimo
60th	sexagésimo
70th	septuagésimo
80th	octogésimo
90th	nonagésimo
100th	centésimo
200th	ducentésimo

at full speed
a todo correr

no sooner said than done
dicho y hecho

birds of a feather flock together
Dios los cría y ellos se juntan

every cloud has a silver lining
no hay mal que por bien no venga

a chip off the old block
del tal palo tal astilla

out of sight, out of mind
ojos que no ven, corazón que no siente

practice makes perfect
la práctica hace maestro

many hands make light work
muchas manos facilitan el trabajo

better late than never
más vale tarde que nunca

at first sight
a primera vista

in the short term
a corto plazo

in the long run
a la larga

on the other hand
por otra parte

in my opinion
a mi juicio

in fact
de hecho

in other words
dicho de otro modo

First names   Nombres de pila

First names	Nombres de pila
Alexander	Alejandro
Andrew	Andrés
Anthony	Antonio
Bernard	Bernardo
Charles	Carlos
Christopher	Cristóbal
Edward	Eduardo
Francis	Francisco
George	Jorge
Henry	Enrique
James	Jaime
John	Juan
Joseph	José
Lawrence	Lorenzo
Louis	Luis
Martin	Martín
Michael	Miguel
Nicholas	Nicolás
Paul	Pablo
Peter	Pedro
Philip	Felipe
Raymond	Ramón
Thomas	Tomás
Vincent	Vicente
Alice	Alicia
Anne	Ana
Catherine	Catalina
Charlotte	Carlota
Deborah	Débora
Eleanor	Leonor
Elizabeth	Isabel
Ellen	Elena
Emily	Emilia
Esther	Ester
Frances	Francisca
Josephine	Josefina
Louise	Luisa
Margaret	Margarita
Mary	María
Matilda	Matilde
Ophelia	Ofelia
Patricia	Patricai
Pauline	Paula
Rachel	Raquel
Rose	Rosa

Susan	Susana
Sylvia	Silvia
Veronica	Verónica

Signs of the Zodiac Los signos del Zodíaco

Aquarius	el Acuario
Pisces	el Piscis
Aries	Aries
Taurus	el Tauro
Gemini	el Géminis
Cancer	el Cáncer
Leo	el Leo
Virgo	la Virgo
Libra	la Libra
Scorpio	el Escorpión
Sagittarius	el Sagitario
Capricorn	el Capricornio

Prepositions and conjunctions Las preposiciones, los adverbios y las conjunciones

against	contra
at	en
between	entre
for	para, por
from	de
in	en, dentro de
of	de
on	en, sobre
to	a
with	con
without	sin
above	arriba
down	abajo
under	debajo de
in front of	delante de
opposite	enfrente
forward	adelante
behind	detrás de
backwards	atrás
close to	junto a
near	cerca de
far from	lejos de
before	antes de
after	después, tras
here	aquí
there	allí

inside	dentro
within	adentro
outside	fuera
where	donde
during	durante
except	excepto
towards	hacia
until	hasta
according to	según
now	ahora
often	a menudo
then	entonces
never	nunca
always	siempre
at once	en seguida
soon	pronto
still	todavía
already	ya
like	como
how	cómo
neither... nor...	ni... ni...
either... or...	o... o...
and	y
but	pero
why	por qué
because	porque
if	si
yes	sí
no	no
well	bien
badly	mal
quickly	de prisa
slowly	despacio
enough	bastante
when	cuando
too	demasiado
more	más
less	menos
much	mucho
nothing	nada
nobody	nadie
never	nunca
perhaps	quizás, acaso
once	una vez
instead of	en vez de
often	a menudo
at times	a veces

Spanish Phrases

Getting Started

Everyday words and phrases

Yes
Sí
see

Please
Por favor
por fa-bor

Yes, please
Sí, por favor
see, por fa-bor

Thank you
Gracias
gra-thee-as

No
No
no

Excuse me
¡Perdón!
pair-don

No, thank you
No, gracias
no, gra-thee-as

Good
Bueno
bway-no

OK
Vale
ba-lay

I am very sorry
Lo siento mucho
lo syen-to moo-cho

Being understood

I do not speak Spanish
No hablo castellano
no a-blo kas-te-ya-no

It does not matter
No importa
no eem-por-ta

I do not understand
No entiendo
no en-tyen-do

I do not mind
No me importa
no may eem-por-ta

Can you find someone who speaks English?
¿Puede encontrar a alguien que hable inglés?
pwe-day en-kon-trar al-gee-en kay a-blay een-glays

Please repeat that slowly
Por favor repítame eso lentamente
por fa-bor, re-pee-ta-may e-so len-ta-men-tay

Can you help me, please?
¿Puede ayudarme, por favor?
pwe-day a-yoo-dar-may, por fa-bor

Greetings and exchanges

Hello
Hola
o-la

Hi
Hola
o-la

Good evening
Buenas tardes
*bway-nas **tar**-des*

Good morning
Buenos días
*bway-nos **dee**-as*

Good night
Buenas noches
*bway-nas **no**-ches*

Good-bye
Adiós
*a-dee-**os***

It is nice to meet you
Encantado / Encantada de conocerle
*en-kan-**ta**-do / en-kan-**ta**-da day ko-no-**thair**-lay*

How are you?
¿Qué tal estás?
*kay tal es-**tas***

I am very well, thank you
Muy bien, gracias
*mwee byen, **gra**-thee-as*

It is good to see you
Me alegro de verlo
*may a-**le**-gro day **bair**-lo*

There are five of us
Somos cinco
*so-mos **theen**-ko*

This is — my son
Este es — mi hijo
*es-tay es — mee **ee**-ho*

— my husband
— mi marido
*— mee ma-**ree**-do*

This is — my daughter
Ésta es — mi hwija
*es-ta es — mee **ee**-ha*

— my wife
— mi esposa
*— mee es-**po**-sa*

My name is . . .
Me llamo . . .
*may **ya**-mo . . .*

What is your name?
¿Cómo te llamas?
***ko**-mo tay **ya**-mas*

I am a student
Soy estudiante
*soy es-too-dee-**an**-tay*

I am on holiday
Estoy de vacaciones
*es-**toy** day ba-ka-**thyo**-nes*

I live in London
Vivo en Londres
***bee**-bo en **lon**-dres*

You are very kind
Es usted muy amable
*es oo-**sted** mwee a-**ma**-blay*

You're welcome!
¡De nada!
*day **na**-da!*

See you soon
Hasta pronto
*a-sta **pron**-to*

I am from   — **America**
Soy de   — los Estados Unidos
soy day   — *los es-**ta**-dos oo-**nee**-dos*

   — **Australia**
   — Australia
   — *ow-**stra**-lee-a*

   — **Britain**
   — Gran Bretaña
   — *gran bre-**tan**-ya*

   — **Canada**
   — Canadá
   — *ka-na-**da***

   — **England**
   — Inglaterra
   — *een-gla-**te**-ra*

   — **Ireland**
   — Irlanda
   — *eer-**lan**-da*

   — **New Zealand**
   — Nueva Zelanda
   — ***nway**-ba the-**lan**-da*

   — **Scotland**
   — Escocia
   — *es-**ko**-thee-a*

   — **South Africa**
   — Sudáfrica
   — *soo-**da**-free-ka*

   — **Wales**
   — Gales
   — ***ga**-les*

Common questions

Where?
¿Dónde?
don-day

Where is...?
¿Dónde está...?
*don-day es-**ta**...*

Where are...?
¿Dónde están...?
*don-day es-**tan**...*

When?
¿Cuándo?
***kwan**-do*

What?
¿Qué?
kay

How?
¿Cómo?
***ko**-mo*

How much?
¿Cuánto?
***kwan**-to*

Who?
¿Quién?
kee-en

Why?
¿Por qué?
por kay

Which?
¿Cuál?
kwal

How long will it take?
¿Cuánto tardará?
kwan**-to tar-da-**ra

How can I contact American Express / Diners Club?
¿Cómo puedo contactar la oficina de American Express / Diners Club?
*ko-mo **pwe**-do kon-tak-**tar** la o-fee-**thee**-na day American Express / Diners Club*

What is the problem?
¿Cuál es el problema?
*kwal es el pro-**blay**-ma*

Do you know a good restaurant?
¿Conoce algún buen restaurante?
*ko-**no**-thay al-**goon** bwen res-to-**ran**-tay*

Do you mind if I . . . ?
¿Le importa que yo . . . ?
*lay eem-**por**-ta kay yo . . .*

What is wrong?
¿Qué ocurre?
*kay o-**koo**-ray*

What time do you close?
¿A qué hora cierran?
*a kay **o**-ra thee-e-ran*

Where can I buy a postcard?
¿Dónde puedo comprar una postal?
*don-day **pwe**-do kom-**prar** oo-na po-**stal***

Where can I buy currency?
¿Dónde puedo cambiar dinero en efectivo?
*don-day **pwe**-do kam-**byar** dee-**ne**-ro en e-fek-**tee**-bo*

Where can I change traveller's cheques?
¿Dónde puedo cambiar cheques de viaje?
*don-day **pwe**-do kam-**byar** che-kays day bee-**a**-hay*

Where can we sit down?
¿Dónde podemos sentarnos?
*don-day po-**day**-mos sen-**tar**-nos*

Where is the toilet?
¿Dónde están los servicios?
*don-day es-**tan** los sair-**bee**-thee-os*

Who did this?
¿Quién ha hecho esto?
*kee-**en** a e-cho **es**-to*

Who should I see about this?
¿Con quién debería hablar sobre esto?
*kon kee-**en** de-be-**ree**-a a-**blar** so-bray **es**-to*

Will you come also?
¿Va a venir usted también?
*ba a be-**neer** oo-**sted** tam-**byen***

Asking the time

Spain is on GMT plus one hour in the winter and GMT plus two hours in the summer. The 24-hour clock is commonly used in Spain. *See also* Numbers, page 373.

What time is it?
¿Qué hora es?
*kay **o**-ra es*

  It is — nine-thirty pm (21:30)
Son — las veintiuna trenta
*son — las bain-tee-**oo**-na **trayn**-ta*

  — six-fifteen pm (18:15)
— las dieciocho quince
*— las dee-eth-ee-**o**-cho **keen**-thay*

  — a quarter past ten
— las diez y cuarto
*— las **dee**-eth ee **kwar**-to*

  — a quarter to eleven
— las once menos cuarto
*— las **on**-thay **me**-nos **kwar**-to*

  — after three o'clock
— después de las tres
*— des-**pwes** day las tres*

— **nearly five o'clock**
— casi las cinco
— *ka-see las **theen**-co*

— **twenty-five past ten**
— las diez y veinticinco
— *las **dee**-eth ee bain-tee-**theen**-ko*

— **twenty-five to eleven**
— las once menos veinticinco
— *las **on**-thay **me**-nos bain-tee-**theen**-ko*

— **eleven o'clock**
— las once
— *las **on**-thay*

— **five past ten**
— las diez y cinco
— *las **dee**-eth ee **theen**-ko*

— **half past ten**
— las diez y media
— *las **dee**-eth ee **me**-dee-a*

— **five to eleven**
— las once menos cinco
— *las **on**-thay **me**-nos **theen**-ko*

— **ten o' clock**
— las diez
— *las **dee**-eth*

— **ten past ten**
— las diez y diez
— *las **dee**-eth ee **dee**-eth*

— **twenty past ten**
— las diez y veinte
— *las **dee**-eth ee **bain**-tay*

— **twenty to eleven**
— las once menos veinte
— *las **on**-thay **me**-nos **bain**-tay*

It is — **early**
Es — temprano
*es — tem-**pra**-no*

— **late**
— tarde
— ***tar**-day*

— **one o'clock**
— la una
— *la **oo**-na*

— **midday**
— mediodía
— *me-dee-o-**dee**-a*

— **midnight**
— medianoche
— *me-dee-a-**no**-chay*

at about one o'clock
sobre la una
*so-bray la **oo**-na*

at half past six
a las seis y media
*a las says ee **me**-dee-a*

at half past eight exactly
a las ocho y media en punto
*a las **o**-cho ee **me**-dee-a en **poon**-to*

in an hour's time
dentro de una hora
***den**-tro day **oo**-na **o**-ra*

in half an hour
dentro de media hora
***den**-tro day **me**-dee-a **o**-ra*

soon
pronto
***pron**-to*

this afternoon
esta tarde
*es-ta **tar**-day*

this evening
esta tarde
*es-ta **tar**-day*

At the Airport

Iberia is Spain's main airline, operating both international and domestic flights. They have several direct flights daily from London Heathrow and Gatwick to Madrid and from London Heathrow to Barcelona. There are also flights from Heathrow to a total of thirty destinations, including Bilbao, Alicante, Granada, Gran Canaria, Málaga, Palma, Seville, Tenerife and Valencia. Iberia also operate flights from Manchester to Madrid and Barcelona, plus Alicante, Bilbao, Seville, Valencia and a number of other destinations.

British Airways run daily flights to Madrid and Barcelona from Heathrow as well as a daily flight to Madrid and six flights a week to Barcelona from Gatwick. Other BA services include a daily flight from Gatwick to Málaga, three flights a week from Gatwick to Jerez, and a twice-weekly flight from Heathrow.

Popular holiday destinations are served by charter airlines. Cheap flight-only tickets are available from tour operators.

Arrival

Here is my passport
Aquí está mi pasaporte
a-kee es-ta mee pa-sa-por-tay

How long will this take?
¿Cuánto tardará esto?
kwan-to tar-da-ra es-to

I am attending a convention
Voy a asistir a un congreso
boy a a-see-steer a oon kon-gre-so

I am here on business
Estoy aquí en viaje de negocios
es-toy a-kee en bee-a-hay day ne-go-thee-os

I will be staying here for eight weeks
Me quedaré aquí ocho semanas
may kay-da-ray a-kee o-cho se-ma-nas

We are visiting friends
Estamos visitando a amigos
es-ta-mos bee-see-tan-do a-mee-gos

We have a joint passport
Tenemos un pasaporte familiar
te-nay-mos oon pa-sa-por-tay fa-mee-lyar

How much do I have to pay?
¿Cuánto tengo que pagar?
kwan-to ten-go kay pa-gar

I have nothing to declare
No tengo nada que declarar
no ten-go na-da kay de-kla-rar

I have the usual allowances
Tengo los artículos permitidos
ten-go los ar-tee-koo-los pair-mee-tee-dos

This is for my own use
Esto es para mi uso personal
es-to es pa-ra mee oo-so pair-so-nal

Common problems and requests

Can I upgrade to first class?
¿Puedo cambiar mi billete a primera clase?
pway-do kam-byar mee bee-ye-tay a pree-me-ra kla-say

I have lost my ticket
He perdido el billete
ay pair-dee-do el bee-ye-tay

I have missed my connection
He perdido el vuelo de enlace
ay pair-dee-do el bway-lo day en-la-thay

Please give me back my passport
Devuélvame el pasaporte, por favor
de-bwel-ba-may el pa-sa-por-tay, por fa-bor

The people who were to meet me have not arrived
No ha llegado la gente que iba a recibirme
no a ye-ga-do la hen-tay kay ee-ba a re-thee-beer-may

Where can I find the airline representative?
¿Dónde puedo encontrar al representante de la compañía aérea?
don-day pwe-do en-kon-trar al re-pre-zen-tan-tay day la kom-pan-yee-a a-air-ay-a

Where do I get the connecting flight to Santiago?
¿Dónde puedo enlazar con el vuelo a Santiago?
don-day pwe-do en-la-thar kon el bway-lo a san-tee-a-go

Where is	**— the bar?**
¿Dónde está	— el bar?
don-day es-ta	*— el bar*

— the departure lounge?
— la sala de embarque?
— la sa-la day em-bar-kay

— the information desk?
— la oficina de información?
— la o-fee-thee-na day een-for-ma-thyon

— the transfer desk?
— el mostrador de transbordos?
— el mos-tra-dor day trans-bor-dos

Where is	**— the toilet?**
¿Dónde están	— los servicios?
don-day es-tan	*— los sair-bee-thee-os*

Is there a bus into town?
¿Hay autobús a la ciudad?
eye ow-to-boos a la thee-oo-dad

How long will the delay be?
¿Cuánto se retrasará?
kwan-to say re-tra-sa-ra

I was delayed at the airport
Me entretuvieron en el aeropuerto
may en-tray-too-byair-on en el a-air-o-pwair-to

My flight was late
Mi vuelo se retrasó
mee bway-lo say re-tra-so

I was held up at immigration
Me entretuvieron en el control de pasaportes
may en-tray-too-byair-on en el kon-trol day pa-sa-por-tes

Luggage

Where is the baggage from flight number . . . ?
¿Dónde están los equipajes del vuelo número . . . ?
don-day es-tan los e-kee-pa-hays del bway-lo noo-me-ro . . .

I have lost my bag
He perdido la bolsa
ay pair-dee-do la bol-sa

These bags are not mine
Estas bolsas no son mías
es-tas bol-sas no son mee-as

Are there any baggage trolleys?
¿Hay carritos de equipaje?
eye ka-ree-tos day e-kee-pa-hay

Can I have help with my bags?
¿Puedo obtener ayuda para llevar el equipaje?
pwe-do ob-te-nair a-yoo-da pa-ra ye-bar el e-kee-pa-hay

Is there any charge?
¿Hay que pagar algo?
eye kay pa-gar al-go

I will carry that myself
Esto lo llevaré yo mismo / misma
es-to lo ye-ba-ray yo miz-mo / miz-ma

My baggage has not arrived
No ha llegado mi equipaje
no a ye-ga-do mee e-kee-pa-hay

Where is my bag?
¿Dónde está mi bolsa?
don-day es-ta mee bol-sa

It is — a large suitcase
Es — una maleta grande
es — oo-na ma-lay-ta gran-day

    — a rucksack
    — una mochila
    — oo-na mo-chee-la

    — a small bag
    — una bolsa pequeña
    — oo-na bol-sa pe-ken-ya

No, do not put that on top
No, no ponga eso encima de todo
no, no pon-ga e-so en-thee-ma day to-do

Please take these bags to a taxi
Por favor lleve estas bolsas a un taxi
por fa-bor, ye-bay es-tas bol-sas a oon tak-see

Careful, the handle is broken
Cuidado, el mango está roto
kwee-da-do, el man-go es-ta ro-to

This package is fragile
Este paquete es frágil
es-tay pa-ke-tay es fra-heel

At the Hotel

Hotels and hostales

Spain classifies all its hotels and similar accommodation with a star rating that reflects their facilities and amenities rather than the comfort or style of the individual establishments, so a tower block hotel could be rated with four stars and a fine old *hacienda* with the character and atmosphere that makes it uniquely Spanish may score only two or three stars, or even fewer. These are official government ratings and should be clearly displayed at the entrance with gold stars on a blue plaque. They should also appear on the standard tariff sheet, which must be displayed at reception.

Prices are generally quoted per room rather than per person and VAT (IVA) is added to the bill.

Accommodation is divided into several categories but for the purpose of ratings there are two main divisions – hotels and *hostales*. Hotels are star-rated on a one-to-five scale, although there are some hotels whose level of luxury is distinguished by a separate GL (*Gran Lujo*) rating.

Hostales (or pensions) are cheap hotels, rather like boarding houses, are rated on a one-to-three scale, ranging from fairly basic but mostly having a shower and some having a lavatory and bath to frugal with cold water.

The kind of accommodation is also classified and described by initials that precede the star rating. If an hotel or *hostal* does not have facilities for meals other than breakfast, it is described as a *residencia*. A place that provides apartment-like suites with self-catering facilities, together with many of the public facilities that you would expect of an hotel, is called an *aparthotel*.

The Spanish Tourist Office (*Oficina Nacional Española*), 57–58 St James's, London SW1A 1LD, can provide full lists of hotels and hostales.

Paradores

In 1926 the Marqués de Vega-Inclán, the Royal Tourist Commissioner to King Alfonso XIII, established the first of Spain's state-run hotels, Paradores. Now there are well over eighty hotels under the Paradores Nacionales banner. They offer an authentic taste of Spain, since many occupy historic buildings, including castles, palaces, monasteries and other buildings of interest. There are also many modern Paradores in the chain, and all the old ones are equipped with modern facilities.

They are liberally scattered throughout Spain, with the accent on places of outstanding natural beauty or of historical interest. Apart from the furnishings and decor being typically Spanish, the Paradores make a feature of regional specialities in their cuisine.

Reservations and enquiries

I am sorry I am late
Siento llegar tarde
*syen-to ye-**gar** **tar**-day*

I have a reservation
Tengo una reserva hecha
***ten**-go **oo**-na re-**sair**-ba **ay**-cha*

I shall be staying until July 4th
Me quedaré hasta el cuatro de julio
*may ke-da-**ray** a-sta el **kwa**-tro day **hoo**-lee-o*

I want to stay for 5 nights
Quiero quedarme cinco noches
*kee-e-ro ke-**dar**-may **theen**-ko **no**-ches*

Do you have a double room with a bath?
¿Tiene una habitación doble con baño?
*tee-e-nay **oo**-na a-bee-ta-**thyon** **do**-blay kon **ban**-yo*

Do you have a room with twin beds and a shower?
¿Tiene una habitación con camas gemelas y ducha?
*tee-**e**-nay **oo**-na a-bee-ta-**thyon** kon **ka**-mas he-**may**-las ee **doo**-cha*

Do you have a single room?
¿Tiene una habitación individual?
*tee-e-nay **oo**-na a-bee-ta-**thyon** een-dee-bee-**dwal***

I need — a double room with a bed for a child
Necesito — una habitación doble con una cama para un niño
*ne-the-**see**-to — **oo**-na a-bee-ta-**thyon** **do**-blay kon **oo**-na**ka**-ma **pa**-ra oon **neen**-yo*

— a room with a double bed
— una habitación con cama doble
*— **oo**-na a-bee-ta-**thyon** kon **ka**-ma **do**-blay*

— a room with twin beds and bath
— una habitación con camas gemelas y baño
*— **oo**-na a-bee-ta-**thyon** kon **ka**-mas he-**may**-las ee **ban**-yo*

— a single room
— una habitación individual
*— **oo**-na a-bee-ta-**thyon** een-dee-bee-**dwal***

— a single room with a shower or bath
— una habitación individual con ducha o baño
*— **oo**-na a-bee-ta-**thyon** een-dee-bee-**dwal** kon **doo**-cha o **ban**-y*

How much is — full board?
¿Cuánto es — la pensión completa?
*kwan-to es — la pen-**syon** kom-**play**-ta*

— half-board?
— la media pensión?
*— la **me**-dee-a pen-**syon***

How much is it per night?
¿Cuánto cuesta por noche?
*kwan-to **kwes**-ta por **no**-chay*

Does the price include room and breakfast?
¿Están incluidos en el precio la habitación y el desayuno?
*es-**tan** een-kloo-**ee**-dos en el **pre**-thee-o la a-bee-ta-**thyon** ee el des-a-**yoo**-no*

Does the price include room and all meals?
¿Están incluidos en el precio la habitación y todas las comidas?
*es-**tan** een-kloo-**ee**-dos en el **pre**-thee-o la a-bee-ta-**thyon** ee **to**-das las ko-**mee**-das*

Does the price include room and dinner?
¿Están incluidos en el precio la habitación y la cena?
*es-**tan** een-kloo-**ee**-dos en el **pre**-thee-o la a-bee-ta-**thyon** ee la **thay**-na*

Can we have adjoining rooms?
¿Nos puede dar habitaciones contiguas?
*nos **pwe**-day dar a-bee-ta-**thyo**-nes kon-**tee**-gwas*

Are there other children staying at the hotel?
¿Hay más niños hospedados en el hotel?
*eye mas **neen**-yos os-pe-**da**-dos en el o-**tel***

Are there supervised activities for the children?
¿Hay actividades vigiladas para los niños?
*eye ak-tee-bee-**da**-des bee-hee-**la**-das **pa**-ra los **neen**-yos*

Can my son sleep in our room?
¿Puede dormir mi hijo en nuestra habitación?
*pwe-day dor-**meer** mee **ee**-ho en **nwes**-tra a-bee-ta-**thyon***

Do you take traveller's cheques?
¿Acepta cheques de viaje?
*a-**thep**-ta **che**-kays day bee-**a**-hay*

Which floor is my room on?
¿En qué piso está mi habitación?
*en kay **pee**-so es-**ta** mee a-bee-ta-**thyon***

Do you have a fax machine?
¿Tiene fax?
tee-e-nay faks

Do you have a laundry service?
¿Tienen servicio de lavandería?
*tee-e-nen sair-**bee**-thee-o day la-ban-de-**ree**-a*

Do you have a safe for valuables?
¿Tiene caja fuerte para objetos de valor?
*tee-e-nay **ka**-ha **fwair**-tay **pa**-ra ob-**he**-tos day ba-**lor***

Do you have any English newspapers?
¿Tiene periódicos en inglés?
*tee-e-nay pe-ree-**o**-dee-kos en een-**gles***

Do you have a car park?
¿Tienen aparcamiento?
*tee-e-nen a-par-ka-**myen**-to*

Do you have a cot for my baby?
¿Tiene una cuna para el bebé?
*tee-e-nay **oo**-na **coo**-na **pa**-ra el be-**bay***

Do you have satellite TV?
¿Tiene antena parabólica?
*tee-e-nay an-**te**-na pa-ra-**bo**-lee-ka*

What is the voltage here?
¿Qué voltaje hay aquí?
*kay bol-**ta**-hay eye a-**kee***

Is there— a casino?
¿Hay — casino?
   *eye — ka-**see**-no*

       — a hairdryer?
       — secador de pelo?
       *— se-ka-**dor** day **pay**-lo*

       — a lift?
       — ascensor?
       *— as-then-**sor***

       — a minibar?
       — minibar?
       *— mee-nee-**bar***

       — a sauna?
       — sauna?
       *— **sow**-na*

       — a swimming pool?
       — piscina?
       *— pees-**thee**-na*

       — a telephone?
       — teléfono?
       *— te-**le**-fo-no*

       — a television?
       — televisión?
       *— te-lay-bee-**syon***

— a trouser press?
— plancha para pantalones?
— *plan-cha **pa**-ra pan-ta-**lo**-nes*

Is there a room service menu?
¿Hay menú para el servicio de
  habitaciones?
*eye me-**noo pa**-ra el sair-**bee**-thee-o day a-bee-
  ta-**thyo**-nes*

Is there a market in the town?
¿Hay algún mercado en la ciudad?
*eye al-**goon** mair-**ka**-do en la thee-oo-**dad***

Is there a Chinese restaurant?
¿Hay algún restaurante chino?
*eye al-**goon** re-sto-**ran**-tay **chee**-no*

Is there an Indian restaurant?
¿Hay algún restaurante indio?
*eye al-**goon** re-sto-**ran**-tay **een**-dee-o*

Is this a safe area?
¿Es ésta una zona segura?
*es es-ta **oo**-na **tho**-na se-**goo**-ra*

Where is the socket for my razor?
¿Dónde está el enchufe de la máquina de
  afeitar?
***don**-day es-**ta** el en-**choo**-fay day la **ma**-kee-
  nee-ya day a-fay-**tar***

Is the voltage 220 or 110?
¿Es el voltaje de doscientos veinte o de
  ciento diez?
*es el bol-**ta**-hay day dos-thee-**en**-tos **bain**-tay o
  day thee-**en**-to dee-**eth***

What time does the hotel close?
¿A qué hora cierra el hotel?
*a kay **o**-ra thee-e-ra el o-**tel***

What time does the restaurant close?
¿A qué hora cierra el restaurante?
*a kay **o**-ra thee-e-ra el re-sto-**ran**-tay*

When does the bar open?
¿Cuándo se abre el bar?
***kwan**-do say **a**-bray el bar*

What time is — breakfast?
¿Á qué hora es — el desayuno?
  *a kay **o**-ra es — el des-a-**yoo**-no*

— dinner?
— la cena
— *la **thay**-na*

— lunch?
— la comida?
— *la ko-**mee**-da*

Service

Can I charge this to my room?
¿Puede cargar esto a mi cuenta?
*pwe-day kar-**gar es**-to a mee **kwen**-ta*

Can I dial direct from my room?
¿Puedo marcar directamente desde mi
  habitación?
*pwe-do mar-**kar** dee-rek-ta-**men**-tay **dez**-day
  mee a-bee-ta-**thyon***

Can I have a newspaper?
¿Me da un periódico?
may da oon pe-ree-o-dee-ko

Can I have an outside line?
¿Me da línea, por favor?
*may da **lee**-nay-a, por fa-**bor***

Can I have my wallet from the safe?
¿Puedo sacar mi cartera de la caja fuerte?
*pwe-do sa-**kar** mee kar-**tair**-a day la **ka**-ha
  fwair-tay, por fa-**bor***

Can I have the bill please
¿Puede darme la factura, por favor?
*pwe-day **dar**-may la fak-**too**-ra, por fa-**bor***

Can I hire a portable telephone?
¿Puedo alquilar un teléfono portátil?
pwe-do al-kee-lar oon te-le-fo-no por-ta-teel

Can I make a telephone call from here?
¿Puedo hacer una llamada telefónica desde
  aquí?
*pwe-do a-thair oo-na ya-ma-da te-le-fo-nee-ka
dez-day a-kee*

Can I send this by courier?
¿Puedo enviar esto por mensajero?
pwe-do en-byar es-to por men-sa-hair-o

Can I use my charge card?
¿Puedo utilizar mi tarjeta de pago?
pwe-do oo-tee-lee-thar mee tar-hay-ta day pa-go

Can I use my personal computer here?
¿Puedo utilizar aquí mi ordenador
  personal?
*pwe-do oo-tee-lee-thar a-kee mee or-de-na-dor
pair-so-nal*

Can I use traveller's cheques?
¿Puedo utilizar cheques de viaje?
pwe-do oo-tee-lee-thar che-kays day bee-a-hay

Can we have breakfast in our room, please?
¿Podemos desayunar en la habitación, por
  favor?
*po-day-mos des-a-yoo-nar en la a-bee-ta-
thyon, por fa-bor*

**Can you recommend a good local
restaurant?**
¿Puede recomendar un buen restaurante
  cercano?
*pwe-day re-ko-men-dar oon bwen re-sto-ran-
tay thair-ka-no*

I want to stay an extra night
Quiero quedarme una noche más
kee-e-ro ke-dar-may oo-na no-chay mas

Do I have to change rooms?
¿Tengo que cambiarme de habitación?
ten-go kay kam-byar may day a-bee-ta-thyon

I need an early morning call
Necesito que me llame por la mañana
  temprano
*ne-the-see-to kay may ya-may por la man-ya-
na tem-pra-no*

I need — a razor
Necesito — una maquinilla de afeitar
*ne-the-see-to— oo-na ma-kee-nee-ya day a-
fay-tar*

    — some soap
    — jabón
    — ha-bon

    — some toilet paper
    — papel higiénico
    — pa-pel ee-hyen-ee-ko

    — some towels
    — toallas
    — to-a-yas

I need to charge these batteries
Tengo que cargar estas pilas
ten-go kay kar-gar es-tas pee-las

I want to press these clothes
Quiero planchar esta ropa
kee-e-ro plan-char es-ta ro-pa

Is there a trouser press I can use?
¿Hay prensa para pantalones que pueda
  usar?
*eye pren-sa pa-ra pan-ta-lo-nes kay pwe-do
oo-sar*

Please fill the minibar
Por favor, llene el minibar
por fa-bor, ye-nay el mee-nee-bar

Please leave the bags in the lobby
Por favor, deje las bolsas en el vestíbulo
por fa-bor, de-hay las bol-sas en el bes-tee-boo-lo

Please send this fax for me
Por favor, envie este fax de mi parte
por fa-bor, en-bee-ay es-tay faks day mee par-tay

Please turn the heating off
Apague la calefacción, por favor
a-pa-gay la ka-le-fak-thyon, por fa-bor

**Please, wake me at 7 o'clock in the
 morning**
Por favor, llámeme a las siete de la mañana
*por fa-bor, ya-may-may a las see-e-tay day la
 man-ya-na*

Where can I send a fax?
¿Dónde puedo enviar un fax?
don-day pwe-do en-byar oon faks

Can I have — my key, please?
¿Puede darme — mi llave, por favor?
pwe-day dar-may — mee ya-bay, por fa-bor

— an ashtray?
— un cenicero?
— oon the-nee-thair-o

— another blanket?
— otra manta?
— o-tra man-ta

— another pillow?
— otra almohada?
— o-tra al-mo-a-da

— some coat hangers?
— algunas perchas?
— al-goo-nas pair-chas

— some notepaper?
— papel de cartas?
— pa-pel day kar-tas

Has my colleague arrived yet?
¿Ha llegado mi compañero?
a ye-ga-do mee kom-pan-ye-ro

I am expecting a fax
Estoy esperando un fax
es-toy es-pe-ran-do oon faks

My room number is 22
El número de mi habitación es el veintidós
*el noo-me-ro day mee a-bee-ta-thyon es el
 bain-tee-dos*

Please can I leave a message?
¿Puedo dejar un mensaje, por favor?
pwe-do de-har oon men-sa-hay, por fa-bor

Problems

Where is the manager?
¿Dónde está el gerente?
don-day es-ta el he-ren-tay

I cannot close the window
No puedo cerrar la ventana
no pwe-do the-rar la ben-ta-na

I cannot open the window
No puedo abrir la ventana
no pwe-do a-breer la ben-ta-na

The air conditioning is not working
No funciona el aire acondicionado
no foon-thyo-na el eye-ray a-kon-dee-thyo-na-do

The room key does not work
No funciona la llave de la habitación
*no foon-thyo-na la ya-bay day la a-bee-ta-
 thyon*

The bathroom is dirty
El cuarto de baño está sucio
el kwar-to day ban-yo es-ta soo-thyo

The heating is not working
No funciona la calefacción
no foon-thyo-na la ka-le-fak-thyon

The light is not working
No funciona la luz
no foon-thyo-na la looth

The room is not serviced
La habitación no está preparada
la a-bee-ta-thyon no es-ta pre-pa-ra-da

The room is too noisy
La habitación es demasiado ruidosa
la a-bee-ta-thyon es de-ma-sya-do roo-ee-do-so

There are no towels in the room
No hay toallas en la habitación
no eye to-a-yas en la a-bee-ta-thyon

There is no hot water
No hay agua caliente
no eye a-gwa ka-lee-en-tay

There is no plug for the washbasin
No hay tapón en el lavabo
no eye ta-pon en el la-ba-bo

Checking out

I have to leave tomorrow
Tengo que irme mañana
ten-go kay eer-may man-ya-na

We will be leaving early tomorrow
Nos iremos mañana temprano
nos ee-ray-mos man-ya-na tem-pra-no

Could you have my bags brought down?
¿Podría hacer que me bajen las bolsas?
po-dree-a a-thair kay may ba-hen las bol-sas

Could you order me a taxi?
¿Puede pedirme un taxi?
pwe-day pe-deer-may oon tak-see

Thank you, we enjoyed our stay
Gracias, hemos disfrutado de nuestra
  estancia
*gra-thee-as, ay-mos dees-froo-ta-do day nwes-
  tra e-stan-thee-a*

Other Accommodation

Apart from hotels, hostales and paradores, other accommodation options in Spain include self-catering apartments (*aparthotels*) or villas, camping and hostelling. Many of the major tour operators have a self-catering programme of villas and apartment as well as hotel holidays, or you can book your own through the Spanish Tourist Office (*Oficina Nacional Española*), 57-58 St James's, London SW1A 1LD.

Self-catering

Self-catering has become a popular alternative to hotel accommodation in Spain. Most of what's on offer is modern, but standards can vary quite significantly. Although individual villas are available for rent through several tour operators, most of the self-catering accommodation available is in either apartments or small villas within a complex.

Most apartments will provide only basic cooking facilities. You should have enough crockery, cutlery, pots and utensils to see you through simple meals, but there are rarely any electrical gadgets to make life easier. Cookers may be little more than a couple of electric rings - don't assume that facilities such as ovens will be available.

Prices of self-catering packages generally depend on the number of occupants staying in the apartment. It is common to count sofa beds as sleeping space for two of your party. On a two-week holiday this can make your apartment seem cramped, so check how your party is going to be accommodated.

Villa complexes, or *urbanizaciones*, can be found all along the Mediterranean coasts as well as in the Balearic Islands and in the Canary Islands. Although most are booked through package arrangements, you may be able to arrange a booking on the spot. Villa complexes are unlikely to accept a booking of less than a week, but apartments and aparthotels will often agree to shorter stays. In villas you may be asked to pay a deposit on top of the rental charges. Charges usually include services such as gas and electricity, but be sure to confirm this. Maid service is usually provided only weekly, but it is sometimes possible to arrange additional service and also baby-sitting.

Renting a house

We have rented this villa
Hemos alquilado este chalé
ay-mos al-kee-la-do es-tay cha-lay

Here is our booking form
Aquí tiene nuestra reserva
a-kee tee-e-nay nwes-tra re-sair-ba

We need two sets of keys
Necesitamos dos juegos de llaves
ne-the-see-ta-mos dos hway-gos day ya-bes

Can I contact you on this number?
¿Puedo contactarle en este teléfono?
pwe-do kon-tak-tar-lay en es-tay te-le-fo-no

Where is the bathroom?
¿Dónde está el baño?
*don-day es-**ta** el **ban**-yo*

How does this work?
¿Cómo funciona ésto?
*ko-mo foon-**thyo**-na es-to*

I cannot open the shutters
No puedo abrir los postigos
*no **pwe**-do a-**breer** los po-**stee**-gos*

Can you send a repairman?
¿Puede enviar alguien a reparar?
pwe**-day en-**byar** al-gee-en a re-pa-**rar

Is the water heater working?
¿Funciona el calentador de agua?
*foon-**thyo**-na el ka-len-ta-**dor** day a-gwa*

Is the water safe to drink?
¿El agua es potable?
*el **a**-gwa es po-**ta**-blay*

Is there any spare bedding?
¿Hay ropa de cama de más?
*eye **ro**-pa day **ka**-ma day mas*

The cooker does not work
No funciona la cocina
*no foon-**thyo**-na la ko-**thee**-na*

The refrigerator does not work
No funciona el frigorífico
*no foon-**thyo**-na el free-go-**ree**-fee-ko*

The toilet is blocked
El inodoro está atascado
*el een-o-**do**-ro es-**ta** a-ta-**ska**-do*

There is a leak
Hay un escape
*eye oon es-**ka**-pay*

We do not have any water
No tenemos agua
*no te-**nay**-mos **a**-gwa*

When does the cleaner come?
¿Cuándo vienen a limpiar?
kwan**-do bee-e-nen a leem-**pyar

Where is the fuse box?
¿Dónde están los plomos?
*don-day es-**tan** los **plo**-mos*

Where is the key for this door?
¿Dónde está la llave de esta puerta?
*don-day es-**ta** la **ya**-bay day es-ta **pwair**-ta*

Around the house

bath
baño
ban-yo

bathroom
cuarto de baño
***kwar**-to day **ban**-yo*

bed
cama
ka-ma

brush
cepillo
*the-**pee**-yo*

can opener
abrelatas
*a-bray-**la**-tas*

chair
silla
see-ya

cooker
cocina
ko-thee-na

corkscrew
sacacorchos
sa-ka-kor-chos

cup
taza
ta-tha

fork
tenedor
te-ne-dor

glass
vaso
ba-so

inventory
inventario
een-ven-ta-ryo

kitchen
cocina
ko-thee-na

knife
cuchillo
koo-chee-yo

mirror
espejo
es-pe-ho

pan
sartén
sar-ten

plate
plato
pla-to

refrigerator
frigorífico
free-go-ree-fee-ko

rubbish
basura
ba-soo-ra

sheet
sábana
sa-ba-na

sink
fregadero
fre-ga-dair-o

spoon
cuchara
coo-cha-ra

stove
estufa
es-too-fa

table
mesa
may-sa

tap
grifo
gree-fo

toilet
inodoro
een-o-do-ro

vacuum cleaner
aspirador
as-pee-ra-dor

washbasin
lavabo
la-ba-bo

Camping

With a coastal climate conducive to being out of doors for much of the day, it's not surprising that camping is popular on the Mediterranean coasts, which is where most of Spain's 700-plus camp sites are located, particularly in the north, on the Costa Brava and Costa Dorada. But camping isn't restricted to the mainland. There are sites on both the Balearic and Canary Islands. Most sites are open only during the summer months, but some of those in areas of more favourable climate are open all year round.

Camping in Spain is for the most part restricted to camp sites. All camp sites are rated in categories from one (first class) to three (third class), depending on the facilities and services provided. Category one is the top of the range - in addition to the basic facilities of showers, toilets and a laundry, there should be a shop on the site, selling general goods, and a public telephone.

You can expect some of the sites in the top two categories to have shade, but this may well be at a premium during the hotter months, when the shady spots will be snapped up first.

Many camp sites will have some sort of café or restaurant to give you a break from the barbecue. It's worth finding out exactly what catering there is, since it could be quite a walk to the nearest resort or village.

All sites should have a post box and first-aid facilities, and bottled gas (usually Camping Gas only) is available at all but the most basic of places. Some of the better sites will have recreational facilities, including swimming pools and tennis courts. Very few camp sites have tents or equipment for hire.

Some will have holiday chalets and cabins to let.

Rates for camp sites are based on a 24-hour period, starting at midday. There are usually reductions available for long stays.

The Spanish Tourist Office (*Oficina Nacional Española*), 57-58 St James's, London SW1A 1LD, can provide you with information. It's worth booking in advance if you plan to visit Spain during the busy summer months. Once in Spain, the *Guía Oficial de Campings*, available in bookshops, gives details of most sites, and local tourist offices can give you information on the nearest sites.

Camping carnet

A camping carnet provides not only an alternative to your passport as identity but also gives third-party insurance cover. Many camp sites still prefer you to have a carnet, although you should no longer be refused entry, as was once the case. They are available from both the AA and RAC.

Camping rough

You can camp on open ground, with the owner's permission, but not in mountainous regions or on beaches. And there are other rules: you are not allowed to camp within a kilometre of a town or village, near a national monument or within 150 metres of a main road or a drinking water supply; camps are restricted to a maximum of three tents and no more than ten people; you are allowed to stay in any camp for a maximum of three days; campfires are not permitted within 200 metres of a main road. (Fire is a major risk during the dry summers, and extreme care should be taken.)

Taking a caravan

Taking a caravan across the Channel can be expensive. It is worthy studying closely the available options on the various ferry services and Le Shuttle. Most companies

charge according to length, although some also consider the height. Surprisingly, some peak-time ferry sailings have cheap rates for caravans, and several companies provide a substantial discount on return bookings.

If you're planning on taking a caravan, bear in mind that roads can get very congested in the summer, particularly along the Mediterranean coast, and that crossing the wide central plateau in searing summer heat can be quite an ordeal. It's worth considering either a late spring or an early autumn break. Only some camp sites allow caravans, usually the bigger and more expensive ones.

Speed limits for cars towing caravans differ from the standard limits for cars. They are:

Built-up areas: 60 kph (37 mph)
Single lane: 70 kph (43 mph)
Dual carriageway: 80 kph (49 mph)
Motorways: 80 kph (49 mph)

Note that cars with caravans and trailers are charged approximately twice the toll of cars on motorways. Be sure to include your caravan or trailer in your Green Card arrangements before setting off.

Useful camping questions

Can we camp in your field?
¿Podemos acampar en su terreno?
po-day-mos a-kam-par en soo te-ray-no

Can we camp near here?
¿Podemos acampar cerca de aquí?
po-day-mos a-kam-par thair-ka day a-kee

Please can we pitch our tent here?
¿Podríamos montar la tienda aquí?
po-dree-a-mos mon-tar la tee-en-da a-kee

Can we park our caravan here?
¿Podemos aparcar la caravana aquí?
po-day-mos a-par-kar la ka-ra-ba-na a-kee

Do I pay in advance?
¿Tengo que pagar de antemano?
ten-go kay pa-gar day an-tay-ma-no

Do I pay when I leave?
¿Tengo que pagar al salir?
ten-go kay pa-gar al sa-leer

Is there a more sheltered site?
¿Hay algún lugar más resguardado?
eye al-goon loo-gar mas res-gwar-da-do

Is there a restaurant or a shop on the site?
¿Hay alguna tienda o restaurante en el camping?
eye al-goo-na tee-en-da o re-sto-ran-tay en el kam-peen

Is there another camp site near there?
¿Hay algún otro camping cercano?
eye al-goon o-tro kam-peen thair-ka-no

Is this the drinking water?
¿Es ésta el agua potable?
es es-ta el a-gwa po-ta-blay

The site is very wet and muddy
El terreno está muy húmedo y lleno de barro
el te-ray-no es-ta mwee oo-me-do ee ye-no day ba-ro

Where are the toilets?
¿Dónde están los servicios?
don-day es-tan los sair-bee-thee-os

Where can I buy gas?
¿Dónde se puede comprar gas?
don-day say pwe-day com-prar gas

Where can I have a shower?
¿Dónde puedo ducharme?
don-day pwe-do doo-char-may

Where can we wash our dishes?
¿Dónde podemos fregar los platos?
don-day po-day-mos fre-gar los pla-tos

Around the camp site

air mattress
colchoneta hinchable
*kol-cho-**nay**-ta een-**cha**-blay*

backpack
mochila
*mo-**chee**-la*

bottle-opener
abrebotellas
*a-bray-bo-**te**-yas*

bucket
balde
***bal**-day*

camp bed
cama plegable
***ka**-ma ple-**ga**-blay*

camp chair
silla plegable
***see**-ya ple-**ga**-blay*

can-opener
abrelatas
*a-bray-**la**-tas*

candle
vela
***bay**-la*

cup
taza
***ta**-tha*

fire
fuego
***fway**-go*

flashlight
linterna
*leen-**tair**-na*

fly sheet
toldo impermeable
***tol**-do eem-pair-may-**a**-blay*

folding table
mesa plegable
***may**-sa ple-**ga**-blay*

fork
tenedor
*te-ne-**dor***

frying pan
sartén
*sar-**ten***

ground sheet
suelo impermeable
***sway**-lo eem-pair-may-**a**-blay*

ground
suelo
***sway**-lo*

guy line
viento
*bee-**en**-to*

knife
cuchillo
*koo-**chee**-yo*

mallet
mazo
***ma**-tho*

matches
cerillas
*the-**ree**-yas*

pail
cubo
***koo**-bo*

penknife	**stove**
navaja	hornilla
*na-**ba**-ha*	*or-**nee**-ya*
plate	**tent peg**
plato	clavija
***pla**-to*	*kla-**bee**-ha*
rucksack	**tent pole**
mochila	mástil de tienda
*mo-**chee**-la*	*ma-**steel** day tee-**en**-da*
shelter	**tent**
refugio	tienda
*re-foo-**hyo***	*tee-**en**-da*
sleeping bag	**thermos flask**
saco de dormir	termo
sa**-ko day dor-**meer	***tair**-mo*
spoon	**torch**
cuchara	linterna
*koo-**cha**-ra*	*leen-**tair**-na*

Hostelling

Most Spanish hostels belong to the Red Española de Albergues Juveniles (REAJ) and are listed in the annual directory published by Hostelling International. Rates vary dependng on the season and whether you are under 26. You do not always need a Hostelling International membership card, but may have to pay more without one. The address of REAJ is Calle José Ortega y Gasset 71, 28006 Madrid.

Is there a youth hostel near here?
¿Hay algún albergue juvenil cercano?
*eye al-**goon** al-**bair**-gay hoo-be-**neel** thair-**ka**-no*

Can we stay here five nights
¿Podemos quedarnos aquí cinco noches?
*po-**day**-mos ke-**dar**-nos a-**kee theen**-ko **no**-ches*

Can we stay until Sunday?
¿Podemos quedarnos hasta el domingo?
*po-**day**-mos ke-**dar**-nos **a**-sta el do-**meen**-go*

Here is my membership card
Aquí está mi tarjeta de socio
*a-**kee** es-**ta** mee tar-**hay**-ta day so-**thee**-o*

I do not have my card
No tengo mi tarjeta
*no **ten**-go mee tar-**hay**-ta*

Can I join here?
¿Puedo hacerme socio aquí?
*pwe-do a-**thair**-may so-**thee**-o a-**kee***

Are you open during the day?
¿Está esto abierto durante el día?
*es-**ta** a-bee-**air**-to doo-**ran**-tay el **dee**-a*

Can I use the kitchen?
¿Puedo utilizar la cocina?
*pwe-do oo-tee-lee-**thar** la ko-**thee**-na*

What time do you close?
¿A qué hora cierran?
a kay o-ra thee-e-ran

Do you serve meals?
¿Sirven comidas?
seer-ben ko-mee-das

— **to take away?**
— para llevar?
— *pa-ra ye-bar*

Childcare

Can you warm this milk for me?
¿Puede calentarme esta leche?
pwe-day ka-len-tar-may es-ta le-chay

Do you have a high chair?
¿Tiene alguna silla alta?
tee-e-nay al-goo-na see-ya al-ta

Is there a baby-sitter?
¿Hay una canguro?
eye oo-na kan-goo-ro

Is there a cot for our baby?
¿Hay alguna cuna para nuestro bebé?
eye al-goo-na coo-na pa-ra nwes-tra be-bay

Is there a paddling pool?
¿Hay piscina para niños?
eye pees-thee-na pa-ra neen-yos

Is there a swimming pool?
¿Hay piscina?
eye pees-thee-na

Is there a swing park?
¿Hay parque de columpios?
eye par-kay day ko-loom-pyos

I am very sorry. That was very naughty of him
Lo siento mucho. Ha sido una travesura suya
lo syen-to moo-cho. A see-do oo-na tra-be-soo-ra soo-ya

It will not happen again
No volverá a ocurrir
no bol-bair-a a o-koo-reer

How old is your daughter?
¿Cuántos años tiene su hija?
kwan-tos an-yos tee-e-nay soo ee-ha

My daughter is 7 years old
Mi hija tiene siete años
mee ee-ha tee-e-nay see-e-tay an-yos

My son is 10 years old
Mi hijo tiene diez años
mee ee-ho tee-e-nay dee-eth an-yos

She goes to bed at nine o'clock
Se acuesta a las nueve
say a-kwe-sta a las nwe-bay

We will be back in two hours
Volveremos dentro de dos horas
bol-bair-ay-mos den-tro day dos o-ras

Where can I buy some disposable nappies?
¿Dónde puedo comprar pañales desechables?
don-day pwe-do kom-prar pan-ya-les des-e-cha-bles

Where can I change the baby?
¿Dónde puedo cambiar al bebé?
don-day pwe-do kam-byar al be-bay

Where can I feed my baby?
¿Dónde puedo dar de comer al bebé?
don-day pwe-do dar day ko-mair al be-bay

Getting Around

Opening hours

Local tourist offices vary widely but are usually open Monday to Friday from 9.00 or 10.00am until 1.00 or 2.00pm. They close for lunch and re-open at 4.30pm until 7.00pm.

Post offices (*oficinas de correos*) are open in the mornings and again from 5.00pm to 7.00pm Monday to Friday and on Saturday mornings. Stamps (*sellos*) are also available from tobacconists (*estancos*) and from hotels.

Banks are open Monday to Friday from 8.30am to 2.00pm and on Saturdays from 9.00am until 1.00pm.

Museums open usually at 9.00 or 10.00 am but close for lunch. Some (but not all) reopen in the late afternoon. Many are closed all day on Mondays.

Most offices, shops and museums are closed on public holidays (*see* page 474).

Asking for directions

Where is — the art gallery?
¿Dónde está — el museo de arte?
don-day es-ta— el moo-say-o day ar-tay

— the post office?
— el correos?
— el ko-ray-os

— the Tourist Information Service?
— la Oficina de Turismo?
— la o-fee-thee-na day too-reez-mo

Can you tell me the way to the bus station?
¿Puede indicarme el camino a la estación de autobuses?
pwe-day een-dee-kar-may el ka-mee-no a la e-sta-thyon day ow-to-boo-ses

I am lost
Estoy perdido / perdida
es-toy pair-dee-do / pair-dee-da

I am lost. How do I get to the Carlos Quinto Hotel?
Estoy perdido / perdida. ¿Cómo se llega al Hotel Carlos Quinto?
es-toy pair-dee-do / pair-dee-da. Ko-mo say ye-ga al o-tel Kar-los Keen-to

Can you show me on the map?
¿Puede indicarme en el mapa?
pwe-day een-dee-kar-may en el ma-pa

May I borrow your map?
¿Puede prestarme el mapa?
pwe-day pre-star-may el ma-pa

We are looking for a restaurant
Estamos buscando un restaurante
es-ta-mos boo-skan-do oon re-sto-ran-tay

Where are the toilets?
¿Dónde están los servicios?
don-day es-tan los sair-bee-thee-os

I am looking for the Tourist Information Office
Estoy buscando la Oficina de Turismo
es-toy boo-skan-do la o-fee-thee-na day too-reez-mo

I am trying to get to the market
Quiero ir al mercado
kee-e-ro eer al mair-ka-do

Can you walk there?
¿Se puede ir andando hasta allí?
say pwe-day eer an-dan-do a-sta a-yee

Is it far?
¿Está lejos?
es-ta lay-hos

I want to go to the theatre
Quiero ir al teatro
kee-e-ro eer al tay-a-tro

Is there a bus that goes there?
¿Hay algún autobús que vaya allí?
a-ee al-goon ow-to-boos kay ba-ya a-yee

Where do I get a bus for the city centre?
¿Dónde puedo coger el autobús al centro de la ciudad?
don-day pwe-do ko-hair el ow-to-boos al then-tro day la thee-oo-dad

Is there a train that goes there?
¿Hay algún tren que vaya allí?
eye al-goon tren kay ba-ya a-yee

Directions - by road

Where does this road go to?
¿Adónde va esta carretera?
a-don-day ba es-ta ka-re-tair-a

Do I turn here for Jaca?
¿Tengo que girar aquí para Jaca?
ten-go kuy hee-rar a-kee pa-ra ha-ka

How do I get onto the motorway?
¿Por dónde se entra a la autopista?
por don-day say en-tra a la ow-to-pee-sta

How far is it to Toledo?
¿Qué distancia hay a Toledo?
kay dee-stan-thee-a eye a to-lay-do

How long will it take to get there?
¿Cuánto se tarda en ir allí?
kwan-to say tar-da en eer a-yee

I am looking for the next exit
Busco la siguiente salida
boos-ko la see-gee-en-tay sa-lee-da

Is there a filling station near here?
¿Hay una gasolinera aquí cerca?
a-ee oo-na ga-so-lee-nair-a a-kee thair-ka

Is this the right way to the supermarket?
¿Es éste el camino al supermercado?
es es-tay el ka-mee-no al soo-pair-mair-ka-do

Which is the best route to Pamplona?
¿Cuál es la mejor carretera para Pamplona?
kwal es la me-hor ka-re-tair-a pa-ra Pam-plo-na

Which is the fastest route?
¿Cuál es la carretera más rapida?
kwal es la ka-re-tair-a mas ra-pee-da

Which road do I take to Segovia?
¿Qué carretera debo coger para Segovia?
kay ka-re-tair-a de-bo ko-hair pa-ra se-go-bee-a

Directions - what you may hear

Vaya — hasta . . .
by-a — a-sta . . .
You go— as far as . . .

— allí
— a-yee
— over there

— a la izquierda
— a la eeth-kyair-da
— left

Atraviese la calle
a-tra-bee-ay-say la ka-yay
Cross the street

— a la derecha
— a la de-ray-cha
— right

Siga las señales a . . .
see-ga las sen-ya-les a . . .
Follow the signs for . . .

Vaya hacia . . .
by-a a-thya . . .
You go towards . . .

— el próximo cruce
— el prok-see-mo croo-thay
— the next junction

Está— en el cruce
es-ta — en el croo-thay
It is— at the crossroads

— la autopista
— la ow-to-pee-sta
— the motorway

— a la vuelta de la esquina
— a la bwel-ta day la es-kee-na
— around the corner

— la plaza
— la pla-tha
— the square

— bajo el puente
— ba-ho el pwen-tay
— under the bridge

Siga todo recto
see-ga to-do rek-to
Keep going straight ahead

— después del semáforo
— des-pwes del se-ma-fo-ro
— after the traffic lights

Gire a la izquierda
hee-ray a la eeth-kyair-da
Turn left

— junto al cine
— hoon-to al thee-nay
— next to the cinema

Gire a la derecha
hee-ray a la de-ray-cha
Turn right

— en el siguiente piso
— en el see-gee-en-tay pee-so
— on the next floor

Tiene que dar la vuelta
tee-e-nay kay dar la bwel-ta
You have to go back

— frente a la estación de ferrocarril
— fren-tay a la es-ta-thyon day fe-ro-ka-reel
— opposite the railway station

Coja la primera carretera a la derecha
ko-ha la pree-mair-a ka-re-tair-a a la de-ray-cha
Take the first road on the right

Coja la carretera de Simancas
*ko-ha la ka-re-**tair**-a day see-**man**-kas*
Take the road for Simancas

Coja la segunda carretera a la izquierda
*ko-ha la se-**goon**-da ka-re-**tair**-a a la eeth-**kyair**-da*
Take the second road on the left

Hiring a car

The large international car hire firms all operate in Spain as well as local companies, and there is a wide range of cars available at differing prices. In theory you will need an International Driving Permit or a European Union driving licence but in practice a driving licence from any major country is sufficient. The basic hire charge excludes third-party insurance, VAT (IVA) and collision damage waiver. You must be over 21 and have held a driving licence for at least two years. You will usually have to pay by credit card. It is often worth arranging car hire in advance through an international firm or a fly-drive deal.

I want to hire a car
Quiero alquilar un coche
*kee-e-ro ul-kee-**lar** oon **ko**-chay*

I need it for 2 weeks
Lo quiero para dos semanas
*lo kee-e-ro **pa**-ra dos se-**ma**-nas*

Can I hire a car?
¿Es posible alquilar un coche?
*es po-**see**-blay al-kee-**lar** oon **ko**-chay*

Can I hire a car with an automatic gearbox?
¿Puedo alquilar un coche con cambio automático?
*pwe-do al-kee-**lar** oon **ko**-chay kon kam-**byo** ow-to-**ma**-tee-ko*

Please explain the documents
Por favor, explíqueme los documentos
*por fa-**bor**, eks-**plee**-kay-may los do-koo-**men**-tos*

We will both be driving
Conduciremos los dos
kon-doo-thee-ray-mos los dos

Do you have — a large car?
¿Tiene — un coche grande?
*tee-**e**-nay — oon **ko**-chay **gran**-day*

— a smaller car?
— un coche más pequeño?
*— oon **ko**-chay mas pe-**ken**-yo*

— an automatic?
— un coche con cambio automático?
*— oon **ko**-chay kon kam-**byo** ow-to-**ma**-tee-ko*

— an estate car?
— una furgoneta?
*— oo-nu foor-go-**nay**-la*

I want to leave the car at the airport
Quiero dejar el coche en el aeropuerto
*kee-e-ro de-**har** el **ko**-chay en el a-air-o-**pwair**-to*

I would like to leave the car at the airport
Me gustaría dejar el coche en el aeropuerto
*may goo-sta-**ree**-a de-**har** el **ko**-chay en el a-air-o-**pwair**-to*

Is there a charge per kilometre?
¿Se cobra el kilometraje?
*say **ko**-bra el kee-lo-me-**tra**-hay*

Must I return the car here?
¿Tengo que devolver el coche aquí?
***ten**-go kay de-bol-**bair** el **ko**-chay a-kee*

Can I pay for insurance?
¿Puedo pagar un seguro?
*pwe-do pa-**gar** oon se-**goo**-ro*

Do I have to pay a deposit?
¿Tengo que pagar algún depósito?
*ten-go kay pa-**gar** oon de-po-zee-to*

How does the steering lock work?
¿Cómo funciona el antirrobo?
*ko-mo foon-**thyo**-na el an-tee-**ro**-bo*

I would like a spare set of keys
Me gustaría tener un juego de llaves de repuesto
*may goo-sta-**ree**-a te-**nair** oon **hway**-go day ya-bes day re-**pwes**-to*

Where is reverse gear?
¿Dónde está la marcha atrás?
*don-day es-**ta** la **mar**-cha a-**tras***

Where is the tool kit?
¿Dónde está la caja de herramientas?
*don-day es-**ta** la **ka**-ha day e-ra-**myen**-tas*

Please show me how to operate the lights
Por favor, enséñeme cómo manejar las luces
*por fa-**bor**, en-sen-yay-may **ko**-mo ma-ne-**har** las **loo**-thes*

Please show me how to operate the windscreen wipers
Por favor, enséñeme cómo manejar los limpiaparabrisas
*por fa-**bor**, en-sen-yay-may **ko**-mo ma-ne-**har** los leem-pya-pa-ra-**bree**-sas*

By taxi

Taxis are easy to find in major towns and resort areas. They are distinguished by a green light on top and/or by colouring – black or white, with a broad stripe on the side. In cities, taxis can be hailed in the street – they display a *libre* sign if available for hire. Rates are reasonable and normally metered. Agree the fare first when this is not the case.

Where can I get a taxi?
¿Dónde puedo tomar un taxi?
*don-day **pwe**-do to-**mar** oon **tak**-see*

Take me to the airport, please
Lléveme al aeropuerto, por favor
*ye-bay-may al a-air-o-**pwair**-to, por fa-**bor***

The bus station, please
La estación de autobuses, por favor
*la es-ta-**thyon** day ow-to-**boo**-ses, por fa-**bor***

Please show us around the town
Por favor, enséñenos la ciudad
*por fa-**bor**, en-**sen**-yay-nos la thee-oo-**dad***

Please take me to this address
Por favor, lléveme a esta dirección
*por fa-**bor**, ye-bay-may a es-ta dee-rek-**thyon***

Could you put the bags in the boot, please?
Puede meter las bolsas en el maletero, por favor
*pwe-day me-**tair** las **bol**-sas en el ma-le-**te**-ro, por fa-**bor***

Turn left, please
Gire a la izquierda, por favor
*hee-ray a la eeth-**kyair**-da, por fa-**bor***

Turn right, please
Gire a la derecha, por favor
*hee-ray a la de-**ray**-cha, por fa-**bor***

Wait for me please
Espéreme, por favor
*es-**pe**-ray-may, por fa-**bor***

Can you come back in one hour?
¿Puede volver dentro de una hora?
*pwe-day bol-**bair** **den**-tro day **oo**-na **o**-ra*

Please wait here for a few minutes
Por favor, espere aquí unos minutos
*por fa-**bor**, es-**pe**-ray a-**kee** **oo**-nos mee-**noo**-tos*

Please, stop at the corner
Por favor, pare en la esquina
*por fa-**bor**, **pa**-ray en la es-**kee**-na*

Please, wait here
Espere aquí, por favor
es-pe-ray a-kee, por fa-bor

I am in a hurry
Tengo prisa
ten-go pree-sa

Please hurry, I am late
Dése prisa por favor, se me ha hecho tarde
day-say pree-sa por fa-bor, say may a e-cho tar-day

How much is it per kilometre?
¿Cuánto cuesta por kilómetro?
kwan-to kwes-ta por kee-lo-me-tro

How much is that, please?
¿Cuánto es eso, por favor?
kwan-to es e-so, por fa-bor

Keep the change
Quédese con el cambio
kay-day-say kon el kam-byo

By bus

All significant towns and villages are connected by bus services. They are cheap but slow.

Does this bus go to the castle?
¿Este autobús va al castillo?
es tay ow to boos ba al ka-stee-yo

How frequent is the service?
¿Con qué frecuencia es el servicio?
kon kay fre-kwen-thee-a es el sair-bee-thee-o

What is the fare to the city centre?
¿Cuánto es al centro de la ciudad?
kwan-to es al then-tro day la thee-oo-dad

Where should I change?
¿Dónde tengo que cambiar?
don-day ten-go kay kam-byar

Which bus do I take for the football stadium?
¿Qué autobús tengo que coger para el estadio de fútbol?
kay ow-to-boos ten-go kay ko-hair pa-ra el es-ta-dee-o day foot-bol

Where do I get the bus for the airport?
¿Dónde puedo coger el autobús para el aeropuerto?
don-day pwe-do ko-hair el ow-to-boos pa-ra el a-air-o-pwair-to

Will you tell me when to get off the bus?
¿Me dirá cuándo bajarme del autobús?
may dee-ra kwan-do ba-har-may del ow-to-boos

When is the last bus?
¿Á que hora es el último autobús?
a kay o-ra es el ool-tee-mo ow-to-boos

By train

Spain's national railway, RENFE, runs a variety of services that will deliver you to your destination at quite different speeds and levels of comfort.

At the top of the scale is the *Talgo* service, which operates between major cities, with links to France. They are fast, modern, air-conditioned trains. If you have time on your hands, less money or maybe just a sense of romance, there are cheaper and slower services. *Rápido* trains stop only at main stations and, despite their name, are not necessarily fast. The slowest trains of all, *Regionales*, travel between provinces within a region and never miss a stop.

Bookings on RENFE trains can be made through European Rail Travel Ltd and American Express. RENFE operates various discounts, including reductions for travel on Blue Days (*Días Azules*), which are over half the days of the year. If you are anticipating a lot of train travel, you can buy a *Tarjeta Turística*, which you can use for four to ten days' travel within a two-month period.

Inter-Rail cards for passengers under 26 are accepted on Spanish services. You will have to pay part of the fare on some trains, such as the Talgo service. The adult version of the Inter-Rail card is not accepted in Spain.

Car-carrying services operate between various Spanish cities under the name *Auto-Expreso*.

Can I buy a return ticket?
¿Puedo comprar un billete de ida y vuelta?
*pwe-do kom-**prar** oon bee-**ye**-tay day **ee**-da ee
 bwel-ta*

A return (round-trip ticket) to Barcelona, please
Un billete de ida y vuelta a Barcelona, por favor
*oon bee-**ye**-tay day **ee**-da ee **bwel**-ta a bar-the-**lo**-na, por fa-**bor***

A return to Paris, first class
Un billete de ida y vuelta a París, en primera clase
*oon bee-**ye**-tay day **ee**-da ee **bwel**-ta a pa-**rees**, en pree-**mair**-a **kla**-say*

A single (one-way ticket) to Lisbon, please
Un billete de ida a Lisboa, por favor
*oon bee-**ye**-tay day **ee**-da a leez-**bo**-a, por fa-**bor***

A smoking compartment, first class
Compartimento de fumadores, primera clase
*kom-par-tee-**men**-to day foo-ma-**do**-res, pree-**mair**-a **kla**-say*

A non-smoking compartment, please
Compartimento de no fumadores, por favor
*kom-par-tee-**men**-to day no foo-ma-**do**-res, por fa-**bor***

Second class. A window seat, please
En segunda. Asiento de ventana, por favor
*en se-**goon**-da. a-**syen**-to day ben-**ta**-na, por fa-**bor***

Can I take my bicycle?
¿Puedo llevar mi bicicleta?
*pwe-do ye-**bar** mee bee-thee-**klay**-ta*

Is this the platform for Zaragoza?
¿Es éste el andén para Zaragoza?
*es **es**-te el an-**den** pa-ra tha-ra-**go**-tha*

What are the times of the trains to Paris?
¿Cuál es el horario de trenes para París?
*kwal es el o-**ra**-ree-o day **tre**-nes pa-ra pa-**rees***

How long do I have before my next train leaves?
¿Cuánto tiempo tengo antes de mi próximo tren?
*kwan-to tee-**em**-po **ten**-go **an**-tes day mee **prok**-see-mo tren*

Where can I buy a ticket?
¿Dónde puedo comprar un billete?
don-day pwe-do kom-prar oon bee-ye-tay

Where do I have to change?
¿Dónde tengo que cambiar?
don-day ten-go kay kam-byar

Where do I pick up my bags?
¿Dónde se recogen los equipajes?
don-day say re-ko-hen los e-kee-pa-hays

Can I check in my bags?
¿Puedo facturar el equipaje?
pwe-do fak-too-rar el e-kee-pa-hay

I want to leave these bags in the left luggage
Quiero dejar estas bolsas en la consigna
kee-e-ro de-har es-tas bol-sas en la kon-seeg-na

How much is it per bag?
¿Cuánto es por cada bolsa?
kwan-to es por ka-da bol-sa

I shall pick them up this evening
Las recogeré esta tarde
las re-ko-hair-ay es-ta tar-day

I want to book a seat on the sleeper to Paris
Quiero reservar una plaza en coche-cama a París
kee-e-o re-sair-bar oo-na pla-tha en ko-chay-ka-ma a pa-rees

Is there— a left-luggage office?
 ¿Hay — consigna de equipajes?
 eye — kon-seeg-na day e-kee-pa-hes

 — a buffet car (club car)?
 — coche bar?
 — ko-chay bar

 — a dining car?
 — vagón restaurante?
 — ba-gon re-sto-ran-tay

 — a restaurant on the train?
 — coche restaurante en el tren?
 — ko-chay re-sto-ran-tay en el tren

Where is the departure board (listing)?
¿Dónde está el tablón de salidas?
don-day es-ta el ta-blon day sa-lee-das

What time does the train leave?
¿A qué hora sale el tren?
a kay o-ra sa-lay el tren

Do I have time to go shopping?
¿Tengo tiempo para ir de compras?
ten-go tee-em-po pa-ra eer day kom-pras

What time is the last train?
¿A qué hora es el último tren?
a kay o-ra es el ool-tee-mo tren

When is the next train to Seville?
¿Cuándo sale el siguiente tren para
 Sevilla?
*kwan-do sa-lay el see-gee-en-tay tren pa-ra se-
 bee-ya*

When is the next train to Valencia?
¿Cuándo es el siguiente tren para
 Valencia?
*kwan-do sa-lay el see-gee-en-tay tren pa-ra
 ba-len-thee-a*

Which platform do I go to?
¿A qué andén tengo que ir?
a kay an-den ten-go kay eer

Is this a through train?
¿Es éste un tren directo?
es es-tay oon tren dee-rek-to

Is this the Madrid train?
¿Es éste el tren de Madrid?
es es-tay el tren day ma-dreed

Do we stop at Vigo?
¿Paramos en Vigo?
pa-ra-mos en bee-go

What time do we get to Burgos?
¿A qué hora llegamos a Burgos?
a kay o-ra ye-ga-mos a boor-gos

Are we at Durango yet?
¿Hemos llegado a Durango?
ay-mos ye-ga-do a doo-ran-go

Are we on time?
¿Llegaremos a la hora prevista?
ye-ga-ray-mos a la o-ra pray-bee-sta

Can you help me with my bags?
Puede ayudarme con el equipaje?
pwe-day a-yoo-dar-may kon el e-kee-pa-hay

Is this seat taken?
¿Está ocupado este asiento?
es-ta o-koo-pa-do es-tay a-syen-to

May I open the window?
¿Le importa si abro la ventana?
lay eem-por-ta see a-bro la ben-ta-na

My wife has my ticket
Mi esposa tiene mi billete
mee es-po-sa tee-e-nay mee bee-ye-tay

I have lost my ticket
He perdido el billete
ay pair-dee-do el bee-ye-tay

This is a non-smoking compartment
Éste es un compartimento de no fumadores
es-tay es oon kom-par-tee-men-to day no foo-ma-do-res

This is my seat
Éste es mi asiento
es-tay es mee a-syen-to

Where is the toilet?
¿Dónde está el servicio?
don-day es-ta el sair-bee-thee-o

Why have we stopped?
¿Por qué hemos parado?
por kay ay-mos pa-ra-do

Driving

Driving in Spain offers some rewarding experiences, with excellent touring country in regions as far apart as the Pyrenees and Andalucía. But you should pay particular attention to preparations. It is a big country, temperatures can be high and roads can be rough.

Standards of driving in Spain are not high, and it is important to expect unpredictable behaviour from other drivers. In country areas, expect the roads to be used by slow-moving vehicles without lights and farm animals.

Any long-distance continental trip implies the need for some preparations – adjusting headlights, fitting a GB plate, getting an insurance Green Card, and so on. For Spain there are some special needs.

Holders of a green UK licence must also have an International Drivers Permit (IDP). Pink EU licences are fully recognised.

In the event of a serious accident, you may be arrested and/or your car may be impounded. By taking a Bail Bond – a guarantee of a substantial cash payment if you abscond – you are more likely to avoid confinement. Bail Bonds are available from motoring organisations.

A spare set of light bulbs and a red warning triangle are obligatory. If you wear glasses, you must carry a spare set in the car. Carrying a first aid kit and a fire extinguisher is also recommended. Basic spare parts are worth taking for cars of non-European origin.

Choosing which way you get to Spain is likely to depend on various factors, such as how much time you have, what sort of budget you are on, whether you want to include a tour of France, and how much of a problem will be presented by long periods of driving.

If you are going to Barcelona, for example, you could opt for 24 hours on the ferry from Plymouth to Santander followed by a 720-kilometre (450-mile drive). Taking a short Channel crossing or using Le Shuttle through the Channel Tunnel instead will leave you with 1375 kilometres (860 miles) to drive to your destination but probably at a lower total cost. For a compromise on cost and driving time, the Portsmouth-St Malo route would leave a little over 1120 kilometres (700 miles) to reach Barcelona.

The roads

Some main roads are dual carriageways but most are not. On the major routes, roads are usually in reasonable condition, although they can be narrow in places, and it is not uncommon to find abrupt corners at the end of long straight sections. Hazardous mountain roads have acute hairpin turns and do not necessarily have crash barriers. In some relatively undeveloped areas, even main roads can be slow going, with few opportunities for overtaking. Some busy roads have become notorious for accidents. The N340, which runs the length of the Mediterranean coast from Barcelona to the Costa del Sol, claims many lives each year.

Spain has relatively few motorways (*autopistas*). Motorways currently exist along the northern Costas of the Mediterranean coast, from the border to Alicante. On the Atlantic coast, motorways run from the

French border to Bilbao and a little way inland to Burgos, and there is a motorway link from here across to Barcelona on the Mediterranean.

Most motorways are subject to tolls. These can be paid by cash or credit or debit card, which you put through a machine. Tolls, which can be heavy, can be avoided by looking for the *peaje* (toll) sign then finding an alternative road.

Motorway services, both for refuelling and refreshments, are fairly regularly distributed. You can expect to find them about every thirty to fifty kilometres. For assistance on the motorways, emergency phones are generally available every two kilometres.

If you need a map, Michelin publishes a map covering Spain and Portugal and six larger scale regional maps covering Spain. They are accurate, up-to-date and available both in the UK and in Spain.

The rules

- driving on the right – this is relatively easy to adapt to, but extra care is needed when joining a road in circumstances that may encourage you to revert to UK habits – when joining a quiet road, say.
- priority to the right – in the absence of any other indications, priority at intersections is given to traffic coming from the right. Intersections where traffic on a minor road gives way to that on a major one normally have a 'Stop' or give-way sight, 'Ceda el paso'.
- speed limits – the standard limits for cars are:

built-up areas – 50 kph (31 mph)
single carriageways – 90 kph (56 mph)
dual carriageways – 100 kph (62 mph)
motorways – 120 kph (74 mph)

  If you are overtaking outside a built-up area, you can exceed the speed limit by a maximum of 20 kph (12 mph) to do so.

- the minimum age for driving in Spain is eighteen.
- overtaking outside built-up areas requires the use of the horn as well as indicators. In built-up areas, where horns may be used only in cases of emergency, you should flash your headlights.
- safety belts are obligatory, if fitted. Children should travel in the rear seats.
- as in the UK, spare petrol must be carried only in approved containers.
- use dipped headlights when driving in built-up areas.
- drink-driving is subject to the same blood-alcohol limit as in the UK.
- fines – Spanish police can, and do, levy on-the-spot fines. You can be fined for many offences – speeding, breaking traffic rules, failing to have a correct GB sticker, and so on.

Traffic and weather conditions

Are there any hold-ups?
¿Hay atascos?
eye a-tas-kos

Is the traffic heavy?
¿Hay mucho tráfico?
eye moo-cho tra-fee-ko

Is the traffic one-way?
¿Es sentido único?
es sen-tee-do oo-nee-ko

Is there a different way to the stadium?
¿Hay otro camino al estadio?
eye o-tro ka-mee-no al es-ta-dee-o

Is there a toll on this motorway (high way)?
¿Esta autopista es de peaje?
es-ta ow-to-pee-sta es day pay-a-hay

What is causing this traffic jam?
¿Qué está causando este embotellamien to?
kay es-ta kow-san-do es-tay em-bo-te-ya-myen-to

What is the speed limit?
¿Cuál es el límite de velocidad?
kwal es el lee-mee-tay day be-lo-thee-dad

What time does the car park close?
¿Cuándo se cierra el parking?
kwan-do say thee-e-ra el par-keen

When is the rush hour?
¿Cuándo es la hora punta?
kwan-do es la o-ra poon-ta

Do I need snow chains?
¿Necesito cadenas para la nieve?
ne-the-see-to ka-day-nas pa-ra la nee-e-bay

Is the pass open?
¿Está el paso abierto?
es-ta el pa-so a-bee-air-to

Is the road to Segovia snowed up?
¿Está nevada la carretera a Segovia?
es-ta ne-ba-da la ka-re-tair-a a se-go-bee-a

When will the road be clear?
¿Cuándo estará la carretera despejada?
kwan-do es-ta-ra la ka-re-tair-a des-pe-ha-da

Parking

Parking is usually controlled by local signs. Always park the car facing in the direction of the traffic. Which side of a one-way street you may park depends on the house numbers and which day of the month it is. On even dates you should park on the even-numbered side of the street and conversely for odd dates. In a 'blue zone' (*zona azul*), parking requires a disc or ticket permits – usually obtainable from shops such as tobacconists or from hotels, and travel agencies – and is generally restricted to an hour and a half.

Is it safe to park here?
¿Es seguro aparcar aquí?
es se-goo-ro u-par-kar u-kee

Can I park here?
¿Puedo aparcar aquí?
pwe-do a-par-kar a-kee

Do I need a parking disc?
¿Necesito ficha de aparcamiento?
ne-the-see-to fee-cha day a-par-ka-myen-to

Where can I get a parking disc?
¿Dónde puedo obtener una ficha de aparcamiento?
don-day pwe-do ob-te-nair oo-na fee-cha day a-par-ka-myen-to

Where do I pay?
¿Dónde tengo que pagar?
don-day ten-go kay pa-gar

Where is there a car park (parking lot)?
¿Dónde hay un aparcamiento?
don-day a-ee oon a-par-ka-myen-to

How long can I stay here?
¿Cuánto tiempo puedo permanecer aquí?
kwan-to tee-em-po pwe-do pair-ma-ne-thair a-kee

Do I need — coins for the meter?
¿Necesito — monedas para el parquímetro?
ne-the-see-to — mo-nay-das pa-ra el par-kee-me-tro

— **parking lights?**
— luces de posición?
— *loo-thes day po-zee-**thyon***

At the service station

If you plan on touring remote areas, it is worth topping up the tank whenever it gets down to a quarter full. Beware of fuel stations closing on public and religious holidays (*see* page 474). You may need to be quite resourceful to find fuel in that event. Sometimes marina fuel pumps can help out.

   Spain employs petrol octane standards that closely match those used in the UK. 'Gasolina' or 'normal', which has an octane rating of 92, is equivalent to our 2-star. 'Súper', with an octane rating of 97, is the same as our 4-star. Unleaded petrol – 'gasolina sin plomo' – is widely available. Diesel fuel is called 'gasóleo'.

Do you take credit cards?
¿Acepta tarjetas de crédito?
*a-**thep**-ta tar-**hay**-tas day **kre**-dee-to*

Can you clean the windscreen?
¿Puede limpiar el parabrisas?
*pwe-day leem-**pyar** el pa-ra-**bree**-sas*

Fill the tank please
Llene el depósito, por favor
*ye-nay el de-**po**-zee-to, por fa-**bor***

     25 litres of   — unleaded petrol
Veinticinco litros de   — gasolina sin plomo
*bain-tee-**theen**-ko **lee**-tros day — ga-so-**lee**-na*
                  *seen **plo**-mo*

                — **2 star**
                — normal
                — *nor-**mal***

                — **4 star**
                — súper
                — ***soo**-pair*

                — **diesel**
                — gas-oil
                — *ga-**zoil***

I need some distilled water
Necesito agua destilada
*ne-the-**see**-to **a**-gwa de-stee-**la**-da*

Check the tyre pressure, please
Revise la presión de los neumáticos, por favor
*re-**bee**-say la pre-**syon** day los nay-oo-**ma**-tee-kos, por fa-**bor***

The pressure should be 2.3 at the front and 2.5 at the rear
La presión debería estar en dos coma tres en los delanteros y dos coma cinco en los traseros
*la pre-**syon** de-be-**ree**-a es-**tar** en dos **ko**-ma tres en los de-lan-**tair**-os ee dos **ko**-ma **theen**-ko en los tra-**sair**-os*

   Check — the oil
    Revise — el aceite
*re-**bee**-say — el a-**thay**-ee-tay*

           — **the water**
           — el agua
           — *el **a**-gwa*

Breakdowns and repairs

If you take out some form of breakdown insurance, the documents you are given will explain how to get help if your car goes wrong. Otherwise you will probably need to find the nearest garage, although RACE (Real Automóvil Club de España, the Spanish Royal Automobile Club) has a breakdown centre that members of foreign motoring organisations can use. On a motorway you should find an emergency phone about every two kilometres.

Can you give me — a push?
¿Puede — empujarme?
*pwe-day — em-poo-**har**-may*

— a tow?
— remolcarme?
*— re-mol-**kar**-may*

Can you send a recovery truck?
¿Puede enviar un camión grúa?
*pwe-day en-**byar** oon ka-**myon** groo-a*

Can you take me to the nearest garage?
¿Puede llevarme al garage más cercano?
*pwe-day ye-**bar**-may al ga-**ra**-hay mas thair-**ka**-no*

Is there a telephone nearby?
¿Hay algún teléfono cercano?
*a-ee al-**goon** te-**le**-fo-no thair-**ka**-no*

Can you find out what the trouble is?
¿Puede encontrar el problema?
*pwe-day en-kon-**trar** el pro-**blay**-ma*

Can you give me a can of petrol, please?
¿Me da un bidón de gasolina, por favor?
*may da oon bee-**don** day ga-so-**lee**-na, por fa-bor*

Can you repair a flat tyre?
¿Puede reparar una rueda desinflada?
*pwe-day re-pa-**rar** oo-na roo-**ay**-da des-een-fla-da*

Can you repair it for the time being?
¿Puede repararlo provisionalmente?
*pwe-day re-pa-**rar**-lo pro-bees-yo-nal-**men**-tay*

Can you replace the windscreen wiper blades?
¿Puede cambiar las paletas del limpiaparabrisas?
*pwe-day kam-**byar** las pa-**lay**-tas del leem-pya-pa-ra-**bree**-sas*

My car has broken down
Mi coche se ha averiado
*mee **ko**-chay say a a-be-ree-**a**-do*

My car will not start
Mi coche no arranca
*mee **ko**-chay no a-**ran**-ka*

Do you have an emergency fan belt?
Tiene una correa de ventilador de emergencia?
*tee-**e**-nay **oo**-na ko-**ray**-a day ben-tee-la-**dor** day*
*e-mair-**hen**-thee-a*

Do you have jump leads?
¿Tiene cables puente de batería?
*tee-e-nay **ka**-bles **pwen**-tay day ba-te-**ree**-a*

Do you have the spare parts?
¿Tiene los repuestos?
*tee-e-nay los re-**pwe**-stos*

I have a flat tyre
Tengo un pinchazo
***ten**-go oon peen-**cha**-tho*

I have blown a fuse
Se me ha quemado un fusible
*say may a ke-**ma**-do oon foo-**see**-blay*

415

I have locked myself out of the car
He cerrado el coche con las llaves dentro
ay the-ra-do el ko-chay kon las ya-bes den-tro

I have locked the ignition key inside the car
He dejado la llave de contacto dentro del coche
ay de-ha-do la ya-bay day kon-tak-to den-tro del ko-chay

I have run out of petrol
Me he quedado sin gasolina
may ay ke-da-do seen ga-so-lee-na

I need a new fan belt
Necesito una nueva correa de ventilador
ne-the-see-to oo-na nway-ba ko-ray-a day ben-tee-la-dor

I think there is a bad connection
Creo que hay una mala conexión
kray-o kay eye oo-na ma-la ko-nek-syon

Is there a mechanic here?
¿Hay algún mecánico aquí?
eye al-goon me-ka-nee-ko a-kee

The engine has broken down
Se ha averiado el motor
say a a-be-ree-a-do el mo-tor

There is something wrong
Hay algún problema
eye al-goon pro-blay-ma

There is something wrong with the car
Algo va mal en el coche
al-go ba mal en el ko-chay

Will it take long to repair it?
¿Tardará mucho en repararlo?
tar-da-ra moo-cho en re-pa-rar-lo

Is it serious?
¿Es grave?
es gra-bay

My windscreen has cracked
Se me ha rajado el parabrisas
say may a ra-ha-do el pa-ra-bree-sas

The air-conditioning does not work
No funciona el aire acondicionado
no foon-thyo-na el a-ee-ray a-kon-dee-thyo-na-do

The battery is flat
La batería está descargada
la ba-te-ree-a es-ta des-kar-ga-da

The engine is overheating
El motor se recalienta
el mo-tor say re-ka-lyen-ta

The exhaust pipe has fallen off
Se ha caído el tubo de escape
say a ka-ee-do el too-bo day es-ka-pay

There is a leak in the radiator
Hay una fuga en el radiador
eye oo-na foo-ga en el ra-dee-a-dor

Accidents and the police

Spain has three police forces. The Guardia Civil, who wear green uniforms, deal with law enforcement on the roads and in rural areas. The Policía Local, who wear blue and white uniforms, patrol within towns and can be approached about any difficulties. The Policía Nacional, who wear blue uniforms, guard public buildings and in all substantial towns man the *comisaría* (police station), where crimes may be reported. In addition, the autonomous communities of the Basque country, Catalonia, Galicia and Valencia have their own police forces. Telephone 091 for the Policía Nacional, 092 for the Policía Local.

There has been an accident
Ha habido un accidente
*a a-**bee**-do oon ak-thee-**den**-tay*

We must call an ambulance
Tenemos que llamar a una ambulancia
*te-**nay**-mos kay ya-**mar** a oo-na am-boo-**lan**-thee-a*

We must call the police
Tenemos que llamar a la policía
*te-**nay**-mos kay ya-**mar** a la po-lee-**thee**-a*

What is your name and address?
¿Cuál es su nombre y direción?
*kwal es soo **nom**-bray ee dee-rek-**thyon***

You must not move
No debe moverse
*no **de**-bay mo-**bair**-say*

Do you want my passport?
¿Quiere mi pasaporte?
*kee-e-ray mee pa-sa-**por**-tay*

He did not stop
Él no paró
*el no pa-**ro***

He is a witness
Éste es testigo
***es**-tay es te-**stee**-go*

He overtook on a bend
Él adelantó en una curva
*el a-de-lan-**to** en la **coor**-ba*

He ran into the back of my car
Él chocó con la parte trasera de mi coche
*el cho-**ko** kon la **par**-tay tra-**sair**-a day mee **ko**-chay*

He stopped suddenly
Él se paró de repente
*el say pa-**ro** day re-**pen**-tay*

He was moving too fast
Él iba demasiado rápido
*el **ee**-ba de-ma-**sya**-a-do **ra**-pee-do*

Here are my insurance documents
Aquí está la documentación del seguro
*a-**kee** es-**ta** la do-koo-men-ta-**thyon** del se-**goo**-ro*

Here is my driving licence
Aquí está mi permiso de conducir
*a-**kee** es-**ta** mee pair-**mee**-so day kon-doo-**theer***

I could not stop in time
No he podido parar a tiempo
*no ay po-**dee**-do pa-**rar** a tee-**em**-po*

I did not see the bicycle
No vi la bicicleta
*no bee la bee-thee-**klay**-ta*

I did not see the sign
No vi la señal
*no bee la sen-**yal***

I did not understand the sign
No entendí la señal
*no en-ten-**dee** la sen-**yal***

I am very sorry. I am a visitor
Lo siento mucho. Soy turista
*lo **syen**-to **moo**-cho. Soy too-**ree**-sta*

I did not know about the speed limit
No sabía lo del límite de velocidad
*no sa-**bee**-a lo del **lee**-mee-tay day be-lo-thee-**dad***

How much is the fine?
¿Cuánto es la multa?
*kwan-to es la **mool**-ta*

I have not got enough money. Can I pay at the police station?
No tengo suficiente dinero ¿Puedo pagar en la comisaría de policía?
*no **ten**-go soo-fee-thee-en-tay dee-ne-ro. **Pwe**-do pa-gar en la ko-mee-sa-**ree**-a day po-lee-**thee**-a*

I have not had anything to drink
No he bebido nada
*no ay be-**bee**-do **na**-da*

I was only driving at 50 km/h
Sólo iba a cincuenta por hora
so-lo ee-ba a theen-kwen-ta por o-ra

I was overtaking
Estaba adelantando
es-ta-ba a-de-lan-tan-do

I was parking
Estaba aparcando
es-ta-ba a-par-kan-do

My car has been towed away
La grúa se ha llevado mi coche
la groo-a say a ye-ba-do mee ko-chay

That car was too close
Ese coche venía demasiado cerca
e-say ko-chay be-nee-a de-ma-sya-do thair-ka

The brakes failed
Los frenos fallaron
los fray-nos fa-ya-ron

The car number (license number) was...
La matrícula del coche era...
la ma-tree-koo-la del ko-chay ay-ra...

The car skidded
El coche derrapó
el ko-chay de-ra-po

The car swerved
El coche giró bruscamente
el ko-chay hee-ro broo-ska-men-tay

The car turned right without signalling
El coche giró a la derecha sin señalizar
el ko-chay hee-ro a la de-ray-cha seen sen-ya-lee-thar

The road was icy
La carretera estaba congelada
la ka-re-tair-a es-ta-ba kon-he-la-da

The tyre burst
El neumático reventó
el nay-oo-ma-tee-ko re-ben-to

Car parts

accelerator
acelerador
a-the-le-ra-dor

aerial
antena
an-tay-na

air filter
filtro de aire
feel-tro day eye-ray

alternator
alternador
al-tair-na-dor

antifreeze
anticongelante
an-tee-kon-he-lan-tay

axle
eje
e-hay

battery
batería
ba-te-ree-a

bonnet
capó
ka-po

boot
maletero
ma-le-te-ro

brake fluid
líquido de frenos
lee-kee-do day fray-nos

brakes
frenos
fray-nos

bulb
foco
fo-ko

bumper
parachoques
pa-ra-cho-kes

car phone
teléfono de automóvil
te-le-fo-no day ow-to-mo-beel

carburettor
carburador
kar-boo-ra-dor

child seat
silla de niño
see-ya day neen-yo

choke
estárter
e-star-tair

clutch
embrague
em-bra-gay

cylinder
cilindro
thee-leen-dro

disc brake
freno de disco
fray-no day dee-sko

distributor
distribuidor
dees-tree-boo-ee-dor

door
portezuela
por-tay-thway-la

dynamo
dinamo
dee-na-mo

electrical system
sistema eléctrico
see-stay-ma e-lek-tree-ko

engine
motor
mo-tor

exhaust system
sistema de escape
see-stay-ma day e-ska-pay

fan belt
correa del ventilador
ko-ray-a del ben-tee-la-dor

foot pump
bomba de pie
bom-ba day pee-ay

fuse
fusible
foo-see-blay

fuel pump
bomba de carburante
bom-ba day kar-boo-ran-tay

fuel gauge
indicador de carburante
een-dee-ka-dor day kar-boo-ran-tay

gear box
caja de cambios
ka-ha day kam-bee-os

gear lever
palanca de cambios
pa-lan-ka day kam-bee-os

generator
generador
he-ne-ra-dor

hammer
martillo
*mar-**tee**-yo*

hand brake
freno de mano
*fray-no day **ma**-no*

hazard lights
luces de emergencia
***loo**-thes day e-mair-**hen**-thee-a*

headlights
faros
fa-ros

hood
capó
*ka-**po***

horn
bocina
*bo-**thee**-na*

hose
manga
***man**-ga*

ignition
contacto
*kon-**tak**-to*

ignition key
llave de contacto
***ya**-bay day kon-**tak**-to*

indicator
intermitente
*een-tair-mee-**ten**-tay*

jack
gato
***ga**-to*

lights
luces
***loo**-thes*

lock
cerradura
*the-ra-**doo**-ra*

oil
aceite
*a-**thay**-ee-tay*

oil filter
filtro de aceite
***feel**-tro day a-**thay**-ee-tay*

oil pressure
presión de aceite
*pre-**syon** day a-**thay**-ee-tay*

petrol
gasolina
*ga-so-**lee**-na*

points
platinos
*pla-**tee**-nos*

pump
bomba
***bom**-ba*

radiator
radiador
*ra-dee-a-**dor***

rear-view mirror
espejo retrovisor
*es-**pe**-ho re-tro-bee-**sor***

reflectors
reflectantes
*re-flek-**tan**-tes*

reversing light
luz de marcha atrás
*looth day **mar**-cha a-**tras***

roof rack
baca
***ba**-ka*

screwdriver	**steering wheel**
destornillador	volante
des-tor-nee-ya-dor	*bo-lan-tay*
seat	**stoplight**
asiento	luz de freno
a-syen-to	*looth day fray-no*
seat belt	**sun roof**
cinturón de seguridad	techo solar
then-too-ron day se-goo-ree-dad	*te-cho so-lar*
shock absorber	**suspension**
amortiguador	suspensión
a-mor-tee-gwa-dor	*soo-spen-syon*
silencer	**tools**
silenciador	herramientas
see-len-thee-a-dor	*e-ra-myen-tas*
socket set	**towbar**
juego de llaves de tubo	barra de remolque
hway-go day ya-bes day too-bo	*ba-ra day re-mol-kay*
spanner	**transmission**
llave inglesa	transmisión
ya-bay een-glay-sa	*trans-mee-syon*
spare part	**trunk**
repuesto	maletero
re-pwe-sto	*ma-le-te-ro*
spark plug	**tyre**
bujía	neumático
boo-hee-a	*nay-oo-ma-tee-ko*
speedometer	**warning light**
velocímetro	luz de advertencia
be-lo-thee-me-tro	*looth day ad-bair-ten-thee-a*
starter motor	**wheel**
motor de arranque	rueda
mo-tor day a-ran-kay	*roo-ay-da*
steering	**windscreen**
dirección	parabrisas
dee-rek-thyon	*pa-ra-bree-sas*

windscreen wipers
limpiaparabrisas
leem-pya-pa-ra-bree-sas

wrench
llave inglesa
ya-bay een-glay-sa

Road signs

Alto
al-to
Stop

Dirección única
dee-rek-thyon oo-nee-ka
One way

Aparcamiento sólo para residentes
a-par-ka-myen-to so-lo pa-ra re-see-den-tes
Parking for residents only

Estacionamiento de automóviles
es-ta-thyo-na-myen-to day ow-to-mo-bee-lays
Car park

Camino particular
ka-mee-no par-tee-koo-lar
Private road

Estacionamiento prohibido
es-ta-thyo-na-myen-to pro-ee-bee-do
No parking permitted

Ceda el paso
thay-da el pa-so
Give way

Obras
o-bras
Roadworks

Centro ciudad
then-tro thee-oo-dad
Town centre

Paso prohibido
pa-so pro-ee-bee-do
No through road

Circule por la derecha
theer-koo-lay por la de-ray-cha
Keep to the right

Peaje
pay-a-hay
Toll

Deslizamientos
des-lee-tha-myen-tos
Icy roads

Peligro
pay-lee-gro
Danger

Despacio
des-pa-thee-o
Drive slowly

Prohibido el paso
pro-ee-bee-do el pa-so
No thoroughfare

Desviación
des-bee-a-thyon
Diversion

No entrar
no en-trar
No entry

Desvío
des-bee-o
Diversion

Eating Out

Dining in Spain is as much a reason for a social gathering as it is a matter of satisfying bodily needs or gastronomic indulgence. It is not something to be hurried. Despite the bustle of waiters scurrying around, you will rarely feel rushed in a restaurant - indeed, it is often an effort to extract the bill. Note, however, that in the big coastal resorts hotel meals are normally served buffet-style with international menus often presented in pictures.

There is a variety of options for eating out, but the uniquely Spanish one is the *tapas* bar. *Tapas* are small, savoury dishes of practically anything tasty - fish, squid, meats, olives, cheeses, vegetables, and so on. Select one or two small portions (*porciones*) for a snack or a selection of bigger portions (*raciones*) to make up a meal. The bars specialising in *tapas* are usually modest places, although some in the cities are beautifully tiled. You may eat your chosen delicacies at the bar over a beer or at a table (perhaps outside in a tourist area). *Tapas* are also served wherever snacks are likely to be in demand - in hotels, *bodegas* (wine cellars) *tabernas* (bars) or *tascas* (inns).

Away from the main resorts, main meal times are later than in most other countries. Lunch is the main meal of the day, mostly taken from about 2.00pm and often preceded by tapas. Restaurants open for lunch usually from 12.30 or 1.00pm until 3.30 or 4.00pm. They re-open from about 7.30pm but do not do much business before 9.00pm. In cities, they will still be receiving diners at midnight.

In restaurants you will normally be encouraged to order *à la carte*, although there should also be a fixed menu of the day available. Menus are often broken down into kinds of dish - meat, fish, eggs, for example - rather than into courses.

Reservations

Should we reserve a table?
¿Deberíamos reservar mesa?
de-be-ree-a-mos re-sair-bar may-sa

Can I book a table for four at 8 o'clock?
¿Podría reservar una mesa para cuatro para las ocho?
po-dree-a re-sair-bar oo-na may-sa pa-ra kwa-tro pa-ra las o-cho

Can we have a table for four?
Una mesa para cuatro, por favor
oo-na may-sa pa-ra kwa-tro, por fa-bor

I am a vegetarian
Soy vegetariano / vegeteriana
soy be-he-ta-ree-a-no / be-he-ta-ree-a-na)

We would like a table — by the window
Nos gustaría una mesa — junto a la ventana
nos goo-sta-ree-a oo-na may-sa — hoon-to a la ben-ta-na

— on the terrace
— en la terraza
— en la te-ra-tha

Useful questions

Are vegetables included?
¿Se incluye verdura?
*say een-**kloo**-yay bair-**doo**-ra*

Do you have a local speciality?
¿Tienen alguna especialidad local?
*tee-e-nen al-**goo**-na es-peth-ya-lee-**dad** lo-**kal***

Do you have a set menu?
¿Tiene un menú del día?
*tee-e-nay oon me-**noo** del **dee**-a*

What do you recommend?
¿Qué me recomienda?
*kay may re-ko-**myen**-da*

What is the dish of the day?
¿Cuál es el plato del día?
*kwal es el **pla**-to del **dee**-a*

What is the soup of the day?
¿Cuál es la sopa del día?
*kwal es la **so**-pa del **dee**-a*

What is this called?
¿Cómo se llama esto?
*ko-mo say **ya**-ma es-to*

What is this dish like?
¿Cómo es este plato?
*ko-mo es es-tay **pla**-to*

Which local wine do you recommend?
¿Qué vino local recomienda?
*kay **bee**-no lo-**kal** re-ko-**myen**-da*

Do you have fruit?
¿Tiene fruta?
*tee-e-nay **froo**-ta*

How do I eat this?
¿Cómo se come esto?
*ko-mo say **ko**-may es-to*

Is the local wine good?
¿Es bueno el vino local?
*es **bway**-no el **bee**-no lo-**kal***

Is this cheese very strong?
¿Es muy fuerte este queso?
*es mwee **fwair**-tay **es**-tay ke-so*

Is this good?
¿Está bueno esto?
*es-**ta bway**-no es-to*

What is this?
¿Qué es esto?
*kay es **es**-to*

Ordering your meal

The menu, please
El menú, por favor
*el me-**noo**, por fa-**bor***

I will take the set menu
Tomaré el menú del día
*to-ma-**ray** el me-**noo** del **dee**-a*

Can we start with soup?
¿Podemos empezar con sopa?
*po-**day**-mos em-pe-**thar** kon **so**-pa*

I like my steak — very rare
Me gusta — muy poco hecho
*may **goo**-sta — mwee **po**-ko e-cho*

— rare
— poco hecho
*— **po**-ko e-cho*

— medium rare
— medianamente hecho
*— me-dee-a-na-**men**-tay e-cho*

— well done
— bien hecho
— *bee-**en** e-cho*

I will take that
Tomaré eso
*to-ma-**ray** e-so*

Could we have some butter?
¿Puede traernos mantequilla, por favor?
*pwe-day try-**air**-nos man-te-**kee**-ya, por fa-**bor***

That is for me
Eso es para mí
*e-so es **pa**-ra mee*

We need some bread, please
Nos hace falta pan, por favor
*nos **a**-thay **fal**-ta pan, por fa-**bor***

Could we have some more bread please?
¿Puede traernos más pan por favor?
*pwe-day try-**air**-nos mas pan, por fa-**bor***

I will have salad
Yo tomaré ensalada
*yo to-ma-**ray** en-sa-**la**-da*

Can I see the menu again, please?
¿Puedo volver a ver el menú, por favor?
*pwe-do bol-**bair** a bair el me-**noo**, por fa-**bor***

Ordering drinks

The wine list, please
La lista de vinos, por favor
*la **lee**-sta day **bee**-nos, por fa-**bor***

Black coffee, please
Café solo, por favor
*ka-**fay** so-lo, por fa-**bor***

We will take the Rioja
Tomaremos el Rioja
*to-ma-**ray**-mos el ree-o-ha*

Can we have some (still / sparkling) mineral water?
¿Nos puede traer agua mineral (sin gas / con gas)?
*nos pwe-day try-**air** a-gwa mee-ne-**ral** (seen gas / con gas)*

A bottle of house red wine, please
Una botella de vino tinto de la casa
*oo-na bo-**te**-ya day **bee**-no **teen**-to day la **ka**-sa*

Coffee with milk, please
Café con leche, por favor
*ka-**fay** kon le-chay, por fa-**bor***

A glass of dry white wine, please
Un vaso de vino blanco seco, por favor
*oon **ba**-so day **bee**-no **blan**-ko **se**-ko, por fa-**bor***

Some plain water, please
Agua natural, por favor
*a-gwa na-too-**ral**, por fa-**bor***

Another bottle of red wine, please
Otra botella de vino tinto, por favor
*o-tra bo-**te**-ya day **bee**-no **teen**-to, por fa-**bor***

Two beers, please
Dos cervezas, por favor
*dos thair-**bay**-thas, por fa-**bor***

Another glass, please
Otro vaso, por favor
*o-tro **ba**-so, por fa-**bor***

Paying the bill

Can we have the bill, please?
¿Puede traernos la cuenta, por favor?
pwe-day try-air-nos la kwen-ta, por fa-bor

I haven't enough money
No tengo suficiente dinero
no ten-go soo-feeth-yen-tay dee-ne-ro

Is service included?
¿Está el servicio incluido?
es-ta el sair-bee-thee-o een-kloo-ee-do

This is not correct
Esto no es correcto
es-to no es ko-rek-to

Is tax included?
¿Están los impuestos incluidos?
es-tan los eem-pwe-stos een-kloo-ee-dos

This is not my bill
Ésta no es mi cuenta
es-ta no es mee kwen-ta

Is there any extra charge?
¿Hay algún cargo adicional?
a-ee al-goon kar-go a-deeth-yo-nal

You have given me the wrong change
Me ha dado mal los cambios
may a da-do mal los kam-bee-os

Complaints and compliments

This is cold
Esto está frio
es-to es-ta free-o

Can I have the recipe?
¿Puede darme la receta?
pwe-day dar-may la re-thay-ta

This is not what I ordered
Esto no es lo que he pedido
es-to no es lo kay ay pe-dee-do

The meal was excellent
La comida estaba excelente
la ko-mee-da es-ta-ba eks-the-len-tay

Waiter! We have been waiting for a long time
¡Camarero! Estamos esperando desde hace mucho tiempo
*ka-ma-rair-o! Es-ta-mos es-pe-ran-do dez-day
a-thay moo-cho tee-em-po*

This is excellent
Esto está buenísimo
es-to es-ta bwe-nee-see-mo

Food

Spanish food has an earthy richness, with pronounced flavours enhanced by different herbs and spices. There are some common factors across the country – the wide use of olive oil and garlic, for example – but also marked regional variations in the types of dishes and styles of cooking. There are relatively few national dishes, and only a handful have become internationally known – *tortilla* (omelette), *paella*, *gazpacho* and little else, but there is a good deal more to discover.

Stews (*cocidos*) and hotpots are the mainstay of much of the everyday Spanish diet, combining pulses such as rice or chickpeas with vegetables, meats, poultry and seafood, all enriched with peppers, herbs and spices. They make filling meals, particularly given the generous proportions of most Spanish servings – a feature of their hospitality.

But restaurant meals are much more sophisticated than this, at least in areas where there is the necessary affluent clientele. If food is your real passion, pack your brolly and head north to the Basque country, where gastronomy is alive and well.

The Spanish have a pronounced sweet tooth and have concocted many kinds of delicious sweet breads, pastries and sweetmeats, which they consume at every opportunity through the day, starting at breakfast with *churros* - sausage-shaped fritters - and *suizos* - sugar-topped sweet rolls.

Regional specialities

The Atlantic coast - the north coast, from Galicia across to the Basque country, has a mild, wet climate that ensures rich pastures for grazing and lots of fresh vegetables. The seafood too is about Spain's finest, and the cuisine reflects the quality of the produce used.

Galicia has the greatest reputation for seafood, its ports supplying much of the rest of Spain. Octopus is a speciality, and the large prawns are irresistible. Galicians use either seafood or meats cooked with onions to fill their pies, called *empanadas*. Other dishes to look out for are *lacón con grelos*, a combination of salted ham, turnips and spicy *chorizo* sausages, and *caldo gallego*, which includes beans and cabbages in a meaty stew.

Asturias is famous for its *fabada* – so much so that it exports the rich meaty stew based on *fabes* (white beans). Fish is again a speciality, with excellent salmon and a fish stew known as *caldereta*. Try also the *merluza a la sidra*, hake cooked in cider.

The food of the **Basque country** is superb. Seafood and sauces are the Basques' forte, subtly combined in dishes such as cod cooked with peppers and onions - *bacalao a la vizcaína* – or cod in garlic and oil – *bacalao al pil-pil*. Also worth trying is sea bream – *besugo*. Some of the local specialities include baby eels – *anguilas* – which are fried in oil spiced with hot peppers and garlic. *Marmitako* (tuna stew) is also popular, as is the hake dish *kokotxas*.

South of the Pyrenees – meat replaces fish and seafood as the central element in the popular dishes of the regions south of the Pyrenees. The wine regions of Rioja and Navarra both have individual styles of cooking. Some of Rioja's most memorable dishes are those that involve cooking a variety of meats in red peppers and asparagus. Game is an important part of Navarra's cooking, drawing influences from both the Basques to the north and the Aragonese to the south. A popular home-grown dish of the region is trout cooked with ham – *trucha a la Navarra*.

Aragon – meats are the staple diet of the Aragonese, usually served with a rich red-pepper sauce called *chilindrón*. Another tasty dish is *magras con tomate*, using fried ham and a tomato-based sauce.

Catalonia's distinctive dishes have benefited from its position on the French border, laying it open to both French and Italian influences. Sauces are part of the attraction. Look out for *ali-oli*, made from olive oil and garlic beaten into a paste, and *picada*, made from almonds, pine nuts, garlic and parsley. Seafood is important. This is one of the best areas to try *zarzuela de mariscos* – mixed seafood stew - and Tarragona is noted for *romesco*, a distinctive sweetish sauce served with fish.

A simple, satisfying dish is *pan con tomate* – bread smeared with tomato and olive oil. As elsewhere in Spain, spicy sausages play an important part in the diet. Try *butifarra*, especially when served with *mangetes* (white beans). On the coast, you should try the mixture of chicken and lobster, and in Barcelona seek out the filling local *cocido* called *escudella* – it includes meat balls, a range of meats, pulses, vegetables and spices. Farther south, rice dishes are popular – *arroz a banda* is just rice cooked in a fish broth, which can be superb.

Catalonians are keen on cakes. Among the sweet delicacies are *torteles* (*tortells* in Catalan) – filled rings of sweet bread – and *buñuelos* – fried puffs.

The southern Costas – paella originates from Valencia, and you should find some excellent examples in its home territory. As in the rest of Spain, *cocidos* are a major part of the everyday diet. Some to look out for are *cocido de pelotas* – meat in cabbage, chickpeas and potatoes – and *arroz con costra*, which includes chicken, rabbit, black pudding and more chickpeas.

Murcia is also strong on rice dishes. Try the fish one, *arroz al caldero*. Look out also for *menestra*, a vegetable stew. And for fish, try *mújol* (mullet), especially the roe.

Jijona is famous for its *túrron* – hard or soft nougat.

Andalucia is less distinguished in its cooking than some other regions, but it nevertheless gave birth to Spain's most famous soup, *gazpacho*. Fried fish – *pescaíto frito* - is a popular part of the diet, and from the land of flamenco comes *huevos a la flamenca* - eggs, ham, tomato, asparagus, *chorizo* and peppers.

Sweet specialities include *polvorones* – shortbread cookies – and *mostachones* – almond buns.

The meseta – in the central plateau regions, roast meats such as suckling pigs are popular. So are *cocidos* with lots of pulses, particularly chickpeas. Despite being landlocked, the central region still manages to produce some notable seafood dishes, drawing on the bountiful seas off Galicia. *Bacalao al ajo arriero* is one – cod cooked in garlic. Soups too are popular. Try some of the *sopas castellanas*, usually a type of meat broth.

If you like pork, ham or sausages, head for **Extremadura**. *Chorizos* take on myriad forms here, and the *Montánchez* ham is famous all over Spain. *Cocidos* are slightly less popular than in other regions. *Migas* is a tasty fried mixture of soaked bread, bacon and peppers.

A favourite sweet delicacy from **Ávila** is *yemas de Sta Teresa* – sugared egg yolks.

The Canary Islands – two of the most popular local dishes on the Canaries are again stews – *gofio* and *puchero canario*. Many dishes will be accompanied by the dressing known as *el mojo*, made of oil, vinegar, spices and garlic. The Canaries are one of the best places to sample *mazapanes* – marzipan cakes.

On the **Balearic Islands**, apart from an abundance of seafood, there are several meat dishes to try. *Sobrasada*, a peppery pork sausage, is one of the most common. On Majorca, try the enormous puff pastries, *ensaimadas*, and the sweet flans, *cocas*.

Menu reader

aceite
a-thay-tay
oil

aceitunas
a-thay-too-nas
olives

acelga
a-thel-ga
chard

aguacate
a-gwa-ka-tay
avocado

ajo
a-ho
garlic

albahaca
al-ba-a-ka
basil

albaricoques
al-ba-ree-ko-kes
apricots

albondigas
al-bon-dee-gas
meatballs

alcachofa
al-ka-cho-fa
artichoke

almejas
al-may-has
clams

apio
a-pee-o
celery

arroz con leche
a-roth kon le-chay
rice pudding

asado / asada la parrilla
a-sa-do / a-sa-da la pa-ree-ya
grilled

atún
a-toon
tuna

berenjena
be-ren-hay-na
aubergine

berro
be-ro
watercress

berza
ber-tha
cabbage

bizcocho
beeth-ko-cho
sponge cake

bocadillo
bo-ka-dee-yo
sandwich (with French-style bread)

bogavante a la marinera
bo-ga-ban-tay a la ma-ree-nair-a
lobster cooked in Galician style

bollos de pan
bo-yos day pan
bread rolls

budín
boo-deen
pudding

buñuelos
boon-yoo-ay-los
doughnuts

caballa
ka-ba-ya
mackerel

caballa en escabeche
ka-ba-ya en es-ka-be-chay
marinated mackerel

cabezas de cordero al horno
ka-bay-thas day kor-dair-o al or-no
roast head of lamb (Aragon)

calabacín
ka-la-ba-theen
courgette

calabaza
ka-la-ba-tha
squash

calamares
ka-la-ma-res
squid

caldo
kal-do
broth

caldo de pollo
kal-do day po-yo
chicken broth

caldo de vaca
kal-do day ba-ka
beef broth

callos
ka-yos
tripe

cangrejo de río
kan-gre-ho day ree-o
crayfish

carne
kar-nay
meat

carne asada
kar-nay a-sa-da
grilled meat

carne de vaca en asador
kar-nay day ba-ka en a-sa-dor
braised beef

castañas asadas
kas-tan-yas a-sa-das
roast chestnuts

cebollas
the-bo-yas
onions

cebollinos
the-bo-yee-nos
chives

cerdo asado
thair-do a-sa-do
pork roast

cerezas
the-ray-thas
cherries

chalotes
cha-lo-tes
shallots

champiñones
cham-peen-yo-nes
mushrooms

champiñones al ajillo
cham-peen-yo-nes al a-hee-yo
mushrooms with garlic

champiñones en salsa
cham-peen-yo-nes en sal-sa
mushrooms in sauce

chirivía
chee-ree-bee-a
parsnip

chorizo
cho-ree-tho
hard pork sausage

chuleta de cerdo
choo-lay-ta day thair-do
pork chop

chuleta de cordero
choo-lay-ta day kor-dair-o
lamb chop

chuleta de ternera
choo-lay-ta day tair-nair-a
veal cutlet

churros
choo-ros
fritters

ciruelas
thee-roo-ay-las
plums

cochinillo asado
ko-chee-nee-yo a-sa-do
roast suckling pig (Castile)

cocido de alubias
ko-thee-do day a-loo-byas
bean stew

cocido madrileño
ko-thee-do ma-dree-len-yo
meat stew with vegetables

coles de Bruselas
ko-les day broo-say-las
Brussels sprouts

coliflor
ko-lee-flor
cauliflower

compota de manzana
kom-po ta day man-tha-na
apple compote

conejo con caracoles
ko-ne-ho kon ka-ra-ko-les
rabbit with snails

conejo estofado
ko-ne-ho e-sto-fa-do
stuffed rabbit

cordero en asador
kor-dair-o en a-sa-dor
mutton on the spit

dátiles
da-tee-les
dates

ensalada
en-sa-la-da
salad

ensalada de maíz
en-sa-la-da day my-eeth
corn salad

ensalada de patata
en-sa-la-da day pa-ta-ta
potato salad

ensalada de pepino
en-sa-la-da day pe-pee-nee-yo
cucumber salad

ensalada de tomate
en-sa-la-da day to-ma-tay
tomato salad

ensalada mixta
en-sa-la-da meek-sta
mixed salad

ensaladilla rusa
en-sa-la-dee-ya roo-sa
Russian salad

. . . en salsa
. . . en sal-sa
. . . in sauce

escarola
e-ska-ro-la
chicory

espaguetis
es-pa-ge-tees
spaghetti

espárragos
es-pa-ra-gos
asparagus

espinacas
es-pee-na-kas
spinach

estragón
es-tra-gon
tarragon

fabada
fa-ba-da
bean and pork stew (Asturias)

faisán
fy-ee-san
pheasant

filete
fee-le-tay
fillet steak

filete de merluza
fee-le-tay day mair-loo-tha
hake fillet

filete de vaca
fee-le-tay day ba-ka
beefsteak

flan
flan
crème caramel

frambuesas
fram-bway-sas
raspberries

fresas
fray-sas
strawberries

fresas con nata
fray-sas kon na-ta
strawberries and cream

fruta con nata montada
froo-ta kon na-ta mon-ta-da
fruit with whipped cream

gazpacho
gath-pa-cho
cold soup with cucumber, tomato, garlic etc

granada
gra-na-da
pomegranate

grosellas negras
gro-se-yas ne-gras
blackcurrants

guisado de carne
gee-sa-do day kar-nay
beef stew

guisado de pollo
gee-sa-do day po-yo
chicken stew

guisantes
gee-san-tes
peas

habas
a-bas
broad beans

helado
e-la-do
ice cream

hierbabuena
yair-ba-bway-na
mint

hoja de laurel
o-ha day low-rel
bayleaf

huevo pasado por agua
way-bo pa-sa-do por a-gwa
soft boiled egg

huevos con jamón
way-bos kon ha-mon
eggs with ham

huevos con tocino
way-bos kon to-thee-no
eggs with bacon

huevos fritos
way-bos free-tos
fried eggs

huevos revueltos
way-bos re-bwel-tos
scrambled eggs

jamón serrano
ha-mon se-ra-no
cured ham

judías verdes
hoo-dee-as bair-des
French beans

langosta
lan-go-sta
lobster

langostinos rebozados
lan-go-stee-nos re-bo-thu-dos
scampi

lechón en asador
le-chon en a-sa-dor
suckling pig on the spit

lechuga
le-choo-ga
lettuce

lengua
len-gwa
tongue

limón
lee-mon
lemon

macedonia de frutas
ma-the-do-nee-a day froo-tas
fruit salad

maíz
my-eeth
sweet corn

mantequilla
man-te-kee-ya
butter

manzana asada
man-tha-na a-sa-da
roast apple

manzanas
man-tha-nas
apples

mejillones
me-hee-yo-nes
mussels

melocotón
me-lo-ko-ton
peach

melón
me-lon
melon

merluza en salsa verde
mair-loo-tha en sal-sa bair-day
hake in parsley sauce

mermelada
mair-me-la-da
jam

morcilla
mor-thee-ya
black pudding (= blood sausage)

mousse de chocolate
moos day cho-ko-la-tay
chocolate mousse

nabo
na-bo
turnip

naranjas
na-ran-has
oranges

natillas
na-tee-yas
custard

oca
o-ka
goose

ostras
o-stras
oysters

ostras fritas
o-stras free-tas
fried oysters (Galicia)

paella
py-e-ya
paella

pasta
pa-sta
pasta

patas de rana fritas
pa-tas day ra-na free-tas
fried frog legs

patatas a la riojana
pa-ta-tas a la ree-o-ha-na
potatoes, tomatoes and haricot beans (Rioja)

patatas asadas
pa-ta-tas a-sa-das
roast potatoes

patatas bravas
pa-ta-tas bra-bas
spicy fried potatoes

patatas fritas
pa-ta-tas free-tas
French fries

patatas troceadas y verdura con mayonesa
*pa-ta-tas tro-thay-a-das y bair-doo-ra kon my-o
nay-sa*
potatoes and vegetables with mayonnaise

pato
pa-to
duck

pato relleno con manzanas
pa-to re-yay-no kon man-tha-nas
roast duck with apples

pavo
pa-bo
turkey

pepinillo
pe-pee-nee-yo
gherkin

pepino
pe-pee-no
cucumber

pera
pay-ra
pear

perdiz en chocolate
pair-deeth en cho-ko-la-tay
partridge with a chocolate sauce (Navarra)

perejil
pe-re-heel
parsley

perifollo
pe-ree-fo-yo
chervil

perrito caliente
pe-ree-to kal-lee-en-tay
hot dog

pescado
pes-ka-do
fish

pescado en escabeche
pes-ka-do en es-ka-be-chay
marinated fish

pierna (de cordero, etc)
pee-air-na (day kor-dair-o, etc)
shank (of lamb, etc)

pimiento rojo
pee-myen-to ro-ho
red pepper

pimiento verde
pee-myen-to bair-day
green pepper

pimientos rellenos
pee-myen-tos re-yay-nos
stuffed peppers

piña
peen-ya
pineapple

plátano
pla-ta-no
banana

pollo cocido / asado
po-yo ko-thee-do / a-sa-do
baked / roasted chicken

pollo frito/rebozado
po-yo free-to/re-bo-tha-do
fried/breaded chicken

pomelo
po-me-lo
grapefruit

puerros
pwe-ros
leeks

puré de patatas
poo-ray day pa-ta-tas
mashed potatoes

queso
ke-so
cheese

queso manchego
ke-so man-chay-go
la Mancha cheese

rábanos
ra-ba-nos
radishes

remolacha
re-mo-la-cha
beetroot

riñones guisados
reen-yo-nes gee-sa-dos
stewed kidney

romero
ro-mair-o
rosemary

salchicha
sal-chee-cha
sausage

salmonete
sal-mo-ne-tay
mullet

salsa de cebolla
sal-sa day the-bo-ya
onion sauce

salsa de manzana
sal-sa day man-tha-na
applesauce

salsa de pimiento verde
sal-sa day pee-myen-to
green pepper sauce

salsa de tomate
sal-sa day to-ma-tay
tomato sauce

salsa de vino
sal-sa day bee-no
wine sauce

salvia
sal-bee-a
sage

sandía
san-dee-a
watermelon

sandwich de jamón
san-weech day ha-mon
ham sandwich

sardinas
sar-dee-nas
sardines

sepia
se-pee-a
cuttlefish

sopa de ajo
so-pa day a-ho
garlic soup

sopa de crema de champiñones
so-pa day kray-ma day cham-peen-yo-nes
cream of mushroom soup

sopa de fideos
so-pa day fee-day-os
noodle soup

sopa de frijoles
so-pa day free-ho-les
kidney-bean soup

sopa de guisantes
so-pa day gee-san-tes
pea soup

sopa de pollo
so-pa day po-yo
chicken soup

sopa de puerros
so-pa day pwe-ros
leek soup

sopa de tomate
so-pa day to-ma-tay
tomato soup

tallarines de huevo
ta-ya-ree-nes day way-bo
egg noodles

tarta
tar-ta
cake / pie

tarta de almendra
tar-ta day al-men-dra
almond cake

tarta de limón
tar-ta day lee-mon
lemon meringue

tarta de manzana
tar-ta day man-tha-na
apple cake

tomates
to-ma-tes
tomatoes

tomillo
to-mee-yo
thyme

tortas
tor-tas
thin pancakes

— con chocolate
— kon cho-ko-la-tay
—with chocolate

— con mermelada
— kon mair-me-la-da
—with jam

tortilla española
tor-tee-ya es-pan-yo-la
Spanish omelette

trucha
troo-cha
trout

trucha cocida
troo-cha ko-thee-da
boiled trout

trucha frita
troo-cha free-ta
fried trout

uvas
oo-bas
grapes

verduras
bair-doo-ras
vegetables

vinagre
bee-na-gray
vinegar

yogur
yo-goor
yoghurt

zanahoria
tha-na-o-ree-a
carrot

Wine

As in France and Italy, there is a system of specified wine names in Spain, which may be applied only to wines produced from particular areas, in particular ways, using particular grapes. The Spanish system does not attempt to pin down the geographical origin with any precision. The area covered by a single Denominación de Origen (DO) may be enormous. There are only thirty demarcated regions, compared with over three hundred in France. The regulations are also somewhat general. The result is that DO status does not mean a great deal and that the reputation of individual producers is the key to identifying good wine.

Since joining the European Union, Spain has gained another wine classification - vinos de la tierra – along the lines of the French vins de pays system. The regulations specify grape varieties (up to a point) and minimum alcohol levels.

Spanish winemaking has improved a lot in recent years, but the biggest revolution has been in white winemaking. Most exported whites are now made fresh and fruity, if rather neutral in flavour, taking after the main white grapes, the Airén and the Viura. Reds from the Penedés and Rioja can be extremely good.

Wine regions

Catalonia – the most important wines of Catalonia in the northeast are from Penedés, the area inland from the coast south of Barcelona. The reds – particularly those based on the non-native Cabernet Sauvignon - rival the wines of Rioja, but the area is also the major producer of Cava – Spain's sparking wines fermented by the Champagne method. The areas southwest of Penedés (Priorato, Tarragona, Terra Alta) produce some weighty reds.

Navarra – west of Catalonia – shares the northern flank of the Ebro valley with Rioja but until recently did not achieve the quality or status of its neighbour. Now there are excellent reds to be had – both light wine for drinking young and heavier, barrel-aged ones. Recent white vintages are satisfactorily zippy.

Rioja is easily the best known of Spain's wine regions. South of Navarra, it is divided into three areas straddling the River Ebro. It is from Rioja Alta and Rioja Alavesa (scenic, hilly, upstream areas, north and south of the river) that the best of the wines originate. The flat, hot Rioja Baja produces heavier wines often used to bolster the more delicate reds from upstream. The maturing of wines, especially the reds, in oak casks is the region's distinctive feature, giving a pronounced vanilla flavour.

Galicia – in the northwest, this area's proximity to Portugal's *vinho verde* country is reflected in its sharp white wines.

Ribera del Duero – north of Madrid, this medium-sized DO area – 'the banks of the Duero' - is realising its potential for the production of fine reds.

Rueda - this region north of Madrid is traditionally known for sherry-style wines made from the Palamino grape but it now produces mainly fresh, nutty white table wines from the native Verdejo grape.

La Mancha and Valdepeñas – these two areas south of Madrid together form by far the largest wine-producing region in the country, making some very agreeable reds and whites. Although they may lack the subtleties of Riojas and Penedés, there are some *reservas* and *gran reservas* worth attention.

Sherry – from in and around Jerez in the far south (or indeed from Spain in general) – bears little relation to the sweetened products sold in volume in Britain.

There are two basic varieties of sherry. *Fino* is pale and dry with a pronounced tang that comes from a natural yeast (*flor*) that forms on the surface of the wine in the barrel. Only light, fresh, fine wines are susceptible. An *amontillado* starts out as *fino* but is aged until the *flor* dies. Although deeper in colour, it is still dry. *Olorosos* are richer in colour but also dry, made from heavier wines more heavily fortified, without the formation of *flor*.

Wine label reader

abrocado
a-bro-ka-do
medium sweet

almacenista
al-ma-the-nee-sta
unblended sherry with distinctive flavours

amontillado
a-mon-tee-ya-do
aged *fino* - darker, deeper but still very dry

blanco
blan-ko
white

bodega
bo-day-ga
wine cellar (wherever wine is made, stored or sold)

brut
broot
dry

cava
ka-ba
wine made by the Champagne method

clarete
kla-re-tay
light red

criado y embotellado por . . .
kree-a-do ee em-bo-te-ya-do por . . .
grown and bottled by . . .

(de) crianza
(day) kree-an-tha
aged in wood

dulce
dool-thay
sweet

embotellado de origen
em-bo-te-ya-do day o-ree-hen
estate-bottled

espumoso
*es-poo-**mo**-so*
sparkling wine

fino
fee-no
pale, very dry sherry made from the
lightest wines, to be drunk cool and young

generoso
*he-ne-**ro**-so*
aperitif or dessert wine

gran reserva
*gran re-**sair**-ba*
top quality Rioja wine, aged for longer
before sale than *reserva* but capable of
further ageing. The meaning may be
different for wines from outside Rioja

manzanilla
*man-tha-**nee**-ya*
form of fino

nuevo
nway-bo
young wine

oloroso
*o-lo-**ro**-so*
dark sherry made from richer wines and
more heavily fortified but still dry

reserva
*re-**sair**-ba*
selected Rioja wine from a good vintage,
aged for a minimum period before sale, at
which point it is generally ready to drink

rosado
*ro-**sa**-do*
rosé

seco
say-ko
dry

semi-seco
*se-mee-**say**-ko*
medium dry

sin crianza
*seen **kree**-an-tha*
not aged in wood

tinto
teen-to
red

Other drinks

agua mineral
a-gwa mee-ne-ral
mineral water

aguardiente
a-gwar-dee-en-tay
brandy

aguardiente de cerezas
*a-gwar-dee-**en**-tay day the-**ray**-thas*
cherry brandy

aguardiente de manzanas
*a-gwar-dee-**en**-tay day man-**tha**-nas*
apple brandy

anís
*a-**nees***
anis

café
*ka-**fay***
coffee

439

café americano
ka-fay a-me-ree-ka-no
large black coffee

café con hielo
ka-fay kon ye-lo
iced coffee

café con leche
ka-fay kon le-chay
white coffee

café escocés
ka-fay es-ko-thes
coffee with whisky and ice cream

café instantáneo
ka-fay een-stan-ta-nay-o
instant coffee

café irlandés
ka-fay eer-lan-des
Irish coffee

café sólo
ka-fay so-lo
small black coffee

una caña
oo-na kan-ya
a small glass of draught beer

carajillo
ka-ra-hee-yo
coffee with a dash of brandy

capuchino
ka-poo-chee-no
cappuccino

cerveza
thair-bay-tha
beer

cerveza embotellada
thair-bay-tha em-bo-te-ya-da
bottled beer

cerveza enlatada
thair-bay-tha en-la-ta-da
canned beer

una cerveza grande
oo-na thair-bay-tha gran-day
a large beer

cerveza negra
thair-bay-tha ne-gra
stout

champán
cham-pan
champagne

coca-cola
ko-ka-ko-la
coke

un coñac
oon kon-yak
a brandy

cortado
kor-ta-do
coffee with a dash of milk

descafeinado
des-ka-fay-na-do
decaffeinated coffee

horchata
or-cha-ta
tiger nut milk

licor
lee-kor
liqueur

limonada
lee-mo-na-da
lemonade

manzanilla
man-tha-nee-ya
camomile tea

naranjada
*na-ran-**ha**-da*
orange drink

pacharán
*pa-cha-**ran***
a type of sloe gin

ron
ron
rum

sangría
*san-**gree**-a*
fruit cup with wine

sidra
see-dra
cider

soda
so-da
soda water

té
tay
tea

té con leche
*tay kon **le**-chay*
tea with milk

té con limón
*tay kon lee-**mon***
lemon tea

tónica
to-nee-ka
tonic water

un vaso de vino blanco
*oon **ba**-so day **bee**-no **blan**-ko*
a glass of white wine

un vaso de vino tinto
*oon **ba**-so day **bee**-no **teen**-to*
a glass of red wine

vermut
*bair-**moot***
vermouth

vino rosado
***bee**-no ro-**sa**-do*
rosé wine

zumo de albaricoque
***thoo**-mo day al-ba-ree-**ko**-kay*
apricot juice

zumo de manzana
***thoo**-mo day man-**tha**-na*
apple juice

zumo de melocotón
thoo**-mo day me-lo-ko-**ton
peach juice

zumo de naranja
***thoo**-mo day na-**ran**-ha*
orange juice

zumo de uva
***thoo**-mo day **oo**-ba*
grape juice

Out and About

The weather

The northern coastal regions catch all the rain clouds coming off the Atlantic, making this area wet and often windy. Relatively little rain crosses the mountains to the elevated central plateau where the climate can be harsh, with blisteringly hot summer days and freezing winter nights. In winter, much of the Pyrenees may be snowbound. (There is skiing here and in the very high Sierra Nevada in the extreme south.) The Mediterranean coasts enjoy milder climates of hot dry summers and cool damp winters. The Canaries have reliably sunny summers and warm winters.

Is it going to get any warmer?
¿Va a hacer más calor?
ba a a-thair mas ka-lor

Is it going to stay like this?
¿Va a continuar así?
ba a kon-tee-nwar a-see

Is there going to be a thunderstorm?
¿Va a haber tormenta?
ba a a-bair tor-men-ta

Isn't it a lovely day?
¿No es éste un día maravilloso?
no es es-tay oon dee-a ma-ra-bee-yo-so

It has stopped snowing
Ha parado de nevar
a pa-ra-do day ne-bar

It is a very clear night
Hace una noche muy despejada
a-thay oo-na no-chay mwee des-pe-ha-da

It is far too hot
Hace demasiado calor
a-thay de-ma-sya-do ka-lor

It is foggy
Hay niebla
eye nee-e-bla

It is raining again
Está lloviendo de nuevo
es-ta yo-byen-do day nway-bo

It is very cold
Hace mucho frío
a-thay moo-cho free-o

It is very windy
Hace mucho viento
a-thay moo-cho bee-en-to

There is a cool breeze
Hay una brisa fresca
eye oo-na bree-sa fre-ska

What is the temperature?
¿Qué temperatura hace?
kay tem-pe-ra-too-ra a-thay

It is going— to be fine
Va — a hacer bueno
ba — a a-thair bway-no

— to be windy
— a hacer viento
— a a-thair bee-en-to

— to rain
— a llover
— a yo-bair

— to snow
— a nevar
*— a ne-**bar***

Will it be cold tonight?
¿Hará frío esta noche?
*a-**ra** free-o es-ta **no**-chay*

Will the weather improve?
¿Va a mejorar el tiempo?
*ba a me-ho-**rar** el tee-**em**-po*

Will the wind die down?
¿Va a amainar el viento?
*ba a a-my-**nar** el bee-en-to*

On the beach

Can we change here?
¿Podemos cambiarnos aquí?
*po-**day**-mos kam-**byar**-nos a-**kee***

Can you recommend a quiet beach?
¿Puede sugerir una playa tranquila?
*pwe-day soo-he-**reer** oo-na **ply**-a tran-**kee**-la*

Is it safe to swim here?
¿Es seguro nadar aquí?
*es se-**goo**-ro na-**dar** a-**kee***

Is the current strong?
¿Hay mucha corriente?
*eye **moo**-cha ko-ree-**en**-tay*

Is the sea calm?
¿Está la mar tranquila?
*es-**ta** la mar tran-**kee**-la*

Can I rent — a sailing boat?
¿Puedo alquilar — un barco de vela?
*pwe-do al-kee-**lar**— oon **bar**-ko day **bay**-la*

— a rowing boat?
— un bote de remos?
*— oon **bo**-tay day **re**-mos*

Is it possible to go— sailing?
¿Es posible — salir a navegar?
*es po-**see**-blay — sa-**leer** a na-be-**gar***

— surfing?
— hacer surf?
*— a-**thair** soorf*

— water skiing?
— hacer esquí acuático?
*— a-**thair** e-**skee** a-**kwa**-tee-ko*

— wind surfing?
— hacer windsurf?
*— a-**thair** ween-soorf*

Is the water warm?
¿Está el agua templada?
*es-**ta** el a-gwa tem-**pla**-da*

Is there a heated swimming pool?
¿Hay alguna piscina climatizada?
*eye al-**goo**-na pees-**thee**-na klee-ma-tee-**tha**-da*

Is there a lifeguard here?
¿Hay algún salvavidas aquí?
*eye al-**goon** sal-ba-**bee**-das a-**kee***

Is this beach private?
¿Es privada esta playa?
*es pree-**ba**-da es-ta **ply**-a*

When is high tide?
¿Cuándo toca marea alta?
***kwan**-do **to**-ka ma-**ray**-a **al**-ta*

When is low tide?
¿Cuándo toca marea baja?
***kwan**-do **to**-ka ma-**ray**-a **ba**-ha*

Sport and recreation

Can I rent the equipment?
¿Puedo alquilar el material?
pwe-do al-kee-lar el ma-te-ree-al

Can we go riding?
¿Podemos ir a montar a caballo?
po-day-mos eer a mon-tar a ka-ba-yo

Can we — play tennis?
¿Podemos — jugar al tenis?
po-day-mos— hoo-gar al te-nees

— play golf?
— jugar al golf?
— hoo-gar al golf

— play volleyball?
— jugar al voleibol?
— hoo-gar al bo-lee-bol

Where can we fish?
¿Dónde podemos pescar?
don-day po-day-mos pe-skar

Do we need a permit?
¿Necesitamos permiso?
ne-the-see-ta-mos pair-mee-so

Entertainment

How much is it for a child?
¿Cuánto cuesta para un niño?
kwan-to kwe-sta pa-ra oon neen-yo

How much is it per person?
¿Cuánto cuesta por persona?
kwan-to kwe-sta por pair-so-na

How much is it to get in?
¿Cuánto cuesta la entrada?
kwan-to kwe-sta la en-tra-da

Is there   — a disco?
  ¿Hay   — alguna discoteca?
   eye   — al-goo-na dee-sko-tay-ka

— a good nightclub?
— algún buen club?
— al-goon bwen kloob

— a theatre?
— teatro?
— tay-a-tro

Are there any films in English?
¿Hay alguna película en inglés?
eye al-goo-na pe-lee-koo-la en een-gles

Two stalls tickets, please
Dos entradas en butacas, por favor
dos en-tra-das en boo-ta-kas, por fa-bor

Two tickets, please
Dos entradas, por favor
dos en-tra-das, por fa-bor

Is there a reduction for children?
¿Hay descuento para niños?
eye des-kwen-to pa-ra neen-yos

Sightseeing

Are there any boat trips on the river?
¿Hay excursiones en barco por el río?
eye ek-skoor-syo-nes en bar-ko por el ree-o

Are there any guided tours of the castle?
¿Hay alguna visita con guía al castillo?
eye al-goo-na bee-see-ta kon gee-a al ka-stee-yo

Are there any guided tours?
¿Hay visitas con guía?
eye bee-see-tas kon gee-a

What is there to see here?
¿Qué hay para ver aquí?
kay eye pa-ra bair a-kee

444

What is this building?
¿Qué es este edificio?
kay es es-tay e-dee-fee-thee-o

When was it built?
¿Cuándo se construyó?
kwan-do say kon-stroo-yo

Is it open to the public?
¿Está abierto al público?
es-ta a-bee-air-to al poo-blee-ko

What is the admission charge?
¿Cuánto cuesta la entrada?
kwan-to kwes-ta la en-tra-da

Can we go in?
¿Podemos entrar?
po-day-mos en trar

Can we go up to the top?
¿Podemos subir hasta arriba?
po-day-mos soo-beer a-sta a-ree-ba

Can I take photos?
¿Puedo hacer fotos?
pwe-do a-thair fo-tos

Can I use flash?
¿Puedo utilizar flash?
pwe-do oo-tee-lee-thar flas

How long does the tour take?
¿Cuánto dura la excursión?
kwan-to doo-ra la ek-skoor-syon

Is there a guide book?
¿Hay alguna guía turística?
eye al-goo-na gee-a too-ree-stee-ka

Is there a tour of the cathedral?
¿Hay visita a la catedral?
eye bee-see-ta a la ka-te-dral

Is there an English-speaking guide?
¿Hay algún guía que hable inglés?
eye al-goon gee-a kay a-blay een-gles

Is this the best view?
¿Es ésta la mejor vista?
es es-ta la me-hor bee-sta

What time does the gallery open?
¿A qué hora abre la galería?
u kay o-ra a-bray la ga-le-ree-a

When is the bus tour?
¿Cuándo es la visita en autobús?
kwan-do es la bee-see-ta en ow-to-boos

Souvenirs

Have you got an English guidebook?
¿Tiene alguna guía turística en inglés?
tee-e-nay al-goo-na gee-a too-ree-stee-ka en een-gles

Have you got any colour slides?
¿Tiene diapositivas en color?
tee-e-nay dee-a-po-zee-tee-bas en ko-lor

Where can I buy postcards?
¿Dónde puedo comprar postales?
don-day pwe-do kom-prar po-sta-les

Where can we buy souvenirs?
¿Dónde podemos comprar recuerdos?
don-day po-day-mos kom-prar re-kwair-dos

Going to church

When visiting a church, dress appropriately. Do not wear shorts or short skirts, and ensure that your shoulders are covered.

If you are just sightseeing, it is advisable to arrange to visit when there is not a religious service in progress.

Where is the — **Catholic church?**
¿Dónde está la — iglesia Católica?
don-day es-ta la — *ee-glay-see-a ka-to-lee-ka*

    — **Baptist church?**
    — la iglesia Bautista?
    — *la ee-glay-see-a bow-tee-sta*

    — **mosque?**
    — la mezquita?
    — *la meth-kee-ta*

    — **Protestant church?**
    — iglesia Protestante?
    — *ee-glay-see-a pro-te-stan-tay*

    — **synagogue?**
    — la sinagoga?
    — *la see-na-go-ga*

What time is mass?
¿A qué hora es la misa?
a kay o-ra es la mee-sa

I would like to see   — **a priest**
Me gustaría hablar con   — un sacerdote
may goo-sta-ree-a a-blar kon — *oon sa-thair-do-tay*

    — **a minister**
    — un pastor
    — *oon pa-stor*

    — **a rabbi**
    — un rabino
    — *oon ra-bee-no*

Shopping

Most shops in smaller towns tend to follow the traditional pattern of the siesta, closing from lunchtime until 4.00 or 4.30pm, then staying open until 7.00pm or later. In the cities and in the busy resorts, however, you will find many shops and department stores stay open all day. Most shops are closed on public holidays (*see* page 474).

General phrases and requests

How much does that cost?
¿Cuánto cuesta eso?
kwan-to kwes-ta e-so

How much is it — per kilo?
¿Cuánto cuesta — por kilo?
kwan-to kwes-ta — por kee-lo

— **per metre?**
— por metro?
— *por me-tro*

How much is this?
¿Cuánto es esto?
kwan-to es es-to

Have you got anything cheaper?
¿Tiene algo más barato?
tee-e-nay al-go mas ba-ra-to

Can I see that umbrella?
¿Puedo ver ese paraguas?
pwe-do bair e-say pa-ra-gwas

No, the other one
No, el otro
no, el o-tro

Can you deliver to my hotel?
¿Puede entregármelo al hotel?
pwe-day en-tre-gar-may-lo al o-tel

I do not like it
No me gusta
no may goo-sta

I like this one
Me gusta éste
may goo-sta es-tay

I will take — this one
Tomaré — éste
to-ma-ray — es-tay

— **that one**
— ése
— *e-say*

— **the other one**
— el otro
— *el o-tro*

— **that one over there**
— aquél de allí
— *a-kel day a-ye*

Where can I buy some clothes?
¿Dónde puedo comprar ropa?
don-day pwe-do kom-prar ro-pa

Where can I buy tapes for my camcorder?
¿Dónde puedo comprar cintas para el camcórder?
don-day pwe-do kom-prar theen-tas pa-ra el kam-kor-dair

447

Where can I get my camcorder repaired?
¿A dónde puedo llevar a reparar el
  camcórder?
*a **don**-day **pwe**-do ye-**bar** a re-pa-**rar** el kam-
  kor-dair*

Where is — the children's department?
¿Dónde está — el departamento infantil?
*don-day es-**ta** — el de-par-ta-**men**-to een-fan-
     teel*

— the food department?
— el departamento de comestibles?
*— el de-par-ta-**men**-to day ko-me-**stee**-
    blays*

I am looking for a souvenir
Estoy buscando un recuerdo
*es-**toy** boo-**skan**-do oon re-**kwair**-do*

Do you sell sunglasses?
¿Venden gafas de sol?
***ben**-den **ga**-fas day sol*

Can I have — a carrier bag?
¿Puede darme — una bolsa?
*pwe-day **dar**-may   — **oo**-na **bol**-sa*

— a receipt?
— un recibo?
*— oon re-**thee**-bo*

— an itemised bill?
— una cuenta detallada?
*— **oo**-na **kwen**-ta de-ta-**ya**-da*

Can I pay for air insurance?
¿Puedo pagar un seguro aéreo?
*pwe-do pa-**gar** oon se-**goo**-ro a-**air**-ay-o*

What is the total?
¿Cuánto es el total?
kwan**-to es el to-**tal

Do you accept traveller's cheques?
¿Acepta cheques de viaje?
*a-**thep**-ta **che**-kays day bee-**a**-hay*

I do not have enough currency
No tengo suficiente cambio
*no **ten**-go soo-fee-**thyen**-tay **kam**-bee-o*

I do not have enough money
No tengo suficiente dinero
*no **ten**-go soo-fee-**thyen**-tay dee-**ne**-ro*

I would like to pay with my credit card
Me gustaría pagar con tarjeta de crédito
*may goo-sta-**ree**-a pa-**gar** kon tar-**hay**-ta day
  kre-dee-to*

Please forward a receipt to this address
Por favor, envíe un recibo a esta dirección
*por fa-**bor**, en-**bee**-ay oon re-**thee**-bo a **es**-ta
  dee-rek-**thyon***

Please wrap it up for me
Por favor, envuélvamelo
*por fa-**bor**, en-**bwel**-ba-may-lo*

There is no need to wrap it
No hace falta envolverlo
*no a-**thay** **fal**-ta en-bol-**bair**-lo*

Please pack this for shipment
Por favor, envuelva esto para envío
*por fa-**bor**, en-**bwel**-ba **es**-to pa-ra en-**bee**-o*

Will you send it by air freight?
¿Lo enviará por avión?
*lo en-bee-a-**ra** por a-**byon***

Buying groceries

Supermarkets and small grocery stores proliferate, but shopping is more fun in local markets. Most towns and major centres have markets – usually mornings only, Monday to Saturday – with fresh fruit, vegetables and meat at prices that are likely to be lower than those in the shops (and often open to bargaining).

We need to buy some food
Tenemos que comprar comida
*te-**nay**-mos kay kom-**prar** ko-**mee**-da*

I would like — a kilo of potatoes
Me da — un kilo de patatas
*may da — oon **kee**-lo day pa-**ta**-tas*

— a bar of chocolate
— una barra de chocolate
*— **oo**-na **ba**-ra day cho-ko-**la**-tay*

— 100 g of ground coffee
— cien gramos de café molido
*— thee-**en gra**-mos day ka-**fay** mo-**lee**-do*

— two steaks
— dos filetes
*dos fee-**le**-tes*

— 5 slices of ham
— cinco lonchas de jamón
*— **theen**-ko **lon**-chas day ha-**mon***

— half a dozen eggs
— media docena de huevos
*— me-dee-a do-**thay**-na day **way**-bos*

— half a kilo of butter
— medio kilo de mantequilla
*— me-dee-o **kee**-lo day man-te-**kee**-ya*

Can I have — some sugar, please?
¿Puede darme — azúcar, por favor?
*pwe-day **dar**-may — a-**thoo**-kar, por fa-**bor***

— a bottle of wine, please?
— una botella de vino, por favor?
*— **oo**-na bo-**te**-ya day **bee**-no, por fa-**bor***

— a kilo of sausages, please?
— un kilo de salchichas, por favor?
*— oon **kee**-lo day sal-**chee**-chas, por fa-**bor***

— a leg of lamb, please?
— una pierna de cordero, por favor?
*— **oo**-na pee-**air**-na day kor-**dair**-o, por fa-**bor***

— a litre of milk, please?
— un litro de leche, por favor?
*— oon **lee**-tro day **le**-chay, por fa-**bor***

Groceries

baby food
comida para bebés
*ko-**mee**-da **pa**-ra be-**bes***

biscuits
galletas
*ga-**yay**-tas*

bread
pan
pan

butter
mantequilla
*man-te-**kee**-ya*

cheese
queso
ke-so

coffee
café
*ka-**fay***

cream
nata
na-ta

eggs
huevos
way-bos

flour
harina
a-ree-na

jam
mermelada
mair-me-la-da

margarine
margarina
mar-ga-ree-na

milk
leche
le-chay

mustard
mostaza
mo-sta-tha

oil
aceite
a-thay-tay

pepper
pimienta
pee-myen-ta

rice
arroz
a-roth

salt
sal
sal

soup
sopa
so-pa

sugar
azúcar
a-thoo-kar

tea
té
tay

vinegar
vinagre
bee-na-gray

yoghurt
yogur
yo-goor

Meat and fish

beef
carne de vaca
kar-nay day ba-ka

chicken
pollo
po-yo

cod
bacalao
ba-ka-la-o

fish
pescado
pe-ska-do

ham
jamón
ha-mon

herring
arenque
a-ren-kay

kidneys
riñones
*reen-**yo**-nes*

mussels
mejillones
*me-hee-**yo**-nes*

lamb
cordero
*kor-**dair**-o*

pork
cerdo
***thair**-do*

liver
hígado
***ee**-ga-do*

sole
lenguado
*len-**gwa**-do*

meat
carne
***kar**-nay*

veal
ternera
*tair-**nair**-a*

At the newsagent's

English newspapers are readily available in major cities and tourist resort areas. They are generally a day late, and the quality dailies are expensive. You can get cheaper, locally published, English-language papers in many resort areas.

Do you sell — English paperbacks?
¿Vende — libros de bolsillo en inglés?
ben**-day — **lee**-bros day bol-**see**-yo en een-**gles

— **postcards?**
— postales?
— *po-**sta**-les*

— **a local map?**
— un plano de la localidad?
— *oon **pla**-no day la lo-ka-**lee**-dud*

— **a road map?**
— un mapa de carreteras?
— *oon **ma**-pa day ka-re-**tair**-as*

— **coloured pencils?**
— lápices de color?
— *la-**pee**-thes day ko-**lor***

— **drawing paper?**
— papel de dibujo?
— *pa-**pel** day dee-**boo**-ho*

— **felt pens?**
— rotuladores?
— *ro-too-la-**do**-res*

— **street maps?**
— planos de ciudad?
— *pla-nos day thee-oo-**dad***

I would like some postage stamps
Me da sellos de correos
*may da **se**-yos day ko-**ray**-os*

Do you have — English books?
¿Tiene — libros en inglés?
*tee-e-nay — **lee**-bros en een-**gles***

— **English newspapers?**
— periódicos en inglés?
— *pe-ree-o-dee-kos en een-**gles***

I need — some writing paper
Necesito — papel de cartas
*ne-the-**see**-to — pa-**pel** day **kar**-tas*

— **a bottle of ink**
— una botella de tinta
— *oo-na bo-**te**-ya day **teen**-ta*

— **a pen**
— un bolígrafo
— *oon bo-**lee**-gra-fo*

— **a pencil**
— un lápiz
— *oon **la**-peeth*

— **some adhesive tape**
— cinta adhesiva
— ***theen**-ta a-de-**see**-ba*

— **some envelopes**
— sobres
— ***so**-bres*

At the tobacconist's

Do you have — cigarette papers?
¿Tiene — papel de fumar?
tee-**e**-nay — pa-**pel** day foo-**mar**

— **a box of matches**
— una caja de cerillas
— *oo-na **ka**-ha day the-**ree**-yas*

— **a cigar**
— un cigarro
— *oon thee-**ga**-ro*

— **a cigarette lighter**
— un mechero
— *oon me-**chair**-o*

— **a gas (butane) refill**
— una carga de gas
— *oo-na **kar**-ga day gas*

— **a pipe**
— una pipa
— *oo-na **pee**-pa*

— **a pouch of pipe tobacco**
— una petaca de tabaco de pipa
— *oo-na pe-**ta**-ka day ta-**ba**-ko day **pee**-pa*

— **some pipe cleaners**
— unos limpiapipas
— *oo-nos leem-pya-**pee**-pas*

Have you got — any American brands?
¿Tiene — marcas americanas?
tee-e-nay — ***mar**-kas a-me-ree-**ka**-nas*

— **any English brands?**
— marcas inglesas?
— ***mar**-kas een-**glay**-sas*

— **rolling tobacco?**
— tabaco de liar?
— *ta-**ba**-ko day lee-**ar***

A packet of ... please
Un paquete de ... por favor
*oon pa-**ke**-tay day ... por fa-**bor***

— **with filter tips**
— con filtro
— *kon **feel**-tro*

— **without filters**
— sin filtro
— *seen **feel**-tro*

At the chemist's

As in Britain, you can get drugs from a chemist (*farmacia*) during shopping hours. Rotas of chemists open at other times are posted in their windows and published in local papers.

Do you have toothpaste?
¿Tiene pasta de dientes?
tee-e-nay pa-sta day dee-en-tes

I need some high-protection suntan cream
Necesito una crema solar de alta protección
ne-the-see-to oo-na kray-ma so-lar day al-ta pro-tek-thyon

Can you give me — a headache?
something for
¿Puede darme — el dolor de cabeza?
algo para
pwe-day dar-may — el do-lor day
al-go pa-ra   ka-bay-tha

— **insect bites**
— las picaduras de insectos?
— *las pee-ka-doo-ras day een-sek-tos*

— **a cold**
— un catarro
— *oon ka-ta-ro*

— **a cough**
— tos
— *tos*

— **a sore throat**
— dolor de garganta
— *do-lor day gar-gan-ta*

— **an upset stomach**
— mal del estómago
— *mal del e-sto-ma-go*

— **toothache**
— dolor de muelas
— *do-lor day mway-las*

— **hay fever**
— fiebre del heno
— *fee-e-bray del ay-no*

— **sunburn**
— quemadura de sol
— *ke-ma-doo-ra day sol*

Do I need a prescription?
¿Necesito una receta?
ne-the-see-to oo-na re-thay-ta

How many do I take?
¿Cuántas tengo que tomar?
kwan-tas ten-go kay to-mar

How often do I take them?
¿Con qué frecuencia tengo que tomarlas?
kon kay fre-kwen-thee-a ten-go kay to-mar-las

Are they safe for children to take?
¿Los niños pueden tomarlas sin riesgo?
los neen-yos pwe-den to-mar-las seen ree-ez-go

Medicines and toiletries

antihistamine
antihistamínico
an-tee-ee-sta-mee-nee-ko

antiseptic
antiséptico
an-tee-sep-tee-ko

aspirin
aspirina
*a-spee-**ree**-na*

bandage
vendaje
*ben-**da**-hay*

bubble bath
espuma de baño
*e-**spoo**-ma day **ban**-yo*

cleansing milk
leche limpiadora
*le-chay leem-pya-**do**-ra*

conditioner
suavizante
*swa-bee-**than**-tay*

condom
preservativo
*pray-sair-ba-**tee**-bo*

contraceptive
anticonceptivo
*an-tee-kon-thep-**tee**-bo*

cotton wool
algodón hidrófilo
*al-go-**don** ee-**dro**-fee-lo*

deodorant
desodorante
*des-o-do-**ran**-tay*

disinfectant
desinfectante
*des-een-fek-**tan**-tay*

eau de Cologne
agua de colonia
*a-gwa day ko-**lon**-ya*

eye shadow
sombra de ojos
som-bra day o-hos

face powder
polvos
pol-bos

hair spray
laca para el cabello
*la-ka pa-ra el ka-**be**-yo*

hand cream
crema de manos
kray-ma day ma-nos

insect repellent
repelente de insectos
*ray-pe-**len**-tay day een-**sek**-tos*

laxative
laxante
*lak-**san**-tay*

lipstick
barra de labios
ba-ra day la-bee-os

mascara
rímel
ree-mel

moisturiser
loción hidratante
*lo-**thyon** ee-dra-**tan**-tay*

mouthwash
antiséptico bucal
*an-tee-**sep**-tee-ko boo-**kal***

nail file
lima de uñas
lee-ma day oon-yas

nail varnish
esmalte de uñas
*es-**mal**-tay day oon-yas*

nail varnish remover
quitaesmalte
*kee-ta-es-**mal**-tay*

perfume
perfume
pair-foo-may

plasters
tiritas
tee-ree-tas

razor blades
hojas de afeitar
o-has day a-fay-tar

sanitary towels
compresas
kom-pray-sas

shampoo
champú
cham-poo

shaving cream
espuma de afeitar
es-poo-ma day a-fay-tar

soap
jabón
ha-bon

suntan lotion
bronceador
bron-thay-a-dor

talc
talco
tal-ko

tampons
tampones
tam-po-nays

tissues
Kleenex
klee-neks

toilet water
colonia
ko-lon-ya

toothpaste
pasta de dientes
pa-sta day dee-en-tes

Shopping for clothes

I am just looking, thank you
Sólo estoy mirando, gracias
so-lo es-toy mee-ran-do, gra-thee-as

I do not like it
No me gusta
no may goo-sta

I like it
Me gusta
may goo-sta

I will take it
Lo llevaré
lo ye-ba-ray

I like — this one
Me gusta — éste
may goo-sta — es-tay

— that one there
— aquél
— a-kel

— the one in the window
— el que está en el escaparate
— el kay es-ta en el e-ska-pa-ra-tay

I would like — this suit
Quiero comprar — este traje
kee-e-ro kom-prar — es-tay tra-hay

— **this hat**
— este sombrero
— *es-tay som-**brair**-o*

I would like one — **with a zip**
Quisiera uno — con cremallera
*ke-see-**air**-a **oo**-no* — *kon kre-ma-**yair**-a*

— **without a belt**
— sin cinturón
— *seen then-too-**ron***

Can you please measure me?
¿Puede medirme, por favor?
*pwe-day me-**deer**-may, por fa-**bor***

Can I change it if it does not fit?
¿Puedo cambiarlo si no me vale?
*pwe-do kam-**byar**-lo see no may **ba**-lay*

Have you got this in other colours?
¿Tiene éste en otros colores?
*tee-e-nay **es**-tay en o-tros ko-**lo**-res*

I take a large shoe size
Uso una talla de zapato grande
*oo-so **oo**-na **ta**-ya day tha-**pa**-to **gran**-day*

I take continental size 40
Uso la talla cuarenta europea
*oo-so la **ta**-ya kwa-**ren**-ta ay-oo-ro-**pay**-a*

Is it too long?
¿Es demasiado largo?
*es de-ma-**sya**-do **lar**-go*

Is it too short?
¿Es demasiado corto?
*es de-ma-**sya**-do **kor**-to*

Is there a full-length mirror?
¿Hay algún espejo de cuerpo entero?
*eye al-**goon** es-pe-ho day **kwair**-po en-**tair**-o*

Is this all you have?
¿Es esto todo lo que tiene?
*es **es**-to **to**-do lo kay tee-e-nay*

It does not fit
No me vale
*no may **ba**-lay*

It does not suit me
No me queda bien
*no may **kay**-da byen*

May I see it in daylight?
¿Puedo verlo a la luz del día?
*pwe-do **bair**-lo a la looth del **dee**-a*

Where are the changing (dressing) rooms?
¿Dónde están los probadores?
*don-day es-**tan** los pro-ba-**do**-res*

Where can I try it on?
¿Dónde puedo probármelo?
*don-day pwe-do pro-**bar**-may-lo*

Have you got — **a large size?**
¿Tiene — una talla grande?
tee-e-nay — *oo-na **ta**-ya **gran**-day*

— **a small size?**
— una talla pequeña?
— *oo-na **ta**-ya pe-**ken**-ya*

What is it made of?
¿De qué material es?
*day kay ma-te-ree-**al** es*

Is it guaranteed?
¿Tiene garantía?
*tee-e-nay ga-ran-**tee**-a*

Will it shrink?
¿Encogerá?
*en-ko-hair-**a***

Is it drip-dry?
¿Es de lava y pon?
*es day **la**-ba ee pon*

Is it dry-clean only?
¿Es de limpiar en seco sólamente?
*es day leem-**pyar** en **se**-ko so-la-**men**-tay*

Is it machine washable?
¿Es lavable a máquina?
es la-ba-blay a ma-kee-na

Clothes and accessories

acrylic
acrílico
a-kree-lee-ko

belt
cinturón
theen-too-ron

blouse
blusa
bloo-sa

bra
sujetador
soo-he-ta-dor

bracelet
pulsera
pool-say-ra

brooch
broche
bro-chay

button
botón
bo-ton

cardigan
chaqueta de punto
cha-kay-ta day poon-to

coat
abrigo
a-bree-go

corduroy
pana
pa-na

cotton
algodón
al-go-don

denim
tela vaquera
tay-la ba-kair-a

dress
vestido
be-stee-do

dungarees
pantalón de peto
pan-ta-lon day pay-to

earrings
pendientes
pen-dee-en-tes

espadrilles
alpargatas
al-par-ga-tas

fur
piel
pyel

gloves
guantes
gwan-tes

handbag
bolso
bol-so

handkerchief
pañuelo
pan-yoo-ay-lo

hat sombrero *som-**brair**-o*	**polyester** poliéster *po-lee-**e**-stair*
jacket chaqueta *cha-**kay**-ta*	**pullover** pulóver *poo-**lo**-bair*
jeans vaqueros *ba-**kair**-os*	**purse** monedero *mo-ne-**dair**-o*
jersey jersey *hair-**say***	**pyjamas** pijama *pee-**ha**-ma*
lace encaje *en-**ka**-hay*	**raincoat** impermeable *eem-pair-may-**a**-blay*
leather cuero ***kwair**-o*	**ring** anillo *a-**nee**-yo*
linen lino ***lee**-no*	**sandals** sandalias *san-**da**-lee-as*
necklace collar *ko-**yar***	**scarf** bufanda *boo-**fan**-da*
nightdress camisón *ka-mee-**son***	**shirt** camisa *ka-**mee**-sa*
nylon nylon *nee-**lon***	**shoes** zapatos *tha-**pa**-tos*
pants (women's) bragas ***bra**-gas*	**shorts** pantalón corto *pan-ta-**lon** **kor**-to*
petticoat combinación *kom-bee-na-**thyon***	**silk** seda ***say**-da*

skirt
falda
fal-da

slip
enagua
e-na-gwa

socks
calcetines
kal-the-tee-nes

stockings
medias
me-dee-as

suede
ante
an-tay

suit (men's)
traje
tra-hay

suit (women's)
traje de chaqueta
tra-hay day cha-kay-ta

sweater
suéter
swe-tair

swimming trunks
bañador
ban-ya-dor

swimsuit
traje de baño
tra-hay day ban-yo

T-shirt
camiseta
ka-mee-say-ta

terylene
terylene
te-ree-le-nay

tie
corbata
kor-ba-ta

tights
medias
me-dee-as

towel
toalla
to-a-ya

trousers
pantalón
pan-ta-lon

umbrella
paraguas
pa-ra-gwas

underpants (men's)
calzoncillos
kal-thon-thee-yos

velvet
terciopelo
tair-thee-o-pe-lo

vest
camiseta
ka-mee-say-ta

wallet
cartera
kar-tair-a

watch
reloj
re-loh

wool
lana
la-na

zip
cremallera
kre-ma-yair-a

Photography

I need a film — for this camera
Quiero una película — para esta cámara
kee-*e*-ro **oo**-na pe-
lee-koo-la — **pa**-ra **es**-ta **ka**-
ma-ra
— for this camcorder
— para este camcórder
— **pa**-ra **es**-tay kam-
kor- dair
— for this cine-camera
— para esta cámara de
cine
— **pa**-ra **es**-ta **ka**-ma-ra
day **thee**-nay
— for this video camera
— para este video
cámara
— **pa**-ra **e** s-tay bee-
day-o-**ka**-ma-ra

Can you develop this film, please?
¿Puede revelar esta película, por favor?
*pwe-day re-be-**lar** es-ta pe-**lee**-koo-la, por fa-**bor***

I would like this photo enlarged
Quiero que amplíen esta foto
*kee-**e**-ro kay am-**plee**-en **es**-ta **fo**-to*

I would like two prints of this one
Quiero dos copias de ésta
*kee-e-ro dos **ko**-pyas day **es**-ta*

When will the photos be ready?
¿Cuándo estarán las fotos?
***kwan**-do es-ta-**ran** las **fo**-tos*

I want — a black and white film
Quiero — una película en blanco y negro
*kee-e-ro — **oo**-na pe-**lee**-koo-la en **blan**-ko ee
ne-gro*

— **a colour print film**
— una película en color
— **oo**-na pe-**lee**-koo-la en **ko**-lor

— **a colour slide film**
— una película de diapositivas en
color
— **oo**-na pe-**lee**-koo-la day dee-a-po-zee-
tee-bas en ko-**lor**

— **batteries for the flash**
— pilas para el flash
— **pee**-las **pa**-ra el **flas**

Camera repairs

I am having trouble with my camera
Tengo un problema con la cámara
***ten**-go oon pro-**blay**-ma kon la **ka**-ma-ra*

The film is jammed
La película está atascada
*la pe-**lee**-koo-la es-**ta** a-ta-**ska**-da*

There is something wrong with my camera
Le ocurre algo a mi cámara
*lay o-**koo**-ray **al**-go a mee **ka**-ma-ra*

Where can I get my camera repaired?
¿Dónde puedo llevar la cámara a reparar?
don**-day **pwe**-do ye-bar la **ka**-ma-ra a re-pa-**rar

Camera parts

accessory
accesorio
*ak-the-**so**-ree-o*

blue filter
filtro azul
feel**-tro a-**thool

camcorder
camcórder
*kam-**kor**-dair*

cartridge
carrete
*ka-**re**-tay*

cassette
cassette
*ka-**se**-tay*

cine-camera
cámara de cine
*ka-ma-ra day **thee**-nay*

distance
distancia
*dee-**stan**-thee-a*

enlargement
ampliación
*am-plee-a-**thyon***

exposure
exposición
*ek spo-zee-**thyon***

exposure meter
fotómetro
*fo-**to**-me-tro*

flash
flash
flas

flash bulb
bombilla de flash
*bom-**bee**-ya day flas*

flash cube
cubo de flash
koo-bo day flas

focal distance
distancia focal
*dee-**stan**-thee-a fo-**kal***

focus
foco
fo-ko

image
imagen
*ee-**ma**-hen*

in focus
enfocado
*en-fo-**ka**-do*

lens cover
tapa de objetivo
*ta-pa day ob-he-**tee**-bo*

lens
objetivo
*ob-he-**tee**-bo*

negative
negativo
*ne-ga-**tee**-bo*

out of focus
desenfocado
*des-en-fo-**ka**-do*

over-exposed
sobreexpuesto
*so-bray-eks-**pwes**-to*

picture
fotografía
*fo-to-gra-**fee**-a*

print
copia
ko-pya

projector
proyector
*pro-yek-**tor***

red filter
filtro rojo
*feel-tro **ro**-ho*

reel
rollo
ro-yo

shade
sombra
som-bra

shutter
obturador
ob-too-ra-dor

shutter speed
velocidad de obturación
be-lo-thee-dad day ob-too-ra-thyon

slide
diapositiva
dee-a-po-zee-tee-ba

transparency
transparencia
trans-pa-ren-thee-a

tripod
trípode
tree-po-day

viewfinder
visor
bee-sor

wide-angle lens
granangular
gra-nan-goo-lar

yellow filter
filtro amarillo
feel-tro a-ma-ree-yo

At the hairdresser's

I would like to make an appointment
Quisiera reservar hora
kee-see-air-a re-sair-bar o-ra

I want — a haircut
Quiero — cortarme el pelo
kee-e-ro — kor-tar-may el pelo

> **— a trim**
> — cortarme las puntas
> *— kor-tar-may las poon-tas*

Not too much off
No quite demasiado
no kee-tay de-ma-sya-do

Take a little more off the back
Quite un poco más por detrás
kee-tay oon po-ko mas por de-tras

> **Please cut my hair — short**
> Por favor, córteme — corto el pelo
> *por fa-bor, kor-tay-may — kor-to el pe-lo*

> **— fairly short**
> — bastante corto
> *—ba-stan-tay kor-to*

> **— in a fringe**
> — con flequillo
> *— kon fle-kee-yo*

That is fine, thank you
Está bien, gracias
es-ta byen, gra-thee-as

I would like — a perm
Quisiera — una permanente
kee-see-air-ra — oo-na pair-ma-nen-tay

> **— a blow-dry**
> — secar con secador
> *— se-kar kon se-ka-dor*

> **— my hair dyed**
> — teñirme el pelo
> *— ten-yeer-may el pe-lo*

— **my hair streaked**
— mechas en el pelo
— *may-chas en el pe-lo*

— **a shampoo and cut**
— lavar y cortar
— *la-**bar** ee kor-**tar***

— **a shampoo and set**
— lavar y marcar
— *la-**bar** ee mar-**kar***

— **a conditioner**
— un suavizante
— *oon swa-bee-**than**-tay*

— **hair spray**
— laca de pelo
— *la-ka day **pe**-lo*

The dryer is too hot
El secador está demasiado caliente
*el se-ka-**dor** es-**ta** de-ma-**sya**-do ka-lee-**en**-tay*

The water is too hot
El agua está demasiado caliente
*el **a**-gwa es-**ta** de-ma-**sya**-do ka-lee-**en**-tay*

Laundry

Is there a launderette nearby?
¿Hay alguna lavandería cercana?
*eye al-**goo**-na la-ban-de-**ree**-a thair-**ka**-na*

How does the washing machine work?
¿Cómo funciona la lavadora?
*ko-mo foon-**thyo** na la la-ba-**do**-ra*

How long will it take?
¿Cuánto tardará?
kwan**-to tar-da-**ra

Can you — clean this skirt?
¿Me puede — limpiar esta falda?
*may **pwe**-day — leem-**pyar** es-ta **fal**-da*

— **clean and press these shirts?**
— limpiar y planchar estas camisas?
— *leem-**pyar** ee plan-**char** es-tas ka-**mee**-sas*

— **wash these clothes?**
— lavar esta ropa?
— *la-**bar** es-ta **ro**-pa*

This stain is — oil
Esta mancha es — de aceite
*es-ta **man**-cha es— day a-**thay**-ee-tay*

— **blood**
— de sangre
— *day **san**-gray*

— **coffee**
— de café
— *day ka-**fay***

— **ink**
— de tinta
— *day **teen**-ta*

This fabric is delicate
Esta tela es delicada
*es-ta **tay**-la es de-lee-**ka**-da*

I have lost my dry cleaning ticket
He perdido el resguardo de la tintorería
*ay pair-**dee**-do el rez-**gwar**-do day la teen-to-re-ree-a*

Please send it to this address
Por favor, enviélo a esta dirección
por fa-bor, en-bee-ay-lo a es-ta dee-rek-thyon

When will I come back?
¿Cuándo puedo volver?
kwan-do pwe-do bol-bair

When will my clothes be ready?
¿Cuándo estará mi ropa lista?
kwan-do es-ta-ra mee ro-pa lee-sta

I will come back— later
Volveré — más tarde
bol-bair-ay — mas tar-day

— in an hour
— dentro de una hora
— den-tro day oo-na o-ra

General repairs

This is — broken
Esto está — roto
es-to es-ta — ro-to

— damaged
— averiado
— a-be-ree-a-do

— torn
—estropeado
— e-stro-pay-a-do

Can you repair it?
¿Puede repararlo?
pwe-day re-pa-rar-lo

Can you do it quickly?
¿Puede hacerlo rápidamente?
pwe-day a-thair-lo ra-pee-da-men-tay

Have you got a spare part for this?
¿Tiene alguna pieza de repuesto para esto?
tee-e-nay al-goo-na pee-ay-tha day re-pwe-sto pa-ra es-to

Would you have a look at this please?
¿Puede mirar esto, por favor?
pwe-day mee-rar es-to, por fa-bor

Here is the guarantee
Aquí está la garantía
a-kee es-ta la ga-ran-tee-a

At the post office

Post offices (*oficinas de correos*) are open in the mornings and again from 5.00pm to 7.00pm Monday to Friday and on Saturday mornings. They can be found in most centres. Stamps (*sellos*) are also available from tobacconists (*estancos*) and from hotels.

12 stamps please
Doce sellos, por favor
do-thay se-yos, por fa-bor

I need to send this by courier
Necesito enviar esto por servicio de
  mensajero
*ne-the-see-to en-byar es-to por sair-bee-thee-o
  day men-sa-hair-o*

I want to send a telegram
Quiero enviar este telegrama
kee-e-ro en-byar es-tay te-le-gra-ma

I want to send this by registered mail
Quiero enviar esto por correo certificado
*kee-e-ro en-byar es-to por ko-ray-o thair-tee-
  fee-ka-do*

I want to send this parcel
Quiero enviar este paquete
kee-e-ro en-byar es-tay pa-ke-tay

When will it arrive?
¿Cuándo llegará?
kwan-do ye-ga-ra

How much is a letter — to Britain?
¿Cuánto cuesta una carta — a Gran
                 Bretaña?
kwan-to kwes-ta oo-na — a gran bre-tan-ya

— to the United States?
— a los Estados Unidos?
— a los e-sta-dos oo-nee-dos

Can I have six stamps for postcards to Britain?
Me da seis sellos para postales a Gran
   Bretaña
may da says se-yos pa-ra po-sta-les a gran bre-tan-ya

Can I have a telegram form, please?
¿Puede darme un impreso de telegrama,
   por favor?
pwe-day dar-may oon eem-pray-so day te-le-gra-ma, por fa-bor

Using the telephone

Most phone numbers have six digits, usually written in three groups of two. Madrid, Barcelona and a number of other towns have seven-digit numbers.

The ringing tone on Spanish phones is a slowly repeating long tone rather than a double ring.

Area codes, which you dial before the local number when calling one area from another, have two or three digits, the first of which is always 9.

To phone Spain, dial 00 34 to access the country, then dial the area code, leaving off the initial 9. Then dial the local number. To phone Britain from Spain, dial 07 and wait for a high-pitched tone before dialling the country code, which for Britain is 44. Then dial the British area code without the first 0, then your number.

Public phone boxes accept 5, 25, 50 and 100 peseta coins. Most public phones have a groove on top to hold coins and a digital display of how much credit remains. Calling from a public phone is far cheaper than calling from a hotel bedroom – hotels are entitled to make a heavy service charge. In big cities, you can also make calls from central telephone offices (*locutorios*), where you pay for the call – plus a service charge – after you have made it.

Can I use the telephone, please?
¿Puedo utilizar el teléfono, por favor?
pwe-do oo-tee-lee-thar el te-le-fo-no, por fa-bor

Can I dial direct?
¿Puedo marcar directamente?
pwe-do mar-kar dee-rek-ta-men-tay

Can you connect me with the international operator?
¿Puede conectarme con la operadora internacional?
pwe-day ko-nek-tar-may kon la o-pe-ra-do-ra een-tair-na-thyo-nal

Have you got any change?
¿Tiene cambio?
tee-e-nay kam-bee-o

How do I use the telephone?
¿Cómo se utiliza el teléfono?
ko-mo say oo-tee-lee-tha el te-le-fo-no

How much is it to phone to London?
¿Cuánto cuesta llamar a Londres?
kwan-to kwes-ta ya-mar a lon-dres

I must make a phone call to Britain
Tengo que llamar a Gran Bretaña
ten-go kay ya-mar a gran bre-tan-ya

I need to make a phone call
Tengo que hacer una llamada
ten-go kay a-thair oo-na ya-ma-da

What is the code for the UK?
¿Cuál es el código del Reino Unido?
kwal es el ko-dee-go del ray-no oo-nee-do

I would like to make a reversed charge call
Deseo hacer una llamada a cobro revertido
de-say-o a-thair oo-na ya-ma-da a ko-bro re-bair-tee-do

The number I need is…
El número que necesito es…
el noo-me-o kay ne-the-see-to es…

What is the charge?
¿Cuánto es?
kwan-to es

Please, call me back
Por favor, devuelva mi llamada
por fa-bor, de-bwel-ba mee ya-ma-da

I am sorry. We were cut off
Lo siento. Se ha cortado
lo syen-to. Say a kor-ta-do

What you may hear

El número no funciona
el noo-me-ro no foon-thyo-na
The number is out of order

Está comunicando
es-ta ko-moo-nee-kan-do
The line is engaged (busy)

Estoy intentando conectarle
es-toy een-ten-tan-do ko-nek-tar-lay
I am trying to connect you

Hable, por favor
a-blay, por fa-bor
Please go ahead

Hola, soy el director
o-la, soy el dee-rek-tor
Hello, this is the manager

Le voy a pasar con el señor Smith
lay boy a pa-sar kon el sen-yor Smith
I am putting you through to Mr Smith

No puedo obtener este número
no pwe-do ob-te-nair es-tay noo-me-ro
I cannot obtain this number

Changing money

Banks are open Monday to Friday from 8.30am to 2.00pm and on Saturdays from 9.00am until 1.00pm.

Can I contact my bank to arrange for a transfer?
¿Puedo contactar a mi banco para pedir una transferencia?
*pwe-do kon-tak-**tar** a mee **ban**-ko **pa**-ra pe-deer oo-na trans-fe-**ren**-thee-a*

Has my cash arrived?
¿Ha llegado mi dinero?
*a ye-**ga**-do mee dee-**ne**-ro*

I would like to obtain a cash advance with my credit card
Quisiera un anticipo en metálico con mi tarjeta de crédito
*kee-see-**air**-ra oon an-tee-**thee**-po en me-**ta**-lee-ko kon mee tar-**hay**-ta day **kre**-dee-to*

This is the name and address of my bank
Éste es el nombre y la dirección de mi banco
*es-tay es el **nom**-bray ee la dee-rek-**thyon** day mee **ban**-ko*

Can I change	**— these traveller's cheques?**
¿Puedo cambiar	— estos cheques de viaje?
*pwe-do kam-**byar***	— *es-tos **che**-kays day bee-a-hay*

— these notes (bills)?
— estos billetes?
— *es-tos bee-**ye**-tes*

Here is my passport
Aquí tiene mi pasaporte
*a-**kee** tee-e-nay mee pa-sa-**por**-tay*

What is the rate of exchange?
¿A cuánto está el cambio?
*a **kwan**-to es-ta el **kam**-bee-o*

What is the rate for	**— sterling?**
¿A cuánto está el cambio	— de la libra esterlina?
*a **kwan**-to es-**ta** el **kam**-bee-o*	— *day la **lee**-bra es-tair-**lee**-na*

— dollars?
— del dólar?
— *del **do**-lar*

What is your commission?
¿Cuánto es la comisión?
*kwan-to es la ko-mee-**syon***

Health

To receive medical treatment under the Spanish health service, you will need to get an E111 form from a post office before you travel. Take a photocopy of it and, if you need treatment, show the doctor the original and hand over the copy. Even if you do have an E111, you should not go without travel insurance.

As in Britain, you can get drugs from a chemist during shopping hours. Rotas of chemists open at other times are posted in their windows and published in local newspapers.

All dental treatment is private; your travel insurance may cover emergency treatment.

In an emergency, call the operator for a telephone number; your accommodation may also be able to help. If you need urgent hospital treatment, E111 arrangements entitle you to treatment in public wards of state hospitals. Show your E111 form immediately to avoid being charged.

What's wrong?

I need a doctor
Necesito un médico
*ne-the-**see**-to oon **me**-dee-ko*

Can I see a doctor?
¿Puedo ver a un médico?
***pwe**-do bair a oon **me**-dee-ko*

He / she is hurt
Está herido / herida
*es-**ta** e-**ree**-do / e-**ree**-da*

He / she has been badly injured
Está malherido / malherida
*es-**ta** mal-e-**ree**-do / mal-e-**ree**-da*

He / she has burnt himself / herself
Se ha quemado
*say a ke-**ma**-do*

He / she has dislocated his / her shoulder
Se ha dislocado el hombro
*say a dees-lo-**ka**-do el **om**-bro*

He / she is unconscious
Está inconsciente
*es-**ta** een-kons-thee-**en**-tay*

He / she has a temperature
Tiene fiebre
*tee-**e**-nay fee-**e**-bray*

He / she has been bitten
Tiene una mordedura
*tee-**e**-nay **oo**-na mor-de-**doo**-ra*

My son has cut himself
Mi hijo se ha hecho cortado
*mee **ee**-ho say a e-cho kor-**ta**-do*

My son is ill
Mi hijo está enfermo
*mee **ee**-ho es-**ta** en-**fair**-mo*

I am ill
Estoy enfermo / enferma
*es-**toy** en-**fair**-mo / en-**fair**-ma*

I am a diabetic
Soy diabético / diabética
*soy dee-a-**be**-tee-ko / dee-a-**be**-tee-ka*

I am allergic to penicillin
Soy alérgico / alérgica a la penicilina
*soy a-**lair**-hee-ko / a-**lair**-hee-ka a la pe-nee-thee-lee-na*

I am badly sunburnt
Tengo quemaduras de sol
ten-go ke-ma-doo-ras day sol

I am constipated
Estoy estreñido / estreñida
es-toy es-tren-yee-do / es-tren-yee-da

I cannot sleep
No puedo dormir
no pwe-do dor-meer

I feel dizzy
Estoy mareado / mareada
es-toy ma-ray-a-do / ma-ray-a-da

I feel faint
Me siento mareado / mareada
may syen-to ma-ray-a-do / ma-ray-a-da

I feel nauseous
Siento náuseas
syen-to now-say-as

I fell
Me he caído
may ay ka-ee-do

I have a pain here
Me duele aquí
may dwe-lay a-kee

I have a rash here
Tengo un sarpullido aquí
ten-go oon sar-poo-yee-do a-kee

I have been sick
He estado vomitando
ay es-ta-do bo-mee-tan-do

I have been stung
Tengo una picadura
ten-go oo-na pee-ka-doo-ra

I have cut myself
Me he cortado
may ay kor-ta-do

I have diarrhoea
Tengo diarrea
ten-go dee-a-ray-a

I have pulled a muscle
Tengo un tirón en un músculo
ten-go oon tee-ron en oon moo-skoo-lo

I have sunstroke
Tengo insolación
ten-go een-so-la-thyon

I suffer from high blood pressure
Tengo la tensión alta
ten-go la ten-syon al-ta

I think I have food poisoning
Creo que tengo una intoxicación de alimentos
*kray-o kay ten-go oo-na een-tok-see-ka-thyon
    day a-lee-men-tos*

It is inflamed here
Esto está inflamado
es-to es-ta een-fla-ma-do

My arm is broken
Me he roto el brazo
may ay ro-to el bra-tho

My stomach is upset
Tengo mal de estómago
ten-go mal day e-sto-ma-go

My tongue is coated
Tengo la lengua sucia
ten-go la len-gwa soo-thya

There is a swelling here
Tengo hinchazón aquí
ten-go een-cha-thon a-kee

I have hurt — my arm
Me he hecho daño en — el brazo
may ay e-cho dan-yo en   — el bra-tho

— my leg
— la pierna
— la pee-air-na

It is painful — to walk
Me duele al — caminar
may dwe-lay al — ka-mee-nar

— to breathe
— respirar
— re-spee-rar

— to swallow
— tragar
— tra-gar

I have — a headache
Tengo — dolor de cabeza
ten-go — do-lor day ka-bay-tha

— a sore throat
— dolor de garganta
— do-lor day gar-gan-ta

— an earache
— dolor de oído
— do-lor day o-ee-do

I am taking these drugs
Estoy tomando estos medicamentos
es-toy to-man-do es-tos me-dee-ka-men-tos

Can you give me a prescription for them?
¿Puede hacerme una receta para ellos?
pwe-day dar-may oo-na re-thay-ta pa-ra e-yos

I am on the pill
Estoy tomando la píldora
es-toy to-man-do la peel-do-ra

I am pregnant
Estoy embarazada
es-toy em-ba-ra-tha-da

My blood group is …
Mi grupo sanguíneo es …
mee groo-po san-gee-nay-o es …

I do not know my blood group
No sé el grupo sanguíneo que tengo
no say el groo-po san-gee-nay-o kay ten-go

I need some antibiotics
Necesito antibióticos
ne-the-see-to an-tee-bee-o-tee-kos

Do I have to go into hospital?
¿Tengo que ir al hospital?
ten-go kay eer al o-spee-tal

Do I need an operation?
¿Tengo que operarme?
ten-go kay o-pe-rar-may

At the hospital

Here is my E-111 form
Aquí está mi formulario E-111 (ciento once)
a-kee es-ta mee for-moo-la-ree-o thee-en-to on-thay

How do I get reimbursed?
¿Cómo me van a reembolsar?
ko-mo may ban a ray-em-bol-sar

Must I stay in bed?
¿Tengo que estar en la cama?
ten-go kay es-tar en la ka-ma

When will I be able to travel?
¿Cuándo podré viajar?
kwan-do po-dray bee-a-har

Will I be able to go out tomorrow?
¿Podré salir mañana?
po-dray sa-leer man-ya-na

Parts of the body

ankle
tobillo
to-bee-yo

arm
brazo
bra-tho

back
espalda
es-pal-da

bone
hueso
we-so

breast
pecho
pe-cho

cheek
mejilla
me-hee-ya

chest
pecho
pe-cho

ear
oreja
o-ray-ha

elbow
codo
ko-do

eye
ojo
o-ho

face
cara
ka-ra

finger
dedo
de-do

foot
pie
pee-ay

hand
mano
ma-no

heart
corazón
ko-ra-thon

kidney
riñon
reen-yon

knee
rodilla
ro-dee-ya

leg
pierna
pee-air-na

liver
hígado
ee-ga-do

lungs
pulmones
pool-mo-nes

mouth
boca
bo-ka

muscle
músculo
moos-koo-lo

neck
cuello
kwe-yo

nose
nariz
na-reeth

skin
piel
pyel

stomach
estómago
e-sto-ma-go

throat
garganta
gar-gan-ta

wrist
muñeca
moon-yay-ka

At the dentist's

I have to see the dentist
Tengo que ir al dentista
ten-go kay eer al den-tee-sta

I have a toothache
Tengo dolor de muelas
ten-go do-lor day mway-las

Are you going to fill it?
¿Va a empastarme?
ba a em-pa-star-may

I have broken a tooth
Me ha roto una muela
may a ro-to oo-na mway-la

Will you have to take it out?
¿Tendrá que sacármela?
ten-dra kay sa-kar-may-la

My false teeth are broken
Se me han roto los dientes postizos
say may an ro-to los dee-en-tes po-stee-thos

Can you repair them?
¿Puede reparármelos?
pwe-day re-pa-rar-may-los

My gums are sore
Me duelen las encías
may dwe-len las en-thee-as

Please give me an injection
Póngame una inyección, por favor
pon-ga-may oo-na een-yek-thyon, por fa-bor

That hurts
Eso duele
e-so dwe-lay

The filling has come out
Se me ha caído el empaste
say may a ka-ee-do el em-pas-tay

This one hurts
Me duele ésta
may dwe-lay es-ta

For Your Information

The seasons

spring	primavera *pree-ma-bair-a*
summer	verano *be-ra-no*
autumn	otoño *o-ton-yo*
winter	invierno *een-byair-no*

Times of the year

in spring	en la primavera *en la pree-ma-bair-a*
in summer	en el verano *en el be-ra-no*
in autumn	en el otoño *en el o-ton-yo*
in winter	en el invierno *en el een-byair-no*

Months

January	enero *e-nair-o*
February	febrero *fe-brair-o*
March	marzo *mar-tho*
April	abril *a-breel*
May	mayo *my-o*
June	junio *hoo-nee-o*
July	julio *hoo-lee-o*
August	agosto *a-go-sto*
September	setiembre *se-tee-em-bray*
October	octubre *ok-too-bray*
November	noviembre *nob-yem-bray*
December	diciembre *deeth-yem-bray*

Days

Sunday	domingo *do-meen-go*
Monday	lunes *loo-nes*
Tuesday	martes *mar-tes*
Wednesday	miércoles *mee-air-ko-les*
Thursday	jueves *hwe-bes*
Friday	viernes *bee-air-nes*
Saturday	sábado *sa-ba-do*

Dates

on Friday	el viernes *el bee-air-nes*
next Tuesday	el martes próximo *el mar-tes prok-see-mo*
last Tuesday	el martes pasado *el mar-tes pa-sa-do*
yesterday	ayer *a-yair*
today	hoy *oy*
tomorrow	mañana *man-ya-na*
in June	en junio *en hoo-nee-o*
July 7th	el siete de julio *el see-e-tay day hoo-lee-o*
next week	la semana que viene *la se-ma-na kay bee-e-nay*
last month	el mes pasado *el mes pa-sa-do*

Public holidays

When a holiday falls on a Tuesday or Thursday, the day between it and the weekend is usually declared a *puente* (bridge) and taken off as well.

Most shops, offices and museums are closed on the following days.

January 1, New Year's Day
Año Nuevo
*an-yo **nway**-bo*

January 6, Epiphany
Día de Reyes
*dee-a day **ray**-es*

Maundy Thursday
Jueves Santo
*hwe-bes **san**-to*

Good Friday
Viernes Santo
*bee-**air**-nes **san**-to*

May 1, May Day, Labour Day
Día del Trabajo
*dee-a del tra-**ba**-ho*

24 June, St John's Day
Día de San Juan Batista
*dee-a day san hwan ba-**tee**-sta*

Corpus Christi Day (2nd Thursday after Pentecost - late May or early June)
Corpus Christi
*kor-poos **kree**-stee*

25 July, St James's Day
Día de Santiago Apóstol
*dee-a day san-**tya**-go a-po-**stol***

15 August, Assumption
Asunción
*a-soon-**thyon***

12 October, Columbus Day
Día de la Hispanidad
*dee-a day la ee-spa-nee-**dad***

1 November, All Saints Day
Todos los Santos
*to-dos los **san**-tos*

6 December, Constitution Day
Día de la Constitución
*dee-a day la kon-stee-too-**thyon***

8 December, Immaculate Conception
Inmaculada Concepción
*een-ma-koo-**la**-da kon-thep-**thyon***

25 December, Christmas Day
Navidad
*na-bee-**dad***

Colours

black
negro
ne-gro

blue
azul
*a-**thool***

brown
marrón
*ma-**ron***

cream
crema
kray-ma

fawn
beis
bays

gold
dorado
*do-**ra**-do*

green
verde
bair-day

red
rojo
ro-ho

grey
gris
grees

silver
plateado
pla-tay-a-do

orange
naranja
na-ran-ha

tan
color canela
ko-lor ka-nay-la

pink
rosa
ro-sa

white
blanco
blan-ko

purple
morado
mo-ra-do

yellow
amarillo
a-ma-ree-yo

Common adjectives

bad
malo
ma-lo

difficult
difícil
dee-fee-theel

beautiful
hermoso
air-mo-so

easy
fácil
fa-theel

big
grande
gran-day

fast
rápido
ra-pee-do

cheap
barato
ba-ra-to

good
bueno
bway-no

cold
frío
free-o

high
alto
al-to

expensive
caro
ka-ro

hot
caliente
ka-lee-en-tay

little
poco
po-ko

long
largo
lar-go

new
nuevo
nway-bo

old
viejo
bee-ay-ho

short
corto
kor-to

slow
lento
len-to

small
pequeño
pe-ken-yo

ugly
feo
fay-o

Signs and notices

abierto
a-bee-air-to
open

aduana
a-dwa-na
Customs

agencia de viajes
a-hen-thee-a day bee-a-hes
travel agency

agotado
a-go-ta-do
sold out

agua potable
a-gwa po-ta-blay
drinking water

alarma de incendios
a-lar-ma day een-then-dee-os
fire alarm

ambulancia
am-boo-lan-thee-a
ambulance

aparcamiento sólo para residentes
a-par-ka-myen-to so-lo pa-ra re-see-den-tes
parking for residents only

área de fumadores
a-ray-a day foo-ma-do-res
smoking area

ascensor
as-then-sor
lift (elevator)

banco
ban-ko
bank

bienvenido
byen-be-nee-do
welcome

bomberos
bom-bair-os
fire brigade

caballeros
ka-ba-yair-os
gentlemen

cajero
ka-hair-o
cashier

caliente
ka-lee-en-tay
hot

camino particular
ka-mee-no par-tee-koo-lar
private road

carril de bicicleta
ka-reel day bee-thee-klay-ta
cycle path

cerrado
the-ra-do
closed

cerrado por la tarde
the-ra-do por la tar-day
closed in the afternoon

circule por la derecha
theer-koo-lay por la de-ray-cha
keep to the right

colegio
co-le-hee-o
school

compartimento de fumadores
kom-par-tee-men-to day foo-ma-do-res
smoking compartment

cuidado
kwee-da-do
caution

cuidado con el perro
kwee-da-do kon el pe-ro
beware of the dog

desviación
des-bee-a-thyon
diversion

emergencia
e-mair-hen-thee-a
emergency

empujar
em-poo-har
push

entrada
en-tra-da
entrance

entrada gratuita
en-tra-da gra-twee-ta
no admission charge

entre sin llamar
en-tray seen ya-mar
enter without knocking

equipaje
e-kee-pa-hay
baggage

está prohibido hablar al conductor mientras circula
es-ta pro-ee-bee-do a-blar kon el kon-dook-tor myen-tras theer-koo-la
it is forbidden to speak to the driver while the bus is moving

frío
free-o
cold

horario
o-ra-ree-o
timetable

hospital
os-pee-tal
hospital

información
een-for-ma-thyon
information

libre
lee-bray
vacant

lista de precios
lee-sta day pre-thee-os
price list

llame
ya-may
ring

llame por favor
ya-may por fa-bor
please ring

llegadas
ye-ga-das
arrivals

no entrar
no en-trar
no entry

no pisar el césped
no pee-sar el thes-ped
keep off the grass

no tocar
no to-kar
do not touch

ocupado
o-koo-pa-do
occupied

oferta especial
o-fair-ta es-peth-yal
special offer

oficina de objetos perdidos
o-fee-thee-na day ob-he-tos pair-dee-dos
lost property office

papelera
pa-pe-lair-a
litter

peligro
pe-lee-gro
danger

peligro de incendio
pe-lee-gro day een-then-dee-o
danger of fire

peligro de muerte
pe-lee-gro day mwair-tay
danger of death

permitido sólo para...
pair-mee-tee-do so-lo pa-ra...
allowed only for...

policia
po-lee-thee-a
police

prohibida la entrada
pro-ee-bee-da la en-tra-da
no trespassing

prohibido asomarse
pro-ee-bee-do a-so-mar-say
do not lean out

prohibido el paso
pro-ee-bee-do el pa-so
no thoroughfare

prohibido fumar
pro-ee-bee-do foo-ma
no smoking

prohibido hacer fotos
pro-ee-bee-do a-thair fo-tos
no picture taking

rebajas
re-ba-has
sale

recuerdos
re-kwair-dos
souvenirs

reservado
re-sair-ba-do
reserved

salida
sa-lee-da
exit

salida de emergencia
sa-lee-da day e-mair-hen-thee-a
emergency exit

salidas
sa-lee-das
departures

se alquila
say al-kee-la
to let (for hire)

se vende
say ben-day
for sale

señoras
sen-yo-ras
ladies

sólo empleados
so-lo em-play-a-dos
employees only

sólo para uso externo
so-lo pa-ra oo-so ek-stair-no
for external use only

teléfono
te-le-fo-no
telephone

timbre de alarma
teem-bray day a-lar-ma
communication cord

tirar
tee-rar
pull

veneno
be-nay-no
poison

venta de liquidación
ben-ta day lee-kee-da-thyon
closing down sale

In an Emergency

What to do

Spain has three police forces. The Guardia Civil, who wear green uniforms, deal with law enforcement on the roads and in rural areas. They do not enjoy a great reputation for helpfulness. The Policía Local, who wear blue and white uniforms, patrol within towns and can be approached about any difficulties. The Policía Nacional, who wear blue uniforms, guard public buildings and in all substantial towns man the *comisaría* (police station), where crimes may be reported. In addition, the autonomous communities of the Basque Country, Catalonia, Galicia and Valencia have their own police forces. Telephone 091 for the Policía Nacional, 092 for the Policía Local.

If you suffer a loss or theft, report the incident to the police and obtain a copy of the report. If your passport is stolen or lost, inform the nearest British Consulate so that they can issue you with temporary papers.

For assistance with fires, refer to local directories or call the operator.

Call — the fire brigade
Llame — a los bomberos
*ya-may — a los bom-**bair**-os*

— the police
— a la policía
*— a la po-lee-**thee**-a*

—an ambulance
— a una ambulancia
*— a **oo**-na am-boo-**lan**-thee-a*

Get a doctor
Busque a un médico
***boos**-kay a oon **me**-dee-ko*

There is a fire
Hay un incendio
*eye oon en-**then**-dee-o*

Where is **— the British consulate?**
¿Dónde está — el consulado británico?
don**-day es-**ta *— el kon-soo-**la**-do bree-**ta**-nee-ko*

— the police station?
— la comisaría de policía?
*— la ko-mee-sa-**ree**-a day po-lee-**thee**-a*